Strategic Survey
2001/2002

Published by
OXFORD
UNIVERSITY PRESS
for
The International Institute for Strategic Studies
Arundel House
13–15 Arundel Street
London WC2R 3DX
United Kingdom

The International Institute for Strategic Studies

Strategic Survey 2001/2002

Published by
OXFORD
UNIVERSITY PRESS

for
The International Institute for Strategic Studies
Arundel House, 13–15 Arundel Street,
London WC2R 3DX, United Kingdom

This publication has been prepared by the Director of the Institute and his Staff, who accept full responsibility for its contents, which describe and analyse events up to 5 April 2002. These do not, and indeed cannot, represent a consensus of views among the worldwide membership of the Institute as a whole.

First published ....May 2002

ISBN 0-19-851665-7
ISSN 0459-7230

Strategic Survey (ISSN 0459-7230) is published annually by Oxford University Press.

Payment is required with all orders and subscriptions. Prices include air-speeded delivery to Australia, Canada, India, Japan, New Zealand and the USA. Delivery elsewhere is by surface mail. Air-mail rates are available on request. Please add sales tax to prices quoted. Payment may be made by cheque or Eurocheque (payable to Oxford University Press), National Girobank (account 500 1056), credit card (MasterCard, Visa, American Express), direct debit (please send for details) or UNESCO coupons. Bankers: Barclays Bank plc. PO Box 333, Oxford, UK, code 20-65-18, account 00715654.

Claims for non-receipt must be made within four months of dispatch/order (whichever is later).

Please send subscription orders to the Journals Subscription Department, Oxford University Press, Great Clarendon Street, Oxford, OX2 6DP, UK. *Tel* +44 (0)1865 353907. *Fax* +44 (0)1865 353485. *e-mail* jnl.orders@oup.co.uk

Strategic Survey is distributed by Mercury International, 365 Blair Road, Avenel, NJ 07001, USA. Periodical postage paid at Rahway, New Jersey, USA, and additional entry points.

US POSTMASTER: Send address corrections to *Strategic Survey*, c/o Mercury International, 365 Blair Road, Avenel, NJ 07001, USA.

Abstracted and indexed by: Reasearch Base Online, PAIS.

PRINTED IN THE UK by Bell & Bain Ltd, Glasgow.

Contents

List of Tables and Maps

Strategic Survey Online

Members of the IISS can access *Strategic Survey 2001–2002* online at http://www.iiss.org/pub/stratsur.asp. The address for subscribers is http://www3.oup.co.uk/stsurv, where they will first need to register using their subscriber number.

Perspectives

For most of 2001, world affairs stumbled along, as they had for most of the post-Cold War nineties. The consuming issues were Iraq; the Middle East; missile defence and European worries about American unilateralism; proliferation of weapons of mass-destruction (WMD); free trade and globalisation; AIDS in Africa; and peacekeeping worries in the face of persistent insurgencies and fraught peace processes across the globe. On 11 September 2001, terrorists in Osama bin Laden's al-Qaeda network steered two hijacked passenger airliners into the World Trade Center in New York and another into the Pentagon outside of Washington DC, and crashed a fourth – probably bound for the White House – in western Pennsylvania. Over 3,000 people representing over 40 nationalities – most of them Americans and virtually all of them civilians – were killed. By signalling the mass-casualty intent and capabilities of transnational Islamic terrorists, and their resistance to deterrence or political suasion, the event transformed international affairs. While international security was cast into disarray, international relations acquired a new, if grimly realist, clarity. America had been shown to be vulnerable at home. US security was at stake. If the US were not able to respond in an effective manner to the act of war perpetrated on its own territory, the US and its friends would become fair game. To re-affirm US global leadership, Washington would need to move towards extroversion and engagement. In building a new coalition against terrorism, it would, in effect, define a new series of alliance relationships in the pursuit, as Washington sees it, of self-defence under Article 51 of the United Nations Charter. The members of that alliance would be selected largely according to how states responded to American counter-terrorist requirements.

The end of globalisation?

The eleventh of September also starkly exposed globalisation as something both more and less than it had appeared. On the one hand, it was more than lower communication and transport costs and better-integrated economies, questioned only by dispersed enclaves of traditional farmers or middle-class anti-capitalists in search of a noble cause. Globalisation also enabled transnational networks of terrorists with apocalyptic objectives to operate. On the other hand, it was less than an inexorable and all-enveloping force destined to consolidate what Francis Fukuyama has deemed 'the end of history'. The persistence of old-fashioned geopolitics and ancient forms of international violence has shown that we live not in a monolithic globalised world but in three different global geopolitical time zones.

To be sure, there is the postmodern world of the networked society and globalisation, where a premium is placed on transparency, information-sharing and communication, and the economic opportunities that flow from them. The erosion of international barriers through these processes discourages conflict among those who benefit from it. But international society is also characterised by the resilience of the 'modern' twentieth-century world, where balance of power, alliances and secrecy remain important to preserve national interests and to deter conflict between powers that retain different strategic outlooks. Conflicts in the Middle East and in Asia suggest the attractive methods of postmodern diplomacy: confidence building and transparency. The threat and possible application of force retain a role, and balances of power make the use of force possible. Finally, there are the pre-modern outposts, inhabited until October 2001 by the Taliban in Afghanistan and still by Hizbullah in Lebanon, where religious solidarity and mysticism motivate and govern politics and where there is little productive economic life outside the agricultural domain. The capacity to use mobile phones or watch CNN in these places does not colour the fact that they operate from dramatically different sources of political legitimacy and different motivations for political and military action.

The trend is towards a more postmodern globalised world, but dealing with the vestiges of the pre-modern, while maintaining the order of the modern has become the over-arching strategic challenge. The complexity of these intermingling worlds resides in the fact that those who hail from pre-modern outposts, use the instruments of the postmodern globalised world – finance and instant communication – and the armaments of the modern world – weapons of mass destruction as well as conventional weapons – to advance atavistic goals. In confronting pre-modern adversaries, it was important to minimise the risk of foreclosing their integration into the modern and postmodern worlds – of creating, in Samuel Huntington's phrase, a 'clash of civilisations'.

US engagement

From the early stages of the global US-led mobilisation against terrorism, there were strong signs that Washington had taken this exhortation to heart. Rather than go it alone, the US quickly built a multi-layered counter-terrorism coalition that would operate in the military, intelligence and law-enforcement spheres. That said, the war in Afghanistan against the Taliban – al-Qaeda's host and abettor – that began less than a month after the 11 September attacks resulted in a swift, decisive military victory. That effort dismantled the Taliban and allowed an agreeable transitional government to be installed. It also disrupted al-Qaeda's operations by forcing bin Laden to flee, killing several of his highest-level advisers, and forcing others to disperse. It proceeded with the critical diplomatic and logistical assistance of Pakistan – until 11 September the Taliban's one state supporter – as well as that of Russia, Uzbekistan and Tajikistan. And it did not produce the mass outcry of the Muslim 'street' that many predicted. Yet battlefield detentions and law-enforcement operations, intense though they were, yielded at best 1,000 or so al-Qaeda members – a tiny number against the 15-20,000 estimated to have passed through al-Qaeda's training camps in Afghanistan. As the 23 December 2001 attempt by British Muslim Richard Reid to blow up a jet bound from Paris to Miami demonstrated, there are still active and willing al-Qaeda members dispersed throughout Western society.

Washington and its coalition partners appear to understand that the campaign against terrorism will be one of containment waged on a number of fronts, perhaps less on the military one than others. After Afghanistan, the US was reluctant to use force on possible al-Qaeda hosts such as Somalia and Sudan, preferring diplomatic, preventive and law-enforcement approaches to apprehending terrorists and compromising their networks, as well as limited military assistance in the cases of the Philippines, Yemen and Georgia. Given the different levels and types of engagement required, the definition of victory in this war will be hard to articulate in advance and the public perception of victory may arise prematurely. On 12 September, *Le Monde*'s headline may have read, 'We are all Americans now', but sustaining a coalition against an enemy depends on maintaining a constant image of the ever-present threat and perpetual evil against which one must fight. Except for fleeting exposure to bin Laden by way of videotapes he has occasionally supplied to the al-Jazeera news network in Qatar, al-Qaeda is essentially an anonymous, faceless enemy. If bin Laden is killed, turns out to be dead already or otherwise disappears from the scene, the terrorist networks that he has inspired and spawned are likely to remain active. The US faces an enormous challenge in keeping allies and newfound friends focused on a war that may appear to conform to a purely American agenda. Indeed, the transatlantic differences in threat perceptions prevalent before 11 September began to return in early 2002, as some European capitals appeared to relax counter-terrorism postures while the US remained on highest alert.

Coalition challenges

The coalition-building that the US accomplished immediately after 11 September – without an institutional base like NATO – was impressive. But as the counter-terrorism campaign settled from a high-profile military operation to decapitate al-Qaeda into a more protracted American effort to plug multiple sources of vulnerability, even transatlantic support began to show signs of strain. Differences increased when President Bush labelled

Iraq, Iran and North Korea the 'axis of evil' in his January 2002 State of the Union address. Contributing factors were the United States' choice not to use NATO in the Afghanistan war – despite its invocation of Article 5 for the first time ever – and its manifest preference for 'coalitions of the willing' that it could decisively lead with less consultation than NATO would require. It is possible that NATO will be marginalised as a military alliance, and become a military services organisation on which members can draw on a case-by-case basis. The upshot would be less comprehensive involvement in a wider array of military operations – perhaps including 'out-of-area' deployments. In any event, maintaining a wider counter-terrorist coalition will require an intensity of diplomacy and degree of cooperation with culturally different powers that is unprecedented.

The US engagement in the Middle East has taken on even greater diplomatic significance in the new strategic context. US support for Israel combined with Israel's aggressive retaliatory policy against Palestinian violence tends to push young Muslims with dim expectations of their own governments towards terrorism, and makes it politically difficult for those governments to extend counter-terrorist cooperation to the West. Thus, it is incumbent on Washington to stay closely engaged in the Israeli–Palestinian conflict. Improving US–Russian relations received a boost from shared concerns about Islamic terrorism. But differences of view could have sharper diplomatic consequences as the US puts itself psychologically on a war footing. Moscow may, for example, grow uneasy with any lingering US military presence in Central Asia. It may also resent Western criticism over its prosecution of operations against Chechen rebels, which may increase if the US decides not to move against Iraq and the counter-terrorism effort becomes less military. China too supported US-led action in Afghanistan on account of its own Islamic terrorist problems, but it will continue to position itself as a strategic competitor to the US. Neither Moscow nor Beijing is likely to back regime-changing US military action against Iraq. Thus, the coexistence of a broad political coalition and a narrow military one will likely produce periodic stresses in diplomatic support for the campaign against terrorism.

Beyond counter-terrorism

Yet the US agenda now encompasses more than just counter-terrorism. That concern has animated an equally strong anxiety about the spread of weapons of mass destruction. The eleventh of September showed that non-state actors like al-Qaeda were willing to use such weapons to inflict massive casualties. Those weapons are available mainly from state actors. Thus, the 'axis of evil' speech should be read in part as reminding the world that 11 September has not made the US so naïve or tunnel-visioned as to think that 'roguery' or conduct 'of concern' is confined to non-state terrorists.

The growing prospect of US military action against Iraq – which has not been clearly connected to 11 September – confirms this policy evolution. So does the Bush administration's reiteration of the existing US policy of targeting small nuclear weapons against ostensibly non-nuclear actors to foster a more credible and powerful deterrent against biological or chemical WMD attacks.

Indeed, as the counter-terrorism effort becomes routinised, and if it is successful enough to forestall large-scale attacks in the short term, the Bush administration's focus on state actors and WMD could have a more dynamic and potentially revolutionary effect on international relations than counter-terrorism itself. Regime-change in Iraq, for instance, could change the alignment of strategic relationships in the Middle East and the Gulf; the defeat of al-Qaeda would not. Furthermore, the WMD threat could re-invigorate the military utility of nuclear weapons by prompting the development of a new generation of less destructive ones.

Imperfect intelligence

Both counter-terrorism and WMD policy place a premium on intelligence that will not be easy to pay. Preparations for the 11 September attack were made in the US. The conspiracy emerged abroad, in European and Central Asian countries that still were not, in the main, the conspirators' countries of origin. The new terrorism threat is therefore substantially a diaspora problem. This means that there is a vital connection between domestic and foreign intelligence collection. The link is pivotal not just because of its indispensability, but because of the problems it poses both for liberal societies and their governments. Law enforcement agencies want to prosecute; intelligence agencies want to collect information for policy and operational purposes. Interior ministries gather evidence at home, while clandestine services operate abroad. Thus, separate arms of government seek crucial information for incompatible purposes. These problems are not easily resolved without infringing the civil liberties governments are supposed to be protecting from terrorist attack. In the months following 11 September, lawmakers in the US and Europe appeared to strike a workable, if controversial, preliminary balance.

Serious substantive, as well as social, intelligence challenges remain. The US and other governments had forms of strategic warning of the 11 September attacks, but probably no tactical warning. The eleventh of September was not a case like the 1973 Arab–Israeli War, when entrenched beliefs prevented decision-makers from understanding the significance of the accurate intelligence before them. Yet, although human agents are the best instruments for determining intentions and revealing operational planning, they are difficult to insert – particularly into a network of religiously driven terrorists culturally distinct from their adversaries. Technical intelligence, on the other hand, provides a predictable yield, even if the product is limited in the nature of insights it can provide. Thus, real-time surveillance provided by *Predator* and *Global Hawk* unmanned aerial vehicles facilitated the effort to track down and neutralise al-Qaeda in general, but did not allow US and British forces to zero in on bin Laden in particular.

It is clear that no one country can gather all the intelligence it needs, and that intelligence-based warnings are by nature ambiguous. The US and its friends and allies must therefore move from a threat-based system to a vulnerability-based one. This will call for, among other things, a greater degree of information-sharing among governments. Although bilateral channels usually sufficed for sharing information between police forces and intelligence services before 11 September, the global scope of terrorist activity will necessitate new relationships and creative approaches to information sharing. The need to share intelligence for protection of critical infrastructure is equally urgent. Key information as to a cyber-attack, for example, will almost certainly lie outside the borders of the victimised country. Achieving a high level of cooperation was relatively easy in the immediate aftermath of 11 September, but within six months – when no major attacks occurred – it showed signs of waning. Even in the presence of an extraordinarily grave transnational threat, shedding the institutional reluctance to share intelligence has proven difficult for all governments – not least, the United States. Against sustained US demands, Belgian and German authorities complained in late 2001 that they were getting little in return. Perceived 'global unilateralism' on the part of the US will only make the problem tougher.

Venues that could facilitate cooperation include the Group of Eight industrialised nations plus Russia (G-8), which has been a highly useful arena for counter-terrorism cooperation since the mid-1990s, NATO and the EU, but new arrangements may be required to capture countries outside of these organisations. There has been some movement in this direction in the Association of South-east Asian Nations, in a region where Islam is becoming more conservative. Other areas may pose greater challenges. Sub-Saharan African countries are generally resistant to the encroachment of radical Islam and appear willing to extend cooperation, but lack effective regional organisations through which it might be marshalled. Arab and Islamic countries often have highly effective intelligence and security services, but are reluctant to share them with traditional Western adversaries. Nevertheless, the US was able to win limited cooperation from several such countries – notably Sudan and Syria – after 11 September.

The economic front

The attack on the world's financial centre, and the human and intellectual capital it contains, threatened to have a significant adverse impact on the global economic environment. It came amid a marked slowdown in the US, a correction in world financial markets and the bursting of the information-technology (IT) bubble. A sharp deterioration in US investor and consumer confidence – the dominant engines of global growth since the mid-1990s – deepened an international economic downturn. Japan was in no position to take up the slack, while emerging economies – many of which were over-exposed in the US market or had export baskets that were too narrowly focused on IT goods – lacked the fiscal resources and healthy financial sectors needed to effect a return to healthy growth. The scale of the problem demanded sustained coordinated action by the world's leading central banks, as well as the G-8, to shore up confidence and stabilise nervous markets. This did not fully materialise. The US Federal Reserve Bank was proactive, cutting interest rates even more steeply than it had been following 11 September, and to some extent buoyed markets and staved off negative economic growth in the US. The European Central Bank, however, was hobbled by institutional limitations and a stubborn commitment to price stability at the expense of stimulus. Although there were positive signs of a US recovery by early 2002, lingering uncertainty seemed likely to inhibit its momentum and improvement in Japan and Europe appeared likely to lag.

The global recession exposed weaknesses in emerging-market economies – notably that of Argentina, which erupted in street violence amid a liquidity crisis in late 2001 – suggesting that the International Monetary Fund might need to rethink its macroeconomic prescriptions for such economies. It also appeared likely that the Bretton Woods institutions would become, to an extent, re-politicised, as Pakistan and Turkey were promised hefty assistance for strategic reasons despite sluggish economic reforms. Policymakers also grappled with the question of whether to maintain the freedom of movement of goods and individuals on which today's world economy fundamentally relies, or to take steps that would limit this freedom in order to ensure greater physical security of people and property. The Bush administration decisively adopted the first option, allocating $38 billion for a homeland security plan designed unambiguously to secure rather than close US borders by better coordinating the activities of border-control agencies and drastically improving aviation security to encourage people to resume flying. Due mainly to 11 September, the volume of air passengers and freight fell by 6% in 2001 – the first drop since 1991 – but showed signs of returning to pre-11 September levels by early 2002. Further, 11 September had a lower-than-expected overall effect on international trade, which depends predominantly on slow maritime shipments – a less attractive means of delivery to terrorists.

Any other business?

Many of the pre-11 September problems have remained insuperable and some have been ameliorated. To be sure, there have been developments completely unconnected to 11 September. In February 2002, Angolan government forces killed rebel leader Jonas Savimbi, a persistent 'spoiler' of peace efforts there, paving the way to a cease-fire in late March. In the opposite direction, Zimbabwean President Robert Mugabe has crudely used the counter-terrorist moment as a lame pretext for repressing a brave and legitimate political opposition. Hindu–Muslim ethnic violence flared in India, killing over 500 people in February and March. Well-calibrated European and American diplomacy in Macedonia appeared to contain residual instability in the Balkans. But very few strategic issues, it seems, have been unaffected by the attacks. The eleventh of September probably strengthened the US case for ballistic missile defence. Some argued that it was ineffective against asymmetric attacks like those on the World Trade Center and the Pentagon. But stronger voices retorted that the mass-casualty intent reflected in those attacks showed that new enemies would use missiles with WMD payloads if they could get them from countries like Iran, Iraq and North Korea. The one qualification is that the marginal cost for an effective defence could drain resources needed for transforming the US military from the Cold War model designed to fight two major theatre wars to a more agile force for combating terrorism. Suggesting the need for the latter, the Afghanistan campaign has been prosecuted in significant part by special-operations soldiers and unmanned aerial vehicles. Indeed, the proposed US defence budget submitted by President Bush in February 2002 would hold missile-defence funding steady rather than increasing it.

Signs of American unilateralism nevertheless resurfaced after a brief honeymoon of pre-Afghanistan coalition-building. On the trade front, President Bush appeared unfazed by the new premium on transatlantic and trans-Pacific solidarity when, in March 2002, he authorised high protective tariffs mainly on European, Russian and Asian steel, risking a trade war. Before 11 September, in July 2001, the US had rejected the enforcement protocol for the Biological Weapons Convention. In December 2001 the Bush administration announced that the US would unilaterally withdraw from the Anti-Ballistic Missile Treaty in June 2002, and the US continued to resist the ratification of the Comprehensive Test-Ban Treaty. Washington's refusal to treat as prisoners-of-war suspected al-Qaeda and Taliban members detained in Afghanistan and taken to the US Marine base in Guantanamo Bay, Cuba, also re-emphasised the American opposition to the International Criminal Court and its scepticism about international treaties in general. Yet the US also moderated perceptions of unilateralism by promising Russia a written arms reduction agreement by May 2002 and leaving open the possibility of repatriation for some of the detainees.

Third World problems – AIDS and famine in sub-Saharan Africa, instability in Angola and the Democratic Republic of Congo, and the increasingly ominous unrest in Zimbabwe – suffered from strategic inattention in the short term, and were not helped by the inability of regional leaders to pick up the diplomatic slack. But in the long term, there is an enduring strategic need to bring more parts of the developing world into the modern and even postmodern worlds in order to inoculate them against terrorist cooptation as well as to moderate north–south economic differences. Nowhere is this need more acute than in the Arab world. In countries such as Egypt and Saudi Arabia, burgeoning young and restless populations dissatisfied with their governments confront declining incomes, making them fertile ground for al-Qaeda recruiters. These countries have become increasingly disengaged from the global and regional economy. The exigency of reversing this trend for the sake of international security may prompt a higher degree of engagement on the part of the Bretton Woods institutions and the World Trade Organisation, as well as bilateral foreign assistance programmes.

The US predilection against peacekeeping intensified, and the world's other capable armies at least lowered the priority of peacekeeping in favour of possible coalition operations. But the apparent need for such operations dropped off after Afghanistan, and the importance of nation-building as a long-term counter-terrorism tool gained recognition. A clearer division of military labour – with the US carrying the burden of offensive and large-scale military engagements, and lesser militaries filling defensive roles, mopping up and nation-building – also emerged. From these developments, brighter long-term prospects for peacekeeping may have arisen. Peace-keeping in Afghanistan remains a more immediate problem. The 4,700-strong British-led contingent operates only in Kabul and is barely sufficient to secure Hamid Karzai's transitional government, which has found forging a consensus among the country's factions a difficult task. A peacekeeping force suitable for the whole country would require at least five times as many troops. Thus, the US may find it necessary to marshal and support more peacekeepers to create better conditions for the national conference (*loya jirga*) scheduled for June 2002, at which Afghani factions are supposed to blueprint a permanent government. As much as the US wants to avoid being drawn into Afghanistan, leaving a power vacuum there that could attract terrorists is unacceptable.

On the strictly political side, less tolerance for threatened or actual violence appeared to advance peace processes in Northern Ireland, where the Provisional Irish Republican Army made a token disarmament gesture in October 2001 that nonetheless reinvigorated political reconciliation. In Sri Lanka, the government and the Tamil Tigers agreed to a formal bilateral cease-fire in February 2002 for the first time since 1995, paving the way to face-to-face peace talks. As of 5 January 2002, the brutal Revolutionary United Front in Sierra Leone had handed over nearly 20,000 weapons to UN troops in Sierra Leone. At the same time, it was clear that the general disinclination of insurgencies to use terror as a means to their political ends was merely tactical rather than strategic. As the dust settled in lower Manhattan, in February 2002 violence surged from Maoist terrorists in

Nepal and Marxist ones in Colombia. The Basque separatists of Euskadi ta Askatasuna continued their campaign of political violence unperturbed by 11 September, although it also galvanised the French and Spanish counter-terrorism authorities. While the events of 11 September compelled Arab governments to crack down on Islamic terrorism, they probably, on balance, inspired those terrorists to greater mayhem. Witness the 13 December attack on the Indian parliament by Kashmiri Muslim separatists; the kidnap and despicable murder in January of *Wall Street Journal* reporter Daniel Pearl; and the rise in Palestinian suicide-bombings.

Strategie Oblige

Containing and ultimately defeating terrorism is a formidable task, offering as much scope for disagreement as for cooperation. Yesterday's sense of emotional solidarity is today's shared political burden. It needs to be handled with economic finesse, political savvy, military firmness and moral resolve in careful balance. In the early stages of the containment effort bilateral relationships between the United States and allies, friends, tentative coalition partners and old adversaries will be most important. In this sense, 11 September has re-affirmed that the state remains the basic and indispensable constituent of the international system. At the same time, the US will need to make strides in coordinating with an ever more ambitious EU Common Foreign and Security Policy if it is to be successful in maintaining European backing and assistance on the counter-terrorism front. Conversely, for many Europeans, the new extroversion demanded of them will require a much higher level of engagement. By early 2002, most governments appeared reconciled to the fact that a networked threat like the one posed by al-Qaeda called for a networked international system that would pool information resources and harmonise national objectives.

During the Cold War, the US and its allies could not afford to have desultory foreign policies. Neither can they now. The intensity of US engagement on the counter-terrorism and WMD issues into 2002 has buoyed a more moral and ideological element in US foreign policy. The words 'evil', 'faith' and 'God' crop up with conspicuous frequency in Bush's public discourse. His terms of reference – 'either you are with us or you are with the terrorists' – have a black-and-white cast. In his trip to China in February 2002, to the surprise of many US analysts who consider a confrontational approach to China on human rights counter-productive, Bush publicly criticised China for suppressing the right of Christians to worship. He also spoke of the American conviction to advance 'liberty paired with law'. Such phrases reflect careful deliberation, and a recognition that the US and its allies cannot rely only on realpolitik and hardnosed assessments of clear-and-present dangers in executing foreign policy in an epoch of ill-defined threats from multiple directions. But while this idealistic emphasis may help provide focus for grand strategy, it is no more a substitute for it than was Ronald Reagan's 'evil empire' characterisation of the Soviet Union. Grand strategy requires resolute application as well as high purpose. And it is, once again, an obligation.

Strategic Policy Issues

Big Bang: 11 September and US Non-proliferation Policy

On taking office, the Bush administration clearly identified the proliferation of nuclear, biological and chemical (NBC) weapons and ballistic missiles to 'rogue regimes' as the primary security threat facing the United States. Driven by intellectual conviction and a political desire to distinguish itself from the Clinton administration, the Bush presidency emphasised missile defence and deterrence as the primary means of dealing with this threat and downplayed the value of traditional non-proliferation instruments, such as multilateral arms control, export controls and diplomacy. Within a few months, however, the Bush administration began to soften this stark view, and stressed that missile defence and deterrence were part of a comprehensive non-proliferation strategy, which included these three traditional instruments. Prior to 11 September, the administration also began to put its own stamp on specific non-proliferation agreements and programmes bequeathed to it by the Clinton administration.

On North Korea, Washington decided to support existing agreements to limit Pyongyang's nuclear and missile programmes, but in June 2001 announced a tougher position for future negotiations. On China, the administration decided to adopt the November 2000 agreement between the US and China to control Chinese missile-related exports, but moved quickly to impose sanctions in early September 2001 against Chinese entities that continued to provide missile assistance to Pakistan. In contrast, the administration was intent on lifting sanctions against India and Pakistan imposed for their nuclear tests in 1998. Cooperative threat reduction programmes with Russia and efforts to constrain Russian nuclear and missile assistance to Iran were subject to lengthy internal reviews. On Iraq, Washington sought to build support for 'smart sanctions', but there was sharp internal debate on overall strategy towards Saddam Hussein.

The 11 September terrorist attacks, the subsequent anthrax scare and the successful war against the Taliban regime and al-Qaeda in Afghanistan had four major effects on the Bush administration's emerging policies to prevent and respond to the proliferation of nuclear as well as chemical and biological weapons (CBW), and ballistic missiles. First, they reinforced the administration's pre-existing emphasis on defence and deterrence as the primary instruments of non-proliferation policy and created domestic and international political conditions that facilitated these efforts. In addition, Washington dramatically increased existing efforts to strengthen homeland defence against the threat of terrorists armed with weapons of mass destruction (WMD). Second, without changing the administration's basic scepticism towards multilateral arms control, Washington began to search for ideas to enlist existing multilateral treaties to help deal with the threat of non-compliance by 'rogue regimes' and terrorists seeking WMD. Third, the administration reversed its previously lukewarm attitude towards cooperative threat reduction programmes with Russia and began to focus greater attention on the problem of Russian nuclear and missile-related transfers to Iran. Fourth, and most important, the administration was emboldened to adopt a tougher policy towards the 'rogue regimes' – newly christened the 'axis of evil' – that emphasised regime change over containment. Iraq is the test case for this new strategy.

Defence and deterrence: from Clinton to Bush

The Bush administration's emphasis on defence and deterrence to deal with proliferation threats has its roots in the Clinton administration. Drawing on the lessons of the Gulf War and the possibility that the US might find itself in conflict with an adversary armed with CBW and short-range missiles, the Clinton Pentagon stepped up efforts to develop theatre missile defences and announced a doctrine of 'counter-proliferation', which was primarily intended to protect troops against CBW attack but also contemplated pre-emptive attacks to destroy WMD facilities. Building on statements made by the US during the Gulf War, the Clinton administration also adopted (though it did not broadcast) a more ambiguous negative security assurance, indicating that the US would not rule out the use of nuclear weapons to respond to a CBW attack. Finally, following the 1998 North Korean missile test, the Clinton administration responded to domestic pressure and sought to reach agreement with the Russians to amend the 1972 Anti-Ballistic Missile (ABM) Treaty to allow for development of a limited national missile defence system.

These measures created unease among US allies in Europe that the US was pursuing a more 'unilateralist' and military non-proliferation policy that threatened to undermine multilateral arms control, which many Europeans saw as the primary non-proliferation tool. The Clinton administration, however, was also active in pursuing traditional multilateral efforts, including indefinite extension of the Non-Proliferation Treaty (NPT); strengthening of International Atomic Energy Agency (IAEA) safeguards and Nuclear Supplier Group (NSG) export controls;

completion of the Comprehensive Test Ban Treaty (CTBT); ratification of the Chemical Weapons Convention (CWC); and establishment of the Organisation for the Prohibition of Chemical Weapons (OPCW). The Clinton administration also made efforts to negotiate an inspection protocol for the Biological Weapons Convention (BWC) and to develop an International Code of Conduct (ICOC) for missiles and a Fissile Material Cut-Off Treaty (FMCT).

Toward the end of the Clinton administration, the momentum of multilateral arms control began to flag. Despite its general support for these efforts, the administration rejected the International Landmines Convention in 1997 on national security grounds, primarily the need to deploy landmines in the Korean Peninsula. Following the defeat of the CTBT in the Senate and the administration's movement towards national missile defence, China and several other countries refused to allow initiation of FMCT negotiations at the Conference on Disarmament in Geneva unless the US accepted negotiations on a treaty limiting the military use of space. This was unacceptable to Washington. As a result, the Conference on Disarmament became locked in stalemate, unresolved at the time of writing.

The Bush administration came to office with a strong political impetus to pursue a strategy that emphasised defence instead of multilateral efforts, rather than defence in addition to multilateral efforts. During the Clinton years, US support for some multilateral instruments became highly politicised and enmeshed in partisan politics between the White House and the Republican Congress. The ratification of the CWC degenerated into a bruising battle that split the Republican Senate, and the CTBT went down to stunning defeat. The administration's approach to limit missile defences and efforts to preserve the ABM Treaty were denounced as sacrificing US security. During the presidential campaign, candidate Bush announced his opposition to the CTBT, while candidate Gore said that his first act if elected would be to re-submit the CTBT to the Senate for ratification.

Underpinning this political debate was the conviction among key officials on the incoming Bush team that the proliferation of WMD and ballistic missiles was widespread and inevitable. As expressed by the Rumsfeld Commission on Missile Proliferation in July 1998, hostile regimes are bound to acquire WMD and ballistic missiles to threaten the US and its allies. The events of 1998 – nuclear tests by India and Pakistan, and missile tests by North Korea and Iran – were cited to support the contention that non-proliferation efforts have failed. Moreover, this argument runs, 'rogue regimes' cannot be reliably deterred by threats of massive retaliation because idiosyncratic and irrational dictators, once they acquire a small force of WMD-armed ballistic missiles, would be prepared to confront the US and its allies. In this view, multilateral regimes cannot be effective against such countries determined to acquire WMD and violate their treaty commitments. At best, the traditional non-proliferation tools of treaties, export controls and diplomacy are delaying tactics. At worst, they are dangerous, creating a false sense of security, distracting energy and attention away from the urgent need to strengthen missile defences and providing a means for countries to obtain technology for secret WMD programmes under cover of international treaties.

In addition, the incoming Bush team believed that some international instruments, such as the CTBT and BWC protocol, weakened US defence and deterrence capabilities, and therefore potentially contributed to proliferation and the risk that WMD might be used against the US and its allies. From this perspective, whatever value the CTBT has in terms of prohibiting testing by other countries is far outweighed by the danger that it would undermine the credibility of US nuclear forces and therefore could lead states under the US nuclear umbrella to seek their own nuclear capabilities. Similarly, the BWC protocol was seen as providing very little value in detecting covert biological weapons, while potentially exposing US bio-defence secrets and commercial interests to international inspections. (Many experts and agencies in the Clinton administration shared this sceptical view of the BWC protocol.)

After taking office, however, the Bush administration soon realised that its case for missile defence would be stronger – and more palatable to allies – if it was presented as part of broader comprehensive strategy that included support for multilateral arms control. Thus, by the summer of 2001, even though the Bush administration reiterated its firm opposition to the CTBT and decided to reject the BWC protocol, it also declared its strong support for existing treaties like the NPT and CWC and supported negotiation of new instruments, such as the FMCT and an international code of conduct for missiles. On paper at least, the Bush administration's 'comprehensive approach' to combat proliferation was not conceptually different from the Clinton administration's strategy, although there were obvious divergences on specific issues, such as the CTBT.

Like the Clinton administration, the Bush administration argued that multilateral arms-control treaties helped to limit proliferation and provide an international basis for rallying political coalitions, but, by themselves, could not stop a determined proliferator, such as Iraq or North Korea. On this basis, the Bush administration, like its predecessor, argued that the US needed to pursue limited missile defence to strengthen deterrence and prevent 'blackmail'. The difference between the two administrations is one of conviction. The Clinton administration truly believed that multilateral arms control played an important part in dealing with proliferation threats, but was deeply conflicted about the wisdom of missile defence. In contrast, the Bush administration is deeply committed to the need for missile defence, but dubious about the real value of multilateral arms control.

Bin Laden kills the ABM Treaty

Although most Bush arms-control experts preferred outright withdrawal from the ABM Treaty, the administration realised that it could better limit opposition to missile defence if it first made (or at least appeared to make) a serious effort to negotiate an agreement with Russia to amend the ABM Treaty. For their part, the Russians signalled that they were anxious to reach an agreement to relax constraints in the ABM Treaty on missile defence testing and limited deployments, in exchange for preserving some limits on the US missile defence programme. Whether the administration was actually prepared to strike a deal with Russia or was just going through the motions before withdrawing from the ABM Treaty was unclear. The events of 11 September settled the issue. The attacks dramatically increased the American public's sense of vulnerability and completely undercut efforts by Senate Democrats to challenge the administration's desire to withdraw from the ABM Treaty. For the average American, it didn't matter that the attack came in the form of civilian airliners rather than ballistic missiles. All defences had to be strengthened against these irrational enemies, who appeared willing to do anything to attack America. As a result, domestic opposition to the administration's approach on missile defence, especially Senate Democrat opposition to withdrawal from the ABM Treaty, was virtually mute.

Internationally, Russian President Vladimir Putin's strategic decision to side with Washington in the campaign against global terrorism gave the US more confidence that it could walk away from the ABM Treaty without damaging other aspects of the US–Russian relationship, including an agreement on reducing offensive strategic weapons, which candidate Bush had announced as an important objective. This calculation proved correct.

Even though an agreement with Moscow to amend the ABM Treaty appeared achievable, Washington decided to exercise its preference to kill the ABM Treaty, announcing in December 2001 its intention to withdraw. Russia's reaction was decidedly mild. Rather than provoking a new arms race between the US and Russia, presidents Bush and Putin seem on track to announce a new agreement during their summit in Russia on 23–26 May 2002 to reduce deployed strategic weapons to between 1,700 and 2,200. In a concession to Russia, the agreement will take the form of a legally binding document (though probably not a treaty), although Washington is determined to resist any Russian pressure to impose legally binding limits on the US missile defence programme or any requirement to destroy warheads and delivery vehicles retired from the 'deployed' strategic forces. Moscow, anxious to demonstrate that its new partnership with Washington is producing concrete results, is likely to concede on the main issues, although there will probably be face-saving formulations in the form of political declarations.

Beijing, seeking to improve ties with Washington (after the EP-3E spy-plane incident in April 2001) and line up for the counter-terrorism campaign, also chose not to pick a public fight over the US decision to withdraw from the ABM Treaty, especially after Washington declared that its proposed missile defence programme was not directed against China. In private, Chinese officials had no faith in US assurances, but seemed confident that they could take the necessary measures to preserve their strategic deterrent in the context of China's ongoing nuclear modernisation programme, while avoiding any appearance of a nuclear arms race with the US. As opposition from Moscow and Beijing to missile defence withered, those in Europe who opposed missile defence held their tongues.

The Nuclear Posture Review: old nukes in new bottles?

The leak of the Bush administration's Nuclear Posture Review (NPR) in March was greeted with protest and criticism that the US was lowering the nuclear threshold and increasing the risk of further proliferation. In fact, much of the NPR was not new. The contingency of using nuclear weapons against countries that used CBW against the US was established during the Clinton administration, although the 2001 NPR may mark the first time that the Department of Defense has made the political mistake of listing the countries in writing and sending it to Congress.

Some elements of the NPR, however, are new and represent another indication of the Bush administration's emphasis on defence and deterrence in responding to proliferation threats. In particular, the NPR proposes to study the development of a new generation of specialised low-yield nuclear weapons to destroy hardened underground WMD facilities. In the view of the Bush administration, such weapons would strengthen deterrence by making use of nuclear weapons more credible. At the same time, development of such weapons will eventually increase pressure for the US to resume nuclear testing, which is advocated by some Bush officials.

Homeland defence to the rescue

The 11 September attacks shocked the American public, but experts inside and outside government have long been concerned about the increasing threat of mass-casualty terrorism from non-state actors. The main worry of the expert community, however, was terrorist use of weapons of mass destruction – especially biological weapons – not civilian airliners crashing into buildings. Nevertheless, the 11 September attacks reinforced America's sense of vulnerability to terrorist WMD attacks, and this fear was reinforced by the subsequent anthrax attacks through the US postal system. In addition, as al-Qaeda facilities were overrun in Afghanistan, further details emerged of al-Qaeda's quest for biological, chemical and nuclear weapons, although – as far as can be determined from publicly available information – these efforts were unsuccessful. In particular, al-Qaeda's attempts to acquire nuclear materials or weapons seemed amateurish, and it apparently fell prey to con men and scam artists purporting to sell nuclear materials on the black market. Biological and chemical weapons seemed a more plausible threat, although the lethality of these weapons would vary greatly depending on the particular agent and delivery system used.

In the wake of these developments, Washington mounted more intense efforts to deal with the threat of WMD terrorism. Clearly, sufficient intelligence to enable preventive actions was the best antidote, but, as 11 September and the anthrax scare illustrated, it was very difficult for intelligence and enforcement agencies to obtain advance information about attacks that terrorist groups or individuals planned to conduct. Moreover, traditional deterrence was not an effective defence against groups that sought to conceal the origin of their attacks and were motivated by messianic beliefs. Accordingly, Washington placed great emphasis on bolstering 'homeland defence', which included efforts to detect and intercept potential terrorist attacks and manage the consequences of such attacks if they took place. To implement this policy, President Bush appointed former Governor Tom Ridge to head a new Office of Homeland Defense in the White House to coordinate US government efforts, and sought nearly $40 billion in additional spending to bolster homeland defence against terrorism. As of April, it is too early to judge the effectiveness of these efforts.

Making multilateral arms control useful

The eleventh of September did not fundamentally alter the Bush team's basic scepticism about the usefulness of multilateral arms control in dealing with 'real' proliferation threats: countries like Iraq, Iran and North Korea that are prepared to violate their treaty commitments. In some respects, the strong alliance solidarity against terrorism made it easier for Washington to follow its natural instincts on multilateral arms-control issues because other countries wanted to minimise public disagreements while working together against the common enemy of global terrorism. At the contentious BWC Review Conference in Geneva in November 2001, for example, many US allies were furious at Washington for making last-minute demands that scuttled the meeting, but there was little official outcry because most capitals did not want to distract attention from the counter-terrorism front.

At the same time, however, the administration has begun to look for new ways to employ multilateral regimes against both the 'old' proliferation threat of rogue regimes and the 'new' proliferation threat of terrorists armed with WMD. In part, this was driven by the tactical need to deflect criticism against the US for opposing multilateral arms-control efforts, such as the BWC protocol. But it also reflected a genuine interest in Washington to mobilise all means available (even weak ones) in the campaign against terrorism.

At the BWC Review Conference, for example, US officials began to identify compliance with treaty commitments (a traditional American issue) as the most important element of multilateral arms control, even publicly identifying five countries that it suspects of violating the BWC. Having focused on compliance as the critical issue for the BWC, but rejected the protocol that was intended (however imperfectly) to plug this gap, Washington proposed a number of alternative measures to strengthen compliance. Unfortunately, most of these measures were even weaker than the protocol itself, and in any event, the sour collapse of the conference prevented agreement on any way forward. With the BWC Review Conference scheduled to 'resume' in November 2002, a critical issue is whether Washington and its allies can put aside their bitter disagreement over the enforcement protocol and reach agreement to work on a new menu of alternative multilateral measures. Even if these measures are not adopted by the conference, it would demonstrate that Washington is trying to find ways to strengthen the BWC in place of the protocol.

In the CWC context, the Bush administration finds itself locked in a messy battle to remove the Director General of the OPCW, José Bustani, for fiscal mismanagement of the organisation. Washington's unhappiness with Bustani began during the Clinton administration, but reached breaking point in December 2001, when Bustani, in a report to the UN General Assembly, sought to blame the organisation's financial crisis on late contributions from member-states, including the US. The US campaign to replace Bustani is supported by the Western group, who are also fed up with him, but Bustani refuses to go quietly, and has the support of Russia and many non-aligned countries. Assuming Bustani is eventually forced to resign, it will give the US and its supporters an opportunity to increase financial contributions to the OPCW and strengthen management. Once order is restored, the administration – in keeping with its emphasis on compliance – will need to decide whether to begin using the 'challenge inspection' provisions of the CWC against suspected violators, such as Iran. (During the Clinton administration, the US publicly accused Iran of violating the CWC, but the US has never asked the OPCW for a challenge inspection of suspect chemical weapons stocks or production facilities.)

In contrast to the BWC and CWC, the Bush administration has no major difficulties with the nuclear regime. IAEA Director-General Mohammad El-Baradei is highly thought of in Washington, and the administration plans to provide increased financial and technical support to the Agency, which will be critical in addressing nuclear proliferation concerns in Iraq, Iran and North Korea. Perhaps alone among international arms-control agreements, the US–IAEA enhanced safeguards protocol (negotiated during the Clinton administration) will probably be submitted to the Senate for ratification. Reflecting new fears that terrorists are seeking to acquire materials for nuclear or radiological weapons, the US is also supporting efforts to strengthen the

Convention on the Physical Protection of Nuclear Materials. The administration is even prepared to give the IAEA more authority to enforce the Convention. Ironically, some European countries resist this 'multilateral' approach for fear it will arouse public opposition to nuclear energy.

Finally, the administration appears to have the solid game plan and good working relations with the key countries and multilateral groups needed to manage the NPT review process, which gets under way with a preparatory meeting in New York in April and continues with annual meetings until the Review Conference in 2005. As at the 2000 Review Conference, the US is likely to emphasise the importance of compliance (both North Korea and Iraq have violated the NPT) and stress the need to strengthen IAEA safeguards and (in light of 11 September) protection of nuclear material. Although the US will come in for some criticism from the disarmament crowd for its Nuclear Posture Review and rejection of the CTBT, as of April 2002, there appeared to be little appetite for a major blow-up.

On balance, the multilateral arms-control landscape does not make a pretty picture. The CTBT is dead for now. FMCT negotiations are blocked. The BWC protocol negotiations are finished. The OPCW is in crisis. Only the nuclear regime (the NPT and IAEA) appears to be functioning well. With the US opting out of many efforts, supporters of multilateral arms control will need to decide whether to hunker down and wait for a new American administration with different views or seek to continue multilateral arms-control efforts without US participation or support.

New support for Cooperative Threat Reduction

Coming into office, several key Bush officials had a lukewarm attitude towards cooperative threat reduction (CTR) programmes with Russia. These programmes – to assist Russia in destroying strategic weapons, secure and dispose of fissile material and chemical weapons and help find alternative employment for Russian weapons scientists – were initiated under the administration of George H. W. Bush and substantially expanded under Clinton. Although CTR programmes had substantial bipartisan support in Congress (not least because they provided government funding to important constituencies), there was vocal opposition among some Republican members. For these critics, CTR programmes were viewed as inefficient and wasteful, and, even worse, potentially subsidising Russia's military. Moreover, some criticised extending 'aid programmes' to Russia while Moscow was at the same time selling sensitive military equipment and hardware to countries such as Iran.

After taking office, the Bush administration began a comprehensive review of these CTR programmes. The intention was clearly to look for ways to cut rather than expand them. Before 11 September, it appeared that many programmes would be sustained at current or slightly lower levels of funding, while a few big-ticket items, such as plutonium disposition (which was closely identified with President Clinton), were slated for restructuring or total elimination. After 11 September, however, the administration did an about-face. The new alliance with Moscow against terrorism removed many of the political objections to providing assistance to Russia. Even more important, Washington's concern that al-Qaeda was seeking WMD for use against the US prompted the administration to make even greater efforts to prevent leakage of materials or expertise from Russia, which remained the most likely source from which terrorists might obtain such assistance. The president's fears in this regard were reportedly heightened by an intelligence report in November 2001 – later judged to be inaccurate – that al-Qaeda had managed to obtain a tactical nuclear weapon from Russia and was shipping it to New York City.

Congress had made the connection between 11 September and CTR before the administration. In December 2001, it voted to increase funding for CTR programmes by $120 million in its fiscal year (FY) 2002 emergency supplemental budget, over the administration's objections. By early 2002, however, the Bush administration overcame its initial reservations. Completing its policy review, it decided to proceed with existing programmes, including plutonium disposition, and is seeking $1.04bn for CTR programmes in its FY2003 budget request, which is 37% higher than the previous year's appropriation. In addition, having long complained that European partners could be more generous on CTR, Washington is seeking larger European contributions.

At the same time, the Bush administration has turned its attention to the perennial problem of Russian nuclear and missile assistance to Iran. The Clinton administration invested tremendous energy to stem this flow of technology, but with only mixed results. The Russian government proclaimed that it opposed any assistance to Iran's ballistic missile programme. It promised not to provide sensitive nuclear technology and even established comprehensive export control laws and regulation, although implementation was sporadic and incomplete. Whether by choice or inefficiency, Moscow did not mount a sustained effort to stop the sale of sensitive technology to Iran by companies and individuals. Moreover, by the end of the Clinton administration, Moscow had openly renounced earlier pledges to limit the sale of conventional arms and nuclear power reactors to Iran.

The incoming Bush administration also opposed these Russian transfers to Iran, but the administration was slow in coming up with a plan to deal with the threat and, in any event, Washington's initial agenda with Moscow was dominated by strategic issues and later, after 11 September, cooperation in the campaign against global terrorism. Washington is now pressing Moscow to cease all missile and nuclear assistance to Iran, and threatening to impose sanctions against any Russian entities that provide such assistance. In theory, the good personal relationship that has developed between presidents Bush and Putin, and improved overall relations between the US and Russia post-11 September, point to favourable conditions for tackling this problem, but it remains to be seen whether the administration can produce concrete results.

Fresh start in South Asia

The 11 September attacks provided the US with new opportunities in South Asia. For the Clinton administration (like earlier administrations), South Asia presented a nearly hopeless proliferation quandary. After the 1998 nuclear tests by India and Pakistan, the US imposed legally mandated economic sanctions against New Delhi and Islamabad, marshalled strong international pressure against the two nuclear powers and engaged in lengthy negotiations to cap, if not roll back, their nuclear and missile programmes. By the end of the Clinton administration, it was clear that these efforts had largely failed. Although India and Pakistan were observing a moratorium on additional nuclear tests, New Delhi seemed determined to develop a 'minimum nuclear deterrent' against China, and Pakistan was equally determined to maintain its own nuclear deterrent against India. With the 1999 Kargil incident, Washington's attention shifted from non-proliferation to preventing a war between India and Pakistan that could quickly escalate to nuclear use. As a result, most in Washington agreed that economic sanctions had outlived their usefulness.

For the incoming Bush team, the primary focus of South Asia policy was improving relations with India, which some saw as a potential counterweight to China. Pakistan, with its missile deals with North Korea and efforts to sell missiles to the Middle East, was seen as a quasi-'rogue state'. The administration quickly decided to lift nuclear sanctions against India – and perhaps Pakistan – but was debating the best way to remove sanctions without appearing to abandon its non-proliferation policy. The eleventh of September dramatically changed the South Asian strategic landscape. Facing a critical decision, President Musharraf of Pakistan responded to American pressure and blandishments and decided to back the US and abandon the Taliban if it refused to give up Osama bin Laden. Though disappointed by the resurrection of good relations between Islamabad and Washington, India also saw opportunities in the counter-terrorism campaign to pressure Pakistan (with American help) to end support for the Kashmiri jihadists and thus end the rebellion in Kashmir. In the wake of these developments, Washington was able to lift most of the nuclear sanctions against India and Pakistan without protest from the non-proliferation community.

Immediately after 11 September, US non-proliferation policy in South Asia focused on more immediate concerns, including the security of Pakistan's nuclear forces and contacts between Pakistani nuclear scientists and al-Qaeda. Although these specific concerns have abated, the possibility that individual Pakistani scientists might attempt to sell sensitive nuclear technology to willing buyers remains a serious risk. More broadly, Washington continues to espouse nuclear and missile 'restraint' for India and Pakistan, but there seems little chance that India and Pakistan will stop producing more nuclear material and weapons or developing longer-range missile-delivery systems. Instead, the primary focus of US efforts is on convincing New Delhi and Islamabad not to deploy 'operational' nuclear weapons, which could increase the risk of escalation in a crisis. This concern for crisis stability became especially acute in late 2001, when India and Pakistan were once again at loggerheads over Kashmir following a December 2001 terrorist attack on the Indian parliament. Mobilising forces along the line of control in Kashmir and the border with Pakistan, India proclaimed that Pakistan's nuclear forces would not stop it from attacking unless Pakistan handed over suspected terrorists and ceased support for Kashmiri militants. The tension was temporarily defused by US and UK diplomatic efforts and a dramatic speech by President Musharraf in January vowing to end all support for terrorism from Pakistani territory. As of April 2002, however, the risk of conflict remains high. Under domestic political pressure, New Delhi may launch a limited attack across the line of control if, in spring 2001, it finds that infiltration of terrorists from Pakistan into Kashmir has continued.

Dealing with rogues: containment and regime-change

On the non-proliferation front, the most important effect of 11 September and the subsequent campaign against global terrorism has been on the issue of dealing with 'rogue states' pursuing WMD. Here, too, there is both continuity and change. Under President Clinton, the US identified Iraq, Iran and North Korea as the most dangerous proliferation threats to US interests. Senior officials expended more time and energy dealing with the so-called 'hard cases' than with any other aspects of non-proliferation policy. The Clinton administration's approach, however, was tactically very different from that of the Bush administration. After the Gulf War, the US sought to deal with Iraq's WMD threat through a combination of intrusive UN inspections backed by the threat of military force, attacks against suspect WMD-related facilities when inspections failed in December 1998 and covert attempts to mount a coup against Saddam Hussein. Beneath the official policy of containment, Washington's real objective was to change the regime, which was seen as the best chance to remove Iraq's WMD threat, although the US did not, under prevailing political conditions, have the means to achieve this objective.

Towards Iran, Washington sought a diplomatic opening to negotiate WMD issues, especially after the election of ostensibly reformist President Mohammed Khatami in 1997, and encouraged its European allies to press Tehran to comply with its obligations under the NPT, CWC and BWC and limit its ballistic missile programme. In the meantime, the US made strenuous efforts (with mixed results) to delay Iran's WMD progress by cutting off the supply of sensitive technology and materials from countries such as Russia, China and North Korea. By the end of the Clinton administration, however, many experts were increasingly doubtful that the so-called 'moderates' in Tehran were willing or able to reverse Iran's long-term efforts to acquire nuclear weapons.

To deal with North Korea, the US pursued a diplomatic strategy. It wielded carrots and sticks to achieve the 1994 Agreed Framework to freeze North Korean plutonium production and the 1999 moratorium on long-range missile tests, and sought to negotiate a broader deal to end North Korean missile exports and limit its indigenous missile programme. In essence, Washington's strategy was to contain and limit the North Korean threat through a combination of military deterrence and diplomatic and economic inducements (principally, the construction of two light-water nuclear reactors and the provision of fuel oil pending their completion), while anticipating that the North Korean regime would eventually evolve or (more likely) collapse from within.

Coming into office, the Bush administration was highly critical of the Clinton administration's efforts to deal with these rogue states. The nuclear deal with North Korea, for example, was attacked as 'rewarding' proliferation and helping to prop up a dangerous regime by submitting to 'blackmail'. Moreover, critics argued, the strategy was bound to fail because the North Korean regime could never be trusted to abandon its WMD programmes completely. Clinton's policy towards Iraq was sharply attacked both from the left (who argued that the administration had needlessly sacrificed UNSCOM inspections) and from the right (who argued that the administration had denied assistance to the Iraqi National Congress and missed a chance to overthrow Saddam). Despite general agreement in the Bush administration that proliferation to and by 'rogue states' was America's greatest security threat, there were different views on how to deal with specific cases. On North Korea, some officials favoured a continuation of the Clinton negotiations to limit North Korea's nuclear and missile programme, while others felt strongly that such deals were ineffective and even immoral. After a policy review, the administration announced a compromise in June 2001. It decided to continue to fund the existing agreements and send humanitarian assistance to the North, but toughened its position for further negotiations. The North, however, refused to resume talks on these terms.

The most substantial internal policy debate, however, focused on Iraq. Officials agreed that the most effective way to remove Iraq's WMD threat was to remove Saddam Hussein and replace him with a government in Baghdad prepared to honour Iraq's international treaty commitments and UN Security Council resolutions requiring Iraq to disclose and abandon its various WMD programmes. They disagreed, however, on the urgency of achieving this result and whether it was attainable without a massive commitment of US forces. Some Bush officials believed that more than a decade of containment had substantially weakened Saddam's conventional and WMD capabilities and argued for more effective containment through smart sanctions and the return of UN inspectors. Other officials argued that containment had failed. Saddam had clearly not abandoned his ambitions to acquire WMD and dominate the region. The sanctions were porous and the inspectors had been kicked out. From this perspective, it was critical to remove Saddam immediately, before he could reconstitute enough of his WMD capabilities to preclude US options. To overthrow Saddam, Washington needed to throw its support behind the Iraqi opposition – including military backing.

The events of 11 September and the subsequent war in Afghanistan significantly altered the terms of the debate in three ways. First, they created a grave sense of peril in Washington that terrorists might obtain WMD with the assistance of hostile states, such as Iraq. There were unsettling hints of contacts between Iraqi officials and al-Qaeda operatives, and widespread speculation (doubtful in hindsight) that Iraq had a hand in the subsequent anthrax scare. The 11 September attacks drove home the saliency of the threat of mass-casualty terrorism. Documents obtained in al-Qaeda hideouts in Afghanistan provided vivid details that al-Qaeda was seeking nuclear, chemical and biological weapons. Upon analysis, it seemed that al-Qaeda's efforts to obtain WMD were largely unsuccessful, but that assessment was construed as merely emphasising the point that terrorists were most likely to obtain WMD through state assistance. Moreover, if rogue dictators are hard to deter, fanatical terrorists are even worse. As 11 September demonstrated, terrorist groups like al-Qaeda would use any weapon they could get their hands on.

Second, the shock of 11 September created much stronger public willingness in the United States to use military force to eliminate America's enemies. The reaction was comparable to that following the Japanese attack on Pearl Harbor. In dealing with Saddam, Clinton did not have public support for the option of large-scale military action to remove him. Thanks to bin Laden, President Bush does. Third, the relatively easy victory over the Taliban regime strengthened the case for those advocating a similar approach to overthrow Saddam Hussein. There are, of course, many differences between Afghanistan and Iraq, such as the lack of an Iraqi equivalent to the Northern Alliance, much stronger Iraqi military capabilities and greater resistance from frontline Middle Eastern and Gulf states to serve as bases for US military operations. Nonetheless, the Afghanistan campaign demonstrated that unpopular dictatorial regimes could crack with relatively little force; some speculated that perhaps even a strong show of force would be enough to trigger a coup against Saddam.

The US effort to extend the war against global terrorism to 'rogue regimes', however, got off to a rocky start with President Bush's 'axis of evil' State of the Union message on 29 January 2002. The president tried to draw a connection between three countries pursuing WMD (Iraq, Iran and North Korea) and the threat that these countries would provide WMD to terrorist groups willing to use such weapons against the United States. As many critics pointed out, Iraq, Iran and North Korea do not constitute an 'axis' or alliance in any meaningful sense. Moreover, the extent to which these three governments actually support terrorism varies widely and there is no hard evidence that they have provided WMD to terrorists. In particular, most observers doubt that Baghdad was behind the 11 September attacks or the subsequent anthrax scare.

Finally – and most importantly – many realised that the 'axis of evil' formulation threatened to distract attention from and complicate the immediate objective of toppling Saddam. The Europeans, who had rallied to America's side after 11 September, were shocked and confused by what they saw as an unjustified expansion of the war against terrorism. It appeared to many European allies that success in Afghanistan had gone to Washington's head, and the US was threatening to embark on extremely risky military adventures. Tehran, which might be quietly supportive of an American move to remove Saddam, was suddenly alarmed that Iran was next on the 'axis of evil' hit list after Iraq. After the president's speech, administration officials clarified that the US was still prepared to begin dialogue with North Korea and hoped that reformist forces in Iran would produce a more moderate government. Iraq, they made clear, was the only case where the US is contemplating military force to change the regime.

Iraq: ousting Saddam Hussein

As of early April 2002, the administration was making a systematic effort to lay the groundwork for an attack on Iraq, especially were it to continue to refuse to cooperate with UN inspectors and comply with UN Security Council resolutions to disclose and disarm its WMD programmes. In the face of this threat, Baghdad had begun to hint that it would allow the resumption of UNMOVIC inspections, now headed by Hans Blix, a former director of the IAEA. Most observers believed that if the UNMOVIC inspectors were truly allowed complete access (as required under the various UNSC resolutions), it would substantially limit (although not totally eliminate) Iraq's ability to pursue WMD programmes. Even with the best inspections, it would not be possible to confidently account for every drop of BW or CW agent or every avenue of secret nuclear research, but robust inspections would make it very difficult for Iraq to conduct large-scale production of CBW, nuclear materials or ballistic missiles without timely detection.

Other observers, however, contended that the value of even the most intrusive inspections in Iraq would be minimal. After more than a decade of playing cat-and-mouse, they argued, Saddam has perfected techniques for defeating UN inspections. According to some press reports, for example, Iraq's biological weapons programme has taken to the road, using mobile labs for research and production. In contrast, UNMOVIC was untested. Even under the best estimates, it would take months before Blix and his new team of inspectors would be operational and even longer (perhaps as much as a year) before Blix could report to the UN Security Council whether Iraq had provided sufficient cooperation to suspend sanctions, as called for in Security Council Resolution 1284. Indeed, hawks in Washington feared that Saddam would slip the noose by accepting the return of UN inspectors. As long as Iraq appeared to be cooperating with inspections, it would be extremely difficult for the US to justify a military attack, although efforts to increase support for the Iraqi opposition could continue. Even worse, in this view, Saddam might allow sufficient cooperation to create pressure in the Security Council to suspend sanctions, in which case he would be in an even stronger position to secretly revive his WMD capabilities.

It is more likely, however, that Iraq will continue to reject inspections or tactically play along with UNMOVIC inspections to buy time and try to defuse the US military threat, before eventually returning to its past pattern of 'cheat and retreat'. In that case, the US will have a clear *casus belli*. Outside the region, few countries will have much sympathy if Saddam ignores all warnings and continues to violate Security Council resolutions. A key issue for Washington is whether to seek a last Security Council ultimatum demanding that Iraq allow inspections and comply with the Security Council's disarmament requirements. On one hand, such a resolution would give the US a legal basis for building a political coalition to support US actions, and blunt criticism that the US is acting arbitrarily. On the other hand, Washington does not want to concede the principle that it needs another resolution and, more practically, is uncertain whether it can make a deal with Moscow, Paris and Beijing to support such a resolution, given that they have significant economic interests in Iraq. All three, however, have hinted that they are willing to abandon Saddam if they receive adequate assurances that the new Iraqi government will respect those interests.

The situation inside the region is more complex. As Vice-President Cheney learned on his March 2002 tour of the Middle East, the US must address the profound fear in the region that a war against Iraq in the absence of an Israeli–Palestinian peace process will be destabilising to many Arab regimes. This gives Washington a very strong incentive at least to limit the violence in Palestine and Israel, and the best way to limit violence is to resume peace negotiations. In addition, the US will need to present a convincing case that it has a credible plan (and political commitment) to preserve Iraqi territorial integrity, help the Iraqi people and establish a stable government after Saddam is overthrown. Many governments are looking at US actions in Afghanistan as a test of whether the US has such a commitment. Finally, and perhaps most difficult, Washington cannot prosecute a war unless it strikes deals with key frontline states like Turkey, Kuwait, Saudi Arabia and the Gulf states. Unless these governments are willing to make bases available to the US, any military campaign would be difficult, if not impossible, to prosecute effectively.

If the US does attack Iraq with the intent of overthrowing the regime, the risk that Saddam will use WMD appears high. Unlike the Gulf War, when US war aims were limited and Saddam was deterred by threats of massive retaliation, Saddam would presumably have nothing to lose by threatening or using whatever WMD capability he has left as a last resort to deter or disrupt an attack. Although much is unknown, Iraq's capabilities appear to be much less now than they were at the time of the Gulf War. As far as is known, Iraq's nuclear weapons programme was shattered by the Gulf War and subsequent inspections, although Iraq retains its nuclear teams and expertise. Even without further disruptions, it would probably take years for Iraq to produce nuclear weapons. Similarly, Iraq's ballistic missile programme has been seriously degraded, although Baghdad may retain a few operational *Scud* missiles that could be launched with CBW warheads. In fact, CBW are the greatest threat. In addition to the CBW capabilities that Iraq was able to salvage from UNSCOM inspectors, Baghdad has rebuilt dual-use facilities destroyed in the 1998 *Operation Desert Fox* strikes and presumably has been able to replenish some chemical and biological stocks over the past three years.

Iran: Is proliferation inevitable?

Although Iraq is clearly the first priority, the outcome there could have a direct impact on efforts to convince Tehran to end or limit its WMD programmes. Unlike Iraq, Iran has not yet demonstrably violated its treaty commitments, although it appears to be pursuing (at a minimum) a 'break out' strategy for NBC weapons. In its nuclear programme, for example, Tehran faces a choice between continuing to develop its nuclear infrastructure and capacity to produce fissile material under IAEA safeguards or proceeding with a nuclear weapons programme in violation of its NPT commitments. There appears to be some internal debate within Tehran on these issues. The dominant view apparently sees real or potential enemies – Iraq, Israel and the United States – that support the need for acquiring WMD. Others, however, see the danger of proceeding with programmes that would attract international pressure and even military attack.

Arguably, a successful outcome in Iraq – whether real disarmament under UN inspections or replacement of Saddam with a government prepared to comply with Iraq's treaty commitments – might help tip the balance in favour of those in Tehran arguing for restraint. In principle, elimination of the Iraqi WMD threat could reduce one of the key Iranian motivations for acquiring WMD and set an example for avoiding actions that would make Iran a target of international pressure. At the same time, if Tehran feared that the US was intent on forcing regime change in Iran, it might strengthen those arguing that only nuclear weapons and long-range missiles could deter American pressure. In practice, much will depend on the outcome of Iran's complex internal political struggle. In meantime, as this struggle plays out, it is clearly critical to delay Iran's acquisition of sensitive technologies, especially nuclear and missile technology from Russia.

North Korea: malign neglect

North Korea is a fundamentally different case from Iraq because US options to use military force or even overthrow the regime are much more constrained. Unlike Iraq, North Korea has formidable conventional forces, robust (if primitive) ballistic missile capabilities and possibly one or two nuclear weapons. Moreover, US allies in East Asia strongly oppose the use of force or even efforts to 'strangle' North Korea by cutting off its vital outside assistance. Seoul, in particular, was alarmed by the inclusion of North Korea in the 'axis of evil', and Pyongyang, predictably, responded with harsh rhetoric of its own against the Bush administration.

After the president's 'axis of evil' speech, however, senior US officials stressed that the US was still ready for dialogue with Pyongyang, and President Bush praised Kim Dae Jung's sunshine policies during his subsequent trip to Asia. As of early April 2002, however, the Bush administration appeared to be basically content with the status quo. It was getting all the benefits of the freeze on plutonium production and missile tests without the unpleasantness of actually negotiating with Pyongyang. As a result, Washington has continued to provide funds to the Korean Peninsula Energy Development Organization (KEDO), even though the US decided in March 2002 (for the first time) not to certify that North Korea was complying with the Agreed Framework. Administration officials explained that Washington did not believe the North had violated the Agreed Framework, but wanted to send a strong signal to Pyongyang that it should begin cooperating with the IAEA to account for undeclared plutonium.

In late March 2002, Pyongyang decided to launch an effort to break the diplomatic stalemate it had largely created. Resuming North–South talks,

North Korea invited South Korean Senior Advisor Lim Dong Won to Pyongyong to discuss a range of North–South agreements that might be pursued in the waning months of Kim Dae Jung's presidency. In addition, Pyongyang accepted Washington's long-standing offer to resume bilateral discussions, although North Korea remains suspicious of the Bush administration's intentions and wary of its tougher negotiating position. The pressing question is whether talks between Washington and Pyongyang resume and bear fruit or the North, following a familiar pattern, provokes a crisis to force the US to pay attention. While 2002 could be stable as North Korea awaits the outcome of South Korean elections, 2003 could be the year of living dangerously. The North has already declared that its missile-test moratorium is up for renewal in 2003 and signalled that it wants 'compensation' for delays in the replacement nuclear energy project, which was targeted for completion in 2003. At the same time, the North remains heavily dependent on foreign assistance to survive, and knows that it would risk a cut-off if it provokes a crisis – especially given China's obvious preference for peace and quiet on its border.

Washington also faces a dilemma. On one hand, it has no realistic option to destroy the North Korean regime without risking an extremely destructive war on the Korean Peninsula. On the other hand, many in the Bush administration are viscerally opposed to diplomatic engagement with the North, and their opposition has hardened in line with the tougher attitude towards 'rogue regimes' post-11 September. For now, the administration seems content to treat North Korea with malign neglect, perhaps hoping that the regime will collapse by itself before Washington needs to make any hard choices.

A crystallised but still untested non-proliferation policy

The 11 September terrorist attacks have clarified and strengthened US non-proliferation policy in several key ways. First, they reinforced the Bush administration's predilection to emphasise defence and deterrence as the most important elements of its non-proliferation policy. Second, while not changing the administration's basic scepticism about the value of multilateral regimes, the attacks have animated a search for a more positive agenda, including the need for measures to deal with WMD terrorist threats and stronger compliance measures. Third, the administration has been persuaded of the value of CTR programmes. Finally, and most importantly, the conditions have been created for a more assertive policy to deal with rogue states, especially Iraq. Whether such a policy is sustainable hinges critically upon how US plans for regime change in Baghdad play out.

US Homeland Security: New Focus on Vulnerability

The 11 September attacks have prompted a drastic shift in the United States' conception of national security. For the first time since 1814, the American heartland was attacked. The vulnerability of its people, transportation networks and economic lifelines was exposed. No longer were oceans a buffer against attack, and no longer was military superiority sufficient to deter it. In addition to maintaining the capacity to respond to identifiable threats, preferably before they are carried out, the United States must now minimise vulnerabilities to ill-defined threats.

Reflecting this new priority, in his State of the Union address on 29 January 2002, President George W. Bush stated that the United States' 'first priority' was 'the security of our nation', and announced that the new budget would 'protect our homeland' in addition to winning the war on terrorism and reviving the economy. A week earlier, Bush proposed, in his fiscal year (FY) 2003 budget, $37.7 billion for homeland security – nearly double the FY2002 allocation of $19.5bn for domestic security.

Military power

In what former Secretary of Defense William Cohen called the 'superpower paradox', overwhelming US military superiority appeared only to ensure that attackers would practise asymmetric warfare to neutralise it. While the military campaign in Afghanistan is an important element of the US-led counter-terrorism campaign, and like operations can preempt terrorism if American intelligence has clues about pending attempts that may originate from overseas, military power has only limited relevance to homeland defence. There are, however, three special areas in which military power will affect homeland security.

First, and most importantly, the 11 September attacks highlighted the importance of air supremacy in US airspace. After 43 years of defending against external aerospace threats to North American air sovereignty, on 11 September the mission of North American Air Defense Command (NORAD) – originally created to provide early warning of airborne nuclear attacks – expanded to include defence against a domestic airborne threat under *Operation Noble Eagle*.

According to NORAD's chronology, within six minutes of Federal Aviation Administration (FAA) notification of the first hijacking – just as the first airliner was reaching the south tower of the World Trade Center in lower Manhattan – two Air National Guard F-15 *Eagle* air defence interceptors out of Otis Air National Guard Base in Falmouth, Massachusetts, received their scramble order. These two F-15s were about 100km from Manhattan – about eight minutes' flying time – when the second airliner struck the north tower. Twelve minutes after NORAD's notification by civilian air-traffic controllers at Reagan National Airport of a third airliner's hijacking, the Pentagon was struck. Two Air Force F-16 *Fighting Falcons* based at Langley AFB in Hampton, Virginia, were airborne at 9:35 a.m., within six minutes of notification from the FAA that American Flight 77 had been hijacked. They were approximately 160km (12 minutes' flying time) from the Pentagon when it was hit. These F-16s were in position over Washington when they were redirected to intercept United Flight 93, and were about 160km from the airliner en route to intercept it when the airliner crashed in western Pennsylvania; thereafter they were redirected to fly combat air patrols over Washington DC. Air National Guard fighter jets from the District of Columbia, Oregon, and Ohio were subsequently scrambled for various air missions over US air space, while F-16 fighters from Texas and the District of Columbia escorted Air Force One on 11 September when the president returned to Washington from Florida. The president authorised military aircraft that morning to intercept and shoot down hijacked airliners that did not respond to signals, and more than 100 aircraft from 26 bases were soon on alert, with fighter aircraft reportedly flying combat air patrols over some 30 US cities.

After this initial response had been implemented, the Defense Department moved swiftly to transform NORAD into an interoperable, interagency force consisting of active military and National Guard units, US and Canadian military aircraft and US Navy ships, with streamlined rules of engagement for hostile acts over domestic airspace. Its standing alert posture increased from 20 fighters at seven bases to over 100 aircraft at 26 (and later, 30) bases, and operational tempo was raised significantly. Whereas Air National Guard fighters were conducting about 80% of the air-patrol missions, active Air Combat Command tactical aircraft were also involved in establishing orbits in case other hijacked aircraft showed up in the FAA system. Also deployed were Atlantic fleet ships operating in support of NORAD. Aircraft carriers – including the USS *George Washington*, which was off New York – and guided missile destroyers were moved into the waters near New York and Washington to support the air-defence mission. The 26th Marine Expeditionary Unit was placed on alert, and the civil support unit of the Joint Task Force, based in Fort Monroe, Virginia, was marshalled and an assessment team dispatched to New York City. Following NATO's 12 September invocation of Article 5 of the North Atlantic Treaty, five NATO Airborne Early Warning aircraft were seconded to the US to assist in the aerospace warning and control mission. Continuous combat air patrols were conducted over Washington DC and New York, while random patrols were conducted over other metropolitan areas and key infrastructure, and in support of presidential travel and other significant public events such as the Winter Olympics; command-and-control, airborne early warning and tanker aircraft also were surged to support the 24-hour-a-day operations.

During the year prior to 11 September, Air Force fighters had scrambled only seven times in US airspace, in some cases only for exercises. In the three months from 11 September to 10 December, an estimated 13,000 missions had been flown, with NORAD jets responding 207 times to unidentified aircraft, planes violating restricted air space and in-flight emergencies. In 92 of these cases, jets on alert on the ground were scrambled to respond, while in the other 115 cases, NORAD diverted jets that already were in the air flying combat air patrols. By this time, the operation involved 250 aircraft and 11,000 people, including maintenance crews, pilots for 100 F-15 and F-16 fighter jets, AWACS and tanker crews, and the number of bases on alert had grown from 26 to 30. National Guard units that once flew five or six sorties a month were flying more than 100. The total cost for the first three months of operations was estimated at about $324 million, and the projected cost for FY2003 was $1.2bn.

Under NORAD's new remit, rules of engagement for interdicting hijacked commercial airliners were streamlined, giving regional commanders the authority to approve shoot-downs if time did not permit the president or other senior leaders to be contacted. Portable air control radars also were positioned to respond more rapidly to FAA requests for assistance. On 19 December, although combat air patrols still were being flown, the FAA lifted its restrictions on the airspace around 30 cities, enabling private aircraft to once again fly in these areas; however, restrictions remained over the eastern Boston–New York–Washington corridor. AWACS surveillance planes continued to provide tracking information and vectored the fighter intercepts. By late December 2001, estimates as to the number of air reservists and guard personnel who had been activated for air-defence duties under the First Air Force and NORAD ranged from 11,000 to 22,000. Despite this significant mobilisation, US Central Command, based at MacDill Air Force Base in Tampa, Florida – the very command responsible for prosecuting the campaign against terrorism in Afghanistan – was unaware of the unauthorised flight of a private plane through its own airspace until after it had crashed into a building in downtown Tampa. NORAD's readjustment, then, may not yet be complete.

Second, ballistic missile defence (BMD) is a fundamental element of homeland defence, and remains an important part of the Bush administration's defence agenda. The 11 September attacks, however, fuelled arguments, advanced mainly by Democrats, that asymmetrical threats were more salient than those from ballistic (or cruise) missiles and that homeland-defence areas other than BMD therefore merited a greater share of resources. Reinforcing this point is a Central Intelligence Agency

(CIA) National Intelligence Estimate, released on 10 January 2002, indicating that the United States is more likely to sustain a terrorist attack with weapons of mass destruction (WMD) by way of ships, trucks or airplanes than an attack by a foreign state using long-range ballistic missiles. Yet the mass-casualty intent revealed by 11 September suggests that terrorists themselves may try to acquire missiles despite the operational and cost disadvantages, and the missile threat from rogue states has not disappeared. Thus, budget disputes in Congress centred on allocations for missile defence versus homeland counter-terrorism measures. Against the massive increase for homeland security in the administration's FY2003 budget, the missile defence allowance merely held steady at $8.3bn. This tension is likely to continue.

Third, reserve units may be used to guard especially vulnerable elements of critical infrastructure. For example, National Guard units are being more heavily used to help secure the country's 103 nuclear power plants, and may assist the Federal Emergency Management Agency (FEMA) and other agencies in handling terrorism-related civil emergencies. By 16 January 2002, 70,180 reservists from all 50 states, the District of Columbia and Puerto Rico had been mobilised.

More generally, on 26 October the Department of Defense announced plans to consolidate homeland security responsibilities and review operational planning for homeland security through the Chairman of the Joint Chiefs of Staff, the Joint Staff and the unified commands. Positions for two new undersecretaries of defence – one for homeland security, the other for intelligence – were under consideration. Finally, the biennial revision to the unified command plan was expected to yield a new unified command consolidating military homeland defence and civil support responsibilities under a single US-based commander-in-chief.

Office of Homeland Security

Most aspects of homeland security, however, are not among the Pentagon's core competencies, and the United States' historical aversion to using military forces at home limits the military's potential homeland security role. To help develop and coordinate myriad non-military components of homeland defence, on 20 September Bush appointed Governor Tom Ridge of Pennsylvania to be the Director of Homeland Security. He and his Office of Homeland Security, based in the White House, have been tasked with crafting a 'coordinated, integrated, and comprehensive national strategy' to combat terrorism. This calls for a mammoth partnership among 46 federal agencies, the 50 states and thousands of local jurisdictions, and the harmonisation of a wide range of professionals including emergency managers, doctors, public health officials, police officers and firemen. Achieving these aims will not be easy or fast. It involves establishing a national strategy for assessing threats; a system for disseminating intelligence about threats, trends and available assistance among state and local officials; coordinating federal, state and local emergency capabilities; fixing training and readiness standards for state and local officials; harmonising private and public medical capabilities; enhancing public-health surveillance systems; and ensuring that a surge capacity for the medical system is at hand.

While these are major responsibilities, Ridge commands little authority and few resources. His appointment is not subject to Senate confirmation, and – although most of his funding requests were met in Bush's proposed FY2003 budget – he has no veto power over budgetary and personnel decisions of the agencies he his charged with coordinating. Many of his staff – who numbered over 80 as of April 2002 – were seconded from other agencies. In the words of one policy analyst, Ridge has only 'a licence to persuade'. In the long term, better mechanisms will have to match authority and responsibility more closely. Behind the scenes, a comprehensive strategy is being built, but it too will call for structural and cultural changes. This integrated strategy will embrace several key elements of national security, including border security, intelligence, law enforcement, airport security and public health programmes.

Border security and 'forward' measures

The most daunting domestic challenge is posed by the porous nature of America's borders and transportation networks, juxtaposed with the lack of redundancy and physical vulnerability of the nation's critical infrastructure. Constructed primarily to serve commercial interests, networks and infrastructure are designed to facilitate travel and trade rather than security. Further, the pressure of globalisation and an ever increasing volume and velocity of trade has overwhelmed the capacities of US border security.

It is difficult to overstate the challenge. With 9m square km of ocean, 152,900km of shoreline, 8,000km of inter-coastal waterways and 14,500km of land borders, the points of entry to US territory are practically limitless. Some 3,700 terminals in 301 ports of entry stretch the capacity of the federal government to maintain control over outside access, to which the virtually uninterrupted volume of illegal narcotics attests. Some 127m cars, 11.5m trucks, 11.6m shipping containers, 2.2m railroad cars, 829,000 planes and 211,000 ships also passed through US borders in 2000. Most of this traffic was concentrated in just a few ports and crossings. Over $8.8bn worth of goods are processed daily at US entry points nationwide, a container every 20 seconds at major US ports. It generally takes five inspectors three hours to conduct a thorough examination of a full 12-metre container or an 18-wheel truck, and border agencies are able to examine only 2% of the cargo that comes into the country. In October 2001, an al-Qaeda suspect was discovered inside a container bound for Canada from Italy that had originated from Egypt. Long before 11 September, US authorities raised concerns that nuclear bomb components could be smuggled into the country in a container.

In 2000, almost half a billion people crossed US borders. On 11 September, the US Border Patrol had only 126 posts and 334 agents covering the 6,379km border between US and Canada, where even existing border stations are secured by only an orange cone when the customs agent or border patrolman is off duty. Most of its 9,000 agents have been assigned to stop illegal immigrants – which number 275,000 annually, between 6m and 11m in total – from crossing the 3,107km Mexican border. The Immigration and Naturalization Service (INS) processed 160,000 deportations in 2000, but there are another 300,000 'absconders' who were ordered deported, but who never left. That year the United States issued 67,742 visas to persons wishing to visit from Saudi Arabia alone; more than half overstayed those visas, but only five were deported. The INS has only 2,000 agents available for interior border and immigration enforcement.

While the pre-11 September policy preoccupations with drugs and illegal immigration may not precisely match counter-terrorism priorities, and the border agencies clearly require more and better trained staff and bigger budgets, border-security problems are to a significant extent organisational. Responsibility for border control is distributed among several agencies. The US Customs Service, the Food and Drug Administration, the Department of Agriculture and the Environmental Protection Agency inspect cargo. The INS, which includes the US Border Patrol, oversees the flow of people into and out of the United States, while the Department of State issues visas authorising their entry and duration of stay. The US Coast Guard is responsible for inspecting ships and securing ports. Their activities are not centrally coordinated, and most of these agencies report to different executive departments of the federal government. Moreover, each agency has remits in addition to homeland defence, and none regards security as its core mission.

The INS has particularly acute problems. Although it is one of the most rapidly expanding federal agencies (with 35,000 employees and a $5.6bn budget in 2002), it remains plagued by outmoded systems and poor organisation. In March 2002, a cruel irony highlighted these problems. Six months after the 11 September attacks, the agency sent second notices approving student visa extensions for two of the dead hijacker-terrorists – including ringleader Mohammed Atta – to the Florida flight school where the men learned how to steer jetliners into skyscrapers. Four senior officials, including the head of INS field operations and its director of international affairs, were summarily dismissed. The bureaucratic foul-up accelerated the agency's internal reform process and prompted questions from Senate Majority Leader Tom Daschle about Ridge's accountability to Congress.

Proposals for better inter-agency coordination – in particular, those of the Hart-Rudman Commission on National Security in the 21st Century and the Advisory Panel to Assess the Capabilities for Domestic Response to Terrorism Involving WMD – have taken root in Congress and are being considered by Ridge. On 14 November 2001, he indicated that he was seriously considering a merger of the enforcement arm of the INS, Customs, the Agricultural Quarantine Inspection programme and the Coast Guard into a single agency, deemed the 'Federal Border Administration' in a white paper prepared in December 2001. Accomplishing this has proven extremely difficult from a bureaucratic and institutional point of view. The Treasury, Justice and Transportation departments are reluctant to relinquish control over the separate elements of homeland security for which they are responsible. On the practical side, they argue that a wholesale reorganisation would needlessly duplicate existing bureaucratic infrastructures and disrupt operations precisely when the highest state of readiness is required. Notably, border security administrative consolidation was not mentioned in Bush's 2002 State of the Union address. By March 2002, the administration was favouring a less ambitious plan under which only the INS and Customs would be combined under the control of the Justice Department.

Operational improvements appear to be more realistic than sweeping structural reforms. But although some progress was made in integrating separate agencies' information systems during the 1990s, they do not yet have fully interoperable databases and communications networks. Data-sharing among them is rendered difficult by outmoded equipment, Congress's cumulative budgetary neglect and legal barriers. Consequently, while the Coast Guard might identify a ship with a suspect history, Customs might have some knowledge of a hazardous cargo on a converging tanker and the INS could possess a few clues about the crew on each vessel, no one agency is likely to command all this information, and no front-line inspector is likely to have ready access to relevant CIA or Federal Bureau of Investigation (FBI) intelligence. This is a critical deficiency. While law-enforcement and intelligence agencies are unsure about how all 19 hijackers entered the country, it is clear that most of them were admitted legally and were still legally inside the United States when they struck.

In the near term, better data-sharing and other improvements in existing agency practices and procedures remain more feasible than a large-scale statutory overhaul of the homeland security system. In the immigration sphere alone, sensible substantive measures could include: more rigorous checking of passports on departure; investing immigration officials with law-enforcement status; giving all INS inspectors access to lists of those ineligible to enter the US and electronic access to consular visa application information; requiring airlines to provide the INS electronically with passenger information in advance of arrival; widening the use of biometric identifying data, already in use on secure green cards and 'laser visas'; implementing automated entry-exit data systems for non-immigrant flyers; and establishing a comprehensive monitoring system for international students. Nationwide, safeguards for issuing key forms of identification, such as drivers' licences and birth certificates, could be strengthened.

The 2003 budget authorises funds for several thousand new caseworkers and Border Patrol agents. The Bush administration also requested $380m for a comprehensive entry-exit system and set a target date of September 2004 for establishing a computerised programme that would track hundreds of millions of border crossings a year. But many experts question the feasibility of both developing such a capability and meeting the deadline, and point to the profound effect that a truly comprehensive system could have on the pace of commerce. Advanced biometric identification procedures for visa applicants are under study, as are magnetic swipe-cards, bar-coded vehicle stickers and cards read by radio antennas. Government agencies plan to consult private industry. Although the precise form that any new system will take remained an open question in April 2002, it seemed clear that some ethnic profiling and greater scrutiny of visa applicants would occur. Considerable effort will also be made to track foreign students, although many American universities are uncomfortable serving as monitors.

Given the substantial global dimension of the US economy – the volume of US international trade, in terms of dollars and containers, has doubled since 1990 and will double again between 2001 and 2005 – bilateral and multilateral cooperation is also required to meet homeland security needs. The diplomatic task of winning such cooperation may be eased by the security improvements that it will offer the other countries involved. The US Coast Guard is advocating 'Maritime Domain Awareness', whereby agencies and private industry pool information on inbound ships, cargos, crews and passengers from multiple jurisdictions. Since the US–Canada border is the most porous, it has drawn the closest and most immediate attention. In an accord signed on 3 December 2001, the US agreed to integrate Canadian officials into its new Foreign Terrorist Tracking Task Force, to develop joint units to assess information on incoming passengers and to increase immigration-control personnel assigned to Canada. US and Canadian multi-agency special law-enforcement teams to track terrorists and combat organised crime are also to expand. Other promising reforms include encouraging industry via tax credits and 'fast pass' benefits to promote better security at loading docks, ports and warehouses, conducting background checks on shipping personnel and crews, and establishing an automated database to identify and track shipping and provide updated manifests before entry.

Furthermore, Washington is gently exploiting its leverage over international transportation and commercial networks to enlist the aid of

Asian and European allies to attain 'point-of-origin' cargo security. The primary task is to establish common standards for physical security, reporting and information-sharing for operators, conveyances and cargo, and a multilateral system for enforcing compliance with those standards. Particular measures under consideration include: requiring containers to be loaded in electronically monitored, security-sanitised facilities; affixing global-positioning system transponders and electronic tags to trucks and containers to facilitate tracking; installing theft- and tamper-resistant seals on containers; mandating background checks for personnel processing cargo or vehicles; instituting the use of biometric travel identity cards; and establishing inter-agency data links from point of departure to point of entry. At a February 2002 meeting of the International Maritime Organisation (IMO) in London, the IMO and most of its 161 member states backed US proposals for automatic ship identification systems; security plans for ships, port facilities and offshore terminals; vulnerability assessments; and improving security checks on containers. But they would not support US proposals for background checks and biometric identification devices for seafarers, and were resistant to another American initiative on international sharing of information on the ultimate ownership of vessels.

Sensitivities related to territory and sovereignty, as well as individual liberties, are bound to arise. Washington's approach is therefore low key, and will likely concentrate on global 'megaports' like Hong Kong, Singapore, Hamburg, Antwerp and Rotterdam as locales for international – or at least bilateral – inspection zones. The US Customs Service has proposed installing its own security checks at the ten busiest foreign ports, through which 49% of the containers shipped to the US pass. The idea is that, were these ports to accept the plan, pressure would result on smaller ports to acquiesce to similar controls or risk losing American commerce. Such initiatives are likely to be pursued primarily on a bilateral basis.

Intelligence

Because warnings gleaned from intelligence are by nature ambiguous, the 11 September attacks cannot be laid solely at the door of the intelligence community but rather reflect a security failure writ large. Nevertheless, the attacks did reveal flaws in the US intelligence system that affected homeland security. The main problem is that while the US intelligence agencies are capable of gathering massive quantities of raw data, they are less adept at processing it and developing an in-depth analytic understanding of an increasingly complex and borderless world. Collection consumes 85% of the $30bn intelligence budget, but only 10% of the 'take' is processed. Organisational inefficiencies and inter-agency competition are partly to blame, but there are two more salient deficiencies.

First, there is a severe shortage of intelligence officers with the linguistic, operational and analytic skills needed to assess attitudes in Arab countries and the intentions of their governments. Much of the problem results from a counter-intelligence culture of mistrust, however, and therefore will be difficult to remedy quickly. The 11 September attacks also prompted calls from some quarters for the United States to energise its human intelligence capabilities. These were severely compromised first in the wake of the 1976 Church Report and then following the discovery of senior CIA counter-intelligence officer Aldrich Ames's treason in 1994, when agent-recruitment and other operational restrictions were imposed and several unfortunate appointments in the CIA's Directorate of Operations were made. Since the cultural differences between Western intelligence officers and al-Qaeda terrorists are particularly sharp, and the latter's level of fanaticism is extraordinarily high, effective penetration of al-Qaeda cells remains a daunting task even for unrestricted covert intelligence operations. On the other hand, the fact that a number of Western individuals – such as John Walker Lindh – joined the Taliban suggests that 'humint' may have greater potential to infiltrate Islamic terrorist networks than US officials had previously thought.

Second, imbalances exist between strategic intelligence – which is most relevant to homeland security – and support for military operations. But almost 85% of the intelligence budget falls within the purview of the Secretary of Defense and, given the inertia of vested bureaucratic interests, will likely stay there. This allocation will tend to perpetuate the imbalance. A number of reforms will undoubtedly emerge from ongoing congressional hearings, and the National Security Council is trying to provide better guidance to the CIA and the domestic intelligence organs. Despite an increase in resources, however, priorities among strategic needs, military requirements and domestic security demands have yet to be established.

Law enforcement

Another front in the global war on terrorism is law enforcement. Both the FBI and its parent Department of Justice have been subject to severe criticism in the aftermath of the 11 September terrorist attacks. Prior to the attacks, the FBI had tips that foreign students had signed up for jet simulator training and had little interest in learning about landing. More probing investigations might have given the FBI advance warning about the 11 September hijacking plot, but acting on such information went against the grain of a reactive law-enforcement culture sensitised to social concerns about preserving civil liberties and freedom of action.

To its credit, the FBI immediately swung into action after the attack, sending nearly 4,000 agents into the field on the biggest manhunt since the 1950s. Within days, the FBI had compiled impressive (if belated) dossiers on each of the 19 hijackers of 11 September, and was able to track down their identities, finances, addresses and photographs. It also arrested and detained up to 1,500 potential suspects over the next three months, most of whom were of Middle Eastern origin. About 725 people were detained on immigration violations, but only 100 were charged with criminal offences. Fewer than 30 have been linked to al-Qaeda. But the bureau was very slow to respond to the anthrax attacks via the US mail that occurred in October and November, killing five people and infecting at least 13 others.

FBI Director Robert Mueller III has quickly re-orientated the FBI towards counter-terrorism and domestic intelligence gathering, which will become its primary missions. The bureau will cede some of its minor domestic responsibilities to local officials, while a greater proportion of bank robberies, drug offences, and financial and computer surveillance will be delegated to the Drug Enforcement Agency and the US Treasury Department's Bureau of Alcohol, Tobacco and Firearms. Mueller also wants to alter the FBI's inclination not to share information with other law-enforcement agencies. He must also grapple with limited resources and outmoded information architectures.

To facilitate the collection of domestic intelligence, on 26 October 2001, President Bush signed into law the US Patriot Act. While the dark immediate post-11 September mood – public as well as official – augured substantial curtailments of civil liberties, the new powers are not as extensive as some legal and political analysts had anticipated. For example, law-enforcement access to the content of e-mails remains restricted. Nevertheless, many left-wing liberals and right-wing libertarians consider the law too sweeping. It substantially dismantles the firewall between domestic and foreign intelligence erected in the late 1970s in the wake of the post-Watergate Church Committee investigations of intelligence abuses. The new law will strengthen capabilities in several key areas, including:

- Surveillance. Subject to a four-year sunset provision, court oversight for wiretaps, e-mail tracing, voice-mail retrieval and tracking web-surfing has been reduced. The FBI may subpoena business records and computer records from internet service providers (ISPs) 'to protect against international terrorism or clandestine intelligence activities', and law-enforcement agencies may use 'roving wiretaps' (allowing investigators to listen to all the phones a suspect uses). Federal law-enforcement agencies are permanently empowered to conduct secret searches and need only notify the owner of searched premises after a 'reasonable time'.
- Search warrants. Federal investigators may obtain nationwide warrants to better trace terrorists moving through multiple jurisdictions.

- Detention. Non-citizen terrorist suspects and immigration law violators can be detained for up to seven days for questioning without a hearing. Aliens who are certified to be threats to national security can be detained indefinitely, and those who raise funds for terrorist organisations can be deported.
- Restricted access. Access of non-immigrant aliens to biological and chemical agents may be restricted.
- Money-laundering. US banks can now be ordered to determine sources of suspicious accounts, the Treasury can now apply sanctions against uncooperative countries or banks, and US banks are prohibited from dealing with unregulated offshore 'shell' banks.
- Information-sharing. Information obtained in grand jury proceedings can also be released to US law-enforcement, intelligence and immigration organisations, and domestic law-enforcement agencies and foreign intelligence agencies are now allowed to share information.
- Criminal penalties. Penalties for aiding, abetting or committing acts of terrorism have been made more severe. Terrorism against mass transit networks was added to the list of federal crimes.

Although the Foreign Intelligence Surveillance Act (1978) still requires that government officers seeking wiretaps without probable cause that a crime is being committed demonstrate a foreign connection, the Bush administration is pressuring Congress for the removal of that restriction.

A key building block in countering the evolving network threat could be the collection and analysis of 'information artifacts'. This can probably be done without violating the US Patriot Act's restrictions on access to e-mail or Internet-site content. An information artifact is simply a record of a transaction. An artifact that hints at a plot to use biological weapons could take the form of, say, an electronic bank record of a funds transfer to buy a fermenting tank, a shipper's database entry of an export license for the tank, or an e-mail message in an Internet service provider's server confirming receipt of the tank. That transaction, in turn, constitutes a link in a threat network – that is, an action (e.g., a sale) that connects two or more potentially hostile actors (e.g., a purchaser and a supplier). Since information has made tracks from one part of the network to the other, the intelligence discipline known as 'traffic analysis' can provide clues about the digital activities of a terrorist network. Information artifacts, however, will tend to be highly 'granular' and require significant context to afford effective analysis. Context will consist of other data relating to possible hostile agents that is collected and archived by the law-enforcement and intelligence authorities. Technology capable of monitoring external features of Internet transmissions and 'sniffing' for significant data, such as the FBI's *Carnivore* computer programs and the National Security Agency's *Echelon* surveillance system, already exists. The primary limitation on the preventive (as opposed to reconstructive) potential of this form of intelligence remains the lag between the collection and the analysis of data. There are also so-called 'black crypto' rogue encryption counter-measures available.

Aviation security

The most glaring of the multiple security failures on 11 September was in the aviation sphere. It is easy to see why. The number of commercial airline flights in the United States has doubled in the past two decades, stretching the capacities of existing facilities. There are a total of 25,000 flights a day in the United States, involving almost 650m passengers a year. Before 11 September, security took a back seat to efficiency. The Transportation Department's 'red teams' would routinely enter restricted areas without any badges, and would be challenged only 25% of the time. Similarly, the watchdog Government Accounting Office (GAO) frequently skirted around security screens, and successfully planted weapons on planes at US airports. Although there was a special security screening system in place on 11 September, and nine of the 19 hijackers were singled out, all were ultimately allowed to board airplanes. In 2002, US airports were expected to lose $2–3bn in revenues while having to spend at least $1bn to meet new security requirements. Operational disruptions and increased fines due to a 'zero-tolerance' policy towards security violations imposed additional costs. Between October 2001 and April 2002, nearly 2,500 flights were delayed or cancelled and 156 terminal or concourse evacuations had occurred.

In recognition of these realities, Bush signed the Aviation and Transportation Security Act on 19 November 2001. This measure created a Transportation Security Administration (TSA) to strengthen airport security. The US government has assumed responsibility for personnel and baggage screening at airports, establishing minimum citizenship, education, training and security standards (including criminal background checks) for 31,000 screeners, who were to be hired as federal employees by 17 February and on duty at the nation's 429 commercial airports by November 2002. A federal security manager will be assigned at each US airport. Airlines now have beefed-up access security for their own facilities, and fortified cockpit doors, which are to stay locked for the duration of flights. The government also has reinvigorated its 1970s-era 'sky marshal' programme, placing an armed law-enforcement officer – 'borrowed' from élite branches of existing federal agencies – on some domestic flights, mainly in the Washington DC area. The TSA provides funding for creating a fully professional air marshal service and increasing the marshals' presence on domestic flights. On the ground, airport authorities have started to enforce parking restrictions more rigorously, to perform random intensive identification checks on any individuals present on airport grounds and to require those standing in security lines to be holding airline tickets in their hands.

The most substantial changes to pre-11 September practices that the new law mandates involve luggage and passenger screening. Under the US hub-and-spoke logistical network for air travel, which entails close coordination of connecting flights and finely tuned air-traffic control, a relatively short delay on a given flight can have immense multiplier effects. The basic challenge is therefore to design a virtually fault-proof system that does not produce substantial ground delays. This will not be easy. By 31 December 2002, each airport is supposed to have mass-screening technology in place to screen all checked bags for explosives. It is doubtful that all systems will be up and running by then. In January 2002, only 91 mass-screening machines were in use. An additional 2,200 were needed, at an aggregate cost of $4–5bn, but manufacturing capacity was limited as only two companies produced the heavy machines, and airport floors needed to be reinforced to accommodate them. Nevertheless, as of 18 January, more thorough baggage inspections were required. For the interim between that date and comprehensive mass-screening capability, the Federal Aviation Administration has approved four baggage-screening techniques: use of bomb-sniffing dogs; running luggage through smaller explosive-detecting machines; hand searches; and bag-matching, a procedure long employed in Europe whereby no item can be loaded onto a plane unless its owner is also on board.

Perhaps most significantly, a profiling system known as computerised-assisted passenger screening (CAPS) has been put in place. While the details of the system are classified, it has produced a significantly higher number of passengers considered to be potential threats than the less probing methods employed before 11 September. Bags belonging to passengers flagged by the system are screened by machine, while those owned by persons who are not singled out are sniffed by the dogs or manually searched. Bag-matching is applied to all passengers on originating flights. Even if fully implemented, the new system remains far from foolproof. Matching bags, for instance, would not deter a suicide bomber, and even that measure will not be conducted on some connecting flights. Nevertheless, the TSA's measures have generally been received as providing a relatively high degree of security and a substantial deterrent provided they are substantially implemented. Whether they can or will be remains a soberingly open question. One Israeli aviation security expert, for example, has expressed doubt about the feasibility of universal baggage screening in a country the size of the United States, and recommended more intensive passenger screening in order to streamline the demands on baggage screeners. In early 2002, US aviation authorities began testing a computerised screening system considerably more discerning than CAPS that would link every reservation system in the United States to private and government databases, employing data-mining and predictive software to profile passengers and ferret out potential threats.

Cyber security

Another homeland-security worry is a scenario analysts call a 'Digital Pearl Harbor': a surprise attack on the web of computer networks that undergirds the American economy and government. A cyber-attack might immobilise the Pentagon's ability to communicate with US military forces, siphon billions from the economy, or shut down all the services of a large city. Many computer-attack tools are posted on the Internet, available to anyone with a mouse and a modem. New defensive capabilities, including better encryption, intrusion detection and firewalls are rapidly being developed, but so are viruses and advanced attack tools. The vulnerability of the 'wired' economy is evident. Intrusions on US private-sector computers and Pentagon systems have increased steadily, peaking at 36,000 and 40,000 respectively, in 2001. Other US government systems are routinely visited or probed by foreign assailants.

The major threat will probably come from state-sponsored information-warfare efforts. Chinese military officials, for instance, have written articles about America's vulnerability to 'electrical incapacitation systems', and believe it will be a potentially decisive element in future conflict. Indeed, prompted by the 1 April 2001 collision between a US surveillance plane and a Chinese fighter, Chinese and US hackers for over a month exchanged defacement and denial-of-service attacks on various websites, some of them run by their respective governments. The episode was over-hyped by the media, but did illustrate the ease with which supposedly secure computer assets could be compromised, as did the untraced 13 July 2001 'Code Red' denial-of-service worm attack affecting 280,000 hosts running Microsoft Windows. Numerous computer crimes and intrusions have also been traced to sources in Russia. Although few countries presently demonstrate a strategic-level offensive information-warfare capabilities, in addition to Russia and China, the governments of India, Iran, Iraq, Cuba, Taiwan, Israel, Bulgaria, France, Britain, Canada and North Korea are believed to be attempting to develop them.

US government computer systems do not get passing grades from the GAO. Red teams from the NSA regularly enter government-owned information systems, undetected by system administrators. The Bush administration in October 2001 set up the Office of Cyber-Security, headed by Richard Clarke, within the White House. His effectiveness may be limited by the same budgetary and organisational factors affecting Ridge's.

Moreover, his direct authority is limited to government computers. They are, of course, vulnerable, and shortly after the 11 September attacks Clarke announced plans to set up an ultra-secure computer network, known as 'Govnet', for government agencies and their key partners.

But even greater potential vulnerability resides in the non-governmental infrastructure underlying the power-generation, transportation and financial sectors of the economy. A study by computer-security firm Riptech Inc. released in January 2002 found that attacks monitored weekly at 300 companies totalled 128,678 and increased by 79% between July and December 2001, and that power and energy companies were disproportionately targeted by actions originating in the Middle East. Clarke's challenge is to win the cooperation of private industry, which may be inclined to believe that security is adequate in order to preserve consumer confidence. So far, Clarke's approach has been to rely on consumers' lack of confidence to spur industry to voluntarily implement the government's cyber-security proposals. These include: periodically distributing 'patches' that plug holes in software through which hackers can seize control of computers; monitoring ISP networks for viruses and false Internet addresses; and rendering Internet servers capable of suppressing denial-of-service attacks. Industry has been initially supportive of this non-coercive posture, but if it does not produce results, government pressure will have to increase.

Biological attacks

The congressionally mandated TOPOFF exercise co-sponsored by the US Justice Department and FEMA in early 2000 and the DARK WINTER simulation conducted in June 2001 by several prominent former US officials have highlighted the dire implications of a biological attack. In each exercise, the hypothetical attack was successful because medical and emergency personnel did not know how to diagnose unusual symptoms, and the local medical infrastructure collapsed. Daunting complications also arose with respect to quarantine laws and information management. Analysts assessed that hundreds of thousands could have died had the simulated circumstances been real.

The real anthrax attack that occurred in October and November 2001 showcased many of these problems. Government agencies were surprised at the virulence and lethality of the anthrax spores, which were far more deadly than any individual biologist-cum-terrorist was considered able to produce. The mode of delivery precluded large-scale casualties. Yet medical professionals and biological warfare analysts underestimated the level of the infective dose that could cause death. Government communications procedures were inadequate for reassuring a frightened public. Equally sobering was the insufficiency of medical resources.

Laboratories were unprepared for the volume of work required to test samples for anthrax. Further, US hospitals would have found it difficult to cope with a more sophisticated mass-casualty operation. After a decade of cutting costs to make health care cheaper, they are unlikely to invest independently in the new capacity needed to handle bioterrorist attacks.

Owing to these difficulties, the budget for the federal Centers for Disease Control and Prevention for improving national preparedness for biological events is likely to increase substantially. More broadly, the US government now recognises that, given the ease with which biological weapons can be concealed and a biological attack launched, minimising risks requires a strengthened public health system. Under the auspices of the National Academy of Sciences, the larger science and technology community is mobilising to assess the near-term requirements of federal, state and local agencies. In October 2001, the 80-member inter-agency Technical Support Working Group asked private industry for ideas for combating terrorism, stressing the need to develop methods of detecting chemical and biological weapons before they are released. The group had received 12,000 ideas by March 2002.

Spurred by the anthrax attacks, the Bush administration has made biological terrorism its chief homeland defence priority. In December 2001, the Secretary of Health and Human Services, Tommy Thompson, announced major initiatives for developing a new anthrax vaccine, research on new rapid-response strategies, improving methods of mass diagnosis and tracing vectors of infection. Congress approved $1.4bn for bio-terrorism in the FY2002 budget as well as a $3.7bn supplemental allocation, and in February 2002, the Bush administration requested $5.9bn for FY2003 – a total of $11bn over two years. Congress is likely to approve all requests. The money will be used primarily to improve the national public health system. Specific line-items include: $1.75bn to the National Institutes of Health for basic and applied research; $1.8bn to federal agencies involved in bio-defence; $1.6bn to state and local health care systems; $650m to expand the national stockpile of vaccines and antibiotics (in particular, 300m doses of smallpox vaccine); and $600m to the Pentagon, mainly to develop better release-detection capabilities. The budget also allots $10m to the Centers for Disease Control and Prevention for creating a team of epidemiologists to share information with foreign counterparts and $20m to bolster the centres' Epidemiological Intelligence Service, which was established in 1951 to provide early warning in case of biological warfare.

A delicate balance

Homeland security is an integral element of the larger debate about the proper mix of diplomatic, military and domestic tools required to protect the American people. The most important aspect of homeland security remains the attitude of the American populace. So far, the horror of the atrocities in New York and Washington appears to have galvanised public support for a concerted effort to stamp out, or seriously impede, transnational terrorism. The United States' inexorable connectedness to world events and a global economy militate against a 'Fortress America', its traditions of civil liberty preclude the creation of a police state, and its national determination and military capability promise considerable success in the global campaign against terrorism. The general challenge to the US government is to ensure that such success does not lull the American people back into complacency about the security of their homeland. Barring another attack, claims on finite resources will inevitably grow. The government's task is to make sensible estimates of what threats, flowing from a dauntingly long list of vulnerabilities, warrant investment and focused official action. So far, it appears that, while all areas of homeland security need serious improvement, the greatest vulnerability rests in the public health system's incapacity to handle a biological terrorist attack. The other key areas of vulnerability are border controls and information technology. Ridge's initial assessment and Bush's new budget reflect these priorities.

Transnational Control of Money-Laundering

Spurred by the 11 September terrorist attacks on the United States, governments and international organisations significantly increased efforts in 2001 to enforce financial and banking regulations in an attempt to combat the various forms of financial crimes, including tax evasion, fraud schemes, money-laundering and terrorist financing. These efforts were reflected in the imposition of new due-diligence measures on the private sector, the continued weakening of confidentiality laws, the enforcement of penalties for non-compliance with regulatory efforts and the freezing of assets of organisations tied to terrorist activities. The shock of 11 September may have accelerated the establishment of money-laundering controls by a generation. However, international efforts against money-laundering had already accelerated substantially prior to 11 September as a result of decisions taken in the late 1990s by several organisations, especially the Financial Action Task Force on Money Laundering (FATF), based in Paris.

The FATF's push to upgrade controls on money-laundering entered a new phase in June 2001, when the FATF carried out its threat of sanctioning non-cooperative states by releasing a list of three countries – Nauru, the Philippines and the Russian Federation – for failing to adhere to international efforts to combat money-laundering. Members of the FATF then became obligated to inspect accounts containing funds from the sanctioned jurisdictions, increase scrutiny of future financial transactions and limit bilateral and multilateral aid to the jurisdictions.

In September 2001, after the terrorist attacks, the Bush administration initiated an unprecedented wave of initiatives to hinder the laundering of illicit capital and to curtail the financing of terrorist groups, beginning with the imposition of new economic sanctions against terrorist assets on 23 September. These, in turn, were incorporated into the obligations of all United Nations member states with the passage of UN Security Council Resolution 1373 on 28 September. In October 2001, the US Congress further stepped up pressure on terrorist groups by enacting the International Money-Laundering Abatement and Anti-Terrorist Financing Act (2001). This is a comprehensive money-laundering statute that requires US financial institutions to implement know-your-customer procedures, to investigate offshore banks and financial institutions operating in countries with lax banking controls before opening accounts, and to close accounts with 'shell banks'. The legislation further permits US authorities to freeze suspected illegal funds that depositors have put into bank accounts in other countries, seizing the equivalent amounts in correspondent accounts held by those banks in the US as if the illegal funds were in the US. The Bush administration also significantly increased the budget of the Office of Foreign Assets Control, a division of the US Department of the Treasury, which enforces sanctions against banking and financial institutions that aid terrorist organisations. In a further attempt to disrupt the financing of terrorist groups, the Bush administration froze the assets of 27 entities, including a number of financial institutions, linked to Osama bin Laden's terrorist network al-Qaeda and the Palestinian terrorist group Hamas.

Despite these new measures, cutting off al-Qaeda's terrorist funding through financial controls will be exceedingly difficult for several reasons. First, the organisation's assets are widely dispersed through a web composed of other radical Islamic groups – often disguised – across the Middle East, Asia and Africa. Second, its funding sources are equally broad, and include ostensibly legitimate businesses as well as criminal operations like extortion and drug-trafficking. Even if bin Laden's personal fortune is as much as $30 million, and has partly funded al-Qaeda's activities, al-Qaeda's total assets – built up largely through the diversion of charitable contributions and the proceeds of otherwise above-board businesses based in Somalia and Sudan, among other jurisdictions – dwarf that sum. During the four months following 11 September, about $80m in suspected al-Qaeda assets were frozen and $12.5m seized outright. Yet the organisation is far from being out of business. Finally, the existing US regulatory framework and high threat perception have combined to produce intense scrutiny of possible al-Qaeda laundering schemes.

These factors will thus force the group to seek other, more accommodating hosts for its money. Europe is a prime candidate. More than the US, European countries as well as the European Union (EU) tend to draw distinctions between the military and political wings of terrorist organisations, and to allow the latter to raise and distribute funds unimpeded. As of March 2002, for example, US authorities had shut down the Holy Land Foundation – believed to be a financial conduit to Hamas – while most European countries had not. Arab countries are even more reluctant to inhibit the money-raising capacities of Islamic organisations that are ostensibly charitable. Thus, the diplomatic ability of the US to convince multilateral organisations and national regulators to tighten their financial controls remains in some doubt. Yet it will be a key determinant of the success of transnational efforts to cut off al-Qaeda's financial oxygen.

Laundering on a global scale

Since banking regulators discovered that more than $7 billion of illicit funds had been laundered in the Bank of New York scandal in 1999, security, intelligence and law-enforcement agencies have linked money-laundering activities to a range of international, regional and domestic concerns. For instance, the laundering of illicit profits routinely plays a significant role in the funding of civil conflicts in Colombia and Myanmar, and arms, narcotics, and human trafficking across the globe. Law-enforcement and regulatory agencies also concluded that a series of money-laundering schemes have been responsible for the destabilisation of financial markets in Mexico, the Russian Federation and Turkey in recent years. Furthermore, money-laundering contributes to high levels of political corruption, which undermines political legitimacy, reduces foreign and domestic investments and slows economic growth.

The enormous volume of financial transactions conducted through global banking and non-banking institutions facilitates money-laundering schemes, and hinders effective regulation of banking activities. For example, every day the US financial system handles more than 700,000 wire transfers, valued at over $2 trillion. Determining which of these transactions might be related to money-laundering creates a needle-in-a-haystack problem for both private-sector institutions and for law-enforcement or regulatory agencies. Beyond using banks, criminals successfully launder illicit funds through stock exchanges, trust companies, postal and telegraph offices, casinos, pawnbrokers and other non-credit institutions. Law-enforcement agencies and financial regulators continually uncover acts of money-laundering in financial institutions, but criminals just as quickly respond, shifting the sites, mechanisms and means of laundering funds, transferring them to other jurisdictions, or bribing officials to impede criminal investigations. The World Bank estimates that up to 5% of annual global financial transactions, roughly $800m to $2 trillion, involve the laundering of illicit profits.

Private banks in lax offshore jurisdictions whose principal drawing card is secrecy manage an estimated $27 trillion. A common device offered by such banks, and used by those wishing to shield their assets from regulatory scrutiny and action in other countries, is the so-called correspondent account. The offshore bank opens a 'pay-through' account in its corporate name with a bank in, say, New York. The offshore bank's customer is permitted to draw cheques on or make deposits to his or her individual offshore account via the New York pay-through account, whereupon the offshore bank debits or credits the individual's account. The New York bank doesn't know who the individual is because it is the offshore bank rather than the individual that is the New York bank's customer and pays its fees. Although all the banking is done in the US, the money is technically offshore. A regulator looking to trace the money will hit a dead-end when it reaches the offshore bank's correspondent account by virtue of the offshore jurisdiction's bank secrecy laws. Al-Taqwa, a Switzerland-based Islamic financial network suspected of funnelling funds to al-Qaeda, registered with a Bahamian bank, through which the network has made heavy use of correspondent accounts in established European banks. After the bombings of the US embassies in East Africa in August 1998, US intelligence and law-enforcement agencies reportedly tracked telephone contacts between al-Qaeda operatives in various places and al-Taqwa agents in the Bahamas, but found it difficult to determine how much money was actually transferred in either direction.

International efforts to quell money-laundering

The prominence of international initiatives to discourage money-laundering reflects two major influences: the rise of international governmental organisations and related groups; and the propagation of financially sophisticated transnational non-state actors, including terrorist groups and criminal enterprises. As world markets converge and multinational firms continue to cross-invest in other financial and service sectors, the world will increasingly need better institutional decision-making, better transparency, better sequencing in the liberalisation process and a more secure legal foundation. This effort has been systematically led by technocrats at international financial regulatory bodies rather than by policymakers.

The growing threat that narcotics money laundering posed to governance provided the impetus in 1989 for the creation of the FATF, an inter-governmental body that develops and promotes national legislative and regulatory reforms to combat money laundering. The FATF, currently composed of 29 countries, compiled and issued 40 recommendations regarding record-keeping requirements, mandatory reporting of suspicious or large financial transactions, identification of beneficial ownership and elimination of anonymous accounts, to assist states in combating money-laundering schemes. In 1996, the FATF expanded this system to cover all illicit proceeds, not just those involving narcotics. In 1999, to encourage non-member countries with systemic money-laundering deficiencies to adhere to international norms, the FATF established the Non-Cooperative Countries and Territories (NCCT) initiative. The first annual report by the NCCT, published in June 2000, identified 15 jurisdictions that fail to meet the minimal level of effort with regard to combating money-laundering. The annual list is issued in an attempt to dissuade companies and investors from investing in the blacklisted states. Inclusion subjects the jurisdiction to censure by international regulatory bodies. If it then fails to correct the deficiencies during a probationary period, it is incumbent on Western financial institutions to curtail the jurisdiction's financial transactions. The second-annual NCCT report, published in June 2001, listed 17 non-cooperative states, and threatened sanctions against three of the jurisdictions on the list. To foster the implementation of international anti-money-laundering standards, FATF also established a number of regional anti-money-laundering groups, which have observer status with FATF. Like the FATF, regional groups conduct mutual evaluations of their members and review regional money-laundering trends.

Another multilateral organisation assisting in the fight against money-laundering is the Financial Stability Forum (FSF), established by the Group of Seven (G-7), and composed of finance ministers, central bankers and supervisory officials from 11 nations with advanced financial systems. The FSF, which includes representatives of the International Monetary Fund (IMF) and regulatory bodies such as the Basel Committee on Banking Supervision, was created to examine offshore centres and to assess the quality of their respective regulatory environments offshore. The FSF submitted a survey that required banking, insurance and securities supervisors to evaluate the level of resources devoted to supervision and international cooperation, and the degree of cooperation by individual offshore centres. It then grouped offshore jurisdictions into three categories, from high quality to low quality. Based on the survey results, the FSF identified a number of regulatory and enforcement weaknesses that facilitate the laundering of illicit capital in offshore zones. The FSF passed its data to the IMF, which is currently proposing ways to enhance compliance in offshore centres that are known havens for laundering.

The third international organisation that combats money-laundering is the Organisation for European Cooperation and Development (OECD), which investigates tax evasion and issues guidelines on how states should combat harmful tax practices. The OECD identified a number of tax havens that undermine other nations' tax bases through a lack of transparency, secrecy provisions, permitting foreign customers to be subject to rules different from those applied to citizens and offering no or low effective tax rates. The OECD has placed numerous jurisdictions under review, and required these states to eliminate harmful tax practices through a series of progressive changes by the end of 2005 or face sanctions. If any of these states fail to comply with the OECD directive, each member of the OECD is permitted, through a coordinated defence-mechanism framework, to require comprehensive reporting of all transactions involving the non-complying state, to withhold taxes on certain payments to residents in the state, to terminate all existing double-taxation agreements and to impose charges on transactions involving the state.

Responses to international anti-money laundering initiatives

The FATF, FSF and OECD initiatives reflect the intensified focus of international organisations and national governments on extending anti-money laundering legislation to cover additional persons, products and situations, while developing strategies and mechanisms to implement and enforce anti-money laundering laws and conventions. The responses of individual jurisdictions to these initiatives has varied widely. Some Caribbean and South Pacific opponents of the initiative have urged resistance through formal legal action. However, most tax-haven jurisdictions have responded positively by strengthening their regulatory infrastructures for supervising offshore financial vehicles and service providers, and enacting anti-money laundering laws. A number of these jurisdictions have explicitly committed to addressing FSF concerns, and abolishing or curbing secrecy laws or anonymous accounts. For instance, the Cayman Islands and Bermuda governments have agreed to participate in the OECD harmful tax competition initiative. As part of the initiative, they are to make their tax regimes more transparent and exchange legal information. This agreement exerts considerable pressure on other offshore jurisdictions to adhere to international norms.

A number of the targeted jurisdictions have formed the International Tax and Investment Organization (ITIO). The ITIO has the following aims: to strengthen international cooperation between small and developing economies (SDEs) in tax and investment matters; to assist SDEs in interfacing with international organisations to achieve this end; and to consider the development implications of international tax and investment initiatives. The ITIO evolved out of the work of the OECD–Commonwealth Joint Working Group on Harmful Tax Competition. The experiences of the SDEs in this group persuaded them to band together into a new, inclusive organisation. The Organising Committee was composed of Antigua and Barbuda, Barbados, British Virgin Islands, Cook Islands, Dominica, Malaysia and Vanuatu.

The recent FATF report also produced significant changes in a number of jurisdictions. To avoid sanctions by the FATF, in 2001, Lebanon passed money-laundering legislation, the Seychelles signed a letter of commitment to the OECD to work toward the implementation of international standards to eliminate harmful tax competition, and Liechtenstein hired the accounting firm KPMG to assist in creating an advisory body, which includes members of Interpol and the US Treasury, to help fight money-laundering. These last-minute efforts resulted in Liechtenstein being removed from the FATF 'black-list'. The Seychelles, however, was blacklisted for a second year.

The new US anti-money laundering law included a wide range of new authorities for the US president to seize funds in the US to offset terrorist funds held at the same institutions elsewhere. All US financial institutions are required to close accounts with shell banks based in poorly regulated jurisdictions and to install comprehensive anti-money laundering procedures. The new law extended extraterritorial coverage of predicate offences – including foreign corruption and schemes to defraud foreign governments – and in essence requires any foreign financial institution to respond to document requests from the US government as a condition of doing business in or holding assets in the US.

Less agreement currently exists on substantive tax policies or on procedural compliance and enforcement regimes, although intergovernmental organisations are attempting to develop better ones. The leader in this area is the EU, which has led the battle on exchange of information, breaking secrecy barriers and harmonising tax policy. The OECD harmful tax competition initiative is the latest effort to design, implement, and enforce a tax enforcement sub-regime on a universal basis and at high speed. At the same time, a transnational corruption enforcement regime has developed, spearheaded by the OECD, whose Convention against Transnational Bribery of Public Officials in 1998 finally internationalised the criminalisation of bribery. Broader anti-corruption conventions have been passed by the Council of Europe and the Organization of American States. The Council of Europe Convention, like that of the OECD, uses the mechanism of mutual assessment first developed by the FATF, as the primary means enforcing the regime. Increasingly, these sub-regimes – transnational bribery enforcement, anti-money laundering, tax enforcement and the establishment of a new international financial regulatory architecture – are interacting and converging. At the same time, the insularity and financial opportunism of sovereign governments and the dynamism of international and regional economic developments still present effective means by which illicit actors can evade financial oversight.

Wayward governments: two case studies

A comparison of the recent evolutions of money-laundering regulatory regimes in Ukraine and Cyprus illustrates the impact that economic and political incentives can have on reform efforts. Ukraine has no immediate prospect of joining the EU, and its reform moves have stayed lethargic. Cyprus is a strong candidate for 'first-wave' EU accession, and its efforts have been robust.

Ukraine

Ukraine, which was added to the FATF blacklist in October 2001, is a paradigm case for illustrating how a weak regulatory regime can facilitate the laundering of legal and illegal profits through financial institutions. After the Ukrainian parliament failed to pass comprehensive money-laundering legislation, significant amounts of illicit funds from Ukraine were deposited into financial institutions in the Commonwealth of Independent States, the Middle East, the United States, Western, Central and Eastern Europe, and numerous offshore zones. Poor enforcement efforts by Ukrainian authorities to combat money-laundering prompted representatives from the world's 12 largest banks in October 2000 to place Ukraine (along with the Russian Federation) first among countries transferring dirty money abroad. As of 2001, the Ukrainian Ministry of Internal Affairs estimated that 60,000 criminal groups were involved in fraud schemes, tax evasion and the smuggling of narcotics, women and arms. The Internal Affairs Ministry also concluded that these criminal groups had laundered over $100bn through global financial institutions since Ukraine gained independence in late 1991. The two most important devices employed in Ukraine for laundering money are anonymous bank accounts, which frequently mix legal and illegal proceeds, and 'front' companies, which move money through offshore zones, such as Antigua, the Cayman Islands and the Republic of Nauru. Following the path previously trodden by laundered funds in Russia, Ukrainian laundered funds may then return to Ukraine for the purchase of real estate and state-owned firms. Alternatively, the illicit monies are transferred through correspondent bank accounts and remain abroad.

The decade-old banking system in Ukraine remains largely unregulated. Each bank enforces its own set of regulations. Enforcement of what financial regulations do exist has also been hampered by the overlapping portfolios of law-enforcement bodies that combat money-laundering, such as the Tax Police, the Ministry of Internal Affairs and the State Security Service. The agencies rarely share information, and view one another as competitors rather than allies. Ukraine's legal deficiencies could largely be remedied by the passage of comprehensive draft money-laundering legislation. The draft legislation would establish a wide range of predicate offences related to money-laundering, clarify existing legislation, impose penalties on individuals who violate money-laundering laws and require financial institutions to enforce stringent customer identification provisions and record-keeping requirements. It would also limit banking confidentiality practices, sanction banks that fail to report unusual or suspicious transactions, and compel financial institutions to cooperate in investigations launched by the Ukrainian regulatory authorities. Finally, the legislation would bolster law-enforcement efforts by mandating the formation of a financial intelligence unit to assist in the investigation of money-laundering offences.

Passage of such a law would limit capital flight and meet international standards for combating money-laundering. But enforcement activities in Ukraine cannot work without close cooperation from the National Bank of Ukraine, the country's primary regulator, which to date has placed few controls on banks or exchange houses. Effective regulation would require licensing and oversight of the thousands of unregulated casinos that exist throughout Ukraine, and elimination of the dozens of 'conversion centres' that provide currency-exchange services, and transfer illicit funds that cannot be traced by regulators. As of early 2002, prospects for these reforms were dim, as reform efforts had been diverted by economic difficulties and political scandals. The irony is that failure to impose such reforms tends to perpetuate those very problems. Billions of dollars in income tax revenues have been sent to bank accounts outside of Ukraine. The loss of tax revenue further limits the amount of money available for domestic spending and reduced funding for social welfare programmes and government assistance to the agricultural and industrial sectors, weakening the economy and governance, and creating a vicious circle in which criminals have greater resources than the government.

Cyprus

The EU has been deeply concerned about the entrance of countries that lack rigorous legislative and regulatory frameworks for deterring money-laundering. Cyprus, a well-known haven for laundering money, possesses an offshore financial sector composed of more than 47,000 registered companies. These are casually regulated and routinely transfer large sums of money abroad to other well-known money-laundering centres. One unofficial estimate suggests that the offshore financial sector contributes more than $200m a year to the Cypriot economy. This may explain its continuing disregard for the origin of offshore deposits. In the late 1990s, for instance, former Ukrainian Prime Minister Pavlo Lazarenko transferred significant portions of the $200–250m in allegedly embezzled funds through the Cypriot offshore sector during his term as prime minister.

More recently, domestic and international law-enforcement agencies have concluded that significant amounts of money illegally obtained by former Yugoslavian leader Slobodan Milosevic were laundered through the offshore Cyprus. Both the US and the EU responded to these scandals by placing greater emphasis on reform in Cyprus. In particular, Cyprus received numerous intimations from Brussels that accession to the EU would take place only after more ambitious legislative and regulatory reforms were implemented to assure the assiduous monitoring of the offshore financial sector. The result has been a systematic ratcheting upward of Cyprus' regulatory and enforcement regime; greater scrutiny of the movement of funds involving suspect individuals and organisations from Cyprus to places further east, such as Lebanon; and the attenuation of Cypriot involvement in handling the proceeds of more notorious customers, such as al-Qaeda, Russian organised crime and UN-sanctioned Serbs.

Laundering, the introduction of the euro and EU enlargement

Ironically, while the 'carrot' of EU membership can motivate governments to improve their financial oversight, the pace and degree of economic change in the European system affords money-launderers offsetting loopholes. In particular, in early 2002 the short four-week transition period to monetary union has provided a unique opportunity for criminal groups in the Americas, Asia and Europe to launder illicit profits through European financial institutions. During the transition period, individuals were permitted to exchange money at any bank in the eurozone except Germany, which made it less likely that bank clerks would recognise or scrutinise customers. In addition, confusion from the increased pace of transactions almost inevitably produced bank laxity. To date, it remains difficult to assess the degree to which the conversion of 12 national currencies to the euro has been used to launder funds. It is doubtful, however, financial institutions had the time required to investigate and thwart suspicious or unusual transactions. Moreover, the diverse regulatory regimes of the 12 countries involved have invited short-term regulatory arbitrage, providing criminal groups the opportunity to evade stringent currency-exchange regulations in countries such as Germany by converting currency in countries that possess imperfect monitoring systems for identifying suspicious transactions. Monitoring and assessing the actual laundering of funds through the EU in connection with the transition will be an important job for the EU's analytic law-enforcement arm, Europol, as a means of protecting the EU as its enlargement extends to states whose historic regulatory and law-enforcement competencies have been limited.

The EU's treatment of the Czech Republic reflects Brussels' emerging approach. The EU required the Czech Republic to enact legislative amendments to close several loopholes as a precondition to entry into the EU planned for 2004. Most importantly, EU regulators appealed to the Czech government to identify ownership of anonymous financial accounts, and require customers to declare the origin of the large cash deposits. In an effort to assist Western European regulators, Ceska Sporitelna, the second-largest bank in the Czech Republic, recently launched 'Euro Project,' a task force that will monitor the amount – more than $22.7bn – that could be converted through Czech banks during the conversion period for suspicious transactions. The practical difficulty in making this project effective is evident from the scant resources allocated to the task force by the Czech Republic: the task force has assigned only one full-time employee to investigate potentially fraudulent transactions, which is clearly inadequate for monitoring suspicious transactions during the changeover period.

Other states near EU territory may find themselves even less able to curtail the laundering activities of indigenous criminal organisations. For instance, Albania's transition from a command economy witnessed the establishment of narcotics, arms and women smuggling operations, which were underground during the communist era, in the thriving local black economy. Such operations have been controlled by well-organised criminal groups that oversee major regional smuggling and trafficking operations, and routinely launder their proceeds through Albanian financial institutions. The laundering of illegal profits has been commingled with monies tied to capital flight and tax evasion schemes, which may then be re-invested in the Albanian economy. Although EU regulators have demanded closer regulation of Albanian financial institutions, the Albanian government has had little practical interest in overseeing such flows, so long as funds are returning to Albania for investment in the local economy. In late 2001 and early 2002, law-enforcement agencies in neighbouring countries, including the Italian Guardia di Finanzia and the Turkish National Police, concluded that Albanian money-laundering is a major threat to European financial institutions, and called for immediate reform of the Albanian financial sector. In an effort to quell the intense international criticism, the Albanian government passed comprehensive money-laundering legislation in May 2000, but, as of April 2002, no money-laundering cases had been prosecuted in Albanian courts and no illicit proceeds had been forfeited through judicial action.

The Czech and Albanian cases exemplify the EU's problem as it enlarges. Both potential member states and non-member states in the region have limited capacity against financial crime, yet are increasingly integrated with EU institutions in handling funds. This is a problem that is likely to intensify as the euro becomes a common European currency and as enlargement continues.

The Middle East and the Gulf

Of the $80m in suspected al-Qaeda assets frozen worldwide during the four months following 11 September, about $34m were in the US and $46m overseas. It is clear that al-Qaeda capacity to conduct terrorist operations has been hindered. Furthermore, US investigators examined 61,000 transactions involving more than 90 foreign banks, and gained considerable understanding about how al-Qaeda operatives received money, how and where they were trained to fly, where they lived and whom they contacted. But authorities are unable to say whether the amount frozen constitutes a small fraction or the substantial bulk of al-Qaeda's financial resources. One reason for this uncertainty is that while cooperation from financial authorities in Europe and Asia has been diligent, cooperation from Arab governments has been erratic and uncertain. An appreciable portion of al-Qaeda's funding comes from private donations made by wealthy Saudis to apparent charities. After months of what US officials considered a desultory effort, in late January 2002, Saudi Arabia announced that it was 'urgently implementing' a law to combat money-laundering by moving to freeze 150 suspect bank accounts. But the Saudis provided no details.

The 11 September hijackers received from the United Arab Emirates (UAE) at least $120,000 of the $500,000 believed to have been advanced to them for funding operations. For years, the UAE showed little conviction in implementing financial controls, and considered money-laundering to be primarily a phenomenon associated with drug-trafficking, of which there is very little in the Muslim country. But UAE officials also declined to tighten the screws after the 1998 US embassy bombings in East Africa on the grounds that they could not distinguish between al-Qaeda funds used for such criminal activities and those used for what they regarded as acceptable practices, such as training Islamic rebels in Bosnia and Chechnya. Under US pressure, however, in January 2002, the UAE criminalised money laundering by imposing jail terms of up to seven years and fines as high as $82,000 on those transferring or depositing money in UAE accounts with the intent to conceal its origin. Under the new UAE legal regime, the Central Bank is empowered to exchange information on suspicious accounts with foreign counterparts, and all visitors are required to declare any funds in excess of $11,000 brought in from another country.

Certain Middle Eastern and Asian financial practices, however, are exceedingly difficult to regulate. Moreover, intelligence suggests that al-Qaeda is increasingly apt to use these devices to transfer small sums of money, which is less conspicuous than using more regular means (like wire transfers) to send larger amounts. In particular, the unregulated *hawala* system leaves little trace of money transferred around the world. In its simplest form, a *hawala* system consists of two persons in distant locations communicating by phone, fax, or e-mail. No money is exchanged between the brokers themselves, only between the brokers and the customers, and the broker does not maintain records of the transaction. Honest persons seeking a trusted and inexpensive way to send money abroad often use the *hawala* remittance system, but al-Qaeda operatives, seeking to avoid control and reporting regimes, have exploited *hawala* to send illicit funds to cells around the world. Perhaps the best-known of these is the Somali-owned, Dubai-based firm al-Barakaat, from which US officials estimate al-Qaeda skimmed $25m annually in handling and money-exchange fees charged mainly to diaspora Somalis transferring money to relatives at home. In November 2001, the US froze al-Barakaat's assets and the UAE followed with similar action, seized its records and allowed American authorities to inspect them.

The UAE has since drafted legislation to criminalise certain *hawala* activity. Individuals convicted of an irregular money transfer to finance kidnapping, piracy and terrorism in the UAE could receive a seven-year prison sentence and a $272,000 fine. The chronic lack of convictions related to financial violations in the UAE, however, does little to alleviate fears that *hawala* brokers will continue to operate there. The recent passage of money-laundering legislation in the Philippines, one of the primary recipients of funding from al-Qaeda, may assist in tracking funds al-Qaeda sent to the Abu Sayyaf group and the Moro Islamic Liberation Front. The Philippines, however, lacks adequate resources and personnel to track the laundering of capital in Philippine financial institutions, and will require significant assistance from the international community to assist in the investigation of al-Qaeda assets.

Although US officials believe that countries like Saudi Arabia and the UAE have genuinely increased their scrutiny of financial transactions since 11 September, there remain grave doubts about the durability of their commitment. More generally, the Middle East still lacks serious controls on the placement of funds – in particular, systematic identification of the actual owners of such funds. The Middle East also remains wide open both to the placement of licit funds for illicit purposes, such as terrorist finances, that prove impossible to trace, and to the placement of illicit funds for licit or illicit purposes. The giant gap in placement controls, which includes essentially the entire Middle East and Gulf region (apart from Cyprus, Israel and the UAE, which have significant limits), constitutes an ongoing global vulnerability to terrorist finance and money laundering. For the near term, funds coming out of the Middle East will continue to be difficult to assess. It will be left to international financial institutions to review their movements and uses as well as their origins, in order to analyse money-laundering risk. Name-and-shame exercises by the major international groups are not likely to have much of an impact in the absence of heightened scrutiny of such accounts. Active sharing of information by the US, and strategic regulatory and enforcement actions against suspect funds, will be necessary to bring about greater transparency and certainty in the identification of assets from the Middle East.

The threat of e-commerce

Though numerous states have passed comprehensive money-laundering legislation, a number of countries in the Caribbean and South Pacific are augmenting their limited economies, which are based on tourism and rudimentary agriculture and fishing production, with offshore financial sectors. These offshore sectors utilise Internet-based payment systems that assure anonymity and facilitate the laundering of illicit profits. For example, in late 2000, domestic and international regulators expressed considerable concern after Vanuatu, a Southern Pacific island chain with a population of about 190,000, passed the E-Business Act No. 25 of 2000, which permits proprietors to establish web-based e-commerce sites, and to conduct business from Vanuatu without the need to form an offshore corporation. In essence, the new legislation permits the establishment of a 'cyber-suite': a Vanuatu-based website from which business can be conducted without revealing the identity of company directors and shareholders. Moreover the owner of the cyber-suite does not have to maintain a physical presence in Vanuatu, such as a registered office. The E-Business Act does mandate customer identification and record-keeping requirements, and the filing of suspicious activity reports, but the chronic failure by Vanuatuan regulators to enforce money-laundering legislation provides the owners of cyber-suites, which are frequently leased by virtual banks and other financial institutions, tremendous opportunities for laundering legal and illegal profits.

Another unsettling trend is the concerted efforts by countries throughout the Caribbean to become global centres for Internet gaming, a $10bn global industry. For instance, the island-nation of Dominica, which has been blacklisted by the FATF since June 2000, recently established a regulatory framework that permits offshore operations of Internet gaming through high-speed fibre-optic and satellite facilities. The gaming licence permits the establishment of traditional forms of gaming over the Internet, including table games, slot machines, and video poker and gambling on a wide variety of sporting events, such as basketball, soccer and motor racing. Criminal organisations are attracted to Dominica because on-line gaming companies are exempt from income tax, withholding tax, sales tax and foreign-exchange controls. Western regulators are increasingly concerned that Internet casinos and lax foreign exchange controls on Dominica will facilitate the laundering of illicit profits, and hinder attempts by law-enforcement agencies to determine the origin and transfer of laundered assets.

The anonymity of individuals laundering illicit funds is also protected by a number of jurisdictions that provide information safe havens for international business companies. Information safe havens – an established practice in a number of blacklisted countries, including the Seychelles, Philippines and St Kitts, do not require beneficial owners or shareholders to reveal their identities – shield information that is crucial to law-enforcement agencies investigating alleged acts of money-laundering. Frequently, individuals launder money through information safe havens by establishing a parent company without revealing beneficial ownership and then immediately forming a number of subsidiaries, or 'transacting companies'. Since the identities of individuals controlling the parent firm are protected, the transacting companies appear to be unassociated with the parent firm. Criminal groups routinely use the subsidiaries to launder illicit funds for the parent company. In the handful of instances in which international and domestic regulators have initiated investigations into alleged acts of money laundering, there has been no information available to locate the principal actors involved in the money-laundering scheme.

Outlook

Better surveillance of illicit attempts to hide financial assets is essential, not only to deny terrorists and criminals of the resources they require, but also to trace their movements so as to generate useful intelligence about their modes of operation and to facilitate their apprehension by law-enforcement and counter-terrorism authorities. The achievements of the international regulators, national governments and domestic law-enforcement agencies over the last few years, and particularly since 11 September, have been impressive. In December 2000, over 125 countries signed the UN convention to combat organised crime and prevent money-laundering of illicit profits, and the annual blacklist by the FATF has resulted in the enactment by numerous countries, including the Bahamas, the Cayman Islands and Malaysia, of significant regulatory amendments to prevent money-laundering through domestic financial institutions. Furthermore, the passage of stringent money-laundering legislation in Albania reflects the trend that many countries are following in curtailing money-laundering activities within their borders to avoid penalisation by the World Bank, the IMF and the EU.

Despite such notable successes, money-laundering activities continue to thrive across the globe, as demand for narcotics, prostitution and weapons grows unabated. More can be done by states to combat money-laundering. For example, budgets for financial intelligence units could be increased to ensure ample staffing and training of personnel. The financial intelligence arms of numerous countries, including Cyprus, Latvia, Switzerland and Vanuatu, are grossly under-staffed, and cannot adequately investigate suspicious-activity reports filed by financial institutions, conduct on-site inspections of domestic financial institutions, provide training programmes for financial officers, issue record-keeping and reporting guidelines to financial institutions or shepherd foreign requests for assistance. Domestic law-enforcement and regulatory agencies that oversee offshore jurisdictions must also assure Western regulators that financial institutions are complying with money-laundering legislation. This could be accomplished by increasing the number of unscheduled on-site inspections and sanctioning financial institutions that fail to submit suspicious activities reports with fines and closures. Finally, a number of countries, including Antigua, Dominica, and Vanuatu, must provide better regulation of e-commerce (such as cyber-suites) and Internet gaming to reduce the chance that individuals will launder funds through these largely anonymous forms of electronic financial institutions. Direct pressure can work. In spring 2001, for example, the US prevailed on the Bahamas to revoke al-Taqwa's licence, and in March 2002, the Swiss government initiated an intense criminal investigation of the network at the prompting of US Attorney-General John Ashcroft.

Even with such steps, limitations in government capacity – especially in countries in transition or under non-democratic rule – will continue to create new pockets of opportunity for financial criminals and terrorists. Al-Taqwa, for instance, has continued to do business. Ongoing responses are required of the world's stronger regulators and enforcement agencies. Broadly speaking, the multiplicity of jurisdictions with lax or secretive banking laws and the resistance of some to international oversight suggests that progress in controlling money-laundering at the level of international law will be slow. In the meantime, it may be necessary to look to diplomatic leverage and to national legislation with transnational reach to address the problem. The latter could include nationally imposed sanctions with an extra-territorial dimension, taking a form similar to those imposed under the US Iran–Libya Sanctions Act. Such measures would have to be used selectively. But many jurisdictions that acquiesce in money-laundering are economically dependent on the provision of financial services. This suggests that the threat or imposition of sanctions by economically powerful governments in countries housing large numbers of potential depositors could have a quick and effective deterrent effect, and therefore might not unduly chill international commerce.

Even if sovereign jurisdictions respond to that kind of pressure, or to name-and-shame exercises, it will be difficult for any single country to regulate multinational financial institutions that operate transnationally and can move money instantaneously across national borders. For the most part, such institutions do not knowingly participate in laundering schemes, but they do consider compliance offices a bothersome cost of doing business that exceeds the reputational risk of being exposed as a money-laundering vehicle. To discourage them from inadvertent participation in laundering, following good anti-laundering compliance practices needs to be turned into a commercial advantage. Neither markets nor politics would likely tolerate the imposition of an institutional blacklist on global finance. A more acceptable alternative, proposed by a former US Deputy Assistant Secretary of State for International Law Enforcement, might be a 'white list'. Inclusion on such a list would denote comprehensive adherence to know-your-customer and other anti-money-laundering practices. The honour of membership might not matter to private enterprises seeking financial services. But public international institutions – for example, the UN, the IMF, the World Bank and the EU – could agree to extend preferences to those on the list for handling their funds. Such organisations command sufficient assets to create a powerful positive incentive for larger financial institutions to self-police their operations more effectively.

US Military Transformation after 11 September

In the mid-1980s, American proponents of military reform, led by the iconoclastic long-time Director of the Office of Net Assessment, Andrew Marshall, emphasised that transformation could not proceed from technology alone. Rather, a wholesale 'revolution in military affairs' – encompassing not only new technologies but also innovative operational concepts and novel organisational adaptations – was required to produce quantum improvements in military effectiveness. But while the 1991 war in the Persian Gulf showed signs of revolutionary changes in warfare, virtually all the weapons employed during that war were decades old. Moreover, there was no evidence of any dramatic doctrinal or organisational adaptations reflected in the overall campaign, however successful it proved to be. A decade after the Gulf War, transformation rather than revolution has become the American quest. President George W. Bush, during his election campaign, raised the prospect of 'skipping a generation' of military procurement to exploit new information technologies as a means of implementing true transformation of military capabilities against new, uncertain future threats. Based on the vision articulated by Secretary of Defense Donald Rumsfeld – and formulated by the now-octogenarian Marshall – there appear to be six key elements of military transformation:

- a future vision of warfare;
- the selection of senior leaders willing to implement military reform;
- a willingness to fund so-called leap-ahead technologies;
- the creation of sufficient organisational slack to foster innovation and institutional change;
- the reform of procurement strategy; and
- a divestment strategy that frees up funding for transformational systems.

Change, however, will probably be evolutionary and will occur over a decade, if not two. Among the principal reasons is that the uniformed services are generally reluctant to relinquish old weapons systems and force structures. Based on a historical analysis of Germany's transformation efforts prior to the Second World War, the Bush administration assumed that only 10–15% of the total force might in fact need to be altered to provide the sorts of capabilities that would yield the improvements policymakers were seeking. This led to focusing transformation on rapidly deployable joint task forces to better overcome adversaries' attempts to deny the US access to regions of interest. In June 2001, Rumsfeld reported that a force structure alternative to the two-major-theatre-war force was being tested. But Pentagon officials also wanted to reduce 2.8 out of 10 active Army divisions, 16 out of 61 active US Air Force fighter wings and 1–2 out of 12 carrier battle groups. Both the service chiefs and the Joint Chiefs of Staff continued to oppose reductions, and instead supported maintaining or increasing force structure.

On 5 September, in testimony before the Senate Appropriations Committee, Rumsfeld stated that the US should spend at least 3% of its GDP on defence and repeated his claim that the Department of Defense (DoD) would need a budget of at least $347.2 billion in FY2002 just to cover inflation costs and avoid emergency spending bills – more for modernisation and transformation. These pleas seemed to fall on many deaf ears in the Democrat-controlled Senate. The absence of a clear threat, coupled with the renewed prospect of federal budget deficits, made defence a dark horse in the annual competition for federal resources. The president acknowledged that the nation could ill-afford to pay for all of the weapons programmes then planned. On 10 September, Rumsfeld launched a public counterattack against the Pentagon's bureaucracy. 'The world has [changed], and we have not yet changed sufficiently', he argued. 'The clearest and most important transformation is from a bipolar Cold War world where threats were visible and predictable to one in which they arise from multiple sources – most of which are difficult to anticipate and many of which are impossible to know today'. These threats would make themselves known in the most horrific terms on the very next day, when terrorists from Osama bin Laden's al-Qaeda organisation exploited weaknesses in the US aviation security system and hijacked four separate US commercial aircraft, using them as jet fuel-laden missiles to attack US financial and government targets in New York City and Washington DC.

A new American way of war

Secretary Rumsfeld suggested in September that the campaign against the Taliban and al-Qaeda – *Operation Enduring Freedom* – would be a very different sort of war, and the war in fact departed from the Gulf War, Bosnia and Kosovo campaigns in a number of important ways. To be sure, the war shared with its predecessors the somewhat predictable opening gambit of strikes by cruise missiles, naval and land-based tactical air, and long-range bombers, but it departed from script thereafter. Perhaps the most dramatic evidence that this was a new sort of war was to be found in the images of US Special Forces troops on horseback, with pack animals carrying their gear. Rather than marking a return to nineteenth-century horse cavalry, however, the use of special operations forces facilitated the coordination of attacks with the ground forces of local Afghan commanders. More fundamentally, however, a common communications grid that linked special operations forces who could detect, identify and designate targets to the strike aircraft flying overhead in that engagement zone, resolved some of the operational problems that had limited air power's effectiveness against fleeting targets in past conflicts, including Iraqi *Scud* launchers in the Gulf War, Serb forces threatening Bosnian enclaves from 1992–95 and Serb fielded forces in Kosovo in 1999. Of course, special-operations units were able to operate fairly openly in Afghanistan because opposition was often insubstantial. Nevertheless, the unprecedented integration of ground-air communications represented a revolutionary operational concept, not only from the vantage point of the performance improvements it conferred, but also in breaking down institutional barriers that historically had prevented the integration of special operations forces with conventional capabilities. In this context, Vietnam-era B-52s, 'daisy cutters', cluster bombs, AC-130 gunships, and other weapons were devastatingly effective against Taliban and al-Qaeda forces and cave systems.

The campaign also saw the operational debuts of several advanced weapon systems that were transformational in their own right. The *Predator* unmanned combat aerial vehicle (UCAV) carrying *Hellfire* antitank missiles – operated by CIA or Air Force personnel – offered the promise of strike capabilities of over 24 hours duration ('long-dwell' capabilities) with ongoing targeting and navigational control from the ground ('positive control'), while reducing the risk to pilots. The AGM-86D deep bunker-penetrating air-launched cruise missile – an improvement over the earlier-generation GBU-28 'bunker busters', also used in the campaign and capable of penetrating six metres of concrete – provided a new capability against the increasingly important category of deeply buried targets. *Global Hawk*, *Predator* and other unmanned aerial vehicles (UAVs), also provided real-time targeting information, reducing sensor-to-shooter delays. By the time the conflict was winding down, then, not even the combination of Special Forces on horseback with pack animals and advanced surveillance and targeting systems seemed out of place in the Afghan operating environment.

If it was a different sort of war, it also would be a different sort of peace. Consistently with the new president's complaints during the campaign about his predecessor's penchant for deploying US troops in peace operations and nation building in far-away places, US officials demurred on the question of participating in a peacekeeping operation in post-war Afghanistan. As Vice President Dick Cheney put it: 'We're not eager to have the United States come in and become an occupying power in Afghanistan'. By January 2002, a peacekeeping force – with the UK in the vanguard – was in place. The United States promised to support the operation with a quick-reaction force, as well as intelligence, logistics and other assets, while promising $296 million in aid (part of a multinational package of about $4.5 billion) to nudge the Northern Alliance into joining a broad-based government of national unity. At the same time, by March, persistent insecurity suggested the need to expand the peacekeeping operation beyond Kabul, and stiff al-Qaeda and Taliban resistance resurfaced near the eastern border, necessitating the commitment of over 1,000 American ground troops. But Washington's measured response to potential transnational terrorist threats in Yemen, Somalia, the Philippines and Georgia – involving preventive measures and training assistance rather than direct military engagement – showed that it understood the use of military force to be an extraordinary remedy in the counter-terrorism campaign.

The US defence budget: vision versus readiness

The issuance of the 2001 report of the Quadrennial Defense Review (QDR) on 30 September 2001, coming less than three weeks after the terrorist attacks, reflected little of the original intent to institute a major programme of transformation. To be sure, much of the new transformation vision, including the possibility of establishing a joint task force to focus on the most difficult military challenges, made it into the QDR. Also of note is the replacement of the two-war strategy with a broad set of policy goals designed to give military leaders more flexibility in shaping the future force structure, and the institution of a capabilities-based rather than threat-based process for determining new military requirements. The latter reflects the fact that the US must contend less with who and where the adversary might be than with how the adversary will fight. But aside from these modest shifts in strategy, the QDR produced little in the way of substantive change, particularly when judged against the six elements of transformation noted above.

In turn, the particulars of the FY2003 defence budget, released on 4 February, suggested a commitment to transformation hedged by operational needs, as a number of weapon system programmes that had demonstrated their value in the war in Afghanistan received a boost in the budget. The president requested $379bn for FY2003, which represented an increase of $46bn (about 15%) over the DoD's FY2002 appropriation – the biggest since the Reagan administration. At the macro level, the administration planned significant increases for its modernisation funding – approximately 10% in real terms. Procurement accounts would be increased to $68.7bn, $7.6bn more than in FY2002. And more help for modernisation (if not transformation) was on the way: by FY2007, procurement was projected to increase to $98.9bn, a level much closer to that specified by the Congressional Budget Office than the $60bn target that had prevailed during the Clinton administration. Meanwhile, research, development, test and evaluation accounts would be increased by $5.3bn to $53.9bn, including funding for 13 new 'transformational' programmes that would yield entirely new capabilities. According to Secretary Rumsfeld's 5 February testimony before the Senate Armed Services Committee, transformation priorities included protecting bases of operation and homeland defence; denying enemies sanctuary; projecting and sustaining power in distant theatres; leveraging information technology; conducting effective information operations; and enhancing space operations.

On top of the estimated $10bn in operational costs that were expected for the war on terrorism in FY2003, DoD identified another $9.4bn in longer-term requirements. These included a number of programmes that were both associated with the successful prosecution of the war on terrorism in Afghanistan, and deemed essential to the administration's larger transformation efforts. Among these were expanded precision-guided munitions programmes. A total of $1.1bn would provide for a higher production rate for the Joint Direct Attack Munition (JDAM) and laser-guided bombs; $146m was provided for remanufacture of the tactical *Tomahawk* cruise missile; and another $54m was earmarked for the development of the small-diameter bomb intended to minimise collateral damage, a key transformation theme. Another area of emphasis encompassed UAVs and UCAVs. Funding for UAV programmes such as *Global Hawk* and *Predator* was due to increase from $359.4m in FY2001, to $970.9m in FY2002 and $1.1bn in FY2003. Production of *Predators* was to rise from seven in 2001 to 16 in 2002, to 22 in 2003, while *Global Hawk* production was to increase from zero in 2001 to two in 2002 and three in 2003. Funding for the accelerated development of UCAVs for the Air Force and Navy also was to rise, from $27.8m in FY2001 to $141m in FY2003. Command-and-control and space capabilities, and force protection efforts also were to get a boost. The budget included $2.5bn for battlefield computer networks. Finally, special-operations capabilities were slated for improvement, with on-board sensors to detect and counter missile threats, towed decoys and low-band jammers to defeat radar-guided missiles, and four additional AC-130U gunships.

Whereas the war seems to have once again demonstrated the value of long-range strike capabilities – whether stealthy B-2s, or non-stealthy penetrating bombers and cruise missile launchers such as B-52 and B-1B – DoD tied its theme of 'manoeuvre and air dominance' to the development of an increasingly stealthy tactical fighter force, including the Air Force's F-22 *Raptor*, the Joint Strike Fighter (JSF) and the Navy's F/A-18 *Super Hornet*. Some $4.6bn to build 23 F-22s and start work on 27 more in FY 2003 would be provided, while JSF development funding would rise $1.5bn in 2002 to nearly $3.5bn in 2003. The F/A-18 programme would get $3.3bn for 44 planes. To help finance all of these modernisation efforts, a total of $9.3bn in programme reductions, management improvements and other initiatives were planned.

11 September: more confirmation than catalyst

The war in Afghanistan did not inaugurate new American thinking about warfighting and defence planning. Rather, it accented Rumsfeld's early transformation initiatives. These, while ambitious, had generated resentment among uniformed officers and career Pentagon civilians as an attempt to preempt the normal bureaucratic process. The review process grew unwieldy, expanding to 18 separate study groups, most of them composed of experts outside of the Office of the Joint Chiefs of Staff and the service staffs. But the events of 11 September gave new resonance to an overarching question posed by many transformation advocates: Why can't the sole military superpower exploit its dominant military advantage more effectively? Transformation advocates respond that American dominance is manifested largely in airpower improvements, which are best suited to the defeat of well-known fixed targets and exposed enemy forces in regular wars. American military strengths produce very uncertain advantages in highly asymmetric conflicts. The United States' current campaign against terrorism – particularly the challenges of rapidly bringing forces to bear on the ground in harsh operating environments and identifying and protecting against bioterrorist threats – exemplify precisely the kinds of new challenges against which current US strengths are suspect.

More particularly, 11 September underscored the need for considerably greater flexibility to configure forces to enable them to respond quickly to a variety of diverse contingencies, not just major regional campaigns. Rapid and agile response to emerging threats is a key thematic element in America's transformation vision. In June 2001, the report based on retired US Air Force General James McCarthy's 'transformation study', commissioned by Rumsfeld, had highlighted the importance of projecting force both rapidly and potently to halt aggression, combining precision with speed, and undertaking more parallel, continuous and seamless operations (as opposed to sequential, scheduled and segmented ones). The vision of providing rapid, virtually instantaneous responses to threats stands in marked contrast to the lengthy build-up phases that have preceded all US and coalition military engagements since the end of the Cold War.

The 2001 QDR, though far from revolutionary, did lend some substance to this vision. In particular, it called for the examination of several Standing Joint Task Forces (SJTFs), most prominently one earmarked to execute an 'unwarned, extended-range conventional attack against fixed and mobile targets at varying depths'. This SJTF would focus on a major shortcoming in US defence capabilities: the ability to continuously locate and track mobile targets at any range and rapidly attack them with precision. This would require enhanced intelligence capabilities, including a space-based radar system, more human-intelligence resources on the ground, and improved airborne systems, all of which would be netted together to locate and track critical mobile targets and provide actionable strike information to attack resources in near-real time. Creating such an SJTF is seen as furnishing the 'vanguard' for a transformed American military. It would provide (on top of operational benefits) a test bed for new operational concepts, organisational changes and new technologies in both new organisational entities and legacy forces. The capabilities implied in the SJTF concept do embody a future vision of warfare, and reflect precisely the kind of response options required to cope with the absence of solid warning, the fleeting nature of targets and the need for instantaneous action. But the concept does not address the other five criteria of military transformation – namely, choosing the right senior leaders, developing the required leap-ahead technologies (for example, to support real-time detection and tracking of moving targets), creating organisational flexibility needed to nourish innovation, reforming procurement strategy and divestment to liberate funding for new systems.

Only time will tell how successful the Rumsfeld Pentagon will be in choosing the appropriate leaders, but there is already a certain irony in the selection of a new Chairman of the Joint Chiefs of Staff, Air Force General Richard Myers. The outgoing Chairman, Army General Henry Shelton, came from the Army Special Forces, which arguably makes him eminently qualified to deal with the immediate challenge of rooting out terrorist cells in hostile environments. Myers has specialised in space warfare, a pet area of transformation advocates but not one necessarily relevant to the crisis at hand. Only time will tell, however, whether General Myers – or indeed, Rumsfeld himself – will hand-select a new cadre of transformation-oriented officers and place them in key service and joint-staff posts.

The funding of leap-ahead technologies – with the notable exception of space-based radar surveillance capability – shows little if any progress because the 2001 QDR put off any decisions on divesting major weapons programmes or force structure changes. Moreover, urgent homeland-defence and short-term operational expenditures precipitated by 11 September have crowded out advanced research to a significant extent. On the other hand, the 11 September-inspired plan to create a new unified command consolidating military homeland defence and civil support responsibilities under a single US-based commander-in-chief has also removed those responsibilities from Joint Forces Command (JFCOM). In theory, this leaves JFCOM free to function as an experimental incubator for transformation ideas. General Myers, in his 5 February posture statement to Congress, noted that JFCOM in summer 2002 would coordinate the Millennium Challenge 2002 joint experiment, testing its model of the standing joint force headquarters. More importantly, he stated: 'Joint experimentation is a key element of the transformation process, and we are revising the Unified Command Plan to enable [JFCOM] to focus more time and effort on experimentation and transformation efforts. Naturally, we need to use the lessons from Operation Enduring Freedom in the joint experimentation process to ensure we are prepared for subsequent battles in the war against terrorism'. The tenfold increase in research, development, test and evaluation items in the budget lends substance to this statement's suggestion that JFCOM's role as a catalyst of transformation will become more robust.

At the same time, however, 11 September has made it harder to achieve sufficient organisational slack (within the military services, the Pentagon, and the industrial base) to foster innovation. Even under the most favourable conditions, innovation would be difficult until the military services – particularly their senior leadership – accepted the necessity of fundamental change. It had not done so before 11 September, and the emergence of a new and immediate threat is likely to make it even more cautious about drastic change.

Procurement reform, in turn, will gain appreciable momentum only when the military services bureaucratically accept the transformation process. This is primarily because under Title 10 of the US Code – that is, the codified body of federal statutes governing the armed forces – each military service has procurement responsibility for its major military systems. To the extent that the services remain wedded to service-centric as compared with joint solutions to future warfare, obstacles to integrating modern information technology effectively into the force structure will remain in place. Title 10 authority has fostered a procurement bureaucracy adept at procuring major weapons platforms rather than information systems.

There are several ways to work around Title 10's procurement limitations, however. Before the war, Rumsfeld had publicly complained that nearly a decade after the Gulf War, the US military had encountered the same problem in Kosovo that they had in the Gulf: special operators on the ground could see targets and strike aircraft could hit targets, but they couldn't communicate and operate together. Before 11 September, one of Rumsfeld's initiatives was to improve the linkages between special operators and strike aircraft, and several innovative alternative bureaucratic processes facilitated that initiative. For instance, Advanced Concept Technology Demonstrations (ACTDs), funded jointly by the Pentagon and a specific military user, are designed to quickly inject new technologies into a theatre military setting. The most notable products of the programme are the *Predator* and *Global Hawk* UAVs, which proved so effective against Taliban and al-Qaeda forces. The US Army's Warfighter Rapid Acquisition Program and the US Air Force's Warfighter Rapid Acquisition Process essentially mimic the ACTD process at the service level. The challenge facing Rumsfeld is to broaden these alternative processes to the point where their features become the standard. Accomplishing this will be particularly central to exploiting the huge American advantage in information technology, which results from dynamic, interactive commercial procurement regimes and not from sluggish, stove-piped military ones. But again, success is unlikely without broad bureaucratic acceptance of the underlying transformation goals.

Finally, a transformation-friendly divestment strategy must eliminate major capital investment in military systems thought to fit poorly into America's new military strategy. Such a programme would entail, in particular, phasing out certain Cold War legacy systems in favour of those employing new information or other leap-ahead technologies. As the 2001 QDR demonstrated, the Pentagon's new civilian leadership at this point is unable to make these difficult choices. Instead, it delayed making decisions by setting up additional study panels to investigate future options for such divestment and other critical matters. Moreover, with the proposed FY2003 budget, the Pentagon bowed to service pressure, continuing to fund three new fighter programmes, with cost estimates of $300–500bn over 10 years. These are precisely the kinds of programmes that transformation advocates argue require divestiture to free up resources. At the same time, the proposed budget would allocate $2bn for the Marine Corps' V-22 *Osprey* hybrid airplane/helicopter – a theoretically transformative technology, but one that has been dogged by flight-test failures and controversy. These choices illustrate the tension between transformation and vested interests in the US defence establishment.

Still more to do

In the short term, 11 September has drawn resources for operations away from transformation. But its revelation of new threats and the need for new ways to thwart them broadly favours transformation. Much is made of the unbreakable links among so-called 'platform' advocates, who represent key states and US congressional districts with large workforces having enormous stakes in the continuation of major legacy systems. These advocates include senior military officers and layers of deeply rooted bureaucracy within the civil and military services, government research and development organisations, and the defence industrial base. The fact that the Afghanistan campaign was fought so differently from those preceding it makes it difficult for many such advocates to insist on the primacy of pet systems. But the fundamental transformation challenge is to induce senior military leaders to identify and select junior military officers who will ultimately form the basis for more flexible and original military thinking within the services. The cultures of the respective American military services remain preoccupied with engineering management and administration rather than new theories of warfare and new operational concepts for achieving victory. Future military innovation – built around the notion of network-centric warfare – entails unprecedented real-time collaboration among several military organisations, which therefore must be jointly configured on a more or less permanent basis. Consequently, strong top-down civilian leadership from the Pentagon may be essential to convince the military services of the efficacy of such changes. Rumsfeld's authority to select senior leaders based on their willingness and ability to effect transformation is perhaps his most important lever of change, and 11 September has probably, on balance, enhanced it.

On 11 December, President Bush returned to The Citadel, the military academy in Charleston, South Carolina, where he had two years earlier presented his vision for the future US military, and took up the topic again. The president identified transforming the military as one of three newly 'urgent and enduring priorities for America', along with preventing the proliferation of weapons of mass destruction and their delivery systems, and strengthening 'the advantage that good intelligence gives our country'. The president pointed to the campaign in Afghanistan as a portent of what was to come. 'These past two months have shown that an innovative doctrine and high-tech weaponry can shape and then dominate an unconventional conflict'. He added that 'real-time intelligence, local allied forces, special forces, and precision air power ... has taught us more about the future of our military than a decade of blue ribbon panels and think-tank symposiums'. The 11 September attacks and their aftermath, then, have sharpened and lent credibility to the Bush administration's pre-existing ideas for defence planning and military transformation. The combination of broad support for higher defence budgets and the growing perception that Rumsfeld had it more right than wrong seems likely to ease the implementation of those ideas. But there is still a very long way to go.

Post-Globalisation? Anti-Capitalists in Retreat

The anti-globalisation movement's date of birth as a headline-grabbing phenomenon is usually seen as the World Trade Organization (WTO)'s Seattle summit, held from 30 November to 3 December 1999. In Seattle, the protests turned violent, and transfixed television viewers with scenes of pitched battles between demonstrators and riot police rarely seen in the United States since the anti-Vietnam War protests of the 1960s. The coincidence of disruptive mass protest, then President Bill Clinton's publicly expressed sympathy with their concerns and the failure of the meeting to produce a new global trade round led many protesters to believe that their tactics had worked. In fact, the governments involved did not require such outside stimulus, as they lacked the political commitment to make the compromises needed to launch a new round. Nevertheless, this apparent efficacy fed the protesters' sense of empowerment. Well-planned mass demonstrations became all the rage, and the new standard was one of popular unrest often met with state suppression. In varying degrees, this pattern was followed at the International Monetary Fund (IMF) and World Bank meetings in Prague in September 2000; at a meeting of the World Economic Forum (WEF) in the same month; at the biannual summit of the Asia–Europe Meeting in Seoul in October 2000; at the EU summit in Nice in December 2000; the following month at the WEF conference in Davos in Switzerland; and in April 2001 in Quebec City at a WTO meeting intended to facilitate a Free Trade Area of the Americas.

Who are the anti-globalists?

Driving all of those who call themselves 'anti-globalists' is the perception that the industrialised world is tightening its grip on the world economy: foreign direct investment flows increased from $114.4 billion per year in the late 1980s to $865.5bn in 1999. But the peripatetic participants in these protests need to be distinguished from indigenous – and indeed, more genuine – grassroots anti-globalists. The latter include, among others, the guerrilla movement Ejército Zapatista de Liberacion Nacional, led by 'Subcomandante Marcos' in Mexico's Chiapas state. The Zapatistas movement has violently resisted the dislocations visited on their rural traditions by the Mexican government's economic modernisation plans. Groups with similar motivations, if more moderate methods, could arise in any of a number of regions that, for one reason or another, have been resistant to US-style globalisation – notably, sub-Saharan Africa, South-west Asia, increasingly South-east Asia and the Andean region of South America. Indeed, according to the World Bank, during the 1990s, some two billion people lived in countries in which trade diminished in relation to national income, economic growth flattened and poverty rose. But the rural poor living in those places can't afford plane tickets to Davos. Rather, the worldwide movement, although it sees itself as the champion of the world's poor, is primarily a rich-world phenomenon, with its main bases of support in Western Europe, North America and other prosperous regions such as Australasia. In part, this reflects the greater financial resources and mobility of those in the rich world. But it has also inspired condescension and contempt from mainstream politicians and media, who have tended to regard the protesters as, at best, well-meaning but ideologically pretentious.

This assessment had merit. The protesters purport to represent the interests of the voiceless and powerless, but are in fact unelected dogmatists hampering the get-togethers of statesmen and governments that enjoy real democratic mandates from their electorates. While the interest of the protesters in trade issues and their focus on multinational institutions such as the WTO, the EU and NAFTA has led to their being labelled 'anti-globalists', their existence as a 'movement' is made possible by the globalising technology of the Internet. Many of the protesters also welcome other features of a globalised world, such as the convergence of labour standards. It is capitalism to which they object. But unlike the Cold War-era generation of protesters, they have no economic model to defend in its place. Indeed, some are not even anti-capitalist but rather, to coin an even uglier term, 'anti-neo-liberal': opposed to the harsher, less tempered form of capitalism functioning in the 'Anglo-Saxon' world of the United States and post-Thatcher Britain.

Some of the protesters' motivations are benign, even noble. Before Seattle, at the Group of Eight (G-8) summit of industrialised nations in Birmingham, England, on 15–17 May 1998, 50,000 people had peacefully held hands to surround the site of the meetings to press their call for debt relief as part of the Jubilee 2000 'Drop the Debt' campaign. Jubilee 2000 attracted religious leaders such as the Dalai Lama; celebrities such as the boxer Muhammad Ali and Bono the rock singer; and eventually mainstream politicians such as Gordon Brown, the British Chancellor of the Exchequer. It yielded the biggest petition in history, with 24 million names. Birmingham also brought together previously divergent groups, including a 'blue–green' alliance of 'Teamsters' (trade unionists) and 'Turtles' (environmentalists) – once precluded by the 'blue' belief that 'green' hostility to big business could cost jobs – to lobby against 'fast-track' trade authority for the US president. Most protesters would like to see the massive north–south economic disparities narrowed, and Third World countries liberated from crushing external debt.

But their arguments are also substantively weak, and frequently as selfish as they are selfless. They attack institutions and policies – notably free trade – that offer the best means of realising the ends that they themselves espouse, such as the eradication of worldwide poverty. They have some forceful points to make, but many are contradictory. Western environmentalists and labour activists want to see rules imposed on developing countries that those countries and their people themselves oppose, since industrialisation and sweatshops offer a marked improvement on existing opportunities. There are inherent conflicts of interest – for instance, between anti-globalising European farmers wanting to see local agriculture and an age-old way of life subsidised, and poor-country food-producers who are thereby shut out of big markets.

Despite the appearance of growing legitimacy occasioned by Seattle, then, before 2001 the anti-globalisation movement lacked real influence vis-à-vis states. This is probably because most of the protesters are law-abiding, peaceable citizens. Yet the very fact of their demonstrations was bound to attract what Tony Blair, the British prime minister, called, at the June 2001 EU summit in Gothenburg, a 'travelling circus of anarchists'. The Gothenburg summit came at the end of a visit to Europe by President George W. Bush. A number of Bush's policies attracted opprobrium from a broad range of European political opinion. The most aggravating were his summary public abandonment of the Kyoto Protocol on cutting carbon dioxide emissions in order to reduce global warming (although Congress would not have ratified it in any event), and his insistence on pursuing missile defence in the face, at the time, of fierce Russian and Chinese objections to anything that might undermine the 1972 US–Soviet Anti-Ballistic Missile Treaty, as well as scepticism from his partners in NATO. After Bush had left the summit, the mood descended swiftly from the coarse – featuring collective 'mooning' – to the thuggishly violent. The target of the protests became more generalised, covering the EU itself and then the capitalist system as a whole. Demonstrators – who totalled 20,000 – tried repeatedly to approach the conference hall where EU leaders were meeting, but were constantly driven back by the police. This only furthered the impression of besieged isolation that had become the norm at such get-togethers. Outside the fortifications, 21 policemen were injured, three protesters were shot and wounded, and dozens were arrested. Sweden's second city suffered an estimated $10m in property damage from mass vandalism.

By mid-2001, then, the 'travelling circus' had become a very big tent indeed. There were still earnest Christians pursuing a belated Jubilee; earnest environmentalists; pranksters intent on baring their behinds or dressing up in funny clothes; and stuntmen trained at the Ruckus Society, a California institution that teaches courses in non-violent protesting skills such as 'how to hang yourself from an urban structure' like a billboard. These types seemed to dominate the May Day protests in London on 1 May 2001, which – though met by a massive and pre-emptive police presence prompted by genuine hooliganism the previous year – never appeared close to degenerating into large-scale violence. But more baleful elements were also infiltrating the movement: semi-violent demonstrators armed with marbles to combat mounted police and citrus fruit to withstand tear gas; avowed anarchists; eco-terrorists; Trotskyites of various stripes; and even old-fashioned Stalinists. In the jargon that had grown up around such events, protesters included both 'fluffies' – the peaceful ones, such as the Tutte Bianche, an Italian affiliate of the Wombles (White Overalls Movement Building Libertarian Effective Struggle) – and 'spikies', gathered on an ad hoc basis by 'black bloc' tactics such as arm-linking, who believe in violent confrontation as a way to make a wilfully deaf political system uncork its ears. The violent fringe, for whom the point of the protest was not the cause but the violence used to further it, were in the minority, but, as always, had a disproportionate influence.

The Genoa G-8 summit

Six weeks after the Gothenburg EU summit, on 19–22 July 2001, an even more sobering scene materialised at the G-8 summit in the northern Italian city of Genoa. In Genoa, the two-year trend of worsening violence peaked. More than 200,000 protesters gathered. There were two days of street violence, in which more than 230 people were injured, nearly 300 people were arrested and some $50m worth of property damage was caused. On 20 July 2001, a few hardcore rabble-rousers instigated massive, violent street protests against Italian security forces and paramilitary policemen, who had aggressive rules of engagement. Carlo Giuliani, 23, was shot dead in a Genoa backstreet by an even younger Italian policeman.

That, sooner or later, somebody would get killed, was not a surprise. Giuliani's death, however, did give the 'anti-globalisation movement' its first martyr. Further, it appeared to most observers that excessive force had been used by the Italian authorities: a government inquiry was set up after widespread allegations of unwarranted police brutality, including a raid on a school used as a dormitory for the Genoa Social Forum, an umbrella protest group, and reports of beatings at a police station. These developments muted the threat of outright terrorism that had been burgeoning within the movement, momentarily gave the movement some moral high ground and, on balance, enhanced its credibility. Thus, the events in Genoa seemed to mark a sort of coming of age for the movement. Between 20 July and 11 September, the movement was viewed as an accepted fact of international political life that seemed poised to influence not just the conduct of diplomacy and summitry but also the formation of policy.

The spectacle of Genoa under siege had raised questions about the very future of the G-7/G-8 process. There was talk of turning the meetings into much smaller affairs, held, perhaps, aboard a ship in the middle of the ocean. Already, the WTO's 2001 ministerial meeting was to be held in November in Doha, Qatar. After the street-fighting in Seattle, this venue was chosen not for its ease of access, or possession of facilities for a massive conference attracting tens of thousands of delegates, media and protesters, but for the opposite reasons: that hotel rooms and other amenities were limited and it was relatively easy to curtail the numbers of uninvited guests. In June 2001, a meeting to be held by the World Bank in Barcelona on poverty alleviation was cancelled altogether after violent street protests by anti-globalisation activists.

Governments had also made policy changes. Gordon Brown called on rich countries to double aid from $50bn to $100bn, and US Secretary of State Colin Powell also urged more assistance from them. One of the more defensible demands of many of the protesters – for faster and more generous forgiveness of the foreign debts of the world's poorest countries – has been partially met by the G-7 and the international financial institutions. By November 2001, under the Highly Indebted Poor Countries (HIPC) debt-relief programme, the IMF and the World Bank had finalised debt-relief plans for 24 of the 41 HIPCs and relieved them of $36bn in debt-service obligations. Another, more controversial proposal for the imposition of a tax on foreign-exchange transactions to deter speculation had progressed from the status of an eccentric economic idea promoted by once-obscure French organisation, ATTAC (Association pour une Taxation des Transactions financières pour l'Aide aux Citoyens), to a cause with a mass following, embraced by left-centre political leaders such as Lionel Jospin, prime minister of France. ATTAC itself now boasts 30,000 members, and dispatched about 5,000 to Genoa.

More generally, there was a sense that the governments needed to confront more constructively the fact that while the American economy enjoyed unprecedented expansion, dragging much of the rest of the world in its wake, the way the benefits of this prosperity were spread was unfair, and becoming more so. The *Financial Times* noted: 'just over a decade after the fall of the Berlin Wall and the "end of history" promised by Francis Fukuyama, who argued free-market liberalism had triumphed forever, there is a growing sense that global capitalism is once again fighting to win the argument'.

The impact of 11 September

That article was published on 10 September, when Genoa still resonated. Indeed, the Genoa summit probably would have become the year's most significant transnational event. But a day later, the attacks on the World Trade Center and the Pentagon overshadowed Genoa and almost everything else in international affairs. The attack on some of the most striking symbols of American power and global capitalism was far more spectacular and horrifying than anything anti-globalisers could ever have imagined. In many parts of the rich world, anti-Americanism, and, by extension, anti-capitalism, went out of fashion. The anti-globalisation protest movement seemed winded. Some of the big annual events on its calendar were postponed or cancelled. Others went ahead, including the Doha meeting, which finished the job Seattle had been unable to complete, the launch of a new round of trade talks. There were demonstrations in October and November in a number of European countries; their target, however, was not 'capitalism' or 'globalisation', but the US-led military action in Afghanistan. On 8 October, the day after US bombing began, several thousand people turned out in Rome, Naples and Palermo, and on 14 October, about 20,000 demonstrators coordinated by the Stop the War Coalition in London marched from Hyde Park Corner to Trafalgar Square chanting 'We want peace'. Also on 14 October, 200,000 people – including members of Tutte Bianche and the Greens – marched from Perugia to Assisi in protest of the war, and 70,000 protesters in Calcutta staged a 12-kilometre march. Such efforts were reprised in both Italy and Britain in November. Street-protesters, and the journalists who sustain them, had found another cause.

The semi-annual EU summit that followed Gothenburg was held in Laeken, Belgium, in December 2001. There were, as usual, large-scale protests, staged by ATTAC and other groups calling for a more 'social' Europe. But while cobblestones were ripped up and tear-gas and water cannons used, the demonstrations were less violent than those seen six months earlier. The non-Belgian media and politicians paid little heed. While 11 September broke the movement's seemingly inexorable momentum, however, most of the factors that led to the growth of the anti-globalisation movement persist. The phenomenon will continue to be a major political issue for the governments of the Western democracies, a problem for the hosts of important international gatherings and, in the nervous post-11 September security environment, a concern to intelligence agencies seeking to thwart possible terrorist attacks. A special EU summit concerning economic issues on 15–16 March 2002 in Barcelona drew up to 300,000 protesters. But although there were 62 arrests, the demonstrations were largely peaceful.

The anti-globalisation movement clearly does have some resiliency. Its more extreme elements and the rightward tilt of traditionally left-leaning governments may well inspire the resurgence of left-wing terrorist groups. For example, on 19 March 2002, a faction of the Italian Red Brigades – which had been largely quiescent since the 1980s – assassinated Italian government economic adviser Marco Biagi. Subsequently, the group issued a virulent 26-page communiqué by e-mail, stating that Biagi was killed for representing 'the interests of bourgeois imperialism' and praising 11 September as a model of effective terrorism. At the same time, the anti-globalisation movement itself does not appear to pose a significant threat to the established order. The Biagi assassination also inspired massive street protests against political violence. The immediate challenge to state authorities and 'globalising' multilateral targets is largely an occasional – but nonetheless serious – one of maintaining civil control. Even before 11 September, the Gothenburg and Genoa experiences had prompted substantial and systematic transnational security responses. In July 2001, the EU started work on a database listing suspected protesters, with a view to barring them from entering a country where a protest was planned. Another database would list foreigners, so that third-country nationals could be identified and removed if they had not left within a prescribed time. Such efforts dovetail with heightened anti-terrorist and homeland-security measures – in particular, the push for an EU-wide arrest warrant in pursuit of a 'common area of freedom, justice and security' – taken in the wake of the 11 September attacks. Globetrotting anti-globalists may well be further inhibited by the ongoing high counter-terrorism alert.

Back to Ground Zero

At first glance, the events of 11 September made the anti-capitalist movement look much more dangerous than it had seemed, even after Genoa. They showed how a loose-knit, cellular group with fiercely held beliefs and careful planning and coordination can wreak havoc with the most modest of tools. But, mercifully, there is no sign that the sort of murderous fanaticism demonstrated on 11 September has any constituency among anti-capitalists. Nor, apart from their shared choice as targets of the symbols of capitalist power – the World Trade Center for al-Qaeda, McDonald's restaurants for the protesters – are there many discernible links between their campaign and Osama bin Laden's. Moreover, in assessing the terrorist risk, there is a crude but important distinction between the two groups. Al-Qaeda's devastating but low-tech acts of terrorism relied on the appeal of martyrdom, an appeal heightened by extreme Islam. Suicide was not an incidental effect of 11 September; it was integral to the attacks' effectiveness. One of their most terrifying aspects is the apparently inexhaustible supply of young men emerging from the

Islamic world ready to kill not just large numbers of others, but themselves. Few fellow protesters, on the other hand, envied Carlo Giuliani his early exit from this earth. Nor, as far as is known, were any intent on murder.

John Lloyd, the British writer, has argued that 11 September demonstrates that the anti-capitalist movement is in a blind alley: 'The only political grouping now using the tactics developed by the global movements – sporadic use of violence and oppositionism through uncontrollable and unpredictable networks – is bin Laden's al-Qaeda. In taking the destructive potential of such tactics and strategies to a far more lethal extreme, they have shown that the line of attack developed by the global movements cannot replace the current system of world governance'. Anti-capitalists, of course, bridle at Lloyd's linkage of their strategies with Osama bin Laden's. But 11 September does present a grotesque parody of their techniques of confrontational symbolic protest, and the aftermath does hint at their probable futility. Accordingly, the anti-capitalist movement has been weakened by 11 September. President Bush's stance that 'you are either with us, or with the terrorists' struck a chord with America's natural allies and diminished the acceptability of all civil violence as well as terrorism itself. Thus, anti-globalisation protesters called off as inappropriate training sessions for the 29–30 September 2001 meeting of the IMF and World Bank in Washington, which in the event were postponed for security reasons. While protests at the WEF meeting in New York from 31 January to 4 February 2002 covered a good portion of Manhattan and resulted in 150 arrests, the various incidents included almost none of the extreme violence that had abundantly occurred in previous demonstrations.

Furthermore, al-Qaeda damaged the global economy, which was already tilting into recession. After average 7% growth throughout the 1990s and 12% growth in 2001, global trade was essentially flat in 2001. This reversal of globalisation – even if only temporary – paradoxically takes the wind out of the movement's sails. Less prosperous middle-class populations are likely to have less sympathy with the protesters. Protesters themselves may become more concerned about their own economic security than the fate of the planet. And the non-governmental organisations that have played a central role in organising protests may find it harder to raise funds, many of which ultimately come from the corporations and institutions that anti-globalists attack. Of course, while 11 September has halted the march of the anti-capitalist movement, it has not gone away. Indeed, many of its weaknesses can also be viewed as strengths: its incoherence, inconsistency and internal contradictions are also evidence of the breadth of the coalition it represents. By early April 2002, hundreds of activists from Western European countries had travelled to the West Bank to act as 'human shields' for Palestinian leader Yasser Arafat in protest of Israeli policies. But the movement's future no longer relies largely, as it did before 11 September, on its own internal momentum – on the series of self-reinforcing protests that once seemed self-perpetuating as well.

In its initial phases, the counter-terrorism effort has effectively split the anti-capitalist movement between those who saw American bombing of Afghanistan as a fresh instance of the sort of global assertiveness that they found unacceptable, and those who generally rallied to the American cause. Even in France – arguably the centre of anti-Americanism in Europe – an opinion poll in late September 2001 indicated 63% support for France's participation in US-led military action. Globalisation, as an economic phenomenon, is far from dead. While foreign direct investment in rich countries in 2001 dropped steeply because of depressed equity markets, the decline was small with respect to poor countries. Further, UN and PricewaterhouseCoopers surveys in late 2001 indicated that multinational firms intended to expand international operations notwithstanding 11 September. But if this aggressiveness occurs in concert with a new world trade round – which the World Bank estimates could increase poor countries' GDP by $1.5 trillion and extricate 320m people from poverty by 2015 – the anti-globalisation movement is likely to find even less nourishment from those whose interests it purports to represent. If the trade round is frustrated, there will probably be less for the protesters to complain about. More broadly, 11 September has lowered state and public tolerance for political violence.

The Americas

The 11 September attacks posed unprecedented challenges to foreign and security policymakers in the United States. The primary tasks they had to undertake involved securing the country's territory and rallying nations around the world to help counter the threat of transnational terrorism that had suddenly become so horrifically salient. The first task was essentially insular, the second extrovert. One produced broader domestic surveillance and law-enforcement powers at the expense of individual liberties. The other prompted more proactive engagement of a broad array of coalition candidates. At the same time, President George W. Bush's administration treated the global counter-terrorism campaign primarily as one of self-defence that also coincided with the exigencies of international security. This meant that the US insisted on maintaining maximum operational control over military efforts to thwart terrorism – opting to prosecute the military campaign against terrorism for 'coalitions of the willing' rather than formal military alliances – while exacting an unprecedented level of logistical support and intelligence and law-enforcement cooperation from a wide range of capitals. Aggressively engaged with capitals throughout the world as a consequence of 11 September, at times the US also appeared to practice what European Union High Representative for Common Foreign and Security Policy Javier Solana called 'global unilateralism'.

The events of 11 September preempted the Bush administration's plans to stress relations within the Western Hemisphere early in his term. One immediate effect of the emphasis on homeland security was the dampening of efforts to achieve an accommodation with Mexico on illegal immigrants: although Bush was a pro-immigration president, in the medium term, US border policy would focus more on keeping people out rather than on letting them in. Washington also became less tolerant of terrorist movements in general. While transnational Islamic terrorist groups and those operating in strategically volatile locales like the Middle East and South Asia were most worrying, American officials also appeared to understand that any area plagued by terrorist-driven instability was a potential host for, or abettor to, al-Qaeda and therefore worthy of US attention. As a result of this greater sensitivity to destabilising forces as well as the frustrations of the US-sponsored 'Plan Colombia' anti-drug initiative in the Andes, by early 2002, the Bush administration appeared to favour broadening that initiative to include direct anti-insurgency efforts. Reinforcing this inclination was the collapse of the peace process in Colombia in February 2002, when

Map 1 The Americas

government troops moved to eject the Fuerzas Armadas Revolocionarias de Colombia (FARC – Revolutionary Armed Forces of Colombia) rebel group, after numerous breaches of good faith, from the large enclave ceded to the group pending peace negotiations. The resulting prospect that insecurity could spread throughout the region is likely to produce an even higher level of US law-enforcement involvement and military assistance in the northern Andes. This, in turn, may give rise to more proactive roles from previously reluctant regional actors like Brazil and extra-regional players like the European Union.

The United States' deep interest in security problems in Latin America seemed to contrast with its relative disengagement from economic ones. While Argentina's economic implosion was at bottom the product of bad domestic policies, and the International Monetary Fund (IMF) had extended Buenos Aires an $8 billion bailout loan in August 2001, the US did not support a quick bailout once the government defaulted on $141bn in debt in December 2001. This may have been particularly hurtful when contrasted to the greater largesse extended to an equally inept Turkey for strategic reasons. Argentina appeared to make constructive remedial moves in early 2002, and began negotiations with the IMF in March. Yet Washington's perceived disinterest in its plight has made Buenos Aires less eager to align itself with Washington and has the potential to lead to wider regional coolness towards the US. In 2001, the US administration's priority of free trade in the Western Hemisphere might have held such disaffection in check. But the administration's March 2002 protectionist decision to impose high tariffs on imported steel – though not directed at Latin America – has damaged its free-trade credentials. To ensure that an 'ideological contagion' of insular nationalism and populism does not spread in Latin America, the US may need to exercise proactive diplomatic and economic engagement in the Hemisphere, despite US counter-terrorism preoccupations. In March 2002, Bush pledged to increase the US foreign assistance budget in a speech at the Inter-American Development Bank, reiterated this intention at a UN conference on poverty in Monterrey, Mexico and subsequently visited El Salvador and Peru. This itinerary appeared to reflect his awareness of a nascent US image problem south of the US border, and the importance of restoring momentum to US diplomacy in the Western Hemisphere.

The United States: Maximum Mobilisation, Minimal State

With the horror and anguish of collapsing towers came also a shock of recognition about the nature of the world and of America's place in it. Foreigners, including those who wished America well and shared its anguish, could be bemused by this shock. Who were these Americans who – so long after Pearl Harbor, Vietnam and assorted calamities of the twentieth century – could still proclaim an innocence to be lost? Yet the American intuition was essentially correct. This genocidal strain of anti-Americanism, if not new, was something newly revealed. Osama bin Laden had been clear enough about this for nearly a decade, and had succeeded already in murdering hundreds, but now his words became deeds on an epic scale.

In trying to explain this *jihad* and the hatred behind it, a natural analytical divide opened up between those who thought America had been targeted for what it was and those who thought it was being punished for what it did. Was it American freedom (as President George W. Bush suggested in his first major speech after the attacks) or American power that inspired such fury? The dichotomy was artificial, of course, for American power and foreign policy were complex manifestations of a vast, wealthy society that was at once cosmopolitan and insular, deeply religious in its self-conception while fundamentally secularising in its influence, a status-quo superpower with revolutionary effect around the world. American power, in its economic, cultural, political and military dimensions, was innate; hence 'isolationism' – in the literal sense – had long ago become impossible. By this logic, moreover, there was little or nothing that the United States could do to deflect the enmity, which was inspired by America's existence rather than American policies. It was true, however, that America's strategic presence in the Persian Gulf and Middle East, and its close relationship with Israel, made the US a ready scapegoat for the misery, humiliations and rage of millions of Muslims. It was also true that every US administration since Franklin Delano Roosevelt's – and perhaps before his – had assumed that it was an American mission to make a world in its image. The question after 11 September was how this assumption might change.

The war at home

The direct experience of many living Americans includes the social and political changes wrought by the Second World War, the Cold War and Vietnam. Clearly America would be changed by its war against terrorism;

yet it was difficult to foresee the scope of the change not least because this was a war without any foreseeable end. The political terms of reference of 10 September became inoperative overnight. The question became whether American politics would return in any recognisable form.

That summer before the attack, Americans had faced the anxiety that an economic boom appeared, finally, to be faltering. Politics was strained by the residual bitterness of the disputed election result of the previous November. Democrats in Congress, claiming that President Bush had a strictly limited mandate, and pointing to polls showing that more Americans supported the policies of his defeated opponent, Al Gore, pressed for a co-leadership in the Senate (divided 50–50 with Vice-President Dick Cheney as a tie-breaking Republican vote). They also staged an early show of strength, mustering 42 votes against the nomination of John Ashcroft – a senator aligned with the religious right just defeated in his re-election bid – to be Attorney-General. Ashcroft's nomination was confirmed, 58–42, but Democrats warned that they had demonstrated the power to sustain filibusters against judicial nominees that they deemed too conservative.

Bush quickly won, however, what at the time looked to be the most important battle of his presidency. With help from conservative Democrats, he enacted the massive ten-year tax cut that had featured as the central plank of his campaign platform. In doing so, he said explicitly what Reagan-era tax-cutters had only occasionally implied: tax cuts were part of a Republican project to diminish the federal government by starving it of funds. Bush's victory was impressive, but conservative triumphalism provoked a backlash when, on 24 May 2001, moderate Republican Senator Jim Jeffords – citing the hardball intolerance of the conservative leadership – defected from his party and thereby threw control of the Senate to the Democrats. Bush had campaigned on a promise to end the partisan rancour, but Washington was as polarised as ever.

The events of 11 September stilled this rancour, at least for a time. Aside from some pockets in the academic and cultural left, there was effectively no political dissent from the administration's war aims. Polls showed well over 90% backing for the president's conduct of the war. Democratic leaders rendered immediate and unconditional support.

Initially, to be sure, the administration had to swim against an undercurrent of disquiet regarding the experience and capabilities of a president who, as candidate the previous year, had famously flubbed a challenge to name the president of Pakistan. In the early days of the crisis, there was some scepticism, *sotto voce*, about Bush's ability to take moral command of the stricken nation. On 11–12 September, the president was jetted around the country in line with crisis-contingency plans, addressing the nation only briefly and, it seemed, unsteadily from a couple of air bases. Almost by default, national attention shifted to New York mayor Rudi Giuliani, whose press conferences conveyed authority and blunt compassion in just the right blend. An element of disquiet continued through the months of October and November as the Capitol, congressional offices and, briefly, the Supreme Court were evacuated and a handful of Americans died from mailed anthrax. Various administration officials gave out incomplete or conflicting information about the magnitude of the anthrax threat, creating a generally clueless impression. (By spring of 2002 it was surmised, thought not yet established, that the anthrax murders were the work of a home-grown malefactor without links to al-Qaeda).

Bush recovered his confidence and found his voice quickly, however. In his first major speech after the attacks, delivered to both houses of Congress on 20 September, he struck a convincing balance, stressing the gravity of the threat and voicing confidence that the US would prevail. He included an obviously heartfelt appeal to avoid ethnic and religious scapegoating. This message of religious inclusiveness (which did not, it must be added, have much to offer non-believers) was repeated in high-profile visits to mosques. Aside from a few isolated incidents, an anti-Arab or anti-Islamic backlash failed to materialise.

There was sharper controversy about the extent to which civil-liberty traditions would have to be sacrificed. The administration did not need to remind anyone that a degree of measured paranoia was justified. The 11 September terrorists, though their cells were based in Europe, had travelled with ease among the hundreds of millions crossing the United States' de facto open borders. Some came as 'tourists' and others on student visas, but no one checked if the 'students' actually studied anything upon arrival, while those with tourist visas faced no obstacles to enrolling, for example, in flight school.

After the attacks, the FBI detained some 1,500 foreigners, mostly from Arab and other Islamic countries, and invited some 5,000 others for 'voluntary' questioning. This posed problems for a country where 'racial profiling' – that is, ethnically targeted dragnets – had already provoked anger and numerous lawsuits. (The 'profiling' issue became particularly heated in December 2001 when an Arab-American Secret Service agent, on his way to join President Bush's protection detail in Crawford, Texas, was kicked off the plane by a pilot who complained that his hand-gun declaration form was filled out improperly.) On the other hand, as numerous commentators observed, if the threat is Islamic terrorism, it would waste scarce intelligence resources to investigate Swedish au pairs.

Given the nation's general state of anxiety, the administration's package of anti-terrorist legal changes ran into surprisingly tough opposition from a congressional coalition of right-wing libertarians and liberal Democrats. By the time President Bush signed into law the Orwellian-sounding 'US Patriot Act' (described in detail elsewhere in this survey), these strange bedfellows had forced its substantial amendment. Although the act effectively dismantled the barrier between foreign and domestic intelligence erected in the 1970s and significantly strengthened the surveillance powers of law-enforcement agencies, it included a four-year 'sunset' provision under which its provisions would expire without explicit congressional renewal. This was a significant improvement for those who worried that 'emergency powers' would tend to survive indefinitely – especially for such an open-ended emergency as this one.

Other changes were instituted by executive order: permitting the monitoring, without a judge's warrant, of generally privileged communications between prisoners and their lawyers; allowing the continued detention of foreigners released from custody by an immigration judge; and, most controversially, Bush's order setting up special military tribunals to try suspected terrorists. Attorney-General Ashcroft made no new friends in Congress when he alleged, in Senate testimony, that critics of these measures were giving 'ammunition to America's enemies, and pause to America's friends'. But in March 2002, the administration added detail to the order on tribunals that substantially reassured its critics. Most, but not all, protections afforded criminal civilian defendants in US courts were extended to the suspected terrorists: provision for public trials; rights to counsel, of confronting evidence and against self-incrimination; a burden of proof 'beyond reasonable doubt'; the requirement of unanimous decisions to impose the death penalty (as opposed to the two-thirds required for conviction); and a limited right of appeal to a special three-member review panel. Overall, the Bush-Ashcroft executive orders had highlighted what was true even before 11 September: aliens have very few rights under American law. On the other hand, as liberal commentator Jacob Weisberg pointed out, 'unlike such liberal heroes as Lincoln, Wilson and FDR', Bush had stopped well short of 'grossly infring[ing] the rights of Americans'.

Civil liberties in wartime are rarely a left–right issue. But ideological battles did return to Washington more quickly than many had expected. The Democrats were hoping to repeat their feat of 1992, when the elder President Bush, acclaimed for his Gulf War victory, nonetheless proved vulnerable in domestic politics. (The historical template, of course, was Winston Churchill's dismissal from office by British voters even before the end of the Pacific War.) Democrats expected help from a decade-long shift in voter preferences towards fiscal discipline (an issue that favoured the Democrats after Clinton-era surpluses), away from tax cuts, and for moderate increases in social spending. They also expected the mobilisations of war, by lending renewed prestige to government institutions and strengthening imperatives of social solidarity, to favour their agenda. But this subtle strategy ran into a bolder Republican agenda of relentless tax cuts and government cutbacks powered by Bush's wartime popularity.

The first battle was over a stimulus bill to offset the economic shocks of 11 September, which had included a several-day shutdown of US air traffic, subsequent stress to the airline industry and the ground-zero pall over what had been, for years, a vibrant New York economy. It was unclear at the time whether the US economy was already in recession, but these effects seemed sure to send it there. In response, House Republicans insisted on further tax cuts, most of which, economists pointed out, would kick in long after they might be needed to stimulate consumer spending. Democrats more or less won this battle: the bill coming out of House–Senate conference was heavy on extended unemployment benefits and lighter on tax cuts.

The battle was rejoined, however, with President Bush's February 2002 presentation of his 2003 budget plan. Bush proposed large boosts to military spending – including nearly $40 billion for homeland security – and deep cuts in other programmes, while making his tax cuts permanent. Their ten-year expiration had made it possible to minimise their long-term costs; this pretence was now dropped. Democrats were furious about what they regarded, in E.J. Dionne's words, as 'their own support for Bush's approach to terrorism being repaid by a brazen effort to strip the federal Treasury of resources for a generation and to create a permanent tilt in American politics toward the right'. Aside from issues of social solidarity – no wartime sacrifices, it was claimed, were being demanded of the very rich – Democrats also complained that the resulting additions to the federal debt would leave the country unprepared for the demographic time-bomb of baby-boom retirement. But Democrats had a basic strategic problem: unwilling to test the theory that taxes were no longer the political kiss of death, they were not prepared to make a straight pitch even for freezing the tax cuts at 2002 levels. In any event, Republicans responded by attacking the Democrats, and particularly Senate Majority Leader Tom Daschle, as 'obstructionists'.

The electoral consequences of these battles looked likely to be influenced by two factors. First was the one piece of major news completely unrelated to terrorism: the scandal surrounding the collapse of Enron Corporation. The astonishing tale of deceptive accounting, hidden loss-making 'partnerships' and share-value mania drew a dramatic line under the era of dot.com enthusiasm. And although perhaps tarnishing the memory of a 'Clinton boom', it also seemed a political bonanza for the Democrats: stories of corporate greed, farcically inadequate regulation and hapless employees stuck with retirement funds full of near-worthless Enron stock. But the other factor, the general state of the economy, was starting to look better for the Bush team. Economic data in the spring of 2002 indicated a shallower-than-anticipated recession. If these indicators were true, Democrats would have less traction for their campaign to hold the Senate and win a handful of seats needed to control the House of Representatives in November 2002. In 2004, moreover, a wartime president presiding over a healthy economy could be unbeatable.

Foreign policy: a worldview confirmed

Invoking NATO's Article 5 for the first time in its history, thus declaring the attack on the US to be an attack on the alliance as a whole, American allies showed no sign of moral equivocation. They were, however, understandably nervous about what they were getting into and at the same time hopeful that the common cause against al-Qaeda might be a way to coax the United States back into the multilateral fold. But the Bush administration, while grateful for allied support and determined to knit together a broad coalition against terrorism, had seen nothing in the 11 September attacks to challenge the central premises of its foreign policy. On the contrary, the attacks confirmed a distinct administration worldview and the diplomatic, strategic and military policies that went with it.

Diplomatically, Bush officials took the view that the unifying glue of a counter-terrorist coalition had to be the magnitude of the threat rather than any diplomatic contortions to make American power more palatable to the world. That the United States had been brutally attacked did not seem like a good reason to start compromising as a matter of principle. Thus, Bush was eager to join Russian President Vladimir Putin in forging a common Russian–American assessment of the Islamic terrorist threat, but he was less than keen to save Russian 'face' through an amended Anti-Ballistic Missile (ABM) Treaty. Similar calculations shaped the administration's Middle East policies. The perceived need to calm 'the Arab street' did bring the administration to engage its diplomatic resources for an end to Israel–Palestine violence, against its initial instincts of disengagement from a process that appeared anything but ripe for a settlement. But with Palestinian suicide bombers engaged in essentially the same psychological and operational ritual as the 11 September terrorists, there were limits to how far Bush was going to press Israeli Prime Minister Ariel Sharon to compromise. Bush himself was deeply angered by the interception of a ship smuggling Iranian weapons to the Palestinian Authority. That interception and growing evidence of deepening Iranian involvement in the Israeli–Palestinian conflict was one of the principal factors ending a nascent US–Iranian rapprochement that, for a few weeks in the autumn, seemed to percolate on the edges of the Afghanistan war. In his January State of the Union message, Bush included Iran with North Korea and Iraq as part of the 'axis of evil' against which extreme vigilance was required.

Bush's speech, which greatly unnerved American allies, was a classic expression of the neo-conservative regard for diplomatic niceties. Moral straight talk was to be valued over sophisticated differentiation. The speech did not imply an American attack on Iran or North Korea, but it did set out a strategic bottom line. 'I will not wait on events', declared Bush. 'The United States of America will not permit the world's most dangerous regimes to threaten us with the world's most destructive weapons'.

Iraq was already firmly placed in the category of unambiguous threats. If there was any argument in principle among Bush officials about whether to tolerate Saddam Hussein's continuation in power, 11 September settled it. The Clinton administration too had been dedicated, as a matter of policy, to regime change, but it saw no practical way, beyond containment, to implement that policy. The Bush team came into office with a greater sense of urgency; it included foreign-policy intellectuals who not only had attacked Clinton-style containment, but also had served in the first Bush administration and participated in the decision, wise or not, to stop the Gulf War short of taking Baghdad. These officials included Deputy Defence Secretary Paul Wolfowitz, said to be deeply shaken by the first Bush administration's ultimate lack of support for the Kurdish and Shi'ite uprisings it had encouraged. The idea of a second Bush administration leaving the White House with Saddam still in Baghdad seemed politically and historically distasteful. If there had been conclusive evidence linking Saddam to the 11 September attacks, American forces would already be in Iraq. (In March 2002, some new – albeit still ambiguous – evidence of a link was put forward in a *New Yorker* article, mentioned by President Bush in a press conference.) But the real importance of 11 September was to undermine anyone who might argue against preemptive attack on moral, legal or political grounds. Daschle, the Democratic leader of the Senate, was among those saying that preemption could be justified. Secretary of State Colin Powell started to downplay his implied resistance to an attack. The State Department might still push for acquiring the legitimisation of a UN Security Council resolution before attacking, and French and Russian assent to such a resolution was beginning, in Spring 2002, to look more likely. But whether or not such a resolution could be obtained would not be the decisive factor in White House decision-making.

Bush officials also had reason to believe that their ideas about military policy – that is, regarding proper and improper uses of US military forces – were confirmed by 11 September, but there were complications to that view as the Afghanistan campaign unfolded. A central foreign-policy debate of the 2002 presidential campaign had involved candidate Bush's opposition to the use of American troops for peacekeeping and 'nation-building' in the Balkans and elsewhere. After the new administration came into office, Powell convinced the president that, for the sake of alliance solidarity, there should be no more talk of an early American withdrawal from Bosnia or Kosovo. But the war against terrorism reinforced the logic of an alliance division of labour: American forces to be marshalled against major strategic threats; European forces, lacking the equipment and technology for such contingencies anyway, to concentrate on such unfinished tasks as stabilising the Balkans. There were, to be sure, some European troops fighting in Afghanistan, while US Balkan deployments continued, but the notion of such a division of labour as a long-term proposition seemed palatable – or at least inevitable. Where this logic broke down, however, was in thinking about what would happen to countries like Afghanistan after US forces had dealt with the 'high-end' strategic threat. The US resisted involvement in a peacekeeping force, and indeed, put the brakes on having any international security force for the country beyond Kabul. Instead, the Pentagon undertook to help train an Afghan army. But if this did not suffice to quell warlord lawlessness, it would cast other American interventions in a dimmer light. As the *Washington Post* suggested in a 1 February 2002 editorial, it would be difficult for the US to expect support for attacking Iraq if it left Afghanistan in anarchy.

The Afganistan war also suggested a gradual change in US military culture. Arguments about 1990s interventions in Somalia and the Balkans had dramatised a post-Vietnam reversal of roles, with army commanders markedly more reluctant to deploy ground troops and incur casualties than their civilian masters. At the same time, strong advocates of military transformation in the Rumsfeld Pentagon favoured using smaller ground units adept at special operations and assisted by sophisticated military technology. In the campaign to topple the Taliban, US air power and special-operations troops utilising new information and surveillance technologies supported proxy Northern Alliance forces that took on the bulk of the ground fighting. It was clearly a very successful partnership. But after the Taliban's fall, as the Pentagon turned to hammering the mountain bastions of al-Qaeda holdouts, US tactics fell short. The reliance on marginally motivated Northern Alliance forces for the December 2002 assault on Tora Bora allowed a large number of al-Qaeda members to escape into Pakistan. Osama bin Laden may have been among them. The army, however, was not going to make that mistake twice. In March 2002, in the fiercely fought *Operation Anaconda*, regular army forces went after al-Qaeda fighters holed up around Gardez. Eight American soldiers lost their lives. The Pentagon also appealed, for the first time in this war, for substantial help from a NATO ally, and Britain delivered 1,700 Royal Marines. The elder president Bush may have prematurely announced the end of the 'Vietnam syndrome' in 1991, but it may have truly died 11 years later at Gardez. According to a March *Washington Post*-ABC News poll taken after the eight Americans were killed, nine out of ten Americans still supported the Afghanistan campaign.

Staying in character

Any residual uncertainty about the return of American politics was settled fairly definitely on 5 March 2002, when President Bush announced 30% tariffs on most imports of steel. The reaction from allies was fierce: *Le Monde* headlined its next-day editorial, 'Hypocrite M. Bush', while British Prime Minister Tony Blair called the move 'unwarranted, unacceptable and wrong'. The plight of the US steel industry had been a long-running drama in American trade politics, but President Bill Clinton had resisted offering shelter, reaching instead beyond protectionists in his own party to form a free-trade coalition with Republicans in Congress. This embrace had been costly in political terms. It produced no bankable gratitude from Republicans, and it helped spawn the anti-globalisation campaign by Greens candidate Ralph Nader that arguably lost the Democrats the White House. George W. Bush decided, his free-trade rhetoric notwithstanding, to be more narrowly political, nursing his political advantage in steel-producing states such as West Virginia. For similar reasons, the administration had already decided against keeping a wartime commitment to lower barriers to Pakistani textiles.

These tariff decisions were doubly disappointing for allies and other US partners looking for signs that the global complexities of a war against terrorism would reinforce the cooperative and internationalist tradition in American foreign policy. In this regard, steel was perhaps a more significant indicator than Iraq. After such a devastating attack on the American homeland, no US administration would be inclined to trust matters of core security to multilateral chance. When it came to economics, however, the second President Bush had ample ideological cover – in neo-conservative and establishment-Republican traditions – to pursue the internationalism of his predecessors. Yet the Bush administration rejected the assumptions that had led Clinton-administration treasury secretaries, Robert Rubin and Lawrence Summers, to organise financial rescues for Mexico, Asia and Russia. By contrast, Bush Treasury Secretary Paul O'Neill (though he acceded to State Department and Pentagon pressure to rescue a fiscally inept but strategically vital Turkey) turned the tragedy of Argentina's financial collapse into an object lesson in international *laissez-faire*. 'Nobody forced them to be what they are', said O'Neill, who previously had derided the activist Rubin as 'chief of the fire department'. Although the administration finally did approve, in August 2001, an $8bn IMF loan to Buenos Aires, its price was further deep cuts in public spending at a time when unemployment was soaring. By winter 2001–02, there were riots, the largest loan default in history and a devalued peso. While Argentina's collapse was anticipated and financial contagion therefore contained, the Bush administration's apparent indifference may have damaged US relations with Latin America in general as well as Argentina in particular.

Partially offsetting such isolationist economics, the administration did respond to international criticism of its historically low foreign-aid budget. At a March 2002 poverty summit in Monterrey, Mexico, Bush promised to 'fight against poverty because hope is an answer to terror'. He said he would propose to Congress a 50% increase over three years, bringing the foreign-aid budget to $15bn in 2006. That would still be just 0.13% of American GDP, barely a third of what European Union countries spend on average, and far below the 0.70% goal set by UN Secretary-General Kofi Annan. It was also far below the Marshall Plan commitment (2% of GDP) that the United States was willing to assume at the outset of the Cold War.

But then, the Cold War was a 40-year extension of America's military, economic and moral mobilisation for the Second World War. It entailed whole new fields of strategy (from the balance of nuclear terror to 'hearts and minds' counter-insurgency); a race to the moon; and renewed attention to American social ills (the Kennedy administration, for example, deemed civil-rights inequities at home an intolerable gift to Soviet propaganda abroad). The six months after 11 September were too few to assess whether a comparable mobilisation was likely. Judging by most American wars since 1862, one would expect a more powerful presidency, and a stronger federal government reaching into more areas of American life. During the six months following 11 September, this pattern seemed to be confirmed by the president's executive order for military tribunals to try terrorists, and by the success of Congressional Democrats over Republican opposition in federalising the system of airport security. According to the precedent of 1942–73, these moves would be followed by a massive expansion of national infrastructure and huge increases in public spending. George W. Bush's administration, distinctly more conservative than even Ronald Reagan's, appeared determined to resist that dynamic. With a public approval rating still high at 77% according to an early March 2002 Gallup poll (though down from the 90% he registered immediately after the 11 September attacks), Bush had some chance of success. Yet if the struggle against terrorism remains global in scope and really lasts for a generation or more, then its transforming consequences will be felt long after President Bush joins his father in retirement.

Insecurity in the Andes

If any term characterises the north Andean region of South America in 2002, it is 'uncertainty'. While for most of the 1990s, this region was under significant strain, recent years have seen a deterioration of domestic and regional security. This trend is likely to continue through 2002. While the peace process aimed at ending Colombia's decades-long civil conflict could produce a cease-fire, it could just as plausibly erupt into full-scale conflict. Ecuador and Peru's northern borders are increasingly becoming safe havens for Colombian rebels. Venezuelan President Hugo Chávez's radical reform agenda threatens to provoke widespread civil unrest and a military coup is a possibility. The only significant bright spots in the Andes right now are Ecuador's unexpectedly strong economic turnaround and Bolivia's effective attempts to eliminate illicit coca cultivation. Yet even in these two areas long-term success is not guaranteed. The potential for events to spin violently out of control – above all in Colombia and Venezuela – are real and the threats to regional stability are considerable.

Stalled peace in Colombia

In late 1998, Colombian President Andrés Pastrana granted the Fuerzas Armadas Revolucionarias de Colombia (FARC – Revolutionary Armed Forces of Colombia), Colombia's 18,000-strong Marxist guerrilla group, a 41,440 square-kilometre demilitarised zone (or *despeje*) in return for the FARC's commitment to participate in peace talks aimed at ending the country's decades-long civil conflict, in which over 50,000 people have died since 1963. For almost three years, there was little sign of progress. The FARC were negotiating in bad faith and taking advantage of the *despeje* to train troops, launch military incursions, and cultivate and traffic drugs. In June 2001, however, the Colombian government and FARC agreed to a deal in which the FARC released 242 soldiers and police agents that it was holding prisoner, some for over two years. Yet, any semblance of progress in the stalled peace process was dealt a severe blow when, on 13 August three members of the Provisional Irish Republican Army (IRA) were arrested holding false passports at the Bogotá airport. Colombian authorities suspected them of spending five weeks in the FARC's liberated zone providing bomb-making training, and they were indicted in February 2002. The arrests were particularly shocking to many Colombians, as they suggested that the FARC intended to shift its military strategies from irregular rural warfare to urban terrorism. They also angered Washington, which had presumed the IRA inactive on the basis of advances in the Northern Irish peace process since 1997.

Soon after the IRA episode, on 24 September, the FARC kidnapped Consuelo Araújonoguera, President Pastrana's popular former culture minister, near the city of Valledupar in the department of César. Six days later, her captors shot her at point-blank range while being pursued by the Colombian army. On 29 September, Liberal Party presidential candidate Horacio Serpa was forced to give up a high-profile protest march into the *despeje*, which violated the terms of the agreement that originally allowed for the demilitarised zone. These actions provoked widespread public condemnation of the FARC. Calls for Pastrana to end the peace process increased. He responded with set of harder-line policies. The military increased its operations immediately outside the *despeje*, while the president approved overhead military flights and banned foreigners from entering the zone without government approval. The United States government supported these moves, arguing that under the laws of armed conflict the FARC should be treated not merely as an armed group but as a terrorist organisation, especially following the 11 September attacks.

On 5 October, the government and the FARC signed the 'San Francisco de la Sombra Accord' that permitted the *despeje* to continue until 20 January 2002. However, less than two weeks later, on 17 October, the FARC unilaterally broke off the peace talks in response to Pastrana's refusal to stop the over-flights and the ban on foreign visitors. The FARC agreed in early January to return to the table to discuss the military's presence directly outside the *despeje* and the ban on foreigners, but on 9 January 2002, Pastrana abruptly suspended the peace talks and gave the FARC 48 hours to clear out of the *despeje* before the military moved in. Pastrana ordered thousands of soldiers and scores of light tanks to mass just outside the *despeje*. Following negotiations, a UN-brokered agreement emerged on 20 January whereby the government would extend the *despeje* until April 10, provided that a cease-fire was in place by 7 April. After three years of humiliating diplomacy and more FARC terrorism, Pastrana's resort to brinkmanship appeared to produce results. But during the two weeks following the agreement, the FARC stepped up its campaign outside the *despeje*, killing over 40 soldiers, police and civilians.

On 20 February, the FARC hijacked a Colombian commercial plane carrying 35 passengers, forced it down and abducted a senior senator, Jorge Gechem, who was on board. In a nationally televised address, an enraged Pastrana announced that he would not continue the peace process and insisted that the FARC vacate the *despeje*. The next day, Colombian Air Force planes bombed FARC camps and airstrips in the enclave. A day later, Colombian ground troops began to retake the area. On 24 February, FARC rebels kidnapped presidential candidate Ingrid Betancourt. As of April 2002, five kidnapped parliamentarians remained in rebel hands.

In the next phase of Colombia's conflict, it is likely that the next president of Colombia – to be elected on May 2002 and inaugurated the following August – will take a hard line comparable to President Pastrana's. Any moves towards more aggressive military actions against the FARC will most likely be applauded in Washington, and heightened counterinsurgency assistance could be forthcoming. The growing right-wing, pro-state paramilitary forces of the Autodefensas Unidas de Colombia (AUC – United Self-Defence Forces of Colombia) – which includes many former members of the Colombian military – add a layer of complexity to the situation. They too are involved in drug cultivation, but also protect the population from rebel coercion and enjoy 13% popular support (against 3% for the FARC) according to a February 2002 poll. In a campaign of urban infiltration, the AUC accounted for more than half of the 3,100 'non-combat' killings committed in Colombia in 2001. Salvatore Mancuso, the

AUC's reputed leader, puts the group's strength at 14,000. In a bestselling 'kill-and-tell' autobiography published in February 2002, AUC founder Carlos Castano takes credit for dozens of assassinations – including the 1990 killing of Carlos Pizarro, a popular left-wing presidential candidate – and chronicles the outfit's brutal vigilantism. The AUC was included on the US State Department's list of terrorist organisations in September 2001, and will be targeted in Plan Colombia under the conditions for the 2003 US assistance package. But the AUC remains a public-relations liability for US-backed government anti-insurgency efforts and has inhibited assistance from European countries.

While an all-out conflict between the military and the FARC had been averted as of April 2002 – fatalities were averaging about 40 per week in guerrilla and counter-insurgency operations – it was clear that the Colombian government and public were losing patience with the FARC's violent operations and refusal to compromise at the negotiating table. Thus, right-wing presidential candidate Alvaro Uribe Velez – who has a close relationship with the military and allegedly with the AUC – emerged as the favourite in January 2002, with an approval rating of 59%. Dozens of pro-Uribe candidates were victorious in March 2002 congressional elections. Further, several factors suggest that the FARC may have emerged from the peace process in a more vulnerable state. These include: the strengthening of the Colombian military under Plan Colombia; expanded counter-insurgency assistance from the US; an increase in FARC defections; the marginalisation of a smaller left-wing rebel group, Ejército de Liberacion Naciónal de Colombia (ELN – National Liberation Army of Colombia); and the increase in the number and activity of pro-government paramilitaries and a consequent reduction in the FARC's drug-related revenues. At the same time, the FARC has increased its membership and is not on the edge of military defeat. Thus, it is likely that the rebels will continue to conduct guerrilla operations in angling for a better political deal, but less likely that the political process will be revived in the short term.

The frustrating regional 'war' on drugs

Until 1997, most of the raw coca for making cocaine was cultivated in Peru and Bolivia and smuggled to Colombia for processing. Pastrana's ambitious US-sponsored Plan Colombia, launched in 1999, is intended to stem international drug traffic and to legitimise and revive Colombia's economy (and, tacitly, to help neutralise the FARC). The plan stresses first eradicating coca plantations run by the FARC and the ELN and then developing long-term agricultural alternatives and strengthening local government, the judiciary and civil society. From the outset, the plan's objectives were bold: to halve drug production within six years and provide the long-term security needed for economic and political change. Implementation has been fraught.

Colombia-based organisations supply 90% of the cocaine and a major portion of the heroin sold in the United States. The United States has supplied Colombia with more than 70 helicopters, trained and equipped three special army battalions for anti-narcotics operations, upgraded Colombian Air Force planes and built up its radar and intelligence-gathering capabilities. The military plan has proven difficult to execute for a variety of technical and political reasons. For instance, the border between the north Andean countries and Brazil in the Amazon Basin – a major route for drug smuggling – is difficult to police, and Brazil is resistant to cooperating with US efforts in general and Plan Colombia in particular. But there has been qualified progress on the economic side – in particular, in substituting legitimate crops for coca and thus shrinking the geographical area of illegal activity.

In Bolivia, President Jorge Quiroga – sworn in as Bolivia's new president on 7 August 2001 after Hugo Banzer stepped down on health grounds – reinforced as a central pillar of his tenure Banzer's policy of converting Bolivia from a coca economy to a natural gas economy. In pursuit of that policy, Bolivia's efforts at reducing coca production have been impressive, reducing coca cultivation from 48,600 hectares in 1995 to 14,600 hectares in 2000 and extending US-financed subsidies to farmers to develop replacement crops. The flip-side of this successful initiative has been widespread economic and social displacement, as coca farmers have often been unable or unwilling to either relocate or switch to less lucrative legal crops. The coca farmers have staged frequent roadblocks and other protests that paralyse Bolivia's transportation system. On 23 April 2001, a massive country-wide demonstration took place that called for, among other things, an end to US-sponsored coca eradication efforts. The Bolivian government has refused to accede to the protestors' demands and in October 2001, dispatched 4,000 troops to quell civil unrest in the coca-intensive Cochabamba-Chapare region, lifting the total number of soldiers there to 15,000. Even so, on 15 November, 400 coca farmers ambushed a truck carrying 15 army soldiers in a village in the Chapare region. The ambush resulted in the death of two leaders of coca farmer groups. President Quiroga's term of office will last only until August 2002 and he will not be eligible for re-election. The government's anti-coca policies will be a central issue in the upcoming presidential elections. Already some candidates have announced that if elected they would relax these policies.

The United States has relied even more directly on the Peruvian government for drug interdiction than it has on the Bolivian government. Peruvian Air Force jets have intercepted – and sometimes shot down – planes suspected of transporting coca or coca paste into Colombia. Many US government officials credit ending the Peru–Colombia 'air bridge' as a large factor in the dramatic decrease in coca cultivation in Peru. But this US-backed anti-drug operation led to an international incident when on 20 April, under guidance from a Central Intelligence Agency (CIA) surveillance plane flown by US contractor pilots, a Peruvian Air Force jet shot down an American missionary plane, killing missionary Veronica Bowers and her seven-month old baby. Although the United States completed its investigation into the matter in summer 2001, the tragedy showered unwanted attention on the United States' anti-drug operations in the Andes, and has dampened enthusiasm for intelligence cooperation in Washington and for aggressive US–Peru interdiction policies in both capitals. Nevertheless, drug surveillance flights were scheduled to resume in the second half of 2002 with new safeguards in place.

Even if La Paz and Lima are able to keep a lid on Bolivia's raw coca production, that success is not without perverse results. As US-supported crop eradication and crop substitution efforts reduced the amount of raw coca cultivated in Peru and Bolivia, coca cultivation in Colombia appeared to surge, especially in the southern department of Putumayo, a traditional stronghold of the FARC. In 2000, raw coca cultivation in Colombia stood at about 136,000 hectares, roughly double the amount from five years previous. This is the 'balloon effect': suppress cultivation in one area and it will pop up in another, where anti-drug efforts are lax or differently focused. Crop substitution efforts in Colombia also face serious incentive-related constraints amplified by unemployment (about 18%) and poverty. For example, although 35,000 families in Putamayo signed up for the programme, the non-cash aid (in tools and agricultural supplies) valued at two million pesos ($870) is far less than the cash proceeds of a single coca harvest, of which there would be at least four per year. In early 2002, only 96 of Colombia's 222 coca-growing counties had adopted alternative development programmes. The presence of violent pro-government paramilitaries has further hindered the battle for hearts and minds in the countryside. The upshot is that outward pressures on regional security radiating from Colombia – due to the civil war, anti-drug efforts and continued drug-related regional commerce – are extremely difficult to relieve. These have been most acute in Ecuador and Peru.

On 1 March 2002, the Colombian government announced that as of 1 November 2001, the total amount of coca under cultivation in Colombia was 144,807 hectares, down 11% from the period ending 31 August 2000. But the US State Department's report released on 7 March – based on CIA analysis of satellite imagery – put the figure at 169,800 hectares, a slight increase. US officials reportedly concluded that the alternative development initiative had failed, and planned to rely increasingly on aerial fumigation.

Ecuador feels the heat

Since early 2001, supported by the United States, the Colombian government has significantly increased its military and aerial fumigation efforts in southern Colombia. The proximity of these areas to the Ecuadorian border has meant that the violence and drug trade has become increasingly transnational, a development that prompted the Ecuadorian military to rush 4,000 troops to its northern border. Reports from the region indicate that coca cultivation in northern Ecuador is increasing, Colombian drug traffickers and guerrillas have murdered Ecuadorian officials, and thousands of Colombian civilians have fled to Ecuador.

The Colombian guerrilla groups' growing incursions into Ecuador constitute another regional security concern. On 22 June 2001, the Ecuadorian army arrested a heavily armed suspected FARC commander in the province of Sucumbios. Moreover, reports indicate that the FARC is building support camps on the Ecuadorian side of the border that will allow them to flee as the Colombian military increases its activities. In August 2001, the Ecuadorian military discovered a FARC camp deep in the jungle near the border with Colombia. More troubling still to the Ecuadorian authorities, in January 2002 reports emerged that the FARC was training Ecuadorian rebels from an organisation that participated in violent anti-government protests in Quito in early January. Although so far Ecuadorian military commanders claim to have conducted all operations without US assistance, the United States government is aware of the potential for the conflict in Colombia to spill over into Ecuador. In 2000, Washington approved $62m to upgrade an airstrip in the coastal city of Manta so that it can be used to house 400 US servicemen who will assist in conducting surveillance flights over Colombia. The stated goal is to track drug trafficking, but the base could easily also be used to track Colombian guerrilla movements.

These security worries have intensified against a brighter backdrop of economic improvement in Ecuador. Two years ago, Ecuador was on the verge of political and economic collapse. In 1999, GDP shrank by 7.3% and the value of the nation's currency, the sucre, plunged from 5000 per US$ to 25,000 per US$. Some 400,000 Ecuadorians left the country to find work abroad and public unrest reached alarming levels. This chaotic situation culminated, in January 2000, in a bloodless coup in which the military ousted President Jamil Mahuad and handed over power to Mahuad's vice president, Gustavo Noboa. Noboa immediately announced that he would continue Mahuad's plan to adopt the dollar as the national currency. While many groups in Ecuador roundly criticised Noboa's decision, the results from dollarisation so far have been impressive. Supported by higher oil prices and $2 billion in international loans, Ecuador's GDP grew by 2.3% in 2000. In 2001, the economy was estimated to have grown by 5% and imports on capital goods picked up 52%, reflecting much stronger domestic demand. Unemployment has fallen to 10.4% in January 2002 from 16.8% in January 2000.

Boosting Ecuador's economy is the country's new $1.1bn oil pipeline. Over the next two years, its construction should directly and indirectly create 50,000 jobs and provide a 1% boost to the country's GDP. One innovative idea that the Noboa administration is considering is to use a tax from the new pipeline's oil exports for a stabilisation fund that will help pay the country's foreign-debt obligations.

Yet key structural reforms are still needed. In March 2001, Ecuador's Congress sent a strong message that it would not go along the economic reform path when it rejected a government plan to increase the value-added tax from 12% to 15%, a change that economists consider essential to maintaining a healthy fiscal balance against declining oil revenues.

Impediments to Peru's military reform

Whereas US–Ecuadorian military cooperation is nascent, joint US–Peruvian security activity is well entrenched, having been developed largely during former President Alberto Fujimori's administration. This fact, and the reality that Washington will likely continue to require such cooperation, impose restraints upon current President Alejandro Toledo's plans to reform the military. Upon assuming office on 29 July 2001, he announced plans to appoint civilians to head all branches of the armed forces. Toledo also called on all South American nations to agree to a freeze on the purchase of offensive military weapons. He continued to make waves by pledging to slash defence spending by 15% – an extremely bold move at a time when military loyalty towards his new administration was uncertain.

To a significant extent, Toledo wishes to purge the military of the substantial residual influence of Vladimiro Montesinos, Fujimori's former intelligence chief. In 2000, it transpired that Montesinos had secretly videotaped politicians and other public figures taking bribes or engaging in other illicit activities, and used the tapes for blackmail. Nine hundred persons have already been identified on videotapes as accepting bribes. His power to control public affairs via extortion extended to the media, most likely to Fujimori himself, and preeminently to the security forces. Following public revelations, in September 2000, Montesinos had fled Peru but was arrested in Venezuela on 23 June 2001 by Peruvian authorities and is now imprisoned in Peru. The Toledo administration has been successful in rooting out military officers whom they believe to be corrupt or undemocratic: as of January 2002, of the 77 generals in the national police, 44 had been sent into early retirement. A number of high-ranking members of the armed forces have also been forced to retire.

Yet another barrier to military reform is Peru's increasingly unstable internal security situation. According to a Peruvian intelligence report, 'Plan Colombia is forcing Colombian guerrillas, drug trafficking firms, coca and marijuana growers, as well as gunrunners to Peruvian border villages'. Moreover, in November 2001, Peruvian authorities captured two operatives of Sendero Luminoso (Shining Path) – a Maoist group that was thought to have been largely subdued following the 1992 arrest of its leader Abimael Guzmán – who were involved in a planned attack on the US Embassy in

Lima. The Peruvian government believes that there are roughly 500 members of the group hiding in the jungles of eastern Peru. In early December 2001, Sendero Luminoso attacked an army barracks in the jungle area of Nuevo Progreso. Ideologically nebulous, the current incarnation of Sendero Luminoso is much more involved in the drug trade than was its progenitor in the 1990s, especially in the cultivation of the highly lucrative poppy crop. Some analysts suspect that Colombian drug traffickers are supplying the group with poppy seeds and extending it financial credit in addition to supplying weapons. The Peruvian army has responded by announcing that it will open 100 new rural outposts. On 20 March 2002, a car-bomb exploded outside the US Embassy in Lima, killing nine people. Although none of them were American, President Bush was scheduled to arrive for an official visit three days later. No group claimed credit, but US intelligence officers suspected the Shining Path and Peruvian officials construed the attack as an anti-American statement.

Regime instability in Venezuela

After his election in December 1998, Venezuelan President Hugo Chávez's 'Bolivarian revolution' of massive social and political reform was extremely popular, especially among the country's majority poor. By early 2002, however, Chávez's revolution had lost steam, as his approval rating dropped from 80% to below 30%. Anti-Chávez groups have normally been poorly organised and disparate, but in recent months they have increased their criticisms of the president. Most remarkable was the 10 December 2001 national strike when schools, stores, factories and other businesses remained closed during a 12-hour work stoppage. This strike was notable not just for its high levels of participation, but also because it marked a growing alliance between anti-Chávez elements in business and labour – two groups normally at odds with each other. Chávez responded to the strike by labelling the strike's organisers as a 'corrupt and bastard oligarchy'. He has stated that he is committed to a 'deeper phase' of political and social reforms, including the highly controversial programmes to increase oil royalties and expropriate idle rural landholdings. The land-reform plan has angered ranchers, who may have killed at least a half a dozen peasants – most recently Luis Mora on 10 January 2002. Later in January, a reactive peasants' group, the Bolivarian Liberation Forces, surfaced. Chávez has also threatened to nationalise banks that do not comply with populist lending requirements. Any serious move to implement policies such as these will meet strong opposition from a growing segment of Venezuelan society, including the news media and the Roman Catholic Church.

A central question for 2002 is whether the Venezuelan military will back Chávez's moves, especially if he is forced to declare a state of emergency in order to implement them. Although the military has generally been respectful of civilian rule, Chávez does not have its full support and this could hinder his efforts to move his revolution to a more radical phase. In particular, military officers see Chávez's tilt towards Cuba and an apparent willingness to cooperate with Colombian guerrillas as jeopardising Venezuela's ties with Washington. In late January 2002, a Venezuelan government memorandum was leaked, detailing offers of medical supplies, asylum, transport and petroleum to the FARC in exchange for FARC pledges not to operate in Venezuela or recruit Venezuelans without permission. The revelation that Chávez was offering succour to a group inimical to American and Colombian interests infuriated Washington and Bogotá.

Given Chávez's domestic circumstances, a bloodless military coup is not out of the question. On 7 February 2002, Air Force Colonel Pedro Soto and National Guard Captain Pedro Flores led protests demanding Chávez's resignation and pushing for new elections. The officers relented within a week and reported to their superiors, as ordered. On 18 February, however, Vice Admiral Carlos Molina Tamayo – who had been appointed Venezuela's ambassador to Greece – called for Chávez to step down and urged impeachment were he to refuse, citing the president's ties to 'terrorist Colombian guerrillas'. Less than a week later, Air Force General Roman Gomez Ruiz echoed these calls for Chávez's resignation, citing his corruption and poor management of the military. Chávez has protected himself by forcing dissident officers into retirement and co-opting others by placing them in key civilian government posts. Although US officials have indicated that they would not support a coup, in light of Chávez's flirtations with the FARC, Washington might acquiesce to something along the lines of the removal of Mahuad in Ecuador in 2000, whereby an elected civilian would immediately replace Chávez.

Change, but little improvement, on the horizon

The events of the past year may suggest that Andean security is an oxymoron. With the peace process in Colombia seemingly frozen and levels of violence continuing to increase, there is real concern that Colombia's civil conflict and related drug-trafficking issues could spread beyond its borders into northern Ecuador and Peru, sparking a regional crisis. President Chávez's increasingly precarious position and politically rash behaviour are also prime concerns. A particularly worrisome scenario is one in which he increases his support – at present erratic and difficult to gauge – for Colombian guerrilla groups. An international dispute or conflict could arise if Bogotá perceives that Chávez is providing logistical support or sanctuary to Colombian rebels. The United States remains the major outside player in Colombia. Some European countries, however, have assumed a more prominent role. Daniel Parfait, the

French Ambassador to Colombia, for example, helped broker the January 2002 agreement to extend the *despeje*. The ten 'friendly countries' supporting the peace process are France, Spain, Italy, Norway, Sweden, Switzerland, Canada, Cuba, Mexico and Venezuela. The European Union (EU) committed $293m to support economic and democratic reform in Colombia in an agreement signed on 30 April 2001. But the European tendency to regard the FARC as a more benign group than it really is produced some arguably unhelpful diplomacy, such as the EU's refusal to provide assistance for government military operations and its failure to freeze FARC assets.

Since the United States' $1.3bn in support and military advice and assistance drives Plan Colombia, and the fulcrum of regional security is Colombia's civil war and drug trade, security in the region turns significantly on US policy. Frustration on both counts and looming instability elsewhere in the region has impelled the Bush administration to take a hard look at the United States' Colombia policy. Washington does not appear to be unduly worried that Plan Colombia poses unacceptable risks to regional security, which so far have been tenuously contained. The Bush administration has also maintained a high level of attention in the region, having put forward the $645m Andean Regional Initiative, which Congress approved in December 2001. This programme would continue efforts initiated under Plan Colombia, but also focus more closely on the regional 'balloon effect', whereby suppression of drug activity in one area produces expansion in another. But in light of the lack of progress in the anti-drug campaign, and a growing recognition that the drug and insurgency problems are fundamentally inseparable, the Bush administration does appear to be considering a move away from a narrow anti-drug focus in favour of a more direct and robust application of military counter-insurgency methods. Indeed, the FARC and the ELN were added to the US State Department's list of foreign terrorist organisations in November 2001, and the proactive suppression of transnational terrorist and criminal threats has become an overriding goal of the Bush administration since 11 September. Proposals under consideration include heightened intelligence-sharing on guerrilla activities and training an additional battalion of Colombian troops to serve as a rapid-reaction force to protect infrastructure against guerrilla attacks.

Such moves would require Congress to loosen restrictions limiting the use of US-provided military equipment to anti-narcotics operations, but this would be compatible with the political mood in Colombia. The traditional official taboo in Washington against direct counter-insurgency assistance has been dropped following the 11 September terrorist attacks, and none of the three leading candidates in the June 2002 Colombian presidential elections has stated that he would roll back anti-drug or anti-insurgent cooperation with Washington. President Bush will still probably maintain a tough anti-drug policy in the region, as such a stance is consistent with his conservative domestic agenda. Brussels strongly supported the Pastrana government's termination of peace talks in February 2002. The EU might be more inclined to back US-led anti-drug and anti-insurgency efforts diplomatically and possibly financially. The likely broadening of US policy to encompass a counter-insurgency posture could, in the short-term, intensify rather than relax existing pressures on regional security. The combination of heightened regional instability and external intervention may also prompt more energetic regional mobilisation to tackle insecurity and refugee problems. Brazil, in particular, has given only reluctant support to Plan Colombia, and may now feel moved to complement US efforts precisely in order to limit Washington's involvement. In early March 2002, Brazilian military units stationed at the Brazil–Colombia border engaged FARC rebels in a firefight. At around the same time, FARC rebels robbed and killed two Ecuadorans near the Ecuador–Colombia border. In any event, regional security challenges are likely to persist in 2002 and 2003.

Argentina's Economic Crisis: Contagion or Catalyst?

Argentina, Latin America's third-largest economy, imploded at the end of 2001. This occurred after four years of deepening recession, elections that yielded up a fragile and ultimately dysfunctional governing coalition, two years of bumbling government and a prolonged struggle with the International Monetary Fund (IMF). On 20 December, following a week of demonstrations and over 30 dead, President Fernando de la Rúa resigned, leaving the country in a state of political and economic chaos. Several emergent factors precipitated de la Rúa's fall. Argentina's international debt had expanded, and the IMF – urged on by its principal shareholders – were reluctant to provide a third stand-by facility to bail the country out. The government also froze bank accounts to stop a run on banks at the end of November, provoking citizen outrage. A constitutional successor resigned after a week, having irritated the factions in his own party to the extent that they refused to support him. Riots that caused the death of another 26 people and 13 police brought the third interim president down. Then more rioters broke into the halls of Congress and set fire to the building, causing the fall of the next successor. A commentator in *La Nación* observed that Argentina was living a 'crisis without precedent', and that Argentina's political leadership was playing its last card.

Argentina's implosion reflected, more than anything else, a crisis of its political system and a crisis of governance. De la Rúa had proven to be a weak leader of his own Radical Party (UCR), and was routinely second-guessed by its patriarch Raul Alfonsin. He presided over a minority coalition cobbled together for the sole purpose of winning the presidency. The minority partner in the coalition, the Frente para un Pais Solidario (FrePaSo), ceased to back government policies almost immediately after the team took office and formally backed out of the coalition before the end of the first year, leaving de la Rúa to cope with a Congress whose upper chamber was controlled by the opposition and in whose lower chamber the government coalition held only a tenuous majority. The opposition Justicialist (Peronist) party's purpose, many surmised, was to make the Radical–FrePaSo task of governing as difficult as possible so that voters would be disposed to vote Peronist in 2004, but it was also divided between supporters of former president Carlos Menem and his opponents. Furthermore, Argentina is a federal state, with 14 of its 23 provinces controlled by opposition party governors. Although one of the mantras of IMF and other agencies' demands for fiscal reform has been for the provincial governors to exercise fiscal responsibility at their level as well, few of the governors have been supportive of Buenos Aires's calls for reform. In short, Congress, governors, political parties, and the national and provincial leaderships fiddled while the country economically burned.

A chronicle foretold

The story began a decade ago. In a dramatic and ultimately very successful effort to cure Argentina of inflationary expectations, in 1991 Argentina's Finance Minister Domingo Cavallo decreed the Argentine peso would be held at par with the US dollar. Congress passed a law that permitted the federal government to spend no more than was held in the treasury. The same government embarked on a fire-sale of public enterprises that left Argentina one of the most privatised emerging markets in the world. Although Argentina was a model reformer in Menem's first administration, many of the reforms turned out to be incomplete. Just as the economy began to gather steam, Argentina was hit brutally by the 1995 Mexican peso crisis, which resulted in massive withdrawals of investor cash from emerging markets. Back on track a year later, Argentina began borrowing heavily on the world market, enjoying the favourable assessment of its efforts to stabilise and reform its economy. Unluckily, as Menem entered his second term, no longer needing to win re-election, he succumbed to politicians' worse temptation – buying his historical legacy – and began to spend lavishly. Because Domingo Cavallo, the finance minister who managed to hold Argentina to its convertibility plan, was lionised by international financial markets,

Argentina was able to finance Menem's extravagance through borrowing. Argentina's public-sector debt increased 300% between 1994 and 2000.

Following seven years of positive growth, Argentina entered recession at the end of 1998. Unlike Brazil and Mexico, it never recovered from the 1997 Asian crisis that sparked the withdrawal of international capital from emerging markets. Whereas Brazil devalued its currency in 1998, Argentina's peso – pegged to the US dollar – was left in an unfavourable and ultimately untenable relationship between the two trading partners. Economists of various stripes have repeatedly questioned Argentina's continued adherence to the dollar parity, but Argentines were generally satisfied with the stability it insured and the first-world image that it conveyed. By late 2000, Argentina's country risk premium was rising, threatening the government's plan to stay out of international arrears by swapping near-term debt for longer-term maturities. In November 2000, the IMF, Inter-American Development Bank, World Bank and the US and Spanish governments constructed a support package valued at $39.7 billion, payable over two years. The early results were positive: the risk calculation fell from 1000 to 600 points and Argentina was able to swap some of its debt. The euphoria lasted only a few months, however, and by March 2001, the risk premium had risen again to 900 points.

President de la Rúa sacked his economy minister, Jose Luis Machinea, at the beginning of March and replaced him with the highly regarded Ricardo López Murphy, former director in one of Argentina's most prestigious economic think-tanks. But López Murphy wanted to impose an orthodox austerity programme and neither the president nor his coalition would support him. He resigned two weeks into office, to be replaced by Cavallo, who, it was hoped, would be able to provide the necessary chemistry with the international community to overcome its scepticism. A month after his appointment, the country risk premium stood at 1300. At mid-year 2001, Argentina's domestic production had fallen by 10% over three years and foreign investment had dropped by 30% in the same period. Unemployment remained over 16%, which together with the underemployed – almost everyone in the greater Buenos Aires area – put more than 30% of Argentine workers without adequate jobs. In greater Buenos Aires, 32% of individuals and 23% of households were at or below the poverty line. This produced anger in the once-aspiring middle class. To alleviate investor doubts about Argentina, the IMF approved a disbursement of $8bn in additional credits to strengthen central bank reserves and to support a $30bn debt swap. The Fund's conditions for support included a continuing commitment to zero deficit, addressing the tax-sharing arrangements with the provincial governments and further federal reforms. The agreement brought little relief. Individuals became increasingly concerned that their deposits would be confiscated to cover the government's fiscal problems, which had occurred in 1989 at the height of Argentina's hyperinflation. In the first half of 2001, growing lack of confidence produced capital outflows greater than inflows for the first time since the adoption of peso–dollar convertibility in 1991.

Congress went along with virtually all of Cavallo's prescriptions. The euro was added to the convertibility formula, effectively devaluing the currency slightly. A new competition law, designed to stimulate economic activity and increase tax collection, was passed in March. It created a tax on bank transactions, required all transactions over 1,000 pesos to be conducted by cheque or credit card, and raised import taxes on consumer goods while eliminating them on capital goods. At the end of July, a zero-deficit law was passed stipulating that taxes would go to pay first the interest on the debt, then for payments to the provinces. Remaining government expenditures, including salaries, retirement and pensions, would be paid depending on how much money was left. Public sector salaries (including both civil servants and the military) were cut by 13%. Provincial governors refused to budge on the federal government's obligatory transfers, which totalled more than $1.18bn a year and were not statutorily dependent on tax revenues. Finally, at the end of August, to further strengthen faith in the banking system, Congress passed a 'law of bank deposit intangibility', which amounted to a guarantee that the government could not touch bank deposits, convert them to bonds or in any way affect the interests agreed upon by bank and depositor. The law slowed bank withdrawals.

The IMF provided another payment from its November 2000 package in September 2001 to support Argentina's reserves, but the risk premium continued to march upwards towards 1500 points. By November 2001, the premium stood at 3000 and Argentine unemployment was over 20% of the workforce. Throughout the year, the de la Rúa government's reaction to the growing lack of confidence was to stand by the convertibility formula and to reduce federal public spending drastically. But the large debt-service payments, the deficit in the social security system (which constituted two-thirds of the public sector deficit in 2001) and obligatory transfers to the provinces gave the government little room for manoeuvre. Moreover, tax collections, which are largely dependent on a value-added levy, were sharply down. Finally, the convertibility law would not allow the government to spend more than it held in the treasury.

According to Latinobarómetro's mid-2001 poll, satisfaction with democracy in Argentina fell to 39%, compared to 53% in 1996. This *bronca* – 'funk' in Argentine slang – was manifested most visibly in the parades of pot-banging middle-class citizens protesting the December freezing of savings and subsequent restrictions on cash that could be taken out of bank accounts, and fearing the loss of their life savings. It was manifested most meaningfully in the October 2001 congressional elections, when a relatively low 73% of voters went to the polls in a parliamentary election that would be decisive in determining whether the government would lose its tenuous control of the lower house of the Congress: 21% of those voting cast blank or null (invalid) ballots, signalling voters' displeasure with the entire political class. The elections gave the Peronist party leadership in the Congress and de la Rúa's resignation put a Peronist in the presidency. The elections also signalled the near-demise of the problematic FrePaSo alliance and returned the Radicals to opposition status, where they have traditionally been more comfortable.

After $1.3bn was withdrawn from Argentine banks on 30 November alone, on 1 December, Cavallo announced that since Argentina still had not managed to win the confidence of the international financial system, the government would implement a series of measures – collectively known as the *corralito financero* – over 90 days to stem the flow of capital from the banking system. These measures included limiting withdrawals from bank accounts to only 250 pesos a week, and requiring all other financial transactions to be conducted by cheque or credit card. No one could leave the country with more than $1,000. The public took to the streets. Demonstrations led to Cavallo's resignation on 19 December and de la Rua's the next day. Politicans and protestors called for an end to free-market policies and a return to some 'better' formula of the past. On 23 December 2001, Interim President Adolfo Rodriguez Saa announced that Argentina would suspend payments on $141bn in loans. Argentina had defaulted, its sovereign debt having returned a loss of 68% in 2001.

When Eduardo Duhalde – the fifth president in two weeks – assumed the leadership of a hastily assembled unity government on 1 January 2002, he told the Argentine people: 'The country is broken'. Duhalde did, however, audaciously assert a measure of control. On 1 February, the Supreme Court ruled that the *corralito* was unconstitutional. Fearing a run on deposits, Duhalde responded by partially relaxing the *corralito* (allowing full salary withdrawals in pesos each month and setting a 1,200-peso maximum on other withdrawals of 1,200 pesos a month), suspending all individual lawsuits seeking recovery of bank deposits for six months and moving to impeach the 28 justices of the Supreme Court. His economic team – after establishing a dual exchange-rate regime with a 1.4:1 rate for government transactions in January – also opted for a completely free-floating exchange rate for the first time in a decade. The initial float on 11 February 2002 resulted in a 50% devaluation. In late March 2002, one peso was worth only $0.25. The government also established differential conversion rates for dollar assets and liabilities, the effect of which was to penalise savers and cushion debtors and finance the subsidy by issuing still more government debt.

One of the few positive signals throughout the crisis was the quiescence of the armed forces. The arbiter of Argentine politics for most of the twentieth century, throughout the three weeks of political and economic crisis, the military remained secure in their barracks while the police handled the rioters. The armed forces leadership was approached publicly and privately to intervene. Its response to civilian appeals for military action to 'restore order', however, was 'only when commanded to do so by law of Congress'. Thus, the armed forces leadership demonstrated their clear understanding of the armed forces' objective role in Argentine society. This attitude at least provides political space for democratically driven economic reform.

Regional impact: neither immunity nor fatality

Even leaving aside Argentina's profound problems, 2001 was not a good year for Latin America, not the least because of the deepening recession in the United States. But growth has been variable and sluggish in the region since the Asian market crisis of 1997. Since then, external financing for Latin American growth has been less available, more volatile and on terms that were less favourable than those prevailing in the early 1990s. Foreign direct investment (FDI) contracted sharply in the late 1990s and has not picked up. The United National Economic Commission for Latin America and the Caribbean expects that 2002 will be the third straight year of FDI contraction and the fourth in which overall foreign capital sources will be null or negative for Latin America overall.

For most of the decade prior to 2001, trade among the countries in the Latin American regional bloc expanded by an average of 16% a year, and trade within Mercosur, the Southern Cone's common market, outpaced export expansion to other markets by a threefold factor. Argentina's sluggish growth since 1998 and the deepening recession in the US and other extra-hemispheric partners have had a substantial impact on trade growth in Mercosur. In 2001, intra-Mercosur trade declined by more than 10% for the first time in over ten years. Brazil and Paraguay were most deeply affected, with exports to their partners falling by more than 12% and 18%, respectively. Uruguayan trade with Mercosur fell by nearly 16% in 2001. Even associate member Chile's exports to Mercosur fell by some 5%. Argentina's prolonged recession and the associated drop in imports was the principal cause of the Mercosur decline. Yet because Argentina is not, overall, a country with heavy trade, regional contagion was limited.

Brazil has a major foreign-policy stake in Mercosur in that it provides a counter-balance to the US in inter-regional affairs. Accordingly, while editorials in major Brazilian papers tended to view the Argentine predicament contemptuously, as a product of incompetence, the government has been keen to show solidarity with Buenos Aires. Brazil's own devaluation in 1998 and its successful recovery from its currency float contributed to some of Argentina's difficulties by making Brazilian products much cheaper than Argentina's, and now shield the larger country from an Argentine blowback. Nevertheless, growth in Brazil in 2001 was less than 2%, compared with 4.5% in 2000. Although extra-regional exports expanded aggressively, they could not substitute for the sharp decline in intra-regional trade. Foreign capital in 2001 stood at 34% below total registered in 2000. In the longer term, Brazil could benefit from its neighbour's problems. Investors inclined to venture into Latin America tend to regard Brazil's two-year old experience in controlling inflation as successful and are attracted to its enormous potential market and large consumer base.

Chile, the other major regional economy tied to Argentina's, struggled with but still weathered the contagion effect of the North American and Argentine recessions throughout 2001. Chilean growth fell from 5% in 2000 to just 3% in 2001. For most of the year, Chile saw its exchange rate affected by Argentina's deteriorating country risk, and the central bank was compelled to step in to protect Chile's currency. Investment slowed and unemployment rose over the year. Since Chilean companies own many of Argentina's utilities and other industries, their profits declined from 1998. Chile's unemployment rate, however, has stood up to the regional economic pressure, remaining at around 10%, and up to $10bn in Chilean capital found refuge outside the region from 1998 through 2001. Chile has stayed outside of Mercosur because of differing approaches to exchange rates and trade. Argentina's return to the floating peso will address the first of these concerns, but the spectre of a resurgence in rampant inflation in Argentina will dampen interest in deeper Mercosur engagement for some time.

Bolivia and Paraguay have suffered significant contagion effects from Argentina's meltdown. Both countries trade heavily with Argentina and Brazil and have seen large numbers of their citizens migrate to Argentina in search of better paying jobs. The Argentine press reported that more than 15,000 Bolivians and 9,000 Paraguayan workers (many in construction) returned home for the Christmas holidays in 2001 without jobs in Argentina. (Likewise, some 4,000 Peruvians and 3,000 Chileans went home jobless.) Only a small fraction of these workers are likely to find employment in their own countries. The contagion effect on Paraguayan industries and agriculture was especially severe. Paraguay sells more than 40% of its lumber exports to Argentina, and is especially dependent on the informal (that is, black) market there. Furthermore, Paraguay is a partner with Argentina in the giant Yacireta hydroelectric project, an undertaking that has long been troubled by corruption and now may see new delays because of Argentina's financial difficulties. Bolivia, for its part, has found it necessary to strengthen economic ties to Peru and other countries farther afield.

Uruguay has also been affected. The country had seen Argentine dollars move into its banks, as Argentine deposits increased by 25% over 2001. But by mid-February 2002, one-third of the deposits at the Uruguayan subsidiary of Banco de Galicia, Argentina's largest private bank, had been withdrawn since December 2001. The bank suspended operations there, and the Uruguayan central bank had to take over the subsidiary's operations for 90 days. Furthermore, Argentine tourism, on which Uruguay has become increasingly dependent, dropped by 60% over 2001. Unemployment in Uruguay reached 15% by the end of the year. With a floating peso, Argentine goods will compete more directly with Uruguayan products, while Argentine purchases will fall precipitously, at least in the short term. On 14 February, Standard & Poor's lowered Uruguay's foreign-currency and national currency debt ratings from low investment grade to junk-bond status, owing in part to the economy's close links to Argentina's.

Extra-regional effects

Argentina's relations with its international partners have been strained by the prolonged recession and the political crisis. During the 1990s, European, American and Chilean firms spent billions of dollars in Argentina buying up privatised state enterprises. Spain's exposure was particularly heavy. Its state-owned companies Telefonica, Iberia and Repsol had bought up Argentina's telecommunications, airline and state oil companies at bargain prices, and Spain's private banks have invested heavily in Argentina. Such arrangements have generally been viewed in Argentina as overly favourable to the investors, and the continuing high prices for services – telecommunications, utilities, financing – are among the factors that made Argentina a less attractive investment site than other Latin American countries in the latter 1990s. One of the first acts of the Duhalde government was to try to place a disproportionate share of the burden of devaluation on foreign companies.

Outside investors, however, saw Argentina's problems coming well in advance and therefore discounted anticipated losses effectively. As the economic crisis heightened towards the end of 2001, Spain was one of the first countries to recognise that Argentina's crisis could be contagious in Europe as well as in Latin America if preventive measures were not taken. Two Spanish banks control one-fifth of Argentina's banking system. In the third quarter of 2001, the two Spanish banks set aside nearly $2bn to provision against losses in their Argentine holdings, insulating them from major shocks. In 2001 and early 2002, many Spanish firms, particularly in the energy sector, watched their profits and share prices drop precipitously in significant part because of the Argentine and broader Latin American recessions. Most of the heavily exposed companies negotiated deals with the Argentine government designed to limit losses and remained insulated by demand inelasticity.

Outside investors also did not place great faith in an IMF bailout, and consequently did not continue to invest once the impending crisis became clear. In addition, the foreign companies tended not to be excessively leveraged, which meant that hasty asset sales in other emerging markets generally would not be necessary. The fact that emerging market countries were increasingly adopting floating exchange rates made the sector more stable overall. Finally, in January 2002, Argentine investors, seeking safe havens from currency uncertainties, propped up Argentina's own stock market, which moderated the effect of the crisis on other equity markets. On balance, then, the contagion effect beyond Latin America was well contained.

Taking stock

In assessing the causes of the crisis and contagion effects, it is impossible to separate the impact of the recession in developed country markets, the economic reactions to the attacks in New York and Washington on 11 September, and the final deterioration of the decade-long Argentine bubble. The recession had already caused growth in the region to drop, and Argentina was heading toward crisis before 11 September. The terrorist attacks sapped any remaining investor taste for risk. Political tensions in the region were already up due to the worsening situation in Colombia and political instability in Venezuela, Ecuador and other countries. More broadly, Afghanistan and the international counter-terrorism campaign have occupied full attention of the American and European publics. Latin America – and its economy – disappeared from the global screen in late 2001 and early 2002. Only one Latin American president (Alejandro Toledo of Peru) showed up at the March 2002 World Economic Forum. In previous years, Latin American presidents had used the Forum to tout their countries' suitability for international capital. Commented one Latin American observer: 'We are becoming the invisible continent'.

Yet however 'invisible' Latin America may presently be, in light of all the other factors affecting Latin American economic performance, the Argentine meltdown appears to have had a relatively mild impact. The effect has been felt mainly by its trading partners in Mercosur and on the bottom lines of hundreds of companies that invested in Argentine firms. The impacts are diffused rather concentrated, and Brazil, Argentina's major trading partner, seemed to be bouncing back by April 2002, which may permit it to lead a regional recovery. Mercosur has, if anything, been strengthened politically by the crisis. Brazil's president has given strong moral support to his Argentine counterpart, and even went to far as to vent his anger – and probably that of many Latin American heads of state – at the IMF for dawdling for so long before pulling the plug. More broadly, an awareness has emerged among Argentina's neighbours that none can remain indifferent to its predicament. Political commentators have noted that most Latin American emerging-market countries are susceptible not only to Argentina's economic problems but also to its political malaise. Noted one Chilean author: 'One sees a certain unease among intellectuals with the political transition that has accompanied the neo-liberal economic model'.

That unease may affect Argentine foreign policy, which could in turn affect the region's global perspective. Argentina is only the third-largest economy in Latin America. Yet it has tended to lead Latin America on the external-relations front. Emerging from the 'dirty war' of 1976–82 and the 1982 Falklands debacle, in the early 1990s Carlos Menem openly courted the United States, theorising that Latin American countries should discard staid nationalism in favour of an internationalist foreign-policy personality and make a contribution to international security in 'automatic alignment' with the US. Setting an example for Brazil and Chile, Argentina sent two ships, several cargo planes and 600 soldiers to the Persian Gulf in 1990–91; dispatched a large battalion of 850–900 peacekeepers to Croatia in 1992; and deployed peacekeeping contingents in Cyprus and Mozambique. In international forums, Argentina was the only Latin American country to side consistently with the US on issues like human-rights violations in Cuba.

After economic crisis has unfolded, however, Argentine officials perceived apathy on the part of the Bush administration. Turkey, which had borrowed 1,500% of its IMF drawing quota as of January 2002, continued to receive IMF assistance due to its strategic importance, while Argentina, at 529% of its quota, was cut off. Thus, Argentine officials appeared less inclined to embrace international economic and political forces – including globalisation and the US itself. Argentine Foreign Minister Carlos Ruckauf stated that Buenos Aires would adopt a more 'polygamous' and less extroverted foreign policy, and seek better ties with Brazil and Europe as well as the US. This may, among other things, produce a stronger bloc that could demand greater trade concessions from Washington in exchange for a free-trade agreement, to which Brazil has been particularly resistant. But while Duhalde has appeared to tilt towards protectionism and 'neo-populism', such instincts will tend to be constrained by the practical exigency of remedying Argentina's current economic ills and setting the country right with the international investor community. It needs help from the IMF and, *a fortiori*, from the US. Argentina will have to find a way to substantially lower the interest it is paying its government debt, lower interest rates to its small and medium-size private-sector enterprises, raise tax collections at all levels of government, end its fixed transfers to the provinces, and generate some $10bn in private-sector investments. More importantly, it will have to find competent political leadership to guide it through those difficult policy changes and at the same time restore voter confidence in the Argentine state.

In early March 2002, Duhalde persuaded Congress to approve a budget that cut spending by 14% from the 2001 level, with the approval of the provincial governors. IMF officials also began talks with government representatives in Buenos Aires to establish a new loan programme. The assumptions underlying the budget – 15% inflation, a 5% drop in GDP and a deficit of only 3bn pesos ($750m, assuming 75% devaluation prevailing in late March 2002) – were optimistic; the IMF, having lent $28bn to Argentina in 2001, was not in a generous frame of mind; and the state–provinces financial relationship has been quick-fixed rather than fully restructured. Furthermore, economic officials appeared undecided as to which currency regime to settle on. But the apparent recognition from the governors that they must make financial compromises and the probability of strict IMF economic conditionality may combine to induce Duhalde to resist populist pressures and produce a sustainable and realistic national economic policy. This will require courage and tough decisions on his part. Sooner or later, for example, the *corralito* will have to be abandoned to enable consumer demand to refuel economic growth, and the government will have to commit to a currency and conversion policy. In any event, Duhalde's legitimacy as a leader – and whether he stays in office until scheduled elections in September 2003 – depends on his government's economic performance.

As of early April 2002, however, it was too early to tell whether Argentina would pull out of its tailspin or crash. A *La Nación* front-page headline on 27 March read: 'For Duhalde, the future is measured in days'. Some investment banks predicted an 11.6% contraction in 2002. Discussions with the IMF and debt-restructuring talks had a long way to go, and some analysts expected a bigger write-down than the 40% originally anticipated. Due to the drop in tax revenues, Buenos Aires was forced to join the poorer provinces in printing scrip to pay employees and suppliers. Inflation in February 2002 was 3.1%, and the March figure was expected to be higher. Some Argentine analysts envisaged a social explosion, with the poor joining the middle class in staging massive and increasingly unruly protests. If the economy crashes, the consequences for the rest of the continent could be dire. Not only would it give a negative signal to international investors, but it would send the message to other countries that entrenched Latin American political systems – not just governments – must be radically overhauled or simply abandoned. Countries such as Venezuela appear vulnerable to both the social upheaval and the capital flight that such 'ideological contagion' would entail. Brazil and Colombia are also susceptible to political forces adverse to the free market. On the other hand, leftist and populist politicians lost in 2001 elections in Honduras, Nicaragua and Peru. The salutary aspect of the Argentine crisis is that it has thrown down the gauntlet to Latin American governments, after the heady days of emerging-market growth, to focus more soberly on their long-term responsibilities to their citizens. If Argentina meets this challenge and other Latin American nations heed its progress, a more thoroughgoing brand of free-market democracy could take hold on a continent where voter faith in democratic institutions has declined sharply.

Europe/Russia

Forces coalesced in late 2001 and early 2002 to produce greater stability both within Europe and on its periphery. As the United States and Russia lost interest in the Balkans, Europe duly stepped in and took responsibility for the region. The European Union (EU) and NATO deftly calibrated diplomacy and the threat of force in stabilising Macedonia. The EU came of age as a pacifying political force, brokering a new constitutional arrangement between Serbia and Montenegro and assuming the stewardship of Macedonia. European representatives also managed their missions in Bosnia and Kosovo with skill. Refinements in the Europe–Balkans relationship are still required – for example, in the International Criminal Tribunal for the former Yugoslavia's prosecution of war crimes – but they appear to be quite attainable.

Shared interests in the global counter-terrorism campaign have reinforced Russian President Vladimir Putin's conviction to improve relations with Europe and the US, and planned enhancements of Russia's role in NATO have tamped down tensions over NATO enlargement. Further, transatlantic enthusiasm for 'big bang' NATO enlargement – possibly to include Bulgaria and Romania – has grown, as forging stability in Central Asia and denying the region to transnational terrorists such as al-Qaeda has become a Western strategic priority. The 11 September attacks also increased Turkey's strategic importance, both as a pivotal power in an unruly Central Asian neighbourhood and an example of a successful secular Muslim state. These factors strengthened Turkey's alliance with the US, which some Turks have come to consider an alternative to European relationships. Yet despite standing differences with the EU over political reform and Cyprus, Ankara substantially resolved its differences with Brussels over the European rapid-reaction force's access to NATO assets, and appears unlikely to abandon its European vocation.

The 11 September attacks prompted Western European nations to engage in a more focused search for a coherent strategic role. The global counter-terrorism mobilisation produced unprecedented levels of US–Europe cooperation in the intelligence and law-enforcement areas. Post-11 September transatlantic military affairs are more complicated. Persistently low European defence outlays and a large increase in American defence spending portend the continuation and perhaps even the widening of the US–Europe 'capability gap'. The US preference for informal 'coalitions of the willing' may have decreased the urgency of mustering an operational European rapid-reaction force, which remains

Map 2 Europe/Russia

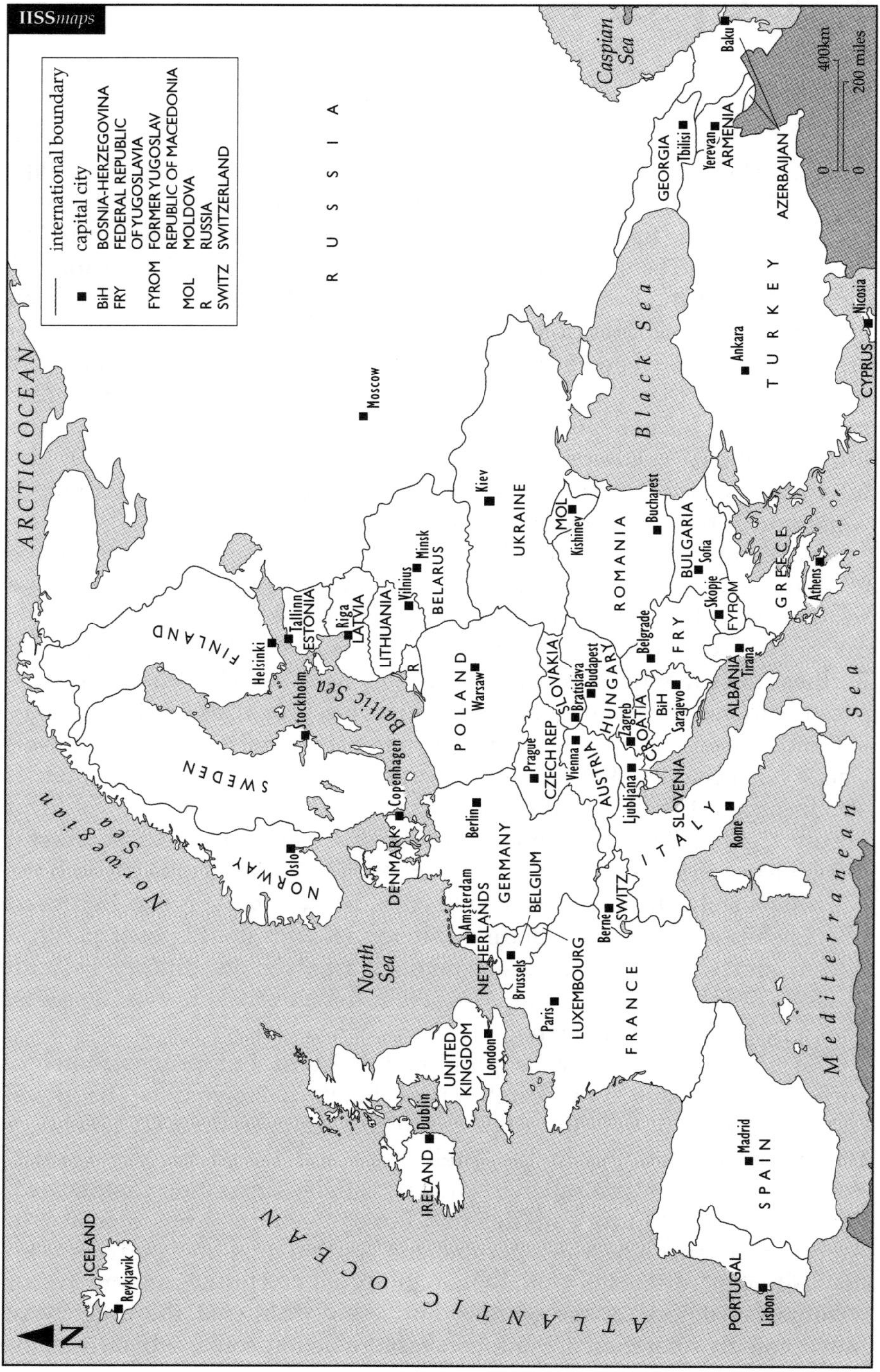

largely notional despite the declaration of operational capability at the December 2001 EU summit in Laeken. At the same time, however, it has increased pressure on European NATO to develop an identity and a set of priorities that are relevant to the counter-terrorism campaign. The allies will need to arrive at a new agreement on the appropriate conceptual military framework for coalition operations, including a more specific understanding about the tasks for which allied armed forces must prepare. At least on the part of those European NATO members most likely to operate militarily with US forces, developing a new allied framework for rapid, high-end, global coalition operations will be desirable. To fulfil this objective, narrowing the capability gap will remain paramount.

In non-military institutional matters, the news was perhaps less spectacular but not, on balance, disheartening. The transition to the euro in January 2002 in 12 of the 15 EU countries did not produce the level of confusion or the volume of shady financial dealings that many anticipated. In making fiscal harmonisation more imminent, however, this development did flag the difficulties some EU members are likely to have with the deepening of EU supranational authority. Such problems could delay the broadening of the EU as well. But EU countries have recognised that their own economic and military security depends to a large extent on that of their neighbours on Europe's periphery, and that they must offer integration to some. Thus, EU governments affirmed their commitment to a speedy conclusion of the accession negotiations with prospective new member states, ideally by the end of 2002.

One serious issue that may arise between the US and Europe is the difference in threat perceptions with respect to terrorism. Europe rallied behind the US immediately after 11 September and a high level of counter-terrorism solidarity and cooperation has continued. But, particularly if al-Qaeda attacks remain subdued, several factors could produce some relaxation in Europe's counter-terrorism posture. These include the fact that the US, not Europe, is al-Qaeda's primary target, and distractions from resurgent domestic terrorist activity in Spain, Italy and possibly the United Kingdom. The transatlantic 'values gap' could also come into play. In March 2002, for example, France threatened to withhold counter-terrorist cooperation with the US if American prosecutors pursued the death penalty for suspected 'twentieth hijacker' Zacarias Moussaoui, a French national. Careful diplomacy may be required to refocus European capitals on the reality that Europe was used as a launching pad for the worst terrorist attack in history, and to drive home the point that, as American territory becomes less vulnerable as a result of a robust homeland security programme, terrorists may find Europe a more attractive target of opportunity. The US, for its part, may discover that policies that reinforce perceptions of American unilateralism – such as the high steel tariffs imposed in March 2002 – make managing the transatlantic counter-terrorism alliance more difficult.

Europe's Evolving Strategic Role

Most European governments were at first uneasy and disoriented with the new Bush administration and its unfamiliar language. It was the shock of 11 September and the strong performance of American political and military leadership in its aftermath that seem to have helped Europeans to reach a clearer understanding of their own responsibility and role in the world. The lesson is that Europeans must move ahead to take charge of their own security but will nevertheless remain dependent on US power in a global context. On its own, in its current state, Europe would be unable to generate a similarly strong, coherent and successful response to an existential challenge.

One reason for this inability is Europe's preoccupation with internal concerns. With a combined population of 379.4 million in 2001, the 15 nations of the European Union (EU) are collectively the world's biggest market in terms of GDP. The EU is also becoming one of two key international political actors, the other being the US. Demography, however, is likely to be Europe's big challenge. Nowhere in Europe except in Turkey is the number of children born to each woman – the fertility rate – high enough to maintain current population levels. The replacement rate is roughly 2.1. In Central, Eastern and Southern Europe, fertility rates are under 1.4. In 2020, about 27% of Europeans are expected to be 60 years or older (up from 21.5 % in 2000), putting additional stress on welfare systems and public budgets, unless immigration and an increased willingness to procreate can mitigate this process of gerontification.

Table 1 **Average number of children per woman to be expected at 1999 reproduction rates** (total fertility rate)

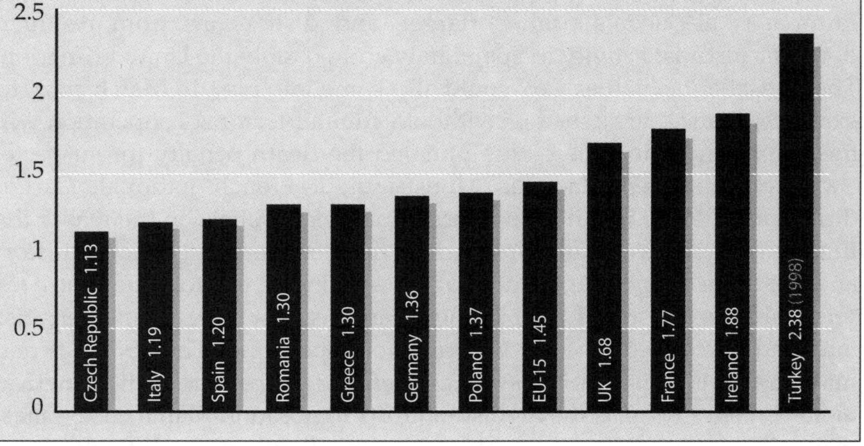

Source: Council of Europe

Aging voters in the EU's wealthier nations are worried primarily about pensions, healthcare, jobs and internal security. Each issue is, in some way, linked to the complex issue of immigration. Currently, the EU takes an annual total net inflow of one million people, mainly into Italy, Spain, Germany and Britain. The popular fear of instability and insecurity gives rise to increased demand for law and order at home. However, it has also helped to build additional support for a positive international role for Europe, geared at preserving a stable political and economic environment.

This more active commitment to wider responsibilities, including international security, found expression in the Declaration of EU heads of state and government made at the December 2001 EU summit in Laeken, Belgium. They recognised that 'Europe needs to shoulder its responsibilities in the governance of globalisation ... resolutely doing battle against all violence, all terror and all fanaticism ... [while] seeking to set globalisation within a moral framework, in other words to anchor it in solidarity and sustainable development'. Even Switzerland's referenda, one in June 2001 on participation in armed peacekeeping forces (including training with NATO), and one in March 2002 on UN membership, reflect this trend. More significantly, European reactions since 11 September convey an increased sense of shared responsibility for international security. According to a Gallup Europe Eurobarometer poll in November 2001, more than half of the respondents in each of the four major EU nations – Britain, Germany, France and Italy – were in favour of sending their troops to fight together with US forces in response to the 11 September attacks. About two-thirds of respondents believed that terrorist actions against their own country were possible. In November 2001, German Chancellor Gerhard Schröder succeeded in winning a vote of confidence from his Social Democrat–Green coalition to send Bundeswehr troops into combat against international terrorism in *Operation Enduring Freedom*, a marked departure from past German abstention. At the same time, Europeans have been eager to point out that in spite of the need to join the military action in this special situation, the 'European model' of preference for non-military tools of crisis prevention and conflict resolution, based on the strengthening of international law, human rights and economic cooperation, remained their distinct credo.

The impact of 11 September

European reaction to the attacks on the World Trade Center and the Pentagon was swift and cohesive. The tone of unconditional support for the US was set by the North Atlantic Council's declaration on 12 September that called upon all NATO members for collective defence against the attack on the US under Article 5 of the Washington Treaty. Transatlantic cooperation among security forces, including a new level of intelligence cooperation, was put into place immediately. This was indispensable, especially given that most of the attackers had been part of terrorist cells in Europe.

For the EU's 'third pillar' – justice and home affairs – the challenge of 11 September meant a return to its origins; in particular, the informal 1975 TREVI group of EU interior ministers to coordinate responses to terrorism. It also proved an impressive demonstration of the progress in European integration in this policy sector. In a special summit meeting on 21 September, EU nations decided to establish a union-wide legal framework for the prosecution of terrorist acts. This includes a broad, agreed definition of terrorism and a common framework to prevent terrorists from finding safe haven in national law-enforcement and extradition loopholes, together with the new European arrest warrant, binding on relevant bodies and mechanisms in all member states, for various crimes, including those typically related to terrorism.

Both elements are to be enshrined in national statutes. Seven EU nations have pledged to implement this arrest warrant by September 2002. In addition, a common EU-wide list of terrorist individuals and groups was established in September 2002 in connection with an immediately binding European regulation, formally adopted on 27 December 2001, to freeze terrorist assets and prohibit support, recruitment and financial services for terrorists throughout the EU. The list gave rise to some disagreement with the US, as it initially did not contain a number of groups whose inclusion the US considered essential.

One currency for (almost) all

The coming of the euro was typical of the slow and methodical way in which the EU achieves success, from the 1970 Werner Plan on economic and monetary union to the 1989 Franco-German understanding that led to the 1992 Maastricht Treaty and its full implementation ten years later. Nevertheless, from a historical perspective, the completion of the European Monetary Union at the beginning of 2002 was the most remarkable event of the year in Europe. The euro has now entirely replaced the national currencies of 12 EU countries, including the German mark and the French franc. It has also already gained wide circulation in South-eastern and Eastern Europe, superseding the mark and to an extent, the dollar. The introduction of 37.5 billion new coins and six billion notes on 1 January turned out to be exactly the kind boost for a European identity that many of its proponents had hoped for. Whereas in November 2001, only 48% of Euro-zone respondents expected the common currency to be a good thing, in January 2002, 60% had come to share that view. The EU's three holdout members are reacting to this success story in different ways. While in Sweden, 57% of the population would now welcome adoption of the euro, the Danes are still undecided and the British remain sceptical. In the UK, only 34% say they would be happy with the euro. On the other hand, according to a Eurobarometer poll taken in February 2002, 70% of respondents in the UK expect that Britain will eventually drop the pound in favour of the euro.

Combining a centralised monetary policy with decentralised national fiscal and economic policies, as with the euro, clearly requires coherent coordination of policies in the euro zone. The price that Europe is required to pay for its common currency is the voluntary weakening of national fiscal policies, as agreed in the EU's Stability and Growth Pact of 1997. Given the political temptations of deficit spending – always hard to reign in once indulged – this binding international regime of fiscal solidarity commits participating nations to balanced budgets. Ironically, Germany – the strongest proponent of this approach – became the first country threatened by a formal EU reprimand for nearly breaching the agreed 3% limit on the annual government deficit in 2001. Germany's government balance was –2.7% of GDP, compared to an EU average of –0.6%. As a consequence, the German federal government brokered a national stability pact in March 2002 with the country's state and local entities and committed itself to a 0.5% reduction in federal expenditures in the next budget.

Similar pressures from Brussels are likely to circumscribe the margin of manoeuvre of European governments for a long time to come, denying states the option to spend substantially more on security and defence, international development and macroeconomic crisis-stability measures. The willingness to pay this price reflects the priority assigned across party lines to the political project of European integration, in the belief that it will be a source of stability and improve problem-solving capacity in the long term. As the conclusions of the EU's Barcelona summit in March 2002 illustrate, this fiscal discipline reinforces a neo-liberal economic agenda that clashes with the social-democrat economic philosophies of many European leaders. Under the neo-liberal agenda, growth and jobs are pursued not through subsidies but by aiming to release entrepreneurial spirit, the forces of innovation and market integration in such fields as transport, energy, financial services and information-technology services. Yet deregulation, especially of the rigid labour markets, remains largely lacking.

Enlarging the EU, stabilising its periphery

The EU faces the three-dimensional task of simultaneously deepening its institutional integration, widening its membership and alleviating the divisions *vis-à-vis* non-members in order not to undermine their reform and stabilisation efforts. EU countries have recognised that they may put their own security at risk if they fail to prevent their neighbours and Europe's periphery from sliding into misery and anarchy. The EU approach has been to offer a mix of integration, development assistance and power projection.

In this role, the EU has become the focal point of the European continent. Increasingly, Brussels also appears able to act in lieu of the US as Europe's pacifier. It has exercised this function among members by offering a legal framework for dispute resolution, but also – in cooperation with NATO, the UN and the Organisation for Security and Cooperation in Europe – in places such as Macedonia, Montenegro and post-conflict Kosovo.

The EU's 'hard border' shifted somewhat east again in 2001. Like citizens from other candidate countries, Bulgarians and Romanians can now enter the EU's Schengen area for up to three months without having to apply for a visa weeks or months in advance. Illicit immigration, trans-border crime and insufficient security cooperation, however, could block further liberalisation. Unlike Brazilians or Malaysians, Europeans from ex-Yugoslav states, Albania, Turkey, Ukraine, Moldavia and Russia continue to be barred by Schengen rules from similar benefits of travel enjoyed by these non-European citizens from former European colonies. Crime and corruption in these borderlands, apparently with some governments' active involvement, and the organised trafficking of illegal migrants into the EU – at least several hundred per day – have been widely perceived as the most serious security threat to the European continent. Resources for long-term commitment to the Balkans region, from troops to investment, are so far only available under the Stability Pact for Southeast Europe. This may have to be complemented by additional efforts, as vital security interests of key states are immediately at stake.

EU governments affirmed their commitment to a speedy conclusion of the accession negotiations with prospective new member states, ideally by the end of 2002. Ten accession candidates – the four Central European Visegrad countries (the Czech and Slovak republics, Poland and Hungary), the three Baltic countries, Slovenia, Malta and Cyprus – are on track for full membership as early as 2004. Internationally, the EU's common foreign and security policy already presents its common positions not only on behalf of members but also accession candidates. Negotiations are organised in 31 separate chapters, representing the elements of the EU's legal and political body of rules (*acquis communautaire*) that must be applied to new members. Even at this late point, not all chapters have been opened with each aspirant country; Romania in particular is far behind others in this respect. Most countries, however, resolved major problems raised in accession negotiations in 2001. These include issues relating to the freedom of movement for persons. In deference to popular sensitivities in current member countries, full labour mobility will only be granted to the new Central and East European member states after a transition period of up to seven years. In 2001, there was also significant progress in justice and home affairs on issues such as border control, police and judicial cooperation, and data protection. It is understood that accession does not necessarily imply immediate inclusion in the Schengen area of borderless travel.

The EU-brokered agreement in November 2001 between Austria and the Czech Republic on additional safety measures for the latter's Temelin nuclear reactor, to become operational in late 2002, allowed closure of the energy chapter with Prague. The threat by Austria's FPÖ – the right-wing, small government coalition party – that Austria would veto Czech accession has since fizzled out, at least for the time being, after a popular initiative launched by the party failed to attract the targeted one million signatures. Negotiations on agriculture – the largest chapter, and politically and financially the most sensitive – had not been finalised with any of the applicants as of early April 2002, in part because current members could not agree on their positions. The Common Financial Framework 2004–06 for the Accession Negotiations, presented by the European Commission in January 2002 on the basis of the budget ceiling that had been earlier approved by member states, foresees a ten-year phased transition for farmers in new member countries for payments of direct subsidies under the EU's future rural development policy. In all likelihood, this controversial issue will play a major role during the remaining negotiations and in subsequent national ratification procedures, especially in Poland.

The Treaty of Nice, with its essential adaptations of the EU's institutional framework that need to be in place before the EU can accommodate additional members, cannot enter into force before Ireland finds a way around the failed 2001 referendum. At the Barcelona summit in March 2002, the Irish government committed itself to seek ratification before the end of the year. Although the traditionally neutral Irish people were concerned about participating in EU defence arrangements, they were far more worried about the EU's bureaucracy and its possible encroachment on Ireland's democratic traditions. In February 2002, the British and German heads of government presented a plan for increased transparency and efficiency in European Council meetings, partially in reaction to the almost farcical horse-trading style of the summit meeting at Laeken. Javier Solana, as Secretary of the Council, characterised existing decision-making mechanisms as dysfunctional, citing, among other factors, the semi-annual rotation of the presidency. In March 2002, the Convention on the Future of Europe, presided over by former French President Valery Giscard d'Estaing, began its proceedings. They are expected to result, by spring 2003, in proposals for constitutional improvements in the EU, potentially in the form of a new constitutional treaty for Europe. Perspectives for major reform initiatives also depend on the outcome of the 2002 elections in France and Germany.

NATO's future: big bang and big crisis?

EU enlargement, while a certain prospect, could slip for a few more years, as it involves complicated legal and economic issues. In contrast, the prospects for a rapid further enlargement of NATO have become more concrete during the last year. Before 11 September, the US administration had been urging further eastward enlargement of NATO to gradually complete the vision of a strategic continuum from the Atlantic via Central Europe and the Baltics and eventually into Russia and Ukraine, allied as a whole with the US. This vision now seems within reach for the first time. Ever since President George W. Bush took a strong position in favour of Baltic NATO membership in the context of his June 2001 trip to Europe, opposition to a big-bang enlargement involving five or more countries has faded, in spite of disappointment with the integration efforts of the three new members admitted in 1999. Remaining fears that Baltic inclusion might unduly bother Russia have lost their salience as a result of Russia's rapprochement with the West since 11 September. Obvious candidates for the next enlargement round to be launched at the Prague summit in November 2002 include Slovenia, Slovakia and the Baltic countries; others, such as Romania and Bulgaria, also merit serious consideration. In the future, even some of the non-aligned EU countries such as Austria – already troop contributors to NATO missions in the Balkans – are likely to seek NATO membership.

On the face of it, an organisation of, say, 26 rather than 19 members will need greater bureaucratic efficiency and institutional decision-making focus to ensure that it does not become a mere talking shop. It would seem to make sense, for example, to endow the NATO Secretary-General with new powers to expedite a consensus on military action more quickly, and to vest him with some financial authority to overcome customary squabbles over matters such as NATO's civilian budget. But such essentially procedural issues will be coloured by a much larger internal substantive debate: whereas the US and the United Kingdom have championed NATO's transformation into a globally operating counter-terrorism alliance, France and Germany are generally opposed to any such metamorphosis. The Prague summit, therefore, will need to face not only questions of enlargement, but also crucial matters of transformation. Since 11 September, influential US officials and politicians have indicated that a big-bang enlargement alone would no longer be sufficient to ensure NATO's ongoing strategic relevance for the US. Instead, an active global military role for NATO in the campaign against terrorism and weapons of mass destruction would be required. If NATO is to remain the natural defence arm of the transatlantic community, they suggest, it needs to be retooled for the most critical threat of the time.

For Europeans, the choice is either to live up to new American expectations and keep the US engaged in NATO, or to keep NATO viable as a functioning military alliance in case the US becomes less and less visible in European defence. In any case, it is unlikely that NATO will turn into a hard-hitting global military machine. A cumbersome allied target review process, further complicated by US restrictions on the sharing of sensitive information that effectively excluded advanced US weaponry from allied planning, probably made Kosovo the last war fought by the US under NATO rules. In Afghanistan, the offer to use NATO as a command framework was rejected. For Europeans, the hub-and-spoke bilateralism implied in the post-11 September US preference for 'coalitions of the willing' – under which US military allies work through US Central Command without being anchored in the institutionalised common experience of NATO – is neither an optimal operational arrangement nor, from a political perspective, an ideal vehicle for sustaining and enhancing Europe's multilateral ability to act. Reaching a consensus on NATO's transformation, then, is not likely to be easy. The different orientations among allies will require a new agreement on the appropriate conceptual military framework for coalition operations, including a more specific understanding about the tasks allied armed forces must prepare for. It is possible that NATO will become less of a military alliance, and more of a military services organisation on which members can draw according to emergent requirements – a kind of military tool kit. At least on the part of those European NATO members most likely to operate militarily with US forces, there will be a desire, building on NATO, to develop a new allied framework for rapid, high-end, global coalition operations.

The other major issue for the Prague summit is an enhanced role for Russia in the alliance. Few would be ready to consider Russian membership, and Russia – aware of its shortfalls in terms of NATO's established membership criteria and abhorring the humiliations of the accession procedure – has not asked for it. But Russian President Vladimir Putin characterised Russia as 'a friendly European country' in his 25 September 2001 speech at the Reichstag in Berlin. In fact, Russia is now widely understood to be an indispensable ally against the new range of transnational threats. The basis for a new Russia–NATO relationship, termed 'NATO at 20', has emerged, with the Russia–North Atlantic Council (RNAC) replacing the Permanent Joint Council (PJC). The new dispensation, in NATO Secretary-General George Robertson's phrase, is more about 'chemistry than arithmetic'. The PJC has employed the 19+1 formula, under which NATO members present a single coordinated position for discussion with their Russian counterparts. In the new council, Russia would have an equal voice with the other 19 NATO members on certain issues, possibly including the campaign against terrorism, WMD non- and counter-proliferation, peace-support operations and countering new threats. RNAC dialogue could also lead to greater cooperation in the military-technical sphere, joint exercises, civil emergency planning, defence modernisation and military restructuring.

Russia would not have a veto over NATO's right to act militarily and would not become a NATO member, and the North Atlantic Council would remain intact. While it would be able to influence agendas and participate in decisions on certain issues, the membership would retain the overriding final authority on an issue if Moscow blocked essential measures. NATO members, however, are increasingly concerned that giving any new NATO–Russia council more powers, even if limited to the counter-terrorist front, could compromise NATO cohesion and freedom of action. Conversely, Russia is still committed to keeping NATO and any other Western institutions from interfering in Russia's own counter-terrorist campaign in Chechnya, and its influential defence industrial lobby would inhibit military cooperation. Nevertheless, both Putin and NATO's civilian leadership want Russia to become more involved in NATO. 'NATO at 20' would, at the very least, add a crucial political dimension to NATO's future role and identity.

ESDP is not European defence

Some might understandably have expected that after 11 September the EU would have grasped the opportunity to boost its much-advertised security and defence ambitions, and in particular the non-military crisis-management and police dimension of European Security and Defence Policy (ESDP). Oddly enough, however, the declaration of the ESDP Police Capabilities Commitment Conference in November 2001 did not even make reference to 11 September. The European Capabilities Action Plan (ECAP) launched by the Capabilities Improvement Conference at the same time, to address shortcomings in military capabilities, has so far only succeeded in giving rise to 16 new expert panels. Strong political guidance on ESDP was nowhere to be found. Even the British government, which launched the ESDP initiative in 1998 at St Malo, was uninterested. In 2002, however, the Spanish presidency made the sensible suggestion that the Helsinki goals should be augmented, with a focus on an instant reaction capability within 48 hours. The EU is scheduled to take over the UN's police operation in Bosnia–Herzegovina in 2003, and may also put its flag on NATO's peacekeeping operation in Macedonia. These prospects constitute added pressure for ECAP operational requirements to be satisfied sooner rather than later

In spite of the near-absence of real progress, ESDP's initial operational capacity was declared at Laeken. The phrasing, however, was cautious: 'the EU is now able to conduct some crisis-management operations'. ESDP's goal was described as being able 'to carry out crisis-management operations over the whole range of Petersberg tasks [i.e. humanitarian and rescue operations, peacekeeping and crisis management including peacemaking], including operations which are the most demanding in terms of breadth, period of deployment and complexity'. This language, even more clearly than before, appears to exclude collective defence from the ESDP agenda. At a time when collective defence against terrorism is firmly on top of the international priority list, this dispensation appeared to imply a strengthened European commitment to NATO as the framework for defence.

One key barrier to a robust ESDP appeared to be resolved in late 2001. Turkey had threatened to use its NATO veto to deny the EU rapid-reaction force (RRF) access to NATO assets unless the EU included Turkey in the decision-making process for any RRF deployment regardless of whether the operation concerned used NATO assets and capabilities. Ankara feared that the RRF might be deployed to support Greece in disputed areas such as the Aegean or Cyprus. On 2 December 2001, however, Turkey surprisingly agreed to a UK-brokered compromise under which Ankara would withdraw its demands in return for a guarantee that the RRF would not be deployed in Cyprus or the Aegean, that Ankara would have a consultative role in ESDP generally and a decision-making and military role in any RRF operations in the region. Greece blocked the agreement at the Laeken summit, but as of April 2002 was prepared to discuss it. Yet, as of early 2002, ESDP was not at the core of the defence policy of European nations. On the contrary, in late 2001 and early 2002, NATO Secretary-General Robertson was increasingly outspoken about Europe's being militarily undersized, dubbing it a military 'pygmy'. He underlined the fact that American critics of Europe's military incapacity are right. Sustaining sufficient troops in the Balkans and living up to additional tasks outside Europe's borders, such as those undertaken in Afghanistan, are stretching Europe's existing armed forces to a degree that could jeopardise mission safety and success.

In 2001, European defence budgets again showed no sign of significant growth, both in constant local currency and in constant dollar terms.

Table 2 **European defence spending** (constant 2000 local currency, in millions)	**2001**	**2002**	**change** (percent)
France (euro)	36,843	36,896	+0.2
Germany (euro)	30,043	30,062	+0.1
Italy (euro)	23,307	24,512	+5.2
Netherlands (euro)	6,910	6,813	-1.4
Spain (euro)	7,616	7,761	+1.9
Sweden (crowns)	45,363	42,590	-6.1
United Kingdom (£)	23,203	23,018	-0.8

Well-known deficiencies remain in key areas: air and sealift; air refuelling; precision-guided munitions; command and control; interoperable secure communications; and intelligence. In addition, the exploitation of advanced technologies, including modelling and simulation, and of networked systems, is lagging behind. Only the UK is investing in defence research and development and procurement at a level comparable to that of the US.

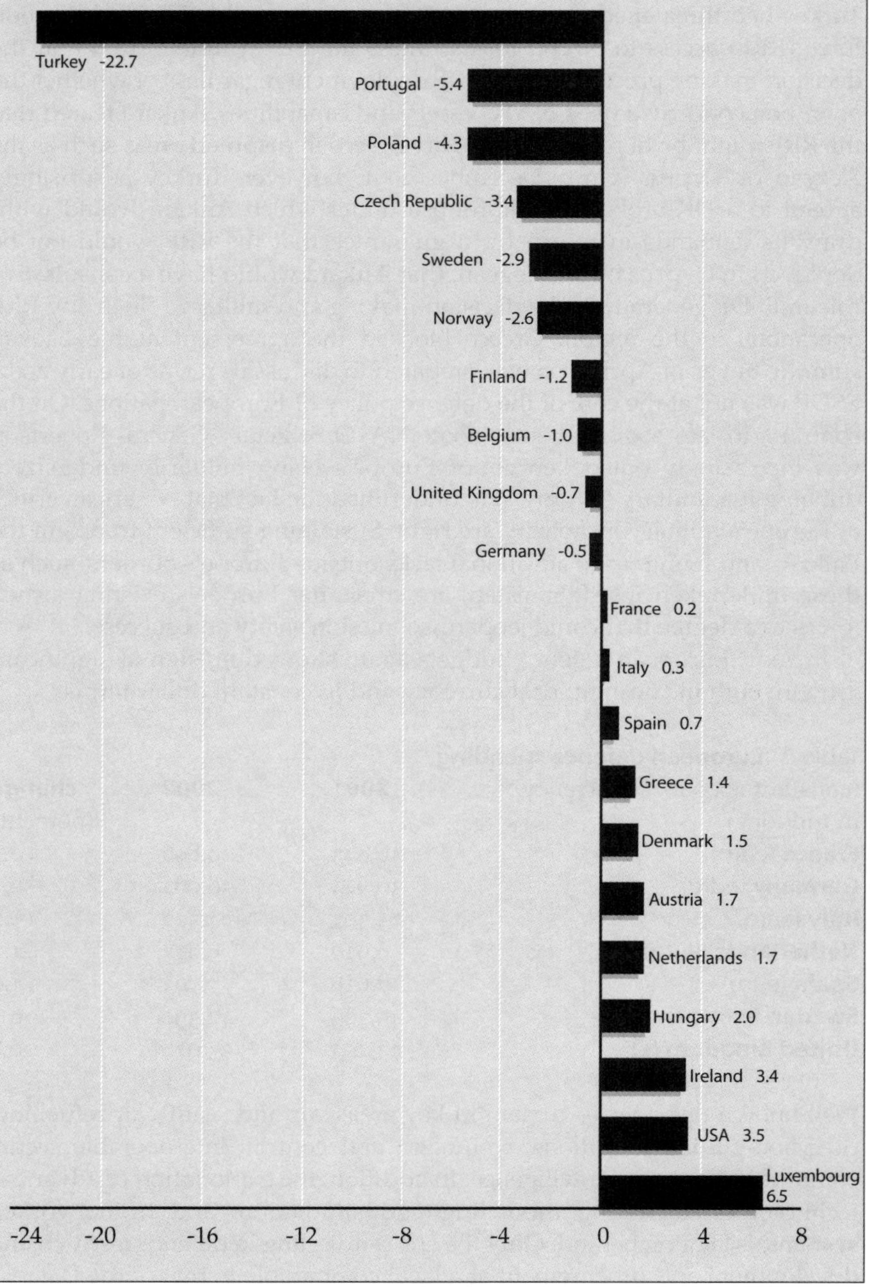
Table 3 **Annual average change in defence spending since 1999**
(in percent, based on constant local currency)
Turkey -22.7
Portugal -5.4
Poland -4.3
Czech Republic -3.4
Sweden -2.9
Norway -2.6
Finland -1.2
Belgium -1.0
United Kingdom -0.7
Germany -0.5
France 0.2
Italy 0.3
Spain 0.7
Greece 1.4
Denmark 1.5
Austria 1.7
Netherlands 1.7
Hungary 2.0
Ireland 3.4
USA 3.5
Luxembourg 6.5
-24
-20
-16
-12
-8
-4
0
4
8

Table 4 **Defence research and development**

(Constant 2000 US dollars)	**2000**	**2001**	**per active soldier**	**2002 (est.)**
France	2.9bn	2.7bn	9,136	2.8bn
Germany	1.1bn	1.0bn	3,086	n/a
United Kingdom	3.1bn	n/a	14,499 (in 2000)	n/a
USA	38.7bn	40.0bn	29,268	46.0bn

Table 5 **Defence procurement**

(Constant 2000 US dollars)	**2000**	**2001**	**per active soldier**	**2002 (est.)**
France	5.0bn	4.5bn	15,437	4.3bn
Germany	3.9bn	3.4bn	10,670	n/a
United Kingdom	8.8bn	8.2bn	38,691	n/a
USA	55.0bn	60.8bn	44,547	59.2bn

On a somewhat more positive note, ongoing military reforms, geared at professionalisation and improved availability of forces, have been proceeding successfully in several European countries. In France and Spain, all remaining drafted conscripts were released from service in 2001. But the apparent fading of ESDP's political fortunes suggests that the success or failure of European defence capability-building efforts, especially with regard to cutting-edge capacities, cannot be gauged primarily by the implementation of ESDP's goals, important though they are for enabling the EU to be a more coherent and forceful actor in international security. Whether European NATO decides to turn the alliance into a power-projecting global force or constrain its functions to European defence in case the US becomes less involved in Europe, the European imperative is to improve military capabilities. The growing transatlantic 'capability gap' and the gulf between operational cultures result, respectively, from unparalleled US investment in advanced defence technology, and the inevitable differences in interest and strategic outlook that arise between the world's only superpower and a group of regionally minded, cash-strapped European NATO states.

The transatlantic future

Stagnating or shrinking procurement funds are causing a severe squeeze, as a small number of ongoing large procurement programmes – in part reflecting past requirements that no longer reflect current priorities adequately – leave little or no room for new programmes geared at new requirements. This situation appears to be particularly severe in Germany. The Airbus Eur18bn A400M transport aircraft programme – the outcome of the two-decade gestation period for a future European large aircraft – has been subscribed to by France, Germany, Spain, Britain, Turkey, Belgium, Portugal and Luxembourg. It has become a key test-case for European defence capability-building efforts, but also adds critically to the long-term procurement budget squeeze. To some extent, the A400M programme owes its existence to long-standing European discontent over cross-subsidies for Boeing from the US defence budget, regarded as a competitive disadvantage for Airbus in the civilian aircraft market. The disproportionately large scale of US defence research-and-development and procurement programmes and budgets, combined with high obstacles for non-US firms that are trying to win US defence contracts, remains a fundamental problem in transatlantic defence and trade relations.

In March 2002, the British government decided to lift the ban on foreign majority ownership of BAE Systems, Europe's biggest defence company, citing increased international investor interest in defence stocks after 11 September. (It remains the case that no individual foreign investor is allowed to hold more than 15% of BAE Systems, and its chief executive must be British.) At the same time, the German government facilitated a major US investment in the cutting-edge submarine manufacturer HDW. With these two developments, the attractive prospect of moving away from protecting national, or European, defence-industrial protectionism towards a strategy that employs market forces to transform US industrial domination into an interlaced transatlantic defence marketplace has been raised again. If US lawmakers were prepared to reciprocate such moves, and amend rules that stand in the way of defence-industrial integration within the Atlantic alliance, the economic, technological and political environment for European military capability-enhancement could improve considerably, as Europeans could benefit from the US market without having to buy American.

With the realisation that it remains in the European interest to cultivate the transatlantic link and be an active partner with the US, the desire to define Europe's identity as an alternative to US leadership has faded considerably. There is a certain revival of the mindset that had originally helped to build the North Atlantic alliance: to make the US-dominated system work to serve Europe's interests – economically, politically and militarily. For this objective to be sustainable, European governments will have to credibly demonstrate respect and influence in Washington. They may also be required to promote a creative makeover of the transatlantic cooperation framework. Accomplishing this goal will be particularly hard when US attention is focused elsewhere. Furthermore, friction on the trade front or the foreign-policy front could impede transatlantic efforts to arrive at the new cohesive and complementary security relationship necessitated by 11 September. The overriding importance of that task, however, is likely to sustain momentum towards NATO enlargement and integrating Europe's regional and global security roles with those of the United States.

Russia's Move Westward

A clearly pro-Western turn in President Vladimir Putin's foreign policy has become one of the most striking features of the global strategic realignment in the aftermath of the 11 September terrorist attacks in the United States. Russia has emerged as an important partner in the US-led international campaign against terrorism. For the first time since the end of Cold War, Russia and the West share important common interests in fighting international terrorism in all its forms. Russia, the US and Europe have all benefited from this new level of partnership, which was particularly evident during the first phase of the global war on terrorism: the US-led military campaign against the Taliban and al-Qaeda in Afghanistan.

Even after a decade of economic decline and the progressive deterioration of its military capabilities, Russia's contribution to the operation was both significant and timely. Moreover, Putin has been surprising in his pragmatic willingness to supersede some of the iron taboos of Russia's post-Soviet foreign and security policy. Putin's agreement to allow the US troops to be deployed in Central Asia and the Caucasus has rendered obsolete the concept of 'post-Soviet space' or 'near abroad' as an area of Russia's exclusive sphere of influence. Putin's apparent acquiescence to the US withdrawal from the 1972 Anti-Ballistic Missile (ABM) Treaty has destroyed the shibboleth that Cold War treaties constitute the 'cornerstone of strategic stability'. Russia's new dialogue with NATO on terrorism effectively ended Russia's insistence on the alliance's 'geographic area of responsibility', partially undermining the basis of Russia's previous geopolitically driven opposition to NATO enlargement. Finally, Putin's decision to authorise Russia's security services to engage in extensive information-sharing with the US has challenged the most conservative elements of Russia's military and security community.

Putin's audacious actions have paid off both internationally and domestically. They have prompted the US and Europeans to re-evaluate Russia's role, providing new impetus to Russia–NATO relations and reinforcing the Western commitment to promoting Russia's economic development and political stability. Domestically, despite criticism from the sidelines by retired military officers and isolated politicians that Putin may be succumbing to the 'Gorbachev syndrome' of unilateral concessions to the West, Putin has enjoyed political and popular support with approval ratings exceeding 70%. There are two major reasons for this outcome. On the one hand, over the past three years, Russia's economic growth has provided enough stability and prosperity for the Russian people for foreign-policy issues to drop to the bottom rung of public concern. On the other hand, growing support for Putin in the West has generated expectations that over the long run, Putin' decisions will advance Russia's international integration and economic development.

Furthermore, the post-11 September convergence of Russian and Western interests did not represent a radical turn, but rather the logical continuation of Putin's push for Russia's modernisation and integration. From the first days of his presidency, Putin indicated his commitment to bringing Russia closer to Europe. Although the initial change was more in style than substance, Putin's foreign policy has since departed from that of his predecessors in reducing the 'rhetoric-per-action' ratio. This has gradually increased the credibility of Russia's diplomatic commitments. Active personal diplomacy on the bilateral level made Putin's extrovert mindset fairly clear, but international opposition to Russia's war in Chechnya, the US election campaign and disagreements between Europe and the US on a number of strategic issues limited Moscow's opportunities to translate its ambitions into a new level of partnership with the West. The eleventh of September presented such an opportunity.

The risks of Putin's turn

Putin's support for the West carries considerable political risks. Domestically, any changes in 2002 and early 2003 in Russia's recent economic trends – which might be prompted by a decline in oil prices or Russia's mounting debt obligations – are likely to provoke changes in public mood. In these circumstances, Russian voters usually turn to foreign-policy issues and Putin's position could be vulnerable to criticism. Internationally, Putin's gamble on Western support has been driven more by the vision of long-term benefits, so it remains essential for Putin to stay the course of partnership with the US and Europe. Putin therefore will have to balance Russia's short-term needs against long-term benefits. Issues on which that balance will be particularly difficult to strike include US military action against Iraq, mounting instability along Russia's border in the Caucasus and the possibility of the protracted presence of US troops in Central Asia.

Putin's policies also face a stiff challenge from Russia's staid bureaucracy. It is ill-equipped to handle an over-ambitious foreign policy agenda. That agenda already includes multilateral negotiations on World Trade Organisation (WTO) accession, new relations with NATO, arms-control talks with the US, a new partnership with the EU, active diplomacy in the UN Security Council with respect to the Middle East and Iraq, as well as a more pragmatic agenda within the CIS framework (in both economic matters and security). Finally, Putin may find it difficult to sustain US and European interest in Russia. In the autumn of 2001, this interest was probably at the highest level in the past decade. Practical payoffs for Russia are likely to come in spring 2002, with a long-anticipated US–Russian summit in Moscow and the new NATO–Russia Council coming on stream.

However, as the partnership between Russia and the West becomes more a matter of routine, Russia is likely to drop to a lower tier on the Western foreign-policy agenda. Thus, Putin is seeking to cement a new place for Russia in the Western community that is both sustainable and influential. His three main objectives are: elevating the role of US–Russian bilateral relations; institutionalising Russia's international role through NATO, the EU and the WTO; and securing Western support for Russia's economic reforms.

Reconciling old and new agendas in US–Russian relations with Russia's contribution to the US-led coalition has been swift and significant. Putin was the first among foreign leaders to call Bush following the 11 September attacks to offer Russia's support. Since that time, Putin has consistently supported the US campaign by providing diplomatic support, sharing intelligence and accepting the US military presence in Central Asia and the Caucasus, despite the growing criticism from Russia's domestic political and military establishment. To preserve its strategic influence in Afghanistan, Russia also increased its military support to the Northern Alliance and gave political backing and humanitarian assistance to the interim administration of Hamid Karzai. However self-interested, these policies were broadly supportive of US policy.

Russia itself has also benefited from the US campaign against al-Qaeda and the Taliban, which had long provided military and financial backing for the rebel commanders fighting Russian troops in Chechnya. Some Western commentators raised questions about Putin's expectations of US rewards for Russia's support. The Russian president has never stated his expectations explicitly, but appears disinclined to demand short-term opportunistic concessions from the US. At the same time, his pursuit of a longer-term strategy of leveraging improved US–Russian relations to promote Russia's integration into the Western economic and security community has caused some frustration among certain Russian politicians, who have accused the US of being unilateralist and applying double standards to Russia. The US has been very slow in sharing intelligence with Russia in regard to Chechen rebel networks. Moreover, although the US muted its criticism of Russia's military campaign in Chechnya during the height of Afghanistan military operations, the US State Department's annual human-rights report, released in March 2002, included sharp criticism of Russia's actions in Chechnya. The State Department so far has also refrained from including Chechen groups on the US list of global terrorist organisations, despite the irony that many Chechen fighters have been involved in fighting US troops in Afghanistan. Finally, Washington has made little effort to keep the Russians regularly informed about US military deployments in Central Asia and the Caucasus, despite the obvious political sensitivity of these actions from Putin's point of view.

Russian–US strategic relations

The Bush administration's caution towards Moscow reflects a bias of long standing. During the US presidential election campaign in 2000, George W. Bush and his team openly discounted Russia's importance and vowed to scale down bilateral cooperation. Bush's administration arrived at the White House with one key commitment in regard to Russia: to develop a new strategic framework in US–Russian relations. This framework was set to incorporate three main issues: de-emphasising the role of the US–Russian arms-control treaties (such as the ABM Treaty and the Strategic Arms Reduction Treaty, or START), which were considered remnants of the Cold War; removing barriers to the United States' development and deployment of limited missile defences; and reasserting US pressure on Russia to curb alleged proliferation practices. Although the two presidents agreed in principle to the linkage between the development of defensive systems, including missile defences, to reductions in offensive nuclear capabilities at the first US–Russian summit in Ljubljana in May 2001, little of substance was added to the US–Russian bilateral agenda there.

Translating that general agreement on changing the offensive–defensive strategic balance into clear commitments has proven difficult. The Bush administration has been reluctant to enter into a legally binding agreement with Russia that could clearly define these limits and to develop a mutually acceptable transparent verification mechanism. In December 2001, President Bush announced that the US would withdraw from the ABM Treaty and proceed with its missile defence programme, regardless of Russian opposition. To reassure Putin and the United States' European allies, Bush had preceded this announcement with a statement of the US intention to undertake unilateral cuts in its strategic nuclear arsenal to the levels of under 2,000 operationally deployed warheads, which is below the limits of the still-unratified START II Treaty. Furthermore, in December 2001, the US Congress voted to increase funding for the Cooperative Threat Reduction (CTR) programme (also known as Nunn–Lugar programme) in Russia above what had already been appropriated for 2002. Congress also approved a $300 million increase for US Department of Energy and State Department non-proliferation programmes in Russia for fiscal year (FY) 2002, and the administration increased its request for FY2003 funding for all CTR programmes for Russia.

At the same time, the administration introduced an additional hurdle to a US–Russian strategic accord by announcing its intention to store rather then eliminate the majority of 5,000 warheads that are expected to be removed from operational deployment. In addition, Russia's concerns have been exacerbated by assertions made by some US analysts that the US may need to resume nuclear testing, which is consistent with the US programme for modernising its nuclear capabilities. Finally, the US Nuclear Posture

Review, which was leaked in March 2002, stated that the US intends to continue targeting Russia as well as some of Russia's neighbours, such as Iran and North Korea, and some of Russia's partners, such as Syria, with its nuclear weapons.

Putin, however, has not allowed any emerging disagreements to blur his vision of a new partnership with the US. This steadiness appears to have prompted a shift in US attitudes towards Russia. Following the US announcement that it would withdraw from the ABM Treaty, President Putin refrained from heavy or sustained criticism of US policy, which a number of European and Asian capitals would have seconded. He has also remained firm on the bilateral nature of the treaty, further limiting European criticism of the US move. His assessment, which appears correct, was that the US stance on the ABM Treaty and missile defence is not open for negotiation due to the overwhelming political consensus behind it in Washington. Accordingly, he issued a statement to the effect that the US plans to develop limited missile defences do not present any immediate threat to Russia's security. Any long-term threats from a more comprehensive missile defence systems, which could reduce the deterrent potential of Russia's aging nuclear weapons, could be overcome by reintroducing multiple independently targetable re-entry vehicles (MIRVs) to Russia's new strategic systems, such as the SS-27 *Topol-M* complexes. This option seems to be acceptable to the US, which is very keen to make it clear to the Russians that missile defences are not being deployed against Russia.

In search of some form of compromise with the US on strategic issues, the Russian government focused bilateral dialogue on translating unilateral commitments on offensive weapons into some form of written political document. The prospects of unilateral and non-transparent cuts in offensive nuclear arsenals had caused some unease not only among influential members of the US Congress, but also among some of the moderate representatives of Bush administration itself. But while the Pentagon was not inclined to negotiate with Russia on any issues related to US nuclear policy, the State Department was more flexible. In addition to the long-term political need to introduce predictability and transparency into the US–Russian strategic dialogue that could survive changes of leadership in the Kremlin and in the White House, there was a growing understanding in Washington that President Putin had to get some quid pro quo for his personal leadership and support for the US global objectives in the campaign against terrorism.

It appears that Moscow's pragmatic arguments in favour of a written agreement, coupled with its support for the campaign against terrorism, have succeeded in influencing US policy. It is likely that, prior to or during Bush's visit to Moscow in May 2002, the US and Russia will sign a statement specifying the number of warheads that both countries will undertake to remove from operational deployment. It should also address the issue of verification, which is likely to be modelled after the system currently in place within the framework of START I. It appears probable, however, that the US will continue to insist that only those warheads that are removed from operational deployment should be open to verification inspections. Russia is seeking to achieve a much greater degree of transparency, and to win some assurances from the US on the number of warheads that are likely to be eliminated completely. In an effort to influence the US decision, Russian Defence Minister Sergei Ivanov has announced that Russia would consider storing some of its own warheads. Unless Russia were to follow a set of procedures and safeguards comparable to those observed by the US, this very costly option could present potential proliferation problems. On a projected 2002 military budget of $9 billion, Russia cannot even afford adequate storage. Accordingly, Russia could use the prospect of storing its warheads to attempt to garner additional CTR funds from the US. But funding the preservation of an arsenal that could be re-operationalised and turned against the US could prove a political problem in Washington.

NATO and Russia: new strategic geometry

Another of Putin's key objectives is to normalise and expand relations with NATO. But while some European leaders and a number of powerful US Senators and Congressmen have favoured considering the possibility of Russia's future membership of NATO, no explicit proposals for enhancing Russia's role in NATO were raised within formal alliance discussions prior to 11 September. The new US administration did not share the European vision of the need to engage Russia more substantially in transatlantic security arrangements, primarily because it did not believe that Russia could make a substantial contribution. European capitals were also concerned that any aggressive proposals that they proffered could reinforce any intention on Russia's part to exploit differences between Europe and the US on a range of issues from the ABM Treaty to NATO enlargement. While a number of these governments shared Russian concerns about US policy, they appeared reluctant to develop a closer security dialogue with Russia while US–Russian relations were effectively put on hold during the first six months of the new US administration.

Post-11 September, the US changed its position significantly. At the November 2001 US–Russian summit in Crawford, Texas, the two presidents pledged to work together and with other NATO members to 'improve, strengthen and enhance the relationship between NATO and Russia, with a view to developing new, effective mechanisms for consultation, cooperation, joint decision and coordinated/joint action'. This commitment, practically in its entirety, was incorporated into the Russia–NATO joint statement following the December 2001 Ministerial meeting of the NATO–Russia Permanent Joint Council (PJC). The two sides agreed that they intend 'that such new mechanisms beyond the current format will be in place for, or prior to, our meeting in Reykjavik in May 2002 or when NATO's foreign ministers meet prior to the Prague summit in November 2002'. At that summit, a number of new members, including the Baltic states, are expected to be invited to join the alliance. The timing will be important, because NATO is keen to provide some political benefits for Putin's pragmatic acquiescence to the next, more difficult, wave of enlargement into the former Soviet space.

The basis for a new Russia–NATO relationship, termed 'NATO at 20', was provided in a letter from British Prime Minister Tony Blair to the NATO heads of state and Secretary-General George Robertson, which put forward an ambitious proposal for replacing PJC with the Russia–North Atlantic Council (RNAC). The PJC has operated under 19+1 formula, with NATO members presenting a single coordinated position for discussion with their Russian counterparts. In the new council, Russia would have an equal voice with the other 19 NATO members on certain issues. Blair's proposal envisages an ambitious new agenda for the RNAC, including the fight against terrorism, WMD non- and counter-proliferation, peace support operations and confronting new threats. It is anticipated that, over time, RNAC dialogue could lead to expanding cooperation in the military-technical sphere (strategic lift, theatre missile defence, communications), joint exercises, civil emergency planning, defence modernisation and military restructuring. This would lead to more interoperable forces that could potentially allow combined peace-support operations. While Blair's proposals emphasised the need to preserve NATO's right to act militarily without Russia's veto, it also set the stage for a meaningful partnership between NATO and Russia.

Blair's proposals, however, have been received with some scepticism, both by some NATO governments and by more conservative elements within Russia's political and military élites. Complicating factors include lingering suspicions left over from the Cold War – which are particularly strong among the new NATO members and candidates – and NATO's own post-11 September identity crisis. Consequently, negotiations on the new format have proceeded with some difficulty. According to NATO Secretary-General Robertson, NATO should 'become the primary means for developing the role of armed forces in helping to defeat the terrorist threat globally'. A closer association between NATO and Russia would make this role more effective. Robertson even went so far as to state that 'intensified NATO–Russia cooperation is a central pillar of the global struggle against terrorism'. However, NATO members are increasingly concerned that giving any new NATO–Russia council more powers, even on the terrorist front, could compromise NATO cohesion and freedom of action. They are wary of granting Russia membership 'through the back door' at a time when Russia's military is far from meeting basic NATO standards, and Russia and NATO continue to disagree both on the definition of terrorism and on which methods of counter-terrorist operations are legitimate. Without common values and inter-operable capabilities, the possibility of joint action and decision-making – even if limited to the fight against terrorism – seems in doubt.

The Russians, for their part, have also expressed some concerns. While they strongly supported Blair's proposal, which would give Russia greater influence over NATO's future evolution, they remain uncommitted to responsibilities that such a role would entail for Russia, both in political terms and in relation to its domestic military reforms. A majority in both the Russian political élites and the Russian public would like to see NATO's identity transformed not towards a greater military role in the global campaign against terrorism, but towards a political organisation in which Russia can play a more equal role. Russia's Ministry of Defence and many members of the Duma have spoken against greater Russian military cooperation with NATO on the grounds that it would entail greater transparency and thus expose many failures of Russia's decade-long programme of military reforms. Moreover, Russia is still committed to keeping NATO and any Western institutions from interfering in Russia's own counter-terrorist campaign in Chechnya. Finally, while Russia has expressed its willingness to engage in greater military-technical interaction with NATO – including the development of European theatre missile defence – there is still a powerful defence industrial lobby that opposes technology-sharing with the West and insists on preserving full control over all domestically produced military equipment.

Despite reservations on both sides, it is clear that an expanding relationship between Russia and NATO is underpinned by NATO's civilian leadership and Putin, who both want to see a Russian seat at NATO's table. It will take time before Russia and NATO can develop the 'culture of cooperation' required for such a relationship to blossom fully. But there are ways in which Moscow could shorten that time. For instance, 'NATO at 20' could present a golden opportunity for Russia to test the waters of European-style multilateral diplomacy, which it has so far avoided by using primarily bilateral channels. Even in the PJC, Russia has lost many opportunities to influence NATO policy simply by refusing to assign a Russian mission to NATO headquarters. Moreover, practical cooperation between Russia and NATO is unlikely to develop through Ministry of Defence channels alone, and would benefit from intelligence-sharing via the Federal Security Bureau, planning joint civil emergency response through the Ministry of Interior and discussing non-proliferation by way of the Foreign Ministry and the Security Council. Military cooperation with the NATO Kosovo Force (KFOR) is set to be scaled down, with Russia announcing its intention to reduce the number of its forces in Kosovo from over 3,500 to 1,000.

Economic challenges

While cooperation on security issues represented one of the main channels for raising Russia's international profile in 2001, Putin was determined to translate it into greater benefits for Russia's economy and domestic reforms. Since the beginning of his presidency, he has consistently promoted Russia's greater integration in multilateral institutions, which include economic organisations such as the EU, WTO and the Group of Eight (G-8). At the same time, Putin has been pursuing a set of radical domestic economic reforms that have brought about greater economic stability, attracted foreign investors and provided Russia with economic levers for developing closer relations with its neighbours, as well as with key partners in Europe and Asia.

In 2001, Russia's economy registered the third consecutive year of real growth. GDP grew by 5.4% in 1999, 9% in 2000 and 5% in 2001. In 2001, growth came at a time of economic recession in all major economic powers, including the US, Europe and Japan. Such economic growth has been accompanied by the growth of real income by 6% in 2001, and by over 15% from 1999 through 2001. This not only increased consumer demand and drew more foreign investment to the retail sector but, most importantly, hastened the creation of a new Russian middle class with a direct stake in the success of Putin's modernisation programme. In addition, from 1999 through 2001, new private small enterprises were established at a rate of 200,000 per year. President Putin has put economic reform at the centre of his domestic agenda, noting that Russia needs to ensure fair rates of economic growth in order to preserve its statehood and 'historical prospects'. These sentiments are shared by increasing numbers of Russians, who are prepared to endorse some apparent concessions by Putin in foreign-policy and security spheres in exchange for greater economic benefits at home.

The West, including the US, has understood this tradeoff and extended to Russia a number of potential economic benefits. Both the US and the European Union (EU) have offered strong political support to Russia's membership in the WTO, though neither is prepared to make it easy for Russia to complete trade negotiations, in which it lacks experience. The introduction of US steel tariffs and EU demands for liberalisation of Russia's aviation industry and service sector, including utilities, insurance and banking, has met considerably greater opposition within Russia than did the US announcement on the withdrawal from the ABM Treaty. At the same time, Putin faces a serious challenge in selling WTO membership to many powerful Russian domestic lobbies and passing the necessary legislation through the Duma to ensure that Russia can join the WTO before January 2005, when more stringent rules come into force.

Putin will need support from his Western partners not only on the WTO and foreign investment, but also in addressing three major concerns facing

Russia in the near future. One of them is Russian debt, which totals about $143bn. While Russia's favourable economic performance allowed it to cover debt obligations in full without borrowing from the International Monetary Fund (IMF) in 2001, it is still carrying a major debt burden. This is due to increase in 2003, when Russia is obliged to start repaying Soviet debts totalling roughly $39bn that were rescheduled by the Paris Club. President Putin has asked both the US and Europeans to help reduce this burden by writing off some part of the Soviet debt, but Germany, which holds the majority of the debt, has been reluctant to do so in light of Russia's economic growth. The US has proposed a debt-for-disarmament swap, under which all Russian appropriations for the disposal of nuclear or chemical weapons under arms-control obligations could be counted against its Soviet debt. This could be significant because Russia has increased its appropriations significantly. In 2001 Russia spent over 3bn roubles on chemical weapons disposal and for that purpose in 2002 appropriated over 6bn roubles – 12 times higher than the total for 1997–2000. But Germany has been reluctant to sign up to this dispensation.

The second economic issue facing Russia is its heavy reliance on the oil sector. Despite of gradual diversification of Russia's economy, oil and gas revenues still constitute around one-third of Russian budget revenues. Total revenues from Russian energy sector exports in 2001 exceeded $52bn. Accordingly, Russia's economic stabilisation from 1998 through 2001 was largely due to stable and high oil prices. As long as oil prices stay above $14 per barrel, the current Russian budget – which underpins Putin's ambitious reform agenda – could be realised. If, however, prices drop below that level, Putin's agenda could be in trouble. At the end of 2001, the US and European recession had contributed to the decline in oil prices, but instability in the Middle East and the threat of US military action against Iraq has kept oil prices higher than expected. Under pressure from the Organisation of Petroleum Exporting Countries (OPEC), Russia agreed to cut its oil exports by 150,000 barrels per day from 1 January to 31 March 2002 to help stabilise oil prices. The pressure from OPEC is understandable, given that Russia is already the second largest oil exporter in the world after Saudi Arabia. In 2001, Russia produced 348m tonnes of oil, including gas condensate, 7.6% more than in the year 2000. However, major Russian oil companies and the government were opposed to extending the cuts beyond March 2002. The subsequent increase in production may put Russia in conflict with OPEC producers. In these circumstances, a heightened commitment from Europe and the US to raise the Russian share of their imports of oil and gas to reduce dependency on the Middle East would serve as a strong indicator of their commitment to Russia's economic stabilisation. This would also be beneficial for the US and Europe. As of March 2002, the EU was currently engaged in a comprehensive 'energy dialogue' with Russia within the framework of the EU–Russia energy charter that was agreed at an EU–Russia summit in Paris in October 2000; while the US was considering increasing imports of Russia's oil.

Russia's third economic challenge is EU enlargement. Unlike NATO enlargement, which constitutes a largely psychological and emotional threat to Russia's security, EU enlargement is likely to impose a real economic price on Russian businesses in dealing with neighbouring states and the EU in general. In early 2002, Russia and the EU were engaged in active dialogue on development of a 'common economic space' concept, but the real cost of enlargement has not been properly understood in either Russia or the EU. It would be particularly high if Russia fails to obtain WTO membership before enlargement takes place. Enlargement will also present some political challenges. In particular, establishing a border regime for residents of Kaliningrad, the Russian enclave wedged between Lithuania, Poland and the Baltic Sea that could be surrounded by EU territory after enlargement, will be politically sensitive. It may also be surrounded by new NATO members. While Russia is paying increasing attention to Kaliningrad issue, the EU is reluctant to make any special exemptions for Kaliningrad residents in the implementation of Schengen regulations imposing stricter border controls on non-members of the EU.

A durable convergence?

For Russia, 2001 was a year of economic success and political stability at home and a heightened international profile through its participation in the US-led campaign against terrorism. These successes were possible largely because of strong conviction and leadership on the part of President Putin. Putin's pragmatic pro-Western policies and his new partnership with the West have raised Russian expectations about a substantial US and European commitment to assist Putin in addressing his domestic challenges, particularly those on the economic agenda. In turn, the US administration has demonstrated increasing willingness to compromise with Russia on strategic nuclear weapons cuts, while bolstering support for CTR programmes.

There remain areas of broad divergence between Russia and the US. The US has included Iran in the 'axis of evil', while Russia has established a strategic partnership with Iran involving exports of conventional weapons worth over $300m a year for five years and cooperation on oil and gas development, and on civilian nuclear power. The United States also is not prepared to endorse many of Russia's counter-terrorist policies. Although the US administration, having launched its own war on terror, has been reluctant to criticise Russia over its recent conduct in Chechnya, many American and European NGOs continue to scold the Russian military for human-rights violations and other excesses in Chechnya. US–Russia tensions over Chechnya could recede. In late March 2002, Russian legislators opened dialogue with rebel politicians with an eye towards prompting political talks between Putin and Chechen rebel leader Aslan Maskhadov. On 29 March, the Russian military command in Chechnya also issued a decree – viewed by Human Rights Watch as a mere 'propaganda step' – designed to curb human-rights abuses. More broadly, however, the US is seeking to establish a new global regime under which the issue of terrorism can no longer be kept as a domestic or even a regional issue. Friction arose in February 2002 between Russia and Georgia over Tbilisi's acceptance of US counter-terrorist military assistance without first consulting Moscow. This global regime is likely to challenge the principle of state sovereignty and to justify more intrusive international oversight on any activities of states and non-state actors that could be linked to terrorism. In particular, US concerns over the proliferation of WMD technologies from Russia could in certain instances make Russia a focus of the US-led counter-terrorism effort rather than a key member of a global anti-terrorist coalition.

Yet Putin's move westward is not founded solely or even mainly on the counter-terrorism campaign, but rather on his deeper and more durable commitment to goals of modernisation and integration. These cannot be achieved without Western cooperation. The very fact that neither the announced US withdrawal from the ABM Treaty nor the 'axis of evil' speech seemed to dilute that commitment is evidence of its strength. Similarly, the US and Europe support greater cooperation with Russia for strategic and philosophical reasons – such as changing the offensive–defensive strategic balance and forging stability in Eastern Europe – that are not limited to a common opposition to terrorism. The next year, then, is likely to see the new partnership between Russia and the West strengthened. Even US military action against Iraq and NATO enlargement to include the Baltic states are unlikely to derail Putin's commitment. It will be fortified if Russia's economy continues to grow and if Russia makes progress towards WTO membership. Both Russia and the West have a stake in making this happen.

Wind-down in the Balkans

Astonishing as it may seem, the Balkans are heading for more stable and prosperous times. In 2001 and early 2002, the three major ingredients that fuelled violence in the region for over a decade have been removed. First, it has become clear that the age of the old nationalist troublemakers in both Yugoslavia and Croatia is truly over: not only have they gone, but the nationalist political infrastructure that sustained their regimes has also evaporated and cannot be recreated. Second, the potential for further territorial disintegration appears to be containable: as of early 2002, no state or splinter nation in the Balkans was in a position to engage in any prolonged warfare. Finally, the divisions between the Europeans and the Americans over policy in the region have largely evaporated: the US has grown more comfortable with the idea of Europeans taking the leadership role, while the Europeans have accepted that the future of this region is ultimately their responsibility, irrespective of how much or how little European armies are engaged in the Balkans. Fulfilling this responsibility will ultimately require the Balkans' full integration into existing European security and economic structures. The absence of nationalist dictators, the sheer exhaustion of all Balkan nations from prolonged warfare and, at long last, a coherent and united Western policy: these are the pillars of the current Balkan stability. For the first time in the region's modern history, the Balkans have begun to be seen as just another poverty-stricken European region that must do better, rather than a continental disease.

The war crimes tribunal: room for improvement

Security in the Balkans remains a relative concept, and a fragile balance. The region's leaders still suffer from a collective amnesia about what has happened to them and what they caused to happen to others during the last decade of warfare. All the nations in the former Yugoslavia accept that crimes were committed by everyone; however, each retains a dogged, self-exculpatory belief that the crimes committed against their own nation were particularly heinous and require a different form of punishment. All the governments in the former Yugoslav space are formally independent, yet utterly dependent on the European Union (EU) and NATO for their perpetuation. The ambivalent attitude towards their immediate past and the client-patron relationship that governs their present – and is likely to govern their immediate future – are the key determinants for the region.

The clearest example of the ambivalent attitude towards the responsibility for the war has been the response of the nations to the ongoing activities of the International War Crimes Tribunal in The Hague. Slobodan Milosevic was arrested and imprisoned in The Hague in June 2001. Many people in Yugoslavia welcomed his trial, which began at The Hague in 12 February 2002, not so much because this represented the ultimate triumph of international law but because Milosevic's disappearance from the national political scene was a prerequisite for meaningful Yugoslav political change. Yet the notion that the tribunal is merely an extension of NATO – the continuation of warfare against the Serbs through other means – remains strong in Serbia.

There are few in Yugoslavia who doubt that Milosevic is guilty of unspeakable crimes, but fewer who accept that he was the most important criminal in the Yugoslav tragedy. The laborious and secretive workings of the tribunal and UN Chief Prosecutor Carla del Ponte, the peremptory, repeated demands by Western governments to hand over suspects, the linkage of economic aid to cooperation with the tribunal, and international lawyers' seeming indifference to Balkan legal procedures and provisions in their quest for a 'higher justice' only add to the sense of dissatisfaction. The feeling of ordinary Serbs in particular, but also of Croats, Bosnian Muslims and Kosovars, is that the tribunal will continue indefinitely, more to expiate the West's guilty conscience than to provide justice in the region. While politicians and military commanders from all the nations are now facing justice, the number of Serbs who were either convicted, arrested or facing arrest dwarfs that of other nationalities.

There are almost certainly more culpable Serbs than others. But the tribunal's almost exclusive public focus on Milosevic in late 2001 and early 2002 has made relations between Western capitals and Belgrade fraught. The strange episode in March 2002 – in which a senior Yugoslav army officer and a US diplomat were arrested in Belgrade for espionage, reportedly on the strength of videotape and audiotape evidence – demonstrated the mutual mistrust between the US and Yugoslavia. The difficulty that Western authorities have encountered in apprehending Bosnian Serb leader Radovan Karadzic and his military commander Ratko Mladic is another indicator of the image problem that the tribunal faces among Serbs. If the tribunal is to be broadly viewed as a fair extension of European justice, it may also be necessary for it to pursue cases against Croats, Bosnian Muslims and ethnic Albanians with the same vigour and publicity with which it is prosecuting Milosevic. This would mean pressing investigations of possible crimes committed by Albanian guerrilla organisations and political leaders in Kosovo, and by Croats responsible for uprooting most of Croatia's ethnic Serbs from Krajina in 1995.

The tribunal probably also needs to be more transparent. The UN Chief Prosecutor operates both an open list of wanted war criminals and a secret list of people indicted for alleged war crimes. The result has been a greater efficiency in apprehending suspects, but also a widespread wariness – particularly among the military commanders in both Croatia and Yugoslavia – about any cooperation with outsiders. If an army general cannot be sure that he will not be arrested when he steps off a plane in any European capital, the opportunities for interaction with the military and security services of the region will remain limited. Correspondingly, if Western governments are not privy to the full list of indictments, few Western politicians will be eager to contemplate a serious engagement with the military of the region, for fear of involvement with potential war criminals. The result has been a continuation of the 'bunker mentality' among the armed forces and security services, particularly in Yugoslavia and Croatia, which not only scuppers any chance for a serious reform in the security sector, but also perpetuates NATO's 'enemy image' in the region. This could have a corrosive effect on regional security.

The 11 September effect

Additional balances between punishing the unacceptable and accepting the unsavoury have also to be struck in dealing with the internal situation in each Balkan state. In this regard, Western engagement looks much more promising, mainly on account of the 11 September attacks. These affected the Balkans in four direct and crucial ways. First, the attacks made it difficult for any European voice to challenge the Bush administration's determination to reduce its military commitment in the Balkans. Second, the Balkans immediately became a political backwater for US policymakers. Central Asia and the Middle East commanded attention, while small bands of marauders in the Balkans, some still with lethal intent but unlikely to threaten the US, were no longer strategically relevant.

Third, Washington's focus on transnational Islamic terrorist networks will mean heightened scrutiny of some of America's closest allies in the Balkans. It is telling that the only major US military effort in the region after 11 September – with the exception of providing continued support for NATO efforts to apprehend war criminals – was the elimination of alleged terrorist networks in Bosnia and the discovery of some links between the region and the recruitment of al-Qaeda fighters. Few if any in Washington believe that Kosovo Albanians or Bosnian Muslims – both still grateful for US military support in their quest for independence – will suddenly provide a fertile ground for anti-American terrorists. The US will continue to support an independent Bosnia and an autonomous Kosovo. It has little tolerance, however, for continued agitation by separatist insurgencies.

Fourth, with US interest in the region waning, Russia's attention has also moved away from the Balkans. Moscow was never entirely sure what it wanted, apart from preventing the US from regarding the region as an extension of its own sphere of influence. Prior to 11 September, Russian influence had been diminishing in every country in the area, apart from its traditional client, Serb-dominated Yugoslavia, where Moscow backed an unappealing and ultimately wrong 'horse': Milosevic. After the Yugoslav dictator's removal from the political scene in October 2000, the Russians had an opportunity to become involved in Macedonia, the next country that appeared to be heading for a disaster, and where NATO, yet again, became involved. For a while, the Russians played their traditional role: as upholders of supposed Slav solidarity against a Muslim 'menace' and as opponents of NATO intervention. Large supplies of Ukrainian-made weapons poured into Macedonia, almost certainly with Moscow's connivance, and the usual dark warnings about another Western-made Balkan war could be heard from the Kremlin. But the events of 11 September changed Russian calculations. Russian President Vladimir Putin was quick to realise that the major strategic games were being played elsewhere, and seized the opportunity to erase a decade of negative and ultimately failed Russian policies in the Balkans. Like the Americans, the Russians are not proposing to ignore the region altogether. But, also like Washington, Moscow no longer regards its presence in the area as either very important or as a symbol of great-power status.

For the first time since communism collapsed on their continent, the Europeans are left to deal with the Balkans largely on their own. They have long accepted that the economic reconstruction of the Balkans was their almost-exclusive responsibility, and have also accepted that any military force in the area will be mostly European. The Albanians of Kosovo and Macedonia, as well as the Bosnian Muslims, used to run to Washington every time they were subjected to political pressure from the Europeans. That route is now barred. The governments in Belgrade and Skopje used to threaten European governments with the prospect of a Russian response; that option has also evaporated. From 11 September onwards, Balkan players became aware that Brussels, not Washington, was the referee, both militarily and politically. The Balkan leaders also realised that the threat of violence no longer worked: Washington's response henceforth would be to crack down hard on whoever started a cycle of violence, regardless of the merits of the case.

A European sphere

The Europeans have taken to their new role with alacrity and, in the process, have achieved a great deal. A clutch of European 'proconsuls' administer Bosnia, Kosovo and Macedonia – three territories that, in effect, have become European colonies. Michael Steiner, a German, runs Kosovo, legally as the UN Secretary-General's Special Representative, but practically with European money and in line with European-dictated priorities. Paddy Ashdown of the United Kingdom is the new UN High Representative in Bosnia. Alain Le Roy, a Frenchmen, dispenses 'advice' in Macedonia as EU Special Representative. Although Le Roy has less extensive powers than the other two, he is the only one to wear the EU hat openly and has exerted considerable influence by drafting local constitutions. Moreover, the message throughout the region is clear: a Frenchman, a German and a Briton – reflecting the ranking European military powers – now manage the fate of Europe's three sick children. Their management verges on quasi-colonial: they decide when and where elections take place, how the EU's Balkan 'colonial service' is to operate and what local leaders are unacceptable and must therefore be removed.

This army of European administrators, hiding behind grandiose names ('coordinator', 'administrator', 'convenor', 'facilitator', 'mediator') designed to convey a sense of both urgency and fairness, work slowly and laboriously, and often without any attention from either individual European governments or public opinion on the continent. It is relatively easy to pinpoint familiar European inefficiency, duplication, waste and the occasional outright financial fraud. But the overall outcome is encouraging. European governments knew all along that territories like Bosnia, Kosovo or Macedonia could survive and eventually prosper only if their entire administration was seized by its bootstraps, and if decisions were imposed on local politicians. For years, the pretence was maintained that Europe's role in the region was merely to suggest good options, to encourage and protect rather than to rule outright. In fact, Europe always had the responsibility and the political power to enforce solutions in the region. It chose to accept the responsibility, but for many years declined to exercise the power. The difference in the last year is that Europe as a whole – including the EU and the European members of NATO – has decided that, if the responsibility is to be discharged properly, then the levers of power must be seized as well. In short, European governments no longer mind being considered 'colonial' in the Balkans, if their job remains essentially that of administering *de facto* European colonies. The results have been almost wholly beneficial, and probably long lasting.

Calmer Kosovo

The Kosovo elections in December 2001 resulted in a relative victory for Ibrahim Rugova, the most moderate local leader. There were serious and prolonged problems about convening a new parliament and forming a new government for the territory. Nevertheless, the remaining ethnic Serbs in Kosovo – up to a tenth of the population – managed to obtain their first formal representation since the 1999 war. Ultimately, a government that includes both Rugova's party and the rival Democratic Party of Kosovo (PDK) was formed. Future difficulties and government crisis are guaranteed, for the political divisions between Rugova and Hashim Thaci, the former head of the rebel Kosovo Liberation Army and now PDK leader, are deep. Nevertheless, the deal allowed a new Kosovo government to start working in March 2001, and was a first step towards the creation of new self-governing institutions. Appointed in January 2002, Michael Steiner, with a staff of 5,000 and a budget of $400 million, has appeared to exercise his influence judiciously.

Outright independence for the province is not envisioned under the UN Security Council mandate that governs the international presence in the territory, while physical incorporation into Serbia – to which Kosovo still belongs – remains unthinkable. Yet there may be more scope for a deal than has been assumed. First, it is not inconceivable that Serbia itself may initiate negotiations over the future status of Kosovo. Such negotiations were precluded as long as the dispute between Montenegro and Serbia remained open. But in March 2002, the two entities reached a constitutional deal whereby Montenegro would acquire greater functional autonomy while maintaining a sovereign link with Serbia in a 'union of states'. If the deal holds – or at least is allowed to operate for a while – Belgrade may find not only an incentive but a legal excuse to engage in negotiations on Kosovo, if only because Serbian leaders could claim that their new constitution left the status of Kosovo unclear. It is also possible that Rugova may participate in such negotiations, provided that the question of independence for his province is clearly one of the items on the agenda. Virtually all of Serbia's current leaders have privately acknowledged not only that Kosovo is lost to them, but also that the re-incorporation would in any event be a political disaster for the Serbs themselves. In short, the Serbs need not fear the encroachment of ethnic Albanians, as there is no appetite either in Kosovo or in neighbouring Albania for the creation of a greater Albanian state. Thus, an independent Kosovo, with European forces at its border with Macedonia and with international guarantees protecting the rights of ethnic Serbs, may be feasible in the medium term.

The real danger in Kosovo was that, as the province remained in a legal limbo, the population would become unruly and yesterday's European liberators would come to be regarded as today's enemies. This danger appears to have been averted. Ibrahim Rugova's good showing in the elections meant that there was a sufficient diversity of views in the province to prevent an outright clash with Kosovo's peacekeepers and administrators. And, in keeping with the new mood, Michael Steiner has not tolerated any resistance to his reforms or obstruction to his administration. The UN police in Kosovo were given new powers to crack down on organised crime. These include the use of wiretapping, covert photography, global positioning devices and forms of electronic surveillance that until then had been prohibited. Greater police efficiency has resulted in the discovery of a secret pipeline pumping fuel across the boundary from Montenegro into Kosovo, and may well be critical in the prosecution of several upcoming war crime trials in the province. Kosovo is unlikely to pose a major security challenge in the near future.

A maturing Bosnia

Similarly, Bosnia is limping along at a livelier clip. In effect, EU policy in that country is to dismantle some of the provisions of the 1995 Dayton Accord informally. The key to this process is to change the Bosnian constitution that, as a result of the Dayton Accord, gave special status to the Serbs as a distinct ethnic group but lumped Muslims and Croats together.

The constitutional reforms – designed to give all three communities equal status – have stalled for a variety of reasons, but there is little doubt that they will ultimately be implemented. Nor is there much doubt that the complicated administrative arrangement imposed on Bosnia – also devised in the hangars of a US military base in Dayton – need to be swept away. Under current arrangements, there is a theoretical possibility for the creation of no less than 13 various governments in Bosnia, and a myriad of other local authorities. This crazy-quilt may have been attractive when the key objective was to reassure every locality, but it makes little sense now that coexistence has become a matter of routine. There remain difficulties in ensuring the cooperation of the Bosnian Serb government, particularly with the extradition of alleged war criminals such as Karadzic and Mladic. But there are indications that these two – and 18 others who have been indicted with them – will soon be handed over or arrested. Prospects for holding new national elections in October 2002, under fresh constitutional provisions, remain good.

The Dayton Accord has become more of a hindrance than a framework for Bosnian stability. It is likely to remain in place, if only because nobody wants another protracted debate about Bosnia's fundamental structures. But the Dayton document will increasingly be ignored as circumstances so require. Before 11 September, the Americans would have resisted such a dispensation; thereafter, Washington has not been particularly interested in even being kept informed of the country's constitutional changes. The big danger for Bosnia was always that Croatia and Serbia, pulling from different directions, would tear the country apart. As in the case of Kosovo, the danger is still there, but it is receding. Croatia has no interest in upholding the supposed rights of ethnic Croats in Bosnia, many of whom supported Franjo Tudjman, Croatia's deceased wartime leader. And Belgrade is no longer interested in allowing the Bosnian Serbs to dictate Yugoslavia's policies. Moreover, Belgrade is in no position to support the Bosnian Serbs financially. The result is that the country's three communities are resigned to continue living with one another, morosely but surely. The EU agreed to take over policing of the country as of January 2003 from the UN's International Police Task Force (IPTF), which numbers 1,800 officers. Like the IPTF, the EU's force would work alongside the NATO-led Stabilisation Force, which numbered 18,000 as of April 2002. The police force will face problems such as migrant smuggling and customs evasion, as well as having to deal with the tensions raised by the return of refugees. Yet these are problems that already affect the EU as a whole, and are no novelty for European police forces.

Macedonia in recovery

A similar situation – combining an unfinished job and a containable threat – has emerged in Macedonia. For much of 2001, the country looked like a classic Balkans disaster: a land split between two nations, unwilling to live with each other or accept any compromise; and an insurgency movement supported from outside with large quantities of weapons. Yet the sense of a disaster in slow motion, of the possibility that the harrowing episodes of Croatia, Bosnia and Kosovo would repeat themselves, ultimately pushed NATO into action. A peace deal brokered by the EU was signed on 13 August 2001, and a NATO-supervised disarmament programme (*Operation Essential Harvest*), designed to garner 3,300 weapons, proceeded in parallel with its implementation. The alliance has justifiably claimed victory in a mission that sought to disarm the Albanian guerrillas and at the same time, force the Macedonian government to give its sizeable Albanian minority new rights and constitutional safeguards. However, this victory was largely for unforeseen reasons.

Despite the official claims to the contrary – NATO announced *Operation Essential Harvest* complete on 25 September 2001 – NATO did not manage to disarm the various groups of ethnic Albanian rebels. Most of the weapons collected by the alliance were old and operationally expendable; the slightly better equipment has, predictably, been stashed away in the mountains adjacent to Macedonia's borders with Kosovo and Albania. Constitutions in the Balkans are generally written in order to sanctify a state of affairs that is already in place, rather than influence or settle a battle that has yet to be concluded. The majority Slav population of Macedonia believes that the current arrangements go too far, while the Albanian minority is not persuaded that what they have achieved is either durable or desirable. But, as in other Balkan states, the protagonists know that this was the maximum that could be achieved at this stage. NATO – and, critically, the US – will not tolerate any new Albanian insurrection. In early 2002, the ability of the various ethnic Albanian movements to capitalise on American goodwill was gone, and probably for good. In early 2001, for example, it appeared that Albanian violence in Macedonia could, at the very least, persuade the West to insist on independence for Kosovo, if only to cut the link between two parts of the same ethnic group. A year later, by contrast, any increase of violence in Macedonia made any change to Kosovo's current legal status less, not more, likely. The Albanians of Macedonia were therefore on their own, and realised that any resort to force would be highly counter-productive.

At the same time, the Macedonian government remained deeply divided about the feasibility of the constitutional arrangement reached in 2001. For a while, it tried to prepare for the next battle by importing large quantities of military equipment from Ukraine. This route was closed off under international political pressure. Ultimately, the authorities in Skopje understood that they could not prevail over the rebels with violence. What they needed was not extra weapons, but Western political and financial support, and a military deterrent in the form of new armed forces, trained for low-intensity warfare. Western support will cease in case of renewed violence, while the retraining of the Macedonian armed forces will take years. New clashes may well resume in the medium term. For the short-term, however, and almost certainly through early 2003, the political conditions for violence are not likely to be present. Furthermore, despite a public dispute on whether the EU should take over the entire military operation in Macedonia from NATO, the reality is that the EU and NATO have displayed exemplary cooperation in Macedonia. A massive aid package of more than EUR500 million was accompanied by heavy and persistent EU and NATO political involvement. Steady and concerted pressure was applied to both protagonists, in equal measures. While the West has committed many mistakes in Macedonia over the course of a decade, it hardly set a foot wrong from early 2001 to early 2002.

Montenegro: successful EU diplomacy

The most spectacular case of EU involvement in the Balkans has been the brokering of a constitutional deal between Montenegro and Serbia, the two remaining components of Yugoslavia. The agreement, signed in Belgrade on 14 March 2002 by Yugoslav President Vojislav Kostunica and his Montenegrin counterpart, Milo Djukanovic, allows the republics to have separate currencies, economic systems and customs services, but maintains their joint foreign and defence policies. A constitution for the new entity, to be known as Serbia and Montenegro, is expected to come into force in late 2002. The agreement contemplates unitary international recognition of the new entity. Its membership in the UN, the EU, the Organisation for Security and Cooperation in Europe and the Council of Europe would be implemented through rotating representatives, while there would be special arrangements for membership in the international financial institutions and some form of proportional representation for diplomatic and consular missions. If Montenegro ultimately elects to leave the 'union of states', international documents (and, presumably, obligations) relating to the Federal Republic of Yugoslavia (FRY) – in particular, UN Security Council Resolution 1244, which concerns Kosovo – will apply in their entirety to Serbia as the FRY's successor.

The EU insisted that the two entities stay connected, fearing that total separation would re-ignite separatist tendencies elsewhere in the former Yugoslavia. While the new arrangement does not meet EU standards for sovereign unity, Brussels described the agreement as 'an extraordinary step forward in stabilising the region'. In fact, it merely postpones a decision on the future of that country as a whole, and the future disposition of Kosovo as well. There is no doubt that the outcome is unsatisfactory to both Djukanovic and to Zoran Djindjic, the Serbian prime minister, both of whom are regarded in the West as progressive politicians. It will also further frustrate the Kosovars. But the agreement does provide a welcome respite to Serbian government leaders, many of whom would be happy if Montenegro went its own way but do not wish to incur nationalist backlash by letting it go.

Federal leaders, on the other hand, along with pro-Serbian groups in Montenegro, may find the agreement a bitter pill. These groups may be tempted to take revenge by stalling the agreement's implementation. There will be abundant opportunity for this, as the agreement lacks much significant detail. Negotiations on the modalities will take months, diverting energies from much needed internal reforms. Moreover, the agreement may never be implemented in full. Djukanovic and Djindjic may even be counting on this outcome. But there is also a reasonable chance that the new hybrid state will gain weight and put down roots over the next three years. And even if this scenario proves impossible, a perfectly acceptable alternative would be a separation in 2005 by mutual agreement, but without disruption or violence. What the agreement has achieved already, however, is focus among local leaders on the paramount task of economic reform. Since the collapse of the Milosevic regime, the dispute between Montenegro and Serbia has been used as an excuse to avoid any painful economic measures; these can no longer be postponed. The final battle between Kostunica and Djindjic has still to be fought. The future of Yugoslavia as a whole and Serbia in particular depends on its outcome. Yet both Serb leaders ultimately know that there is no escape from the necessity of opening up of their society, profoundly reforming its institutions and fully reintegrating Serbia into Europe. If Kostunica triumphs, this process may be slower, since the Yugoslav president still depends on the support of the military and security services. But Yugoslavia's general direction is clear: Belgrade's old bunker mentality is a thing of the past.

NATO and EU enlargement

Just as the EU has finally accepted its heavy political responsibilities in the region, NATO is poised to assume new formal responsibilities in the area. These may extend to the two countries that have carefully avoided being infected by the Yugoslav tragedy, but have also remained outside any supranational institutional framework despite their good behaviour: Romania and Bulgaria. Enthusiasm has grown on both sides of the Atlantic for admitting new countries from Eastern Europe into the alliance. In April 2002, it appeared inevitable that another round of enlargement would take place at the NATO summit in Prague in November 2002. The outstanding issue was how extensive the enlargement would be and how it would be handled. The most challenging determination would be whether Romania and Bulgaria would be invited to join.

The drawbacks to Romania and Bulgaria's integration into NATO are easily identifiable. In terms of territory and size of its population, Romania is the second-largest country in the former communist bloc of Eastern Europe. But it is also among the poorest nations on the continent, and it has repeatedly squandered reform opportunities. Domestically, Bulgaria's government enjoys democratic legitimacy and has succeeded in controlling inflation, but the country remains poor and the political consensus that underpins its economic policies is fragile. Both these Balkan states have large, corrupt and inefficient bureaucracies that have proven incapable of implementing serious administrative and economic reforms. The military in each country remains large relative to the population, but is underpaid and disorganised. While neither army represents a formidable political force likely to impede democracy, what they could materially contribute to NATO is open to question. In Bulgaria's case, three comprehensive military reorganisation programmes have been launched; all have failed. Romania's control over its military is ostensibly better, but even there, the country has had six chiefs of staff in a decade, all appointed and dismissed for political reasons. Romania and Bulgaria fail to meet most of the political, economic and military modernisation criteria of NATO's Membership Action Plans (MAPs).

Since 11 September, however, Bulgaria and Romania's prospects for NATO membership have improved. Central Asia has become one of the American and European strategic focal points in the global counter-terrorism campaign. The area is host to a variety of active and latent transnational threats, including drug-trafficking and organised crime as well as Islamic terrorism. Western energy interests in the region are also seen as increasingly in need of protection. The Black Sea area in particular has served as a staging area for the Afghanistan military effort, for which Bulgaria and Romania have provided significant logistical and peacekeeping support. Accordingly, in March 2002 Washington underlined the desirability of establishing a geographic link to Central Asia and a 'land bridge' between Western and Central European NATO and Turkey via Bulgaria and Romania's admission to the alliance. Both countries have accelerated efforts to streamline and modernise their armed forces in compliance with MAPs. The post-11 September warming of Russian relations with the US and Europe and the prospect of a more substantial role for Russia in NATO have also rendered NATO enlargement less geopolitically problematic.

For European political and strategic reasons as well, Bulgaria and Romania's applications for NATO membership cannot be easily ignored. NATO's first enlargement involved only three countries in central Europe, the most stable region; states in the Baltics or the Balkans were ignored. There is political pressure on NATO to avoid the charge that, the more a country is in need of security, the less likely it is to be admitted into the alliance. Further, some factors suggest that Romania and Bulgaria would make better NATO partners than the Czech Republic and Hungary. Like

Poland, Romania remains in a threatened area, bordering on an unstable Ukraine and a shattered Moldovan republic. Like the Poles, therefore, the Romanians have a stake in contributing to a strong NATO and a need for a relatively large standing army, if only in order to defend their extensive territory. Similarly, Bulgaria faces a latent threat in Macedonia, and will also have every incentive to invest in its security. Thus, the two candidates have strong reasons to contribute adequately to NATO's security and not to be mere consumers of it.

The inclusion of Bulgaria and Romania may also strengthen NATO's internal decision-making capacity. NATO was paralysed in the Balkans for most of its existence because the only two members in the region were Greece and Turkey – two countries that remained preoccupied with their bilateral historical disputes. The Romanians and the Bulgarians have no comparable grievances. Their addition to the alliance will shift NATO's attention to the central challenge in south-east Europe – namely, forging stability in the territory of the former Yugoslavia. There are no regional political barriers, as Greece, Turkey and Hungary all support membership for Romania and Bulgaria.

In terms of EU relations with non-EU Europe, NATO enlargement may be all the more important because the EU is not ready for the Balkans. The only country in the Balkans that is likely to be admitted into the EU in the near future is Slovenia, a state largely irrelevant to the future of the larger region. Romania and Bulgaria are the only two countries that have not been involved in a war in the Balkans and that have behaved relatively well since the collapse of communism in Europe, but that still face the possibility of not being admitted to either the EU or NATO. If their application is rejected at the NATO summit in November 2002, the feeling throughout the Balkans may be that the West remains ready to dispense advice and aid, but unwilling to contemplate embracing the region on equal terms. NATO's promises relating to the region would appear less credible. The patron-client dependency relationship, already a Balkan syndrome, would then be strengthened and with it, a cynical view of Western efforts in the area. But if Romania and Bulgaria do become members of the alliance and prospective members of the EU by the end of the decade, the message to the other countries in the Balkans would be that their European future is bright, provided they continue to refrain from violence and promote economic growth.

A brightening tunnel

Overall, the real challenge for the former Yugoslav space is no longer quelling violence but rather, economic reconstruction. The Yugoslav economy declined by 40% as a result of the war, and unemployment soared to nearly 30%. With a gross domestic product of barely $8bn, Yugoslavia is struggling to finance foreign and domestic debt repayments. The budget deficit in 2001 was about $300m, and is growing. Although there has been a limited recovery, much of economy is operating at only 50% capacity, while there is a huge balance-of-payments deficit amounting to 12% of social product. Inflation is also accelerating, reaching 80% in 2001, compared to 50% in 1999. The World Bank estimates that Yugoslavia will need S4bn in foreign financial assistance from 2002 through 2005. A respected group of Yugoslavian economists have estimated that the total cost of the Kosovo War was $29.4bn in lost output, equivalent to several years' production. The Balkans will remain poorer than the rest of Europe for decades to come. Yet politically they will increasingly resemble the rest of the peaceful continent.

That continent, in turn, appears to be embracing the Balkans more agreeably. For over a decade, the Balkans were a source of discord between NATO and the EU, and between the Europeans and the Americans. Yet in early 2002, it was becoming clear that, in a perverse way, the crisis in the Balkans had also forced both institutions into a new relationship. After being repeatedly humiliated, Europe is now registering its first foreign and security policy victories in the Balkans. More importantly, the two institutions are beginning to divide their responsibilities in an equitable and logical manner, in a way that plays to the strengths of each one and provides stability for the entire area. NATO will remain the ultimate provider of military power, but also the leading force of integration for the more established and stable countries, such as Romania and Bulgaria. The EU will continue to provide most of the economic aid and political impetus, as well as much of the administration and institution-building capacity in the most vulnerable new countries and territories of the region. For the first time in over a century, the Balkans have a realistic chance of being peaceful, as well as an opportunity to eradicate many of the social and political problems that have plagued them.

Turkey: A New Role at Last?

In late summer 2001, Turkey appeared to be in economic and political freefall. Years of mismanagement, corruption and cronyism seemed finally to have taken their toll. The Turkish lira had collapsed in February 2001, forcing the abandonment of Turkey's 14-month old International Monetary Fund (IMF)-backed economic reform programme and plunging the country into its worst recession since 1945. Unemployment and street crime were soaring. Public approval ratings for the ruling tripartite coalition had dipped below 10%. Yet still the government procrastinated, spending more energy on internal turf battles and blocking judicial investigations into allegations of ministerial corruption than on pushing through desperately needed reforms. Internationally, Turkey appeared to be drifting into isolation. In May 2001, after the IMF had approved a further $8 billion in loans for Turkey, Washington had bluntly warned Turkey that it could expect no more bailouts until it put its house in order. Yet far from trying to curry favour with its allies, the Turkish government remained prickly, even confrontational. Nowhere was this more evident than in its relations with the European Union (EU), which had become increasingly strained by Ankara's failure to pass domestic political and economic reforms, its blocking of the European Strategic Defence Policy (ESDP) over the issue of the EU rapid-reaction force's access to NATO assets and its refusal to resume negotiations over the future of Cyprus.

Turkey's embattled position changed after 11 September 2001. Turkey was among the first Muslim countries to condemn the attacks on the United States. When Washington invoked Article 5 of the NATO Charter, it was also the only Muslim country able to make a concrete commitment to Washington's anti-terrorist campaign. The West immediately began to treat Turkey as an asset rather than a liability. The US in particular began to court Ankara, quietly lifting its opposition to the disbursement of more IMF loans and actively encouraging Turkey to act as a bridge between the West and Islamic world. US pundits began to portray Turkey as a role model for other Muslim countries. By late 2001, buoyed by the promise of more IMF funds, the Turkish economy appeared to be emerging from its crisis. Internationally the government basked in the prospect of a new strategic partnership with the US. It had even begun to mend fences with the EU, signing up to a UK-brokered compromise over ESDP and pressuring Turkish Cypriot leader Rauf Denktash to return to the negotiating table.

But change was based on promises and possibilities rather than accomplished fact. By March 2002, reality had begun to kick in. The Turkish government still balked at pushing through painful economic and political reforms, and relations with the EU were, once again, heading for a crisis. Initial predictions that Turkey would play a decisive role in post-Taliban Afghanistan were being scaled down. The vaunted strategic collaboration with the US now looked more image than substance. Nor was there any indication that Muslim countries were anxious to adopt the 'Turkish model'. Indeed, the attacks of 11 September, and the often Manichean rhetoric that followed, appeared to have distracted both the Turkish and Western governments from the real lesson of the turmoil of 2001: that the Turkish political system needed to be extensively overhauled before the country could fulfil its undoubtedly huge potential and become a model for others to emulate.

Economic troubles

In December 1999 the Turkish government had signed a $4bn Standby Agreement with the IMF to support an economic reform programme that sought to reduce the state's role in the economy and curb perennially high inflation. The programme was introduced at the beginning of January 2000. Its centrepiece was a crawling peg exchange-rate policy under which the Central Bank set daily values for the Turkish lira calculated not on realised rates of inflation but on forecasts that retail inflation would fall from 68.8% at end-1999 to 25% by end-2000. The Central Bank faithfully applied its exchange rate programme throughout 2000. But the government was reluctant to relinquish the political leverage afforded by control over large sections of the economy. Most critically, it failed to reform the state banks that were used both to finance populist economic policies and to buy political influence through the provision of soft loans to powerful individuals and interest groups.

Associates of leading politicians had been allowed to establish small boutique banks with a handful of branches, which channelled the profits earned on government paper (which returned 35–40% per year in the late 1990s) into their owners' other business interests. Both inflation and interest rates on government paper fell through 2000. But the government's failure to pass structural reforms meant that by year-end 2000 annual inflation was still 39%. The result was an overvalued Turkish lira and record foreign trade and current account deficits. To address some of the underlying problems, in late 2000 Interior Minister Sadettin Tantan of the Motherland Party (MP) launched Turkey's first-ever anti-corruption campaign. By the end of the year, a string of businessmen and low-level bureaucrats had been put behind bars. But Tantan's efforts to investigate corruption in the state banks were blocked by his ministerial colleagues.

By January 2001, a liquidity crisis had materialised. Commercial banks, which had already seen their earnings eroded by the decline in returns on government paper, nervously awaited an adjustment to the exchange rate policy, aware that any devaluation would increase the cost of repaying their foreign loans. On 17 February 2001, President Ahmet Necdet Sezer, a former jurist and outspoken supporter of Tantan's campaign, announced that he was using the powers vested in him by the Constitution to establish an independent body to audit the state banks. Two days later, before opening a meeting of the Turkish National Security Council, Sezer accused Prime Minister Bulent Ecevit of conniving at corruption by blocking Tantan's investigations. Ecevit angrily retorted that Sezer was exceeding his powers by establishing his own investigative body. Furious, Sezer hurled a copy of the Turkish Constitution across the table at him. Ecevit threw it back, stormed out of the room and announced live on national television that the state had been plunged into a serious crisis.

The Ecevit–Sezer contretemps was the catalyst the markets had been dreading. Over the next three days, stock prices plummeted and overnight interest rates rose to 7,500% as the Central Bank spent $5bn, approximately one-quarter of its total reserves, desperately trying to prop up the Turkish lira. On the evening of 21 February, the government bowed to the inevitable, announcing that it was abandoning the crawling peg policy and allowing the currency to float freely. Over the next two days, the Turkish lira depreciated by 38%. At the end of February, Ecevit invited Kemal Dervis, a 52-year old Turkish vice president at the World Bank, to return to Turkey to oversee the implementation of a new reform programme. On 14 March, Dervis announced a package of 15 measures to reduce state involvement in the economy and encourage foreign investment. Dervis asked the IMF for fresh loans to support the programme, promising that all 15 reforms would be enacted within 15 days. Dervis quickly ran into opposition from Ecevit's coalition partners. Both the ultra-nationalist National Movement Party (NMP) and the centre-right MP suspected that Dervis hoped eventually to succeed the 77-year old Ecevit as head of his Democratic Left Party (DLP) and feared his electoral popularity if the reform programme proved successful. The NMP and MP initiated a discreet smear campaign against Dervis in the media, portraying him as a lackey of the IMF, while delaying the passage of the reforms through parliament. Two months later, most of the reform package had still not been enacted. When, on 16 May 2001 the IMF grudgingly granted Turkey another $8bn in loans, US Treasury Secretary Paul O'Neill warned Ankara it had received its last bailout.

By the beginning of September, Dervis had finally succeeded in passing all but two of his 15 laws. But the economy remained mired in recession with no immediate prospect of an upturn. Annual retail inflation had climbed to 57.5% and was still rising and the Turkish lira was trading at half of its pre-crisis value. Over one million Turks, approximately 5% of the total workforce, were estimated to have lost their jobs over the previous six months. In the first week of September, news of another bailout for Argentina raised hopes that the IMF might also be prepared to loosen its purse strings for Turkey. Privately, US officials insisted that Turkey was much more important strategically than Argentina: the West simply could not afford to allow its economy to collapse. The 11 September attacks on the US proved them right. In late September, IMF officials assured Turkey that more money would be forthcoming. Publicly, the officials claimed that new loans were justified by the successful implementation of Turkey's reform programme. But few in Turkey doubted that the money was a reward for supporting the US counter-terrorism campaign. On 10 October 2001, when parliament granted the Turkish government full war powers, shares on the Istanbul Stock Exchange soared.

In 2001, Turkish gross national product contracted by a worse-than-expected 9.4% in real terms (27.2% in US dollar terms). In March 2002, prospects for a return to growth were pushed back from the third quarter to the final quarter of 2002. Annual interest payments on debt exceeded annual tax revenue for the first time in the country's history. By year-end 2001, annual retail inflation had risen to 68.5%. At the same time, the Turkish lira had stabilised and consumer spending was rising again. The recession seemed to have bottomed out and most analysts expected the Turkish economy to return to growth in the second half of 2002. On 4 February 2002, the IMF formally approved another $16.3bn in loans to Turkey in addition to the $15bn disbursed in 2000 and 2001, making Turkey the largest borrower in IMF history. Yet the Turkish government still appeared to view IMF funds as a solution rather than an opportunity. Dervis's reforms had only reduced, not removed, opportunities for the pursuit of populist economist policies.

More critically, there was still no sign of a change in the political culture that had produced the crisis of February 2001. In April 2001, Interior Minister Tantan had allowed investigators to pursue allegations that his party colleague, Energy Minister Cumhur Ersumer, had rigged state energy contracts. Ersumer was forced to resign on 27 April. In May, Tantan initiated an investigation into allegations of graft involving Turgut Yilmaz, the younger brother of his party boss, MP Chairman Mesut Yilmaz. On 5 June Mesut Yilmaz dismissed Tantan and replaced him with a close aide, Rustu Kazim Yucelen. Although Interior Ministry officials claimed another ministerial scalp on 5 September, when Housing Minister Koray Aydin of the NMP resigned after revelations that his ministry had awarded multimillion-dollar contracts to a company owned by Aydin and his family, gradually the corruption investigations ground to a halt. The coalition partners closed ranks to block applications for the lifting of Ersumer's and Aydin's parliamentary immunity. By March 2002, most of those arrested during Tantan's anti-corruption campaign had either been released or had the charges against them dropped.

Domestic politics: reform and recalcitrance

Islam lay at the heart of the Ottoman Empire. The Sultan's political authority derived from his role as Caliph, the leader of the world's Muslims, while the legal system was based on Islamic *sharia* law. The Turkish republic, which was founded in 1923, though ostensibly secular, did not so much remove religion from public life as replace Islam with another ideology, that of Kemalism, named after Kemal Ataturk, the republic's first president, who died in 1938. Kemalism was heavily influenced by early twentieth-century concepts of authoritarian, state-centred nationalism. Ataturk's ideal society was unified and homogenous, not pluralistic, with the state assuming almost mystical status as the embodiment of the nation. As a result, Turkish laws have traditionally been designed to protect the state rather than safeguard the rights and freedoms of the individual. The process of compliance with the Copenhagen criteria for EU accession, which dominated the domestic political agenda in Turkey in 2001, thus required not only legislative amendments but also a radical change in Turkish political attitudes.

Turkey was named as an official candidate for EU membership in December 1999. On 8 November 2000, the EU published its Accession Partnership Document, setting out the changes required in order for Turkey to join the union. But the Turkish response, a programme of reforms announced on 19 March 2001, fell short of the EU's expectations, avoiding a clear commitment on key issues such as democratisation, cultural pluralism and freedom of speech. By March 2002, despite a number of minor legislative amendments, in practice little had changed; and the Turkish courts continued to be used to combat what were seen as the two main threats to the Kemalist state, namely Kurdish nationalism and political Islam. In addition, a mass hunger-strike by leftist inmates of Turkish prisoners that began in early 2001, in which 48 prisoners had died as of early March 2002, reinforced general perceptions of official Turkish indifference to human rights.

On 22 June 2001, the Turkish Constitutional Court closed the Islamist Virtue Party (VP), the third-largest party in parliament, on the grounds that it had become a centre for anti-secularist activity. There was no suggestion that the VP had advocated the violent overthrow of the Kemalist system. The main charge levelled by the prosecution was that the VP advocated the right of women to wear Islamic headscarves in state institutions. The closure of the VP deepened a conservative–reformist rift in the Islamist movement between followers of 75-year old former Prime Minister Necmettin Erbakan, who had been banned from politics for five years when his Islamist Welfare Party (WP) was itself outlawed in 1998, and a younger generation of activists under the leadership of Tayyip Erdogan, the charismatic 46-year old former mayor of Istanbul. On 20 July, the older generation established the Felicity Party (FP) under the leadership of Recai Kutan, a loyal former aide to Erbakan. On 14 August, the younger generation founded their own party, the Justice and Development Party (JDP) with Erdogan as chairman.

The European Court of Human Rights' validation of the government's 1998 ban of the WP on 31 July 2001 – ostensibly on grounds of human rights – reflected the West's wariness towards Islamist movements in general and reinforced Ankara's secularist policies. By October 2001, however, opinion polls were reporting that if elections were to be held immediately, the JDP would win over 30% of the popular vote, sufficient to enable it to come to power on its own. Erdogan insisted that the JDP was committed to secularism but he remained vague on the policies he would pursue if he came to power, reinforcing Kemalist suspicions that he was secretly planning to establish a state based on *sharia* law. On 9 January 2002, the

Constitutional Court ruled that a four-month prison sentence Erdogan had served in 1999 for allegedly inciting religious hatred by reciting a poem mixing Islamic and militaristic imagery prevented him from ever becoming a member of parliament. The JDP disputed the legality of this ruling, which effectively barred Erdogan from becoming prime minister. The issue was still unresolved in March 2002, although it threatened soon to become academic. Public prosecutors were already investigating other charges against Erdogan, ranging from publicly advocating the abolition of secularism to allegations of graft during his term as Istanbul mayor. In March 2002, Kemalists in the judiciary began new corruption investigations of Islamists, including Erdogan.

There was no indication that the Kemalist establishment was prepared to take a more conciliatory attitude towards its other *bête-noire*, the expression of a distinct Kurdish identity. During the 1990s, Turkey had justified restrictions on freedom of expression and widespread human-rights abuses as an inevitable corollary of its war against the Kurdistan Workers Party (PKK), which was then waging a violent campaign for greater autonomy for the country's 12m Kurds. But the PKK insurgency effectively came to an end with the February 1999 capture of its leader Abdullah Ocalan, who (albeit under the duress of a prospective death sentence) declared a unilateral, open-ended ceasefire in August 1999. By the beginning of 2002, the PKK had officially abandoned the armed struggle and pledged to pursue its goals by purely political means. Yet in March 2002, the Turkish government extended emergency rule in four predominantly Kurdish provinces, even though there had been no serious armed clashes in the region for two-and-a-half years.

Although there was a marked decrease in human-rights violations compared with the mid-1990s, disappearances and extra-judicial killings of suspected Kurdish nationalists continued. On 25 January 2001, two officials from the mainly Kurdish People's Democracy Party (HADEP) disappeared after being taken into custody in the south-eastern town of Silopi. But the Turkish authorities refused even to investigate. In mid-2002, the Turkish Constitutional Court was expected to rule on an application for the closure of HADEP for allegedly threatening the unity of the state by advocating Kurdish cultural rights. In March 2002, the use of Kurdish in broadcasting and education, whether as a medium of instruction or as a foreign language, remained banned. In January 2002, over 2,000 university students were arrested on charges of aiding a terrorist organisation when they staged rallies demanding the right to be educated in Kurdish. Similar charges were also used to justify the banning of numerous books, newspapers, television and radio stations, including, in October 2001, the Turkish-language broadcasts of the BBC World Service and Deutsche Welle.

EU: a brittle betrothal

The West's response to the 11 September attacks on the US reinforced both the Turkish establishment's resistance to reform and its suspicions of the sincerity of the EU's criticism of Ankara's human-rights records. Privately, Turkish officials commented that the US now understood the true nature of terrorism and how justified Turkey's own draconian anti-terrorism policies had been. They also noted that the EU had remained silent as Washington entertained government-sanctioned assassinations, capital punishment and the use of military tribunals for captured Islamist militants, when Brussels had vigorously condemned Turkey for similar measures during its war against the PKK. The net effect on Turkey–EU relations was subtle. Throughout most of 2001, the tension between Turkey and the EU over the slow pace of domestic reform had been exacerbated by what appeared to be impending crises over Cyprus and ESDP. On balance, Ankara seemed to gain sufficient confidence in its geopolitical position to bend a little on three key issues: ESDP, relations with Greece and the Cyprus problem.

ESDP and Greece–Turkey relations

The EU had sought assurance from NATO that, if necessary, the rapid-reaction force (RRF) foreseen by ESDP could have access to NATO assets and capabilities. After some initial misgivings, the EU had reassured most non-EU NATO members, but Ankara remained obdurate, threatening to use its NATO veto to prevent access unless the EU included Turkey in the decision-making process for the RRF's deployment regardless of whether the operation concerned used NATO assets and capabilities. Turkish intransigence was based on the fear that the RRF might be deployed to support Greece in disputed areas such as the Aegean or Cyprus. The EU offered Turkey a consultative role but refused to grant a non-EU member veto power over EU policy.

The EU had set a target of declaring ESDP operational at the EU summit in Laeken on 14–15 December 2001. By late November, with the two sides as far apart as ever, Turkish–EU relations appeared set for a major crisis with severe repercussions for NATO. But, on 2 December 2001, Turkey suddenly signed up to a UK-brokered compromise under which Ankara would withdraw its demands in return for a guarantee that the RRF would not be deployed in Cyprus or the Aegean. The deal was promptly vetoed by Greece. As of March 2002, the issue remained unresolved.

The dispute over ESDP came at a time when a two-year dialogue between Greece and Turkey appeared finally to be bearing fruit. The rapprochement was mainly based on the personal relationship between Greek Foreign Minister George Papandreou and his Turkish counterpart Ismail Cem, who usually visit each other's capitals once a year and often meet on the sidelines of international forums. The two held regular meetings and telephone conversations throughout 2001 and in June their families even briefly vacationed together in the Aegean. On 8 November 2001, Turkey and Greece signed a series of agreements covering the repatriation of illegal immigrants, the creation of a joint emergency disaster unit and confidence-building measures in the Aegean. The first is a significant breakthrough, as an estimated 250,000 illegals arrive in Greece each year, most of them via Turkey. On 12 March 2002, Greek and Turkish diplomats began discussions on applying to the International Court of Justice for a ruling on the delimitation of the continental shelf in the Aegean. But, despite the warmer atmosphere, the two sides still have not agreed on the nature of their more intractable differences, much less formulated possible solutions. For Athens, the continental shelf remained the only dispute. But Ankara still refused to recognise Greece's extension of its airspace to 16 kilometres and alleged that, in the Aegean, Greece was illegally militarising islands and abusing its Flight Information Region. Turkey continued to insist that any attempt to implement what Greece claimed was its legal right to extend its territorial waters from 10km to 19km would be a *casus belli*. Finally, it remains the case that heightened tensions over Cyprus could halt the broader rapprochement.

Cyprus

Since Turkey intervened in 1974 to thwart an Athens-engineered coup designed to unite Cyprus with Greece, the island has been de facto partitioned. While UN troops patrol a 'green line' that separates Turkish and Greek Cypriots, the self-declared 'Turkish Republic of Northern Cyprus' governs the northern 38% of the island, which is secured by 35,000 Turkish troops. Turkish Cypriots constitute roughly 18% of Cyprus' population, Greek Cypriots 78%. Securing the political position of Turkish Cypriots in Cyprus, only 70km from the Turkish mainland and a former Ottoman possession, is to Ankara both a strategic imperative and a nationalist cause. Denktash, in turn, considers EU accession in the absence of an acceptable settlement or Turkish EU membership to amount to Cyprus' unification with Greece – an EU member – 'through the back door'. While most Turkish Cypriots favour EU membership as a means to prosperity, which an international embargo has made impossible for over 25 years, Denktash has moved them to subordinate that goal to his political agenda by raising the spectre of ethnic cleansing under a Greek Cypriot-dominated unitary government. Nevertheless, he appeared willing to re-enter talks without the precondition that Turkish Cypriot sovereignty co-equal to that of Greek Cypriots be recognised – a requirement that had scuppered face-to-face discussion for the previous four years.

At Helsinki in December 1999, in return for being named as an official EU candidate, Turkey agreed that the settlement of the Cyprus problem was not a prerequisite for the accession of the Republic of Cyprus. The EU had already announced that it expected to approve in mid-2002 the membership of the Republic of Cyprus, whose official territory encompasses the entire island and whose Greek Cypriot government is the only one recognised by the United Nations and the EU. Greece has threatened to veto the accession of the Czech Republic, Hungary and Poland if Cyprus is not also included in the 'first wave' of new candidates that are to join the EU in 2003. In terms of adherence to the EU's *acquis communautaire*, Cyprus is among the most qualified of the front-running candidates. Yet on 14 May 2001, Denktash declared that he still saw no reason to resume negotiations, and on 4 November 2001 Ecevit threatened to annex the Turkish Cypriot-administered north of the island if the EU granted accession to the Greek Cypriots.

On 4 December 2001, two days after the resolution of the crisis with the EU over ESDP, Denktash performed a similarly abrupt about-turn by announcing that he was prepared to resume direct negotiations for the first time since 1997 in what threatened to be the final chance to solve the 27-year old Cyprus problem. Denktash and Clerides subsequently met for a series of informal dinners, finally beginning direct negotiations on 16 January 2002. But the initial hopes soon began to fade. It soon emerged that Denktash had only resumed negotiations after being instructed to do so by the Turkish military, concerned that his refusal to do so was making Turkey appear intransigent. But the military had reassured him that Turkey did not expect him to make major concessions. As of March 2002, the talks had achieved little but allowed the two sides to repeat their respective positions, which remained as far apart as ever. The Greek Cypriots maintained that the island must be reunited in a single bi-communal state, while the Turkish Cypriots insisted on a confederal system under which the north would retain its status as a de facto dependency of Turkey.

Inadvertent EU provocation

Hopes for a solution to the Cyprus problem have been premised primarily on the assessment that Ankara was eager to join the EU as soon as possible, and therefore would prevail on Denktash to compromise. The Turkish Cypriot community and leading opposition politicians also prized the prospective benefits of EU membership. Developments in early 2002, perhaps amplified by Turkish self-confidence due to its post-11 September strategic importance, cast doubt on this view, as Turkish relations with the EU took another turn for the worse. The EU had already infuriated Ankara by omitting the PKK and Revolutionary Popular Liberation Party/Front (DHKP-C), a militant leftist urban group, from its list of proscribed terrorist organisations announced on 28 December 2001. On 10 February 2002, Dogu Perincek, a maverick nationalist-socialist politician with links to rogue elements in Turkish intelligence, began publishing e-mail communications between Karen Fogg, the EU representative in Ankara, and her head office in Brussels, in which Fogg spoke candidly about leading members of the Turkish government and forecast that it would be at least ten years before Turkey was ready to accede.

Amid uproar in the nationalist media, the Turkish authorities remained silent. It was five days before government officials condemned Perincek's actions and two weeks before the courts issued an injunction banning publication of the e-mails, by which time they had been exhaustively discussed in the Turkish media. Privately, Turkish officials were adamant that Fogg, an outspoken critic of Turkey's human-rights record, should be withdrawn. Relations deteriorated still further later in the month when an old bugbear of Turkey–EU relations resurfaced. On 28 February 2002, the European Parliament approved a report calling on Turkey to recognise the Ottoman massacres of Armenians in 1915–16 as genocide. EU pressure on Turkey to expand Kurdish political and cultural rights – which appeared to prompt the PKK to rename itself the 'People's Liberation Party' in late March 2002 and seek amnesty for PKK prisoners – is another irritant from Turkey's perspective. On 5 March, Devlet Bahceli, deputy prime minister and chairman of the NMP, declared that EU membership was not Turkey's only option. On 7 March General Tuncer Kilinc, Secretary General of the National Security Council, accused the EU of ignoring Turkey's national interests and suggested it was time for Ankara to look elsewhere, forging closer ties with other countries in the region – in particular, Iran and Russia – while maintaining its alliance with the US. While the Turkish General Staff (TGS) disowned his remarks, they are said to agree privately with his criticisms of the EU. In general, the TGS favours EU membership only on its own terms – that is, without having to fulfil the Copenhagen criteria.

A new strategic partnership with Washington

If Turkey's relations with the EU deteriorated through 2001, by the end of the year ties with the US appeared stronger than at any time since the Gulf War. But prior to 11 September, relations had been cooling. The new Bush administration had declared that it was unwilling to take an active role in solving what it saw as other countries' problems. Not only had it warned Ankara in May 2001 that it could expect no more financial bailouts, but there were tensions over one of the few areas in which Washington appeared to be willing to adopt a more active international role, namely Iraq. Turkey made no secret of its desire for UN sanctions against Baghdad to be lifted and had reopened rail links, tolerated a growth in sanctions-busting trade with Iraq, particularly the steady flow of petroleum products through its sole border crossing at Harbur, and, to Washington's consternation, even announced plans to open a second border crossing. In addition, the Turkish military – traditionally the most pro-American element in the Turkish establishment – had become increasingly frustrated by Washington's failure to press the EU to take a more conciliatory stance over ESDP.

But the attacks of 11 September transformed the relationship. For the US, its alliance with Turkey became a key strategic asset, not so much in terms of logistical and military support but in the propaganda war. Ankara's immediate support for the invocation of Article 5 of the NATO charter, coupled with its offer on 22 September to share intelligence and open its airbases and airspace to US military aircraft, enabled Washington to assure a doubting Muslim world that its anti-terrorism campaign was not directed against Islam. On 10 October, the Turkish parliament went one step further and authorised the hosting of foreign troops on Turkish soil. The US was fulsome in its gratitude, not only supporting a new disbursement of IMF funds but privately offering to write off Turkey's $5bn debts under its Foreign Military Sales (FMS) programme and let Ankara take its pick from a vast array of excess military equipment. US pundits lauded Turkey's loyalty and held up its secular political system as a model for other Muslim countries to emulate.

For Turkish nationalists, such unrestrained praise was proof that at last someone understood them. Unlike the EU, Washington designated the PKK and the DHKP-C as terrorist organisations, had few reservations about Turkey's retention of the death penalty and rarely mentioned Kurdish cultural rights. From the Turkish perspective, the new partnership would be based not just on common interests but on shared values, elevating Turkey to its rightful place as a major player on the international stage and exporting its political system to Muslim countries throughout the world. The first concrete evidence of Turkey's new leading role came in November 2001, when Ankara was asked to contribute a battalion of troops to the International Security and Assistance Force (ISAF) and assume command of the force when the initial British term expired in April 2002. By early 2002, however, reality began to seep in. Turkey dispatched a company of soldiers to Kabul on 15 February 2002, but refused to increase its deployment or take over command of the ISAF without guarantees of financial support and that Turkish troops would not be expected to remain in Afghanistan indefinitely. US military officials announced that they would have to withdraw their offer of a cancellation of Turkey's FMS debts for fear that the Bush administration would be unable to pass such a measure through Congress. As of April, it appeared likely that Turkey would assume ISAF command around June 2002, provided Turkish troops did not have to operate outside Kabul and could use British and German infrastructure, and that allies picked up the bill.

By March 2002, US plans to extend its anti-terrorism campaign beyond Afghanistan had highlighted the limitations of a strategic partnership with Ankara. Despite its repeated claims of cultural and ethnic affinities, Turkey still has little political influence in Central Asia or, with the possible exception of Azerbaijan, in the Caucasus, where the key issue remains the attitude of Moscow rather than Ankara. In the Middle East, Turkey and Syria had nearly gone to war in October 1998 over Damascus's support for the PKK and its provision of sanctuary to Ocalan. Since Syria expelled Ocalan in late 1998, Turkish–Syrian relations have improved. In 2001, Turkey gradually relaxed border controls, and restored rail links to northern Syria, resulting in a steady increase in bilateral trade and cooperation in mineral exploration and agriculture. But tensions remained over Syrian President Bashar al-Assad's refusal to abandon Damascus's claim to the Turkish province of Hatay, which was annexed by Turkey in 1938. Syria also continued to maintain that Turkey's damming of the upper waters of the Euphrates for a massive hydroelectric and irrigation project had produced a dangerous reduction in both the flow and the quality of its main source of fresh water. More broadly, Turkish influence in the Middle East remains circumscribed by Arab suspicions of Ankara's motives and allegiances, particularly its defence ties with Israel. On 27 May 2001, for example, Turkey lodged a reservation on the decision taken at the foreign ministers' meeting of the Organisation of Islamic Conference for Islamic states to boycott Israel. Other Muslim countries also do not appear eager to copy the 'Turkish model'. This should not come as a surprise. Not only have most Muslim countries long been much more sceptical than the West of Turkey's Islamic credentials, but the Turkish system is based on Kemalism, a *sui generis* indigenous ideology that is, by its very nature, non-transferrable.

The issue that offers the greatest scope for strategic cooperation is also the one on which Turkey and the US appear furthest apart – namely, Iraq. As of March 2002, Ankara remained firmly opposed to a military campaign against Iraq, particularly a ground offensive, which it feared would be deeply unpopular domestically and would have a devastating effect on Turkey's tenuous economy by curtailing regional trade and investment and pressuring Turkey with refugees, who had cost the government $1.5m a day during and after the Gulf War in 1991. There were also worries that regime change in Iraq could result in formal autonomy for the Iraqi Kurds, which could in turn refuel secessionist aspirations amongst the country's own restive Kurdish population and necessitate a preventive Turkish military occupation of northern Iraq. This may become a lesser concern. Iraq has proven territorially resilient through decades of instability. Moreover, Iraqi Kurds have benefited from the oil-for-food programme and openly prefer democratic federation in a unified Iraq to secession. The Iraqi Kurds themselves have counselled against US military action without a considered plan for a political transition that would preserve both the economic benefits that flow from Baghdad and its political autonomy in a territorially intact Iraq.

Privately, Turkish officials have admitted that, particularly given its dependence on IMF funding, Turkey would find it difficult to refuse a US request to use facilities such as the airbase at Incirlik in south-eastern Turkey to try to topple Saddam Hussein. Moreover, in Turkish calculations, supporting the US will give Ankara more leverage in shaping the post-Saddam Iraq – in particular, in preventing the creation of a Kurdish state in northern Iraq. Furthermore, it is possible that Turkey, like Saudi Arabia, would candidly favour regime change if it could be assured that the American military commitment would be full-blooded and complemented by a well thought-out political programme.

From new role to final crisis?

At end-December 2001, Turks looking back over the events of the previous 12 months could have been forgiven for seeing 11 September as a *deus ex machina* delivering salvation when all seemed lost. The shock of the appalling attacks on the US had not only jolted the Turkish people out of the introspection and lethargic despair produced by economic recession, but brought in its wake a fresh influx of IMF funds to revitalise the economy and a new international status and strategic importance. But by March 2002, its impact appeared more subtle and insidious.

Since Turkey was named as an official candidate for EU membership in December 1999, reform has become a foreign-policy issue, a means to enter the EU rather than a goal desirable in itself. For most Turks, EU membership was not just the fulfilment of a century-old dream of acceptance as being European or even the best of a number of alternatives; it was their country's only option. In summer 2001, although the Turkish government still resisted change, few Turks doubted the need for political and economic reform. The only question was when and how radical the reform would be. But in the aftermath of 11 September, the pressure for reform lost its momentum and, through IMF funds and foreign praise, suddenly made the old system appear viable. Many Turks began to wonder if perhaps, after all, the conservatives had been right when they argued that all that was needed was a little tinkering with details, not a complete overhaul. In early 2002, ultra-nationalists and conservative members of the Kemalist establishment were already portraying a strategic partnership with the US as an alternative to the EU and using it to delay the reform process. They argued that the EU had no intention of granting Turkey membership, but still demanded sacrifices through painful domestic reforms and concessions on Cyprus. A strategic partnership with the US, on the other hand, required no sacrifices and would transform Turkey into a regional superpower.

There seems little doubt that Turks will eventually understand the limitations of a strategic partnership with the US without healthy European relationships. But time may be short. Although the EU had originally planned to approve Cypriot accession in mid-2002, it subsequently indicated that it might be prepared to delay the announcement until early autumn. But by March 2002, Turkey's reform programme was already months behind schedule and there appeared little prospect of an imminent breakthrough in the Cyprus negotiations. Yet Cyprus' accession without a solution to the Cyprus problem would deliver a severe blow both to Turkish hopes of EU membership and the prospects for domestic reform, with potentially serious consequences for stability both in the country and the region. With the US having already registered its strong support for Turkey, the EU remains the key outside actor for stabilising Turkey's inter-regional position. Ankara's willingness to compromise on the ESDP/NATO issue and its encouragement (albeit cosmetic) to Denktash to negotiate indicate that however serendipitous 11 September may have been for Turkish strategic prestige, Ankara has not abandoned its European vocation. If the EU acknowledges more clearly that Turkey's human-rights record has improved since the PKK cease-fire, and becomes less acquiescent to Greek pressure on Cyprus' accession, some of the damage done by the Fogg revelations could be repaired. Resulting improvements in EU–Turkish relations could then reduce tensions over Cyprus' accession and increase momentum towards Turkey's eventual accession.

Middle East/Gulf

If the collapse of the Oslo process made 2000–01 a bad time for the Middle East, 11 September, the rising violence between the Israelis and the Palestinians, and the increasing likelihood of US military action against Iraq made 2001–02 an even worse one. Osama bin Laden cited Israeli suppression of Palestinians as a pretext for the attacks in New York and Washington. While it is clear that his own motivations are founded on US influence in the Islamic world in general rather than the Israeli–Palestinian conflict in particular, there is little doubt that continued killing in the West Bank and Gaza inspires some of his followers. Israeli–Palestinian tensions have also produced disenchantment with the United States – Israel's principal ally and security guarantor – among key Arab states such as Saudi Arabia and Egypt, and have thus complicated Washington's strategic calculations in the region. Nevertheless, the evolving consensus in US policy circles is that the short-term tremors resulting from US military action to force regime change in Iraq would be worth securing longer-term stability that would result from removing Saddam Hussein's existential regional military and proliferation threat. In particular, that outcome would allow the US to draw down its military presence in Saudi Arabia, which fuels domestic unrest and hence al-Qaeda recruitment in the region. Arab governments, however, would be far less likely to cooperate in such action if fellow Arabs were to continue to die at Israeli hands in the Palestinian territories.

Improving security and advancing a political settlement in Israel and Palestine, then, is essential to the United States' two central post-11 September foreign-policy pillars: counter-terrorism and counter-proliferation of weapons of mass destruction (WMD). While the administration of President George W. Bush initially preferred to avoid a peace brokerage role, in late 2001 and early 2002, the Bush team found this policy bias impossible to maintain. Senior US officials made several intensive and protracted – but as of early April 2002, frustrated – attempts to establish a cease-fire and implement confidence-building measures. It will be necessary for Washington to immerse itself still further in mediation. President Bush appeared to recognise this reality in an important 4 April 2002 statement, issued from the White House, in which he called on the Palestinian Authority to reign in terrorism and on Israel to end its occupation of Palestinian areas, and announced that he would send Secretary of State Colin Powell to the region to engage the parties to the conflict directly. Two salient factors bear on the prospect of American success: Arab diplomacy and Iran's involvement in the Israeli–Palestinian conflict.

Map 3 Middle East/Gulf

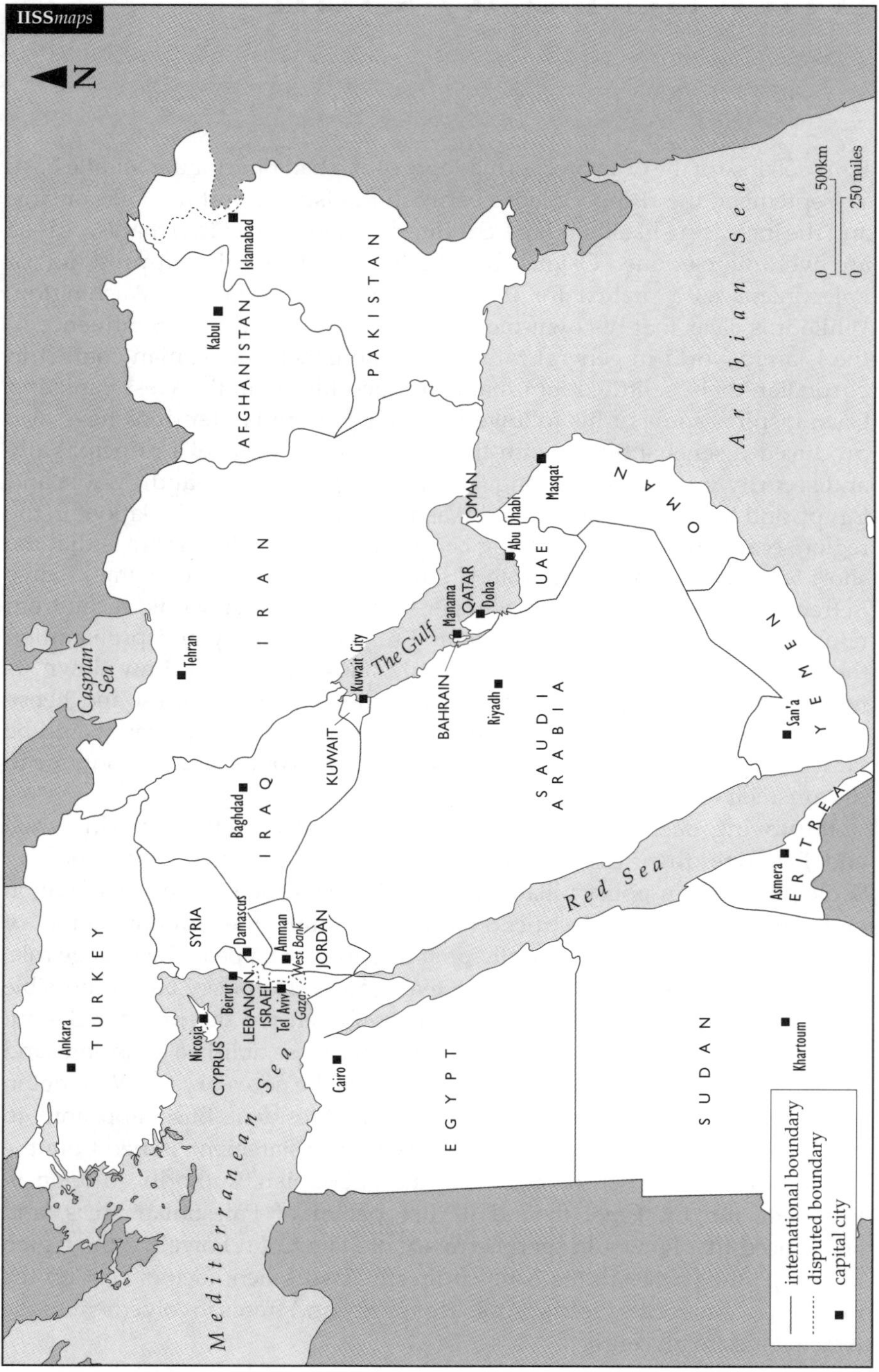

The first factor is positive. At the League of Arab Nations 27–28 March 2002 summit in Beirut, a firm Arab consensus was established behind the Saudi proposal of establishing 'normal relations' (watered down from the 'full normalisation' originally mooted by the Saudis) between Arab governments and Israel in exchange for Israel's withdrawal from the Palestinian territories to pre-1967 borders. While there has been no meeting of minds on this or thorny related issues (such as Jerusalem's sovereignty and the return of Palestinian refugees to Israel), it indicates that some Arab capitals might provide diplomatic support to US-led efforts to forge peace. The second factor, unfortunately, is negative. Iran appears to have become a destabilising player – a 'spoiler' – in the conflict. The principal public indication of this came in December 2001, when Israeli authorities patrolling the Red Sea intercepted a ship – the *Karine-A* – carrying a large shipment of Iranian arms bound for the Palestinian Authority. US and Israeli intelligence agencies have identified deepening links between Tehran and Palestinian leader Yasser Arafat. Furthermore, the well-armed Lebanon-based Hizbullah group, Iran and Syria's proxy, launched terrorist operations against Israelis in early 2002 and has threatened more violence on the Palestinians' behalf. Tehran's provocations in the Middle East, along with its perceived continuation of WMD development, prompted Bush to include Iran with Iraq and North Korea in an 'axis of evil' in his 29 January 2002 State of the Union message. While this may hurt the efforts of reformist elements in Iran to gain greater control of certain government policies, it is likely to have relatively little effect on the Middle East situation, as conservative and reformist leaders alike share a profound animosity towards Israel. But continued Israeli–Palestinian violence could prompt some Arab states to follow Iran's example of materially supporting armed revolt rather than working towards a political solution.

Progress in lowering the level of Israeli–Palestinian violence and reaching a regional accommodation with respect to the conflict would make it more difficult for Iran to pursue disruptive policies. Even if a formal cease-fire is arranged between Israel and the Palestinians, however, residual violence will be inevitable. A wider détente between Israel and the Arab states will be difficult to achieve: beyond the difficult Israeli–Palestinian issues, highly problematic ones, mainly concerning the Golan Heights, remain between Israel and Syria. Syria's support for the Saudi plan was grudging, Libya's wavered within days and Iraq's was immediately followed by calls for Arabs to pull out of the global counter-terrorism coalition and cut oil supplies to the US. A senior Israeli official labelled the Saudi initiative, as presented by the Arab League, a 'non-starter'. The offer of normal relations was also accompanied by support for continued Palestinian resistance and *intifada*. The strategic relationship between the US and Saudi Arabia is undergoing an uncertain transition as a result of 11 September. If the US decides to attack Iraq, the reaction of the Arab 'street' will be difficult to predict and potentially serious. While the US has some diplomatic options for improving relations with the Arab world, they are incremental and long-term. All of these factors suggest that the best that can be hoped for in late 2002 and early 2003 is a tentative diminution in Israeli–Palestinian violence, the maintenance of diplomatic initiatives and the avoidance of a wider war in the Middle East.

The US and the Middle East After 11 September

The events of 11 September spurred the argument – heard in Middle Eastern *diwanat*, satellite television broadcasts and newspaper editorials, and echoed in European salons and broadsheets – that the United States deserved the attacks, or at least should have expected them. Osama bin Laden's own rhetoric, aired on 3 November and 26 December 2001 on the Qatar-based television network al-Jazeera, underscored the presumed logic of this sentiment. He intimated that the attacks resulted from America's policies toward the Islamic, and especially the Arab world. The offending policies included American support for Israel's oppression of Palestinians, Washington's insistence on sanctions against Iraq, and its close relations with Egyptian and Saudi governments that are considered illegitimate in varying degrees by some or perhaps many of their citizens. Bin Laden's public posturing was disingenuous, as it is clear that the United States' overall reach as a superpower – not its specific Middle East policies – inspired the wrath of bin Laden and al-Qaeda's leadership. He first showcased the Palestine question in early 2001, and then probably only as a result of the influence of his second-in-command Ayman al-Zawahiri – the leader of Egyptian Islamic Jihad, which formally merged with al-Qaeda in early 1998. Nevertheless, US policies in the region undoubtedly motivate some of bin Laden's followers.

In any event, 11 September has prompted significant diplomatic developments with respect to the Israeli–Palestinian conflict. President George W. Bush and Secretary of State Colin Powell have affirmed the objective of Palestinian statehood, endorsed the notion of sharing Jerusalem as a capital and spoken of the need to end Israeli 'occupation'. Crown Prince Abdullah of Saudi Arabia has proposed that Israel withdraw to pre-1967 borders in exchange for the normalisation of relations with Arab states. US influence is essential to any solution. Inside the region, however, intellectuals and journalists apprehend the United States as a neo-colonialist power, which makes it the natural target of the passionate anti-colonialism that was once directed at Britain and France. Thus, the 11 September attacks have galvanised more localised elements of anti-Western Islam, which are generally destabilising forces at the domestic and regional level. By default, their tendency is to lash out violently. The United States, the status quo power *par excellence*, is likely to be in for a rough ride in a Middle East on the brink of turbulent and potentially violent change.

The US and the Israeli–Palestinian conflict

The Bush administration followed a hands-off policy in early 2001. When the fact-finding report of former US Senator George Mitchell was published in May 2001, the administration ratcheted up its involvement slightly. The Mitchell Report calls for a cease-fire, a resumption of bilateral negotiations, a freeze on new Israeli settlements, the Palestinian Authority's suppression of terrorism and Israel's relaxation of economic restraints and limitation on its use of lethal force. In June 2001, Central Intelligence Agency (CIA) Director George Tenet was dispatched to the region in an attempt to establish a cease-fire pending the implementation of Mitchell's other recommendations. While he did win a cease-fire agreement, the arrangement broke down within days. In light of this frustration, before 11 September the Bush administration had reconsidered the wisdom of its hands-off policy and was preparing a dramatic re-entry into the process. In the event, re-engagement, which was to have been announced in New York City at the September annual meeting of the United Nations General Assembly, had to be postponed. The exigencies of neutralising al-Qaeda and responding to a domestic anthrax attack made a major diplomatic initiative impractical. Further, to preserve its integrity as a world power, the United States did not want to appear to be meeting the demands of terrorists who had just massacred over 3,000 Americans for fear of inviting attacks from any group harbouring anti-American grievances.

On 2 October 2001, however, President Bush expressed US support for a Palestinian state as 'part of a vision'. Secretary of State Colin Powell subsequently outlined the US plan to move both sides toward a two-state solution with a minimum of violence. In his 19 November 2001 speech, Powell said that Israeli settlement activity must stop because it 'prejudges' and 'preempts' a final settlement, that border closures must end and that the daily humiliation of Palestinians at checkpoints must cease. He also termed Israeli action 'occupation' for the first time. But the Secretary of State reiterated the insistence in earlier Bush administration statements that Palestinian attacks be curtailed – by way of arrests and a policy of non-incitement – before Israel could be expected to resume negotiations. In November 2001, Powell appointed the former commander of US forces in the Near East and South Asia, retired Marine Corps general Anthony Zinni, as Special Middle East Envoy. In December 2001, Zinni and Assistant Secretary of State for Near Eastern Affairs William Burns attempted to arrange a cease-fire with the help of American intelligence monitors and possibly an interposition force made up of American soldiers and perhaps military personnel from other countries acceptable to Israel and the Palestinian Authority. Burns and Zinni failed. The January 2002 shipment of arms from Iran to the Palestinian Authority on the ship the *Karine-A*, interdicted by Israeli authorities, and escalation in the West Bank and Gaza on the part of both sides, cast doubt on ground-up initiatives in general, and chilled further US diplomatic efforts. On 8 March, Sharon dropped his demand for a seven-day cease-fire before entering talks. Immediately thereafter, however, the pace of Palestinian terrorist attacks actually increased; most were perpetrated by the al-Aqsa Martyrs Brigade, a radical offshoot of Arafat's Fatah organisation that claims allegiance to Arafat. Another sustained attempt by Zinni to achieve a cease-fire had proved futile as of 2 April.

Making peace, then, has become even more difficult in early 2002 than it was in early 2001. Between the beginning of the Palestinian *intifada* on 28 September 2000 and 1 February 2002, 1,164 people had died, including 892 Palestinians and 250 Israelis. The violence peaked in early March. In the period 2–10 March, 50 Israelis and over 120 Palestinians died. Insecurity and political dysfunction has made Arafat politically weaker than he was at Oslo and Taba, and less capable of strategic direction, while the Israeli left has been gutted by the failure of Barak's initiative and the former prime minister's maladroit domestic politics. Sharon has also lost credibility. The US has strong reasons – domestic as well as strategic – for actively pushing for peace between Israel and the Palestinians. According to a September 2001 Gallup poll taken after the attacks, 78% of all Americans think that a resolution of the Arab–Israeli conflict should be an important policy goal for their government. In the wake of 11 September, when Americans might have been expected to support pressure from Washington on Israel for concessions to the Palestinians in order to reduce the risk of renewed catastrophic attacks against the US, opinion surveys revealed the opposite reaction. Before the attacks, 41% of those asked expressed support for Israel and 13% for Palestinians. After the attacks, 55% backed Israel, while support for Palestinians dropped by almost half, to 7%. CNN images of Palestinian women ululating in exultation after the World Trade Center attack contributed to this drop. The support for Israel was the highest since Iraq fired *Scuds* at Tel Aviv and Jerusalem in 1991. A corresponding trend appeared among those asked specifically about the peace process. Before 11 September, 74% of the respondents said that America should be neutral; afterward, 63% advocated neutrality. Similarly, after the 11 September attacks, 27% thought that the US should take Israel's side in peace negotiations, compared to the 16% who endorsed this position before the attacks. This reflects overwhelming support for Israel's security across a broad political and religious spectrum in the US.

Even renewed US activism is unlikely to have any effect on al-Qaeda and its sympathisers, since their objective is not a Palestinian state but the obliteration of a politically autonomous Jewish presence in a land they consider to be an exclusively Islamic legacy. What American re-engagement would do is give Arab leaders in Israel's neighbourhood some political cover for the diplomatic, military and intelligence cooperation with the US in the campaign against terrorism; shrink bin Laden's recruitment pool; and remove a pretext for Iran and Syria to confront Israel through Hizbullah. Moreover, by early April 2002, continued Israeli–Palestinian fighting had provoked Israel into re-entering several West Bank towns. If Israeli reoccupation were sustained, a mass emigration of Palestinians into Jordan – disrupting the delicate political balance between Transjordanian 'East Bankers' and Palestinians there – might occur and put pressure on King Abdullah to breach Jordan's 1994 peace agreement with Israel. Peace would remove that pressure and might also spur a Jordanian economic revival rendered impossible by the *intifada*.

Saudi Arabia's tentative introduction in February 2002 of the possibility of a grand bargain – whereby Israel would withdraw to pre-1967 boundaries in exchange for full normalisation of relations with all Arab states – may provide the foundation for a regionally based diplomatic initiative. The idea is not altogether new. In 1981, then Crown Prince Fahd made a similar proposal, and the new proposal builds on longstanding US policy as well as Bush's official endorsement of Palestinian statehood in October 2001. But the proposal did constitute food for thought at a particularly impoverished stage. At the meeting of Arab foreign ministers in Cairo on 9–10 March 2002, all Arab regimes – except for Iraq and Libya, but including Syria – registered official support for the plan. All 22 members of the League of Arab States formally supported the proposal at the 27–28 March 2002 Arab summit in Beirut, but watered the original inducement of 'full normalisation' down to 'normal relations' and also supported Palestinian resistance and the *intifada*. As presented at the summit, the proposal called for the capital of a Palestinian state in East Jerusalem, and called for a 'just' solution to the problem of the return of Palestinian refugees to Israeli territory.

Israel reacted with circumspection and some scepticism. For reasons of strategic depth alone, it would be extremely hard for Israel to agree to leave only a 13-kilometre wide strip of its own territory between the West Bank and the Mediterranean Sea, and the return of the Golan Heights to Syria remains an extremely knotty problem. During Israeli–Syrian peace talks in 1999 and 2000, then Israeli Prime Minister Ehud Barak substantially offered to return the Golan to Syria. But Syria, with Iran, backs Hizbullah, which is based in south Lebanon. Hizbullah has threatened to open a 'second front' from Lebanon and its increased aggression around the Israel-Lebanon border – including the fatal shootings of six Israelis in mid-March 2002 – have given Israel reasons not to reiterate such an offer. These difficulties may not be insoluble. It was also evident from Abdullah's statements that an Israeli withdrawal could be accompanied by border adjustments. But Washington would have to support the initiative and exert pressure on Israel for it to bear fruit.

The question remains how the US might more constructively intervene in the Israeli–Palestinian conflict. Heightened violence in the West Bank and Gaza poses risks to frontline states, and may make it more difficult for the US to win Saudi cooperation in a military campaign against Iraq, which is a top US priority. Another substantial motivating force is the prospective loss of US diplomatic leverage on regional issues. Sharon's aggressive retaliatory policy appears to have backfired, inspiring rather than deterring Palestinian suicide bombers. The Bush administration, however, has not merely stood aloof. Tenet, Zinni and Burns's efforts to achieve cease-fires have attempted to provide a roadmap to the negotiating table: first a cease-fire, then the implementation of confidence-building measures (in particular, arrests of terrorists and intelligence-sharing) under the Mitchell plan. But these efforts have not been fortified with an affirmative basis for negotiations once cease-fires are in place. While Saudi Arabia filled the diplomatic vacuum with a peace proposal, obviously neither Riyadh nor any other Arab capital is an acceptable mediator. The US has little choice but to assume that role. UN Security Council Resolution 1397, passed on 12 March 2002 by a 14–0 vote and sponsored by the US, formally endorsed a Palestinian state. Yet the inglorious end of the Oslo process at Camp David indicates that Washington cannot aim too high, or push the Israelis too hard. On 28 February 2002, in remarks to reporters that he subsequently retracted, White House Press Secretary Ari Fleischer criticised Camp David as a failed attempt to 'shoot the moon' and 'push for an agreement that was not reachable at the time'. A year earlier, US Vice-President Dick Cheney had called the situation in the Middle East a 'mess' that the Bush team had 'inherited' from the Clinton administration.

The grim events of late March and early April 2002 did suggest that the Israelis and the Palestinians were not yet ripe for direct mediation. During the six days from 26 March to 1 April, there were six Palestinian suicide bombings, most of them in Israel and against civilian targets. In response, the Israeli army reoccupied several Palestinian towns in the West Bank. Palestinian gunmen executed 11 alleged collaborators on a single day, indicating the defiant and determined frame of mind prevailing among Palestinians. In Ramallah, the Israelis also resumed and intensified their siege of Arafat's compound, which had begun in January. Although Sharon said that Arafat could attend the late March Arab summit in Beirut, the Israeli prime minister also suggested that he might not be allowed to return to Ramallah. He did not attend the summit, and the US came under criticism from the Arab states for failing to guarantee Arafat's return. Arafat himself called for an international protection force. On 30 March, the UN Security Council, again by a 14–0 vote, adopted Resolution 1402, calling for Israel to pull out of Palestinian areas. On 1 April, Bush took a measured approach – condemning the terrorist attacks but refraining from labelling Arafat a terrorist while asking Sharon 'to keep a pathway open to peace'.

The fact remains that the US is the only outside actor capable of generating the momentum needed to move the process forward. Furthermore, the inability of Israeli and Palestinian leaders to take unilateral steps to diminish spiralling violence suggests that the US may have to assume a mediating role even while hostilities are under way. As of April 2002, pressure was mounting from Congress – in particular, Senators Joseph Biden, Joseph Lieberman and Arlen Specter – for the Bush administration to step decisively between the two antagonists. The risks that some US officials appeared to perceive in doing so – inspiring further Palestinian attacks by arguing Israel's corner on one hand, or appearing soft on terrorism to allies and coalition partners on the other – seem illusory. Most Palestinians already regard the US as hopelessly pro-Israeli in any case. Moreover, the US' European allies and most other coalition partners – in particular, Arab states – would favour a more sympathetic US attitude towards Palestinian violence. Indeed, such an attitude would probably make support for aggressive US counter-terrorist action elsewhere easier to secure. Washington, then, might have to apply sustained pressure on Sharon to withdraw from the West Bank in order to get a reasonably enforceable cease-fire from Arafat. Getting to the negotiation stage will take time and may require Washington to enlist regional actors, including Saudi Arabia, Egypt and Jordan, in concerted diplomatic efforts. The Arab endorsement of the Saudi political proposal suggests that these nations are prepared to assume proactive roles. There is broad agreement that there should be a Palestinian state and that Israel must be secure. The terms under which these objectives could be realised are still unknown, but the records of Camp David and Taba and Clinton's proposals of December 2000 at least provide a frame of reference.

On 4 April 2002, in a potentially pivotal statement issued from the White House, President Bush took these realities on board. Most notably, he called on Israel to end its occupation of the Palestinian territories and cease settlement activity in those territories, and endorsed withdrawal to pre-1967 borders as the basis of agreements between Israel and Syria and Israel and Lebanon as well as Israel and the Palestinian Authority. Citing Arafat's failure to control Palestinian terrorists, he urged the Palestinian Authority make comprehensive efforts to stop terrorism. Bush also characterised the Saudi proposal as 'hopeful' in its recognition of Israel's right to exist. Finally, he announced that Secretary of State Colin Powell would be sent to the region with a broad mandate to consolidate international support for a political solution; directly engage the parties in an effort to achieve a cease-fire and an Israeli withdrawal and implement the Tenet and Mitchell plans; and lay the foundation for resuming political dialogue.

Iraq

Iraq's regime poses a clear threat to its Arab neighbours as well as to the US and its allies. The US defused Saddam Hussein's expansionist military designs by fighting the Gulf War and has since contained his latent threat by enforcing the sanctions regime and the two no-fly zones and pressing for effective weapons inspections. But the massive deployment of American military personnel in Saudi Arabia in 1990 was a key trigger for bin Laden's rage, and a continued US military presence remains an important pretext for his terrorist campaign against the US. The residual presence of 5,000 American troops there also fuels violent dissent (and al-Qaeda recruitment) in Arab countries. Even though the US-led suppression of Iraq is in the immediate security interests of Saudi Arabia and Egypt, it is also seen by their populaces as an extension of an American foreign policy premised on dominating the Middle East and the Gulf in order to protect Israel and oil interests, and one which incorporates a disregard for Muslim lives. Washington would like to disabuse them of this view.

While the United States and Israel naturally perceive Iraq as a mutual enemy, US policy is premised on strategic concerns that extend beyond the protection of Israel or of American oil security. Iraq, from America's perspective, presents the threat of a revanchist dictator in possession of nuclear, chemical and biological weapons, and the means to deliver them. If Iraq's nuclear weapons development programme is not blocked, reasons Washington, it will be all the more difficult to constrain Iranian nuclear ambitions. And if these are unchecked, then at some point Saudi Arabia and possibly the United Arab Emirates will acquire a nuclear capability from a third country. There is no guarantee that a nuclearised Persian Gulf will be stable in a crisis. Stopping Persian Gulf nuclear proliferation by preventing Iraq from gaining weapons of mass destruction (WMD) and especially a nuclear capability, therefore, is a strategic imperative for the United States.

Washington is well aware of the resentment that continued sanctions against Iraq has caused in the region and the strains that the effort to preserve a sanctions regime have produced within the UN Security Council and the Atlantic Alliance. In December 1999, the Clinton administration reluctantly backed the creation of a successor to UN Special Commission on Iraq (UNSCOM). In June 2001, the new Bush administration supported a US–United Kingdom 'smart sanctions' initiative which would have removed most UN restrictions on trade with Iraq to make it as clear as possible that the Iraqis' suffering was due to Saddam's policies, not those of the US. This was never brought to a vote because of Russia's determined opposition. Moscow, with growing economic ties to Iraq, evidently judged then that by siding with Baghdad it would escape Iraqi economic retaliation in a post-sanctions world. In any case, adopting 'smart sanctions' might not have convinced most of the Arab world that US and UK initiatives in the UN were benefiting the Iraqi population. Even without war, from the point of view of most Arabs, whose primary sources of information are their governments, the US and the UK are killing other Arabs. With respect to Iraq, therefore, the battle for hearts and minds in the wider Arab world probably cannot be won.

This recognition is perhaps the dominant factor underlying the commitment of key members of the Bush administration to regime change in Iraq. They have counted the international political costs of a decade of containment and of preserving UN sanctions. In their view, the costs increase as compliance decreases. As long as the Washington is committed to its current Iraq policy, American forces will have to remain in Saudi Arabia, aggravating a delicate political situation there and fuelling resentment over what bin Laden calls military occupation and the alleged desecration of the land of the two holiest mosques in Mecca and Medina. Better, in the administration's evolving view, to destroy the Saddam regime and accept the near-term political risk in order to seize the long-run benefits of an end to the confrontation. The presumed gains would include a halt to Iraq's pursuit of nuclear and other non-conventional weapons, the freedom to withdraw US soldiers from Saudi Arabia, eventual restoration of America's standing in Arab opinion and better relations with Russia and France. At the same time, Saddam's death or infirmity appears unlikely to produce a transition to a materially more cooperative regime, as Saddam has groomed alternative heirs apparent – his youngest son Qusay and his less-favoured oldest son Uday – in his own image. Both would have the loyalty of the Special Security Organisation charged with presidential protection, the division-strength Special Republican Guard deployed in and around Baghdad and the three Republican Guard armoured divisions ringing Baghdad. But all other army divisions are reportedly at only 50% combat effectiveness, and 50% of all equipment lacks spare parts. US 'smart' technology, on the other hand, is smarter and more lethal than it was in 1990–91. Furthermore, as credible military pressure on Iraq mounts, so does the likelihood that indigenous elements will move to eliminate Saddam in order to stave off a US attack.

The apparent success of the US-led war against al-Qaeda and the Taliban has probably made a bold move seem more feasible. As of 30 March 2002, the number of US troops in Kuwait had doubled from 5,500 to 10,500 since 11 September, and there were indications that American computer and communications equipment was being moved from Saudi Arabia to Qatar. This suggested that US Central Command was contemplating military action against Iraq even without Saudi Arabia's support. Building a consensus within the Bush administration on this audacious strategy, however, is proving difficult due to an aversion to near-term risk. During his tour of Middle East capitals in March 2002, Vice-President Cheney encountered solid public Arab opposition to US military action against Iraq in spite of the firm Arab consensus that the region would be better off with Saddam removed from power. Cheney declared that action against Iraq was not linked to progress in resolving the Israeli–Palestinian conflict, but key Arab leaders clearly considered the two closely connected. Although a number of Arab countries (Egypt, Saudi Arabia, Jordan, Bahrain, Kuwait) might acquiesce in US action, the degree of support they would extend remains uncertain. In particular, there is insufficient confidence that Saudi Arabia would permit tactical air operations to be staged from Saudi soil. While Washington can be reasonably certain that the UK will support military action, it is equally certain that major continental powers such as France and Germany will not. Paris and Berlin could raise operational impediments to the US military effort – for instance, by blocking US access to French airspace and the use of the American base in Ramstein for combat operations – and would likely interpose diplomatic obstacles.

In addition, tactical differences within the US administration need to be ironed out. Some administration officials appeared to favour supporting local opposition forces of the Iraqi National Congress (INC) with arms supplies and air power. But some also perceive the INC as insufficiently cohesive, and note that it would face a tougher foe in Saddam's army than the Northern Alliance faced in the Taliban/al-Qaeda forces. An Iran-backed Shi'ite opposition group in southern Iraq has distanced itself from the INC. As of March 2002, the State Department had suspended the INC's US funding, although the State Department Inspector-General was scheduled to re-examine INC books in April or May 2002. Most US military commanders would prefer a decisive application of overwhelming American force on the ground as well as from the air to ensure a swift victory. The US needs time to build up weapons (in particular, precision-guided munitions) depleted in the Afghanistan war and to set the table for a new government in Iraq that accommodates the political and material needs of all Iraqis (particularly the Kurds and Shi'ites), who have come to rely on government rationing. But Bush's 27 November 2001 demand that Iraq permit unimpeded UN inspections immediately suggested that he himself was inclined to take the war to Iraq.

Evidence uncovered in al-Qaeda hideouts in Afghanistan that the group was intent on using chemical weapons, coupled with knowledge of Saddam's support for terrorist groups and mounting indications that he is reconstituting WMD, has injected even greater urgency into the Bush administration's desire to deal with the Iraq problem sooner rather than later. In early March 2002, Iraq suggested that it might be more amenable to arms control by inviting the UK to search for weapons, but most in Washington believe Saddam's intention is only to continue to manipulate inspectors as he has since 1991. Accordingly, through much of early 2002, the US appeared disinclined to seek a more muscular UN Security Council resolution for sanctions and inspections, and certainly considers Saddam's violation of the 1991 resolutions a sufficient basis for using force. Although continued Israeli–Palestinian hostilities would tend to make Saddam less cooperative, the possibility remains that he will decide to fulfil his disarmament obligations on pain of being ousted by the US or worse. In a February 2002 CNN interview, Secretary of State Colin Powell suggested that even in that event, the US would opt for military action. 'The United States' he said, 'believes that the Iraqi people would still be better off with a new kind of leadership that is not trying to hide this sort of development activity on weapons of mass destruction and is not of the despotic nature that the Saddam Hussein regime is'. Such statements may, ironically, underestimate the credibility of American threats. Without inspections, an array of political conditions – Arab opposition, continued violence between the Israelis and the Palestinians, European and Russian objections – would make an attack difficult. If Saddam submits to full inspections, however, these same conditions could make a US attack politically infeasible. The better option would then be to go ahead with inspections. Although they would not guarantee that Saddam would stop reconstituting WMD, the US would retain the option to use force if he were subsequently found to be doing so. In that case, it would be difficult for key Arab states, European capitals and Russia to withhold support for military action.

American support for autocratic regimes

At the same time, the United States would favour continuity over change in relatively cooperative regimes. Washington may nevertheless attempt to effect democratic reform in those regimes. Although this would be difficult to achieve, the effort may be worth undertaking in that it could produce a better popular understanding of US policies among Arabs and at least some firsthand appreciation of American political and economic values. Generating any degree of gratitude to the US for urging the liberalisation of their societies is a more remote possibility.

In the Arab world, the charge that America supports authoritarian regimes generally boils down to alleged complicity in the misdeeds of the Mubarak government in Egypt and the Al Saud ruling family in Saudi Arabia. Perhaps US support for Arafat's autocratic regime will be added to the charge sheet once Palestine accedes to statehood. In US-friendly Jordan, King Abdullah II has promised free and fair parliamentary elections and in 2001 became the first Arab ruler to abolish the ministry of information, although media freedom remains restricted. But, like Iraq, Syria and its Lebanese proxy are outside the American sphere of influence. Ties are thin between the US and Maghreb countries, some of which are moving towards meaningful parliamentary democracy in any case. The Saleh government in Yemen, though accepting limited military counter-terrorist assistance from Washington, is probably doing so mainly to stave off more intrusive US involvement. Most of the Gulf Cooperation Council states are slowly starting to democratise, and the trend appeared to gather momentum after 11 September. Bahrain is being re-invented as a constitutional monarchy, and parliamentary and municipal elections are to be held there in late 2002. Qatar is considering following suit. There are legislative assemblies in Kuwait and Bahrain, and there is one on the way in Oman. (Saudi Arabia, too, has such an assembly, though it is appointed.) Women can vote in Bahrain, Oman and Qatar. In Kuwait, lawsuits being heard by lower courts and a parliamentary bill submitted by liberal members would grant women voting rights, although there is heavy conservative and Islamic militant resistance. Bahrain's Sunni leaders, once notorious for suppression of the Shia majority, have freed political dissidents, suspended special security courts and stopped arbitrary arrests and detention without trial. These governments, of course, may still refuse to change their core policies or seriously dilute their power.

Nevertheless, the two persistently authoritarian governments with which the US is identified, Egypt and Saudi Arabia, are the most powerful Arab governments in the region, and they are increasingly questioned and challenged by the disenfranchised societies over which they preside. Fifteen of the 19 hijackers on 11 September were Saudi nationals, and Mohammed Atta, the operation's ringleader, was Egyptian. Tensions between population and government in these countries imperil US interests. The lesson that Iran taught the United States in 1979 has not been forgotten, but it does not answer the question of what to do about Egypt and Saudi Arabia, now and in the future. In Egypt, the Mubarak government has reduced the space for political action, refused to designate a successor or establish a democratic process by which one might govern with the consent of the Egyptian people, and persecuted secular opposition parties and intellectuals. The Saudi leadership blocks judicial due process and a free press, sharply limits political expression and forbids the practice of non-Islamic religious faiths. It is also resented for skimming off 25% of oil revenues and muscling in on government contracts, though both are done openly within the existing system. These regimes are not, however, utterly savage ones that are somehow beyond redemption, nor have they completely lost popular support. Large segments of each population are not terribly unhappy, and neither state poses a danger to its neighbours. These considerations counsel a conservative US approach to both Egypt and Saudi Arabia.

Egypt

In the case of Egypt, the American interest in democratisation has been reluctantly subordinated to the cause of peace between Israel and the

Palestinians and then, ultimately, between Israel and Syria. The peace process is a higher priority because escalating tensions between Israel and the Palestinians – or Syrians – pose the risk of regional war. Deliberalisation of Egypt under President Hosni Mubarak does not. War would set back Egypt's economy, standard of living and fitful democratisation faster and more comprehensively than would another five years of Mubarak's governance. The same would be true for Jordan, Lebanon and Syria. Moreover, the status quo in the West Bank and Gaza is desperate in a way that life in Egypt is not, even with its widespread poverty and violations of human rights. To be sure, there is a younger generation emerging in Egyptian élites and the ruling National Democratic Party that is pressing for economic modernisation and political democratisation. Using 'steam-release' tactics typical of illiberal regimes, the government validates anti-peace opinion by reinforcing beliefs about Israel that are untrue (as with Mubarak's public allegations that Israel was committing 'mass murder' in the West Bank and Gaza) in order to channel public anger toward Israel and away from harsh socio-economic realities. These have been exacerbated by 11 September. Tourism revenues for the fiscal year ending 30 June 2002 dropped by $2 billion, adding to the domestic pressures of high unemployment (9% officially, but probably closer to 15%) and a high population growth rate of 2.4% per year. Egyptians' desire to assert what they may view as cultural supremacy *vis-à-vis* the West may be checked by a paradoxical but growing desire to Westernise. Nevertheless, US officials do not see appreciable latitude for imposing political conditions on the United States' $1.3bn annual military assistance package and diplomatic support for Egypt.

Egypt might well continue to maintain peace with Israel even without American inducements: restraint is less risky than aggression and therefore preserves Egypt's image as a regional power, which the Mubarak government prizes. The army and the élites perceive going to war as far more disruptive than mere anti-Israeli opinion in the general population. Yet US policymakers do not feel that they can ignore the substantial anti-Israeli sentiment in the Egyptian 'street' and the army's powerful political position, take the army's inclination towards peace with Israel for granted, or be assured of Mubarak's trouble-free succession. Although Mubarak, who is in his early seventies, now has firm control of the government, the army may seek a powerful military figure to succeed him. Alternatively, following the Syrian example, it could acquiesce to a controllable civilian successor (for instance, Gamal Mubarak, one of the president's two sons) who would ensure that its interests were protected. Either way, it is essential from Washington's standpoint that the army continue to support peace with Israel and that the country's economic difficulties be contained. Politically unencumbered US military aid provides the required insurance. In affording Mubarak rough military parity with Israel, that aid also ensures that public opinion against peace with Israel will not gain dangerous momentum. From this perspective, laying down stringent conditions for US assistance to the government would make little sense. Further, reneging on an entitlement of the kind that Washington has maintained to Cairo since the Cold War would become a hugely significant act for which there would need to be dramatic justification.

The US is already reducing its economic aid to Egypt by $40m annually over 10 years. Many in Washington believe that even if the US decided to take a risk and withdraw some or all of its military assistance, publicly distance itself from the Mubarak government and provide moral or other support for the domestic opposition, it would have no practical effect on Mubarak's domestic political programme. Given Egyptians' strong nationalistic streak, these measures would be as likely to alienate them as it would be to persuade them of beneficent US intentions. Furthermore, Mubarak's diplomatic assistance in lowering Israeli–Palestinian tensions and facilitating US military action against Iraq is also central to American calculations. In his visit to the US in early March 2002, Mubarak endorsed the Saudi peace initiative, and urged the US to deepen its engagement in the Israeli–Palestinian conflict. He also indicated his willingness to play a leading diplomatic role, offering to host a Sharon–Arafat summit. While Egypt remains leery of US military action against Iraq, Mubarak did not openly discourage it, merely noting that the US administration took pains to win broad Arab support before the Gulf War began. Although Cairo would not welcome a US move on Iraq, it would be unlikely to jeopardise good relations with Washington by actively opposing it. Finally, for the sake of its own survival, Mubarak's government is resolutely anti-fundamentalist, and Egypt has extended significant intelligence and law-enforcement cooperation to the US since 11 September. For Washington, then, the stakes are too high for hypothesis-testing or policy experimentation. On balance, the risks entailed by an implicit challenge to the legitimacy of Mubarak's government would far outweigh the likely gains. Encouragement towards reform is more likely to come in the form of carrots than sticks – for instance, the free-trade agreement announced by the US in November 2001.

Saudi Arabia

American policy priorities *vis-à-vis* Saudi Arabia are not substantially more opaque than those with respect to Egypt. Both the US and Saudi Arabia will continue to need each other. For the Saudis, there is no substitute for the US security guarantee. For the Americans, there is no substitute for Saudi oil. As of February 2002, Saudi Arabia was producing 7.19 million barrels a day – alongside Russia, the highest output in the world. Even so, the US has already pushed the Saudis to reform. In a cataract of high-level meetings and routine démarches over the past decade, Washington has warned the Saudis about the need for democratisation. Until Crown Prince Abdullah took the reins, these warnings were unheeded. But the Crown Prince himself needed little encouragement to attempt to reduce princely stipends, diversify the economy, cut back on arms purchases, attract foreign direct investment and bring more Saudi youths into the workplace. These have long been his priorities. He has also maintained some slow-motion progress toward freedom of expression and released two prominent Islamic critics of the royal family, Safar al Hawali and Salman al Awdah, from prison. Given his own impulse to meet the concerns of his subjects, there is not much beyond discreet encouragement that the United States can do to accelerate change. Nor would Washington necessarily want to risk pressing too hard. On account of the increasingly Islamist hue of the opposition – in part because the regime permits only the veiled criticism voiced in the mosque – serious political reform might result in theocentric policies inimical to US, and more broadly, Western interests.

The sources of dissent within Saudi Arabia, as in Egypt, admit of only long-term solutions. The principal culprit is a 20-year decline in real gross domestic product per capita, from $15,600 in 1981 to less than half that in 2001. The social services and infrastructure improvements that had been well-funded in past years have been reduced sharply as a consequence of high debt and reduced earnings. The prospect that international trade could fuel economic growth dimmed in 2001, as momentum behind Saudi Arabia's accession to the World Trade Organization (WTO) decreased. Significant Saudi–WTO differences on tariff peaks, sectoral initiatives, market access and tax differentials between foreign and domestic firms remain unresolved. Information – not entirely accurate, but nonetheless damaging – about the immense scale of the royal family's financial self-aggrandisement has begun to circulate more widely. Finally, the education system has increasingly focused on granting degrees in theology and Quranic studies and less on providing Saudi youth with the knowledge and skills that would enable them to get a footing in rapidly changing economic circumstances. Lacking skills, but endowed with a worldview that rejects secular values, these young men are proving to be a problem for Saudi society as well as the United States.

The convergence of the Saudi power transition, the shock of 11 September and US concerns about Saudi unreliability have ushered in an unsettling phase in US–Saudi relations. On the US side, Saudi refusal to permit US tactical aircraft based in Saudi Arabia to be used in attacks against Iraqi targets (even in self-defence), friction and misunderstanding between Washington and Riyadh with respect to the investigations of 1995 and 1996 bombings of American facilities and Saudi reluctance to permit the use of the Kingdom's state-of-the-art Combined Air Operations Center to coordinate US and UK air operations over Afghanistan have sparked resentment. Since

11 September, members of Congress have also criticised the slow Saudi response to US requests that financial flows to al-Qaeda be stopped. Pessimistic news stories about the Al Saud family's stability may also increase pressure for a reassessment of the bilateral relationship. In Riyadh, the de facto transfer of power from the ailing King Fahd to Crown Prince Abdullah that began in 1997 has diminished the cohesion of the family, in which there have always been differences on how to relate to the US and how quickly to pursue the modernisation of legal, regulatory and policy conventions that might be unpalatable to various elements of Saudi society. The events stemming from 11 September will sharpen these internal debates and probably lead some senior princes to recalibrate the costs and benefits of Saudi Arabia's relationship with the US.

Both sides, then, will continue to cast about for alternatives to mutual dependence. Crown Prince Abdullah will try to forge closer ties to Iran and hope for a miracle in Iraq, but Iran itself is in the midst of a fitful transition, and Saddam Hussein is not ready to relinquish control of Baghdad. President Bush will press for exploitation of North American oil deposits to reduce America's dependence on Middle East oil, but geologists do not believe there are significant reserves, economists suspect that extraction will not be cost-effective and a strong environmental lobby rejects drilling in a pristine wilderness. So any American hopes for a swift change for the better in Saudi Arabian domestic governance or stability are likely to be frustrated.

Prospects

Ultimately, it is up to the people of Saudi Arabia and Egypt to win political change and force their rulers to be more accountable for their peoples' woes. Nevertheless, the US is likely to continue to establish discreet contacts with opposition figures to exchange views, offer advice on reform initiatives and criticise violations of civil liberties. In doing so, America will have to bear in mind that these steps could invite the same resentment it has drawn by virtue of its pre-existing relationships with these unpopular governments. Owing to the tendency to displace onto outsiders the causes of internal conditions, many Saudis and Egyptians will perceive any effort to accelerate reform as yet another example of neo-colonial interference.

The lack of journalistic objectivity in the Arab world poses an acute problem for the US. Arab journalists, who often regard themselves catalysts for rallying their populations against globalisation, the United States and Israel, generally reinforce in Arabs factual distortion and self-delusion with respect to the West. Al-Jazeera displayed unusual impartiality from 1996 to 2000, but veered towards partisan, incendiary reportage after the second *intifada* began. It is still difficult to find an accurate accounting of the substantial publicised evidence of al-Qaeda's involvement in the 11 September attacks.

Arabic-language tabloids and their broadcast equivalents often present as 'news' the fanciful notion that Israel destroyed the World Trade Center. While the leading newspapers and broadcasting outlets have been more objective regarding bin Laden and the 11 September attacks, even they have indulged in blatantly false propaganda. *Al-Ahram*, Egypt's leading newspaper, ran an editorial suggesting that the United States had poisoned relief packages and dropped them in minefields in Afghanistan. More broadly, Arab media tend to ignore the fact that Washington has tried diligently for years to forge peace between the Israelis and the Palestinians. The trajectory for US-driven reform is, as a consequence, soberingly flat.

The future of US–Arab relations

In the near-to-medium term, the overall relationship between the United States and the Arab world will be shaped by familiar factors: the Israeli–Palestinian dispute; continuing confrontation between the UN and Iraq; increasing American dependence on Saudi energy; and restrictions on the ability of regional states to cooperate openly with the US due to popular support for bin Laden's cause. Another major factor will be the degree to which the successful suppression of terrorist movements in the region leads to the export of terrorism to the US, as it has from Egypt and Saudi Arabia in the form of al-Qaeda. Trade, which tends to 'thicken' connections between and among states, is likely to grow only in the energy sector. Otherwise, trade will remain limited between the US and the region, as it is within the region itself. Outside of the energy sector, US investment in the region will be constrained by fear of instability, intrusive state sectors, byzantine regulation, underdeveloped banking sectors and fragile physical infrastructure. Adherence to inefficient traditional models of business organisation and failure to devise ways to document clear title for use of property as collateral for business loans will continue to inhibit commercial potential within the region. This commercial pattern will do nothing to foster a greater sense of commonality or good will.

Over the longer term, structural factors will begin to change the character of Middle Eastern societies in ways that will make US–Arab relations even harder to manage for both sides. Between now and 2015, the population of the Middle East is projected to grow by 32%. In the Persian Gulf region, the population of Saudi Arabia will increase 56%, Yemen 67%, UAE 56%, Bahrain 31%, Qatar 87%, Kuwait 60% and Iraq 47%. (Iran, a non-Arab country, will increase 21%.) In the Levant, Gaza will grow by 72%, the West Bank 55%, Israel 20%, Lebanon 19%, Syria 39% and Jordan 44%. Egypt's population will grow by 25%. In the Maghreb, Libya's population will increase 39%, while Morocco's and Algeria's increase by 26% and Tunisia's by 16%. Thus, over the next 15 years, the population in the region will rise from 304 million to 400m (including Iran). The 2–5% population growth rates responsible for this enormous increase will keep the population relatively young, which correlates with political violence. High growth rates also practically mandate low or negative GDP growth, and perpetuate the low status of women, a low standard of living and low literacy rates. As some Middle Eastern governments try to placate Islamist pressure groups by permitting restrictions on the role of women in their societies, these high birth-rates will continue. At the same time, deteriorating educational systems will constrain literacy growth and declining per-capita GDP will be reflected in lower standards of living. According to the World Bank, real per-capita income in the Middle East and North Africa fell by 2% per year between 1985 and 1995 – the largest decline in any developing region in the world.

Even as these ominous demographic changes are taking place, loading weak and increasingly poor states in competition for oil and water with a disproportionately large cohort of unemployable, frustrated young men, political consciousness in the region will grow as options for ruling élites shrink. The burden of coping with these developments rests on both sides. For Arab leaders, the goal must be to build domestic institutions for promoting capital and labour mobility, while permitting greater pluralism. For the US and its allies, as well as multilateral institutions, the goal should be to increase foreign assistance aimed at those who are most disadvantaged by economic and technological change, and to develop infrastructure and institutions that will attract investment. Technical assistance will be needed as well, to help demographically besieged countries develop effective health care, environment and education policies.

Meeting these demands is an enormous enterprise, and requires significant departures from current practices. The industrialised nations devote less than 0.25% of their aggregate gross national product to foreign assistance; the United States, at 0.1%, is one of the least generous. It remains to be seen whether it can make the necessary changes to its foreign policy, or the Arabs to their political cultures. Yet the alternative is increasing mutual disengagement and heightened strategic instability. If these circumstances materialise, given the looming spectre of al-Qaeda and the probable resilience of radical Islamic terrorism beyond bin Laden, both US security and Middle East regional security will be far more difficult to safeguard. Some tentatively encouraging signs have emerged. In March 2002, in Monterrey, Mexico, President Bush announced that he would seek to increase the US foreign assistance budget by 50% by 2006. Egypt's fertility rate appears to be slowing. In Saudi Arabia, since 11 September, Crown Prince Abdullah has been exhorting religious educators to emphasise Islam's tolerance, and has appeared to understand that Saudi schools must better equip the country's youth with practical skills that will make them more employable and build human capital to power economic prosperity. The challenge of reform, though daunting, may therefore be one worth undertaking.

Saudi Arabia in Transition

The Kingdom of Saudi Arabia faced the wrath of Western authorities in the aftermath of the 11 September terrorist attacks on American soil. According to the US Federal Bureau of Investigation (FBI), 15 of the hijackers believed to have taken part in the coordinated suicide missions were Saudi nationals. This claim was quickly disputed by Saudi Interior Minister Nayef bin Abdul Aziz, and at least two Saudis whose names were erroneously included on the FBI's initial terrorist tally sheets received official apologies from Washington. Dozens of others, however, were held and questioned for lengthy periods of time. Osama bin Laden himself is a Saudi national and subscribes to the puritanical Wahhabi form of Islam prevalent in Saudi Arabia, although he was stripped of his Saudi citizenship in 1994.

For much of the year, but especially after 11 September, senior US officials voiced their overall displeasure with Saudi Arabia. They remain aware, of course, that the Kingdom is still critical to US national security because it holds 25% of the world's proven oil reserves. But this truism does not alter the undeniable fact that US–Saudi relations are now severely bruised and that no amount of diplomatic finesse will eliminate the mistrust on both sides. Whether this mistrust will lead to new misunderstandings, or whether they may be replaced with more solid ties, are the key strategic questions facing Riyadh and Washington. Crown Prince Abdullah improved prospects for a warming of US–Saudi relations in February and March 2002 by urging a grand bargain whereby they would normalise relations with Israel in exchange for Israel's full withdrawal from the occupied territories. Such an eventuality seems a long way off, and the Saudi initiative does not directly address the vexing problem of Jerusalem and the holy sites and Palestinian refugees' return to Israeli territory. But the initiative has, in the absence of any other ground-up or regional alternatives, gained momentum. At the 27–28 March 2002 League of Arab States summit, all 22 Arab countries endorsed the proposal. How Saudi officials respond to accusations that they have supported terrorist activities throughout the Muslim world will also shape US–Saudi relations for much of 2002.

The principal transition facing the Kingdom, then, involves its relationship with the US. Yet other major political, social, economic and military transitions have also gathered momentum. Indeed, much of what ails the Kingdom may be traced to its complex socio-economic make-up and the myriad problems that the Kingdom has helped create since its inception in 1932. While Saudi Arabia does not face any imminent risk of instability, it enters the twenty-first century facing a heightened urgency as to how better to provide for its population and secure its role as a source of regional stability.

Political transitions

The most critical internal transition is the succession to the ailing King Fahd. His most likely successor is Abdullah bin Abdul Aziz Al Saud. Crown Prince Abdullah is not one of the 'Seven Sudayris' – King Fahd and his six brothers – on whom popular apprehensions of hypocrisy are focused, but King Fahd's half-brother. His ascension could produce significant changes in Saudi foreign and domestic policies. This prospect, in turn, could precipitate a succession crisis once the winnowing of senior Al Saud family members accelerates. Such an eventuality, however, is not likely to materialise during the next year. Another important transition occurred when the *Majlis al-Shura* (Consultative Council) was enlarged to 120 members at the end of May 2001, and its function became rendering advice rather than merely rubber-stamping government policy. Seventy-five men were appointed for the first time in a move widely perceived as a way of installing technocrats directly into government. While some lower-level members of the royal family have suggested that elections should be held for the Consultative Council, this is not likely to happen in the medium term.

The Saudi security regime experienced a significant and surprising change with the replacement of the Kingdom's intelligence boss Turki bin Faisal in August 2001. Several senior officials in Saudi intelligence left with the affable Turki, who had headed the General Intelligence Directorate since 1977. He was replaced by an Abdullah protégé, Nawwaf bin Abdul Aziz. He is 72 years old, left government as an advisor to the late King Faisal more than 25 years ago and lacks experience in the field of intelligence and security affairs. This suggests that he will remain under Abdullah's substantial control.

These developments have been seen by some observers as an attempt by Abdullah to surround himself with the half-brothers he trusts and to strengthen his position *vis-à-vis* the Seven Sudayris. For example, Prince Nayef Bin Abdul Aziz, the Interior Minister, chairs a number of important committees, some of which include the head of intelligence – now Nawwaf. Because Nawwaf is older than Nayef, it would be difficult under Saudi family protocol for Nayef to command real authority at the meetings of committees on which Nawwaf sits. Abdullah has also appointed some of the less privileged brothers and royal family members to senior posts to consolidate his position. (As these less wealthy princes could not afford to pay bills for water, electricity, telephones and air tickets, Abdullah shelved plans to require princes to do so.)

In the final formation of the 18-member Royal Family Council, the division between the branches of Fahd and Abdullah was also clear, as senior officials began to assign key posts to their children to maintain family influence. Abdullah supported the appointment of the youngest and favoured son of King Fahd, Prince Abdulaziz, as a member of the cabinet and minister of state, to be later promoted to Head of Cabinet Affairs in the Royal court, despite his youth and lack of experience. This precedent paves the way for Nayef to appoint his son Mohammad to the post of Assistant Minister of the Interior for Security Affairs, but also for Abdullah to promote his son Meteeb to the status of a full General and Assistant to the National Guard for military affairs. Accordingly, Prince Sultan, Second Prime Minister and Minister of Defence, pushed to appoint his son Khaled (Chief of Staff of the Joint Arab forces during the Gulf War but sent to an early retirement shortly after the war) to the post of Assistant Minister of Defence for Military Affairs. The stark alignments implicit in these appointments could lead to disputes among the younger cousins.

Economic transitions

According to the *Middle East Economic Digest* (MEED), in 1973, before the beginning of the oil boom, Saudi Arabia had a population of roughly 6.8 million. It grew to 22m (including 5.8m non-Saudis) in 2000. At an annual growth rate of 3.7%, the Saudi population will have nearly doubled between 1990 and 2010. Even conservative World Bank estimates, postulating growth at 3.3%, project a total Saudi population approaching 33.7m in 2010. That, in turn, will add substantial pressures on Riyadh, ranging from ensuring that economic needs are met to accommodating growing political demands.

Likewise, MEED data indicate that in 1973 Saudi Arabia's GDP stood at less than $100 billion, and its per-capita income was less than $2,500. The economy was largely rural and pre-industrial. By 2000, however, according to the Economist Intelligence Unit Saudi GDP had risen to $170bn with per-capita income hovering around $10,000. Yet the latter figure had peaked at $15,000 in 1981. These numbers indicate that a largely agricultural entity has now become a heavily urbanised welfare state with a huge service sector (44.8% of GDP in 1999, against 30.4% for oil and gas, 18.4% for manufacturing and construction, and 6.4% for agriculture). Saudi Arabia faces a critical threat to this welfare state if its economic growth does not outpace its anticipated 3%-plus population growth. Yet real GDP growth averaged only 1.5% from 1996 through 1999, and pockets of genuine poverty have emerged. The only realistic antidote is more liberal economic policies. But despite repeated attempts to diversify, Saudi Arabia remains heavily dependent on oil revenues, which account for around 90% of total export earnings, 70% of state revenues and over 30% of GDP. Without high oil prices – which are unlikely to occur in 2002 – Riyadh will face budget and investment problems, and be unable to fund both its entitlements and development programmes. According to the Saudi American Bank, the Kingdom's domestic public debt was an estimated $630bn, or 99% of GDP, in 2001, and will climb to $675bn, or 109% of GDP, in 2002. The unemployment rate for the Saudi labour force alone reached 15% in 2001 and was projected to stay at that level in 2002.

In the long term, Riyadh will need to encourage rapid diversification and prepare for the day when many subsidies – a significant drain on its unbalanced budgets – are permanently removed. But especially if, as is likely, energy conservation grows and Washington continues to try to shed dependence on Middle East oil, oil income alone will not offset a steady drop in per-capita income. Consequently, Abdullah has continued his efforts to reform the Saudi economy, reduce dependence on foreign labour, encourage private domestic and foreign investment, and open up the nation's economy to help make it globally competitive. To compensate for an anticipated decline in oil revenues, on 15 January 2002 Abdullah indicated that the Kingdom intended to introduce new incentives and guarantees to foreign investors and – particularly in light of losses incurred and increased foreign regulatory scrutiny after 11 September – to Saudis who have chosen to place their capital offshore. International trade – which saw little growth during the 1990s – could also contribute to Saudi Arabia's economic growth, but momentum behind its accession to the World Trade Organisation (WTO) flagged in 2001. The Kingdom has continued to take trade-liberalising steps independent of the WTO accession process. In May 2001, it unilaterally dropped most tariffs from 12% to 5%, and at the December 2001 Gulf Cooperation Council summit agreed with other members to harmonise tariffs at 5% by January 2003. But major Saudi–WTO differences on tariff peaks, sectoral initiatives, market access and tax differentials between foreign and domestic firms have yet to be resolved.

Military transitions

The Saudi leaders were uncomfortable with a strong military before 1990, and retained small force structures. But pressure on the government to form a fighting force capable of defending Saudi Arabia increased after the Gulf War. In the decade since, Riyadh has spent between $18 and $22bn annually on defence. It signed a total of $22bn in new arms agreements between 1991 and 1999, placed massive orders before and during the Gulf War, and took delivery of $76bn worth of kit during the same period. Defence spending rose from $23.6bn in 2000 to $27bn in 2001. Yet the Kingdom's attempted military transition is as fraught as its economic one. Saudi officials' preoccupation in 2002 has been the military's preparedness level. Training above the battalion level is still limited, particularly in combined arms and joint operations. Logistic equipment and stocks are robust, but organisation and training for these military lifelines are inadequate. The regular army's leadership is questionable. The 75,000-strong National Guard can fulfil its specific mandate of protecting the Crown Prince, but little more. Riyadh still lacks the minimum personnel required to defend the country.

The impediments to meeting the manpower requirement are the country's small skilled workforce and the inclination of able-bodied Saudi men to stay outside the military, mainly to manage businesses. Thus, despite high defence expenditures and vast programmes to absorb modern Western military hardware into the Kingdom's armed forces, the Saudi military remains relatively weak against its opponents. To compensate for the chronic manpower shortages, the Saudis have now opened military service to various tribal elements. Unfortunately, tribal and cultural aversions to military service – combined with a lack of technical education – have severely limited Riyadh's abilities to raise a force that is capable of using its sophisticated weapons without massive and unabated outside assistance.

Riyadh boasts the largest modern air force in the Gulf, and the only one in the Persian Gulf region with airborne warning and air control procedures, a major in-air refueling capability and a modern land-based air defence sensor and control network. In 2001, the US approved a $2.7bn package that included spare parts for the Royal Saudi Air Force's entire fleet of F-15s. No longer moved to import skilled pilots from Pakistan or elsewhere, it enjoys solidly average training levels and a high degree of interoperability with US forces, even if some cooperation seemed to deteriorate after US units moved from Dhahran to the isolated al-Kharj Air Base outside Riyadh in 2000. But although the Air Force performs far better than most of its regional competitors, it suffers from inadequate full-aircrew readiness and has only limited capability for joint warfare and marginal proficiency in offensive operations. Saudi Arabia has failed to meet the challenge of subduing internal and regional disturbances. In the end, the 'will to power' and massive expenditures on the military notwithstanding, the Kingdom continues to rely on the American deterrent. Despite the domestic political tensions created by the US presence in Saudi Arabia, a US departure without regime change in Iraq would severely compromise Saudi security.

Domestic political pressures

As the demographic bulge suggests, nearly half of the population is under the age of 15, and 100,000 nationals enter the job market each year. Saudi youths reaching their 20s and 30s – a stage of life that universally brings restlessness and anger – have increased demands for better governance. Those who hanker for more radical action could turn to the likes of al-Qaeda, as a number appear to have done before 11 September. Absent domestic change, the next generation will continue these trends. To maintain stability, the Saudi government will have to perform far better than it has, since without fresh sources of capital, the economy cannot expand fast enough to offer agitated men the welfare lifestyle that they have come to expect as their birthright. Fresh capital means foreign investment, as much of Saudi private wealth is invested overseas and is not put to productive use once repatriated. Although Abdullah is keen on accelerating the return of major Western investors, hurdles – including declining oil prices, attacks on foreigners, perceived regime instability and lack of counter-terrorism cooperation – persist.

The middle classes have the widest exposure to the West through education and travel, and tend to support liberal economic and political reform. But they reject anything approaching radical overhaul and insist on gradual change within the existing system. This means, on the one hand, that the economic tensions facing the government are likely to persist and, on the other, that the political mainstream poses no serious threat to the existing order. Such a threat, however, has emerged from the Islamic right. Political parties are banned in Saudi Arabia, which leaves Islam as the principal outlet for political grievances. The armed three-week occupation of the Grand Mosque in Mecca by hundreds of neo-Ikhwan supporters in November 1979, though put down by the regime, showed the potential for rebellion. After 11 September, dissident clerics warned that any ruler who collaborated with a non-Muslim force in attacking a Muslim country was an apostate, provoking fears of an assassination attempt on a royal family member.

Islamic opposition groups take the view that nationalist government policies on the domestic front enhance Saudi Arabia's standing at the international level, and oppose the regime's pro-Western policies. A violent campaign by opposition groups to end the Western presence on Saudi soil continued for much of 2001. On 15 March, a Briton and an Egyptian were injured at the Jareer Bookshop in Riyadh; on 2 May, an American physician was severely injured in al-Khobar as he opened a letter booby-trapped with a bomb. Incoherently, Interior Ministry officials quickly arrested several Belgian, British and Canadian nationals, accusing them of mostly alcohol-related non-terrorist offences. Unsurprisingly, the bombings continued after those arrested confessed. Another bombing occurred on 6 October – the day before US raids were launched on Afghanistan – in which an American national working for the Halliburton Company, a US technology and construction firm, was killed along with an unidentified expatriate suspected of being an Afghan suicide bomber.

Saudi Arabia and the global counter-terrorism campaign

From an internal Saudi perspective, the 11 September attacks revealed the extent to which some Saudis were ready to defy the government in light of the latter's discreet but sustained support for the United States. Nevertheless, Saudi Arabia's disinclination to assist US counter-terrorism efforts was explicit well before 11 September. On 17 April 2001, Saudi Arabia and Iran signed a security pact to fight crime, drug trafficking and money laundering; it also covered surveillance of borders and territorial waters. Importantly, the accord had neither a military component nor an extradition clause. The absence of such a clause allowed Riyadh to avoid asking for the extradition of Iranians accused by the FBI of involvement in the Khobar Towers bombing in 1996, which led to the deaths of 19 US servicemen. On 21 June 2001, the US Justice Department indicted 14 men (13 Saudis and a Lebanese national) for the bombings. Riyadh apparently was not consulted. The indictments were not well received in the Kingdom, and their parenthetical accusation of 'senior Iranian officials' further embarrassed Abdullah. Interior Ministry statements insisted that the case fell solely within Saudi jurisdiction. Whether or not the indictments were overbearing and insensitive, they brought to the surface internal Saudi dynamics that hindered Abdullah's cooperative agenda with the West in general and the United States in particular. In spite of 11 September, Riyadh has not handed over the three indicted suspects already in Saudi custody or indicated that they would be tried in Saudi Arabia.

Riyadh did take several practical steps to discourage terrorism, including measures to prevent money laundering and ordering banks and other financial institutions to strictly monitor large transactions. But far more serious concerns remained unaddressed. Friday sermons throughout the Kingdom's mosques were hesitant about fully condemning Osama bin Laden, offering support to the coalition to defeat al-Qaeda and the Taliban in Afghanistan but also warning against 'unmeasured' responses. Radical clerics have routinely issued critical statements of the American war in Afghanistan. 'Helping the infidels against Muslims is defecting from Islam', wrote Sheikh Hamoud al-Shuaibi, a radical cleric who died in January 2001, in response to a question on his website. The answer carried the weight of an Islamic religious decree, or fatwa: 'Whoever helps America and its fellow infidels against our brothers in Afghanistan is an apostate', he opined. Such criticism impugns the Saudi government's claim to legitimacy, echoing bin Laden's view of the ruling dynasty as too doctrinaire, too corrupt and too un-Islamic to rule.

Saudi diplomacy, as articulated by Foreign Minister Saud bin Faisal, has been clearer and more conciliatory. The attacks on the United States, he told *Time* magazine in October 2001, were 'a tragedy of such immense proportions that a human response of spontaneous reaction might have been expected, as unwise as it would be. But fortunately, and it is to the great credit of the US administration, the response has been measured. We believe that is the right response. Undoubtedly, the intent of terror is to provoke unmeasured responses ... that bring others into the fray and cause collateral damage that increases the sense of injustice'. In February 2002, Saudi Interior Minister Nayef also admitted that the majority of the hijackers were Saudi nationals after the US government submitted evidence to the Saudi government. And senior US officials frequently acknowledged that Saudi Arabia had extended some counter-terrorist cooperation with the US. But these comments were stressed in few Western media outlets, where past Saudi–Taliban cooperation, developed in the context of the Cold War, was noted with some regularity. Diplomatic relations were finally broken between Riyadh and Kabul on 21 October 2001.

Bad neighbour

Iraq's potential for disrupting Gulf security increased in 2001–02. Saudi–Iraqi relations deteriorated throughout 2001 largely due to continued border skirmishes. In June 2001, Saudi Arabia reported that its border guards had killed an Iraqi soldier during clashes with an Iraqi patrol, which had infiltrated the Kingdom. About two months later, on 25 August 2001, Iraq revealed that its border guards killed a Saudi soldier during clashes with an armed group that had infiltrated into the country. According to a formal Iraqi complaint lodged with the League of Arab States, 'a Saudi armed group of 10 persons infiltrated Iraq and engaged in an exchange of fire with units of its border guards'. It claimed that the Saudis then withdrew, leaving behind a wounded member, named in the written complaint as Saad Mutliq Slibi. According to the letter, he died on his way to hospital in Samawa city, and Iraq's Foreign Ministry contacted representatives of the International Committee of the Red Cross in Baghdad to return his body to Saudi Arabia. The letter also claimed that a Saudi patrol of three vehicles had also entered Iraq's territory and fired at Iraqi border outposts on 25 March 2000.

Dozens of similar incidents were recorded throughout the year as tensions increased. In retaliation, Riyadh seized the Iraqi Pipeline Trans-Saudi Arabia (IPSA), further aggravating relations with Baghdad. But, as irritating as the border skirmishes may have been, what plagued Saudi–Iraqi relations most was the UN-imposed sanctions regime. Unable to shed this albatross, Baghdad vented its frustrations on Riyadh. Riyadh, in turn, complained to Washington about the strains that the suppression of Iraq as well as the plight of the Palestinians imposed on its regional position.

Stormy Relations with Washington

On 15 April 2001, Interior Minister Nayef regretted that the US came 'at the top of the list of countries that have an unfair stance as regards the cause of the Arabs and the Palestinians in particular'. Whether these comments were meant mainly to assuage the growing anti-American sentiment among the Saudi public was difficult to determine. What was irrefutable, however, was that frustration with US Middle East policy remained the primary source of Saudi dissatisfaction with the United States. Abdullah turned down an American invitation to visit Washington in June 2001, professedly to abide by his 'principled stand on behalf of Palestinian rights'. He voiced his bewilderment at international inaction on behalf of the Palestinians while visiting several European capitals. Abdullah insisted that Israeli violence was a 'kind of state terrorism', highlighting the dangers of Israel's 'aggressive attitude in killing people, confiscating land, building settlements and laying economic siege to the Palestinians'. Abdullah called for a more 'balanced US position' to better protect 'vital [US] interests' throughout the region. Riyadh's unrelenting criticisms of Washington necessitated an intervention by George

H. W. Bush, who nurtured special contacts with senior Saudi figures during his own presidency in 1989–93. The former president telephoned Abdullah in June to reassure the Saudi that his son would 'do the right thing'. He reportedly confided to Abdullah that his son's heart was 'in the right place' as far as the conflict between the Palestinians and Israel was concerned. Still, Saudi Arabia's rulers were troubled by Washington's decision to limit its direct involvement in the peace process.

In the immediate aftermath 11 September, Saudi leadership appeared to feel that the US was unfairly singling out the Kingdom as a source of terrorism. Religious and secular elements within Saudi Arabia asserted their support for the government, but set out different implicit conditions for further backing. Aware that the Al Saud ruling family derives its legitimacy from Islam, religious figures claimed that a 'clash of civilisations' was indeed occurring and that the government should defend Islam. But secular leaders, understanding the country's dependence on the West, emphasised that Saudi relations with the West needed to be enhanced with liberal political, social and economic reforms. The US relieved some of the domestic pressure on the Al Saud when, on 2 October 2001, President Bush announced his administration's official support for an eventual independent Palestinian state, reiterating this point in his 10 November speech to the United Nations General Assembly. This emphatic affirmation of what was really the implicit US position came in significant part because the United States needed Arab, especially Saudi, backing in its global campaign against terrorism. With this reality in mind, Riyadh responded cautiously. While Abdullah appreciated Washington's 'inclination to seek a just and comprehensive peace' and pledged to 'exert all efforts to serve security and stability in the region and the world', the Saudi press voiced its suspicions of US motives. Nevertheless, even the Saudis realised that the US could no longer distance itself too far from its own chief executive's declaration supporting the principle of a Palestinian state.

In early October, New York Mayor Rudolph Giuliani upbraided Prince Alwaleed bin Talal for criticising US Middle East policy. The prince had urged Washington to seek 'a more balanced stance toward the Palestinian cause'. Giuliani turned down Alwaleed bin Talal's donation of $10m to the 11 September disaster fund, insisting that 'there is no moral equivalent for this attack'. This rift illustrated the widening gap between Saudi Arabia and the United States. No matter how vociferously the two sides denied the existence of a breach in perceptions of the 11 September attacks, the Saudi position at times appeared to converge on neutrality. To be sure, Saudi Arabia formally condemned the attacks on the US, as well as all other acts of terrorism. But the assumption in Washington was that Riyadh bore some responsibility in light of its past support for the Taliban, its financial assistance to leading Islamist institutions and its fostering of an anti-Western culture through its educational system, for which it offered no apology.

As military action against the Taliban grew nearer, however, the Kingdom's diplomatic importance regained currency. On 4 October 2001, US Secretary of Defense Donald Rumsfeld visited Saudi Arabia to reassure its wary leaders. Rumsfeld underlined the key unwritten alliance between the two countries and pledged to do all he could not to risk undermining the stability of the Kingdom. 'We are respectful of the circumstances of the countries in the region,' he declared. Public pronouncements to the contrary notwithstanding, in prosecuting the war against terrorism Washington placed heavy diplomatic reliance on Saudi Arabia. The revitalisation of official ties, however, was obscured by a broad and sustained anti-Saudi press campaign in the United States. 'One of the disturbing realities clarified by last month's terror attacks is Saudi Arabia's tolerance for terrorism', read an October 2001 *New York Times* editorial that provoked fierce indignation in the Kingdom. 'With Riyadh's acquiescence, money and manpower from Saudi Arabia helped create and sustain Osama bin Laden's terrorist organization', alleged the piece. Interior Minister Nayef refuted the assessment, maintaining that the Kingdom was cooperating with its allies to root out terrorism.

At the same time, Nayef and other senior Saudis were painfully aware of bin Laden's chief grievance, namely, the presence of US military personnel in the Kingdom. Given the domestic and regional pressures facing the Al Saud, Riyadh could no more dismiss this basis for bin Laden's *jihad* than it could opt out of the US-led counter-terrorism effort. Likewise, the diplomatic burden and operational vulnerability inherent in the American presence in Saudi Arabia has induced policymakers to consider effecting regime change in Iraq more seriously, to make a US withdrawal more feasible. While rumours surfacing in mid-January 2002 that the Kingdom had asked the United States to withdraw its 5,000 troops were met with resolute official denials from both Riyadh and Washington, on 26 January White House Chief of Staff Andrew Card acknowledged in a CNN interview that the Saudi government has long expressed its wish that the United States reduce its presence. Whenever that may happen, 11 September has clearly produced unprecedented pressure on both governments to create the conditions required for a US withdrawal.

US–Saudi ties in the balance

Both Washington and Riyadh have managed their numerous differences with aplomb for over 50 years. Throughout 2001, the Saudi–American disagreement over the Arab–Israeli conflict reached unprecedented levels. The Al Saud did not allow that crisis to materially damage long-term Saudi-Western ties, and the fundamentals of the US–Saudi relationship – oil and shared opposition to the Baghdad regime – remain intact. Tracking the 'clash of civilisations' rhetoric inspired by 11 September, however, both Western and Arab commentators have aggravated that relationship by raising fundamental socio-cultural differences. In March 2002, however, Abdullah accepted President Bush's invitation – delivered personally by US Vice-President Dick Cheney during his March 2002 visit to the Middle East – to be Bush's guest at the presidential ranch in Crawford, Texas.

To what extent the Al Saud ruling family is willing to take political risks will be a key strategic question for both Saudi Arabia and the United States in 2002. One test will be whether Saudi Arabia cooperates in supervising Islamic charities suspected of supporting terrorism. A more significant gauge could be whether Riyadh sees fit diplomatically and operationally to support decisive US military action to oust Saddam Hussein with an eye towards securing a subsequent American withdrawal. In March 2002, during Cheney's Middle East tour, Abdullah indicated that Saudi Arabia opposed US military action against Iraq, but pledged to try to persuade Iraq to accept the return of UN weapons inspectors. The use of Saudi bases would be optimal, though probably not essential, for a successful US campaign against Iraq. The consensus among American diplomats is that Riyadh would ultimately acquiesce to their use for combat operations if the US commitment to defeat Saddam were resolute and had the support of the Iraqi people and tensions between the Israelis and the Palestinians were ratcheted down.

The efficacy of US policy in the Middle East, then, is likely to be the most salient factor in Saudi–US relations. In proposing normalised Arab relations in exchange for an Israeli withdrawal to 1967 boundaries and marshalling formal support for this proposal from all 22 members of the League of Arab States at the 27–28 March 2002 Arab summit in Beirut, Abdullah has attempted to provide positive encouragement for more inventive and intensive American efforts to lower tensions between the Israelis and the Palestinians. Abdullah also made it clear to Vice-President Cheney that the Iraq and Israeli–Palestinian issues were intrinsically linked, despite Washington's public position decoupling them. Certainly tangible progress in reducing the level of violence in Israel and the Palestinian territories would help preserve mutual long-term interests. More public American attention to Palestinian concerns and pressure on Israel to relax its requirements for political dialogue and limit retaliatory action could promote that objective. Such measures might also allow Abdullah to introduce sorely needed economic and political reforms that would diminish popular discord over the Kingdom's – and indeed, the United States' – policies.

Garbled Signals from Iran

The year 2001 was eventful for the Islamic Republic of Iran. The main domestic development occurred when the country went to the polls on 8 June and re-elected the incumbent, President Mohammed Khatami. The longstanding conflict between the reformist and conservative camps had dominated the scene prior to the election and continued to do so thereafter. While the reformist camp cannot be seen as monolithic in any sense, it is a popular movement. The conservative camp, however, is essentially institutional, in that its adherents occupy powerful positions in large segments of the state apparatus. At the same time, it enjoys considerable street-level support. The complex relationship between the president, Khatami, and the institutional power in the country, Supreme Leader Ayatollah Khamenei, who controls state structures, makes the Iranian domestic scene complicated, and draws both domestic and international attention away from the key issue of Iran's economic health.

The economy remains in dire shape, a state of affairs aggravated by a severe drought affecting large parts of the country. The one relatively bright spot of Khatami's first presidency was foreign relations, but the external environment from early 2001 onwards proved challenging. For much of 2001, Tehran's energies were focused on bilateral relations with Russia, the Israeli–Palestinian crisis and relations with the United States. After 11 September, this focus switched to the terrorist attacks on the United States, the American response in neighbouring Afghanistan and President George W. Bush's inclusion of Iran in the so-called 'axis of evil'. Indeed, these three events have proved to be the greatest challenge to Iranian foreign policy since the Gulf War of 1991.

Domestic politics

Since Khatami's election to the presidency in 1997, the reformist camp has called for greater political freedoms, easing of restrictive social conventions, greater public accountability and the implementation of the rule of law. The conservatives, on the other hand, view the platform of the reformist camp as an assault on the integrity and security of the Islamic Republic. Many conservatives consider the reformist camp to be inspired by a Western conspiracy to destroy the Islamic Republic and its central religious and governmental institution, the *velayat-e faqih*, or rule of the jurisprudent, whose incumbent is the Supreme Leader, Ayatollah Khamenei. In 1999, there were violent outbreaks and riots in the streets, and the conservatives used the legislative and judiciary to block the reformist agenda. With its victory in the parliamentary elections of February 2000, however, the reformist camp gained control over the *Majlis*, or parliament. The reformists' capture of parliament alarmed but did not cow the conservatives. Reformist parliamentarians, for their part, may have overplayed their hand in attempting to have the *Majlis* use its power to audit the secretive affairs and businesses of institutions such as the Islamic Revolutionary Guards Corps (IRGC) and the *Bassidj*, or Guardians of the Revolution – a 300,000-strong group of young religious militants created by the state to enforce the ways of Islam – which are controlled by the conservatives.

Conservatives continued their attacks on all manifestations of reform, intensifying their offensive as the presidential elections of June 2001 approached. The Council of Guardians – the conservative-dominated watchdog group that vets parliamentary legislation and candidates for public office – vetoed most of the proposed legislation enacted by the new reformist *Majlis*. Beginning in March 2001, the security services and the police rounded up dozens of independent political activists and journalists and carted them off to jail. The Supreme Leader, Ayatollah Khamenei, maintained a policy of prevarication. Sometimes he lent his weight to the reformist camp, at other times he leaned towards the conservative camp. Both he and Khatami appeared to apprehend dangers to stability if the extremists in either camp dominated the political scene.

The political war of attrition waged by the conservatives angered and demoralised President Khatami. Over a three-year period, more than 50 periodicals – the lifeblood of the reformist movement – were banned. Khatami ran for a third term only with reluctance, waging a low-key campaign and continuously stressing the need for prudence, moderation and tolerance. The conservatives showed their strength during the electoral process as well. The Council of Guardians eliminated about 800 aspirants for the presidency, leaving only ten – all conservative men except for Khatami himself. In the event, conservative tactics did not prevent Khatami from winning a landslide victory. After the election, reformists held 189 seats in parliament, radical Islamists 54, independents 42 and religious minorities five. Almost 29 million Iranians voted, and Khatami received almost 22m votes, or about 77% of the total. His share of the vote in 1997 was 70%. It was significant, however, that only about two-thirds of the electorate turned out to vote in 2001 – compared to 80% in 1997 – due to disillusionment with the pace of reforms and with the president himself.

The election appeared to proceed without interference from the mainly conservative power structures. But sniping between reformers and conservatives continued unabated following the election, resulting in a four-day delay in Khatami's inauguration. In his inaugural address of 7 August 2001, Khatami vowed to continue the path towards reform, yet at the same time promised to uphold the Islamic system of the country: 'We have a long and untravelled path before the government and the people. We have no choice but to put the emphasis on the rights and demands of the people in order to make lawful progress and to resolve the country's various problems. We must use all our strength to avoid doing anything against the Islamic *sharia* – God forbid that day'. Khatami remained in a difficult position that he could not easily escape. He had to couple his desire for reform – a policy for which he had a democratic mandate – with the reality of conservative power. This power was made quite evident in the barely concealed warning issued by Ayatollah Mahmoud Shahroudi, the head of the judiciary, in a short impromptu speech prior to President Khatami's inauguration. The Ayatollah said that 'failure to implement the Islamic aspects of the system is a betrayal' and that to neglect or to fail to implement these Islamic aspects 'will be punishable in this world and the hereafter'.

The composition of Khatami's second cabinet indicates his extreme caution. Whereas his first cabinet (1996–2001) included charismatic and outspoken reformers like Ayatollah Mohajerani (who was forced out of office) and Abdollah Nuri (who ran afoul of the judiciary and was imprisoned), Khatami staffed his second cabinet largely with staid and 'quiet' reformers and obscure and lacklustre bureaucrats. His timidity notwithstanding, the conservatives remained on the offensive. From summer 2001 onwards, they made extensive use of the judiciary, which they control, to increase public punishments of those who were alleged to have flouted Islamic morals by wearing Western clothes, consuming alcohol and distributing CDs containing Western rock music. A number of convicted criminals were publicly hanged as well. The government stated that this offensive against corruption and crime was necessary and was supported by the majority of the people. The people, however, were clearly opposed this government crackdown as barbaric. On 16 August 2001, riot police clashed with a large crowd in Tehran that had gathered to object to the public execution of convicted murderer, Vali Hezar-Asb, in a soccer stadium. In October 2001, after the Iranian national soccer team appeared in World Cup qualifying matches, thousands took to the streets for several days of rioting. It was reported that women shed their headscarves and danced to Western music, while others chanted 'death to the mullahs' and 'we love the USA'.

The conservatives were undaunted and turned their attention to cabinet and *Majlis* members, who nominally have immunity from prosecution, in winter 2001–02. On 25 December 2001, reformist legislator Hossein Loqmanian was arrested and imprisoned for allegedly insulting the judiciary on the floor of the parliament. This marked the first time a parliamentarian had been jailed since the 1979 revolution. Oil Minister Bijan Namdar-Zangeneh was summoned to court to hear charges that he had misappropriated and embezzled funds, while Muhsen Mirdamadi, editor of the reformist *Nowruz* newspaper and chairman of the National Security and Foreign Affairs Committee of the *Majlis*, was summoned before Judge Said Mortazavi, who had been dubbed 'butcher of the press' for his role in muzzling freedom of speech. Although massive public outcry forced the Supreme Leader to order Loqmanian's release in January 2002, in February the judiciary ordered more than 60 reformist members (including Khatami's brother) to appear before court on charges of corruption. Simultaneously, closed-door trials of the 60-odd alleged subversives arrested in March 2001 were proceeding. Khatami has said that the trials are unconstitutional, and the head of the Intelligence Ministry has admitted that he knows of no supporting charges. The conservative camp's strategy is apparently to keep the members of the *Majlis* preoccupied with fending off personal attacks, rendering them unable to concentrate on advancing their political and socio-economic programmes. Yet as the various factions of the government become locked in this vital struggle over Iran's future political direction, they risk neglecting a stagnant and threatening economic situation.

The economy – poor prospects

Since the end of the war with Iraq in 1988, there have been various attempts to reform the state-controlled, wartime economy that was characterised by inefficiency, massive waste and corruption. These efforts have been largely unsuccessful. Iran's economic productivity is low and is reflected in high unemployment, which the government states is 'only' 13–15% of the productive population. The actual figure of the unemployed and underemployed may be closer to 30%. Iran's total population stands at 66m and is growing at a rate of about 1.2% per year. The government needs to create jobs for roughly 700,000–800,000 people per year to contain the unemployment problem. Indeed, if economic conditions remain unchanged the government calculates that there will be about five million unemployed Iranians by 2005. Although real GDP grew by 5.6% in 2000-01 – double the previous year's rate – that level is insufficient to meet job-creation needs. The economy is dominated by state-run companies and *bonyads* – charitable foundations controlled by clerics. Accorded monopolistic status, the state companies get preferential treatment, such as subsidies, tax and custom duty exemptions, and low-interest government loans. While the *bonyads* are relatively efficient and are run by business-savvy clerics and *bazaaris* – the traditional mercantile class – the state companies are inefficient, unproductive enterprises run by bureaucratic mediocrities that produce substandard goods.

Khatami's attitude towards economics is not as dismissive as that of the founder of the Islamic Republic, Ayatollah Khomeini, who referred to economics as a matter 'for donkeys'. But during his first term he did not rise to economic challenges. He now appears to understand that he has to devote more time and effort to implementing economic reform during his second term. The 2002–03 Budget Bill, put forward in January 2002, incorporated a number of reforms, including the unification of exchange rates and reductions in consumer subsidies. As these appeared to address concerns lodged by the International Monetary Fund (IMF) in its Article IV consultation with the Iranian government in September 2001, they reflected its inclination towards greater engagement with the international economy. But the State Management and Planning Organisation is chaired by Mohammad Sattarifar, an unbending critic of IMF policies.

Khatami also has to contend with conservatives who have used the Council of Guardians to veto an important law that would have allowed foreign companies to invest in Iran's economic sector and repatriate profits. He faces resistance from the left-wing faction of the reformist camp, which opposes wide-ranging liberal economic reforms that would dismantle much of the public sector and result in increased short-term unemployment. Furthermore, the proposed public budget would be 48.7% higher than the previous one, and 65.7% of it would be allocated to dysfunctional state enterprises. Neither increase indicates the full-blooded commitment to economic liberalisation and privatisation that the IMF deemed necessary to build on the 2000–01 improvements in Iran's fiscal and external positions.

Tehran and Washington

When the Bush administration took office in January 2001, a number of academics, former officials and business professionals in the US had begun to call for an improvement in US–Iranian relations. For example, the Atlantic Council issued a report that set out a roadmap for restoration of relations. Thus, some in Tehran expected positive changes in US–Iranian relations and believed that US economic sanctions would eventually be lifted. But members of the new American administration were not sympathetic to the idea. In early 2001, George Tenet, Director of the Central Intelligence Agency, declared Iran to be one of the biggest proliferation challenges facing the US. In early June 2001, the US indicted those believed to be responsible for the bombing of the US military barracks in 1996 in Khobar Towers in Saudi Arabia. The US has linked Iran to the terrorist blast, though it avoided naming Iranian players suspected of direct involvement. Last but not least, the Bush administration pushed for the renewal of the Iran–Libya Sanctions Act (ILSA), which penalises companies doing more than $20m worth of trade in the two countries' oil sectors. Congress complied in August 2001.

The terrorist attacks on the US on 11 September 2001 relegated Iran's other US-related foreign-policy concerns to the backburner. The Iranian government and both reformist and conservative figures strongly condemned the terrorist attacks. Even more remarkable was the outpouring of sympathy for Americans among Iranians from all walks of life – in stark contrast to other Middle East and Gulf reactions, which ranged from indifference to smug satisfaction that the US was finally getting a taste of violence in its own territory. Although the Iranian leadership warned the US against a policy of 'muscular' reprisal that would lead to another human tragedy in Afghanistan, as the US prepared for war there, a greater readiness surfaced on the part of both Iran and the US to cooperate. Tehran was not displeased that the Taliban regime, with which it almost went to war in 1999, was to face the wrath of American military power, and indicated that it would rescue any American troops or pilots in distress in Iranian territory. Furthermore, Iran became a transshipment point for American wheat into Afghanistan. Not surprisingly, US Secretary of State Colin Powell declared that Iran had been generally helpful in the war against terrorism in Afghanistan. Tehran also pledged over $500m to help rebuild Afghanistan over a five-year period; this is a generous sum, particularly given that Iran already accommodates over one million Afghani refugees.

The late September visit to Tehran by Jack Straw, foreign minister of the United Kingdom – traditionally viewed in Iran as the contemptible ally of the American 'Great Satan' – was perceived by some Western diplomats as an awkward attempt to foster some form of indirect bilateral dialogue between Tehran and Washington. Official multilateral contact between Iran and the United States was facilitated by greater activity on the part of the 'Six-plus-Two' group – the six nations bordering Afghanistan plus Russia and the United States – which was set up in the early 1990s to deal with the Afghanistan problem. But differences between Tehran and Washington over the situation in Afghanistan became readily apparent. Tehran was alarmed by the rapidity of the Taliban defeat and the sudden and rapid emergence of the US as the leading power in Afghanistan, two outcomes that nurtured an essentially pro-American regime under Hamid Karzai. In a meeting in Tehran with UN Secretary-General Kofi Annan in late January 2002, Khatami hoped to dilute the impact of the American presence next door by strongly encouraging the United Nations to continue playing a positive role in bringing about peace and stability and in rebuilding Afghanistan.

The prospect that the US would establish a foothold on Iran's vulnerable border region alarmed both the reformist and conservative camps in Iran. Leading officials with key roles in the Iranian national security establishment viewed the US return to Afghanistan not merely as an incident of the campaign against terrorism, but as part of a broader geopolitical strategy to threaten Iran, suppress Islam and establish a presence adjacent to gas- and oil-rich Central Asia. On different occasions, Defence Minister Shamkhani, IRGC Commander Safavi and National Security Council Chief Hasan Rouhani suggested that the US intended to ensure control of the oil in Central Asia and the pipeline routes for the export of Central Asian oil by stabilising Afghanistan and rendering it preferable to Iran as the site of the required pipelines. The Iranian government may also fear the emergence of a 'secularised' Afghanistan that could ultimately recall its deposed monarchy back to power. Such a development could strengthen the potential for Reza Pahlavi, the son of the monarch deposed in 1979, Mohammed Reza Shah, to inspire political protest in Iran. In 2001, Reza Pahlavi directed satellite television broadcasts from Los Angeles to his homeland calling for non-violent civil disobedience, democracy and the separation of state and mosque. The message was tailored to Iran's huge population of frustrated and restive youth, and it irritated the government.

Against this backdrop, Iran has taken energetic and potentially destabilising steps to safeguard its interests in Afghanistan. Tehran did give its blessing to the Bonn Conference of the various Afghan factions in late November 2001 that led to the establishment of Karzai's transitional government, and indicated its willingness to help in the reconstruction of the devastated country. At the same time, Iran began propping up its former protégé, Ismail Khan, a dissident warlord based in western Afghanistan, with weapons, merchandise and cash. Further, Iranian authorities appeared to allow some fleeing al-Qaeda members into Iran from Afghanistan, and in March 2002 were believed to be providing sanctuary for Abu Musaab Zarqawi, a senior al-Qaeda leader, in Tehran. While sectarian differences between Iranian and al-Qaeda Muslims have been thought to limit the potential for synergy, and Iran supported the Afghani groups opposed to the al-Qaeda and the Taliban, the CIA has not ruled out limited partnerships of convenience. Much of Iran's activity in Afghanistan in early 2002 could be construed as 'spoiler' behaviour: it appears willing to act to ensure that stability does not return to Afghanistan if Iran's security, political and cultural interests there are ignored. In particular, Iran would like to see post-war arrangements that allow Afghani refugees in Iran to be repatriated, as well as restraints enforced by the Kabul government against drug-smuggling and other forms of border insecurity.

President Bush's characterisation of Iran, along with Iraq and North Korea, as a member of the 'axis of evil' in his State of the Union address on 29 January 2002 effectively stopped – and may have reversed – any serious momentum towards improvement of US–Iranian relations. It reflected a decisive political victory of the ideological hawks and the pro-Israeli lobby. Iranian officials reacted immediately and furiously. The most telling comment came from the Iranian Foreign Minister, Kamal Kharrazi, a moderate who had travelled to the United States and met informally with American academics, members of Congress and business executives. He expressed his country's 'strong indignation' and blasted the US for its alleged unconditional support for Israel's policy of 'assassinations, abductions and destruction of entire villages' as well as its purportedly hypocritical policy in the war against terrorism. Washington viewed as destabilising Tehran's support for Ismail Khan in the wake of the American victory in Afghanistan. Reports in early 2002 that some Iranians were negotiating safe passage for al-Qaeda members fleeing from Afghanistan also did not endear Iran to senior Bush administration officials. But these were not the primary factors in Bush's decision to include Iran in the 'axis of evil'. Of greater importance were Washington's sceptical assessments of Iran's internal politics, Iran's perceived support for terrorism in the Middle East, its opposition to the Israeli–Palestinian peace process, its persistent refusal to acknowledge Israel's right to exist and especially the US intelligence assessment that Iran is developing weapons of mass destruction (WMD).

Shrill warnings from the Mossad, Israel's foreign intelligence service, that Iran would become a nuclear power with an operational arsenal by 2005 found a receptive audience in the relatively hard-line Bush administration even before 11 September. Since then, the US has been broadly less tolerant of nations that have not 'put their house in order'. In this light, it is not surprising that the thaw in American–Iranian bilateral relations proved short-lived. According to a US National Intelligence Estimate released in February 2002, Iran has ongoing chemical and biological weapons programmes and could have nuclear capability by the end of the decade. Iran also has a large arsenal of ballistic missiles, including *Shehab*-3 medium-range missiles (scaled-up *Scuds*), and is developing an intermediate-range missile capable of reaching Europe and possibly an ICBM (*Shehabs* 4 and 5, respectively). Press reports in January 2002 indicated that two of Iran's three *Shehab*-3 flight tests had failed, the most recent one in September 2000. Nevertheless, the programmes in place potentially threaten US and allied forces in the Middle East.

The event that probably clinched Iran's membership in the 'axis' was the seizure by Israeli commandos of the ship *Karine-A* on the Red Sea on 4 January 2002. The ship was loaded with 50 tonnes of arms from Iran bound for the Palestinian Authority. These included hundreds of mortars and grenades, antitank weapons, antipersonnel mines, two tonnes of explosives and 62 *Katyusha* rockets capable of reaching most cities in Israel from the Palestinian territories. Washington and Jerusalem accused Tehran of seeking to inflame an already volatile situation in the Palestinian territories. For both Israel and the US, the incident was clear-cut evidence of Tehran's growing addiction to supporting anti-Israeli insurgency in the Middle East in general and a deepening strategic nexus between Iran and the Palestinian Authority in particular. During the 2000 US presidential campaign and the early days of the Bush administration, the Bush team had been inclined to seek warmer relations with Iran, following the Clinton administration's instinct to drop 'dual containment'. The *intifada*, however, stoked radical sentiments in Iran, which had broken with Palestinian leader Yasser Arafat in 1994 over the Oslo accords. In March 2002, press reports indicated that US and Israeli intelligence officials had concluded that Iran had forged an alliance with Arafat over the previous 18 months.

The upshot of the new US assessment was that the *Karine-A* shipment was just the tip of the iceberg; Iran had become a player in the Israeli–Palestinian conflict and appeared to be seeking to 'Lebanonise' the

Palestinian territories. This position reflected a reversal of the official US perception that, apart from supporting Hizbullah's armed opposition to the Israelis in south Lebanon, the Iranians had diminished their support for terrorism around the world after helping to engineer the Khobar Towers bombing in 1996 in Saudi Arabia. The relationship between the Palestinian Authority and Iran is believed to have been consolidated in May 2001 at a clandestine meeting between Arafat and Iranian officials in Moscow. Furthermore, Hizbullah – Iran's protégé, basking in the 'victory' occasioned by the Israeli withdrawal from south Lebanon in May 2000 – is lending support to its Palestinian brethren, and has threatened to open a 'second front'. The group attempted to smuggle *Katyusha* rockets to the Palestinian Authority through Jordan in February 2002; was behind the 12 March 2002 attack on the Lebanon–Israel border in which six Israelis were killed; and has trained Hamas and (Palestinian) Islamic Jihad operatives. The pre-existing relationship between Tehran and Hizbullah provides Iran with a second avenue for influencing the Israeli–Palestinian conflict – and an ideal one for effecting a 'Lebanonisation' strategy. In a television interview on 30 March, Hizbullah Secretary-General Naeem Kassem confirmed that the attacks were in support of Arafat and the Palestinians, and warned the Israelis that they were 'playing with fire'. Although Syria remains Hizbullah's effective landlord, in early 2002 it appeared to be seeking to capitalise on post-11 September counter-terrorism cooperation to establish better relations with the US. As of late 2001, Israeli intelligence sources believed that Hizbullah took its military cue more from Tehran than from Damascus. Iran also appears to finance Islamic Jihad and, less directly or substantially, Hamas.

While US officials generally share the belief that there are significant developments afoot in Iran that could ultimately lead to positive changes, they also see little hope that the stranglehold of the anti-American and anti-Western forces will be broken any time soon. In the Americans' view, the fierce Iranian desire to express independence at any cost will surface in the face of any challenge. Accordingly, in US calculations there is little scope for diplomatically moderating Iran's WMD ambitions, its support for terrorism or its obstructionism and provocation with respect to the Middle East.

Iran's regional diplomacy

Russian–Iranian relations improved significantly in 2001 after several years of stagnation. The stage for a revitalisation of ties was set with the visit of Khatami to Russia in mid-March 2001. Moreover, a major irritant in bilateral Russo-Iranian relations – the Gore–Chernomyrdin memorandum of 1995, which obliged Russia to stop initiating 'destabilising' arms contracts with Iran after 31 December 1999 – was removed when Russian President Vladimir Putin decided to ignore it. This was welcomed by many Russian officials and of course by Iran itself. Defence Minister Ali Shamkhani visited Russia in October 2001 and concluded an arms deal worth $300m over five years with his Russian counterpart. If implemented, it would make Iran the third-largest importer of Russian weapons after China and India.

Iranian diplomacy in South Asia also witnessed dramatic gains in 2001. In mid-April 2001, Indian Prime Minister Atal Bihari Vajpayee made an official visit to Tehran, signing several accords on bilateral trade and commerce and cooperation in the science and energy sectors. Energy-hungry India is particularly keen to improve its access to energy-rich Iran's oil and gas, though Vajpayee downplayed reports that Iran was seeking to cooperate with India in the defence field. Still, Indo-Iranian relations were not all about commerce and trade. Both countries expressed their opposition to the Pakistani-supported Taliban regime and called for the establishment of a broad-based government in Afghanistan. While Khatami focused on the concrete issues that drew Iran and India together, Khamenei tried to interest the Indian Prime Minister in the creation of an 'anti-hegemonic' (read: anti-US) quadrilateral partnership that would also include China and Russia. While India is not interested in such grandiose and provocative notions, it is clear that both Iran and India see their bilateral relations in strategic terms. There are strict limits on how far that relationship will go, given India's own diplomatic and defence interests in expanding warm relations with the US and Israel.

Iranian relations with Iraq, its nearest Arab neighbour, remained troubled throughout 2001. The legacy of hatred engendered by the bloody Iran–Iraq war that ended over a decade ago is difficult to overcome. More particularly, Baghdad continued to support the *Mujahideen-e khalq* organization (MKO), which maintained large and well-stocked military camps along Iraq's border with Iran, from which it launched periodic raids into Iran. In April 2001, Tehran fired a massive barrage of more than 50 surface-to-surface missiles at the camps. About a month later, the main organ of the ruling Baath Party in Iraq, *al-Thawrah* newspaper, issued a long article in which it argued that the Iran's pursuit of a nuclear arsenal constituted an existential threat to pan-Arab security. (In this context, Iraq ironically joins Israel and the United States in drawing attention to the 'danger' posed by Iran's nuclear programme.) Whether Iran favours regime-change or containment with respect to Saddam Hussein is unclear, but logic suggests that his containment as a weak and relatively unthreatening leader would be preferred. Saddam's ouster could lead either to chaos in Iraq, with ominous implications for Iran's security, or to the installation of a weak pro-American regime in Baghdad.

Iran's relations with its various Arab neighbours in the Persian Gulf were essentially static in late 2001 and early 2002. A major bone of contention continues to be three disputed islands between Iran and the United Arab Emirates. In April 2001, Iran did sign a significant cooperation pact with Saudi Arabia on controlling crime, drug trafficking and money laundering, as well as surveillance of borders and territorial waters, but there were no dramatic breakthroughs. Despite a generally positive trend in Iran's relations with its conservative Arab neighbours, it is highly unlikely that any agreement on implementing a regional security system will materialise in the near future. Arab fears of a powerful and domineering Iran, Iraq's unsettled future and the American presence in the Persian Gulf are the main structural impediments. Conversely, the collapse of the Oslo accords and the increased venom in Arab–Israeli relations was a welcome development as far as Iran was concerned. These developments precluded any Arab–Israeli alignment against Iran, which had seemed a genuine possibility in the early to mid-1990s. Iran took the opportunity to tout its support of the Palestinians in their conflict with the Israelis.

The damage to Arab–Israeli relations also enabled Iran to improve or deepen existing relationships with Arab countries further afield than those in the Persian Gulf. Egyptian–Iranian relations – tense for more than 20 years over Egypt's peace with Israel and its providing sanctuary for the deposed Shah – warmed considerably. While full diplomatic relations have not been restored, the two countries continued to nurture trade relationships. Further, each country agreed to reopen the office of its official news agency in the other's capital in December 2001, and in January 2002 the Iranian Foreign Ministry was considering a new name for a Tehran street named after Khaled Eslambouli – Egyptian President Anwar Sadat's assassin. Iran and the new Syrian regime of Bashar al-Assad also reaffirmed a 20-year relationship.

Whither Iran?

The obstructionist power of the conservatives and the political apathy and listlessness over the reformists' impotence prevailed in fall 2001 and winter 2002. That there is a standoff between the two sides is clear. The reformist camp believes has a significant majority of the people behind it, while the conservatives retain firm control of the state's power apparatus. However, there appears to be a growing perception among conservatives that it should not merely rely on its institutional power and must address the needs of the population. For example, while all ten candidates certified by the Council of Guardians to run for the presidency were conservative in their leanings, save for the president himself, only one of the conservative candidates was a cleric. The remainder were lay people who sought to portray themselves as reform-minded. This makeup suggested that a majority in the Council had come to recognise the unpopularity of their more rigid views. One possible result would be an emerging split between enlightened conservatives and the more traditional ones.

The Islamic regime is not in any imminent danger of collapse or overthrow. At the same time, the failure of reform to take root and massive unemployment could result in large-scale outbreaks of urban violence. Iranian women are an increasingly powerful and vocal force, and they have lost patience with the stifling Islamic mores, most of which are directed at them. The religious regime's calls for purity and morality have produced a dangerous cynicism on the part of a restive youth population that increasingly perceives the clerical families as corrupt and hypocritical. This perception was fuelled by the January 2002 trial of three *aghazadehs* – rich sons of powerful clerics – along with 15 others for defrauding state banks out of over $100m. The government, of course, has powerful paramilitary and military forces at its disposal to deal with serious outbreaks of violence and from the mid-1980s the security and military forces have engaged in exercises for putting down such outbreaks. But using state security forces for repression could backfire politically if their leadership or significant numbers of soldiers or police begin to have doubts about shooting and killing the unarmed population. This is a distinct possibility, as many members of the police forces and the military suffer from the same economic difficulties as the general population, and have had to take on second jobs to supplement their meagre salaries.

While it is unclear how the external environment will impact domestic politics in 2002, the deepening chill in US–Iranian relations may work to postpone any showdown between the reformist and conservative camps. It is too facile to state that Bush's State of the Union address was a victory for the conservative camp in Tehran. The fact is that not all conservatives are against a US–Iranian rapprochement, nor are all reformers necessarily enamoured of the US. Reformers and conservatives alike are generally highly nationalistic, and US policies that smack of threats against Iran are likely to unify the two camps in patriotic fervour. Both camps vehemently condemned the American 'axis of evil' characterisation of Iran. There may, however, be material differences between the two sides' responses to the perceived American and Israeli threats against Iran.

Conservatives are more likely to advocate a proactive covert strategy that continues Iran's 'spoiler' role in western Afghanistan and extends more support to Hizbullah and the Palestinians. The reformers are more inclined to counsel caution and the avoidance of any overt action that may provide the US and Israel with the justification to adopt more aggressive policies towards Iran. Nonetheless, they would probably still support continued efforts to acquire more military materiel, enhance Iran's WMD capability and develop closer diplomatic and economic links with the China, Russia and to a lesser extent India. Tehran may also seek to exploit Europe's preference for positive reinforcement to establish beneficial links. The European Union backed Iran's bid for World Trade Organisation membership against Washington's wishes in February 2002. But prospects for progress were dimmed by Iran's rejection in the same month of British

Ambassador David Reddaway on the ground that he was a Jew and a spy, which London denied. Also unhelpful was a mid-February announcement by the ultra-conservative 15th of Khordad Foundation that it had increased the bounty on British writer Salman Rushdie, who was condemned to death in a *fatwa* issued by the Ayatollah Khomeini in 1989.

The Bush administration's decision publicly to stigmatise Iran has delayed any prospective normalisation of Iranian relations with the US. By the same token, it has deferred a decisive ideological confrontation between reformist and conservative elements within Iran. It appears probable that the conservatives still hold the real political power in Iran. On balance, Bush's inclusion of Iran in the 'axis of evil' probably reinforces their capacity to inhibit the reformists. While a spokesman for Khatami said on 18 March 2002 that he would engage in dialogue with Washington, Khamenei, who has ultimate authority over foreign policy, squelched that possibility a day later. As for US policy, Bush has foreclosed warmer relations unless Iran desists from pursuing WMD capability and from supporting Hizbullah and armed Palestinian groups, and he has affirmed confrontation rather than engagement as the US approach. Whether improved US–Iranian relations become a more distinct possibility depends partly on near-term developments in the Middle East and Central Asia. If initiatives aimed at producing Israeli–Palestinian peace – such as the land-for-normalisation idea mooted by Saudi Crown Prince Abdullah in February 2002 – eventually lower tensions between the Israelis and the Palestinians and improve relations between the Arab states and Israel, it would be more difficult for Iran to continue its antagonism towards Israel. If, in turn, the conference of Afghani tribal leaders (*loya jirga*) scheduled for June 2002 yields a multi-tribal permanent government that preserves Tehran's interests, Iranian–US mutual suspicions could also be eased.

The EU is Iran's largest trading partner and has some economic leverage. The EU and European capitals may have a limited but constructive role to play in maintaining a policy of 'critical engagement' with Tehran. Transatlantic relations could likely bear the inevitable stress as long as such dialogue was not accompanied by European behaviour – such as the transfer of dual-use technology or diplomatic acquiescence to Iranian support for Middle East insurgencies – that frustrated US counter-proliferation and conflict-management efforts. Some substantive EU efforts – for example, EU foreign-policy chief Javier Solana's attempt in March 2002 to convince Iran to support the Saudi Middle East peace initiative – will have a low probability of success. But the less tangible benefits to Washington could include insights from allies on Iran's internal situation and ready diplomatic channels through which it could test possibilities for improving relations with Tehran.

Asia

It was a notably dynamic year for Asia as a result of both 11 September and evolving national and regional developments that reached pivotal points. The American-led military campaign in Afghanistan ousted the Taliban and decisively established Central Asia – including the Commonwealth of Independent States – as a durable Western strategic interest. This development complicated the regional calculations of not only Russia, Iran and Turkey but also Pakistan, India, China, Japan and key nations in South-east Asia.

In Pakistan, General Pervez Musharraf's government had little choice but to assist the United States' effort and stood to reap rewards for doing so, but also faced a heightened domestic challenge from radical Islamic groups. The Western coalition's need for Pakistani cooperation downgraded India's status as a US partner, though it regained diplomatic capital when Kashmiri terrorists with Pakistani connections attacked the Indian parliament in Delhi in December 2001, bringing the two South Asian countries to a testy military confrontation in Kashmir. Beijing, stressing perceived threats from militant Islamists within China, supported the action in Afghanistan despite its standing wariness about military intervention. The 11 September attacks put greater pressure than ever on Japan to adopt a more extrovert foreign and security policy, and Tokyo responded positively if cautiously. Links surfaced between al-Qaeda and groups in Indonesia, Malaysia, the Philippines and Singapore, prompting considerable counter-terrorism cooperation with the US from the latter three countries but not from Indonesia. Thailand extended 'unmatched' counter-terrorism cooperation to the US, according to Federal Bureau of Investigation Director Robert Mueller. After a period of comparative strategic neglect, the US presence in South-east Asia expanded markedly from April 2001 to April 2002.

During that period, most Asian countries found themselves in the midst of considerable domestic economic and political transition, turbulence or malaise. China was preparing to impose traumatic economic reforms required by the World Trade Organization, which China joined in December 2001, and faced an uncertain political transition at the 16th Party Congress, scheduled for late 2002. Japan had a charismatic new prime minister in Junichiro Koizumi, but he appeared no more able to make decisive economic reforms than his beleaguered and less reform-minded predecessor, Yoshiro Mori. In India, Prime Minister Atal Behari Vajpayee's

Map 4 Asia

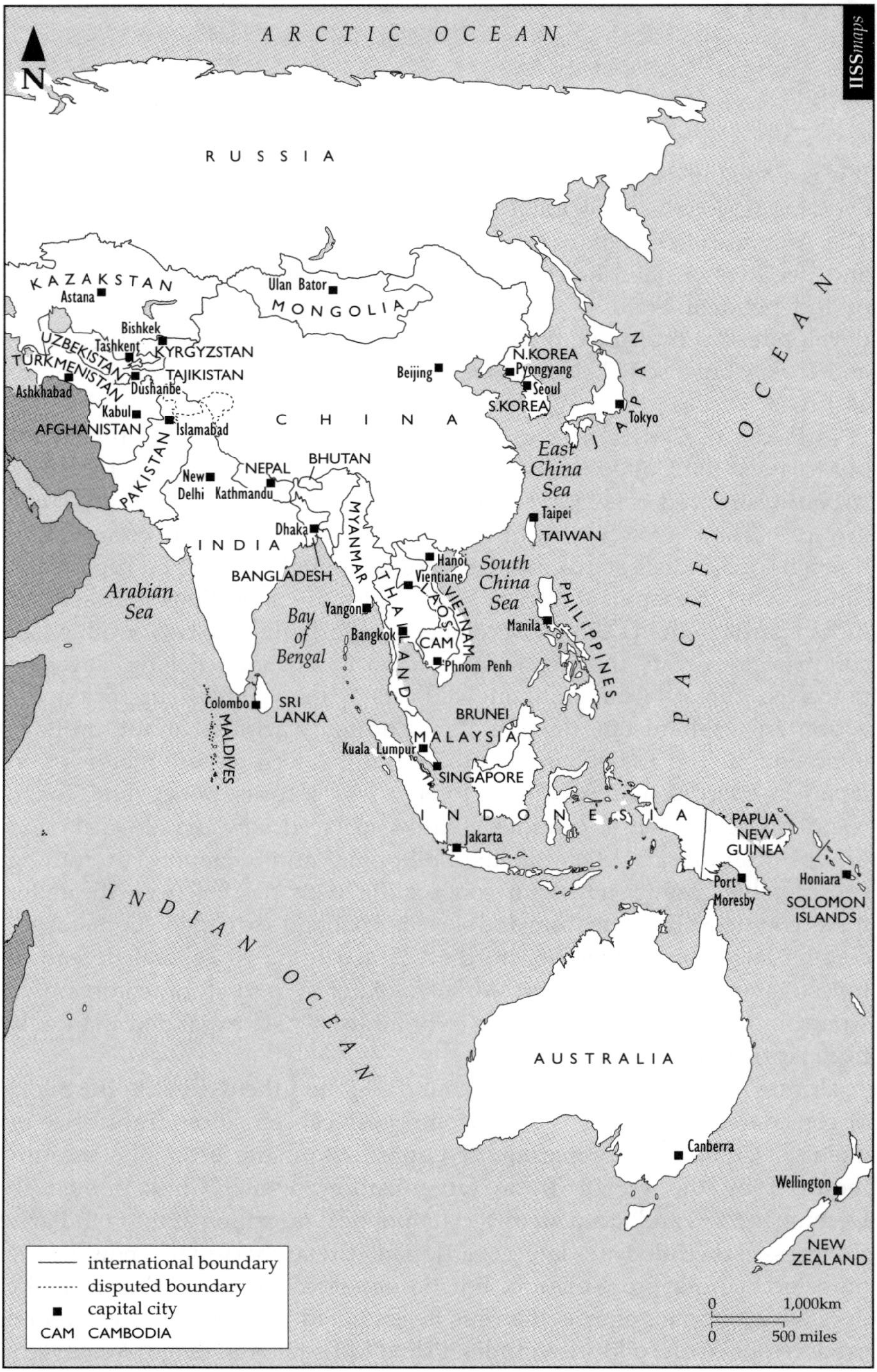
IISSmaps
N
ARCTIC OCEAN
RUSSIA
KAZAKSTAN
Astana
Ulan Bator
MONGOLIA
Bishkek
Tashkent
KYRGYZSTAN
UZBEKISTAN
TURKMENISTAN
Ashkhabad
Dushanbe
TAJIKISTAN
Kabul
AFGHANISTAN
Islamabad
PAKISTAN
CHINA
Beijing
N.KOREA
Pyongyang
Seoul
S.KOREA
JAPAN
Tokyo
East China Sea
NEPAL
BHUTAN
New Delhi
Kathmandu
Dhaka
Taipei
TAIWAN
INDIA
BANGLADESH
MYANMAR
Hanoi
Vientiane
South China Sea
LAOS
VIETNAM
THAILAND
Arabian Sea
Bay of Bengal
Yangon
Bangkok
CAM
Phnom Penh
Manila
PHILIPPINES
PACIFIC OCEAN
Colombo
SRI LANKA
MALDIVES
BRUNEI
MALAYSIA
Kuala Lumpur
SINGAPORE
INDONESIA
Jakarta
PAPUA NEW GUINEA
Port Moresby
Honiara
SOLOMON ISLANDS
INDIAN OCEAN
AUSTRALIA
Canberra
Wellington
NEW ZEALAND
international boundary
disputed boundary
capital city
CAM CAMBODIA
0 1,000km
0 500 miles

ruling coalition became increasingly fractious and incapable of cleaning up corruption and economic inefficiency, while massive ethnic violence called further into doubt his ability to restrain Hindu nationalist radicals within his Bharatiya Janata Party (BJP). Regime change in Indonesia produced a more stable but still tenuous central government with little room to manoeuvre between civilian and military political forces, entrenching the regional political and economic debility of the Association of South-east Asian Nations. In the Philippines, while most were happy to see the corrupt Joseph Estrada replaced by Gloria Macapagal Arroyo, who has proven an adept political survivor, her presidency has been tested by the perennial problems of poverty and rebellion. Under Prime Minister Thaksin Shinawatra, Thailand has experienced an inward nationalist and populist turn that may hinder economic revival. The Korean Peninsula drifted back towards a grim status quo, away from the vision of unification that had seemed so bright at the June 2000 inter-Korean summit. Kim Dae Dung's lame-duck presidency drew to a subdued close, as domestic disillusionment and a lack of US diplomatic support forced him to rein in his 'sunshine policy' *vis-à-vis* North Korea. Pyongyang, angered by its inclusion in President George W. Bush's rhetorical 'axis of evil', threatened to withdraw from the Agreed Framework, though it remains constrained by its dependency on foreign aid.

At the extremes, Nepal saw a sharp upsurge in left-wing terrorist violence, while Sri Lanka witnessed a genuine prospect of peace after nearly 20 years of brutal civil war. In early 2002, hundreds of Nepali Maoist rebels and security forces were killed – including 129 government policemen and soldiers as well as civilians in well-orchestrated attacks on 17 February – bringing to almost 2,500 the total body-count from the conflict, which began in 1996. Counter-terrorism and general strikes by rebel sympathisers are likely to distract the government from critical poverty eradication efforts. Nearly 40% of Nepal's 23 million people live below the poverty line, and the country depends on outside donors for 60% of its economic development costs. To make matters worse, 11 September and the slaying of most of the royal family by the deranged crown prince in June 2001 has depressed the tourist trade, contributing to poor economic growth. Although the US and India are providing limited military assistance, with only 6,000–10,000 security forces against at least 2,000 rebels seeking to overthrow the monarchy, Kathmandu is likely to face a protracted struggle.

In Sri Lanka, a persistent military stalemate, a growing national consensus for peace among both the Buddhist Sinhalese majority and the Hindu Tamil minority, proactive engagement by outside actors, the chilling effect of 11 September and a global crackdown on the separatist Liberation Tigers of Tamil Eelam's (LTTE) external sources of funding combined to produce a bilateral cease-fire on 25 December 2001. On 22 February 2002, the government and the LTTE signed a long-term cease-fire agreement, to be supervised by Norwegian, Swedish, Danish and Finnish monitors. Brokered by Norway, which has commercial interests in Sri Lanka, it was the first formal truce since 1995 in a war that started in 1983 and has claimed close to 65,000 lives. Peace had appeared distant on 24 July 2001, when the LTTE – also known as the Tamil Tigers – audaciously attacked the a military airbase and the adjoining international airport outside Colombo, Sri Lanka's capital, damaging or destroying 14 military and commercial aircraft, shocking hundreds of foreign visitors on holiday and discouraging tourism. Twenty people, including 13 rebels, were killed. But new Prime Minister Ranil Wickremesinghe, whose United National Front coalition came to power in December 2001 parliamentary elections, was more inclined than his predecessor to accord the Tamil minority political equality and greater autonomy if the Tamil Tigers would drop their insistence on sovereignty, which rebel leader Velupillai Prabhakaran may be willing to do.

As of April 2002, the mood music remained upbeat: the economically pressured government proposed slashing defence spending by a third; insurers were contemplating the removal of Sri Lanka's war risk premium; in March, Wickremesinghe had become the first prime minister to visit the largely Tamil city of Jaffna in 20 years; the government eased economic restrictions in Tamil areas; and India, the ranking regional power, as well as the US, had registered strong diplomatic support for the peace process. But there remained considerable obstacles to peace. The LTTE would not make a deal unless the government lifted its ban on the organisation. The radical Marxist People's Liberation Front and the hard-line nationalist Sinhalese Heritage parties were still opposed to any peace accord. President Chandrika Kumaratunga, whom Wickremesinghe replaced as prime minister, had also challenged the prime minister's authority on peace-related matters. Preliminary political negotiations were tentatively scheduled for the first week of May in Bangkok, Thailand.

For the Central Asian states, Afghanistan became a source of seditious ideas, arms and narcotics trafficking in the early 1990s, even before the Taliban took power and allowed the al-Qaeda network to establish itself as a training ground for international terrorism. The most salient radical Islamic threat outside Afghanistan materialised in Uzbekistan in the form of the Islamic Movement of Uzbekistan (IMU). IMU leader Juma Namangani may have been killed in Afghanistan in late 2001, and the camps of the IMU were at least partially destroyed in the US-led military campaign, but the risk that new groups will emerge remains high. Central Asia's burgeoning drug trade has helped fund the perpetuation of militant Islamic groups that have proliferated in Uzbekistan and throughout Central Asia. The largest of these, the Hezb-ut Tahrir, calls for believers to unite and return Islam to the purity of its founding through the creation of a new Caliphate.

To counter the threat to the state, the Uzbek government and others have behaved much like their Soviet predecessors, attempting to dampen the fires of religious ferment by state regulation of religious practice. This marked a reversal of the initial stances adopted by several Central Asian states after they achieved independence, when they saw advantages in according religion a higher status in unstable societies no longer governed along ideological lines. The Hezb-ut Tahrir is outlawed in all of the Central Asian states except Turkmenistan, where it appears to lack a significant presence. Following massive arrests, adherents of the movement have gone underground in Uzbekistan, but their numbers are increasing in the border regions of Kazakhstan and Kyrgyzstan, particularly among unemployed youths who are paid to distribute the movement's religious tracts. These people appear poised to return to Uzbekistan if any opportunity to do so arises. Given Uzbekistan's current demographic and social situation - over half of the country is under 21, and Uzbek youth is generally poorer and less healthy than the previous generation - the potential for such groups to attract new recruits remains high. Comparable vulnerabilities affect the other countries in the region, except Turkmenistan, where there is appreciable poverty but the country's Islamic revival has proceeded through more traditional channels.

The Central Asian states have become valuable to the US and its allies as coalition partners, in terms of both providing logistical assistance for the Afghanistan military campaign and, more broadly, quelling radical Islamic terrorism and other transnational threats in the region. Post-11 September, the Central Asian states are liable to benefit from more direct security relationships with the US. This, in turn, will distance them from Russia and allow them to develop more distinct foreign and security policies. In April 2002, there were US military presences in Tajikistan, Uzbekistan and Kyrgyzstan, and rumours of a possible future US deployment in Kazakhstan. Moreover, the US has signed a long-term security partnership with the Uzbeks, which is likely to ensure, at minimum, continued US investment in the reform of that country's military. There has also been a commitment to increase US spending for upgrading border security throughout the region, and for improved narcotics interdiction.

The US is likely, as well, to continue to nurture relationships with the Central Asian states through increased bilateral foreign assistance (announced by President George W. Bush in Monterrey, Mexico, in March 2002) and through the international financial institutions (IFIs), in which the US is the most influential shareholder. A delegation from Uzbekistan left Washington in late November 2001 with a $100 million aid pledge as well as an additional $50m in US Export-Import Bank credits. In late 2001, the International Monetary Fund (IMF) and the World Bank also promised future assistance to Uzbekistan, which in turn promised to make its currency convertible by 1 July 2002. Visits to Uzbekistan by US Secretary of State Colin Powell in December 2001 and nine US senators in January 2002 produced a new economic cooperation programme involving further US grants and loans. Kyrgyzstan received $93m in poverty-reduction loans from the IMF in December 2001 (probably as an inducement to permit the US to use its airbase in Manas) and another $21m in infrastructure loans and grants from the World Bank in February 2002. Also in February, the IMF and the World Bank met in London to discuss a new initiative, focusing on regional cooperation and including debt reduction, for the CIS.

Greater US and IFI financial involvement in the region could have a catalytic effect on private investment, particularly in oil- and gas-rich Kazakhstan. American investment there could be conditioned on the country's refraining from exporting oil through Iran and opting instead for the new Baku–Ceyhan pipeline that bypasses Russia. While 2001 saw the opening of the Caspian Pipeline Consortium pipeline from the Tengiz field in Kazakhstan to the Russian port of Novorossisk, it also saw Western firms solidifying their commitment to send 'big' Azeri oil through the Baku–Ceyhan pipeline. More broadly, The European Bank for Reconstruction and Development and the Asian Development Bank have made both funding commitments and further promises of aid for projects that will create or expand transport corridors that provide easier and less expensive access to the markets of Europe and Asia. But difficulties in Afghanistan have hampered some of these projects, as have the relative diplomatic isolation of Iran and tensions between India and Pakistan.

The principal challenges of Western engagement in Central Asia are posed by economic dysfunction, corruption (especially that connected to the narcotics trade), illiberal political systems, primitive physical infrastructure and institutional weakness. The Western imperative of eradicating terrorism at its source and Central Asian capitals' shared opposition to radical Islam, however, have given rise to both greater motivation and increased leverage for effecting constructive change. Internationally supported projects that, through conditionality, link strengthening national security to political and economic reform could produce a level of development that dampens the political and religious climate for terrorist recruitment. In turn, economic development could spur much-needed regional cooperation that puts Central Asia on the road to integration into the international system. Whether this salutary sequence will occur may depend on whether Central Asian states perform well in the early stages of IMF, World Bank and bilateral aid programmes inspired by the need to enlist Central Asian states in the counter-terrorism coalition. In any event, the West will probably maintain a considerably higher level of aid to Central Asian states to ensure that the region remains relatively inhospitable to terrorism and other transnational threats, and available to assist possible future Western military operations.

On balance, Asia acquired greater strategic coherence in 2001 and early 2002. Japan's economic woes, China's growing pains and strategic concerns, ASEAN's political and economic disarray and North Korea's continued isolation, of course, will preclude any true concert. But 11 September and China's economic opening have placed a premium on international engagement and regional cooperation in most Asian capitals.

War in Afghanistan

The stage was set for the war against terrorism over the course of the 1990s, as the internal turmoil in Afghanistan permitted Osama bin Laden and his organisation al-Qaeda to establish 28 training camps and headquarters for an international terrorist network of unprecedented scope and sophistication. Though the roots of this terrorist movement extended to the Islamist clerical circles in Saudi Arabia and the anti-Soviet war in Afghanistan, the proximate cause of its rise as a global threat was the sanctuary and support received from the Taliban government in Afghanistan, as well as support from other states and wealthy individuals in the Persian Gulf. From this base of operations in Afghanistan, the preparations for the attacks of 11 September were underway for at least two years before they occurred.

Genesis of the problem

The rise of the Taliban took place in reaction to the aftermath of the Soviet–Afghan war and as a result of Pakistani geopolitical aspirations. When Soviet forces withdrew in early 1989, no arrangements existed for a stable political transition. Resistance commanders and warlords routed most of the forces of the communist regime in a matter of months, leaving only the major cities under Communist control. In late 1991, the disintegration of the Soviet Union severed the lifeline of the Kabul regime, which quickly led to the conquest of the capital by the military forces of the coalition of seven Pakistan-based resistance organisations in early 1992. A weak agreement was reached among these parties on an interim regime, under which executive authority would rotate. During the second rotation, President Burhanuddin Rabbani refused to yield power, while his ministers waged a campaign of assassination and intimidation against competing political groups. Atrocities committed by the regime, particularly against ethnic Pashtuns, further alienated large segments of the population. At the same time, Pakistan's Inter-Services Intelligence agency (ISI), eager to put its favoured Afghan clients into power, unleashed the forces of former

Prime Minister Gulbiddin Hekmatyar on Kabul, ravaging the Afghani capital city with rocket and artillery fire.

With warlords ruling the countryside and warring factions fighting in and around the capital, the Taliban movement, which promised to bring law and order to the country, began to develop momentum from its base around Kandahar. Pakistan's ISI, recognising a geopolitical opportunity, switched its support from Hekmatyar to the Taliban and provided arms, ammunition and transport that enabled the Taliban to sweep north and conquer Kabul by 1996. Even though the remnants of the Rabbani government continued to receive support from Russia and later Iran, the Taliban pressed forward in the west and north, vanquishing warlords and dealing repeated defeats to Rabbani's forces. By 1999, the area under control of what would eventually be called the Northern Alliance was reduced to the Panjsher Valley, a few north-eastern provinces and isolated pockets on the northern approaches to the Hindu Kush. Led by Ahmad Shah Massoud, the military forces of the Northern Alliance had proven ineffective. In light of the brutal record of Rabbani's rule, the movement's political leaders had only a very narrow base of support among the Tajik population. When the last significant towns controlled by the Northern Alliance fell in the late 1990s, many observers concluded that the Taliban had succeeded in securing rule over the country.

The rise of bin Laden and his al-Qaeda organisation was deeply connected with the radicalisation of Afghanistan. In the early 1980s, bin Laden began visiting Pakistan to deliver funds raised in Saudi Arabia to support fundamentalist groups in the Afghan resistance. By 1986, he had moved to Peshawar to operate a programme to train and deploy Arab 'volunteers' who wished to fight in the anti-Soviet jihad. During this period, he made connections with radical Islamists from around the world and forged close ties with his future lieutenants from Islamic Jihad in Egypt. In 1989, he formed al-Qaeda as a vehicle to maintain contacts and coordinate actions among the radical Islamists who had fought in Afghanistan and then returned to their native countries. At the same time, bin Laden had trained sufficient numbers of fighters to deploy units in eastern Paktia province, though they fared poorly in combat against the Soviets. From 1989 to 1996, bin Laden relocated his operations to Sudan and started to launch terrorist attacks around the world. When Sudan forced him to leave in 1996, he returned to Afghanistan, where the ISI introduced him to Mullah Omar, the leader of the Taliban. The two men forged a strong alliance between the two movements. In ensuing years, al-Qaeda provided trained fighters to battle against the Northern Alliance, while the Taliban gave al-Qaeda sanctuary to train terrorists and plan operations.

From this base, al-Qaeda escalated its terrorist operations. During the Clinton administration, the United States initiated covert action and, in retaliation for the August 1998 bombing of US embassies in Nairobi, Kenya and Dar-es-Salaam, Tanzania, carried out cruise missile strikes against al-Qaeda. None of these operations substantially undercut al-Qaeda's effectiveness. By 2001, when the Bush administration took office, al-Qaeda had dozens of training camps in Afghanistan, which accepted recruits from Islamic religious schools (*madrassas*) and radical groups worldwide. At several facilities, it had programmes to research and develop weapons of mass destruction (WMD). Moreover, al-Qaeda had established cells in about 50 countries. Until 11 September, however, US policy dictated only the diplomatic and economic isolation of the Taliban and a constant state of alert with respect to the al-Qaeda threat.

Afghanistan becomes a target

The attacks on 11 September utilised cells and operatives in the Middle East, Europe and the United States. Senior US officials immediately suspected that al-Qaeda was behind the attacks. Within hours, intercepted communications of al-Qaeda operatives confirmed the suspicion, and further intelligence proving the connection was collected from around the world. 'Smoking gun' evidence of bin Laden's complicity in the 11 September attacks emerged when US forces operating in Jalalabad in December 2001 found a videotape dated 9 November depicting bin Laden conversing with a visitor. Bin Laden's statements made it clear that he had advance knowledge of the attacks and knew operational details about them, and he boasted of their success.

In a speech to a joint session of Congress on September 20, President George W. Bush announced that the United States would wage war against those who had struck on 11 September. In an important policy expansion, Bush chose to pursue counter-terrorism not only by law enforcement and intelligence measures but also through a muscular military response. He also declared that he would draw no distinction between terrorists and the states that harboured and supported them. States that continued to support terrorist groups with 'a global reach' would be considered to be 'hostile regimes'. He further explained that this was a new kind of war, requiring the coordinated use of economic, political, intelligence and military instruments of power. Moreover, he warned that it would be a long, protracted and costly conflict.

In September, the Bush administration debated the proper scope for the first phase of the war and the appropriate strategy in Afghanistan. One faction, centred principally in the Defense Department, argued for early action not only in Afghanistan but also against other targets, such as Iraq. It also argued that regime change – toppling the governments of state sponsors of terrorism – was the prerequisite of success. The other faction, in the State Department, contended that the United States should narrowly focus on Afghanistan and equivocated about the need for regime change. Bush opted to maintain a narrow focus on Afghanistan in the first phase of the conflict. Though he had given the Taliban the option of escaping attack by turning over bin Laden and other al-Qaeda leaders, Mullah Omar and the Taliban quickly rejected the offer. As a result, regime change became a central US military objective. With this goal established, US policymakers faced the interrelated and complex political challenges of marshalling international support and navigating Afghanistan's fractured internal politics.

International coalition-building

The horrific nature of the attacks of 11 September enabled the United States to mobilise widespread international support. On 12 September, the UN Security Council approved Resolution 1368, effectively authorising the use of force in response to the events of 11 September. All major powers, including China, denounced the attacks. NATO invoked Article 5 provisions, defining the attacks on the United States as an attack on all members of the alliance. However, US policymakers were intent on building a US-directed 'coalition of the willing', not one involving collective decision-making. The United States would request specific support, consult with coalition members, but reserve decision-making for itself. While NATO acceded to US requests for deployment of AWACS aircraft and other support, only Britain became an immediate close collaborator in Afghanistan. Japan agreed to provide intelligence and logistical support, within its constitutional constraints. Singapore became of key importance in facilitating air-to-air refuelling and providing port facilities to US carriers. Russia provided a significant and unusual quantity of military information.

Coalition-building in the region was operationally more essential than elsewhere, but proved more difficult. Afghanistan, a landlocked, remote and mountainous country, is situated far from US bases and facilities. Even the impressive power-projection capabilities of the US armed forces would be severely tested in this conflict. At the outset of the conflict, the United States had no access to bases or facilities in any of Afghanistan's neighbours. Basing operations in the Persian Gulf was problematic because a US presence threatened to touch on political sensitivities. Bin Laden and the Taliban enjoyed political support among a substantial minority of the population and political élites of certain countries – in particular, US allies Egypt and Saudi Arabia. Saudi Arabia notably declined to authorise the operation of combat aircraft from its air bases. Iran had been anti-US since the 1979 Islamic revolution and subsequent hostage crisis. Although Iran had almost gone to war with the Taliban regime after it had killed ten Iranian diplomats and one Iranian journalist in 1998, Iran refused to grant access to its air space for coalition aircraft, despite diplomatic appeals by Britain.

Washington had better luck with the Central and South Asian states. The US consulted Russia before approaching the states of Central Asia to request base access and overflight rights, and President Vladimir Putin acquiesced to the request. Uzbekistan is not a member of the Commonwealth of Independent States (CIS) Collective Security Treaty (CCST), and therefore did not require CIS approval to grant the US access and overflight rights. It quickly allowed both, albeit with tacit support from Moscow. Kyrgyzstan and Tajikistan, being members of the CCST, had to gain CIS agreement as well as Russian acquiescence. Both states offered the right to transit their airspace. Turkey, unsurprisingly, provided access to air bases for coalition aircraft and other support. The United States also vitally required overflight rights and other forms of cooperation from Pakistan. Within days of 11 September, the United States approached the military government of President Pervez Musharraf with a set of non-negotiable requests, including the right to transit an air corridor to Afghanistan and permission to position search-and-rescue units at Pakistani bases. A difficult internal debate took place in Musharraf's inner council, with leaders of the ISI opposing any support for the US attack on its Taliban clients. However, Musharraf ultimately decided to side with Washington. In response, the United States suspended sanctions imposed after Pakistan's nuclear tests in 1998, restructured bilateral debt and facilitated the release of International Monetary Fund loans. Sanctions against India were simultaneously slackened.

Afghani politics

With coalition support in place, the United States still needed to establish a realistic plan for a transitional government in Afghanistan. This entailed navigating internal Afghani politics. First, it had to establish partnerships and working relationships with anti-Taliban Afghan forces in order to win the war. Second, it had to pave the way for a post-Taliban successor regime that would establish stability and ensure that terrorist organisations could not re-establish themselves in the country after the war. In limited covert operations targeting bin Laden and al-Qaeda before 11 September, the Central Intelligence Agency (CIA) had been providing limited funding to the Northern Alliance and had established connections with certain tribal leaders in southern Afghanistan, including Hamid Karzai, who had friendly relations with Northern Alliance leaders. In navigating internal Afghan politics, US policymakers had two groups with which it felt it could work: the Northern Alliance and the Rome group.

The Northern Alliance, composed of the remnants of the Rabbani government, was the only opposition group with forces in the field. Narrowly based on segments of the Uzbek and Tajik ethnic groups and the mainly Shi'ite Hazara, which together account for about 30% of Afghanistan's population, its military leader was the charismatic Ahmad Shah Massoud. He was killed by two al-Qaeda suicide-bombers posing as Arab journalists on

9 September 2001 in what is widely regarded as the operational prelude to the 11 September attacks. After Massoud's death, the Northern Alliance's top political leaders were two Islamist figures from the anti-Soviet resistance, Rabbani and Abdul Rasul Sayyaf, and one former Uzbek Communist general, Rashid Dostum. Mullah Muhammad Qassam Fahim, who had served as the intelligence chief in Rabbani's government and who had been involved in widespread violence against opposition political groups in the 1990s, assumed command. Estimates indicated that the Northern Alliance had between 10,000 and 15,000 fighters and controlled 5–15% of the country's territory. The alliance's financial and logistical support came largely from Russia and Iran, though additional funds were raised through drug trafficking.

The Rome group was organised around the former king of Afghanistan, Mohammed Zahir Shah, an ethnic Pashtun who resides in Rome. It was composed of royalist elements, pro-Western and moderate elements of the anti-Soviet resistance, technocrats from the pre-Communist government of Afghanistan and leaders of the country's tribal and clan structures. Its social base extended throughout the country but was particularly strong in the Pashtun regions in the south and east. Even before 11 September, their goal was to convene a 'grand national council', or *loya jirga*, that would include representatives of all ethnic and social groups in Afghanistan and would create a provisional government, with the former king as the unifying symbol. In their view, this would enable them to mobilise political and military opposition to the Taliban and facilitate defections among commanders aligned with the Taliban out of expedience rather than ideological conviction. Ultimately, such a strategy would topple the Taliban regime. Much of the political work, particularly establishing contacts with traditional leaders and commanders, had been done over course of several years. From an operational point of view, the major shortcoming of the Rome group was its lack of troops in the field. It had not succeeded in recruiting the support of any major regional power for its programme. Pakistan, in light of its strong support of the Taliban, refused to allow the Rome group to operate in its territory. Despite Congressional support for the Rome process, the Bush administration harboured serious doubts about its capacity to win hearts and minds in Afghanistan.

After 11 September, US officials quickly contacted both the Northern Alliance and the Rome group, but soon chose the Northern Alliance as its principal partner. At first, there was some momentum in favour of fashioning a coalition between the two groups. The Northern Alliance sent commanders to meet with the former king and the Rome group, which was enthusiastic about creating a common front. US officials only half-heartedly pressed for a coalition, while more seriously pursuing military cooperation with the Northern Alliance, including provision of materiel and financial support and the building of an airstrip in Golbahar. In light of this support, as well as even more substantial help from Russia, the leaders of the Northern Alliance opted against a coalition arrangement with the Rome group. The CIA did, however, seek to complement US support for the Northern Alliance by approaching individual commanders aligned with the Rome group, particularly in the Pashtun areas in the south and east. The aim was to preserve the possibility of working with individual Afghan commanders in the combat phase and fashioning a political solution involving the former king after the defeat of the Taliban.

The military campaign

During September and early October, the United States moved forces into the region and secured base access and overflight rights. The first deployments involved naval and air forces. Two aircraft carrier battle groups, the *Carl Vinson* and the *Enterprise*, were already in the Indian Ocean. Two more, the *Theodore Roosevelt* and the *Kitty Hawk*, were soon deployed from ports in Virginia and Japan, respectively. The first three carriers had about 55 strike aircraft and were accompanied by an array of naval combatants, some armed with *Tomahawk* land-attack cruise missiles. The *Kitty Hawk* was reconfigured to carry over 1,000 special-operations soldiers, including elements of the Army 160th Special Operations Aviation Regiment (SOAR), Sea-Air-Land (SEAL) teams, Air Force Special Operations forces, Army Special Forces and other commandos. A dozen special-operations MH-60 *Black Hawks*, a half-dozen MH-47 *Chinook* medium-lift helicopters, and a few MH-53 *Pave Low* helicopters were also on board. A complement of B-52 and B-1 bombers were deployed to the island of Diego Garcia, a British territory. A wide assortment of aerial refuelling, reconnaissance, airborne warning and control system (AWACS)-equipped planes, and other support aircraft flowed into the region as well. Finally, 1,000 troops from the 10th Mountain Division were sent to an airbase in Uzbekistan. US Marines and elements of the 101st Airborne Division would be deployed later in the campaign.

At the same time, the US armed services struggled with how to apply the traditional American approach to war – fielding massively superior forces to overwhelm the enemy – to the forbidding circumstances in this new conflict. There were few valuable targets for US air power, largely because much of the country lay in ruins from 20 years of war and because Taliban forces lacked modern military equipment. The terrorist training camps were evacuated, leaving only empty mud and cement structures. Al-Qaeda terrorists and Taliban fighters, except along the fronts with the Northern Alliance, were dispersed and difficult to distinguish from local populations. Moreover, US planners were wary of a massive deployment of ground forces, both because of the lessons of the Soviet war and because of the imperative to move into other theatres beyond Afghanistan. The strategy that emerged involved air strikes against available targets, building alliances with anti-Taliban Afghani forces, deploying special operations units to improve the capabilities of opposition forces, and creating a highly networked system of manned and unmanned sensors and strike aircraft to execute precision strikes on Taliban military formations.

On 7 October, the United States initiated combat operations against the Taliban and al-Qaeda in Afghanistan. As *Operation Enduring Freedom* (originally, *Operation Infinite Justice,* but changed in response to mainly Muslim complaints that only Allah could dispense such justice) unfolded, US policymakers and military and intelligence operators worked towards six principal objectives: destroying Taliban and al-Qaeda leadership and military capabilities; enhancing the capabilities and supporting the military advances of the Northern Alliance; mobilising opposition to the Taliban in the Pashtun-dominated southern and eastern regions and supporting its military advances; preparing a post-Taliban political settlement among anti-Taliban factions; managing the interests of coalition partners; and providing limited humanitarian relief supplies to Afghan civilians. Often, efforts to achieve some of these objectives were inhibited efforts to achieve others.

The air phase

Operation Enduring Freedom opened with a conventional set of air strikes, designed largely to establish air superiority against an enemy that lacked an air force or integrated air defence. On the first night, strikes were launched by B-1 and B-52 bombers based on Diego Garcia, B-2 bombers based in Missouri, F-14 and F/A-18 strike aircraft based on carriers in the Arabian Sea, as well as with *Tomahawk* land-attack cruise missiles launched from US surface ships and US and British submarines. Concentrated largely around Kabul, Kandahar, Jalalabad and Mazar-e Sharif, the targets included anti-aircraft systems, military headquarters, terrorist camps, military airfields and concentrations of armour and other military equipment, as well as the presidential palace and the national radio and television building. On 7 October, US and British warplanes struck 31 targets. Of these, 17 were Taliban air defences, which were rendered largely ineffective. The next day, 13 targets were struck, disabling all but one of the Taliban's air bases, blinding air defences and pounding a pocket of ground troops and several suspected terrorist training camps. The Garmabak Ghar training camp was destroyed and Shindand Air Base, a remote outpost in west-central Afghanistan that was the second-largest air base used by the Soviets during their 1979–89 war, was damaged. A half-dozen aircraft at Shindand were also struck. No allied planes were engaged in air-to-air combat. At the same time, C-17 transport aircraft operating from Germany dropped 37,000 ration packets to Afghan civilians. C-130 aircraft broadcast radio messages to the Afghan people, while other aircraft dropped propaganda leaflets. Tankers and other support aircraft operated from airbases in the region. Even the intense strikes of the first day were relatively small in comparison to a typical day of the operation in Kosovo and a tiny fraction of the strikes during the first night of *Operation Desert Storm*.

The initiation of military operations bolstered the coalition. NATO committed five AWACS aircraft to patrol US skies, thereby allowing US aircraft to be sent to the Central Asian theatre. Although anti-American protests broke out in Pakistan and other predominantly Muslim countries, the crowds were not as large as feared and were easily managed by authorities. Russian President Putin endorsed the military operations and pledged intelligence support, assistance with search-and-rescue operations, and access to air corridors for humanitarian flights. He also promised to provide arms and supplies to the Northern Alliance. Tajikistan offered access to air corridors and to airbases for intelligence purposes. Turkmenistan provided land and air corridors for humanitarian operations. US Secretary of Defense Donald Rumsfeld reported that US and British warplanes had destroyed 80% of the targets in Afghanistan after two days. Subsequently, sorties tapered off. Despite a moderate amount of anti-aircraft fire, which included a few unguided missiles, US aircraft worked through the available list of targets, including early warning radars, garrisons for ground forces, command-and-control systems, al-Qaeda infrastructure and individual military aircraft or other military equipment that could be identified by pilots. Many targets, such as anti-aircraft missile sites, were not functional and therefore had little value. Though several Taliban leaders were reported killed in the early strikes, most targets had been evacuated. More than 90% of the munitions were precision-guided, compared with 10% in the Gulf War. After most of the fixed targets were destroyed, US commanders focused their air power on 'emerging targets'. Using information from manned and unmanned reconnaissance aircraft and other intelligence systems, commanders fused a common picture of the battlespace and relayed target information electronically to pilots enroute to or loitering in the theatre.

Preparing the ground war

Realising that air power alone would not win the war, US commanders immediately focused on preparing for the ground war. Though the possibility of using large-scale US ground forces was not taken off the table, the first approach was to mobilise and enhance the capabilities of anti-Taliban Afghan forces. In October 2001, US and British special forces and US intelligence operatives worked to strengthen and improve the skills of the Northern Alliance. Russia provided overt and covert assistance. CIA operatives sought to create a Pashtun opposition in southern and eastern

Afghanistan. Meanwhile, diplomats attempted to create a coalition among the Afghan opposition groups, as well as an agreement on a post-Taliban political order.

The estimates of the order of battle among the combatants were imprecise. Most observers believed that the Taliban and al-Qaeda fielded 40,000–60,000 fighters. Afghans accounted for 30,000–50,000, while foreign fighters from a dozen countries totalled perhaps 10,000. In many respects, the military formations of the Taliban and al-Qaeda were integrated and indistinguishable. Because Taliban ranks included commanders aligned with Taliban out of necessity or convenience rather than conviction, most observers believed that the 'hard core' Taliban was smaller than the numbers indicated. The Northern Alliance had between 10,000 and 15,000 fighters. Though the Taliban was better equipped, with functioning armoured personnel carriers (APCs) and tanks, combat between the sides had largely been confined to artillery and rocket exchanges and infantry battles. Command and control was executed through radios, satellite phones and couriers. The Northern Alliance, a coalition of warlords and radical Islamic factions, was often unstable. Though neither side remotely resembled an effective modern military force, the Taliban clearly had had the upper hand in recent years. After the first week of the operation, the air war continued at a lesser pace and without a sharp strategic focus. US aircraft struck such targets as barracks, maintenance shops, and ordnance and fuel depots in and around larger cities. The many al-Qaeda training camps in eastern Afghanistan were destroyed. Air strikes were occasionally launched on convoys or moving troops in the field. 'Bunker busting' bombs were dropped on underground command posts and supply depots, sometimes prompting enormous secondary explosions. AC-130 gunships, armed with machine guns and cannons, were deployed against troops and garrisons.

The Afghani ground combatants faced each other across the Shomali Plain north of Kabul, to the south of Mazar-e Sharif, and in the north-eastern provinces. But while air strikes were conducted on infrastructure targets, US commanders largely withheld attacks on the frontline forces of the Taliban, much to the dismay and frustration of Northern Alliance leaders. There were three reasons for this restraint. First, US policymakers sought to advance the internal Afghani political process before initiating decisive military operations. Pakistani President Musharraf, whose support was indispensable to the war effort, strongly opposed any military strategy that might enable the Northern Alliance to seize Kabul, reportedly even threatening to close Pakistan's airspace to make the point. US policymakers understood that taking the side of the Northern Alliance could alienate anti-Taliban Pashtuns who would be needed to fight in the south and east. Yet American diplomats did not use their enormous leverage to energetically press the Northern Alliance and the Rome group to come to an agreement on a provisional government, instead leaving the negotiations to the UN and the parties themselves. The Rome group had proposed a meeting to create a supreme council that would function as an interim arrangement and would convene a *loya jirga* at a later date to create a provisional government. The Northern Alliance leaders repeatedly promised to the United States that its troops would not attack or seize Kabul. But they delayed acting on the political front, claiming logistical difficulties in sending its delegation to meet with the Rome group. Ultimately, they failed to send a delegation empowered to participate in this process. Though they had not pressured the Northern Alliance to come forward, US policymakers concluded that the fractious Afghans could not come together politically and decided to deal with the problem of post-Taliban Afghanistan after major ground operations were underway.

Second, the United States and Britain needed time to insert special operations forces to assist Northern Alliance units and to mobilise opposition to the Taliban in the south and east. At the outset of the war, reports indicated that US and British special operations forces had already gone into Afghanistan, apparently to conduct reconnaissance and to establish ties with Northern Alliance commanders. These forces were operating from the aircraft carrier *Kitty Hawk*, Khanabad air base in Uzbekistan and the Jacobobad and Pasni bases in Pakistan. Their mission was described as facilitating better coordination among anti-Taliban forces and between Afghan and coalition forces. They were also to improve identification of targets and to plan offensive operations. In addition to infiltrating forces, two or three weeks were needed to complete the airstrip in the Panjsher Valley at Golbahar.

The CIA, which was in charge of US efforts in Pashtun areas, chose to recruit individual commanders and warlords rather than to use the Rome group as a movement to mobilise opposition. CIA officials believed that money and promises of power in post-Taliban Afghanistan could be used to peel away Taliban commanders and governors. The danger of this approach was that Pashtuns would lack a positive political idea, apart from avarice, to motivate the emergence of widespread resistance. Moreover, the CIA proved to have scant knowledge of Pashtun areas, few contacts among key tribal networks and little talent for building up military capacity quickly. The agency did manage to enlist the help of Abdul Haq, a highly respected exiled Pashtun leader. But Haq was also wary of US support, having been received with indifference in Washington in pre-11 September attempts to interest the US government in backing a grassroots rebellion. Declining a CIA offer of money and a satellite telephone, on 22 October, Haq ventured into Afghanistan with a small group of lightly armed supporters to rally Pashtun resistance to the Taliban. On 26 October, however, Haq was captured by the Taliban and publicly hanged. This unfortunate episode demonstrated the volatility of Afghani tribal politics.

Hamid Karzai then became the CIA's favoured client. He began meeting with tribal leaders, but he had little success in mustering followers. CIA operatives also recruited Gul Agha Shirzai, a warlord who had ruled Kandahar before the Taliban. A meeting of tribal leaders and *mujahideen* commanders in Peshawar, organised by Sayed Ahmed Gailani, enabled the CIA to expand its contacts. Cooperating with Pakistan, which placed limits on what political and military activities could take place on its territory, was problematic, particularly in light of suspicions that the ISI had not ceased its support for the Taliban despite Musharraf's replacement of the chief of the intelligence agency. As a result, little if anything was achieved in the south during October.

Third, time was needed for Russia to build up the Northern Alliance. According to press reports, the United States and Russia came to an understanding in mid-October about how Moscow could support the war effort overtly and covertly. Russia openly promised to provide additional arms, equipment and supplies to the Northern Alliance, which had been Moscow's client since the mid-1990s. Vast amounts of support – including T-55 and T-62 tanks, APCs, multiple rocket-launchers, rocket-propelled grenade-launchers (RPGs), assault weapons, ammunition and communications equipment – was delivered covertly through Uzbekistan by ferry across the Amu Darya River and through Tajikistan across the Pyandzh River. In addition, Russia reportedly equipped Uzbek and Tajik special forces, who were inserted into the ranks of the Northern Alliance, and Russians were in command of the tank forces and helicopter gunships that broke down Taliban front lines.

Together, these three constraints produced a lull in the war effort during most of October. Only two significant ground operations were carried out: a special operations assault on a compound frequented by Mullah Omar and an airborne raid by 100 US Rangers on the airport near Kandahar. By mid-October, a review of policy conducted by the US National Security Council recommended an acceleration of the war effort to overthrow the Taliban. According to press reports, the State Department urged caution, while the Defense Department pressed to have a free hand to pursue a military solution. Because of the restraints imposed on US air strikes, Afghans joked that Taliban fighters went to the front lines to escape bombing. On 16 October, Rumsfeld warned, 'I suspect that in the period ahead, that's not going to be a very safe place to be'. The confusion about how to coordinate political developments and military action unnecessarily hindered the early stages of the military campaign. In retrospect, there was never a strong prospect that a southern Pashtun group would coalesce in time to balance the Northern Alliance, which was therefore always likely to bring its credentials as the principal ground force to bear on the political process. In the event, the US came around to this point of view. The Northern Alliance did impose its will on the interim political settlement, though the US and others were able to impose sufficient restraints on Northern Alliance power to achieve a realistic compromise.

Northern Alliance breakthrough

Just as doubts were mounting about the war effort, the tide of battle began to turn. The new policy was to concentrate first on capturing Mazar-e Sharif. Capturing the city would split the Taliban forces on Afghanistan's northern tier. More importantly, it would secure a route for military supplies and humanitarian aid from Uzbekistan via Friendship Bridge into Afghanistan. Then, the United States would focus on cutting off supply lines to all of the Taliban's positions in the north. If successful, the war effort would shift to the Shomali Plains north of Kabul. Dozens of US special forces on the ground would coordinate heavy bombing on Taliban front lines with advances by Northern Alliance ground forces. Progress in the north, it was hoped, would motivate Pashtun tribes in the south and east to take up arms, lest they be left behind.

The political implications of this military strategy raised sensitivities on all sides. Musharraf repeatedly asked for assurances that the Northern Alliance would not be allowed to seize Kabul. Secretary of State Powell provided such assurances, both privately and publicly. At the same time, when their initial hopes that bombing would topple the Taliban faded, Northern Alliance leaders began to fear that the United States would be overly solicitous of Pakistan, cutting them out in the process. Rabbani and his subordinates struggled to win greater recognition from the United States, partly by repeatedly promising not to capture Kabul unilaterally. Senior political and military leaders of the Northern Alliance expressed great frustration over the limited bombing of the Taliban front lines, the limited logistical support of some units and the statements to Pakistan's leaders. Even when US strikes against frontline positions marginally intensified in mid-October, Northern Alliance leaders complained that the bombing was inadequate to enable them to launch a successful offensive.

All of this changed at the end of October and in the first days of November. Heavy bombing ravaged the Taliban front lines outside of Mazar-e Sharif, Kunduz, Taloqan, at the border with Tajikistan, and north of Kabul. Air strikes conducted by B-1 and B-52 bombers more than doubled the pace of bombing, with the number of strike sorties rising from 68 to 100-120 by 7 November. Most of the strikes targeted Taliban forces opposite the Northern Alliance positions at Mazar-e Sharif, near Taloqan, and north of Kabul, and Kandahar and Tarin Kot in the south. F-15E strike aircraft operating from an undisclosed base in the Middle East entered the war. For the first time, anti-personnel cluster bombs and 15,000-pound fuel-air bombs – known as 'daisy cutters' – were employed. Very quickly, 80% of air strikes were focused on the Taliban front lines. While the bombing escalated, its increased effectiveness was attributable to US Special Forces personnel operating as forward air controllers, relaying target information, and using lasers to identify targets precisely. The mood of Northern Alliance leaders, as well as their commanders, became dramatically more upbeat. By 5 November, fierce fighting between Northern Alliance and Taliban forces had begun.

During this period, a debate within the coalition was underway over whether there should be a pause in the bombing. Although regular airdrops of tens of thousands of relief packages had continued, critics noted that some munitions accidentally fell on or near civilian areas, causing fatalities and injuries. Musharraf argued that bombing should be suspended in recognition of the Muslim holy month of Ramadan, which began in late November, lest the campaign be seen as 'a war against the poor, miserable and innocent people of Afghanistan'. Civilian deaths also fuelled some anti-American sentiment in the Muslim world. Aid providers also argued that a pause would permit humanitarian aid to be distributed to an estimated six million people in need of food and other assistance and ease refugee pressure on surround states. But General Tommy Franks, commander-in-chief of US Central Command, argued that advancing unfettered to Mazar-e Sharif would hasten the end of the war and facilitate the delivery of humanitarian aid through Uzbekistan. The fact that much of the aid being delivered in-country was being commandeered by the Taliban reinforced this position. King Abdullah II of Jordan, purporting to speak for the 'too rarely heard Arab majority', said that bombing should proceed despite Ramadan, while others observed that the holy month had not inhibited Arabs from attacking Israel in 1973. European leaders stressed the need for humanitarian relief and voiced anxiety about civilian casualties, but did not seriously challenge the American case for bombing. By the second week in November, events appeared to vindicate that case. A 'tipping point' was reached in the war. Northern Alliance forces, emboldened by the intensified US bombing campaign, seized a number of key Taliban-controlled cities.

At Mazar-e Sharif, the US strategy worked in textbook fashion. Taliban forces outnumbered those of the Northern Alliance by two to one. In late October, Alliance forces under General Rashid Dostum were 80 kilometres south of the city, while other units were far to the east. Using a satellite phone, Dostum had been coordinating air strikes himself. When he was joined by at least a half-dozen Special Forces personnel, the effectiveness of the strikes dramatically increased. Air drops of supplies also improved. By 6 November, Dostum's forces were on the move, leading cavalry charges on horseback in the wake of concentrated bombing by B-52s. Although one offensive was briefly repulsed, Taliban forces lost the city on 9 November, after four days of combined air-land operations. While Northern Alliance forces had made previous advances near Herat and other northern cities, the fall of Mazar-e Sharif produced a domino effect. The United States sought to triple or quadruple the numbers of US special-operations forces with the Northern Alliance to as many as 100 in total. US heavy bombing pounded other Taliban-controlled cities in the north and on the Shomali Plains north of Kabul. This cleared the way for Northern Alliance fighters to capture Samangan, Bamian, Taloqan, Baghlan and Pul-e Khumri on 11 November. Herat and Shindand fell on 12 November. Northern Alliance forces were sweeping Taliban forces out of northern Afghanistan, winning control over the major east-west and north-south highways and preparing the way to turn south to Kabul. Besides isolated pockets of resistance, only Kunduz remained in Taliban hands. Unfortunately, credible reports of summary executions and atrocities emerged after nearly every advance of the Northern Alliance. By 15 November, humanitarian aid was slowly beginning to flow from Uzbekistan into Afghanistan.

The assault on the capital was less straightforward. On 21 October, warplanes had begun bombing the Taliban troops north of Kabul, who there outnumbered the fighters of the Northern Alliance by two to one. By late October, US heavy bombers were focusing on the Taliban fighters who held the trenches in the path of the Northern Alliance. By 8–9 November, the United States had executed the heaviest strikes of the war on those targets. The next day, it was apparent that Taliban forces had been broken or had abandoned their positions. The best assault troops of the Northern Alliance were poised to move. Surprisingly, Taliban forces also fled from Kabul itself. On 10 November, President Bush stated at the United Nations, 'We will encourage our friends to head south, across the Shomali Plains, but not into the city of Kabul itself'. Northern Alliance leaders promised not to enter the city. On 12 November, however, more than 2,000 troops swept into the capital, with these fighters merely relabelled as 'police' and the main force of the Northern Alliance moving into garrisons in and around the city.

Endgame

It took considerably longer to generate comparable progress in the south and east. At the same time, US forces were developing new skills and incorporating more coalition members in operations. Afghanistan was becoming a testing ground for the concept of 'network-centric warfare' – the linking of sensors to create an integrated picture of the theatre and to relay in real time targeting information to strike systems. The sensors included the joint surveillance target attack radar system (JSTARS) and unmanned aerial vehicles such at the *Global Hawk* and the *Predator* that could patrol over targets areas for hours. As bombing intensified in the north, air strikes were carried out against tunnel and cave complexes and against emerging targets – including Mullah Omar's land cruiser – in the south and east. The military capability of the US-led coalition also continued to build. The United States positioned two Marine Expeditionary Units off the coast of Pakistan. The UK deployed one aircraft carrier and one large amphibious helicopter ship to the Arabian Sea and committed more than 4,200 soldiers to the war effort. France also deployed one aircraft carrier and accompanying naval task group, as did Italy later. Germany, France and Italy also made several thousand specialised troops available. Canada, Australia and New Zealand made contributions as well. Kyrgyzstan and Tajikistan gave the coalition access to airbases, thereby enhancing logistic capabilities and enabling the number of land-based strike aircraft involved in the war to increase. Azerbaijan and Armenia granted access to their air space to coalition aircraft. While welcoming offers of broader coalition participation, US commanders kept complete control over operations and carefully selected those offers that were in fact accepted.

The best efforts of the CIA had failed to generate significant Pashtun opposition to or defections from the Taliban. In early October, Karzai had been meeting with tribal leaders in Pakistan. Later in the month, he entered Afghanistan, travelling to Uruzgan province northwest of Kandahar. Yet, he made no progress in any of his meetings. This was partly because he did not have a great stature in the tribal structures of the south and partly because he was asking Pashtuns to attack Pashtuns. It did not help that US bombing in the north was designed to assist a group of leaders who had committed atrocities against Pashtuns in the early and mid-1990s. While Gul Agha Shirzai was sitting in Pakistan, waiting for the United States to further weaken the Taliban, CIA operatives were unsuccessfully trying to buy influence among other tribal leaders and commanders. In early November, the United States sent aircraft to strike Taliban forces zeroing in on Karzai and days later had to send helicopters to extract him before the Taliban could capture him. As weeks passed with no progress, it seemed that the United States had badly miscalculated by trying to recruit individual Pashtun commanders rather than working through the Rome group – and thereby tapping the enormous political appeal of the former king – to mobilise the Pashtun resistance.

After the Taliban abandoned Kabul and days later Jalalabad, the collapse of the regime finally cascaded into predominantly Pashtun areas. Provinces in the west fell based on internal defections. Senior military figures in the Rome group, with minimal coalition support, proceeded to engineer the defection of scores of Taliban commanders in the eastern provinces from Kunar to Kandahar. By late November, Taliban forces had been routed in 27 out of 30 provinces. US special-operations personnel were conducting independent reconnaissance operations and raids, which had succeeded in capturing some al-Qaeda and Taliban leaders. From his redoubt in Kandahar, Mullah Omar issued increasingly desperate calls for his troops to fight. He also declared that while his regime might fall, the Pashtun people 'would do what they have always done and carry on the war from the hills'. Karzai managed to raise several thousand fighters and to approach Kandahar from the north, and Gul Agha Shirzai brought several thousand more from the southeast. Indigenous Taliban forces were melting away into the population, but Arab fighters offered stiff resistance.

In mid-November, the forces of the Northern Alliance had surrounded Kunduz. The city was strategically important, as it straddled the only route apart from the Friendship Bridge from the north into Kabul. It was also the site of the first major training centre for al-Qaeda terrorists – particularly Chechens. There 20,000 Taliban – including several thousand foreign fighters – mounted a final stand. Intermittent talks, mostly with the Afghan Taliban, failed to reach a surrender agreement. US warplanes commenced heavy bombing of the city. On 22 November, Northern Alliance units launched an assault and captured the city two days later. Amid reports of executions and atrocities, Dostum shipped captives to a fortress prison in Mazar-e Sharif, where days later a rebellion broke out in which the US suffered its first combat fatality, a CIA officer interrogating prisoners. The Northern Alliance, assisted by US air strikes, retook the prison, though more than 600 captives reportedly died in the assault.

The fall of Kandahar developed slowly. As chaos and disorder spread in the south and east, Omar stood firm. In mid-November – even as US air strikes pounded Taliban positions, including leadership compounds inside the city – he rejected an offer by two local Pashtun leaders to mediate surrender. Beginning on 26 November, more than 1,000 US Marines established a makeshift airbase, designated Camp Rhino, about 19km south-east of Kandahar on a landing strip built and used by bin Laden. US forces quickly brought in troop transport helicopters, attack helicopters, jump jets and APCs to enhance their capability control routes out of Kandahar and to engage in further raids in the area. A small number of British, German and Australian special-operations troops soon joined the Americans. In early December, US forces escalated the bombing, particularly with B-52s. This had a devastating effect, though one air strike killed three US troops and injured Karzai himself. By 3 December, opposition forces were within 16km of the city. Karzai, as well as other tribal leaders, engaged in an intricate set of negotiations that led to an ambiguous surrender agreement, which left the fate of Omar and foreign fighters unclear. When the Taliban fighters finally laid down their arms on 7 December, Omar and many other Taliban leaders and foreign fighters escaped from the city, though some were subsequently captured by US forces.

Combat efforts then shifted to the White Mountains of south-east Afghanistan near Tora Bora and Khost, where about 1,200 Arab fighters were reportedly hiding in immense warrens of caves and tunnels. US aerial surveillance, expanding networks of informants (some reliable, some deliberately not so) and special-forces raids and reconnaissance dramatically enhanced the available intelligence. American commanders believed that bin Laden himself might be in the area. Special Forces personnel established relationships with local military leaders of the Eastern Shura, who ruled Jalalabad, and mobilised a 1,500-man posse to attack Tora Bora. Heavy bombing with B-52s, as well as fuel-air bombs, cleared the way for the Afghan fighters as they moved from ridge to ridge. Hundreds of Taliban and al-Qaeda fighters were killed or captured, while hundreds more fled, some – reportedly including former Taliban leader Mullah Omar – under the protection of local Pashtun commanders. By early January, seven of the eight most promising cave complexes in Tora Bora had been cleared, and the main focus of the campaign was said to be the area around Khost, a few kilometres from the border with Pakistan in eastern Afghanistan.

The US detained about 525 Taliban and al-Qaeda fighters, sending 300 of them to the US base at Guantanamo Bay in Cuba for interrogation. Unfortunately, however, US commanders had established only porous blocking forces to the east and west, and virtually no blocking force to the south, where Pakistani forces arrived too late to make a difference. As the Afghan fighters advanced, the Arabs withdrew higher and higher into the mountains. For several days, US officers were hopeful that bin Laden and the Arabs were encircled. The Arabs then enticed the Afghans into days of fruitless surrender negotiations. During this critical period, many of the Arabs succeeded in bribing or sneaking their way out of Tora Bora. Subsequent press reports suggested that others, including bin Laden, crossed over the White Mountains on one of the many footpaths into Pakistan, near the town of Parachinar.

Most US and allied commanders believed that the assault on the Tora Bora caves marked the end of the conflict. Some of the fighters who had been allowed to escape from Tora Bora, however, proved more resilient than those commanders had hoped. By early March 2002, largely Arab al-Qaeda and Taliban forces, numbering as many as 1,000 men – later reinforced by up to 500 more – had re-assembled in the Shah-e Kot mountains, about 32km south of Gardez in north-eastern Afghanistan. The US led combat engagement, Operation *Anaconda*, began on 2 March. The al-Qaeda and Taliban forces put up fierce resistance with heavy mortar, RPG and machine-gun fire, leading American and Afghani commanders to speculate that they were protecting bin Laden or his deputy Ayman al-Zawahiri. US bombers and AC-130 gunships and French attack jets pounded the bunkers and caves in which the al-Qaeda and Taliban fighters had taken refuge. But due to the rugged terrain, the dug-in positions of the enemy and snowy conditions that made accurate low-level bombing difficult, American commanders deemed it necessary to deploy around 1,200 US ground troops, including Special Forces and elements of the 101st Airborne Division and the 10th Mountain Division, supported by AH-64 *Apache* and AH-1 *Super Cobra* attack helicopters. About 200 Australian, Canadian, Danish, French, German, New Zealand and Norwegian soldiers also participated.

The number of US forces, allied foreign troops and anti-Taliban Afghani fighters involved in the battle easily exceeded 2,000. In eight days of frequently heavy ground fighting in cold weather, at altitudes of between 2,400–3,300 metres, US-led forces killed between 400 and 800 enemy fighters. Eight American soldiers were killed, and at least 40 wounded. Several local Afghani fighters also died. By 10 March, the al-Qaeda and Taliban forces had been subdued (though not defeated) and 400 US troops were withdrawn, though bin Laden had not been found. As of late March 2002, up to 1,000 al-Qaeda and Taliban fighters were reportedly hiding in Pakistan under the protection of Pashtun tribal leaders. As of March 2002, US forces in-country numbered 5,300, with an additional 60,000 in the region for support. Their mission remained focused on finding bin Laden and neutralising al-Qaeda, and none were deployed for peacekeeping. In March 2002, the UK government designated 1,700 Royal Marines for deployment in Afghanistan in early April for a 90-day mission to assist the American-led effort.

Political contest for power in Kabul

When the Northern Alliance seized Kabul, the leadership of Pakistan became deeply concerned. US policymakers, surprised by the speed of the Taliban collapse, now reportedly exerted intense pressure on Rabbani and the Northern Alliance not to exploit their advantage by creating a new government. Despite these and other efforts, the United States did not succeed in fully levelling the political playing field.

After six years in the wilderness, the leaders of the Northern Alliance, backed by Iran and Russia, aggressively pressed their advantage by way of a three-part strategy. First, they set about creating a political–military *fait accompli*. Northern Alliance leaders immediately seized all of the ministry buildings and proceeded to appoint officials at the senior levels. General Muhammad Fahim became the defence minister, while Yunis Qanconi and Abdullah Abdullah became the interior and foreign ministers, respectively. On 17 November, Rabbani re-asserted his status of head of state, moving into the Arg Palace. Russia and Iran established official presences, and Moscow introduced military advisers under the guise of a humanitarian relief agency. Second, Rabbani and the Northern Alliance sought to derail UN-sponsored meetings to form a broad-based interim administration. At first, they refused to participate at all, offering instead to invite other political groups for discussions in Kabul and hoping to conduct talks under the shadow of Northern Alliance military dominance. Third, Northern Alliance leaders sought to prevent the introduction of international peacekeepers that would dilute their monopoly on the use of force. Mid-November 2001, when Britain sought to introduce 100 troops at Bagram airport as the leading edge of a force of several thousand, Northern Alliance officials forcibly rebuffed the attempt. For several weeks, the US-led coalition was in disarray on this issue, largely because of US reluctance to appear to be involved in nation-building.

Rabbani and the Northern Alliance eventually agreed, albeit reluctantly, to send a delegation to a UN-sponsored meeting in Bonn to negotiate the future of Afghanistan at the end of November. Four Afghani factions participated: the Northern Alliance; the Rome group, which comprises ethnic Pashtuns including Hamid Karzai and the exiled former king; a group of Cyprus-based exiles supported by Iran; and a Peshawar-based group backed by Pakistan. Nineteen countries – including China, Iran, Pakistan and Russia – had observer status at the talks. The negotiations were brokered by UN Special Envoy to Afghanistan Lakhdar Brahimi. His task, as he saw it, was to secure a political settlement, validate whatever transitional arrangement emerged from the talks and shield the political process from outside interference. Anxious to allay Pakistan's fears of a Northern Alliance-dominated polity, Brahimi sought to dilute the Northern Alliance's leverage by dealing with its Uzbek, Tajik and Hazara Shi'ite elements separately.

Yet the Northern Alliance's advantage on the ground profoundly shaped the outcome of the conference, as did Iran's and Russia's consolidation of their respective presences in Kabul. US and UN officials told the Rome delegation that the Northern Alliance must be accorded the three most powerful portfolios – defence, interior and foreign affairs – and that in exchange the Rome group could appoint the chairman of the interim government. However, they refused to permit the Rome group to select its preferred choice for chairman, Abdul Sattar Sirat, who is an ethnic Uzbek. Instead, the chairman had to be an ethnic Pashtun who was 'acceptable' to the Northern Alliance. One figure that met these criteria was Karzai, who was in the eyes of Northern Alliance leaders a weak and pliable personality. Further strengthening their position, the Northern Alliance received 17 of the 30 cabinet positions. (The Rome group was allotted eight, the Cyprus and Peshawar groups one each.) The Northern Alliance also reduced the former king's role merely to presiding over the opening of a future *loya jirga* and limited the role of peacekeeping forces to assisting the interim administration. In turn, Iran convinced the Northern Alliance to accept these terms and persuaded Rabbani to hand over power smoothly to the interim government.

Although this allotment of power was inequitable at the factional level, the ethnic composition of the cabinet – 11 Pashtuns, eight Tajiks, five Hazara, three Uzbeks and three members of other minorities – broadly reflects national diversity. The Bonn agreement also established a sound political process. The interim administration would create an independent commission to organise a *loya jirga*, which would take place within six months. This national assembly would then create a transitional government that would oversee the writing of a new constitution. A permanent government would be selected within two years. The danger, however, was that the Northern Alliance would aggressively use its control over the power ministries and its external support from Russia and Iran either to short-circuit or hijack the political process.

A critical, unresolved issue was the size, composition and role of the international peacekeeping force in Kabul. The force was essential to creating a neutral political setting to shape the future government of Afghanistan, though for weeks US policymakers had seen the issue as a distraction. When the United States finally accepted the need for such a force, the United Kingdom took the lead, pledging to send as many as 6,000 troops. Intent on pre-empting any challenge to his control of the capital, Fahim demanded that the force not exceed a few hundred and be limited to guarding government buildings. In tense negotiations, Fahim ultimately agreed to a force of about 5,000 troops, though he extracted the right to keep his own troops in garrisons in and around the capital and to preserve the role of the Northern Alliance-dominated 'police' force. He also secured concessions to limit the operations of the force to Kabul. On 20 December, the UN Security Council passed Resolution 1386, creating the International Security Assistance Force (ISAF), with the mandate of maintaining security 'so that the Afghan Interim Administration as well as personnel of the United Nations can operate in a secure environment'. Approximately 17 countries were expected to contribute troops. The mandate was initially due to expire in June 2002.

On 22 December, the interim administration took power in an atmosphere of hope and fear. Despite pomp and circumstance, serious tensions and unresolved issues remained. Even though the Northern Alliance held the lion's share of the power, individuals and factions within the alliance were dissatisfied. Rabbani, who complained bitterly that he had to stand aside in the interim administration, staked his claim to the future by refusing to vacate the presidential palace. Sayyaf and several Northern Alliance commanders also denounced the Bonn outcome. Pashtun political figures, members of the Rome group and even Tajiks from Massoud's inner circle decried the fact that power was concentrated in the hands of a tight cohort within the Northern Alliance. Though much work remained to bring stability to Afghanistan, the clear indications were that the rules of the game in Afghan politics were hardly settled and that tumultuous political competition could lie ahead. Security also remained a serious problem. In January, food convoys were being hijacked by bandits. In the northern province of Kunduz, forces loyal to Dostum were in conflict with Rabbani's mainly Tajik *mujahideen*. In February 2002, Abdul Rahman, transport minister in the interim government, was beaten to death at Kabul airport, British patrols in Kabul came under fire and skirmishes were reported between rival militias in Khost. In early April 2002, Kabul police arrested approximately 300 people. The authorities believed that they were connected to Hezb-e Islami, a radical Islamic group headed by Hekmatyar, and suspected them of plotting to assassinate Karzai and the former king and overthrow the interim government.

In November 2001, the UN Development Programme (UNDP) estimated the five-year cost of Afghanistan's reconstruction at $6.5 billion. At a 21 November meeting in Washington chaired by Secretary of State Powell, about 20 donor nations made provisional financial commitments to nation-building. Many of these nations noted that assistance would be dispensed only if a broad-based multi-ethnic government were in place, providing impetus for progress the Bonn conference. In Tokyo on 21 January 2002, about 30 international donors formally pledged about $4.5bn to the effort to rebuild Afghanistan. The European Union (EU) offered $500m and the United States $296m during the first year. Japan promised $500m over two-and-a-half years, including up to $250m during the first year. Iran pledged $560m over five years and $120m during the first year. Pakistan earmarked $100m over five years. As of mid-March 2002, however, very little of the money had actually been paid. In late February, for example, the UNDP noted that only 20,000 of the estimated 240,000 people on the interim government's payroll had received their salaries. This kind of shortfall could have serious consequences in a country with an annual per-capita income of $250 plagued by illicit opium production, to which unpaid workers might turn. The UN was seeking $1.18bn for emergency aid needed before December 2002. In addition, Karzai lamented that even if the money were flowing into the interim government, it lacked the institutions needed to disburse it efficiently. Thus, there was an acute need for technical as well as merely financial assistance.

Even when resources are eventually being smoothly distributed, success in nation-building will require careful consideration of how – and especially to whom – they are allocated. There is likely to be a natural bias among donors in favour of channelling them towards any central administration in Kabul that emerges from the *loya jirga*. But affording a central authority too much control over resources may risk alienating regional leaders, or 'warlords', who consider themselves entitled to co-equal political status, as well as their outside supporters – in particular, Russia and Iran. In view of the decentralised tribal politics that prevail in Afghanistan, the most viable arrangement likely to emerge is a loose confederal system, under which regional leaders perfunctorily recognise Kabul's authority and vice-versa but central and regional authorities have a relatively independent hand in day-to-day governance. Accordingly, donors and multilateral aid-coordinating bodies may need to consider more widely dispersed direct allocations to maintain a stable political balance.

Furthermore, the application of outside assistance cannot be fully exploited unless security is simultaneously established. Karzai has asked for the numerical and geographical mandate of the ISAF, which in March 2002 stood at 4,700 and was largely confined to Kabul, to be expanded. His preference would be for ISAF's mission to include the eradication of banditry and drug-running, and the provision of security in other cities. The rationale is understandable: unless security is extended to larger areas of the country, the unitary government and territorial rule of law that ISAF contemplates cannot arise. The US administration remains divided on the issue, with the State Department in favour of expansion and the Pentagon opposed. Some European capitals believe that the size of the force must be roughly doubled, but may not have the capability or the will to man such an increase. Turkey, with 260 troops in Afghanistan as of early April 2002, was expected to send more troops and take over command of the operation from the British in June 2002, but only on the conditions that it received outside financial support for this undertaking, that Turkish soldiers' activities were restricted largely to Kabul and that the US provided air support.

The US and Karzai, as well as Russia and Iran, support the creation of an all-Afghan national army, which could eventually relieve the country of the need for outside peacekeepers. Given the fractious nature of Afghani internal politics and the fact that no more than 100,000 indigenous combatants were involved in the war, the 250,000-strong multi-ethnic force bruited by Karzai appears unrealistic. Some have argued that broad-based conscription would provide young Afghani men with livelihoods and reduce their dependence on local warlords, thus limiting the warlords' power *vis-à-vis* Kabul. By the same token, however, that dispensation could antagonise and threaten the local leaders, who are unlikely to relinquish control of their own militias. A smaller professional army of no more than 50,000, suggested by the British, would be more feasible and would pose less of a threat to regional leaders. While a national force might not be able to secure Afghanistan without robust outside guarantees, it would at least diminish the need for a foreign military presence and lower related tensions between the US and Russia, Iran and Pakistan. In the long term, a cohesive national army is probably required to stabilise the balance between Kabul and the regional leaders and, therefore, for the peace process to succeed. But one could not be assembled quickly enough to short-circuit the apparent need to expand ISAF.

The extent to which outside powers remain engaged in nation-building is a major uncertainty. The US is expressly disinclined to take the lead, based on the presumed need to mount additional counter-terrorist military operations elsewhere and a general discomfort with protracted peace-keeping engagements ('mission-creep'). In late March 2002, however, Rumsfeld announced plans to send up to 150 Special Forces soldiers to train Afghani recruits for service in a national army to complement training by British and German ISAF troops that was already underway. He also suggested that the US military would remain in Afghanistan for as long as it took to establish security and stability. The United Kingdom made nation-building the centrepiece of its Afghanistan policy, and assumed the inaugural command of ISAF. But given that the UK is likely to participate in any US military action against Iraq, the British government is wary of overstretch and keen on pulling out of Afghanistan sooner rather than later. Other European countries, such as Germany, are reluctant to be drawn in. Iran could destabilise the country if its security, political and cultural interests there are ignored. Tehran wants restraints enforced by the Kabul government against drug-smuggling and other forms of border insecurity and its Afghani allies – in particular, the Hazara and Herat warlord Ismail Khan – treated equitably. Iran has an interest in a stable Afghanistan, which would tend to limit refugees and drug traffic. Russia also has a broad stake in Afghanistan's political success, since it would make the US less likely to establish a long-term military presence in Central Asia, which Moscow considers a Russian sphere of influence. Both Iran and Russia would, on balance, like to see Afghanistan become a viable route for an oil and gas pipeline. But either could regard power politics through Northern Alliance allies, rather than a non-partisan nurturing of political rehabilitation, as the best way of securing their stake in such an eventuality. Given these varying levels and nuances of interest, despite rhetorical acknowledgement of the need to avoid another political vacuum in Afghanistan, a broad-based commitment to nation-building will probably be difficult to sustain.

Prospects for Afghanistan

As of March 2002, the war against al-Qaeda was far from over. Bin Laden and Mullah Omar were presumed still at large, and thousands of al-Qaeda fighters remained in the country. US commanders were committed to staying until the job was done, while regional powers such as Iran and Russia sought to exploit the vacuum of power. The Bonn process, threatened by the winner-take-all politics of the Northern Alliance, appeared fragile. The Northern Alliance may use its dominance in the existing power structure to seize control of the state and find that the Afghan people are too exhausted to resist after a quarter-century of war. Such a development would not, however, unify the country. Instead, local or regional warlords in the southern and eastern regions would maintain sufficient power to avoid subservience to the centre. It is also possible for Afghanistan to revisit the tragic events of the period 1992–1996, when the Rabbani government sought to monopolise power and triggered a disastrous civil war. In the last half century, when one group has overreached and sought to dominate – starting with Communists, extending through the Rabbani government and ending with the Taliban – the outcome has been internal conflict.

Many of the political trend lines were tilting forebodingly in this direction as Hamid Karzai struggled to establish stability before the *loya jirga*, which is scheduled for June 2002. An episode illustrating the delicate ethnic sensibilities Karzai has to navigate occurred during the allied engagement of al-Qaeda and Taliban fighters in north-east Afghanistan in

March 2002. On 7 March, Karzai dispatched from Kabul a 1,000-strong largely Tajik force from the Northern Alliance, equipped with tanks and APCs. Despite their military usefulness, local Pashtun fighters did not want Tajiks defending Pashtun territory for fear that they might stay and lay claim to it. While providing reassurances that they supported the interim administration, Mohammed Ismail, the local Pashtun commander, demanded that the Kabul-based contingent withdraw. American officials were not consulted. The al-Qaeda and Taliban fighters who remain at large in north-eastern Afghanistan constitute another potentially destabilising factor in their capacity to fuel terrorism in Pakistan and the CIS, and to increase the flow of refugees in Pakistan, the CIS and Iran.

To avoid internal conflict, and effect the full implementation of the Bonn agreement, the United States and its allies will need to pressure the Northern Alliance, as well as Iran and Russia, to stand down in their efforts to use the power ministries to tip the political scales in their favour. Another key requirement is to prevent the Northern Alliance from creating police and military forces loyal only to their faction, rather than the nation as a whole. Counterbalancing such a development may call for intensified outside technical and financial support for a professional national army, probably for the most part from the US. The Turks, who will probably assume the leadership of ISAF in June 2002, are inclined to confine its operations largely to Kabul. This may not be sufficient. Washington may not be able to avoid strengthening and extending ISAF and being drawn into the Afghani political reconciliation process. At the very least, it will need to bolster Karzai and the Rome group diplomatically in order to ensure parity *vis-à-vis* the Northern Alliance. Finally, Afghanistan has an ongoing need for international economic support, exacerbated by a devastating earthquake in late March 2002 that killed over 1,000 people and left up to 30,000 more homeless and 80,000 in need of humanitarian relief. Continued and carefully channelled nation-building aid from bilateral and multilateral donors will be essential. Without it, the Afghani people and their leaders may once again opt for illicit means of support from narcotics traffickers or terrorist groups over the rule of law.

India: Another Year of Turmoil

Before the 11 September 2001 terrorist attacks on the United States, India had begun to assume a larger and more favoured role in the eyes of the West, particularly those of the new administration of President George W. Bush.

The Bush administration intended to develop a robust alliance with India, which was deemed a far more reliable and domestically less precarious partner than Pakistan and one which shared a common interest with the US in checking China's strategic ambitions. After 11 September, the US was forced to tilt towards Pakistan in order to ensure its operational and diplomatic cooperation in the US-led campaign in Afghanistan to oust the Taliban and decapitate al-Qaeda. If the American courtship of India was not put on hold, at the very least it was complicated by a serious rival interest. The terrorist attack on India's parliament in New Delhi on 13 December 2001 pushed India and Pakistan to the brink of war, and rendered American diplomacy on the subcontinent even more delicate than it had become by virtue of 11 September.

Relations with the United States

Indo-US relations, which began to improve markedly in 1999 as a result of India's restraint in the Kargil affair, and further after Pakistan fell under military rule, showed considerable prospects for further improvement during 2001. The Bush administration seemed less fixated than its predecessor on limiting the incipient nuclear weapons programmes in India and Pakistan, and thus pursued new avenues of rapprochement. Moreover, some key members of the new president's foreign-policy team were far less sanguine about the China's long-term strategic goals in Asia. In seeking to reshape US regional priorities, they fastened on India as a potential counterweight to China. The Indian political establishment, although unsure about playing this role, recognised an important opportunity to forge a new military and political relationship with the US. Accordingly, the Indian Foreign Ministry provided a cautious and limited endorsement of the US administration's decision in June 2001 formally to abandon the 1972 US–Russian Anti-Ballistic Missile (ABM) Treaty and pursue a national missile-defence programme. Even though the Indian pronouncement on the Bush decision was circumspect, it marked a sea change in Indian attitudes toward American policy initiatives in the global strategic arena. It was all the more significant in that no other major powers expressed genuine sympathy with US plans at the time. Moreover, key members of the ruling coalition did not share the anti-American sentiments of many of their predecessors during the Cold War era. Instead they were intent on forging a new and viable political and military relationship with the United States and other major powers, to raise India's stature in world affairs.

The shifts in the positions of both countries were also manifested in a number of areas of defence cooperation. In July 2001, General Henry H. Shelton, the chairman of the US Joint Chiefs of Staff, visited New Delhi and met his Indian counterpart, Admiral Sushil Kumar. Shelton's visit presaged the revival of the Defence Policy Group, a joint senior military working group that had not met since the US suspended such contacts in response to the Indian nuclear tests of May 1998. The administration also made clear its intention to lift a range of the economic and military sanctions that the Clinton administration had placed on India (as well as Pakistan) following the nuclear tests. The lifting of these sanctions was a precondition to expanded defence cooperation.

After 11 September, as the Bush administration sought to eradicate al-Qaeda and its supporters, the US began to rebuild its ties to the military government of General Pervez Musharraf in Pakistan, in order to take advantage of the latter's geographic proximity to Afghanistan. This development – given the history of positive US–Pakistan relations, often at the expense of US–India ties – caused some misgivings in New Delhi. Nevertheless, key Indian government officials muted their criticisms in an effort not to dissipate the recent bonhomie in Indo-US relations. Foreign Minister Jaswant Singh's statement during Secretary of State Colin Powell's first visit to South Asia in early October – that one did not have to be 'disagreeable to disagree' – exemplified India's new measured-but-principled attitude in its dealings with the United States.

In contrast to the Indian government's behaviour during the Cold War and even after, when non-aligned New Delhi chose not to become embroiled in Washington's troubles, the conduct of Indian leaders after 11 September was diplomatically deft and proactive. They immediately condemned the attacks on the United States and offered both diplomatic and material support to the United States in locating the perpetrators and eliminating their backers. Two factors explain the swift Indian response. First, the regime in New Delhi was intent on neutralising, to the extent possible, Pakistan's efforts to capitalise on its suddenly renewed political and military significance for the United States. Second, the Indian leadership was also quite determined to link its own efforts to suppress the Kashmir insurgency, which has involved a variety of terrorist acts both in Kashmir and elsewhere in India, to the new US 'war against terror'.

Despite the stated willingness of both India and Pakistan to cooperate with the United States in its efforts to vanquish al-Qaeda, decision-makers in Washington remained acutely concerned about a resurgence of tensions between India and Pakistan over the vexed question of Kashmir. These threatened to fray the regional and global counter-terrorist coalition that the United States had carefully knit together in the weeks following 11 September. To calm the situation, Secretary of State Powell visited India and Pakistan in October 2001 and sought to address the conflicting interests of both antagonists. In Pakistan, he counselled Musharraf to restrain the activities of the insurgents who were perpetrating acts of terror in Kashmir. In India, he sought to allay concerns that the US war effort would overlook India's own fight against terrorism.

Continuing the American diplomatic effort to assuage India's unease about United States' renewed military ties with Pakistan, US Secretary of Defense Donald Rumsfeld visited New Delhi in November 2001. During this visit he met Defence Minister George Fernandes, as well as Foreign Minister Singh and the National Security Adviser Brajesh Mishra. Rumsfeld not only discussed the ongoing war against al-Qaeda and the Taliban in Afghanistan, but also broached the possibility of broadening and deepening military-to-military contacts with India. He also signalled the Bush administration's willingness to sell India various forms of defence technology that had long been embargoed, including the General Electric 404 engines for India's much-delayed light combat aircraft prototype. High-level Indo-US consultations continued in the new year with a visit by Fernandes to the United States in mid-January 2002. Although Washington raised concerns about Israel's proposed sales of the *Arrow*-2 anti-tactical ballistic missile system and the *Phalcon* airborne warning and control system, during this visit Fernandes signed the General Security of Military Information Agreement, which would permit the sale of a wider array of military equipment to India in return for India's guarantee of the protection of classified technologies. During his visit, the two sides also formalised a schedule for meetings on counter-terrorism and joint military exercises in the months ahead.

Stasis, corruption and sectarian violence on the domestic front

In Indian domestic politics, the unwieldy coalition in New Delhi inhibited the government from undertaking much-needed but contentious economic reforms. Another factor is the ongoing de facto devolution of central powers to India's states that has been taking place since the Congress Party's decline in the 1990s. This development has made it difficult to establish a party consensus, and the sheer number of parties and interests tends to preclude any sense of coherence. The most difficult arena of the reforms remained India's behemoth public sector, which accounts for over 25% of GDP and a third of gross domestic fixed investment. This sector is rife with inefficiency, featherbedding and sloth. Yet the public-sector employees constitute two-thirds of the organised workforce, making them a formidable political force. Compounding this problem are India's antiquated labour laws, which hobble employers' efforts to rationalise the workforce. Not surprisingly, even when the government managed to muster the requisite mandate to sell off India's perennially loss-making state airlines, Indian Airlines and Air India, it could find no buyers. The coalition regime appears destined to remain fractious for the foreseeable future. Accordingly, significant economic reforms will, in all likelihood, remain stalled. Although government debt is chronically high and the rupee has been weak, the political impact of India's economic troubles has been somewhat cushioned by a projected increase in economic growth from 4.0% to 5.4% in fiscal year (FY) 2001/2002, due mainly to a recovery in the agriculture sector.

Of more immediate concern to Prime Minister Atal Behari Vajpayee's Bharatiya Janata Party (BJP) were the February 2002 elections in Uttar Pradesh – India's largest state, with 166 million people – on which the political fortunes of the regime in New Delhi could pivot. The BJP was in a mortal tussle with its principal local adversary, the Samajwadi Party, a secular group that opposes what is perceived as intolerant sectarianism on the BJP's part. In the event, the critical moment was delayed. The absence of a clear-cut majority, coupled with inter-party squabbling, prevented the formation of a coalition government. Accordingly, the central government invoked its constitutional powers to declare president's rule in this critical and politically volatile state. Under the Indian constitution, the state will be ruled by the central government for six months following the indecisive elections, when new elections, local conditions permitting, will be held.

Sectarianism is especially acute in Uttar Pradesh, and remains a central problem of Indian society. On 27 February 2002, local Muslims in the town of Godhra, in the west Indian state of Gujarat, fire-bombed a trainload of Hindu activists, of whom 58 were killed. Hindu mobs then went on a rampage, attacking Muslim neighbourhoods in the city of Ahmedabad, Gujarat, and setting off a wave of Hindu–Muslim riots that resulted in more than 500 deaths and at least 1,200 arrests. The local police proved unable or unwilling to stop the rioters. As the violence continued, the central government in Delhi dispatched army units, which quickly quelled the rioting. The activists were on their way back from the town of Ayodhya in Uttar Pradesh, where they had been agitating to build a temple on the site of a mosque. Hindu militants had destroyed the sixteenth-century mosque in December 1992. In the wake of its destruction, about 2,000 people had lost their lives in widespread sectarian violence in northern India.

The BJP also lost power in the states of Punjab, Manipur and Uttaranchal in the February 2002 elections, leaving it in control of only four of India's 28 states while Congress held power in 14. According to some analysts, a BJP loss in Uttar Pradesh could trigger a crisis in the national coalition leading to mid-term elections at the national level before the scheduled 2004 elections. Such an outcome would inevitably contribute to further incoherence in both matters of national governance and economic policy-making, as all the members of the existing coalition would focus their attention on the election campaign. Such a development, in turn, could spur a political realignment among opposition parties. Since 1998, under the aloof Sonia Gandhi – widow of assassinated Prime Minister Rajiv Gandhi – the Congress Party has hardly been a major force. Its economic policies amount to little more than reflexive reactions to those of the BJP. Other opposition parties treat it with distrust, and Gandhi has a record of tactical blunders. But Congress – still the second-largest party in India, and strengthened by its February 2002 assembly election victories in Punjab, Manipur and Uttaranchal and its thoroughgoing triumph over the BJP in March 2002 municipal elections in Delhi – could attempt to cobble together a coalition with a group of opposition parties, especially the otherwise dispirited Communists and other regional parties. Such a coalition, however, could have significantly retrograde consequences in the realm of both foreign and domestic policies. A Congress-led coalition dependent upon Communist support could lead to a further slowing of the already near-glacial process of economic reform. (In a New Delhi speech on 28 January, US Ambassador Robert Blackwill blasted India about delays in its second-generation economic reforms, highlighting the disincentives to foreign investors that its bureaucratic red tape – for example, 100 clearances required for investment in a power project – posed and noting that investment flows into India in 2000 were a mere $4.5bn versus $41bn for China.) In the realm of foreign affairs, Indian policy could see a return to the knee-jerk anti-Americanism of the Cold War era. Simultaneously, such a coalition could also attempt to resurrect the moribund third world and non-aligned front, to the detriment of India's critical foreign and economic policy interests.

Corruption revelations continued to plague Vajpayee's government. In October 2001, as India was coping with the aftermath of 11 September, Vajpayee brought back George Fernandes as defence minister to reduce the burden on Foreign Minister Jaswant Singh, who had been tending the Defence Ministry since Fernandes was forced to resign in the spring after an arms-procurement scandal. Fernandes had barely resettled into his old office when yet another defence-contracting scandal embarrassed the regime. A report from the Comptroller and Auditor General's Office, a government watchdog body, revealed that the coffins that the Indian Defence Ministry had purchased to evacuate the bodies of Indian soldiers killed in the Kargil war of May–July 1999 were mostly substandard and had been obtained at exorbitant prices. Once again, the opposition parties sought Fernandes' resignation, but this time he did not step down. The government nevertheless promised to investigate these charges and also to seek financial compensation from the American firm that had supplied the coffins.

Certain issues of national governance will continue to dominate the policy agenda. Chief among them is the fraught question of India's own attempts to deal with domestic terror. In the aftermath of 11 September, after contentious parliamentary debate, the government passed the Prevention of Terrorism Act (POTA). Originally enacted as an ordinance, which lapsed in the 2001 winter session of parliament for lack of support, the statute grants the government extraordinary powers of arrest, detention and surveillance (including wiretapping). Unlike previous acts of parliament, it applies nationwide. Civil libertarians and human-rights groups emphasised that the ordinance not only had the potential to suppress civil liberties but could also be used for partisan purposes. But the fact that India continues to face terrorist attacks both in Kashmir and elsewhere militated in favour of the POTA. Although for over a decade violent attacks in public places had been mostly confined to Bombay and New Delhi, on 22 January 2001, four motorcycle-borne assailants opened fire in the early hours of the morning against the small and poorly armed police picket outside the American Cultural Centre in Calcutta. The attackers killed five policemen and injured 20 others before fleeing the scene. The Indian Home Minister, L. K. Advani, promptly pointed the finger of suspicion towards Pakistan. On the other hand, local American officials, the Calcutta police and the Ministry of Internal Affairs were more circumspect in their assessments. The police, in particular, suggested that the attack in all likelihood was the handiwork of a criminal gang that wanted to avenge the death of one of its members in police custody. They did, however, also suggest that these criminal gangs may have some connections with the underworld in Pakistan as well as that country's Inter-Services Intelligence Directorate (ISI).

Stillborn Indo-Pakistani dialogue

Despite US efforts to calm cross-border rhetoric, tensions with Pakistan continued to revolve around Pakistan's involvement in the Kashmir insurgency. From its roots as an indigenous reaction to Indian political machinations, the insurgency had, since its outbreak in December 1989, settled into a pattern of low-level harassment largely carried out by foreign militants, many of them sponsored by Pakistan in the name of pan-Islamism. In an attempt to create conditions conducive to a political dialogue with the insurgents, the BJP-led coalition government on 19 November 2000 declared, and then repeatedly extended, a unilateral cease-fire within the Indian-controlled portion of Kashmir. The cease-fire bore few tangible results and, under increasing attack from more strident members of his party, Vajpayee allowed it to lapse on 23 May 2001. At the same time, however, he offered to negotiate with Pakistan about the Kashmir issue, thus evincing a willingness to address the festering dispute.

In July 2001, in keeping with his desire to end the conflict in Kashmir, Vajpayee invited Musharraf, who had recently re-styled himself as president rather than simply chief executive of Pakistan, to Agra, the home of the fabled Taj Mahal, for negotiations on the Kashmir dispute, among other contentious matters. The summit was largely an initiative of the Indian prime minister, who was personally committed to improving relations with his country's long-standing adversary. Despite a promising start, the three-day Agra summit broke down without any concrete achievements. The Pakistani leadership accused the more intransigent elements in the BJP of sabotaging the talks. The Indian side, for its part, held that Pakistan's unwillingness to admit its role in supporting the Kashmiri insurgents had led to the collapse of the summit. In all likelihood, the meeting failed to achieve anything because it had been hastily convened and neither side was in a position to make significant concessions. Musharraf could ill-afford to run the risk of making serious concessions on the critical Kashmir issue, given his uncertain domestic position. Vajpayee, in turn, could not make significant progress either without some willingness of Musharraf's part to demonstrate flexibility on the Kashmir question.

After the Agra meeting, the two antagonists lapsed back into an all-too-familiar pattern of mutual recriminations. Even though the Pakistani foreign minister, Abdul Sattar, and his Indian counterpart, Jaswant Singh, publicly stated their commitment to holding further talks, little progress was made in the following months. Musharraf's tenuous political position at home continued to limit his ability to undertake any policy changes on the highly sensitive issue of Indo-Pakistani relations. On the Indian side, the failure of the Agra summit further undermined Vajpayee's efforts to forge a better relationship with Pakistan. His political adversaries, both within and outside his party, roundly attacked him for what in their view amounted to appeasement. Vajpayee was vulnerable to this line of criticism, as he had also been the initiator behind the bold and imaginative 'bus diplomacy' with Pakistan in February 1999, and in the wake of which he had faced the embarrassment of the Kargil invasion of April 1999.

The aftermath of 11 September

The tensions in Indo-Pakistan relations took their most dramatic turn after 11 September. While the terrorist attacks on the United States had no direct link to Indo-Pakistani relations, the apparent links between Osama bin Laden and the terrorists who struck at the United States had a profound impact on ongoing Indo-Pakistani problems. Bin Laden's organisation, al-Qaeda, had taken refuge in Afghanistan in 1998, within two years of the Taliban take-over there. Moreover, it is widely believed that al-Qaeda has links with several of the more radical Islamic groups who were causing mayhem in Kashmir.

Indian officials had for some time sought to characterise the insurgents in Kashmir as terrorists. In the wake of 11 September, they pressed these claims with renewed vigour, seeking to tie their own difficulties in suppressing the insurgency in Kashmir with the newly declared American war on global terror. For the United States, the Indian support was attractive and desirable. But it also placed the United States and its allies in a quandary, since they needed the support of Pakistan to suppress al-Qaeda and the Taliban militarily in Afghanistan. At this critical juncture, preventing a wider rift between India and Pakistan became a priority for the United States and the UK. To this end, the United States dispatched Secretary of State Colin Powell to visit India in October, and British Prime Minister Tony Blair visited the subcontinent twice in this period.

War rears its head on 13 December

The concerted diplomatic efforts to prevent an Indo-Pakistani confrontation – which would undermine the common front against terrorism – suffered a stunning body blow on 13 December 2001, when five armed gunmen attacked the Indian parliament building in New Delhi. In the ensuing gun-battle, all of the attackers were killed, along with nine Indian parliamentary guards and paramilitary troops. No members of parliament were wounded or lost their lives. By tracing cell-phone calls made by the attackers, Indian intelligence agencies concluded that the attackers were members of two terrorist groups, the Jaish-e-Mohammed and the Lashkar-e-Taiba, both Pakistan-based organisations that had been carrying out attacks in Kashmir for several years.

In the wake of this attack on the heart of Indian government, there was extraordinary domestic pressure on the government to take prompt, tough action against Pakistan for its apparent support for these two terrorist organisations. After a careful review of its options, the Cabinet Committee on Security – the apex government body charged with making critical decisions on national security – refrained from taking any precipitate actions. Among other options, they considered, and ultimately rejected, attacking terrorist training camps within Pakistan-controlled Kashmir, large-scale shelling of Pakistani bunkers and military installations along the Line of Control in Kashmir, and swift helicopter strikes against specific military assets within Pakistan. Each of these options, in the assessment of the committee, promised little benefit and held the likelihood of either a larger, protracted war or even potential escalation to the nuclear level.

Faced with no viable military options, New Delhi embarked on a concerted strategy of 'coercive diplomacy' designed to exercise serious political and military pressure on Pakistan without resort to actual war. To this end, India promptly cut all rail, road, and air links to Pakistan, withdrew its high commissioner from Islamabad, limited the diplomatic presence of the Pakistani High Commission in New Delhi, and embarked on a significant military build-up of up to 250,000 troops along the Indo-Pakistani border and the Line of Control. It also asked Pakistan to immediately desist from all support for 'cross-border infiltration', demanded that Musharraf shut down the operations of the Lashkar-e-Taiba and the Jaish-e-Mohammed, and insisted that Pakistan arrest and transfer to India some 20 individuals accused by India of perpetrating acts of terror in India. Finally, the Indian government sought to persuade the great powers – notably the United States, the United Kingdom, France and Russia – that Pakistan had to comply with the Indian demands if India was expected to exercise restraint.

In the new year, India's coercive diplomacy continued in the face of Pakistan's limited willingness to meet India's demands. On 12 January, General Musharraf delivered a speech that went farther than previous Pakistani policies to address India's concerns, but did not wholly satisfy them. Although Musharraf, under tremendous Indian and American pressure, did ban the Jaish-e-Mohammed and the Lashkar-e-Taiba, he categorically declined to abandon Pakistan's support to Kashmiri insurgents and steadfastly refused to hand over the 20 alleged terrorists. But Musharraf did place about 2,000 Islamic radicals under preventive detention and closed down a number of the *madrassas* (Islamic schools) that effectively served as recruiting and training grounds for terrorists – measures that he would not have taken prior to the 13 December attack. In February, Musharraf also began to disband the Afghanistan and Kashmir units of the ISI, which absorbed at least 4,000 of an estimated 10,000 total ISI personnel. The ISI has been Pakistan's principal vehicle of support for the Taliban and for Kashmiri rebels. Some senior ISI officers continue to harbour sympathy for both groups as well as al-Qaeda. Some Western intelligence agencies have considered the ISI a virtual rogue government. Since Musharraf took over the Pakistani government in 1999, however, the agency has been perceived as being more answerable to Islamabad. Musharraf's action appeared to be designed to reassure Washington and Delhi.

While India acknowledged Pakistan's conciliatory moves, Singh stated on 30 January that India would 'wait and watch' to see whether Pakistan's steps to end cross-border terrorism were effective before bilateral dialogue could occur. India maintained its substantial troop presence along the Line of Control and the international border, despite pleas from the United States and the United Kingdom that it ratchet down the tensions.

Further, General Sunderajan Padmanabhan, the Chief of Staff of the Indian Army, caused alarm when, in a press conference in early January, he stated that if Pakistan attacked any Indian assets whatsoever with nuclear weapons, India would retaliate in kind. Senior political leaders in India did little to allay any misgivings that Padmanabhan's remarks may have aroused. At the end of January, India successfully test-fired an *Agni*-2 intermediate-range missile, which can carry a nuclear payload and, with a range of about 700 kilometres, is capable of hitting targets in Pakistan. Successful tests of a longer-range version of the missile had been conducted in April 1999 and January 2001. Although Indian spokespersons were quick to assert that the missile test had been long planned, Pakistani leaders construed the test as an attempt on the part of the Indian political establishment to cower them into meeting India's demands. The *Agni*-2 test was followed five days later by a test of the short-range *Trishul* missile.

Peering ahead

The future of India's economic reforms will depend in large measure upon the unfolding political fortunes of the BJP-led coalition. Unless the BJP manages to consolidate its hold in Uttar Pradesh and thereby bolster its national standing, the reforms could continue to stall indefinitely. Such an outcome would bode ill for India's efforts to make a meaningful dent on endemic rural and urban poverty. It would concomitantly undermine India's hopes for emerging as a significant power in Asia and beyond.

Strategically, the coming year on the subcontinent holds both promise and peril for India, Pakistan and the United States. Unless Pakistan evinces some willingness to address India's concerns about cross-border infiltration, the Indian political leadership, despite American and other external pressures, will undertake, few, if any, efforts to address the grievances of the Kashmiris. As a consequence, the insurgency in Kashmir would continue to exact a deadly toll in both blood and resources. The United States and its allies, for their part, will be loath to press Musharraf to undertake further actions against the Kashmiri *mujahideen* groups as long as they need his cooperation to continue regional operations against al-Qaeda. At the same time, Washington will continue to regard India as a more stable and reliable regional partner than Pakistan in the longer term. Although Musharraf's professed agenda of secularisation and planned parliamentary elections by October 2002 suggest greater stability and a check on fundamentalism in Pakistan, Pakistan's prospective 'partial democracy' will remain a complicating factor in its foreign relations and the country will continue to cede the moral high ground to India. On 5 April 2002, Musharraf announced that he would seek a mandate supporting the campaign against terrorism and domestic reforms and extending his rule for a five-year term by way of a referendum, probably in May 2002, rather than multi-party elections. Condemned by the two main political parties and lawyers as undemocratic, this controversial dispensation would allow Musharraf to bypass Pakistan's constitutional requirement that the head of state be elected by both houses of Parliament. While the United States will naturally counsel Indian military restraint, it is unlikely to exert heavy pressure on India to relax its 'wait and watch' posture if Musharraf does not stop cross-border terrorism.

On balance, a deadlock is likely to prevail in Indo-Pakistani relations through 2003. This paralysis could adversely affect India's efforts to broaden and deepen its political and military relationship with the United States. Longer-term, strategic stability on the subcontinent will depend on whether Musharraf stays in power. A coup is unlikely, as is a military revolt or a popular uprising, but he remains vulnerable, like Anwar Sadat in 1981, to an assassin's bullet. In that case, Pakistan would probably retrench to a more anti-secular, anti-American posture. But assuming he is given time to implement his ideas for secular and political reform, he may be able to reshape the Kashmir issue as one of people rather than territory. This would involve convincing the Pakistani populace to relinquish Pakistan's demand for a plebiscite on Kashmir's sovereignty in favour of requiring simply that Kashmiri Muslims be accorded human rights and reinforced autonomy. Such a shift would constitute a basis, at least, for bilateral dialogue. Provided Musharraf can further deliver on promises to curb cross-border terrorism, India might be willing to respond with civil reforms that would meet Pakistan's modified requirements, which in turn could lead to a draw-down of military deployments around the Line of Control and stabilise mutual deterrence. Developments along these lines are needed if India is to get over its obsession with Pakistan and become the major power it seeks to be – and that Washington would like it to be.

China's Constrained Ambitions

The US-led campaign against terrorism has presented China with a rare opportunity to establish common strategic interests with its rivals and enhance its status and security in Asia. But the leadership has responded with diffidence. It appears too preoccupied with political and economic challenges at home to play an imaginative role in shaping the post-11 September world order. These challenges are considerable, and include the five-yearly Communist Party congress to be held in late 2002, as well as adjusting to China's entry into the World Trade Organization (WTO) in December 2001. Skilful management will be required to avoid disrupting the country's social and political order.

In 2002, maintaining stability will be China's foremost priority. In its external relations, this primarily means avoiding conflict with the United States and Taiwan. President Jiang Zemin does not want the 16th Communist Party Congress to be overshadowed by a crisis such as that of April 2001, when an American EP-3E surveillance aircraft collided with a Chinese fighter plane off the southern Chinese coast. China has toned down its hostile rhetoric towards Taiwan's ruling Democratic Progressive Party (DPP), and has even suggested that it would like to establish contact with it. Beyond the congress, however, greater uncertainty will arise in China's foreign policy as new leaders, less experienced in foreign affairs, try to consolidate their power and Jiang's influence wanes.

11 September and Sino-US relations

Even before the 11 September terrorist attacks, China was clearly intent on improving relations with the United States and healing the divisions caused by the plane collision and President George W. Bush's strong expressions of support for Taiwan. Many Chinese officials felt that their country's response to the EP-3E incident had been excessively militant. President Jiang was particularly anxious to create a harmonious atmosphere for a summit in October of the Asia-Pacific Economic Cooperation (APEC) forum in Shanghai. This was to be the biggest gathering of foreign leaders on Chinese soil since the communist takeover in 1949. It was due to be followed by a state visit by Bush to Beijing, and the two countries' first formal summit in three years. China felt that whatever its differences with America, its diplomatic prestige would be enhanced by ensuring these meetings went smoothly.

As Chinese officials saw it, 11 September provided a welcome pretext to step up their efforts to improve relations with the United States. Even though Bush decided to postpone the bilateral summit and attend only the APEC gathering, China was delighted that he was able to take any time at all away from directing the counter-terrorism campaign. President Jiang's meeting with Bush in the margins of APEC focused on cooperation in the counter-terrorism campaign, rather than on their many disputes over issues ranging from American plans to deploy anti-ballistic missile defences to human rights and Taiwan. The two leaders agreed to work towards a 'constructive relationship of cooperation' – not quite the 'strategic partnership' that President Bill Clinton had aimed for, but more cordial than the 'strategic competition' with China that President Bush had anticipated during his election campaign.

China's response to post-11 September developments, however, was hamstrung not only by the country's focus on domestic problems, but also by its traditional reluctance to adjust foreign policy in response to sudden external change. While China's stand-back approach to world affairs served the country well during the collapse of communism in the Soviet Union and Eastern Europe a decade earlier, it was less beneficial in the rapidly changing strategic environment of 2001. China's unconvincing and belated attempt, weeks after the terrorist attacks, to portray its far western region of Xinjiang as a hotbed of al-Qaeda-trained Muslim separatism failed to match, for example, Russian President Vladimir Putin's achievements in diverting Western attention from Russian military action against Muslim guerrillas in Chechnya.

During the 1980s, before the Tiananmen Square unrest, the US and China shared a security objective – the containment of the Soviet Union – which enabled the two countries to put aside their differences over other issues. Too much has changed since then – from the collapse of the Soviet Union and the Beijing massacre of 1989 to the democratisation of Taiwan and China's extensive military modernisation in the 1990s – for the two countries to turn back the clock. In the build-up to President Bush's state visit to Beijing in February 2002, however, some Chinese officials privately argued that a new communiqué be adopted by the two countries (following the three they issued between 1972 and 1982) in order to establish new guidelines for the Sino-US relationship in the post-Cold War, post-11 September era. Former senior US State Department official Richard Holbrooke also argued in favour of a 'fourth communiqué'. But the Bush administration brushed aside such suggestions, not wishing to tie its hands, alarm America's friends in the region (especially the Taiwanese), or disrupt the relationship with arguments over the drafting of such a document.

Since 11 September, China's efforts to mend fences with the United States – though well-received in Washington and important for the cohesion of the counter-terrorism coalition – have not fundamentally altered the relationship. China's decision to share with the United States detailed intelligence on the Taliban and al-Qaeda, though reminiscent of their cooperation in the 1980s and in stark contrast to its grudging neutrality in the Gulf War of 1991, is limited to the conflict in Afghanistan and constitutes the minimum necessary to satisfy the US administration. A wider campaign, particularly were it to target a country with which China has cordial relations, such as Iran or North Korea, would not elicit such a response. The visit to Beijing by Iraq's deputy prime minister, Tariq Aziz, in January 2002, clearly signalled China's opposition to any extension of the campaign to Iraq. These Sino-US differences were exacerbated when Bush lumped together all three countries as constituting an 'axis of evil' in his 30 January 2002 State of the Union message. On his visit to Beijing on 21 February, Bush mollified Jiang somewhat by enlisting his help in approaching North Korean leader Kim Jong Il, but Jiang would not support US military action against Iraq or accede to US demands that China stop selling ballistic-missile technology to nations like Iran and North Korea as well as Pakistan.

Jiang is partly restrained by widespread anti-American feeling within the party and particularly among the security forces. Memories still persisted of the bombing of the Chinese Embassy in Belgrade in 1999 by American planes, not to mention more recent incidents such as the aircraft collision and President Bush's decision in May 2001 to offer Taiwan the island's biggest arms package from the US in a decade (including weaponry deemed particularly threatening by Beijing, such as eight diesel submarines and four *Knox*-class frigates). Anti-US feelings were evident in the response of some ordinary Chinese to the terrorist attacks in America. Many Chinese Internet users – mainly young, better-educated, males – posted messages on bulletin boards suggesting that America had got what it deserved.

The military action in Afghanistan also appeared to violate the most vigorously proclaimed tenet of China's foreign policy: non-interference in the internal affairs of other countries. Although China's official relationship with the Northern Alliance, which supported the US-led intervention, gave it a pretext to set aside this scruple, China would find it much more difficult to support the United States were it to extend the counter-terrorism campaign to a country whose government Beijing recognises.

Both Russia and China were muted in their response to President Bush's decision, announced in December 2001, to withdraw from the Anti-Ballistic

Missile (ABM) Treaty. At least in theory, the implications of this move are far greater for China, with its tiny arsenal of strategic nuclear weapons, than they are for Russia, whose much larger stockpile would be able to overwhelm any American missile defence system. But Russia's decision not to take a stand on the issue left China – reluctant to stand alone against the US – able to make only desultory criticisms of the American decision. A more robust response by China could have included the suspension of dialogue with the US on missile proliferation issues. Beijing had already warned that it might pull out of such talks in response to Washington's decision, in September 2001, to impose sanctions on two Chinese firms for allegedly supplying missile-related technology to Pakistan. In late November, however, the two sides held their highest-level arms control talks since President Bush took office. The discussions in Washington failed to make any obvious progress. But despite the US indication at the talks that it would withdraw from the treaty, the meeting did not break down in acrimony.

One reason may be that in practice, America's deployment of missile defence systems is unlikely to be as threatening to China's nuclear deterrent as China has sought to convey. China has long been aware of the likelihood of American deployment of missile defences as well as of the vulnerability of its silo-based strategic missiles to preemptive strikes. These missiles are stored separately from their volatile liquid fuel and therefore require considerable preparation time before launch. In recent years, China has worked to develop road-mobile solid-fuelled missiles and to increase the size of its strategic arsenal in order to be sure of penetrating any American defences and ensuring a second-strike capability. President Bush's plans for a national missile-defence system would not substantially affect these efforts. In their attempts to assuage Chinese concerns about this, US officials have implicitly recognised the legitimacy of China's desire for an effective nuclear deterrent – an acknowledgement that is certainly welcome to Chinese leaders. Of greater concern to Beijing than any anti-missile system designed to defend the American homeland is the possibility that such a similar system might be used to protect Taiwan. The US refusal to rule out such a possibility could pressure China to curb its missile build-up on the coast facing the island.

On balance, despite limited counter-terrorism cooperation between China and the United States and Beijing's somewhat more pragmatic approach to missile defence, there has been no sign of change in the fundamental concerns of both countries with respect to each other's long term strategic positions and intentions. The US Quadrennial Defense Review, published on 30 September 2001, diplomatically avoided explicit mention of China, but clearly had China in mind when it mentioned the possibility that 'a military competitor with a formidable resource base will emerge in the [South-east Asian] region'. China also views with some disquiet the strengthening of American security relationships with countries around its borders, from Central Asia, Afghanistan and Pakistan through to the Philippines (where US troops have been dispatched to 'train' Philippine forces engaged in action against Abu Sayyaf guerrillas), Taiwan and Japan (which dispatched naval vessels to the Indian Ocean to provide non-combat support in the Afghanistan campaign). With his visit to India in January 2002, Prime Minister Zhu Rongji tried to restore some balance in big-power alignments on the subcontinent by strengthening ties with New Delhi.

The visit to Beijing by President Bush in late February 2002 helped to satisfy China's desire for recognition as a world power by the United States (it was Bush's second visit to the country in five months), but did little to remove underlying causes of tension between the two countries. In public at least, Bush failed to reiterate Washington's commitment to the three Sino-US accords of the 1970s and 1980s that China regards as the basis of the relationship. Instead, he pledged support for the Taiwan Relations Act of 1979 that commits Washington to helping Taiwan maintain the ability to defend itself from any attack by the mainland. No agreement was reached on the proliferation of Chinese missile technology, which Washington alleges has continued despite a pledge by Beijing in November 2000 to stop the export of equipment that could be used in the production of nuclear-capable missiles. In a speech at Qinghua University in Beijing on 22 February, Bush also publicly criticised China's human-rights policies – particularly those on religious freedom.

Less than a month after Bush's trip, new signs of strain over Taiwan appeared, with Beijing reacting furiously to an unofficial visit to the US by Taiwan's defence minister, General Tang Yiau-ming – the first such trip by a top Taiwanese defence official in two decades. On 11 March 2002, General Tang attended a conference in Florida, where he met senior US officials, including Deputy Secretary of Defense Paul Wolfowitz. The visit is likely to have jeopardised the position of pragmatists in the Chinese leadership who have been arguing that a less belligerent posture towards Taiwan might encourage the island to accept the idea of eventual reunification. The pragmatists' stance was clearly set out by the Deputy Prime Minister Qian Qichen in January 2002, when he suggested that only a handful of members of Taiwan's ruling Democratic Progressive Party were committed to independence.

China's regional concerns

American military involvement in a region of growing importance to China also has clear regional strategic implications. The conflict in Afghanistan highlighted the weakness of the Shanghai Cooperation Organisation (SCO), a group established in 1996 as the 'Shanghai Five' at China's urging, with the aim of combating terrorism and separatist movements in Central Asia.

China had hoped the now six-nation partnership, which also includes Russia, Uzbekistan, Tajikistan, Kyrgyzstan and Kazakhstan, would strengthen its influence over security affairs in the region and keep American power at bay. But the SCO's response to the 11 September attacks and subsequent events was distinctly muted. In fact, its members offered varying degrees of practical bilateral support to the US, including the use of military bases in the frontline states of Uzbekistan and Tajikistan. Although the US has tried to reassure China that it does not plan to maintain a long-term military presence in Central Asia, doubts remain in Beijing.

Yet China also has some reason to be grateful for the American intervention in Afghanistan. It shares international concerns about the impact of radical Islam on security in Central Asia, particularly on its own Muslim population in Xinjiang. But little evidence has been revealed of any organisational links between the Taliban or al-Qaeda in Afghanistan and militants in Xinjiang. China says about 1,000 Xinjiang residents have received covert military training in Afghanistan, but it is likely that the majority of these would have been deployed against the Northern Alliance or in the war in Chechnya rather than in China. China may also have deliberately exaggerated such links in order to justify harsher repression of the separatists.

The campaign against terrorism has exposed the limitations of China's relationship with Russia, which the two countries had been nurturing as a counterweight to American power. In July 2001, Sino-Russian ties had appeared to reach a new height with the signing in Moscow by Presidents Jiang and Putin of a new treaty of friendship. This was the first treaty between the two countries since the 1950s. Jiang and Putin also jointly expressed their opposition to any changes in the ABM Treaty. But apart from sales of Russian weaponry to China (boosted in January 2002 by an agreement to sell two more *Sovremenny*-class destroyers to the Chinese navy), Moscow–Beijing ties have remained largely at the rhetorical level. China was probably little surprised, though doubtless discomfited, by the rapid strengthening of US–Russian ties after 11 September, as well as by signs of closer cooperation between Russia and NATO.

An emerging strategic rivalry between China and Japan also shows no signs of abating in the wake of 11 September. On the military level, to appear compliant with counter-terrorism goals, China did not publicly oppose Japan's decision to send warships to the Indian Ocean. But officials were clearly worried that this might set a precedent for a broader, more extrovert Japanese security role. China is also concerned about growing momentum in Japan to revise Article 9 of its 'peace constitution' to permit a more robust military posture, and a dispute between the two countries arose in December 2001 over the recovery of a suspected North Korean espionage vessel sunk by the Japanese navy inside China's economic exclusion zone. Diplomatic ties were badly strained in August 2001 by Japanese Prime Minister Junichiro Koizumi's visit to the Yasukuni shrine dedicated to Japan's war dead. China saw this as a tribute to those responsible for Japan's brutal occupation of parts of China in the 1930s and 1940s. As much of the world's attention focused on terrorism and how it might define the future security environment, China's relationship with Japan remained enmeshed in antagonisms of the distant past. In late September, Koizumi succeeded in making amends for his Yasukuni trip by paying a visit – at Beijing's insistence – to the site of Japan's invasion of China in 1937.

The notion that China will soon compete with Japan for regional economic leadership is grounded in justifiably pessimistic assessments concerning problems in Japan's banking sector and public finances, as well as the essentially dysfunctional Japanese bureaucratic and political system that has hindered crisis management and is unable to produce imaginative policies. But the debate is often also informed by unduly optimistic appraisals of China's current economic circumstances and future prospects. China's economy remains one-quarter the size of Japan's. Unlike China, Japan is technologically highly advanced. Its corporations have acquired interests and established cross-border production structures that extend far beyond East Asia's emerging markets and penetrate into the core of the area of the Organisation for Economic Cooperation and Development. Few of China's companies are globally competitive, much of its industry is unsophisticated and its main banks are technically insolvent. Unlike China, Japan is in global terms a major source of foreign aid and investment. It is also a net international creditor, and its markets absorb more imports than China's. The yen acts as an international reserve currency next to the dollar and euro, whereas China's *renminbi* is not even fully convertible. Actual indications of competition for leadership are hard to find. China's proposal for the creation a free-trade area with ASEAN in the next ten years may be intended to fend off Japan. But the sluggish pace of trade liberalisation within ASEAN members at present, a possible Chinese reluctance to throw their doors even further open while absorbing competitive shocks of WTO-related tariff reform, and the limited trade complementarities between China and its South-east Asian neighbours cast doubt on the success of the enterprise.

ASEAN's enthusiasm for the free-trade proposal can be read as an indication of its desire to 'get in on the action' in China, while demonstrating to the outside world that ASEAN is going places and thinking big. For China, pledging an essentially theoretical commitment to free trade represents an inexpensive means of demonstrating solidarity with neighbours hit by the downturn in the United States, and may indeed, have more to do with US–China competition than China–Japan competition. What matters more than actual instances of competition for regional economic leadership between China and Japan is the perception among East Asian countries that relative economic performance will translate into relative political clout in the future, and that ASEAN foreign policy must therefore become favourable to China. But ASEAN's warmth towards China will be inhibited by suspicions about China's strategic intentions, particularly in the South China Sea. Conversely, China remains wary of regional efforts to draft a code of conduct governing maritime territorial disputes in the area. ASEAN members probably will also recognise that, no matter how rapid China's annual growth, it would be in no position to take up the regional economic slack if Japan were to enter into the kind of deep crisis that some predict (and others advocate as a form of 'creative destruction'). Thus, China is unlikely to develop regional economic leadership in the foreseeable future.

Calculated extroversion, fraught domestic adjustments

China's foreign and domestic policy decisions will be considerably influenced in the coming years by two of the country's proudest achievements in 2001 – joining the WTO and winning its bid to host the Olympic Games in Beijing in 2008. WTO membership will bind China more closely to the norms governing relations between free-market economies, including Taiwan, which itself joined the WTO in January 2002. The desire to host a successful Olympic Games will encourage China to avoid diplomatic ructions that could mar the event, particularly in the year or two before it. China wants the Olympics to be a celebration of its coming of age as a world power and it wants Taiwan to celebrate with it. Efforts to win over hearts and minds in Taiwan are therefore likely to be intensified in the build-up to the games.

In the meantime, China faces the arduous task of phasing in, mostly over a 3–5 year period, the market-access reforms which it agreed to undertake in return for membership of the WTO (to which it acceded on 11 December). To date, China's economic reforms have consisted of the gradual introduction of incentive structures and market mechanisms to a formerly planned economy. The process of opening up to the outside world has, since 1979, led to vast inflows of foreign investment and China's emergence as a major trading power. However, in critical areas of the economy, such as the state enterprise and banking sectors, reforms have not been sufficiently far-reaching, raising doubts about the sustainability of a rapid pace of growth under circumstances of gross inefficiency and resource misallocation. The immediate benefits of membership will come in the form of increased inward investment and associated gains in access to foreign skills and technology. Other assumed benefits, however, may be slow to materialise. For example, while many new foreign investments will be export-oriented, tariff liberalisation will in the first instance lead to a surge in imports and a consequent deterioration in China's trade balance.

The competitive pressures resulting from WTO membership in the short-term will likely make China's structural problems all the more glaring, and the process of economic adjustment is likely to be difficult. But, over the longer-term at least, such pressure should provide the impetus to reform. A major question concerns the extent to which the central authorities in Beijing can forge ahead in creating a trade regime that is consistent, on a national basis, with the general non-discriminatory spirit and specific demands of the WTO. It will not be helped by the de facto devolution of political power to interests in the provinces that has so far occurred under the economic reform programme. The weakness of China's judicial system, and the effective absence of the rule of law as conceived in the West and elsewhere, will also clash with the rules-based approaches of the WTO. Beijing's aim, which also serves its broader political objectives, will be to find ways of re-centralising powers to achieve policy consistency across China. Faced with the prospect of economic dislocation as foreign competition bites, meanwhile, China's political controls seem destined to tighten to guard against social unrest.

Although WTO membership promises a variety of long-term economic gains, the process of adjusting to greater foreign competition will produce unwanted short-term side-effects. Prominent among these will be a rise in unemployment in urban areas, especially where the dependence on increasingly unhealthy state-owned enterprises (SOEs) is disproportionately large (such as in the 'rust belt' of the north-eastern provinces). The challenges posed by unemployment could be even more pressing in the rural economy, where 200 million agricultural workers are already thought to be unnecessary. Agriculture will be particularly hard hit by competition from imports, and it seems likely that phenomenon of immense labour migration flows to urban areas will pick up. This could lead to further social tensions and crime in China's urban areas. On the other hand, coastal urban areas will generally be better placed to compete, because they have much more established links to the international economy, and because they have placed greatest emphasis on creating the conditions – in terms of physical and human infrastructure – needed to capture foreign investment. Elsewhere, the onus will be on the government to facilitate the rapid growth of the private sector as a means of absorbing the unemployed. Another thorny priority in containing urban unrest will be the creation of welfare facilities to compensate for the loss of health, accommodation, pension and educational entitlements previously afforded by SOEs.

While the Communist Party is likely to be blamed for adverse effects of WTO membership, its growing detachment from day-to-day management issues will make it harder for the party to claim credit for its benefits. So far, however, protests in rural and urban areas alike, though increasing, have proven manageable and have not revealed grand political intentions or organisational sophistication. On balance, the disruption caused by accession to the WTO probably does not pose a serious threat to party rule in the short term. The party continues to have control over the military, the media and the bureaucracy. Although the emergence of the non-political but highly organised Falun Gong has revealed some glaring deficiencies in the public security apparatus, there are few channels for dissent in China, and the party has been adept at nipping protests in the bud.

Notwithstanding considerable economic and social growing pains, China is likely to seek ways of increasing its economic domination of Taiwan while continuing to develop the capability to subdue Taiwan militarily. Yet Beijing will remain suspicious of Taipei's desire to use the WTO as a forum for resolving bilateral economic disputes between Taiwan and China and thereby promoting its independent identity. In Beijing's view, any problems between Taiwan and the mainland should be treated as internal, domestic affairs beyond the purview of any international body. Thus, China is likely to exploit the two sides' entry into the WTO to encourage Taiwan to remove barriers to economic integration between the two sides, including a ban on direct transportation and trading links. Such integration, China believes, will strengthen the mainland's economic leverage over the island. Relations between China and Taiwan in 2002 and 2003 will remain vulnerable to the vicissitudes of the two sides' domestic politics.

Taiwan's parliamentary elections on 1 December 2001 considerably strengthened the political position of the pro-independence DPP, but the party still lacks an outright majority in the legislature. China has appeared more inclined since the elections to accept the reality of the DPP's political dominance in Taiwan and the strong possibility that President Chen Shui-bian will be re-elected in 2004. While it will likely continue to shun Chen himself, China strongly hinted in January 2002 that some form of dialogue with DPP members might be possible. According to state media, Vice-Premier Qian Qichen, Beijing's top foreign-policy official, stated: 'We believe there is a difference between the majority of Democratic Progressive Party members and the extremely small number of die-hard "Taiwan independence" elements. We welcome them, under an appropriate status, to come and look around and to pay visits to further understanding'. In the build-up to the 16th Congress, however, Chinese leaders will be preoccupied with political manoeuvring at home. During this period, they are likely to be reluctant to resume the semi-official talks that Beijing broke off in 1999 in response to what it saw as separatist remarks by Taiwan's then president, Lee Teng-hui. China still insists that Taiwan accept the notion of 'one China' before talks restart. Leaders anxious to display their political strength at the upcoming congress are unlikely to suggest any compromise on this point.

The 16th Party Congress

This congress – likely to be held in October 2002 – will be the most important political gathering in China since President Jiang was appointed party chief in the wake of the Tiananmen Square protests of 1989. It will formally select a new Communist Party Central Committee, which in turn will select a new Politburo and party chief. These appointments will in fact be decided in secret in advance of the congress. Jiang is currently engaged in a tough struggle with his colleagues as he tries to ensure that as many of his protégés as possible secure places in the new leadership. The new party general secretary is all but certain to be Vice-President Hu Jintao, who was selected as Jiang's successor by the late Deng Xiaoping. Jiang, however, has a closer relationship with Zeng Qinghong, the head of the party's Organisation Department. It is likely that Zeng's power will be strengthened at the congress (with promotion to the Politburo's Standing Committee) and that he will rival Hu for influence in the coming years. At the annual session of China's parliament, the National People's Congress, in early 2003, Hu will almost certainly take over Jiang's concurrent position as state president. Zeng would be a likely candidate to assume the vice-presidency.

Signs of heightened political tension in China have already emerged as the congress approaches. These include: the sudden departure of Shanghai's popular mayor Xu Kuangdi in December 2001; small demonstrations on the streets of Beijing against corruption allegedly involving the family of China's second-highest ranking Communist official, Li Peng; and unusually public attacks by hardliners in 2001 against President Jiang's moves to admit private entrepreneurs into the party. None of these suggest any greater political dislocation than would normally be expected before a congress – an event which has historically entailed significant leadership changes.

Little is yet known about how Vice-President Hu would lead the country. He has kept a low profile and expressed no opinions in public that deviate from Jiang's. It is widely believed that Jiang wants to retain his position as chairman of the Central Military Commission even after Hu takes over as party chief and president. Keeping the military position would enable Jiang to play a role similar to that of Deng after the latter's semi-retirement at the 13th Congress in 1987. Deng's military clout proved crucial in the suppression of the anti-government unrest in 1989 and in the subsequent installation of Jiang as party leader. But Jiang lacks Deng's authority and military expertise. His efforts to promote his close associate Zeng have aroused widespread opposition within the party élite, who regard Zeng as belonging to Jiang's 'Shanghai faction' of privileged cronies. China is therefore entering a period of heightened political instability.

Social and economic volatility, political inexperience

The 16th Congress is also taking place against a background of unusually severe social dislocation caused by rapid economic change. Chinese officials readily admit their concern about a growing gap between rich and poor, rising unemployment, sluggish growth in the countryside, endemic corruption and persistent deflation. The country's GDP growth rate in 2002 is likely to be lower than the 7.3% officially recorded in 2001, which in turn was down on the 8% growth rate of 2000. Many Chinese economists believe 7% is the minimum growth necessary to provide enough jobs to prevent serious social disorder. Furthermore, although China's accession to the WTO marks a major step in integrating the country into the international trading system, it remains partially excluded from global capital markets. This self-imposed exclusion is driven largely by concerns about the potentially destabilising macroeconomic impact of high-volume flows of short-term capital (in the form of portfolio investment) into and out of China. With its dysfunctional banking system and under-regulated stock markets, China's exclusion is something it can ill afford over the long-term. As noted, corruption and unemployment are already triggering increasingly frequent protests in poorer urban and rural areas. The new leadership will therefore remain preoccupied with the maintenance of social stability for the foreseeable future.

How it will manage remains a major uncertainty. China's government has sought to entrench its political legitimacy through the pursuit of economic modernisation and the defence of China's national interests, national sovereignty and various territorial claims – all of which are to some extent seen as being under threat. But most recently China seems to have gained a more nuanced understanding of nationalism as a force which – by raising public expectations of China's international influence, foreclosing foreign-policy flexibility through its inherently absolutist nature and establishing exacting standards for government performance – has enormous potential to complicate governance. The April 2001 spy-plane crisis between China and the United States demonstrated the ease with which officially sanctioned patriotic indignation in China could evolve and escalate into expressions of aggressive nationalism and, subsequently, into criticisms that Beijing was being far too soft in dealing with the US. In this sense, it is perhaps unsurprising that Beijing should have actively toned down its official responses in January 2002 to the bugging of China's US-made presidential aircraft. This reflected the pragmatic decision that little was to be gained by supporting further outpourings of Chinese public anger at the risk of wounding a Sino-US relationship that was beginning to heal by virtue of the new opportunities offered by the global campaign against terrorism.

Yet China's external relations could become less predictable in the coming few years. Hu has little experience of handling foreign policy matters. He has never visited the United States and has rarely met American visitors, though it was announced during Bush's February trip to Beijing that he would go to Washington before October 2002. His experience with Russia is hardly more profound – he made his first visit to the country only in October 2001. The new generation of leaders will have to deal with growing public demands for assertive positions *vis-à-vis* the United States, Japan and Taiwan in particular. Such demands were particularly evident in 1999, when widespread protests erupted following the bombing of the Chinese Embassy in Belgrade. Hu, like Jiang and Deng, is likely to try to keep nationalistic demands from upsetting the country's long-term foreign policy goal of maintaining a peaceful external environment in order to allow China to focus on domestic economic development. But with Jiang's influence likely to decline sharply in the next couple of years, and Hu's skills untested (particularly in military affairs, in which he has little experience), other countries will need to be alert to the possibility of sudden fluctuations in China's external and domestic policies.

Japan: New Security Challenges, Same Economic Problems

The year 2001 was a dramatic one for Japan, dominated by a series of policy-making peaks and troughs in the spheres of national security and economic management. The high hopes associated with the new reforming cabinet of Junichiro Koizumi were a welcome antidote to the cynicism and despondency generated by the previous Mori administration. While defence and security issues were addressed pragmatically and swiftly, in part as a consequence of catalysing post-11 September pressures overseas (especially in the United States) and at home, achievements in the economic context seemed more rhetorical than substantive. To the alarm of many outside observers, it remained uncertain by early spring 2002 whether the government would be able to extricate the country from a morass of depressing economic statistics. Potential conflicts between the goals of structural reform and combating deflationary pressures have raised fears that the cabinet lacks both a sense of urgency and a coherent vision for economic recovery. Even assuming that it is, in fact, possible to generate such a vision, it is uncertain whether the government has sufficient institutional and executive authority to challenge the vested political and bureaucratic interests that threaten to condemn Japan to a half-hearted reform strategy that may be 'too little, too late'.

Enhanced US–Japan security cooperation

Prospects for a more vigorous and clearly defined Japanese foreign policy increased in 2001 with the advent of new administrations in Washington and Tokyo. George Bush's inauguration as president in January 2001 and Junichiro Koizumi's surprise selection as Liberal Democratic Party (LDP) president and prime minister in April created an opportunity for a closer and more harmonious relationship between two countries that have consistently emphasised the importance of their bilateral partnership, but which have, in recent years, frequently diverged over trade and economic issues. Bush's inauguration was preceded by the publication in October 2000 of a much commented-upon bipartisan National Defense University study calling for a more 'mature partnership' with Japan involving, among other things, closer military cooperation, wider sharing of defence technology and intelligence cooperation, the lifting of Japan's long-standing prohibition on participation in 'collective security' initiatives, and recognition by Washington that a more independent and proactive Japanese foreign policy need not conflict with American diplomatic priorities. With some of the report's principal authors assuming leading positions in the new administration, and with senior NSC, State Department and Defense Department positions occupied by experienced Japan-specialists, it was widely expected that relations between Tokyo and Washington – particularly in the security field – would become more constructive and cooperative.

Such expectations appear to have been well founded. Although senior Japanese foreign ministry officials were worried initially that a more unilateral and uncompromising stance under Bush might exacerbate relations with China and marginalise Japanese efforts to normalise and improve relations with North Korea, such concerns were in part offset by enhanced bilateral cooperation and extended dialogue. Early in 2001, a series of unanticipated crises threatened to impose severe strains on Japanese–American relations. These included: the arrest in January of an Okinawa-based US marine on sexual molestation charges; undiplomatic and disparaging references to local politicians by the senior US marine commander in Okinawa contained in an e-mail leaked in February; an unscheduled port visit to Sasebo by a US nuclear-powered submarine in April; and the crash-landing in Japan of an American F-16 fighter plane in April as well.

In potentially the most damaging episode of all, on 9 February 2001, a US Navy submarine and a Japanese fishing vessel collided, resulting in the death of nine Japanese nationals. Swift apologies by senior Bush administration officials (as well as a public expression of remorse by the commander of the submarine, who was later forced to resign), the convening of an open and transparent Navy Court of enquiry into the submarine collision, the involvement of Japanese Defense Agency (JDA) officials in the salvaging of the fishing vessel, and a joint decision to establish a memorial to the victims of the accident, all helped to diffuse what might easily have developed into a damaging source of tension between the two countries.

Progress at the local level helped during the year to enhance bilateral relations between Washington and Tokyo. While criminal incidents involving US marines continued to intensify local irritation with the large American military presence in Okinawa, at senior levels of government both the American and Japanese participants appeared to 'manage' such tensions. The time-span for the maintenance of US bases in Okinawa remains unresolved. Keiichi Inamine, the governor of Okinawa, hopes to limit the US presence to 15 years, and both governments are in the process of re-examining the Status of Forces Agreement that defines the terms under which US troops are present in Japan. Nevertheless, the Japanese government's April 2001 decision to close an industrial waste incinerator alleged to be polluting the US airbase at Atsugi gratified the US military. In addition, before leaving office in April 2001, and despite his unpopularity, former Prime Minister Mori was able to win approval for the continued use of Okinawa land for US bases. Finally, the Japanese government's decision on 27 December 2001 to relocate the US marine heliport at Futenma to an offshore facility near East Nago city has helped to contain a number of basing controversies.

Throughout the year, an American stress on the importance of dialogue also appears to have been helpful in assuaging Japanese fears about undue American pressure. For example, US Deputy Secretary of State Richard Armitage visited Tokyo on 8 May 2001 to discuss overall US missile defence plans and theatre missile defence (TMD) cooperation with Japan – an issue actively under consideration between the two countries since 1999. Despite not being able to meet with Japanese Foreign Minister Makiko Tanaka (a non-event that provoked considerable media commentary), Armitage's visit was successful in apparently reassuring a Japanese government that has remained wary of being tied into a development programme with the Americans. The system under consideration is the US Navy's new Sea-based Midcourse Defense TMD system, successor to the Navy Theater Wide programme that ended in December 2001. Japan's worry is that the system risks a regional arms race or worse, given its mobile and flexible character, involving Japan in a future conflict with China over Taiwan. Underlining its commitment to maintaining a degree of operational autonomy in this area, the Japanese government in early April 2001 opened its Cabinet Satellite Information Center. This is arguably a necessary stage in developing the intelligence and monitoring expertise that TMD requires. Japan's capability in this area will doubtless be enhanced by the planned launch in March 2003 of four surveillance satellites. While Prime Minister Koizumi expressed general support for TMD, JDA Director-General Gen Nakatani was careful to point out on 22 June 2001 that any future Japanese TMD system would be operated independently by Japan and used exclusively for its own defence.

At the same time, the role of Japan's security forces has substantially expanded in the wake of the 11 September terrorist attacks. The passage in late October 2001 of legislation allowed Japan's Self-Defense Forces (SDF) to provide logistical, rear-echelon support to US and UK forces in the Indian Ocean, as part of the wider campaign against terrorism. Prime Minister Koizumi responded swiftly to the September events. On 19 September, he announced a seven-point assistance plan. In early October, the despatch of Japanese C-130 transport planes to airlift relief supplies to Afghan refugees in Pakistan was approved. On 9 November, two Japanese destroyers and a supply-ship were sent to the Indian Ocean, initially for a two-month deployment. These decisive actions reflected the Koizumi cabinet's desire to avoid the hesitation and indecision associated with Japan's response to the 1990–91 Gulf War. Moreover, they represent a significant change in official Japanese security policy, and may suggest a shift in government and public attitudes, as well as presage an improvement in Tokyo's ability to respond to international crises.

The October 2001 counter-terrorism legislation – although operative for only a two-year period – broke new ground in three critical areas by:

- entitling SDF personnel to use small arms, not only to protect themselves but also individuals or facilities in their charge;
- ensuring that the SDF should be used to protect both US and Japanese military installations within Japan;
- expanding the duties of Japan's Coast Guard forces beyond coastal surveillance, to include firing directly at hostile vessels intruding into Japanese maritime waters.

Officially, these new provisions restrict SDF personnel to providing logistical support in exclusively non-combat areas. However, it is questionable – given the wide-ranging nature of the anti-terrorism initiative – whether such a precise distinction between combat and non-combat areas can be maintained. This uncertainty, coupled with the wider coalition-based nature of the anti-Taliban campaign, opens the door for a reassessment and qualification (either explicit or implicit) of the long-standing prohibition on participation in collective security initiatives that has governed Japanese security policy for much of the post-Second World War period. Already, there have been suggestions across the political spectrum in Japan that the collective security ban is outdated and ought to be removed. In May 2001, the JDA formally argued for a constitutional revision or reinterpretation of this restriction; younger conservative Diet representatives from both the LDP and the Democratic Party of Japan (DPJ) – the main opposition party – have been vocal in demanding a change. In September 2001, even former Prime Minister Kiichi Miyazawa – a noted 'dove' on security issues – publicly called for a removal of the ban. Moreover, a March 2002 poll conducted by the *Yomiuri Shinbun*, Japan's largest newspaper, revealed that 71% of all Diet members are in favour of constitutional change and 54% support changes to allow Japan to exercise its right to collective self-defence. Thus, there is considerable momentum for Japan to strengthen its security posture via regional avenues. On 13 February 2001, JDA Director-General Nakutani indicated that the time could be ripe for North-east Asian security arrangements, and expressed support for a regional alliance similar to NATO. Japan planned to present an initiative for such an arrangement at the first International Institute for Strategic Studies' Asia Security Conference: the Shangri-La Dialogue, scheduled for 31 May–2 June 2002 in Singapore.

Throughout 2001 and early 2002, there was much to suggest that Japanese security policy was becoming more focused and coherent, and less encumbered by the normative and ideological taboos that have in the past prevented Japanese governments from addressing the country's security needs in a pragmatic fashion. Koizumi has, on a number of occasions, publicly called for a revision of Article 9 of the Japanese constitution – the 'peace clause' restricting Japan to a non-offensive security posture – while also arguing that Japan's Self-Defence Forces should be unambiguously viewed as a standing army. Reflecting the LDP government's intention to reconsider its overall security policy, press reports indicated in early August 2001 that the Koizumi cabinet was reviewing the country's National Defense Program Outline (NDPO). Last reassessed in 1995, the NDPO sets the framework for Japan's mid-term defence plans. The anticipated new outline would, among other things, re-orient Japan's SDF southwards towards Kyushu and Okinawa as a means of tackling potential security challenges from Korea and the Taiwan Strait.

In March 2002, the review process reached a new stage. Legislation was drafted that intended to address emergency situations involving wholesale attacks on the nation. In its original form, and with support from the prime minister, the legislation was originally supposed to contemplate a broad range of contingencies, including wholesale terrorist assaults as well as conventional military attacks. In an effort to avoid bureaucratic turf-wars and jurisdictional disputes between the JDA and the National Police Agency, however, the government chose to restrict the scope of the legislation to invasions by a foreign power. Nevertheless, the proposed measures envisage a much more clearly centralised decision-making role for the prime minister, supported by a counter-measures headquarters and allowing for concentrated intelligence-gathering and power to issue instructions to local authorities and utility companies. To an outside observer, these changes might not seem especially controversial. But given the well-developed and historically informed aversion to centralised leadership in Japan, they are likely to provoke considerable domestic debate.

The impetus for this change in direction has been growing since the late 1990s, in the wake of a series of high-profile security challenges faced by

Japan – most notably North Korea's 1998 launch over Japan of a medium-range *Taepodong* ballistic missile. The most recent expression of regional assertiveness on the part of Pyongyang – the December 2001 surprise incursion into Japanese territorial waters of a North Korean spy ship and its subsequent scuttling in the face of a Japanese Coast Guard challenge – has reinforced the impression of Japanese vulnerability and strengthened the hand of those calling for a stronger, executive-led crisis management system. Washington is likely to welcome these changes. While taking care not to appear to meddle in Japan's decision-making process, Armitage has expressed Washington's clear support for a lifting of the ban on collective security participation, and US officials in general have publicly been very supportive of Japanese efforts to reinforce the country's security preparedness. Indeed, Washington shared intelligence with Tokyo during the North Korean spy-ship crisis in December and on 10 December, US Assistant Secretary of State for Intelligence and Research Carl Ford indicated that the US would be willing to defend Japan's Senkaku Islands in the event of an emergency. This positive tone has been matched on Japan's side by a sympathetic attitude on security matters. Japan quietly backed the US response to the April 2001 collision between a US EP-3 surveillance aircraft and a Chinese fighter plane. Given that the American plane had originally been based in Okinawa, Tokyo's support was of critical importance in shaping Washington's response to Beijing in the ensuing diplomatic crisis.

Volatile relations in North-east Asia

If Tokyo's ties with Washington were largely positive during 2001, relations between Japan and its immediate neighbours were, and continue to be, far more unpredictable. Historical tensions and trade conflicts have, in particular, imposed strains on Japanese ties with China and both of the Koreas.

Sino-Japanese relations

The approval in February 2001 by Japan's Ministry of Education of a controversial new middle-school history textbook representing the Pacific War as a war of liberation and asserting that Japan's pre-war annexation of Korea was a legally justifiable and stabilising act, generated official protests from Beijing. Similarly, public statements in the same month by Hosei Norota, a leading LDP politician, suggesting that there was a legitimate basis for Japan's wartime actions, provoked official Chinese criticism that Japan was attempting to 'beautify' a war of aggression and was insensitive to the feelings of the Chinese people. Japanese claims that the textbook-screening process did not represent an official endorsement of a particular point of view failed to deflect Chinese criticism. The controversy over historical responsibility was exacerbated following Koizumi's decision, on 13 August 2001, to visit the country's Yasukuni Shrine commemorating Japan's wartime dead. The memorial is inextricably associated in the minds of Japan's neighbours with the country's military past. Bilateral relations had already been strained by the Japanese government's decision on April 20 to grant a visa to former Taiwanese President Lee Teng-hui to visit Japan to receive medical treatment for a heart condition.

Koizumi's controversial shrine visit was motivated by his wish to adhere to a previous campaign pledge, by the need to accommodate conservative pressures at home and indeed by the imperative not to appear overly susceptible to foreign pressure. Despite various attempts by the Japanese government to diffuse tensions with China by sending senior LDP envoys to Beijing, the history controversy did not dissipate until Koizumi visited Beijing on 8 October 2001. During the visit, he issued a fulsome apology, or *owabi* – the first by a post-war Japanese prime minister. Bilateral relations improved further after a constructive meeting between Koizumi and PRC President Jiang Zemin at the Asia-Pacific Economic Cooperation summit in Shanghai on 21 October 2001.

Overlaying and complicating these high-profile disagreements were bilateral tensions resulting from repeated incursions during the year by Chinese naval vessels into Japan's exclusive economic zone. These occurred despite an earlier agreement in February 2001 establishing a prior notification system regulating China's putative 'research activities' in Japanese waters. Japan's longstanding concerns about China's military build-up (reflected in a 17% expansion in defence spending for fiscal year 2001), which was highlighted in the 1 March 2002 Strategic Survey of Japan's National Institute for Defense Studies, further increased tensions. Trade relations were also strained during the year by a series of tit-for-tat protectionist measures, with China levying increased tariffs on imports of Japanese automobiles, cell phones and air conditioners in June 2001 in retaliation for temporary Japanese safeguards imposed on Chinese leeks, mushrooms and straw matting.

Personalities and shared economic interests were significant in alleviating some of these bilateral stresses. Koizumi's visits to China helped to secure Chinese acceptance of Tokyo's support for Washington's counter-terrorism campaign. Even amid the political fallout associated with Koizumi's Yasukuni visit, Chinese Foreign Minister Tang Jiaxuan was quick to point out in interviews with the Japanese media that China continued to place great importance on its relationship with Japan. Common economic interests, epitomised by the surge in Japanese investment into China in the final quarter of 2001, particularly in the cell-phone and automobile industries, helped to bind the countries closely together, despite a 10% reduction in Japanese Overseas Development Assistance (ODA) announced in June 2001.

In late December 2001, China lifted its retaliatory sanctions against Japan, and the two countries agreed to establish structures for bilateral mediation of trade disputes. In the military sphere, the two governments agreed, in November 2001, to reciprocal warship visits. This economic cooperation was not restricted to a bilateral context. On 5 November, Koizumi, Jiang and Kim Dae Jung of South Korea, meeting at Brunei for the 'ASEAN plus 3' gathering, established a new trilateral forum for cooperation between their economic, foreign and finance ministers. Progress of this sort – while not necessarily trumpeted – provided a promising basis for continuing cooperation in 2002. On balance, this made for an auspicious beginning for the thirtieth anniversary of the 1972 normalisation of Sino-Japanese relations.

Japan and the Korean Peninsula

Tensions over textbooks and official Yasukuni visits similarly disrupted relations between Japan and South Korea. Seoul withdrew its ambassador in protest against Japanese actions, President Kim refused to receive delegations from Tokyo and in July the South Korean government suspended military exchanges, froze Japanese money transactions and suspended plans to open its market to Japanese cultural products. Once again, personal intervention ultimately helped to diffuse tensions and Koizumi's 15 October 2001 visit to Seoul, combined with an apology, mollified South Korean élites, paving the way for the establishment of a bilateral textbook panel on 20 October. Symbolic concessions and gestures by Japan, including a ruling by a Kyoto district court in August requiring the Japanese government to pay $375,000 in compensation to 15 South Korean survivors of a 1945 ship explosion, also helped to in improve the bilateral mood. By the end of the year, the two countries were able to weather a number of potential disagreements associated with the misfiring of a South Korean ballistic missile in a test near Japan and a vigorous but ultimately unsuccessful South Korean claim for fishing rights close to Japan's Northern Territories. Amid the turmoil over historical interpretations, both countries remained largely aware of wider common strategic priorities – sending representatives to participate in the regular Trilateral Coordination and Oversight Group meetings – a critical context for discussion between the US, Japan and South Korea on how best to enhance security on the peninsula.

At the opposite end of the peninsula, Japanese ties with Pyongyang remained frosty throughout the year, with little indication of pragmatism on North Korea's part. With public opinion in Japan exercised by the issue of Japanese 'abductees', allegedly kidnapped by North Korea during the 1970s and 1980s, bilateral ties remain limited and problematic and were further set back by a Japanese police investigation in November 2001 of the activities of Chosen Soren (the association of North Korean residents in Japan) for suspected embezzlement. Relations soured further following intemperate claims by Pyongyang that Tokyo's launch of its H-2 space rocket was an effort by Japan to develop an independent launch capability for nuclear weapons, and reached their nadir in the wake of the intrusion by a North Korean spy ship into Japanese waters in late December 2001. In the face of continued unwillingness by North Korea to grant access to International Atomic Energy Association inspectors, the year was rounded off by a Japanese government announcement that construction work on two light-water nuclear reactors in North Korea would be delayed by six years. Japan's scope for constructive engagement with Pyongyang via the Korean Peninsula Energy Development Organisation remains limited. At the same time, Tokyo remains concerned about its relative inability to exert leverage over North Korea on security threats that are of immediate relevance to Japan – such as the risks associated with short-range missiles and chemical and biological weapons – but which are not explicitly addressed in bilateral talks between Washington and Pyongyang, and between Seoul and Pyongyang.

Partially reinvigorated regionalism

In the face of limited bilateral opportunities in North-east Asia, Japan has increasingly turned its attention towards South-east Asia. Koizumi's tour of the five founding nations of the Association of South-east Asian Nations (ASEAN) in January 2002 was, in some respects, an attempt to recreate the positive rhetoric of 'heart-to-heart' diplomacy associated with the Fukuda Doctrine of the late 1970s. The prime minister's claim to be 'acting together' and 'advancing together as sincere and open partners' is relatively uncontentious, and reasonably well supported by Tokyo's promotion of a five-point initiative embodying education and human resource development, intellectual and cultural exchange, and by a Japan–ASEAN Comprehensive Economic Partnership. Yet, while China is a long way from rivalling Japan as the dominant regional economy, the initiative was a relatively ineffectual attempt to offset China's growing economic influence in the region. Japanese business interest is increasingly directed towards China and away from South-east Asia. Moreover, Japan's own economic weakness means that it can no longer serve as a model for its South-east Asian partners as it did in the 1970s, and reductions in its ODA budget substantially undercut its regional clout. Moreover, Tokyo's commitment to free trade is highly qualified because of domestic political pressures, as reflected in the exemption of agricultural products from its 13 January 2001 Free Trade Agreement with Singapore. There is little evidence of a genuine long-term and comprehensive regional free trade-initiative among senior Japanese officials.

This is not to say that Japan lacks opportunities to strengthen its hand regionally. Tokyo's announcement in October last year of plans to despatch 700 SDF troops to East Timor as part of an expanded peacekeeping operation is an encouraging sign of constructive regional engagement, as is the government's cooperation with the Philippines in October 2001 anti-piracy exercises off Manila Bay. Similarly, Tokyo's success in hosting the post-conflict Afghanistan reconstruction conference in January 2002 highlights not only Japan's mediating skills but its ability to generate substantial financial support for international humanitarian initiatives. (The conference produced $4.5bn in assistance pledges, including $500m from Japan.) But such programmes – worthy as they undoubtedly are – remain *ad hoc* and do not imply an overarching and long-term Japanese regional strategy.

Reformer on the ropes

There is little doubt that Koizumi's election as LDP leader represented a sharp departure – both in terms of style and substance – from the norms of conservative party politics in Japan. In the face of haemorrhaging support rates for the party and its leader, younger LDP parliamentarians and prefectural chapters (aided by rule-changes enhancing their influence) broke with convention and voted overwhelmingly for Koizumi, rather than backing the traditionally dominant faction headed by party heavyweight and former prime minister, Ryutaro Hashimoto. This strategy of opting for an apparently unconventional, telegenic and plain-speaking iconoclast in an effort to boost party popularity in the run-up to elections for Japan's Upper House paid off handsomely. The LDP secured an overwhelming 53 out of 55 seats in the June 2001 contest for Tokyo's prefectural assembly, and in the July Upper House elections, garnered a creditable 64 seats, comfortably surpassing its pre-election target of 61 seats. The party did well in both rural and urban constituencies, reversing a trend since 1998 for LDP support to be increasingly concentrated in rural areas. 'Koizumi fever' not only helped win back support from younger voters and the key floating-voter constituency, it also produced long political coat-tails for more conventional and traditional LDP candidates.

Given his weak factional base in the party, Koizumi has had to be creative in parlaying his undoubted public popularity into political influence. He has accomplished this mainly by assiduously presenting himself as a reformist and by intentionally distancing himself from the party that he heads. This involved departing – with the exception of junior ministerial levels – from the longstanding tradition of forming a cabinet broadly reflective of the balance of factional strength within the party. Early in his tenure as prime minister, Koizumi emphasised the political 'pain' of administrative restructuring and deregulation, and threatened to 'destroy' the LDP if it failed to support his reform agenda. In a similar manner, Koizumi has also proposed the direct election of the prime minister as a means of strengthening the hand of the political executive. Both this last proposal and the threat of party destruction should be viewed as cosmetic rather than substantive. The practical challenges of revising the constitution to allow for a directly elected prime minister, who would invariably challenge the sovereignty of parliament, are formidable, suggesting that Koizumi is only partially committed to such an institutional change, calculating instead that this popular gambit will place his old-guard, traditionalist opponents within the party on the defensive in the eyes of public opinion.

The prime minister's unprecedented popularity – ranging between 70% and 80% approval levels for much of 2001 – can also be linked to his avoidance of ideological pigeon-holing. Endorsing a district court ruling supporting the interests of leprosy patients, promoting the virtues of flexible child-care provision and appointing a record number of women to cabinet (including popular but unconventional figures like Makiko Tanaka as foreign minister) have all won Koizumi plaudits from progressive groups. By contrast, his support for constitutional revision and the redefinition of Article 9, as well as his visit to the Yasukuni shrine, bolstered his standing among conservatives. Maintaining this ideological ambiguity has involved walking a fine line, and the promotion of concrete reforms has invariably generated a backlash from certain quarters.

Koizumi has committed himself to 'integrating' party and cabinet, and in the process has directly challenged policy-making conventions in place for the best part of 40 years. The dominance of the LDP Policy Affairs Research Council (PARC) and the party political convention that requires all participating members to endorse a policy proposal before it is taken up and promoted by cabinet has long acted as a check on prime ministerial authority. (PARC's head, Taro Aso – a possible future leadership challenger to Koizumi – has mounted a rear-guard action to protect the party's dominance in the face of Koizumi's centralising pressure.) The relevance of the PARC is particularly important in the context of the wider debate over deregulation and Koizumi's commitment to check and reverse the pattern of pork-barrel politics and the channelling of increasingly scarce financial resources towards costly and unproductive construction projects. Old-guard LDP members have traditionally relied on the PARC to solicit government backing for construction and other vested interests – for example, in the state postal system - and therefore have been particularly energetic in seeking to block Koizumi's reforms. In the face of this opposition, the prime minister has been able to capitalise on the administrative reforms put in place by his predecessors. In a manner that echoes the reform initiatives of the 1980s under Prime Minister Yasuhiro Nakasone, Koizumi has increasingly turned to independent advisory bodies to establish a more explicitly top-down decision-making structure. Skilful reliance on the recently created Council on Economic and Fiscal Policy (CEFP) has, for example, helped to diminish the authority of the Ministry of Finance in budgetary policy.

Yet there have been practical limits to the prime minister's ability to centralise decision-making authority. To begin with, he has had difficulties recruiting dedicated cabinet-level assistants, and there is still a tendency for executive-level decisions to be made outside rather than within Cabinet. Such informal decision-making has the advantage of flexibility, but it does not suggest the establishment of a clear, authoritative and unambiguous concentration of power in the hands of the prime minister. Moreover, it is clear that at certain critical junctures, Koizumi has been forced to compromise with some of his party rivals. The decision, for example, to sack Foreign Minister Tanaka in January 2002, in the wake of a damaging series of disagreements between her and senior Foreign Ministry officials, has been seen as an opportunity for conservative forces within the party to reassert their authority. In the process, Koizumi's popularity was sharply undercut – collapsing almost by half from approximately 80% to 53% in the space of a few weeks and weakening his ability to present himself as a genuine and effective reformer. His declining public credibility has been reinforced by the impression that he has been happy to rein in reform in the interest of maintaining unity within the governing coalition. The government's ultimately abortive attempt in autumn 2001 to modify the electoral system – by reintroducing a multimember-based, single non-transferable voting arrangement was widely seen as motivated by political expediency (in that it would bolster the position of the smaller members of the governing coalition) rather than an expression of political principle.

Tanaka's sacking has continued to damage the government. It was accompanied by the forced resignation of Muneo Suzuki, a senior LDP official and former parliamentary vice-minister associated with foreign policy. Suzuki's alleged involvement in influence-peddling and possible perjury in testimony before the Diet has opened the government to sharp criticism from the opposition parties and undermined its reformist image, as has the exposure in March 2002 of a tax evasion scandal implicating Koichi Kato, a senior LDP faction leader seen as broadly sympathetic towards Koizumi's reform agenda. Nevertheless, Koizumi appears politically secure in the near term. Whereas Suzuki and Kato were potential leadership rivals, there are no other strong challengers within the LDP. Hashimoto – Koizumi's most obvious rival – has been recently hospitalised with a heart ailment and the Hashimoto faction is increasingly unwieldy and demoralised. The more strident LDP critics of Koizumi, such as Shizuka Kamei and Takami Eto, are irritants but unlikely to launch a leadership bid, particularly since Koizumi's term as party president runs until the autumn of 2003 and there is no prospect of a general election until 2004. Koizumi can also take comfort from real divisions and confusion within the opposition camp. The DPJ is involved in its own leadership wrangling, with disagreements between its president, Yukio Hatoyama, and the Secretary-General, Naoto Kan. DPJ approval ratings are close to single figures and the party has suffered from appearing divided both on post-11 September security issues and on the larger economic debate over deregulation versus reflation.

Continuing economic uncertainty

The economic policy front has been the area in which Koizumi has persistently faced the greatest challenges and where concern – both within and without Japan – has been most pronounced. Throughout 2001 and the early part of 2002, US officials consistently made clear their worries regarding the state of the Japanese economy. Colin Powell, during his Secretary of State confirmation hearings in January 2001, acknowledged that Japan's economic circumstances had a direct bearing on America's national security, while Alan Greenspan, Chairman of the Federal Reserve, warned the Senate Finance Committee in early April 2001 of the dangers to the US of continuing economic stagnation in Japan. Such concerns have been widely echoed throughout the private sector and among international organisations. The International Monetary Fund has called for increased structural reform in Japan's banking and corporate sectors, and in early December, Moody's downgraded its rating of Japanese government bonds from Aa3 to Aa2, the poorest ranking for any of the world's leading industrial countries. A similar note of lack of confidence in Japan's financial sector was sounded in late November 2001, when Merrill Lynch Japan announced its partial withdrawal from the Japanese market.

Tokyo's response to these developments has been two-pronged, focusing on structural reform and deregulation as well as putting together a series of packages to tackle the seemingly intractable problem of deflation. Yet, the government has appeared to place greater emphasis on the former rather than the latter, with some likening Koizumi to President Herbert Hoover because of the prime minister's apparent preoccupation with reducing the size of the government's ballooning national debt and his pledge in 2001 to limit government bond issues to a maximum of 30 trillion yen. Since the 1980s, demographic pressures arising from the greying of Japan's population have made Japanese finance ministry bureaucrats increasingly concerned about the costs of meeting expanding welfare and retirement costs, as well as the rising interest payments generated by increased bond sales.

Koizumi can claim to have achieved some notable, albeit modest, successes. In the construction sector, the government is gradually fostering greater access for foreign firms by introducing a system comparable to Britain's Private Finance Initiative. In February 2002, new legislation created an external advisory committee to counsel the prime minister on how best to facilitate the privatisation of Japan's four public highway corporations. Similarly, in early March, the government faced down strong opposition from a number of LDP legislators to introduce legislation reforming Japan's medical insurance system by raising the proportion of medical fees levied on salaried workers from 20% to 30%. Yet the government still faces major obstacles. Critics have argued that a long-term solution to the burgeoning cost of medical care requires the provision of substantial incentives to the private sector to take over the costs of an overly debt-ridden public system. Road privatisation faces considerable opposition not only from LDP legislators but also from vested interests in the bureaucracy and local government. In other areas, such as post office privatisation, the coalition of opposing interests is especially strong. In the critically important banking sector, the scale of the bad debt remains enormous – some 6 trillion yen ($45 billion) for the fiscal year ending in March 2002 – and is compounded by differences between the Bank of Japan and the CEFP on the appropriateness of using new injections of public money to bail out weak financial institutions. Similarly, tax reform, which is a key means of addressing the problem of declining land prices, remains mired in controversy. The government's Tax Commission is not due to report on medium and long-term reform proposals until September 2003.

If restructuring is facing difficulties, the same is also true of the government's anti-deflationary policies. In late May 2001, the Ministry of Economy, Trade and Industry announced a 15-point plan to expand employment, increase patents and enhance labour flexibility. Yet by late November the unemployment rate was pushing 5.5% – a post-war high. In anticipation of George Bush's visit to Tokyo in mid-February 2002, the Koizumi cabinet went further by passing a second supplementary budget focusing on urban renewal, environmental protection, science and education and the costs of the aging society. The plan was calculated to have a net stimulus effect of 4.1 trillion yen ($31 billion). But financing needs were met through revenue from the sale of former government Nippon Telegraph and Telephone (NTT) corporation shares. Public concern over the rise in this 'hidden debt' may depress consumer spending and this, together with pressures on local governments to retrench fiscally, may have had a dampening effect on the overall stimulus.

Although the government introduced a further package of specific anti-deflationary measures on 27 February, intended to address the non-performing loan problem, these were widely criticised as inadequate and overdue. An easing of monetary policy by the Bank of Japan and indications that the government had been seeking to talk down the yen from early 2002 may have helped to stimulate demand via the external account, which a recovery in American economic fortunes would also encourage. But such changes were only partial correctives, and in early spring 2002 the government appeared to be pulling back on its anti-deflation strategy. The February packages had, in part, been prompted by fears of a 'March financial crisis'. A resurgence in the Nikkei stock average to close to 12,000 points in March (compared to the 9,900 level recorded on 12 February) suggested that the government's approach might have worked in the short term. Yet this rebound is largely credited to technical changes restricting short sales by speculators rather than any improvement in the economic fundamentals. Capital investment continued to decline sharply and while the government might have been able to breath a sigh of relief there was little to suggest that the 'real economy' was experiencing a genuine upturn. In general, the prognosis for the economy remains pessimistic, with falling private-sector investment, a declining trade surplus and high-profile bankruptcies in the latter half of 2001 (such as that of Aoki Corporation) adding to the country's deflationary woes.

A mixed prognosis

In the medium-term, the government faces both opportunities and obstacles. Domestically, there are some straws in the wind for Japan's opposition parties, in the wake of news of a possible alliance between the DPJ and the Liberal Party, headed by Ichiro Ozawa – ex-LDP Dietman, high profile reformer and committed iconoclast. Yet the DPJ remains fractious, and its ability to act as a focal point for popular disaffection remains in doubt. Although Hiroshi Nakada, a fledgling reform-minded candidate, beat Hidenou Takahide, the LDP-backed incumbent in the mayoral election in Yokohama on 31 March 2002, the DPJ had not officially backed Nakada due to infighting among local party members. Nevertheless, the LDP feared a 'domino effect' in three elections scheduled for April 2002, including the gubernatorial contest in Kyoto. But the opposition camp appears unable to land any decisive punches against the government. Rather, the Koizumi cabinet's major challenge is maintaining the confidence of an electorate increasingly prone to disillusionment with the political process. Koizumi's rise to the prime ministership generated comparable enthusiasm and high hopes to that which surrounded the selection of Morihiro Hosokawa in 1993 at the head of the first non-LDP coalition government since 1955. Hosokawa's administration was short-lived, lasting a mere eight months. Koizumi will require considerable political courage, ingenuity and economic good fortune to ensure that his government does not suffer a similarly swift and decisive reversal of fortune.

The opportunities for Japanese foreign-policy breakthroughs remain limited. Sino-Japanese relations remain testy but manageable. Yoriko Kawaguchi, the new Japanese foreign minister, has commissioned a report on restructuring Japanese assistance to Russia, but with Moscow rigidly inflexible on the long-standing Northern Territories dispute with Japan, there is little prospect of a thaw in Russo-Japanese ties. Although relations with Pyongyang have warmed up a degree or two following indications from the North Korean Red Cross that the North Korea may be more flexible on the abduction issue, Koizumi appears content to maintain a firm line with the North if only because Japanese domestic opinion is ill-disposed to compromise.

In security policy, the new legislative agenda offers the prospect of a new security activism that represents a genuine departure from the post-war consensus. In autumn 2002, the government is due to introduce a new package of security measures (paralleling the March 2002 legislation dealing with foreign invasions) and intended to deal with large-scale terrorist attacks (encompassing nuclear, chemical and biological as well as conventional threats), maritime incursions and cyber-terrorism. This is bound to provoke controversy and debate, not only between the government and the opposition, but also internally, between the LDP and its small but influential coalition partner, Komeito, which is generally dovish on security issues. Similarly controversial is the question of possible Japanese support for any future action against Iraq. There are unconfirmed reports that during Bush's February 2002 visit to Japan, Koizumi pledged official backing, in the form of rear-area support should the US undertake such military action.

Despite the important shift in public opinion towards a more active Japanese stance on security issues, it is doubtful that popular sympathy would extend to support of US intervention in Iraq. Already, there are potential points of divergence between the US and Japan. Washington's abrogation of the 1972 Anti-Ballistic Missile Treaty and its decision to abandon talks on the enforcement protocol of the 1972 Biological Weapons Convention sit uneasily alongside Japanese efforts to promote arms control and its support for confidence-building measures in general. In the new security environment, at the United States' urging, Japan will inevitably become more extrovert, most likely in the areas of maritime anti-piracy and counter-terrorist interdiction and peacekeeping. But its approach to more regionally provocative issues – such as TMD, the amendment of the 'peace constitution' and force projection – will probably remain highly circumspect.

South-east Asia: Regime Stabilisation and Terrorism Concerns

Poor economic performance linked to persistent weakness in corporate governance, public finance and the banking sector has continued to plague South-east Asia's states, and the US slowdown and Japan's recession have combined to dim hopes of an export-led recovery. During 2000 and 2001, inward investment declined considerably, deterred by perceptions of high political risk (largely because of persistent instability in Indonesia) and diverted to more attractive destinations in North-east Asia (mainly China). Escalating concern over the regional and international linkages of domestic militant Islamic groups in the wake of the 11 September attacks has exacerbated the risk factor and further undermined hopes of economic recovery. Lacking the means of stimulating domestic economies over sustained periods, South-east Asian countries will come under increasing pressure to enhance their attractiveness to investors, reducing tariff and non-tariff barriers to goods and services, fostering inter-regional trade and investing in human and physical infrastructure.

While there has been some progress towards free-trade arrangements within South-east Asia and the broader region, a proposed trade liberalisation pact with China has raised geopolitical as well as economic dilemmas. Domestic political developments during 2001 – notably the presidential successions in the Philippines and Indonesia, the judicial vindication of Thailand's prime minister and the disintegration of Malaysia's opposition coalition – brought greater medium-term predictability to the regional political scene. Yet the turbulent confrontations that accompanied these developments also highlighted frailties in state institutions such as legislatures, courts and armed forces. At the same time, divergent national perspectives and lingering distrust among members of the Association for South East Asian Nations (ASEAN) over security matters have limited the scope of regional cooperation in the face of new security challenges.

Indonesia: a new beginning or continuing disarray?

Indonesian President Abdurrahman Wahid became increasingly beleaguered during the first half of 2001, facing criticism for his erratic political style, reputed cronyism, failure to repair the economy and inability to control escalating communal violence and separatism. Responding to the impeachment process begun by the People's Consultative Assembly in February 2001, and reinforced in April by another censure vote, in May that year, Wahid attempted to secure the armed forces' support for the declaration of a national emergency and the dissolution of parliament. In the event, military commanders repudiated Wahid's attempt to avoid impeachment. Most favoured his replacement by Vice-President Megawati Sukarnoputri, who had cultivated their support. In late May, parliament voted overwhelmingly to begin impeachment proceedings on 1 August. Wahid's final efforts to retain power included three cabinet reshuffles between early June and early July, when he again threatened to declare an emergency, dissolve parliament and call new elections unless the Assembly abandoned plans for impeachment proceedings. When Wahid attempted to implement these threats on 23 July, the Assembly quickly convened and voted by 591–0, with 104 abstentions, to substitute Megawati as president. After several days, Wahid conceded defeat.

None of the problems that had plagued Indonesia when Wahid took power in October 1999 had been resolved; some had become more serious. Most importantly, Wahid's preoccupation with political survival had distracted him and his government from focusing on reviving the economy. Relations with the International Monetary Fund, a benchmark for foreign investors' attitudes towards the country, remained fraught. Wahid also failed to assert civilian control over the armed forces. There had been no significant progress towards enforcing justice on military perpetrators of past abuses or ending the armed forces' repressive territorial role or their commercial activities. Another failure was Wahid's inability to control growing separatism and communal conflict. Secessionist impulses in Aceh and Irian Jaya remained strong. Hard-line military policies in these two provinces often contradicted Wahid's preference for political solutions. Violence between ethnic and religious groups had raged in Ambon, North Maluku, Central Sulawesi and Kalimantan. In several cases Laskar Jihad, a Java-based Islamic militia, had exacerbated conflicts with little response from the government or security forces. Although separatist forces capable of challenging Jakarta did not appear to coalesce in any of the areas of tension, Indonesia's potential disintegration continued to worry not only Indonesian politicians, but also other governments in South-east Asia and beyond.

The fact that the succession to Wahid was largely peaceful relieved most Indonesians and foreign observers. However, fears that Megawati might prove no more effective than Wahid were soon confirmed. Megawati's mandate was stronger, but as vice-president she had displayed little political skill, particularly in her handling of ethnic and religious strife and other pressing regional emergencies, for which Wahid had assigned her a leading role. She did not enjoy a parliamentary majority, and from the beginning, her government was vulnerable to pressure from the same political and military interests that helped bring her to power. Some of the Muslim politicians who had helped install Megawati still distrusted her due to her gender and lack of Islamic credentials. The strength of alternative political views was clear in the Assembly's selection of Hamzah Haz, chairman of the Partai Persatuan Pembangunan (PPP, the United Development Party), an Islamic group, as vice-president. Like the leaders of other Islamic parties, Hamzah had campaigned for a constitutional amendment that would apply *sharia* law to all Muslim Indonesians. Relations between Hamzah and the avowedly secular Megawati were uneasy from the beginning. But to ensure her survival until the next parliamentary and presidential elections in 2004, Megawati needed a modus vivendi with the Islamic leaders. In return for their support and agreement not to challenge the secular state ideology of *Pancasila*, Megawati conceded greater freedom for Islamic practices. She also needed to accommodate military interests: though the defence minister was again a civilian, she appointed four retired generals to her cabinet.

Megawati demonstrated some skill in reconciling conservative and reformist political objectives, and her initial six-point programme highlighted not only her objective of maintaining national unity but also continued military reform and democratisation. By October 2001, however, key cabinet ministers' lack of urgency in pursuing the economic, political and security objectives that she had set was becoming clear. Shortcomings in Megawati's own leadership – particularly her lack of involvement in day-to-day affairs and her excessive delegation to ministers – were also evident. The deepening global recession combined with the economic and security implications of the 11 September attacks made a weak new government's tasks even more difficult. Moreover, many Indonesians soon came to believe that Megawati's administration – which has failed to bring corrupt officials and bankers to court – was defending the Suharto-era ruling élite's decadent interests.

Despite widespread disappointment within and outside Indonesia over her government's performance, Megawati is likely to survive as president until 2004. She will probably continue to avoid confrontation with parliament and the military by not pressing too hard for reform. Indonesia's political leaders still appeared to be interested, above all, in exploiting their government positions to accumulate funds and popular support in advance of the 2004 elections. The armed forces' fear of negative domestic and international reactions, and the presence of moderate reformers in its senior ranks, imply that military intervention against Megawati is unlikely. Indonesian politics, then, will continue to be characterised by weakness and ineffectiveness at the political centre. Megawati's government will attempt to muddle through, economically and politically, but the country's multi-dimensional (economic, social, political and security) crisis will persist, with secessionism and communal violence continuing to plague the country's periphery.

The Philippines: threats to Arroyo and trouble in the south

The ousting of President Joseph Estrada in January 2001 and his replacement by former Vice-President Gloria Macapagal Arroyo (like Indonesia's Megawati, a former president's daughter) did not immediately bring political stability to the Philippines. Estrada's arrest on charges of economic plunder in late April provoked large-scale riots in Manila by poor Filipinos who idolised the former president as a champion of the downtrodden. Opposition politicians apparently encouraged the disturbances, hoping to take advantage of the chaos to seize power. Nevertheless, the Armed Forces of the Philippines (AFP) remained loyal to Arroyo, who responded to the crisis with resolution, declaring a 'state of rebellion' in the capital and ordering the arrest of suspected plotters, including Senators Juan Ponce Enrile and 'Gringo' Honasan and former national police chief, Panfilo Lacson.

However, Arroyo – whose legitimacy as president remained in question because of the coercive manner of her succession to Estrada – balanced her tough approach with measures designed to placate her detractors. She visited Estrada and protestors who had been arrested in jail. Enrile, Honasan and Lacson were allowed to continue campaigning for the Senate in the run-up to the 14 May mid-term elections. After the elections, in which government-supported candidates won eight Senate seats out of 12 contested, Arroyo announced plans to 'heal the nation', such as soft loans and educational scholarships for the poor. In December, Arroyo proposed further measures – including a renewed land reform initiative and an expanded national health programme – to relieve poverty as part of a broader economic recovery package.

Many Filipinos remained unconvinced by Arroyo's efforts to portray herself as 'pro-poor', seeing her instead as representing the interests of the small privileged class that had traditionally produced the country's political élite. By mid-2001, concerns were being voiced over her husband's alleged corruption. By December, support for the president was falling, reflecting widespread concerns over declining living standards. At the year's end, another impending coup attempt involving active and retired military officers was rumoured. Though Arroyo dismissed the notion of a serious threat, she reportedly established a high-level committee to coordinate efforts to contain rumoured anti-government conspiracies. While former president Fidel Ramos has become impatient with her economic policies and has considerable influence with the security forces, he has repeatedly denied involvement in any ploy to overthrow Arroyo. Guingona has also been pressured to state his loyalty publicly. If such conspiracies exist, they may be designed to achieve shifts in policy rather than regime change. Right-wing military elements and Estrada supporters may have been responsible for several bomb scares in Manila in March 2002.

The government's most important security concerns were in the south. In May 2001, Arroyo announced that her administration was 'at war' with the small Islamic rebel group, Abu Sayyaf, which had recently seized 20 hostages (including three US citizens). However, Arroyo ended Estrada's policy of 'all-out war' against the 12,000-strong Moro Islamic Liberation Front (MILF), which had continued to fight even after the larger Moro National Liberation Front (MNLF) and Manila signed a peace settlement in 1996. In August, the government and the MILF agreed to a cease-fire, which was to be monitored by Libyan, Indonesian and Malaysian representatives of the Organisation of Islamic Countries (OIC). The ceasefire allowed the MILF and MNLF to form a united front in subsequent peace negotiations with Manila. Tangible developmental benefits and an improved autonomy arrangement for Muslim-populated parts of the south will be needed if the cease-fire is to be followed by a viable settlement.

The fragility of security in the south became clear in November 2001, when a new outbreak of fighting between the communist New People's Army and the AFP left 28 dead. Soon afterwards, an armed MNLF faction answering to Nur Misuari, governor of the Autonomous Region of Muslim Mindanao, attacked an AFP base on the island of Jolo. The dead numbered more than 100, mostly rebels. Misuari, reputedly corrupt and ineffective, had been ousted as MNLF leader in May 2001, and Manila had already refused to endorse him as governor for a second term. Following the attack, the Philippine government suspended Misuari from the governorship and Malaysian security forces captured him as he fled to Sabah. Subsequently, MNLF forces loyal to Misuari took 81 civilians hostage during intense fighting with the AFP in the port city of Zamboanga, but soon surrendered them in exchange for safe passage. Malaysia deported Misuari to the Philippines in early January 2002, despite Arroyo's concerns that this might stimulate further unrest, a position apparently borne out in mid-January when rioting and an attack on AFP troops by former MNLF personnel who had been integrated into the police left 36 dead on Jolo. In March 2002, evidence emerged of a new alliance between MNLF renegades and the MILF, aimed at attacking government targets in Mindanao. Reports also linked the MILF to bomb attacks in Manila in December 2000 and to international terrorism. These new concerns cast a shadow over the peace talks.

Thailand: Thaksin survives and conservative forces gain strength

Thailand gained a new prime minister, Thaksin Shinawatra, a rich businessman and former police lieutenant-colonel whose Thai-Rak-Thai (Thai-Love-Thai) party won a huge parliamentary majority in January 2001. He initially advocated nationalistic policies in response to continuing economic difficulties, projecting himself as a dynamic leader personally concerned with helping the country's poor. During 2001, however, it became clear that some of his populist campaign promises (for example, to give $23,800 in development funds to each village) were lacking in substance.

Weeks before his election victory, the National Counter-Corruption Commission (NCCC) had found Thaksin guilty of concealing assets while he was deputy premier in 1997. He became prime minister knowing that within months the Constitutional Court might uphold this verdict and enforce a five-year ban on his political activity, which would require him to relinquish the premiership. However, against a background of predictions by Thai-Rak-Thai MPs that there might be bloodshed if the corruption charge were upheld, and rumours of bribery, in early August 2001 the Constitutional Court acquitted Thaksin by a vote of 8–7.

Given his overwhelming parliamentary backing, which was reinforced by the merger between Thai-Rak-Thai and the New Aspiration Party in January 2002, and by the entry of one of the remaining two opposition parties into the government, Thaksin could remain in power until at least 2005, when the next general election is due. This prospect concerned political reformers and foreign investors alike, as Thaksin was already showing signs of political authoritarianism as well as economic nationalism. Following his acquittal, the prime minister promised to use constitutional amendments to restrict the powers of the NCCC and Constitutional Court, both key elements of the liberal governance established by the 1997 Constitution. At the same time, it was clear that Thaksin's government sympathised with local vested economic interests and was unlikely to allow the degree of liberalisation necessary for economic revival – in particular, loosening restrictions on foreign ownership of Thai companies. In early 2002, the police drafted a law restricting the right to freedom of assembly. The government also expelled critical foreign journalists and took measures to restrict local news media.

There were also signs that efforts to entrench military professionalism and civilian control over the armed forces might be under threat. In June 2001, a military-sponsored draft of the new People's and State Security Protection Bill affronted liberal reformers. Ostensibly intended to combat international crime, the draft allowed the security forces to conduct searches without warrants and prescribed heavy penalties (including life imprisonment) for vaguely defined 'national security' offences. In August, a reshuffle of senior army posts, apparently influenced by Thaksin, promoted conservative officers at the expense of military reformers, although the highly professional army commander-in-chief, General Surayud Chulanont, remained in his post.

Under Thaksin, Thai foreign policy has become more narrowly focused on supporting Thai business interests. Reversing the tense relationship with Myanmar, which had culminated in a serious border clash between the two countries' armies in February 2001, the new administration in Bangkok prioritised the promotion of commerce (notably natural resource concessions) over political and security concerns. Visits by Thaksin and Defence Minister Chavalit Yongchaiyudh to Yangon in July 2001, and by Khin Nyunt, first secretary of Myanmar's military junta, to Bangkok in September 2001 reflected the thawing relationship. The traditional emphasis placed on strengthening ties with China, meanwhile, has been reinforced by Thaksin's commerce-conscious administration. While Thaksin's regional emphasis has meant some distancing from the US, after a meeting with US Federal Bureau of Investigation Director Robert Mueller III in March 2002, the prime minister announced that the FBI would train Thai security forces in countering terrorism and other transnational threats, and confirmed a high level of US–Thai security cooperation.

South-east Asia and the campaign against terrorism

For several months before the 11 September attacks, South-east Asian governments as well as Washington were growing increasingly concerned over links between local Islamic groups and international terrorist sponsors. In mid-May 2001, Malaysian police arrested nine members of a militant organisation, the Kumpulan Mujahideen Malaysia (KMM, Malaysian Mujahideen Group). Those arrested – some of whom had fought in Afghanistan and Ambon – were implicated in the murder of a Christian politician, attacks on a church and a Hindu temple, and plans to kill

Americans in Malaysia. The Malaysian authorities discovered bomb-making equipment and claimed that the group may have planned large-scale terrorist attacks and was possibly 'linked' to bin Laden and the Taliban. However, the fact that most of those arrested were connected with Parti Islam Semalaysia (PAS, the Islamic Party), which had been posing an increasingly serious threat to the government since becoming the leading opposition party in 1999, prompted speculation that political as well as security factors motivated the government's clampdown.

By August 2001, Washington was expressing concern over the allegedly high level of al-Qaeda-related activity in Indonesia, and warning that terrorists could target US interests there. In July, a suspected al-Qaeda team from Yemen had arrived in Indonesia on a mission to attack the US embassy in Jakarta, but fled after becoming aware of an Indonesian surveillance operation. It later became clear that before 11 September, US intelligence agencies had anticipated that al-Qaeda would mount its next major attack in South-east Asia.

In August, there were further arrests in Malaysia and evidence emerged of KMM involvement in terrorist bombings in Indonesia. At the beginning of September, Malaysian Prime Minister Mahathir Mohamad claimed that militant Islamic fundamentalists were planning to establish a pan-regional Daulah Islamiah Nusantara (Sovereign Islamic Archipelago) subsuming Malaysia, Muslim-populated parts of Indonesia and the southern Philippines. Anti-terrorist cooperation was high on the agenda in bilateral meetings in late August involving Indonesia's Megawati, Malaysia's Mahathir, the Philippines' Arroyo and Singaporean Senior Minister Lee Kuan Yew.

After 11 September, South-east Asian governments already concerned over Islamic terrorism and maintaining close economic, political and security ties to the West were predisposed to heed US calls for cooperation against bin Laden's terrorist network. From Washington's viewpoint, evidence that hijackers in the US attacks had held meetings in Malaysia, and rumours that bin Laden had already or might soon take refuge in Indonesia, as well as tentative evidence of links between him and local terrorists, indicated the potential importance of South-east Asia in the burgeoning US-led struggle against al-Qaeda and its allies. The region emerged as a significant 'second front' in the conflict.

The Philippines, hoping to secure US economic and military assistance, was the most supportive South-east Asian state, with President Arroyo claiming that she was prepared to 'go every step of the way' with Washington. Allowing US ships and aircraft to refuel en route to the conflict zone in South-west Asia to prosecute the war in Afghanistan was an important contribution, while a planned new bilateral logistics agreement offered even greater US access to Philippine naval and air bases. During a visit by Arroyo to Washington in November, the United States offered Manila $100 million in military and economic aid as well as $1 billion worth of trade benefits. The military aid, including helicopters and infantry weapons, was intended for use initially against Abu Sayyaf, whose hostages still included two Americans.

Arroyo declined a US offer to deploy forces to engage Abu Sayyaf directly. However, she effectively acknowledged the Philippine military's operational shortcomings by agreeing to the United States' despatch of 650 troops, including 160 special-forces personnel, to Zamboanga for a six-month exercise commencing in January 2002. The US troops were tasked not only with training Philippine forces, but also with observing them in action against Abu Sayyaf on nearby Basilan Island and offering tactical advice. They were allowed to return fire if attacked. This was the first major US military deployment to the Philippines since the Subic Bay naval base closed in 1992. It provoked opposition from Filipino leftists and nationalists, including anti-Arroyo senators and Vice-President Teofisto Guingona, who claimed that it might violate constitutional prohibitions on the establishment of foreign military bases and foreign soldiers joining combat on Philippine soil. However, a Philippine National Security Council meeting in late January effectively confirmed congressional and cabinet support.

Concerned by reports that 17 of bin Laden's bodyguards were planning to enter the Philippines, and might already have landed on Basilan, during February and March 2002 US forces became more directly involved in operations there, using helicopters to conduct night reconnaissance missions and evacuate Philippine army casualties. On 22 February, a US helicopter crashed, killing 10 Special Forces soldiers; it had not, however, come under hostile fire. In mid-March, Philippine officials claimed that the US wished to increase its military presence in the south to almost 1,500 troops.

The 11 September attacks also alarmed Singapore's government. In recent years, US–Singapore security relations had become very close, despite the lack of a formal alliance. In March 2001, for example, a US Navy carrier battle group docked at Singapore's new Changi Naval Base for the first time. As the US confronted the challenge of Islamic terrorism, Singapore's strategic alignment and its predominantly Muslim-populated regional environment placed it in the front line. On 23 September, Prime Minister Goh Chok Tong proclaimed that Singapore stood with the US, despite 'regional and domestic sensitivities to manage', and soon afterwards the government revealed that Singapore was providing logistical and other support for increased numbers of transiting US aircraft and ships, including air-to-air refuelling and port facilities for aircraft carriers, during the Afghanistan military campaign. Some sections of the moderate Malay Muslim population (15% of Singapore's total) aired grievances in early 2002 about their position in society and accused the government of being insufficiently inclusive. The government has responded with calls for racial harmony.

In early January 2002, based in part on intelligence gleaned by the United States from detainees in Afghanistan, Singapore's government announced that in December its Internal Security Department had arrested 15 people (all but one of them Singaporeans) in December in connection with a terrorist plot to mount devastating attacks on local targets, including US military personnel and businesses as well as the US, British, Australian and Israeli diplomatic missions. Those detained were ethnic Malays or Muslims of Indian or Pakistani descent; all but two belonged to the local branch of Jemaah Islamiah (Islamic Group), an Indonesia-based clandestine organisation linked to the KMM and allegedly aligned with al-Qaeda. Some detainees had received terrorist training in al-Qaeda camps in Afghanistan. Subsequently, in mid-January, the Philippine police arrested five suspected Jemaah Islamiah members, including an Indonesian who may have acted as a regional intermediary for al-Qaeda, and seized explosives and weapons apparently intended for the Singaporean terrorists. But with the alleged masterminds of Jemaah Islamiah still at large in Indonesia, in February 2002 Senior Minister Lee Kuan Yew claimed that Singapore continued to face a terrorist threat.

Malaysia's domestic problems with militant Islam and the need to demonstrate to foreign investors that it was not a hotbed of violent extremism led its government, a week after 11 September, to promise full cooperation with the United States in fighting terrorism. There were limits on Malaysian support, however. Fearing a backlash among local Muslims, during October 2001 Mahathir and his government registered their opposition to the US attacks on Afghanistan. Nevertheless, it was clear that counter-terrorist cooperation had facilitated substantial improvements in US-Malaysian relations after a period of strain following Washington's disapproval of the treatment of disgraced deputy premier Anwar Ibrahim in 1998. The Malaysian government's stance on terrorism also brought domestic political benefits. In early October, PAS reacted fiercely to the US offensive in Afghanistan by declaring *jihad* against America and stating that the United States was the 'mother of all terrorists', precipitating the exit of the second-largest anti-government party, the Democratic Action Party, from the opposition coalition. The government's attempts to equate PAS with the Taliban and to connect it with the KMM now seemed less far-fetched to many non-Muslim Malaysians, strengthening the ruling coalition's hold on power.

In December 2001 and January 2002, 23 more Muslim militants were arrested in Malaysia. These new detainees belonged to a group that the Malaysian authorities termed 'KMM 2'. It was apparently closely connected with Jemaah Islamiah in Singapore, for which it allegedly secured large quantities of explosives. US sources alleged that at least one detainee had hosted those 11 September conspirators who had visited Malaysia during 2000. According to Malaysia's police, as many as 200 more dangerous militants were still at large. By late January, there was growing evidence that both the KMM and Jemaah Islamiah were directed by Abu Bakar Bashir, a religious teacher and leader of the Majelis Mujahidin Indonesia (MMI, Indonesian Mujahideen Council), who may have acted on behalf of al-Qaeda. Fearing for the country's international image, Malaysia's government sought to refute allegations of direct links between those arrested in Malaysia in August 2001 and the 11 September attacks, denying that its territory had been used for planning the attacks on the US. In March 2002, the government claimed that no al-Qaeda cells were based in the country. Malaysia's position thus contrasted with Singapore's, which stressed the close relations between Jemaah Islamiah and al-Qaeda.

Despite $650m in US economic assistance and Megawati's promise of counter-terrorism help when she met President George W. Bush in Washington a week after 11 September, counter-terrorist cooperation in Indonesia was less forthcoming. This was primarily due to Megawati's need to appease domestic Muslim political forces and the reluctance of some senior military officers to take action against militant groups. Even before the US attacked Afghanistan, militant Muslim groups began a campaign of anti-American demonstrations and intimidation of US businesses and citizens. The air strikes led some religious leaders to call on the government to suspend diplomatic ties with Washington. Vice-President Hamzah Haz, who had earlier claimed that the 11 September attacks would 'cleanse the US of its sins', went further and demanded an end to the war. Even among politically moderate Muslims, there was concern over the war. Megawati accordingly requested the US to limit its military operations.

In November 2001, US Deputy Secretary of Defense Paul Wolfowitz brought matters to a head, warning that Indonesia was 'wide open' to infiltration by al-Qaeda. By January 2002, evidence gained from the arrests in Malaysia and Singapore indeed seemed to indicate that Indonesia's political disarray and lawlessness since the late 1990s may have allowed al-Qaeda to develop close working links with the MMI and related militant groups. US and Indonesian intelligence sources also claimed that al-Qaeda had operated a training camp on the island of Sulawesi. Megawati's government was evidently unwilling to act firmly against local militants and repeatedly cast doubt on allegations that Indonesian groups were linked to al-Qaeda. However, it claimed readiness to take action if concrete evidence connected Indonesians to international terrorism, and did curb anti-US demonstrations and ban Indonesians from travelling to Afghanistan to fight the US. In early January 2002, Jakarta also extradited a terrorist subject to Egypt, with US assistance. After weeks of pressure from Singapore, Malaysia and the United States, in late January 2002, Indonesian authorities questioned Abu Bakar Bashir, who expressed admiration for bin Laden but denied links with al-Qaeda or calling for *jihad* in Malaysia and Singapore. During February and March 2002, further measures were aimed particularly at tracking down a key Jemaah Islamiah suspect, Riduan Isamuddin (usually referred to as Hambali). Intelligence exchanges with Singapore, Malaysia, the Philippines, Pakistan, Australia and Interpol, as well as the US, were intensified.

Although the links between al-Qaeda and Indonesian Islamic groups appear attenuated, Islamic practices in Indonesia are becoming broadly more conservative and the potential for such links is correspondingly increasing. Yet it is not clear that the government is prepared to undertake concerted efforts to uproot al-Qaeda influence, and Washington remains concerned over Jakarta's failure to act more decisively. Resuscitating Washington's military-to-military relations with Jakarta could facilitate greater cooperation, but US legislation prohibits such links until Indonesian soldiers accused of atrocities against political opponents and separatist movements have been brought to justice.

Lacklustre regional cooperation, growing strategic significance

There have been only tentative signs of a reinvigoration of an ASEAN debilitated by expansion, the 1997–98 economic paralysis over the central principle of non-interference in members' domestic affairs and the loss of leadership following from Suharto's political demise. Though ASEAN still plays an important role in reducing the likelihood of armed conflict between its longer-established members by relaxing regional tensions, the intense border fighting between Thailand and Myanmar in February 2001 highlighted the fact that newer members have yet to be socialised into the security regime.

Myanmar's military junta hinted at the possibility of political liberalisation in holding closed-door talks with Aung San Suu Kyi, leader of the opposition National League for Democracy, beginning in October 2000, but progress has been slow. Myanmar continues to be complicit in transnational drug trafficking and remains mired in poverty. The government did not enhance its dismal international standing in announcing, in January 2002, that it would build a nuclear 'research' facility – particularly in light of reports that two Pakistani nuclear scientists linked to bin Laden would be working on the project and the country's history of terrorist infiltration. Laos' similarly authoritarian regime continues to depend on bilateral and multilateral aid for its country's economic subsistence, and is unable to make progress on poverty. In Vietnam and Cambodia, there are somewhat more hopeful signs. Vietnamese political and economic reform will remain slow, but the National Assembly moved towards greater accountability and entrenching the private sector during its tenth session, which ended in December 2001. The country also got an economic boost from the trade agreement with the United States, effective 10 December 2001. As a result of Russia's withdrawal from Cam Ranh Bay in January 2002 after 23 years, Vietnam may also become the object of strategic attention as major powers – particularly India – angle for access.

Cambodian Prime Minister Hun Sen's Cambodian People's Party (CPP) maintained its political domination in February 2002 local elections. The elections were tainted by CPP graft and intimidation – about 20 people, including eight opposition candidates, were killed before the poll – but were accepted as essentially fair by local and foreign observers. Whereas the main opposition Royal Funcinpec party lost ground amid perceptions that it had capitulated to the CPP, the reformist Sam Rainsy Party (named for its leader, a former finance minister) won six of 76 communes and anticipated gains in 2003 parliamentary elections. Following the United Nations' withdrawal in February 2002 from negotiations with Phnom Penh to establish a special war-crimes tribunal to try Khmer Rouge members, the government announced that Cambodian courts would proceed against them. But it is widely anticipated that the courts will be lax and dilatory.

It was Indonesia that posed ASEAN's greatest problem. ASEAN remained powerless and practically irrelevant in the face of Indonesia's continuing large-scale domestic security problems. Nevertheless, terrorism loomed large at ASEAN's annual summit meeting in Brunei in November 2001. While Arroyo had pushed for an 'ASEAN operational agreement' to galvanise multilateral intelligence-sharing, joint border patrols and even peacekeeping, South-east Asian leaders agreed only to strengthen anti-terrorist cooperation in general terms. But Malaysia failed to persuade members to call collectively for a halt to US air strikes on Afghanistan. Over the following months, the Philippines, Indonesia and Malaysia coordinated their maritime patrols with the aim of interdicting terrorist threats, and ASEAN states' army commanders agreed to use counter-terrorist scenarios in their first multilateral command-post exercises. In January 2002, military intelligence chiefs from Malaysia, Singapore, Thailand and Brunei also met to discuss terrorism.

Promoting economic cooperation remained an ASEAN priority. The ASEAN Free Trade Area (AFTA) was launched in January 2002, and the highlight of the 'ASEAN-plus-three' meeting between South-east Asian leaders and their Chinese, Japanese and South Korean counterparts after the Brunei summit was a surprising agreement in principle that an ASEAN–China free trade area should be established within ten years. The agreement reflected ASEAN members' recognition of their excessive dependence on the US and Japanese economies and of China's relative dynamism, and that economic integration with China could help cement regional peace and stability. But given fears among South-east Asian politicians that Chinese exports and cheap labour would eventually overwhelm South-east Asia, and the resistance of South-east Asian business interests to even AFTA's requirements, the viability of the more ambitious China-ASEAN proposal remains unproven. Economic considerations aside, there were also concerns that China's regional leadership and economic dominance in East Asia would subordinate South-east Asia's future political and security relations with Beijing (for example, in relation to conflicting claims in the South China Sea) and cast South-east Asia as a pawn in Beijing's drive for strategic multipolarity. Japan also sought to check its declining economic importance to South-east Asia against China's rising influence. In January 2002, Japanese Prime Minister Koizumi proposed a 'comprehensive economic alliance' and intensified security cooperation with ASEAN.

South-east Asia has entered a new phase of relative political stability. The perception of a common threat from international terrorism may enhance that stability. Thus, while ASEAN itself is unlikely to assume a more concrete security role, counter-terrorist cooperation between ASEAN governments will probably continue to grow. Beginning in December 2001, Indonesia, Malaysia and the Philippines have been running joint naval interdiction operations to hinder terrorism. In February 2002, at ASEAN foreign ministerial sessions in Thailand, the foreign ministers of the three countries signed a comprehensive agreement to facilitate counter-terrorism cooperation and interoperability. At the same time, South-east Asia's strategic significance for the major powers is increasing. China and Japan appear resolved to compete for regional influence in strategic and political as well as economic terms. From the American point of view, the region is arguably the most important locus of anti-Western terrorist activity outside the Middle East and South-west Asia, and Washington will attempt to develop closer security relations with South-east Asian governments in order to combat terrorist groups connected with al-Qaeda. In particular, Washington may persist in its joint campaign with the Philippines against Abu Sayyaf until that group is neutralised. Some South-east Asian governments, particularly in Indonesia, Malaysia and the Philippines, may find difficulty in balancing US demands for closer anti-terrorist collaboration against the danger of losing legitimacy with nationalist and Muslim domestic constituencies. Meanwhile, short- to medium-term economic recovery is not in prospect for any ASEAN member. But the stimulus provided by Beijing's and Tokyo's heightened economic interests in the region and possible bilateral and multilateral rewards for counter-terrorist cooperation may militate to improve South-east Asia's economic outlook.

The Koreas: Returning to Normal

A deepening layer of gloom has settled over the Korean Peninsula once again, blanketing the few, tentative rays of hope that had emanated from the early successes of South Korean President Kim Dae Jung's 'sunshine' policy.

The tensions that had been somewhat attenuated by the summit meeting of the leaders of the two Koreas in mid-2000 returned to their more normal levels. US President George W. Bush included Pyongyang in his 'axis of evil' and North Korea reinvigorated its most vituperative propaganda in response. One probably inadvertent result was to weaken Kim Dae Jung badly as his term of office sputtered towards its close. His policy of engaging the North unravelled; corruption scandals erupted and crept closer to his family; reform of the *chaebol* system slowed and even reversed; the economy, while performing reasonably well, did not improve enough to return prosperity to many companies and workers. The precipitate drop in support for President Kim (from a high of 80% to around 20% by the end of 2001) seemed certain to affect the presidential election to be held in December 2002, boosting the chances of the opposition party and dimming those of Kim's groomed successor.

North Korea not only retreated behind its accustomed barbed-wire mentality when viewing the outside world, but also upended expectations that it was planning an approach to domestic economic reforms along Chinese lines. A flurry of discussion in the North Korean press and a supposedly symbolic visit to Shanghai by North Korean leader Kim Jong Il – where he looked in on the stock market and discussed with his hosts their path from a command economy to their present successful mixed one – proved to be uncertain indicators of the future. There has been no reach for real economic reforms. What passes for economic strategy as well as foreign policy in North Korea remains little more than a search for outside economic aid.

The clouds gather

It has always been clear that unless the United States and South Korea basically agree on an approach to North Korea and thus move in tandem, it will not be possible to entice that economically weak and insecure nation to join the international family of nations. Neither US President Bill Clinton nor President Kim had any illusions about the totalitarian nature of the regime in the North. While making it clear that any North Korean aggression would be forcefully opposed, however, they also moved to assure Pyongyang that they had no hostile intent. Both supported the essence of President Kim's 'sunshine' policy: a policy of gradual détente, nurtured by open discussion without threats and the creation of confidence-building measures.

That policy appeared to be bearing some fruit when the leaders of the two Koreas met at an historic summit in June 2000 in Pyongyang and agreed to work together for reconciliation, cooperation and unification. In the next six months, the two countries held four ministerial-level talks and their defence chiefs met for the first time ever. A few tentative moves toward normalisation occurred. A legal framework to protect investments, avoid double taxation, open bank accounts for financial transactions and settle corporate trade disputes was arranged. Three rounds of exchange visits took place, each involving 200 families (100 from each country) that had been separated by the 1950–53 Korean War. The reunification of members of families who have been torn apart for 50 years was an especially important long-term humanitarian aim for the South, and constituted a highly meaningful breakthrough for the sunshine policy. The South also began work on reconstruction of the railway line that had connected it to the North until it was severed during the war and allowed to decay. At the same time, US–North Korean relations took a turn for the better. Talks on curbing North Korea's missile programme made sufficient progress that then Secretary of State Albright visited Pyongyang in October 2000 in an effort to move the regime towards ending North Korean sales of missiles and missile technology, and freezing its testing and production of missiles with ranges over 500 kilometres. Her mission, however, did not succeed and discouraged Clinton, with little time left in office, from visiting North Korea.

Bush chose not to pursue a further warming of relations unless more cooperation was forthcoming. Both during his campaign for the presidency and when he assumed office, Bush expressed deep scepticism about North Korea's motives and froze discussions until a review of relations that he had established reported its findings. When Kim Dae Jung visited Washington in March 2001, Bush embarrassed him publicly by referring to North Korea's refusal to agree to any verification measures as the reason that he did not believe it could be relied upon to fulfil its end of a bargain. True to its principle of regarding the US and South Korea as two faces for the same entity, Pyongyang extended the chill on its relations with Washington to Seoul. It cancelled a series of planned inter-Korean talks, including the fifth ministerial meeting that was to have taken place in March 2001, put off any discussion concerning family exchange visits, halted plans for combined sporting teams and meets, and generally withdrew to its customary bunker mentality. A six-month diplomatic impasse provided ammunition for the opposition party in South Korea to mount a campaign against Kim Dae Jung's faltering policy of accommodation with the North, specifically by calling for a vote of no-confidence against Kim's Minister of Reunification Lim Dong Won, who had been the author of the sunshine policy. In what most observers believed was a typically inept (and unsuccessful) effort to turn the tide, North Korea, the night before the vote was to take place, offered to reinstate high-level talks. Although Lim fell, ministerial talks were renewed, with the Southern team headed by the newly enfranchised Minister of Unification Hong Soon Yong. They took place in Seoul on 16–18 September, producing another round of reunions for 100 separated families from each side scheduled for October. The sixth ministerial talks were also scheduled for that month.

The North abruptly and unilaterally postponed the scheduled exchanges on 12 October, less than a week before they were to take place. Pyongyang offered the lame justification that the declaration by South Korea of a security alert as a counter-terrorist measure after the attacks of 11 September made it too dangerous for civilians to fly between the two countries. Pyongyang conveniently ignored the fact that it had agreed to the exchanges after the alert was announced, and that as late as 9 October, it was still discussing the lists of those to be exchanged. Despite its demands that Seoul lift its security alert, North Korea maintained that it would attend the scheduled sixth ministerial meeting. But it insisted that this meeting and all future ones be held at the Mt Kumgang resort in North Korea rather than in South Korea, or even Pyongyang. Those meetings finally did take place on 9–14 November, after the two sides squabbled for weeks over the venue. If South Korea thought that by giving in to the North's insistence on its desired location it would elicit positive responses from the North's leaders, it was deeply disappointed. The outcome of the talks was completely negative, leaving the two sides farther apart than at any time since the summit meeting in 2000. In hopes of making it easier for North Korea to agree to return to inter-Korean talks, Seoul responded positively to a 17 December special statement from North Korea's Committee for the Peaceful Reunification of the Fatherland calling for the South to take 'drastic steps' to resume a dialogue. It lifted its counter-terrorist security alert that it had established after the 11 September attacks on the World Trade Center. At the same time, Seoul revealed a plan to provide 100,000 tonnes of corn in additional food aid to the North.

This initiative apparently triggered a series of secret meetings, beginning in January 2002, that culminated in an announcement on 25 March that, in an effort to jump-start their stalled diplomatic and security dialogue, South and North Korea were to exchange high-level envoys. Resuming North-South talks, the North Korea invited South Korean Senior Advisor Lim Dong Won to Pyongyong to discuss a range of North–South agreements that might be pursued in the waning months of Kim Dae Jung's Presidency. North Korea probably changed its tune to counter increasing US pressure, which tended to increase its isolation. Japan, in step with the US, had also hardened its position; in reaction, Pyongyang used the opportunity of a visit by Japan's prime minister to Seoul in the previous week to provide, for the first time, details concerning Japanese believed to have been kidnapped during the 1970s and 1980s and held by North Korea. Whether these latest moves by North Korea are merely tactical adjustments to improve its weak position will take time to ascertain, but they were nevertheless welcomed by South Korea. In early April 2002, Pyongyang accepted Washington's long-standing offer to resume bilateral discussions, although North Korea remained suspicious of the Bush administration's intentions and wary of its tougher negotiating position.

A war of nerves

Running parallel with, and contributing to, the increasing difficulties Seoul was having with Pyongyang was a sharp increase in the tension between the United States and North Korea. The Bush administration had completed its long review of the relationship and on 6 June 2001, President Bush unveiled its conclusions. The US, he emphasised, was prepared to resume talks with no preconditions. Washington wished to focus on improved implementation of the Agreed Framework, which had been reached in 1994 and ended the standoff on North Korea's nuclear efforts; on verifiable constraints on missile development; on a ban on missile exports; and on 'a less threatening conventional military posture'. North Korea appeared willing to explore the possibility of renewed talks; on 13 June, Jack Pritchard, the US special envoy for Korean Peace Talks, met with North Korean UN Ambassador Li Hyong Chol to discuss possible arrangements.

Although both the president and Secretary of State Colin Powell reiterated the importance of 'open dialogue', their list of priorities for discussion inevitably appeared to the North Koreans as unacceptable preconditions. The formal response by North Korea on 18 June exposed the differing priorities the two sides had with regard to a proposed dialogue. Pyongyang considered Washington's insistence that the discussion should have North Korean nuclear, missile and conventional weaponry as their centrepiece to be tantamount to a demand that it unilaterally disarm; before it would discuss such matters, the US would have to withdraw its troops from South Korea. In place of the US agenda, it demanded that the talks should revolve around compensation for the delays in construction of the two light-water nuclear reactors that were supposed to be completed by 2003 as part of the Agreed Framework.

This exchange illustrated the chasm that separated the views of the two sides. Although North Korea has largely kept to the letter of the nuclear agreement that it reached with the Clinton administration, as even the present administration and the Central Intelligence Agency have admitted, the Bush administration insisted that new verification measures were required to assure that Pyongyang was not cheating. Kim Jong Il also used a visit by an EU delegation to announce, on 3 May 2001, that North Korea would unilaterally impose a moratorium on new missile tests until 2003, which he renewed during his visit to Moscow in August, but this was insufficient to convince Washington that North Korea was not still the leading missile threat to the US. The North laid out its position with equal clarity. It looked upon the talks as a further opportunity to acquire needed immediate cash aid and in the longer run, to induce the US to lift economic sanctions that precluded loans from international financial institutions.

This divide proved too wide to be bridged. The standoff was worsened when President Bush, in his State of the Union message on 29 January 2002, bracketed North Korea with Iraq and Iran in his 'axis of evil'. Pyongyang's immediate response was an expected flood of vitriolic rhetoric. Less expected was North Korea's cancellation of a visit by four former US ambassadors that it had earlier encouraged. This had been thought originally to be a signal that the North was seeking some way of keeping its channels open to the US despite its cold relations with official Washington. The cancellation was another sharp blow to leaders in the South, who had seen it as a hopeful glint of light in the overall gloom. That gloom was only deepened by President Bush's visit to South Korea on 19–22 February. Kim Dae Jung had hoped that the president would accent the positive during his visit by publicly supporting the sunshine policy and offering again to hold open talks without pre-conditions, while in return South Korea would endorse the US battle against international terrorism. Bush did all that, but also noted that he could not trust a leader who starved his people, and later, during a visit to the highly fortified border, again accused the North of being 'evil'. In an echo of President Reagan's call for the Soviet Union to tear down the Berlin Wall, he also called on the North to remove the barbed wire along the border and allow free access to both sides. Unsurprisingly, this 'sound-bite' diplomacy has not produced a positive response from the prickly leader of North Korea.

The lamest of ducks

The events of 2001 and early 2002 have left Kim Dae Jung's sunshine policy in tatters and have seriously undercut his, and his party's, popularity. In March 2001, his compatriots perceived what they considered his humiliation at the joint press conference in Washington DC, when President Bush aired his scepticism concerning Kim Jong Il's trustworthiness, thus eviscerating the case for Kim's adherence to the sunshine policy. Nearly a year later, when Bush proclaimed the North Korean regime 'evil', President Kim's standing among his fellow citizens plummeted. When Kim Dae Jung had entered the Blue House in February 1998 and articulated his engagement policy toward the North, four out of five Korean voters had been enthusiastic supporters of the effort to entice North Korea into discussions of confidence-building measures and eventually, unification. By the end of 2001, support for Kim Dae Jung's handling of the policy had dropped to about one in five. Business leaders were among the most dissatisfied, as they perceived investing in North Korea as yielding insufficient returns. Hyundai's six-year, $940 million tourism venture on Mt Kumgang led to the conglomerate's bankruptcy. Surveys with more nuanced questions showed that a sizable plurality still believed in a fairly robust open policy toward the North. According to a Gallup poll taken in early 2002, 29% of South Koreans support the sunshine policy, 15% oppose it and 42% think it has 'some problems' calling for modification. But public confidence in the capacity of Kim himself to orchestrate the sunshine policy has been lost.

Although Kim was always more popular abroad than at home (in December 2000 he was accepting toasts from the Nobel Peace Prize committee), his domestic descent from grace has been remarkably precipitous. As the shine was rubbed off Kim's policy toward the North, other domestic problems surfaced that might otherwise have been finessed. Kim had come to office proclaiming that he would run a squeaky-clean administration, insisting on the highest probity for those who worked for the government. In 2001, however, prosecutors have pursued a serious bribery scandal that involved a former top aide to President Kim. Even more damaging is that the case has raised questions concerning the role of two of the president's sons. The accusations have been a major embarrassment for the president at a time of dwindling popularity and as his term of office draws to a close. Kim cannot, under the rules of the South Korean constitution, run for a second five-year term, but he had hoped to smooth the way for a successor from his Millennium Democracy Party (MDP) to win the elections due in December 2002. With his anti-corruption drive unfulfilled and unravelling, and his hopes for a breakthrough in relations with the North at a dead end, there remained only the plans to reform the economic structure to provide a solid plank for the MDP in the elections.

Yet in 2001 there were clear signs that the huge conglomerates (*chaebols*) were poised to recover the freedom of action that had been stripped from them earlier in the name of reform. After four years of restraints imposed by the government after the crisis years of 1997–98, the government's Fair Trade Commission appears ready to grant exceptions to the rule that no group or company can invest more than 25% of its assets in other companies. In addition, the requirement, imposed by President Kim Dae Jung in 1999 that companies must cut their debt-to-equity ratio to no more than 2–1, is increasingly ignored. The difficulty is that reform is easier when it recognised as very necessary, as it was in the collapse of the economy back in 1997, or when there is a surge of economic growth to cushion the pain of reform, as there might have been in 1999–2000 as the economy was making a strong comeback. In 2000, real GDP rose by 8.6%; during 2001, it dropped back to nearer 3%. Kim's critics complain that his timing has been off.

As Kim looked ahead to the election at the end of 2002, there was not much to be cheerful about. Yet he could point to the extraordinary achievement of a summit meeting with North Korea's paramount leader, the exchange of a number of separated families, to an economic recovery sufficient to have repaid the $19.6 billion that it borrowed from the IMF during the economic crises on 1997 and to having built up a very healthy reserve. The position he took was that a robust improvement in the economy during 2002, as he expected, would sweep whoever was the candidate of his party, the MDP, to office. For this to be more than a professional politician's public face of optimism would require a significant improvement indeed. A series of polls up to the end of February 2002 indicated that Lee Hoi Chang, President of the Grand National Party (GNP) and widely considered to be the favourite to become the candidate of the opposition party, would easily defeat any of the candidates that Kim's ruling party might field. Even the best of the lot only came within 10 points of Lee's lead. Rhee In Je, who appeared in early March to have the inside track over eight other candidates for the nomination in the MDP primary to be held in March and April 2002 (a first-time imitation of American party political practice) had run for president in 1997. Prior to that, he had been a senior member of the ruling New Korea Party (now called the Grand National Party), served as Minister of Labour and governor of Gyeonggi province. He bolted the party when it gave its nomination for president to Lee Hoi Chang, formed a small party (the New People's Party) and put himself forward as its candidate for president. Although he ran a distant third in the race, his five million-odd votes may have thrown the election to Kim Dae Jung, who surpassed Lee Hoi Chang, the candidate of the New Korea Party (NKP), by only 390,000 votes.

Rhee is very much the pragmatist. Having left the NKP, encouraged the development of a new party and lost his election bid, he then merged his small party with Kim Dae Jung's party, the National Congress for New Politics, constituting what has become the MDP. At the end of March 2002, he was facing an unexpectedly strong challenge from Roh Moo Hyun, a lawyer who had come from far behind to be a leader in the polls. Unlike Rhee, who has not been able to top Lee Hoi Chang's popularity, Roh would be expected to beat Lee out. Whichever of the two becomes the presidential candidate for the MDP, the candidate's prospects in the general election will depend on developments in the political scene set in motion by Park Geun Hye. Park bolted the opposition party on 28 February 2002, accusing Lee Hoi Chang of 'imperialistic' leadership, saying the party hampered reformists' efforts to promote democracy and transparency, and to end autocratic party rule and 'backroom' politics. This move vastly complicates the election picture. The daughter of Park Chung Hee, who ruled South Korea with an iron fist for almost 20 years until he was assassinated by his head of intelligence, Park has gained considerable popularity as nostalgia for her father's rule rises against the backdrop of Kim Dae Jung's falling popularity and the continuation of an economic slowdown. Park Geun Hye was a vice-president of the GNP until her defection, but only a first-term member of parliament with little political experience. All the signs were that she would soon join forces with a number of older, more experienced politicians to form a new party and launch herself as its presidential candidate.

Who would gain most in that event was very much an open question. Kim Dae Jung and the MDP originally encouraged Park's ambitions, thinking that she would take votes from Lee Hoi Chang and thus help the cause of the MDP candidate. But the earliest polls taken after her decision to leave the GNP for greener pastures suggested that while she would indeed attract votes that would have gone to Lee, she would also deprive Rhee In Je or any other possible MDP candidate of support. During the run-up to the presidential election in December, rapidly changing South Korean politics are likely to leave the outcome very much in doubt.

A kind of stability

In contrast to South Korea's messy democracy, North Korean politics leave no question about political transition. After a hesitant start when his father Kim Il Sung died in 1994, bequeathing the leadership of the country to him, Kim Jong Il has consolidated his power and remained firmly in command. His sixtieth birthday was elaborately celebrated on 16 February 2002, illustrating both his continuing grip on power and a picture of status-quo normality at the top of the heap. Hailed as the 'sun of the twenty-first century' and saluted for his 'immortal deeds', adulation for the 'Dear Leader' is approaching that which was extended to his father.

Kim Jong Il's 'immortal deeds', however, did not include calling a Korean Workers Party conference to lay out plans for future development, which some observers suggested would be a fitting method of marking his birthday. There has been no party conference for over 20 years and no indication that the North Korean leadership has any idea of how to meet the disastrous economic situation they face. Suggestions had surfaced during Kim Jong Il's visit to China in January 2001 that he was contemplating following China's successful example of how to move from the smothering embrace of a command economy to the more open and effective structure of a free economy. He had visited the Shanghai stock market and various showpieces of China's move to a market economy and spent much time asking leading questions of his hosts. But this ostensible interest appears to have been mainly for show, with the North Korean press obviously under instructions to cover it heavily. Since then, there have been no clear signs that North Korea was really interested in testing free-market waters.

Yet the need has never been greater. The North Korean economy continues to sink, slowly but inexorably. Per-capita annual income is about $750, and foreign debt stands at $12bn. There has been no improvement in the food-supply chain and there will not be until there is a drastic and fundamental change in both the structure of agriculture and of the industries that should supply the tools, from fertiliser to tractors, necessary for improvement. Most of the population subsists on a near-starvation diet, and it is only the supply of food from abroad that keeps that famine at bay. Despite the political tensions between Washington and Pyongyang, the US provides the largest chunk of such aid, followed by China and Japan. The

UN has been seeking pledges for 673,500 tonnes of food to assure a minimum supply to supplement the production of the collapsed state-run farm industry. By the end of February 2002, foreign governments had pledged 25% of the demand, although the US had promised to maintain its usual contribution of 300,000 tonnes a year.

Much of Kim Jong Il's efforts have gone into trying to beg, borrow or wheedle cash and aid from abroad. For a leader who had spent most of his life totally out of the public view, he was unusually active both in travelling abroad and receiving visitors at home. He visited China in January, took a slow train across the trans-Siberian railroad (a 10-day journey) for a return visit to President Vladimir Putin in Moscow in August 2001, and met with a stream of visitors, some from the many countries that established diplomatic relations with North Korea after the summit meeting relaxed the South Korean opposition to such normalisations. During 2001, North Korea was recognised and exchanged diplomats with the Netherlands, Belgium, Canada, Spain, Germany, Luxembourg, Greece, Brazil, New Zealand, Turkey and the European Union. During the visit to Russia, Kim wrangled an agreement from Putin that Russia would connect the Trans-Siberian railway with North Korea, and there were suggestions that this would include freight links between the two countries. Chinese President Jiang Zemin made a visit to Pyongyang in September. Although no joint communiqué was issued, suggesting that little of substance was discussed or concluded, China has continued to be among the major providers of aid to Pyongyang. When the Norwegian Prime Minister visited in January 2002, he noted that Norway was looking for ways to aid North Korea in its search for an improvement in its energy requirements, perhaps by helping to refurbish its hydroelectric plants. But all of these are merely tokens when set against the overwhelming need for economic restructuring. There is little indication that anyone in leadership circles in the North has begun to think in this direction.

From dreams to dismay

Momentum behind attempts to remove the divide on the Korean Peninsula from near the top of every list of the most dangerous military standoffs in the world slowly dissipated during 2001. The euphoria that had greeted the long-delayed meeting of two leaders of North and South Korea had been overblown from the start. But even more sober appreciations of what progress could be expected proved far off the mark. Part of the problem lay with Kim Jong Il, whose vacillations and erratic behaviour made it difficult for Kim Dae Jong to continue to offer carrots while requiring little or nothing in return. Now that his popularity has plummeted, the opposition is emboldened to lead an attack on his audacious policy towards the North, even though they have no affirmative policy of their own to bring forward.

Should they prevail in the December 2002 elections, their candidate for president will likely align himself much more closely with President Bush's visceral distrust of Kim Jong Il and his insistence that the Northern leadership accommodate US views before there can be any improvement in the diplomatic atmosphere. By the end of February 2002, relations between the United States and North Korea had assumed the tone that prevailed in the last days of the Cold War. Although the US continued to talk of engagement, it was what many observers have called 'hawkish engagement'.

The pressing question is whether the president's muscular language has left room for even that kind of engagement. Neither of the two possible alternatives – ignoring North Korea or increasing pressure to the point where, if Pyongyang responds aggressively, it might lead to military action – seems very palatable. A number of existing timetables make ignoring the North difficult. Pyongyang has indicated that 2003 will be a critical 'year of decision'. According to Kim Jong Il, North Korea's moratorium on long-range missile tests only extends until 2003; at that point, Pyongyang will review its options to extend the moratorium or resume missile testing. In addition, the Agreed Framework specifies 2003 as the 'target date' for the completion of the first light-water reactor (LWR) that Korean Peninsula Energy Development Organisation (KEDO) – the multinational consortium created under the Agreed Framework – is building in North Korea in exchange for North Korea's suspension of plutonium production. However, the project is already running many years behind schedule, and Pyongyang has threatened to pull out of the Agreed Framework and resume plutonium production if it is not 'compensated' for these delays in the nuclear energy project. Furthermore, North Korea is required to account for plutonium that it produced before 1994 only after a 'significant portion' – defined as the major non-nuclear components – is completed. KEDO's current estimate is that this will not happen until around 2005. Finally, a new and probably more conservative government will take office in Seoul in January 2003, marking the official demise of Kim Dae Jong's sunshine policy.

The danger of continuing to ratchet the tensions upwards is that North Korea will live up to its reputation for creating a crisis in order to force the US and its allies to come to terms with it. For example, Pyongyang could seek to exploit an actual or prospective US military move on Iraq by airing exaggerated rhetoric about an imminent attack on South Korea, spiced with threats to resume missile tests and plutonium production. Its hope would be to force the US and South Korea to soften their positions and continue (or expand) assistance that is vital to the Pyongyang regime's survival. At the same time, Pyongyang's room for manoeuvre is limited. Because it is heavily dependent on foreign assistance for survival, it will need to weigh the risks that provoking a crisis could easily backfire by terminating assistance or – even worse from the North's standpoint – provoking a US military attack. Moreover, Pyongyang will need to carefully heed the views of Beijing, which does not want a crisis on the peninsula.

The Bush administration also faces a dilemma. On one hand, many senior officials believe that the US should not be helping to prop up the 'evil' North Korean regime through diplomatic deals and assistance. In this view, a far more effective and enduring strategy for ending the North Korea WMD threat is to isolate, starve and destroy the regime, as in the case of Iraq. On the other hand, in contrast with Iraq, US military options against North Korea are much more problematic. Although the US and its allies would certainly prevail in the end, North Korea could inflict very heavy damage and casualties on South Korea, including Seoul, which is within artillery range. Moreover, North Korea has a much more robust arsenal of ballistic missiles than Iraq, as well as biological, chemical and possibly even nuclear weapons, which it would presumably be prepared to use as a last resort if its survival were at risk. Finally, Washington would find it very difficult to convince its allies in the region, much less China, to support a high-risk strategy of pressure against Pyongyang.

For these reasons, the Bush administration, like its predecessor, may find that it has little choice but to pursue diplomatic options with the North, no matter how distasteful and difficult. Clearly, the North would prefer to make a deal. The issue for 2003 is whether both sides' rational interests in pursuing a diplomatic approach take hold or Pyongyang's penchant for risk-taking and Washington's deep distrust and hostility towards the North combine to create a crisis that nobody wants.

Africa

While sub-Saharan Africa was among the regions least affected by 11 September, many of its profound political, economic and humanitarian problems have persisted or worsened in 2001–02. Poverty and AIDS remained the scourges of the continent. Roughly 45–50% of sub-Saharan Africans live below the poverty line – a far higher proportion than in any region of the world except South Asia. Of the world's 25 most AIDS-ridden countries, 24 are in Africa, where seven countries have infection rates above 20%. Among the most heavily infected are South Africa (20%) and Botswana (38.5%) – two of the continent's most otherwise promising economies. This state of affairs will exacerbate poverty by at once reducing the skilled workforce and increasing public-spending needs, and corrode stability and security by hollowing out civil services and armies. The World Bank estimates that AIDS will reduce GDP by up to 20% in some states over the next ten years. These factors will raise the probability of state failure, rendering states more vulnerable to 'hijacking' by transnational criminals or terrorists. Dealing with these prospects calls for a level of Western engagement and a public-health mobilisation that have not yet materialised.

At the same time, most quadrants of sub-Saharan Africa showed possibilities of progress as well as confirmations of gloom. In an election marred by the ruling party's systematic corruption of the political process, Zimbabwean President Robert Mugabe won a six-year term in March 2002. Despite condemnation as well as diplomatic and economic isolation by virtually all major powers, the refusal of regional leaders – in particular, South African President Thabo Mbeki – to seriously question the election result helped Mugabe to remain unrepentant for his coercive land seizures and gross economic irresponsibility. Whether popular upheaval or state repression carries the day is a key question for southern African stability in 2001–02. In civil war-riven Angola, on the other hand, a single military development may have increased the potential for peace. Jonas Savimbi – leader of the rebel Unión Nacional para la Independencia Total de Angola (UNITA) – was killed on 22 February 2002 in an attack by government forces. The government sought to capitalise politically on the resulting disarray in UNITA's leadership, declaring a unilateral cease-fire and meeting rebel leaders for peace talks in mid-March in the small Angolan town of Luena.

Luanda's objective is to persuade UNITA to disarm and join the mainstream political process, pursuant to the 1994 Lusaka peace agreement

Map 5 Africa

IISSmaps
N
Mediterranean Sea
Red Sea
ATLANTIC OCEAN
INDIAN OCEAN
Rabat
MOROCCO
Algiers
Tunis
TUNISIA
Tripoli
ALGERIA
LIBYA
Cairo
EGYPT
WESTERN SAHARA
Ad Dakhla
MAURITANIA
Nouakchott
SENEGAL
Dakar
GA
Banjul
Bissau
G-B
Bamako
MALI
NIGER
Niamey
Ouagadougou
BURKINA
GUINEA
Conakry
Freetown
SIERRA LEONE
Monrovia
LIBERIA
CÔTE D'IVOIRE
Abidjan
GHANA
Accra
TOGO
Lomé
BENIN
Porto Novo
NIGERIA
Abuja
CHAD
Ndjamena
SUDAN
Khartoum
ERITREA
Asmera
DJIBOUTI
Djibouti
ETHIOPIA
Addis Ababa
SOMALI REPUBLIC
Mogadishu
CAMEROON
Yaoundé
Malabo
EQ. G.
SÃO TOMÉ & PRÍNCIPE
CENTRAL AFRICAN REPUBLIC
Bangui
Libreville
GABON
CONGO
Brazzaville
Kinshasa
Cabinda (ANGOLA)
DEMOCRATIC REPUBLIC OF CONGO
UGANDA
Kampala
KENYA
Nairobi
RWANDA
Kigali
BURUNDI
Bujumbura
Dodoma
TANZANIA
Dar es Salaam
Luanda
ANGOLA
Lusaka
ZAMBIA
MALAWI
Lilongwe
MOZAMBIQUE
Harare
ZIMBABWE
MADAGASCAR
Antananarivo
NAMIBIA
Windhoek
BOTSWANA
Gaborone
Pretoria
Mbabane
Maputo
SWAZILAND
Maseru
LESOTHO
SOUTH AFRICA
Cape Town
international boundary
disputed boundary
capital city
GA GAMBIA
G-B GUINEA BISSAU
EQ G EQUATORIAL GUINEA
0 1,000km
0 500 miles

abandoned by Savimbi. Although exiled leaders derided the talks as a 'farce', the loss of Savimbi's charismatic leadership has shrunk the rebel group's options. While UNITA still raises money from illicit diamonds, sanctions have diminished revenues and UNITA faces food and supply shortages. By virtue of the country's large oil output (more than 850,000 barrels per day), the government's resources are abundant. The balance may have shifted decisively in favour of normalisation. On 31 March 2002, senior government and UNITA representatives signed a preliminary cease-fire agreement in Luena, witnessed by representatives of the UN, the United States, Russia and Portugal. The deal included amnesty for UNITA rebels for crimes committed during the civil war, which was unanimously approved by the Angolan parliament on 2 April. The cease-fire was finalised by the two sides in Luanda on 4 April. The government's next major challenge may be resolving internal rivalries within the ruling Movimento Popular da Libertação de Angola (MPLA) that are liable to surface in the absence of the unifying phenomenon of war. Reformers (and most voters) will seek a more equitable allocation of oil revenues, while MPLA conservatives will be reluctant to dismantle the patronage networks from which they have benefited. Pressure from international donors could prove decisive in swinging the odds towards the reformers. But post-conflict tasks, such as resettling about three million displaced people and pacifying rebel holdouts, will remain major challenges to the state.

In West Africa, somewhat surprisingly, the situation has improved. Liberian President Charles Taylor's regime has been and continues to be the principal 'spoiler' in the region. But international sanctions designed to inhibit trade in illicit 'conflict diamonds', heightened outside scrutiny after 11 September and an emerging indigenous insurgency appeared to dampen Liberia's support for Sierra Leonean and Guinean rebels. Refugee flows became more manageable, and Liberia, Guinea and Sierra Leone signed an agreement in early March to repatriate refugees and supply assistance to displaced persons. The Revolutionary United Front (RUF) in Sierra Leone also found it more difficult to resist UN, government and pro-government forces, and its attempt to take control of some of Guinea's diamond fields was rebuked with decisive military action from Conakry. Between May 2001 and January 2002, the 17,000-strong UN Mission in Sierra Leone (UNAMSIL) collected weapons from 45,844 ex-combatants, including 18,354 from the RUF, and 39,220 ex-combatants registered to receive demobilisation payments. On 11 January, UNAMSIL force commander Lieutenant-General Daniel Opande of the Nigerian army declared disarmament complete and the war over. But Sierra Leone still faced a shortfall of $12 million for reintegrating ex-combatants, and a residual threat from an RUF splinter – the 'Independent RUF' – led by Sam Bockarie. Liberia's growing internal instability, while diverting Taylor's attention from Sierra Leone, could produce new regional instability. In early February, a rebel movement, the

Guinea-based Liberians United for Reconciliation and Democracy, moved to the outskirts of Monrovia, prompting Taylor to declare a state of emergency. This situation could re-ignite tensions between Liberia and Guinea.

Consolidating peace continued to be a frustrating task in the Democratic Republic of Congo. But the level of violence did not increase appreciably, and the cease-fires and withdrawals by national armies that began in February 2001 pursuant to UN Security Council Resolution 1341 have substantially held. Among pro-government forces, Namibia and Angola no longer had troops in Congo in March 2002. About 11,000 Zimbabwean troops remained there, but mainly to pursue and safeguard economic mineral and timber interests granted to Mugabe by the Kabila government. On the anti-government side, Uganda sent troops to towns near the Congolese border to quell ethnic violence in January and February 2002, but this was done at the request of the UN Mission in Congo (MONUC). Rebel action supported by Rwanda in March was more provocative. The Rwanda-backed Congolese Rally for Democracy seized the strategic port of Moliro to preempt its recapture by government forces. Nevertheless, the group agreed to withdraw if MONUC would send troops to ensure that the port remained neutral. Clashes among rebels, which hold nearly half of the country, and pro-government militias have continued. MONUC fields only 3,500 cease-fire monitors and is too small to enforce a cease-fire. This makes political progress all the more essential. On this front there were mixed signals. Peace talks that had resumed in Sun City, South Africa, on 25 February 2002, stalled over the Moliro episode, but were reconvened in Lusaka, Zambia, on 3 April.

In the Horn of Africa, a sober and tenuous status quo prevailed. The Ethiopia–Eritrea border dispute remained non-violent, though only barely. Sudan extended counter-terrorist cooperation to the US. The peace process involving the Muslim government of Sudan and the Christian/animist southern rebels developed momentum and produced a cease-fire in the Nuba Mountains (though not in the south) as a result of the proactive outside efforts of the US, the European Union and European capitals. The government's refusal to stop aerial bombardment in the south, however, jeopardised progress. The failed state of Somalia was the focus of intense US attention in late 2001 and early 2002 as a possible host for al-Qaeda. Washington concluded that the threat was not actionable and settled on a preventive rather than an intrusive approach. Kenya's problems are more subtle but nonetheless ominous. After ruling the country for 23 years, President Daniel arap Moi is constitutionally required to relinquish his rule after elections that must occur before the end of 2002. Moi belongs to the relatively small Kalenjin tribe, and as of March 2002 had not named a successor. Eager to exploit the opportunity to acquire power long denied them, Kenya's two largest tribes – the Kikuyus and the Luos – appeared to be violently jockeying for position. The 1992 and 1997 multiparty elections in Kenya were marred by tribal violence, but did not spill over into large-scale civil unrest. With the competition more open now than it has ever been, that possibility may be less remote.

On the island of Madagascar in the Indian Ocean, a tentatively bloodless civil conflict unfolded in late 2001 and early 2002. Opposition leader Marc Ravalomanana appeared to have won the December 2001 election with 52% of the vote, but incumbent Didier Ratsiraka capriciously ordered a runoff. The move sparked a general strike. Ravalomanana refused to participate in the runoff. In a 'popular coup' on 22 February 2002, he was nominated president by his supporters; a Supreme Court judge swore him in at a stadium in front of 200,000 people. Ratsiraka declared martial law, and mass protests ensued. As of March, Ravalomanana's supporters had control of the capital city of Antananarivo. He was paying civil servants' salaries and had encountered little resistance from the military. But Ratsiraka set up a second capital in Toamsina on the coast, cut off supplies to Antananarivo and appeared to secure the support of five of six provincial governments.

There are quiet indications that sub-Saharan Africa is managing better. Despite prohibitively small UN contingents in Ethiopia–Eritrea and Congo, violence in these places did not spin out of control. The peacekeeping force in Sierra Leone, though fortified by Britain's aggressive support in late 2000, undertook the demobilisation programme under Nigerian leadership. Angola and Namibia have opted out of the Congo war, while Uganda and Rwanda have shown greater restraint. Sudan's government, though still highly problematic, has appeared more inclined to end its international isolation in cooperating with the US-led counter-terrorism campaign and with peace initiatives aimed at ending Sudan's civil conflict. Madagascar's political process was fraught but non-violent. Failed and failing states – such as Somalia and Zimbabwe, respectively – remain serious threats to stability. It is possible, however, that 11 September will redound to Africa's benefit in this regard. The West's long-term strategic interest in depriving terrorists of safe havens may animate greater economic and political involvement in the region to remedy or forestall state failure and, perforce, greater attention to the devastating problems of poverty and AIDS. A potential vehicle for that involvement may be the New Partnership for African Development (NEPAD) – an initiative devised by the United Kingdom, South Africa, Nigeria and Algeria to secure aid from Western donors for economic development by establishing clear economic and political conditions for such assistance. NEPAD was approved in principle at the June 2001 Group of Eight summit in Genoa and is to be further refined at the June 2002 summit in Kananaskis, Canada. The initiative sets a target of $64 billion in aid.

Repression and Dysfunction in Zimbabwe

By intensifying a bitter struggle to retain power, President Robert Mugabe pushed Zimbabwe still further into economic collapse and political repression in 2001 and early 2002. Militias organised by the state waged a violent campaign against the opposition Movement for Democratic Change (MDC), while white farmers were dispossessed in a wave of illegal land seizures. Mugabe's bitter struggle to hold power in Zimbabwe culminated with his victory in the presidential polls held from 9–11 March 2002. After the most violent election campaign in Zimbabwe's post-independence history, Mugabe won 56% of the vote, compared with 42% for Morgan Tsvangirai, his challenger from the MDC.

Zimbabwe's crisis began in February 2000, when Mugabe unexpectedly lost a referendum on a new constitution. From that moment onwards, Zimbabwe was rocked by political violence. June 2000 saw a narrow victory for the ruling Zimbabwe African Peoples' Union – Patriotic Front (Zanu-PF) party in a parliamentary election condemned by international observers as neither free nor fair. Yet the events of 2001 marked a new and crucial stage in Zimbabwe's descent. Mugabe has confounded even the most pessimistic forecasts. His actions have three profoundly disturbing aspects. First, he has made peaceful political change almost inconceivable. Second, Mugabe has made no effort whatsoever to arrest the catastrophic decline of Zimbabwe's economy – on the contrary, the situation has worsened. So great is the damage that there is no possibility of economic recovery in the medium term without a large injection of international capital – highly unlikely without quick and radical political and economic reform. Third, despite the devastating consequences of Mugabe's rule, there was no determined or effective effort by regional African leaders to curb his excesses prior to his re-election and there remains little prospect of this taking place in its immediate aftermath.

State-sponsored domestic terror

The MDC is a multi-ethnic alliance of trade unionists, professionals and middle-class business people, organised country-wide. The party is committed to the rule of law, wants orderly land reform and espouses economic recovery by way of liberalisation and privatisation that is consistent with the policies of the international financial institutions. This platform is at thoroughly odds with Mugabe's policies.

In 2001, Zanu-PF's violent crackdown against the MDC continued unabated. Some 41 political killings were recorded, bringing the total to 88 since February 2000. About 20,000 people suffered assault, torture, rape or abduction at the hands of Zanu-PF militias during 2001. On 28 June, another 2,030 white-owned farms were listed for seizure by the government, bringing the total to 4,593, or 90% of all white-owned properties. About 1,000 farms were still occupied by Zanu-PF supporters, following the illegal land invasions of 2000. A 'fast track' resettlement scheme, which Mugabe made his flagship policy, had been launched on 15 July 2000. Although the Supreme Court ruled this programme illegal on 10 November 2000, Mugabe simply ignored this judgement and pressed ahead with land seizures, unmoved by heavy international criticism of his disregard for the rule of law.

Mugabe's coercive land policy is the central component of his carefully planned drive to hold power. Rhetorically, he characterizes the MDC as a 'pawn' of former colonial power the United Kingdom; allegedly neo-colonial institutions such as the International Monetary Fund (IMF), the World Bank, and the European Union (EU); and the predominantly white South African political opposition (the Democratic Party). Tactically, Mugabe uses a simple 'carrot and stick' approach. Mugabe offers white-owned land to his supporters as a reward for keeping him in office. Seizing farms affords him sweeping powers of patronage, which he has skilfully manipulated to reinforce his position. Moreover, the mobs that occupy farms have also been encouraged to wage a brutal campaign against anyone suspected of supporting the MDC. The ongoing political violence is designed to demonstrate the penalties of backing the opposition. Zanu-PF supporters can expect land, while Mugabe's opponents live under daily threat of violence. By forcing every Zimbabwean to confront this simple balance of risk and reward, Mugabe has sought to secure his dominance. The 'carrot and stick' approach remained key to all of Mugabe's actions in the run-up to the presidential election.

May 2001 saw the last weeks of an attempt to bring this method of campaigning into the capital, Harare, and Zimbabwe's second city, Bulawayo, both strongholds of the MDC. Zanu-PF mobs raided about 300 businesses and charities, many of them linked to the tiny white community, comprising about 0.3% of the population. Money was extorted from their owners and distributed to any employees who backed the ruling party. Meanwhile, those suspected of harbouring MDC sympathies were assaulted. The intention was to extend the rural terror campaign, centred on occupied farms, into the cities. Yet this new offensive failed to damage the MDC's urban support. During the June 2000 parliamentary poll, the opposition, led by Morgan Tsvangirai, achieved 75% of the vote in Harare and Bulawayo, and might have won a parliamentary majority had it not been for the 20 unelected seats allotted to Zanu-PF. Almost a year later, on 14 May 2001, at the height of Zanu-PF's urban offensive, the town of Masvingo staged a mayoral election and the MDC held this level of popularity by taking 71% of the vote. The new campaign was quietly abandoned, though not before the numerous factories and offices were stormed by gangs, dealing yet another blow to Zimbabwe's tattered image as an investment destination.

A government-imposed overnight rise of 74% in the price of petrol on 13 June 2001, with the accompanying increase in bus fares, probably ended any chance Mugabe had of rolling back the MDC's support in the cities. From that moment onwards, all Zanu-PF's efforts were focused on ensuring the loyalty of the rural areas, where 70% of Zimbabwean voters live. This meant resettling white-owned farms as swiftly as possible. On 25 July, Mugabe used his address at the official opening of parliament to claim that 100,000 black families had been given land. This was almost certainly an exaggeration, but the task of placing Zanu-PF supporters on formerly white-owned land became the government's central priority. On 28 July 2001, Mugabe tried to apply a veneer of legal legitimacy to the confiscation of white-owned land when he enlarged the Supreme Court from five justices to eight. All three new judges on the Supreme Court bench had strong links to Zanu-PF. The resolutely independent Chief Justice, Anthony Gubbay, had already been hounded out of office on 2 March and replaced with Godfrey Chidyausiku, a former Zanu-PF minister. By packing the Supreme Court, Mugabe managed to neutralise the last restraint on his power. He also moved decisively towards blocking international media coverage of Zimbabwe. The last British newspaper correspondent resident in Harare was forced to leave on 30 June 2001, while the BBC was banned from the country from July onwards.

With Zimbabwe largely closed to international scrutiny, the efforts by Zanu-PF militias to sow terror in the rural areas were stepped up. On 6 August 2001, a clash between white farmers and squatters occupying their land was used as a pretext for the jailing of 21 landowners and random attacks on whites in the town of Chinhoyi. By 9 August, this had escalated into a full-scale looting spree, involving perhaps 4,000 Zanu-PF supporters, working in organised gangs. By 15 August, 45 farms in the Doma and Mhangura areas had been looted and destroyed, forcing the evacuation of 350 people. Scores of black farm-workers were assaulted and hundreds driven from their homes. This large-scale operation succeeded in imposing Zanu-PF's dominance over a swath of Zimbabwe's agricultural heartland.

Mugabe's actions were neither surprising nor, in political terms, irrational. Rather, they were guided by his overriding wish to hold onto power. Without violence, intimidation and illegal land seizures, he stood little chance of containing the MDC's challenge. Throughout autumn 2001, Mugabe stepped up the seizure of white-owned land. On 9 November, he issued a decree that amended the Land Acquisition Act of 1992 to provide that any farmer in receipt of a 'section eight occupation order' had three months to pack up and leave. In the meantime, the landowner was confined to his home and barred from working the farm, and the resettlement of his land could begin immediately. There was no avenue for appeal. Perhaps 1,000 farmers –

accounting for 90% of white-owned commercial farmland – had already received these orders and Mugabe's decree was worded to apply retrospectively.

The newly packed Supreme Court fulfilled the opposition's worst expectations on 4 December, when a panel of five justices – four of them new arrivals – ruled that Mugabe's land acquisitions were legal. All of the adverse judgements previously made by the court were reversed, while the government was given full authority to proceed with dispossessing white farmers. In announcing the ruling, Chief Justice Chidyausiku declared that land reform was a matter of 'social justice and not, strictly speaking, a legal issue' – precisely the words that Mugabe had employed all along.

Economic collapse, political perversity

As land seizures gathered pace in late 2001, Zimbabwe's agriculture-based economy imploded. White-owned commercial farms provided, directly or indirectly, almost half of Zimbabwe's entire gross national product, over 40% of its export earnings and homes and employment for 300,000 families. The Zimbabwe dollar, worth $1.50 at independence, as of January 2001 was worth only 2 cents in the official market and one-sixth that in the parallel market. By early 2002, farm productivity had dwindled to insignificance, and no adequate substitute was available. Moreover, the massive disruption to commercial agriculture inevitably meant that Zimbabwe would face food shortages. A report by the United Nations Food and Agricultural Organisation released in July 2001 calculated that Zimbabwe faced a deficit of 579,000 tons of maize in 2001–2002. To avoid a famine in the early months of 2002, before the harvest in May, Zimbabwe would therefore be compelled to import this amount. But its economic crisis meant that no hard foreign currency was available to cover the cost, so Mugabe was forced to call for food aid. Only supplies by the UN's World Food Programme (WFP) saved Zimbabwe from a self-inflicted famine in early 2002.

In Mugabe's mind, this abject strife was a price worth paying for regime security. To further minimise the risks of losing power, he took additional steps against the MDC. In fact, he came close to banning the MDC altogether. On 5 November, Cain Nkala, an official of the War Veterans' Association, a central part of the Zanu-PF structure, was murdered in Bulawayo. His death was blamed on the MDC and a Zanu-PF mob rampaged through the city and burned down the opposition party's regional headquarters. Dozens of MDC activists were rounded up and placed behind bars on flimsy charges. By late November, the party in the Matabeleland region had been effectively shut down. Mugabe gave Nkala a state funeral on 18 November. In his eulogy, he attempted to cast himself as a dutiful partner in the post-11 September global counter-terrorism campaign, branding the MDC and white farmers 'terrorists' no less than 20 times. 'The MDC perpetrators of violence and crimes against humanity and their international sponsors should also know their days are numbered. The time is now up for the MDC terrorists', Mugabe said. Despite this rhetoric, he stopped short of proscribing the opposition. But at Zanu-PF's annual Congress, held in Victoria Falls on 14-15 December 2001, he did the next worst thing. In two belligerent and incendiary speeches, he readied his supporters for a 'real physical fight' with the MDC and then told Zanu-PF: 'This is war against the MDC, total war, when the order comes the guns must be ready and their trajectory true'. Violence directed against his opponents claimed five lives in December alone.

In early 2002, Mugabe presented parliament, where Zanu-PF holds 93 of 150 seats, with a package of laws that sought in effect to remove the last remaining democratic freedoms in Zimbabwe. A Public Order and Security Act passed on 10 January outlawed criticism of the president, gave the police sweeping powers of detention without trial and forced the MDC to apply for official permission before holding any rallies. A General Regulations (Amendments) Act passed on the same day banned independent observers from covering the presidential election, and outlawed voter-education programmes run by civic groups. The new law also stripped all Zimbabweans living abroad – except soldiers and diplomats, who were assumed to back Mugabe – of the right to vote. Everyone else faced unprecedentedly stringent requirements for voter registration. City dwellers were ordered to produce proof of residence, in the form of title deeds, rental agreements or utility bills. For many people living in poverty-stricken townships, this effectively constituted disenfranchisement. In the rural areas, the new rules required village chiefs to vouch for everyone registering to vote. As each headman is paid a grant by the government and almost all support Zanu-PF, none would be likely to certify anyone suspected of backing Tsvangirai. The Access to Information and Protection of Privacy Bill – passed on 31 January, and watered down at the insistence of moderate senior Zanu-PF members – restricted foreign correspondents working in Zimbabwe to covering specified events for limited time periods and made illegal their reporting on deliberations of the cabinet or other government bodies. The law also required all local journalists to apply for licences from the Information Minister, who has sole discretion. The clear intention of this law was to shut down Zimbabwe's tiny but outspoken independent press before the election. Although the Supreme Court overturned a number of these provisions on 27 February, the government largely ignored the ruling. By executive fiat, Mugabe decided to use government election monitors and ballot counters, imposed the proof-of-residency requirements and barred expatriate Zimbabweans (except government employees) from voting.

Militias organised by the state escalated a brutal crackdown on the MDC, claiming at least 33 lives between 1 January and polling day on 9 March. More than 20,000 people were forced to flee their homes, with tens of thousands beaten, tortured, raped or abducted. The total number of political killings recorded in Zimbabwe since the onset of Zanu-PF's official terror campaign in February 2000 stood at 125 when Mugabe's re-election was announced. The election itself saw irregularities and outright ballot stuffing. The number of polling stations in Harare, where Tsvangirai enjoys overwhelming support, was cut by up to 50%. The authorities chose to combine the presidential poll with the elections for Harare's new mayor and the city's council. Thus, multiplying the ballot papers threefold while halving the provision of polling stations was a recipe for administrative chaos.

Predictably, queues stretched for miles as people in Harare waited to vote. Some waited for 18 hours on both voting days and were still unable to participate. After an urgent application from the MDC, the High Court ordered a third day of voting. But the government failed to comply with this ruling in full. Polling stations opened six hours late on 11 March and were forcibly closed while thousands waited to vote. Riot police dispersed the queues with tear gas and baton charges. The clear intention was to disenfranchise Tsvangirai's urban stronghold. This tactic succeeded. The final turnout in Harare was 41%, well below the national figure of 55% and lower than that of any other province. By contrast, turnout in Mashonaland Central province – Mugabe's heartland, where the number of polling stations had been increased by half – was 69%, the highest in the country. This remarkable variation in turnout alone explains Mugabe's victory, but was guaranteed by other measures. The government printed seven million ballot papers, although Zimbabwe has fewer than 5.6m registered voters. The evidence suggests that many of the extra 1.4m papers were used to inflate Mugabe's total.

In the constituency of Tsholotsho, MDC polling agents counted 12,000 people casting their votes. Yet the official result put the turnout at 21,941. Mugabe mysteriously won this seat, although it had voted for the MDC in the parliamentary polls of June 2000 by a margin of 70%. In the neighbouring constituency of Bubi-Umguza, MDC agents at 19 mobile polling stations counted 137 voters. When its ballot boxes were opened at the counting centre, they yielded 1,137 votes and Mugabe won the seat. Discrepancies of this sort were recorded across Zimbabwe. Ballot rigging, violence and intimidation combined to ensure Mugabe's victory by 1,685,212 votes against Tsvangirai's 1,258,401 – a relatively slender margin of 426,811 votes.

Regional diplomatic futility

The looting and destruction in Doma and Mhangura drew wide international criticism, including some from Mugabe's African neighbours. Momentarily abandoning his customary timidity with respect to Zimbabwe, on 7 August 2001, President Thabo Mbeki of South Africa talked of the need to 'avoid economic meltdown in Zimbabwe'. One week later, he was instrumental in ensuring that Mugabe lost his chairmanship of the Organ on Politics, Defence and Security of the Southern African Development Community (SADC) during a summit in Lilongwe, the Malawian capital. Mugabe had used his leadership of this committee to increase his regional influence and lend an appearance of legitimacy to Zimbabwe's intervention in the Democratic Republic of Congo (DROC)'s civil war in August 1998.

Pretoria's mounting frustration with Mugabe was also demonstrated by Tito Mboweni, Governor of the South African Reserve Bank, on 22 August, when he said: 'The wheels have come off [Zimbabwe]. The situation has become untenable when it is seen that the highest office in the land seems to support illegal means of land reform, land invasions, the occupation of land, beating up of people, blood flowing everywhere'. Yet South Africa still hoped that Mugabe could be influenced through diplomatic channels. At Mbeki's urging, a committee of seven Commonwealth foreign ministers, including those from Britain and Zimbabwe itself, was formed to resolve the crisis. On 6 September, this group met in Abuja, the Nigerian capital, and agreement was reached after eight hours of talks. Mugabe, represented by Zimbabwe Foreign Minister Stan Mudenge, agreed to 'restore the rule of law to the process of land reform' and 'take firm action against violence and intimidation'. Zimbabwe gave a 'commitment to freedom of expression' and agreed that 'there will be no further occupation of farm lands'. Mugabe reaffirmed his adherence to the Commonwealth's statement of democratic principles embodied in the Harare declaration of 1991. In return, British Foreign Secretary Jack Straw held out the prospect of paying £36 million for land reform if these conditions were met.

British officials hailed the Abuja agreement as Mugabe's last chance to pull Zimbabwe back from the brink and restore normality. But the Abuja accord was dead before the ink was dry. Mugabe made no effort whatever to observe the deal, which he had signed purely as a short term expedient to head off international criticism. In the six weeks after it was signed, over 800 violent incidents were recorded on occupied farms, and police remained equally unwilling to act. Zanu-PF supporters invaded another 100 properties. Despite Mugabe's professed 'commitment to freedom of expression', the BBC remained banned from Zimbabwe and foreign correspondents still found it impossible to visit the country. Routine harassment of the MDC continued unabated.

On 22 December 2001, US President George W. Bush signed into law the Zimbabwe Democracy and Economic Recovery Bill, empowering Bush to impose targeted sanctions on Mugabe and senior figures in his regime, freezing their assets and enforcing travel bans unless Zimbabwe holds free and fair elections. British Prime Minister Tony Blair labelled Mugabe a 'disgrace' on 23 January 2002. On 28 January, the EU invoked Article 96 of its Cotonou free trade agreement and announced that it would impose personal travel and financial sanctions on Zanu-PF leaders unless Zimbabwe permitted international election observers to be effectively deployed, allowed the media access, stopped attacks on the opposition and held a free and fair election. On 18 February, the EU imposed targeted sanctions, freezing any assets senior Zimbabwean officials may hold in the EU and banning them from visiting any EU member state. The US followed suit with financial sanctions of its own on 19 February, and a travel ban on Mugabe and his closest aides on 23 February.

Unfortunately, Southern Africa's leaders did not match this solid consensus in the developed world. Mbeki and other senior South African officials, to their credit, stated publicly that South Africa would 'no longer defend Mugabe' and that the Zimbabwean had 'lost the plot'. On 27 November, the South African leader warned: 'If people are being beaten, clearly there cannot be a free election in Zimbabwe'. Mbeki added that 'civil conflict' could be sparked by an unfair contest. Mugabe's allies played the race card, responding with an article in *The Herald*, Harare's official daily, on 4 December that accused Mbeki of bowing to 'white pressure' and 'betraying Zimbabwe'. In the event, Mbeki did not back his words with action. Although South Africa supplies Zimbabwe with over 50% of its electricity and 30% of its fuel, Mbeki made no attempt to use this leverage over Mugabe. Nor did he explicitly endorse the expressed concerns of Western leaders, or echo criticisms of Mugabe voiced by pre-eminent South Africans such as Nelson Mandela and Bishop Desmond Tutu.

Mbeki appeared to be constrained by an array of paralysing factors that includes: domestic sensitivities to land reform; the South African left's accusation that he would be pandering to white interests; the prospect that the MDC's ascendancy would lend too much encouragement to South African trade unions; fear of triggering an influx of refugees; and an inflexible and blinkered commitment to solidarity with African 'liberation groups'. Other countries in the region also declined to act for some of the same reasons. Indeed, a visit by SADC foreign ministers to Harare on 10 December resulted in a public statement of full support for Mugabe and the remarkable claim that the situation in Zimbabwe was 'much improved'. Shortly before the Zimbabwe election began, at a summit of Commonwealth leaders held from 5–8 March in Coolum, Australia, Mbeki and other African leaders refused to support Britain's request that the Commonwealth suspend Zimbabwe. Responding to criticism, Mbeki wrote in an online letter issued by the ANC that 'those inspired by notions of white supremacy are free to depart [the Commonwealth] if they feel that membership of [sic] the association reduces them to a repugnant position imposed by inferior blacks'.

Within three days of the announcement of Mugabe's victory on 13 March, Canada, Australia, New Zealand and Switzerland announced that they would follow the EU's and the United States' lead with 'targeted' sanctions of their own. The US and Britain declined to recognise the outcome of the election, while Denmark broke off diplomatic relations with Harare. A consensus was forged among nations in the developed world that Mugabe's re-election would not be afforded legitimacy. Once again, this was not matched by a similar consensus among African countries. Five African heads of state, including President Joaquim Chissano of Mozambique, usually considered a friend of the West, attended Mugabe's inauguration in Harare on 17 March.

Despite the overwhelming evidence of impropriety, international observers differed markedly in their assessments. The Commonwealth observer team, led by General Abdusalami Abubakar, the former Nigerian ruler, issued a damning report, saying that the contest was held in a 'climate of fear'. Norwegian observers said that the election was neither free nor fair. The Zimbabwe Election Support Network, a coalition of civic groups, condemned the poll as a 'violation of every democratic standard'. But observer teams from Nigeria, Malawi, Kenya and Tanzania gave the election a clean bill of health. Most crucially of all, the South African observers described the outcome as 'legitimate', even though two members of their team had earlier been caught up in an attack on an MDC office carried out by members of Mugabe's Zanu-PF party.

The South African election observers' certification of the Zimbabwe election as free and fair led Mbeki to indicate that he was willing to recognise Mugabe's victory. Jacob Zuma, South Africa's deputy President, visited Harare on 14 March and publicly congratulated Mugabe. But Mbeki was under conflicting pressures. At the March 2002 Commonwealth summit, he had been placed on a three-member committee that was mandated to decide the organisation's response to the Zimbabwean election. The other members were John Howard, the Australian Prime Minister, and President Olusegun Obasanjo of Nigeria. When the Commonwealth observer team condemned the election, they made it exceedingly difficult for this committee to reach any conclusion other than that Zimbabwe should be suspended from the club of former British colonies. Nevertheless, in a last-ditch effort to keep Mugabe within the fold, Obasanjo and Mbeki flew to Harare on 18 March. During a two-hour meeting, they asked Mugabe to form a government of national unity, according Tsvangirai a senior position. But Mugabe dismissed this suggestion. Having failed to secure any offer from Zimbabwe that could avert suspension from the Commonwealth, Mbeki and Obasanjo agreed with great reluctance to Zimbabwe's suspension on 19 March after a meeting with Howard in London.

The single most important factor that pushed Mbeki towards endorsing Zimbabwe's suspension was the future of the New Partnership for African Development (NEPAD), a regional initiative to attract anti-poverty assistance. This can only succeed with Western support, and Tony Blair made it clear to Mbeki during a telephone call on 19 March that no help would be forthcoming unless Mugabe's regime was isolated. But after being pushed into this course of action, Mbeki swiftly revealed his ambivalence. Shortly after his return to Pretoria, the South African cabinet met on 22 March and publicly endorsed the conclusion of its observer team that Mugabe's re-election was legitimate. Some observers took Mbeki's approval for Zimbabwe's Commonwealth suspension as a sign that he had finally lost patience with Mugabe. In fact, the evidence suggests that Mbeki has still failed to reach a coherent policy over Zimbabwe. He has managed to endorse the reports of two election observer teams that reach diametrically opposing conclusions. He has both congratulated Mugabe on his re-election and approved Zimbabwe's suspension from the Commonwealth. Mbeki has moved from tacitly supporting Mugabe to having no identifiable policy whatsoever.

Dismal prospects

The continual failures of leadership on the part of Mbeki and the entire SADC region came as Zimbabwe recorded the worst macroeconomic statistics in Africa. By the end of 2001, inflation had risen to 97.9% and unemployment to 60%, while the economy contracted by a further 8%, making it the fastest-shrinking in the world except Turkey's. At this rate of decline, the country faces complete de-industrialisation by 2004. The second-largest economy in the SADC is steadily imploding, with potentially devastating consequences for the region. An estimated 300,000 Zimbabwean economic migrants illegally entered South Africa or Botswana in 2001. The food shortages inflicted by Mugabe's land policies can only increase the risk of a mass population movement. On 14 December, the WFP announced that 558,000 Zimbabweans were in need of immediate food aid. Judith Lewis, the WFP's regional director, said: 'We need to start delivering food to thousands of hungry people as fast as possible. People are really struggling to survive and they're resorting to selling off meagre belongings as a last option to buy food'. If the economic collapse continues, refugees could rise into the millions, with the attendant risk of destabilising Mugabe's neighbours.

Mugabe has garrisoned himself against these pressures. General Vitalis Zvinavashe, commander of the Zimbabwe Defence Forces, announced on 10 January that the military would not accept a president who had 'not fought in the liberation struggle'. This was a coded reference to Morgan Tsvangirai and a clear warning that the army would overthrow him if he came to power. To consolidate the support of the security forces, in January 2001, Mugabe reportedly doubled their pay. Oil credits provided by Libyan President Muammar Gaddafi financed the raise. There were also indications that Mugabe bulked up security – hence the intimidation factor – for the March presidential elections by redeploying to Zimbabwe some of the 11,000 Zimbabwean troops deployed in the DROC in support of the Congolese government and to guard mining concessions extended to Mugabe by that government.

Although Tsvangirai probably would have won an untainted election, the environment of fear and intimidation meant that Tsvangirai had little chance of defeating Mugabe in the March 2002 election. Prompted by MDC voters' bravery against repression in the June 2000 parliamentary elections, increasing political violence has driven the MDC underground in large areas of Zimbabwe. The party's organisational base has been shattered and its supporters are increasingly fearful. Further, the package of repressive laws passed in January 2002 has made it practically impossible for the opposition to function.

Mugabe's re-election has created an unsustainable and deeply damaging situation in Zimbabwe, from which no escape route is apparent. Despite the open support of some African countries, Mugabe lacks international legitimacy. This means that Zimbabwe cannot hope for the resumption of aid from bilateral donors or international financial institutions. But in the absence of outside help, the country's disastrous economic decline, which is likely to see GDP slump by at least 12% in 2002, will continue unchecked. It will be difficult for the 78-year old Mugabe to serve out a six-year term over a devastated country. Unless he changes course, 2002 is likely to witness the ultimate collapse of Zimbabwe's economy and more food shortages, as well as Mugabe's total international isolation. Regional diplomacy – most importantly, on South Africa's part – has proven cosmetic, fleeting and impotent, and is likely to remain tame. The Bretton Woods institutions were shown to have little leverage over Mugabe, and have had no major programmes in Zimbabwe since 1999. The Commonwealth finally suspended Zimbabwe after the March election. The EU and the US imposed targeted sanctions. But Mugabe has shown no substantial sign of adopting moderation in the face of prior sanctions and is more likely to take the view that irregular sources of money and power – Libya's largesse, business interests in the DROC – can keep him in power.

Particularly in light of the diplomatic fecklessness of Zimbabwe's neighbours and the aggressive US stance against terrorism, it would appear that Washington could do more to thwart Mugabe than merely threaten to impose targeted sanctions and issue perfunctory official exhortations that Zimbabwean elections should be free and fair and that the government should respect the rule of law. His tactics border on state terrorism and imperil regional security, and the United States would be less inclined to accept this state of affairs in strategically vital areas like the Middle East. One feasible American option might be to establish firmer diplomatic contacts with the MDC and openly support the group. Another would be to rally regional diplomatic pressure more proactively. Both would raise the political risks of repression for Mugabe.

Yet Mugabe has made it abundantly clear that peaceful political change will not be permitted, and he would not easily buckle even under heavy American pressure. Economic implosion and wider international pressure could force Mugabe from office, à la Mobutu in 1997, and spur free and fair elections. A new regime would attract investment and aid as well as strong diplomatic support. Otherwise, Mugabe's political agenda leaves for Zimbabwe's opposition only the options of continued subjugation or disruptive change. In the wake of the tainted March 2002 presidential elections, the MDC is riper for precipitating such change than it was following the June 2000 parliamentary elections. Then MDC supporters at least apprehended the additional prospect of orderly reform by virtue of the 2002 presidential election. After the latter election, that prospect no longer existed, as Mugabe's term is for six years. Furthermore, by securing an apparently doctored videotape in which Tsvangirai purportedly contemplates 'eliminating' Mugabe, Mugabe has preserved a pretext for trying the opposition leader for treason, which carries the death penalty. If the MDC stages a revolt against Mugabe, he could attempt to use the army to suppress it. Political allegiances in the military, however, appear to be divided between Zanu-PF and the MDC, and there is no guarantee that the army would be willing to inflict massive civilian casualties. Either humanitarian disaster or a further deterioration in security could prompt aggressive outside diplomatic, economic or even military intervention. In any event, Mugabe's sustained excesses have made Zimbabwe's political and economic rehabilitation a long-term project.

The Horn: Old Wars, New Terrorism

The Horn of Africa remained afflicted by weak political structures, resource scarcities and violent conflict on several fronts in 2001. Unrest continued in Sudan and Somalia and, while a tenuous cease-fire held along the Ethiopia–Eritrea border, renewed potential for internal conflict rose within both countries. Further, internal struggles fed off interstate rivalries and conflict between states complicated domestic relations. The 11 September attacks further complicated the situation. Actors in the region manoeuvred to promote themselves as important allies in the global campaign against terrorism. Significant international attention focused on Somalia as a possible safe haven for terrorists and as a potential target for US military action following the war in Afghanistan. Ethiopia, and to a lesser extent Kenya, perceived opportunities to use counter-terrorism as a rationale for actions against domestic opponents. While the global counter-terrorism campaign threatened to escalate conflict in Somalia, the new focus may encourage moves toward peace in Sudan as leaders in Khartoum seek to undo their past associations with Osama bin Laden and al-Qaeda and with other terrorist organisations.

Somalia: factionalism and links to terrorism

In the collapsed state of Somalia, tentative movement towards greater order was countered by more enduring forces of disorder and violence. In Mogadishu, the Transitional National Government (TNG) – set up following the Arta peace conference in Djibouti in August 2000 – faced leadership struggles and could not construct a working administration, despite recognition by the United Nations. Ethiopia opposed the TNG and raised concerns about Islamic groups linked to the regime. In October 2001, the Transitional National Assembly passed a no-confidence vote and President Adbulkassim Salad Hassan named Hassan Abshir Farah the new prime minister. This would-be national government, however, failed to extend its authority outside of a portion of Mogadishu, Somalia's putative capital and largest city. The TNG could not open Mogadishu's airport or seaport, and scandals involving international aid and corruption weakened the regime's support. Hopes that the TNG could serve as the basis for a new national government faded by year's end without the emergence of a clear alternative.

The TNG was challenged on a number of fronts. Political order in Somalia had devolved to a series of regional administrations in the 1990s, and each of these resisted the TNG. In north-west Somalia, the self-proclaimed independent Republic of Somaliland continued to reject incorporation into a united state and remained relatively stable and well, if minimally, administered. President Mohamed Ibrahim Egal remained on good terms with bordering Ethiopia, sharing Addis Ababa's concerns about Islamic groups and the TNG. In the north-east, the self-proclaimed regional administration in Puntland also remained autonomous, although its relative stability came under threat in 2001, when Puntland leader Abdullahi Yusuf's authority faced a challenge from Jama Ali Jama and armed clashes ensued. Some in Puntland regard Abdullahi Yusuf as being imposed and supported by Ethiopia, with whom he shares concerns about Islamic groups. In the southwest, Hasan Mohamed Nur 'Shurgudud' controls Bay and Bakool through a separate administration.

In southern Somalia, the TNG is opposed by a loose alliance of convenience among a number of clan-based factional leaders – though not necessarily the clans themselves, either militarily or socially – who formed the Somali Reconciliation and Restoration Council (SRRC), based in the southern town of Baidoa, in March 2001. The SRRC includes factional leaders in Puntland and Bay and Bakool, as well as others who have maintained militias and shifting zones of control since the collapse of central authority in the early 1990s. Somaliland's leaders have not joined the SRRC. Talks between the TNG and the SSRC took place in Nakuru, Kenya, in December 2001. An agreement was announced, but the potential for broad and workable reconciliation was jeopardised by boycotts, competition for leadership among the factions and Ethiopia's opposition to any process that included the TNG. Violence and hostage-taking continued to plague Mogadishu and southern Somalia, and the leaders of armed factions persisted in their pursuit of the politics of armed coercion. Humanitarian assistance declined in 2001, while famine returned following poor rains.

Following the 11 September attacks on the United States, Washington turned its attention to possible links between al-Qaeda and Somalia. Washington placed al-Itihaad (the Islamic Union), an indigenous Somali Islamic movement, on its list of terrorist organisations, and in November closed the Somali bank and remittance firm al-Barakaat and seized its assets. The actions reflected growing US concern that Somalia was a potential host for bin Laden and other al-Qaeda members fleeing Afghanistan, and preceded American intelligence probes and preventive action in and around Somalia. The possibility that Somalia would become the next arena for Washington's global war on terrorism received heated media attention in late 2001, as the military phase of the struggle in Afghanistan wound down.

Accurately assessing the terrorist threat in Somalia, however, has been made difficult by propaganda wars among parties eager to use the campaign against terrorism to advance competing agendas. A number of Somali factions in the SRRC have cast the TNG as another Taliban-type government, and would like to be recognised as a force in the Northern Alliance mould that could take power with the assistance of the US military. Thus, several factional leaders have alleged that al-Qaeda members fleeing Afghanistan were entering Somalia, and that the TNG had links to al-Qaeda and al-Itihaad. The TNG insisted that there were no terrorists operating within Somalia. Abdullahi Yusuf Ahmed similarly accused Jama Ali Jama, his rival for leadership in Puntland, of being a fundamentalist with ties to international terrorists.

Ethiopia too regards the TNG as a haven for al-Itihaad and supports the SRRC. It has valid strategic reasons for fearing radical Islam in Somalia, as Ethiopia continues to be challenged by armed groups (such as the Oromo Liberation Front) seeking independence for the ethnic Somali-inhabited Ogaden region of the country, some of which have had tactical links to al-Itihaad. Al-Itihaad itself claimed credit for bomb attacks in Addis in 1996. Numerous reports in late 2001 indicated that Ethiopian forces were present in Puntland and elsewhere in southern Somalia, and Ethiopia made clear to Washington its willingness to intervene against Islamic organisations in Somalia. Kenya's key interest is to stem refugee traffic, contain radical Islam and, to a lesser degree, relax Western scrutiny of its own problematic political transition. Nairobi has offered the use of Kenyan territory as a possible staging point for counter-terrorist operations in Somalia.

In fact, al-Itihaad does not appear to pose an immediate transnational threat. Al-Itihaad had controlled some territory in southern Somalia, imposed

Islamic *sharia* courts that brought a degree of order, and operated some training camps for al-Qaeda in the early 1990s. But the group failed to consolidate power – largely because it attempted to work independently of dominant clan structures, and Ethiopian soldiers substantially destroyed the camps in the late 1990s. Thus, a campaign to bomb marginally functional or defunct terrorist camps in 2001–02 made little sense. Although there may be a few individuals in Somalia with links to al-Qaeda, prospects for a US-manned *Black Hawk Down*-style snatch operation to arrest such individuals are remote – due in significant part to the difficulty in obtaining reliable real-time intelligence and the associated risk. More aggressive military action, like aerial bombing, could induce any al-Qaeda members to disperse across Somalia's border and would engender anti-American resentment among Somalis.

Based on these considerations – and an exploratory 9 December visit by up to ten American civilians with faction leaders and possibly Ethiopian military officers in Somalia – by January 2002 it appeared that Washington had determined that the al-Qaeda presence in Somalia was negligible. The United States settled on a preventive posture of air surveillance (including the use of US Navy P-3 surveillance aircraft and *Predator* unmanned aerial vehicles over Somalia) and naval interdiction using dozens of US and other ships positioned in the Arabian Sea. As of late March 2002, a 160-strong German contingent and a 140-strong British unit, both based in Mombasa, Kenya, were assisting the US with air surveillance. Preserving the option of military intervention, the US also positioned three amphibious assault ships – each with a 1,200-strong Marine Expeditionary Unit – near the Somali coast and analysed the feasibility of deploying Central Intelligence Agency personnel and special forces. Nevertheless, were a meaningful al-Qaeda presence to emerge in Somalia, the United States would probably be more inclined to discreetly encourage Ethiopia or pro-American SRRC factions – perhaps with US operational support – to remove it than to take extensive military action itself. In roughly sequential order, then, US counter-terrorist options in Somalia include: freezing assets; surveillance and interdiction; support for indigenous groups or Ethiopian troops opposed to al-Qaeda and al-Ittihad; and, if there were reliable intelligence indicating a terrorist presence, limited and surgical direct military action. The US appears to have ruled out any major military engagement in Somalia.

Despite US restraint, there remains significant potential for terrorist activity in Somalia. Since its suppression by Ethiopia and hostile Somali factions in the late 1990s, al-Itihaad has sought to work within clan-based structures and institutions in Puntland and the TNG. Al-Itihaad members have positioned themselves in the courts and have established schools and health clinics as a way to influence Somali social and cultural development. Somalis may also be involved in funding al-Qaeda. Al-Barakaat was a critical part of the Somali money-transfer network based on the informal *hawala* system by which diaspora Somalis sent money to those in Somalia and vice-versa. Washington believes that the bank has been used to funnel money to al-Qaeda, though the bank's founder (based in Dubai, United Arab Emirates) has denied the charges. The flow of money into Somalia – which reportedly totalled up to $500 million a year – declined by 50% following the bank closure. Al-Itihaad and al-Qaeda may be relatively minor players in this complex mix, but Washington's interest in combating global terrorism is likely to keep its attention fixed on Somalia. Factions in the SRRC will probably keep trying to curry favour with the United States to re-start that flow and deliver other rewards for counter-terrorism cooperation. The regime in Somaliland and the fractured administration in Puntland are also seeking to assert and expand their influence, as is Ethiopia. Because the TNG appears more susceptible to radical Islam, however, its prospects for viability seem to have faded.

Sudan: old terrorist links, modest prospects for peace

Sudan saw yet another year of warfare in 2001. As the balance of power shifted to the north and as oil revenues provided new resources and Khartoum worked its way out of international isolation, a new peace initiative emerged. With a new US Special Envoy and a greater sense of urgency in Khartoum following 11 September, scenarios for peace received more serious attention and a window of opportunity may be slightly ajar. But in order for the new process to move forward, it will require substantial and coordinated international attention and resources, and it remains unclear that the major powers are willing to grant Sudan such priority. Furthermore, thorny questions relating to new institutions and revenue sharing suggest that any peace process will be long and difficult.

The Sudanese government remained divided. In late 1999, President Omar Bashir broke with Hassan al-Turabi – Sudan's religious leader and Bashir's long-time ally in the National Islamic Front (NIF) – and appeared to make significant attempts to normalise Sudan's relations with the West and cleanse its reputation as a leading state sponsor of terrorism. In the ensuing competition for a domestic power base, key NIF leader and vice-president Ali Taha sided with Bashir, thereby isolating Turabi. The government entered into talks with traditional political parties and Umma Party leader Sadiq al-Mahdi left the opposition National Democratic Alliance (NDA) and returned to Khartoum, although he refused to join the government. In an effort to remain a relevant political player, Turabi signed an agreement with the Sudan People's Liberation Army (SPLA) in February 2001 and subsequently was arrested and his supporters purged and harassed. In November 2001, Democratic Unionist Party leader Ahmed al-Mirghani returned to Sudan after 12 years of exile in Egypt, further dividing the opposition. Bashir was thus able to strengthen his control over the government in 2001.

Following the 11 September attacks, Washington re-focused on Khartoum's past close relationship with Osama bin Laden. Bin Laden was based in Sudan between 1991 and 1996, until he was expelled and moved to Afghanistan, and a number of leaders in Khartoum had deep connections with his network. In 1998, the US struck with cruise-missiles a Sudanese factory believed to produce chemical weapons. Anxious to avoid being branded a state supporter of terrorism as it had been in the past, Khartoum offered its support to Washington's anti-terrorist campaign. Sudan reportedly arrested a number of suspected terrorists, and 200–300 intelligence files were delivered to US State Department officials in November. Partially as a result, Washington abstained from a United Nations vote in late September 2001 removing sanctions that had been placed on Sudan in response to its involvement in the assassination attempt against Egyptian leader Hosni Mubarak in 1995.

While Khartoum made halting diplomatic progress both before and after 11 September, the Sudanese civil war that has raged since 1983 between the Islamic government and Christian-animist southerners of the SPLA seeking self-determination continued to devastate the southern part of the country. The conflict also affects the Nuba Mountains in the south-central region, where dissident Muslim rebels are represented by both the NDA and the SPLA. Oil production fundamentally changed the nature of the conflict in the late 1990s, with the government gleaning an estimated $500m in revenues in 2000. This allowed the regime to increase its defence expenditures by more than a third, from about $424m in 1999 to roughly $580m in 2000 and 2001. This infusion of new resources shifted the military advantage to the north. The peace process under the auspices of the Intergovernmental Authority on Development (IGAD, a regional organisation in the Horn of Africa) stalled in 2001, and was drained of momentum by an alternative Libyan–Egyptian Joint Initiative. The SPLA failed to sustain actions outside of its southern areas of control and did not seriously disrupt oil production. Rebel forces faced further difficulties as the supportive 'frontline states' of Ethiopia, Eritrea, and Uganda, all tired of the war and faced more urgent security problems at home, and as European and other countries pursued 'constructive engagement' with the regime.

Similarly, as US President Bill Clinton's efforts to isolate Sudan had shown few results, President George W. Bush appointed former Republican Senator John Danforth as his Special Envoy to Sudan in September 2001, suggesting both that the administration was looking to start a new policy in Sudan and that domestic groups within the United States (mobilised around issues of religious persecution of Christians and slavery) would continue to press for engagement. Danforth travelled to the region in November 2001 and urged a four-point confidence-building agenda to improve conditions for negotiation. The four points – humanitarian access to the Nuba Mountains, a ceasefire to allow aid to other 'zones of tranquillity' in the country, an end to the aerial bombardment of civilians and an end to kidnappings and slavery – were a reasonable starting point, but carried the risk that unfulfilled expectations of quick change after 18 years of war might dash hopes further. The United Kingdom and Norway supported the initiative with shuttle diplomacy between leaders in both the north and south.

In January 2002, Sudanese opposition and government leaders met in Burgenstock, Switzerland, and agreed to a six-month cease-fire in the Nuba Mountains – the longest ever agreed by the government. The cessation is being internationally monitored (albeit not by those from 'unfriendly' countries, and subject to delays and suspensions) and backed by deliveries of humanitarian assistance and development aid. Within days, however, numerous, largely government violations had occurred. The SPLA did not agree to a cease-fire in the south. The government offered a one-month cessation on all anti-rebel aerial bombardment, with an exemption for 'self-defence', but the United States rejected it as inadequate. Given that the government appeared intent on using air attacks to displace civilians from oil-producing areas, any durable government commitment of restraint was unlikely in any event. In February 2002, in response to SPLA harassment of oil-drilling activities, the Sudanese government conducted at least three bombing and strafing operations, including a major attack on Bieh, site of a World Food Programme relief drop, on 20 February. This incident, in which at least 24 were killed, seriously aggravated Sudanese relations with both the US and European countries, prompting American hard-liners to push for a tough response (such as providing surface-to-air missiles to the SPLA). Washington suspended its mediation of peace talks, which placed the Nuba Mountains cease-fire at risk. In early March, however, direct US pressure on Khartoum produced a pledge to investigate the bombing and institute flight-control safeguards. In mid-March, the government and the rebels agreed in principle to monthly breaks in fighting during which humanitarian aid could be delivered. The reality appears to be that both Khartoum and the SPLA regard a comprehensive cease-fire as the outcome, rather than a precondition, of the peace process. Thus, despite frustration on that score, there remains some room for negotiation.

One much-discussed framework for peace, supported by Danforth, would be a loose confederal structure with two separate constitutions. A secular constitution would protect the rights of Sudanese in the southern part of the country, where Muslims are a minority, while the system of Islamic *sharia* law, which the government has attempted to impose throughout Sudan since 1989, would apply in the mainly Muslim north. The SPLA would be reconstituted into 'national formations and local defence forces'. The group also, however, contemplates a right of self-determination for southern Sudanese and those living in the Abyey and the Nuba Mountains areas after an interim transitional period under the confederal system. This holds out the possibility of secession. Khartoum would not accept such a result. Washington would also resist it, as Egypt, an important ally, is opposed to multiple states controlling the Nile. Other issues, most notably ownership and revenue sharing from oil production, would need to be resolved as well.

Danforth is likely to step down as Special Envoy in April 2002, but he may have made a lasting impression on the peace process. In particular, he has indicated that he favours a unified Sudan and does not consider separation a realistic option for the south. He has also suggested a softer US position on religion–state separation, stating that Muslims are entitled to a national government that reflects their faith. These effective concessions to the Sudanese government may reflect wider US strategic priorities (such as catering to Egypt's sensibilities), and an inclination to reinforce Bashir's normalising impulses (in particular, post-11 September intelligence sharing and law-enforcement cooperation). US Undersecretary of State John R. Bolton noted on 19 November that Sudan had shown 'growing interest' in acquiring biological weapons, indicating that a backslide to terrorism by Khartoum remains an active US worry. But the concessions have displeased the southern rebels, and appear to have produced greater solidarity among them. In January 2002, SPLA leader John Garang signed a reconciliation agreement in Nairobi with Riek Machar, the leader of a faction that broke from the SPLA in 1991. If Danforth's initiative fails, Sudan could return to heavy fighting and American Christian-right backers of the SPLA may renew efforts to increase support the rebel group. The US government probably would not respond favourably for fear of inducing Khartoum to discontinue counter-terrorism cooperation or, worse, to tilt again towards bin Laden and al-Qaeda. Although the United States might not resume proactive mediation efforts in the short term, it would support a continuation of the process by the UK or Norway.

Ethiopia–Eritrea: shaky peace, domestic challenges

The December 2000 cease-fire in the brutal border war between Ethiopia and Eritrea has held, although underlying grievances kept the two countries polarised and deeply suspicious of each other. While the 4,200-member United Nations Mission in Ethiopia and Eritrea (UNMEE) force operated in the 25-kilometre wide Temporary Security Zone along the disputed border and de-mining operations began, Eritrea refused to sign a status-of-forces agreement or to recognise the southern boundary of the zone and restricted UN movements in adjacent areas. In September 2001, the United Nations extended UNMEE's mandate for another six months, until 15 March 2002, and in March 2002, still another six months to 15 September 2002. That mandate, under UN Security Council Resolution 1320, issued 15 September 2000, calls for both countries 'to fulfil all their obligations under international law, including the agreement on cessation of hostilities'; empowers UNMEE to chair a military coordination committee to facilitate that objective; authorises the deployment of up to 4,200 troops, including 220 military observers; and urges that de-mining proceed.

In early 2002, the UN planned to send a high-level delegation to manage tensions anticipated from the border delimitation decision. Questions relating to repatriation of prisoners of war and the larger issue of compensation remained contentious. Despite UN efforts, confidence-building measures such as the resumption of direct flights between Asmara and Addis Ababa were not implemented. The UN-facilitated Military Coordination Commission met regularly and served as the only mechanism for direct contact between Ethiopia and Eritrea. In mid-November 2001, Ethiopian President Meles Zenawi alleged that Eritrea was building up its troops along the border and that Ethiopia was prepared to meet the growing threat. UNMEE observers refuted the charges and both sides accused UNMEE of 'appeasement'. Armed conflict, however, was avoided.

The Boundary Commission established to demarcate the border held meetings in December 2001 in The Hague and received testimony from both parties. The commission, composed of two members nominated by each side and one neutral member, planned to announce a decision on 13 April 2002. Rising tensions in late 2001 may become more heated when the commission makes its border announcement, whereupon opposition groups will be likely to exploit the decision to challenge the incumbent regimes. In February 2002, a spokesman from the Tigray People's Liberation Front (TPLF) – the central party in Ethiopia's ruling coalition – stated that Ethiopia would not be bound by an unjust border decision. Under the Algiers peace agreement signed in December 2000, the decision is supposed to be binding. Subsequent demarcation on the ground will, in any case, be a protracted process requiring extensive de-mining. The UN does not contemplate withdrawing UNMEE until the Boundary Commission's work is done.

In the aftermath of the war, significant domestic challenges occurred in both regimes. The Ethiopian regime, while reasonably secure, is still seeking to construct a viable coalition that is sufficiently inclusive to maintain stability and foster democratic consolidation. The Ethiopian People's Revolutionary Democratic Front (EPRDF) government faced its most substantial test since it took power in 1991. Violent student demonstrations and a police crackdown early in 2001 were reminiscent of the campus activism that preceded the overthrow of Emperor Haile Selassie in 1974. More substantively, the TPLF, the core of the multi-ethnic EPRDF coalition, erupted into two rival factions in March 2001. The schism was severe, splitting the TPLF Central Committee down the middle, with high-level, veteran leaders on both sides. The core differences related to Ethiopia's policy toward Eritrea, as the opposition faction accused Meles of failing to capitalise on Ethiopia's military advantage to punish Eritrea. Other contentious issues included economic policy, corruption and party procedures.

Meles weathered the storm, at least in the short term, although the question of the regime's support base remained open to question. With his base in the Tigray heartland in jeopardy, Meles took advantage of his strong position within the security forces and support within the broader EPRDF coalition to successfully outmanoeuvre his rivals within the TPLF, who restricted their focus to their colleagues within the party. He restructured his cabinet and charged a number of former TPLF loyalists and supporters with corruption. Twelve senior central committee members and their supporters were purged, including former defence minister Siye Abraha, the party's number two official Tewolde Wolde Mariam, and the president of the regional state of Tigray, Gebru Asrat.

The battles within the TPLF had ripple effects throughout the EPRDF, however, and the Oromo People's Democratic Organization (part of the EPRDF coalition) also saw purges and recriminations that raised questions about the inclusion of the largest single ethnic group within the ruling regime. Several prominent Oromos, including President Negaso Gidada, resigned their positions and other leaders were expelled from the party and charged with corruption. The Oromo Liberation Front, the Ogaden National Liberation Front and the Sidama Liberation Front claim to be engaged in an armed struggle against the EPRDF regime, but nearly all of the country remains firmly within government control. Repression of opposition groups, particularly in southern Ethiopia, escalated, but Meles ended the year by consolidating his regime while the opposition remained fractured and ineffective. Steady economic growth at about 7% forecast for 2002–03, positive marks from the International Monetary Fund on poverty-reduction and IMF-approved debt relief may ease Meles' political burden. A shared interest with the United States in suppressing militant Islamic networks – sharpened since 11 September by US concern with Somalia's Islamic elements – could also redound to Ethiopia's benefit.

Domestic strain in Eritrea is the most serious since before its independence from Ethiopia in 1994, as the ruling movement is beset by increased demands for economic reform and a more open political system. Prompted by President Isaias Afewerki and his People's Front for Democracy and Justice (PFDJ)'s continued delays in effectuating a democratic transition, in March 2001, a group of 15 senior officials in the party and government signed an open letter that criticised Isaias – accusing him of 'conducting himself in an illegal and unconstitutional manner' – and calling for greater democracy and a meeting of the National Assembly. The letter was leaked, and eleven of those who signed were arrested on 18 September 2001. Three other signatories, including Defence Minister Mesfin Hagos, remained overseas to avoid arrest. The official media referred to the dissidents as traitors who had 'committed crimes against the sovereignty, security, and peace of the nation', a capital offence under Eritrean law.

Subsequent repression of dissent included the closure of all privately owned media, the sacking of the chief justice in August after he complained about executive interference in the judiciary, and a clampdown on students at the University of Asmara after they criticised conditions in the camps that housed students participating in the government's mandatory summer work programme. In August 2001, the university student council president was arrested and 2,700 student protesters rounded up to be sent to a desert camp near Massawa, where two died of heatstroke. Elections scheduled for December 2001 were postponed until mid-2002. In the aftermath of this wave of unrest, donor criticism grew, leading to the expulsion of the Italian ambassador in October and the temporary withdrawal of other EU diplomats. Italy, the former colonial power, was Eritrea's biggest donor. The United States joined the European Union in criticising the government and two Eritreans working for the US embassy were arrested the next day. In January 2002, Denmark announced it intended to end its aid to Eritrea, citing human-rights concerns, while in February, the European Parliament blasted the 'authoritarian' trend in Asmara. If donors continue to freeze assistance, and Eritrean diaspora hold back remittances in protest, economic growth could drop from a projected 7–8% to 3–5% in 2002–03, offsetting the 'peace dividend' resulting from a drop in defence expenditure from 38% of GDP during the war to 9% in 2002–03. Such poor economic performance, against more optimistic predictions, is likely to fuel further political dissent.

Eritrean dissidents, led by the popular former Defence Minister Mesfin Hagos, launched an opposition party from exile known as the Eritrean People's Liberation Front Democratic Party (EPLFDP) in January 2002. The EPLFDP claimed to be the legitimate inheritor of the legacy of the liberation struggle, but its presence within Eritrea and its ability to operate under current political circumstances were difficult to determine. The contest for control of Eritrea will continue in 2002. It is not likely to proceed smoothly. Issues of long-postponed political reform and the outcome of the border demarcation process may provide grievances that opposition elements can seize upon to undermine Afewerki's regime, but he is likely to resist them with determination. On 1 February 2002, the National Assembly met for the first time since September 2000 and adopted a resolution outlawing political parties. As of March 2002, elections had not been scheduled, and no electoral law had been enacted.

Looking ahead

The Horn of Africa will continue to face challenges to stability and political development over the coming year. Although increased instability with potential spillover effects in Ethiopia and Kenya could result if Somalia became the target of major US-led international action against terrorism,

Washington appears to have concluded that no such action would be justified. In any event, none of the principal actors within Somalia have demonstrated the ability to forge political authority sufficient to overcome the deeply rooted divisions within the state. In Sudan, though a new peace process offers some hope of ending the war, issues relating to new governmental structures, power and revenue sharing, the democratisation of all parties, and the institutionalisation of the rule of law remain daunting. While a return to large-scale war between Ethiopia and Eritrea is not likely, ongoing tensions and unresolved underlying issues are likely to require the continued presence of UN peacekeepers. The announcement of the border decision may spark internal political opposition in both states, as opposition groups air grievances relating to the cost of the war in relation to the scant benefits of the outcome.

On balance, the global counter-terrorism campaign may have brightened prospects for the Horn. Heightened post-11 September concern in Washington about the Horn's susceptibility to militant Islam is likely to produce more sustained US engagement in the region. That engagement will probably have a diplomatic, intelligence and law-enforcement focus in the short term – keying on Somalia and Sudan, and enlisting Ethiopian assistance – but may acquire a broader and more substantial economic dimension over time in the interest of forging political stability.

West Africa: Mixed News

After a decade of some of the most savage warfare on the African continent, peace has finally been attained in Sierra Leone. Despite this welcome development and the continued presence of the world's largest United Nations peacekeeping mission, the UN Mission in Sierra Leone (UNAMSIL), serious questions abound about the durability of peace in Sierra Leone and elsewhere in the war-torn Mano River Union. Although Charles Taylor remains the principal 'spoiler' in West Africa, Liberia's warlord-president has not had a good year. Bitter regional enemies, hostile UN commissions and a plethora of negative press reports have fuelled attacks against him on both the military and the diplomatic front. Taylor is losing on both. Moreover, cowed by the scorn heaped on the Liberian government in 2001 for stoking regional war through its backing of the Revolutionary United Front (RUF), and by the emerging links between the West Africa conflict-diamond trade and transnational terrorist organisations, Taylor's two key allies, Burkina Faso and Libya, have reduced their support. Likewise, increased scrutiny post-11 September has turned up the heat on Taylor's criminal non-state partners who are at the heart of the guns-for-conflict-diamonds enterprise. Weakened but not defeated, Taylor limps on, fighting a domestic uprising in the north of Liberia and threatening to disrupt both the crucial May 2002 elections in Sierra Leone and peace in Guinea. While few doubt Taylor's will and ability to survive, his capacity to destabilise and spread warfare in West Africa has finally been compromised.

Better prospects in Sierra Leone

The key factor in subduing Taylor is the demise of the RUF, the Sierra Leonean rebel force that, along with Sierra Leonean rebel leader Foday Sankoh in 1991, Taylor helped to father. This ragtag rebel group became Taylor's conduit for criminal activity and his most effective tool, mining conflict diamonds in eastern Sierra Leone and funnelling them into Taylor's export pipeline in exchange for money and weapons transited through Monrovia. The RUF's fall can be tied to several developments, but most notably to the vigorous intervention of the British, who first entered the fray during the summer of 2000 to buttress a wobbly UNAMSIL that had found itself at the mercy of the rebels. Following the rescue of UNAMSIL personnel from RUF captors, the British systematically stepped up military and diplomatic pressure on the rebels, training and equipping a reconfigured Sierra Leone Army (SLA) while pressuring the UN to deploy a more robust international force.

Thus, by early 2001, the RUF faced mounting pressure from a fortified, British-backed UNAMSIL. In response, they focused on establishing the border region of Guinea as a redoubt, striking out at refugees, civilians and the Guinean military with the aim of destabilising their adversary in Conakry, President Lansana Conté, and taking control of some of Guinea's diamond fields. But the RUF's move against Guinea produced a vicious riposte from Conté, who unleashed the full might of the Guinean military in ground assaults using French- and American-supplied hardware and supported by warplanes and helicopter gunships. The Guinean armed forces drove the RUF into Sierra Leone. Meanwhile, in Liberia, pressure mounted on Charles Taylor with the imposition of UN Security Council Resolution 1343, passed on 7 May 2001, calling for the immediate cessation of support to the RUF and other armed groups in the region, imposing an arms embargo on the Liberian government and prohibiting the international sale of diamonds and travel by senior Liberian leaders and their spouses. These penalties strengthened the UN arms embargo imposed on Liberia in November 1992 and bilateral US economic sanctions on arms and travel. At the same time, a flood of damning reports emerged, linking Taylor to the RUF, gross human-rights abuses and various criminal enterprises.

Guinea's military resistance and Taylor's debility left the RUF with few tactical options. At the same time, Taylor was feeling the heat of the international community in Monrovia. With the noose tightening on the RUF, thousands of fighters streamed into UN demobilisation centres to surrender their weapons and foreswear future violent conflict, each receiving $152 and various services in exchange. Throughout this period, peaceful Sierra Leoneans and the international community held their collective breath. UN administrative setbacks and various instances of RUF backsliding suggested the rebels could return to the bush and resume their 10-year campaign of killing and terrorising civilians. During the second half of 2001, however, the demobilisation effort gained momentum. By January 2002, all the major concentrations of fighters in Sierra Leone had surrendered and disarmed. So when Sierra Leonean President Tejan Kabbah declared the war over in January 2002, more than 45,844 ex-combatants – 27,490 from the pro-government Civil Defence Forces and 18,354 from the RUF – had handed in 15,000 weapons and 1.3 million rounds of ammunition. In a decade of civil war, some 43,000 had been killed and hundreds of thousands had been displaced, raped or mutilated.

Taylor's terrorist ties

Taylor's links to Foday Sankoh and the RUF have been known since the inception of the rebel movement in 1991. But the depth of the association and its foundation on the diamond smuggling network did not become clear until the late 1990s, when press reports emerged connecting Taylor to illicit diamond sales from Sierra Leone for weapons transited through Burkina Faso and Libya. By the summer of 2000, the 'conflict diamond' phenomenon – heavily publicised in 1998 by Global Witness, a small group of British environmentalists and human-rights activists that in 1998 made the connection between illicit diamond sales, warlord Jonas Savimbi and the brutal Angolan civil war – was recognised as applying to the war in Sierra Leone. The bulk of diamonds exported from Liberia originated in Sierra Leone. These revelations, along with images of Sierra Leoneans with severed arms and legs, garnered international attention. In June 2000, the UN passed a resolution demanding that all states move to prohibit the direct or indirect import of rough diamonds from Sierra Leone, and requiring the government of Sierra Leone to implement a certificate-of-origin system for diamond exports. Moral pressure from the UN the Group of 8 (G-8) industrial nations, efforts on the part of diamond merchants (led by De Beers, the world's largest producer and seller) and certification schemes appeared to depress the price of conflict diamonds. But the certification controls could be circumvented, and the trade remained lucrative. Liberia continued selling conflict diamonds. The penalties imposed on Liberia by the UN in early May 2001 and a ban on imports of rough diamonds from Liberia imposed by the US on 23 May 2001 appeared to have a more pronounced effect on Liberia's participation in the conflict-diamonds trade.

The 11 September attacks have broadened and intensified government and media interest in the other possible connections between transnational criminal and terrorist activity. In November 2001, the *Washington Post* ran an exposé alleging that over the previous three years, Osama bin Laden's al-Qaeda terrorist network had made millions on the sale of Sierra Leonean gems. The article outlined al-Qaeda's *modus operandi*, whereby its operatives would buy diamonds from rebels and sell them in Europe for huge profits. The *Post* report has been substantially corroborated in subsequent investigations of Taylor's sanction-busting activities and by high-ranking sources in the American intelligence community. Beginning in July 2001, al-Qaeda diamond buyers began converting their funds into diamonds, a move investigators have suggested is a strong indication that al-Qaeda sought to protect its assets in anticipation of actions by financial authorities to monetary holdings following the 11 September attacks. Reports suggest that the terrorist network may have amassed millions, perhaps ten of millions, of dollars through sales and money-laundering schemes using conflict gems.

The RUF's principal diamond dealer, General Ibrahim Bah, acted as the point of contact with both al-Qaeda and Hizbullah, the Lebanon-based Shi'ite Muslim armed group backed by Iran and Syria that seeks to establish an Islamic state in Lebanon and continues to confront Israel. The Gambian-born Bah was trained in Libya and fought with the Casamance separatist movement in Senegal in the 1970s. He also spent several years in the early 1980s fighting alongside anti-Soviet forces in Afghanistan. Based in Ouagadougou, Burkina Faso, Bah's strongest ties are said to lie with Hizbullah, which has a longer history than al-Qaeda of dealing in West Africa. There are an estimated 120,000 Lebanese living in a number of West African states; most are involved in import–export businesses. Hizbullah is active in all these countries in seeking contributions for its cause among the Lebanese populations. While only a small part of the community is sympathetic to that cause, others support it to keep the network off their backs.

The RUF's connections with al-Qaeda are believed to have solidified in 1998 when Bah arranged for Abdullah Ahmed Abdullah, a top bin Laden adviser, to visit Monrovia. During this visit, Abdullah and Bah were reportedly flown in a Liberian government helicopter to the border with Sierra Leone, where they met with a senior RUF commander and close Taylor associate, Sam 'Mosquito' Bockarie, to discuss buying diamonds on a regular basis. Bah arranged subsequent meetings between Bockarie and Ahmed Khalfan Ghailani and Fazul Abdullah Mohammed, al-Qaeda operatives who initiated the diamonds-for-cash transactions. According to the US Federal Bureau of Investigation, Ghailani is linked to the 1998 bombing of the US embassy in Tanzania and Fazul is head of al-Qaeda's

Kenyan cell. Bah later rented a dwelling in Monrovia to function as a safe house for buyers who, with the complicity of senior Liberian security officials, purchased millions of dollars worth of gems.

The revelations about al-Qaeda and Hizbullah links to the conflict diamond trade in Sierra Leone and Liberia attracted the keen interest of Western officials trying to determine the level of Taylor's non-compliance with UN sanctions as well as those trying to unravel the sources of al-Qaeda revenue. The articulation of an al-Qaeda–RUF nexus thus gave further credence to a hard-hitting UN Panel of Experts' Report on Liberia, published on 26 October 2001. The exhaustively researched report revealed that despite UN sanctions, the Taylor regime had continued to receive weapons imports and had not expelled RUF figures, and that senior officials in the government were violating the UN travel ban. The report also detailed how weapons had been shipped illegally to Liberia from Kyrgyzstan, Moldova, Slovakia and Ukraine with the use of false end-user certificates, most of which cited Guinea as the destination for the arms.

One of the chief international actors behind Liberia's weapons-for-diamonds transactions is Victor Bout, a former Soviet military officer who heads one of the largest weapon-trafficking networks in the world. Based in the United Arab Emirates, Bout's operations rely on a fleet of about 60 aircraft and some 300 pilots. They are used to ferry arms and major weapons systems – mostly bought in the former Soviet bloc, especially in Bulgaria and Romania – around the world, often to countries under arms embargoes. In two instances during July and August 2000, cited by UN investigators monitoring the UN embargoes, Bout's company flew four shipments into Liberia, delivering two combat-capable helicopters, surface-to-air missiles, armed vehicles, machine guns and almost a million rounds of ammunition. Payments were believed to have been made in diamonds from Sierra Leone. The November 2001 *Washington Post* article squares with a matrix of reports connecting al-Qaeda to diamonds purchased in the Democratic Republic of Congo (DRC), tanzanite from Tanzania, gold transited through Dubai and other commodities that the terror group has used to raise money and hide assets.

West Africa's regional war and 11 September

The campaign against terrorism and the emerging links between the RUF, Liberia and terror networks has had an important impact on Liberia's ability to conduct business as usual. To begin with, these connections have heightened the scrutiny exercised by the UN, the US and the rest of the international community on Taylor's regime. Further, as evidence has mounted of Taylor's disregard for sanctions and his dealings with Bout, al-Qaeda and Hizbullah, it has become more and more difficult for his putative abettors to associate with the Liberian president. Two have publicly distanced themselves from him. In December 2001, Burkina Faso President Blaise Campaoré entertained exiled Liberian opposition leaders Ellen Johnson-Sirleaf and Amos Sawyer for three days in Ouagadougou, expressing support for their opposition to Taylor. Similarly, Libyan President Muammar Gaddafi has diplomatically eschewed Liberia and has even presented himself as America's friend, condemning the 11 September attacks as 'horrifying' and reportedly sharing intelligence on al-Qaeda with Washington. The degree to which these gestures were intended merely to garner friendly publicity, however, is uncertain.

With his back against the wall, Taylor ostensibly remains eager to curry favour with the United States. In the wake of the 11 September attacks he wasted no time in condemning al-Qaeda and holding a memorial service for the lost Americans. He even went as far as to instructing his security forces to arrest vendors of bin Laden portraits in Monrovia and to offer the services of his so-called élite Anti-Terrorist Unit for service in Afghanistan. The rhetoric and posturing of the three main sponsors of the West African regional war – Campaoré, Gaddafi and Taylor – should not obfuscate the fact that this troika remains most concerned about the threat posed by UNAMSIL to the RUF's control of the rich diamond fields of eastern Sierra Leone.

Taylor's new domestic distraction

Despite the fragile peace in Sierra Leone, the warfare that has savaged the Manu River Union (MRU) – which includes Liberia, Guinea and Sierra Leone – for more than a decade has again exhibited a 'balloon effect': when effective pressure has tamed insecurity in one zone, new insecurity has popped up in another area. This occurred most recently with the expansion of fighting in northern Liberia and the growth of a little-known rebel faction, Liberians United for Reconciliation and Democracy (LURD). By early 2002, LURD had advanced their insurrection from their stronghold in Lofa country to strike at government posts in Tubmanberg and Klay Junction, just 50 kilometres north of Monrovia. In response, Taylor declared a state of emergency on 8 February. By late March 2002, fighting had reportedly spread to the diamond-mining towns of Gbaama and Camp Smith, about 85km from the capital, and to an area near Liberia's northern border with Guinea.

The intensification of LURD attacks in northern Liberia has had a major destabilising effect on the region. The renewed bloodshed produced more than 60,000 refugees and internally displaced persons from Lofa County and threatened to throw the country into all-out civil war. Over 10,000 refugees have fled to the Ivory Coast, while thousands more have crossed the borders into Guinea and Sierra Leone. Taylor has accused Guinean President Lansana Conté of supporting LURD, and many analysts have concluded that this assessment is correct. Nevertheless, the group's provenance, composition and base of financial support have been difficult to discern. Two things, however, are clear: the chaos and hardship that has devastated the region continues, and Charles Taylor remains at its centre.

Since 1989, when Taylor led a small, irregular group of Libyan-trained opponents to the regime of then President Samuel Doe into Liberia, he has repeatedly and consistently sewn the seeds of violent conflict in the MRU region. Even today, numerous foreign officials and analysts have speculated that Taylor could be behind the LURD – sponsoring the shady rebel group's activities in order to win sympathy from the international community, get out from under UN sanctions and secure a pretext for ignoring calls for democratic reforms prior to the scheduled 2003 presidential elections. Taylor is not above employing such a strategem. But the fighting in northern Liberia –mostly centred in Lofa country – appears to be a led by genuinely dissatisfied Liberians, supported by Conakry and a growing number of Sierra Leonean recruits mostly from anti-RUF militias. Thus, it is more likely that Taylor's meddling and repressive policies at home and in the other MRU states over more than a decade have simply come back to haunt him. LURD appears to be gaining strength and increasing pressure on the Taylor regime. While nowhere close to being an organised and effective fighting force, the rebels have local support in Lofa County as well as the backing of Guinea. Moreover, the Armed Forces of Liberia have put up a weak response to the incursion, often fighting internally and robbing Liberian civilians in zones of conflict. At the same time, Charles Taylor is unlikely to slither out of Monrovia without a fight. Indeed, he is recognised for his prowess as a bush fighter and has said he will burn Monrovia before leaving it. For its part, LURD has pledged to expel Taylor from the country. Either scenario bodes badly for Liberians, as does the continued presence of the kleptocratic Taylor regime.

Elsewhere in the region

Throughout West Africa, security remains a serious preoccupation: in southern Senegal, the rebel movement in the Casamance persists; in Guinea-Bissau, peace has remained elusive since the bloody insurrection in 1999; in Guinea, an illegitimate and corrupt political regime continues to frustrate and repress its citizenry and Africa's largest cohort of refugees (nearly 500,000) remains a potential source of instability; and in Nigeria, the Obasanjo government is struggling to control growing sectarian violence and spreading lawlessness as it tries to prepare the nation for another round of elections in early 2003.

Perhaps one point of light in an otherwise troubled coastal region is the Coté d'Ivoire, which appears to be developing a more stable political landscape. Once a peaceful oasis of relative economic prosperity in the region, the country appears to have weathered the political storm that gathered in the two-year period following the nation's first coup in December 1999. Hundreds died in street violence, and a dangerous religious schism formed between Muslim southerners and Christian northerners, crippling an already weakened economy. But tensions in Coté d'Ivoire receded at the end of 2001, largely because of the National Reconciliation Forum that dominated political discourse during the last three months of the year. This conference was followed by a consultation in early 2002 between the nation's four main political leaders: Henri Konan Bédié, the former president; Laurent Gbagbo, the current president; Alassane Ouattara, a former prime minister and the leading opposition candidate; and General Robert Gueï, the coup leader. Together these politicians appeared to be smoothing out tribal conflict stemming from Ouattara's exclusion as a candidate in 2000 presidential and parliamentary elections on the grounds that he is not of Ivorian descent.

The importance of outside actors

The events of 11 September and revelations about the nexus between the illicit diamond trade and transnational terrorism are likely to mean a sustained level of international law-enforcement and intelligence activity in the region. Such a posture may reinforce Campaoré and Gaddafi's recent disinclination to help Taylor, and enhance the effect of UN sanctions on the conflict diamond trade through asset freezes and other counter-terrorism measures. International pressure on Taylor, combined with the aggressive UNAMSIL demobilisation plan, has also helped make the 'rebel option' a less desirable career choice for young men in Sierra Leone.

West African stability, however, still pivots on the broader MRU situation. Optimism has followed the demobilisation of the RUF in the latter part of 2001 and early 2002, but it could quickly dissipate. Major questions persist about the reliability of the newly constituted SLA. Observers point to the fact that these forces have been under the tutelage of British army trainers for too short a time and have too chequered a past to be deemed truly professional. Furthermore, the emergence of LURD tends to confirm what both Kabbah and Conté have suggested: lasting stability in the MRU will be difficult to attain unless it is approached as a regional problem rather than on a nation-by-nation basis. Thus, additional regional and international diplomatic attention to Liberia's burgeoning internal difficulties may be required to consolidate the gains from the Sierra Leonean peace process.

In this connection, it is salutary that regional actors have stepped in and made considerable peace-making efforts. Throughout the 1990s, Nigeria repeatedly intervened under the auspices of the Economic Community of West African States (ECOWAS) Monitoring Group (ECOMOG) to try to stop fighting in both Liberia and Sierra Leone. Nigeria suffered significant casualties in these efforts and clearly demonstrated its willingness to assume the burden and responsibilities required of the ranking regional power. Its capacities are likely to be strengthened by virtue of the American military training operation completed last year called *Operation Focus Relief* (OFR). The roots of OFR lay in the immediate aftermath of the detention by the RUF of some 500 UNAMSIL troops in Sierra Leone in May 2000. In response to the perceived ineptitude of the UN forces, the US committed $90m to train and arm seven battalions from ECOWAS member states who would then serve in the UNAMSIL mission. Five battalions were composed of Nigerians, and one each was drawn from Ghana and Senegal. Beyond the OFR, in 2001 the US supported the UNAMSIL mission with nearly $190m, which constituted a significant portion of UNAMSIL's humanitarian aid budget. As noted, the peacekeeping mission in Sierra Leone has also benefited critically from the operational and training support of the United Kingdom.

The involvement of al-Qaeda in West Africa illustrates the threat posed to international security by corrupt, weak or collapsed states such as Sierra Leone, Liberia and the DRC, which have proven to be ideal growth media for organised crime networks and terrorist groups and for their cross-fertilisation. If anything, the theoretical interest of outside actors in stabilising West Africa and rendering it less vulnerable to exploitation by transnational criminals and terrorists increased with 11 September and reports of al-Qaeda's involvement in the region. Yet the press of counter-terrorist and other strategic business elsewhere may produce waning involvement in the short term. With residual military counter-terrorist commitments in Afghanistan and the prospect of major military action in Iraq, the US is less engaged than ever in developing-world peacekeeping. As of April 2002, British forces had been drawn down to 300–400 from a high of 1,000 early in 2001. The UN was jarred by allegations in early 2002 that UNAMSIL workers demanded sex from teenage girls in exchange for food. The mission increased its military personnel from 13,000 in October 2001 to 17,000 by March 2002, but UNAMSIL is the UN's largest and, at $600m per year, most costly operation. Although on 28 March 2002, the UN Security Council extended UNAMSIL's mission another six months to 30 September, pressures may mount on the UN to diminish the size of the mission by the end of 2002.

British suggestions that private military companies might fill peacekeeping voids, based on a February 2002 Foreign and Commonwealth Office 'Green Paper' commissioned by the House of Commons, have drawn reactions ranging from scepticism to outrage. Meanwhile, the wild card in Sierra Leonean peace process continues to be the RUF, which says it will participate in the May 2002 elections. Whether or not the group will accept political defeat is an open and therefore troubling question for the entire region. In April 2002, Nigeria had over 3,300 troops deployed in Sierra Leone, while seven other African nations had deployed a total of about 4,500 soldiers. Maintaining stability in West Africa may depend on the willingness of regional powers – in particular, Nigeria – to maintain or increase their commitment to peacekeeping efforts, and continued training and equipping efforts from major military powers such as the US and the UK.

Prospectives

Long before 11 September, the Bush administration had manifested its distaste for peace operations and nation-building. During the presidential election campaign, in a 22 October 2000 interview with the *New York Times*, future National Security Advisor Condoleezza Rice commented that 'we don't need to have the 82nd Airborne [Division] escorting kids to kindergarten'. Elements of the 82nd were then deployed in Bosnia-Herzegovina. Yet the debate over the allocation of military responsibility between the US and Europe in Bosnia did not reach a decisive point. As of March 2002, 6,500 US troops remained deployed in Bosnia and engaged in peacekeeping. Washington would not completely foreclose the possibility of supporting peace operations for fear of encouraging the European Union (EU) to form a duplicative, rather than complementary, rapid-reaction force. European capitals, for their part, could not renounce NATO in favour of the EU force for an array of political reasons, and because of the vast military capability gap between them and the US. The events of 11 September complicated the debate. By politely declining NATO's offer of joint self-defence on its behalf under Article 5, the US entrenched its preference for 'coalitions of the willing' rather than formal military alliances. The war in Afghanistan was conducted from the headquarters of US Central Command in Tampa, Florida, without significant command input from any ally save perhaps for the United Kingdom.

The main effort proceeded swiftly and with very few US casualties. By March 2002, soldiers from the 101st Airborne Division were in Afghanistan. Despite the pleas of Hamid Karzai's transitional government for more peacekeepers to maintain security around Kabul, the 101st – along with Special Forces and elements of the 10th Mountain Division – was tasked only to conduct combat operations against holdout members of al-Qaeda and the Taliban. Although there were over 5,000 US ground troops and another 60,000 American personnel for support in the region, the British-led multinational force of 4,700 was left to handle peacekeeping on its own. From the outset of the Afghanistan campaign, pundits and officials alike had warned against leaving Afghanistan politically vulnerable to co-optation by bad actors once again, as the West had done after the Cold War. Washington acknowledged this exhortation by supporting the Bonn political process establishing Karzai's government and by making a substantial financial contribution (though still only the fourth-largest) to Afghanistan's reconstruction. But any deeper military diplomatic or military commitment was foresworn on the grounds that US assets would be more urgently needed in Afghanistan to finish off al-Qaeda and the Taliban and elsewhere – Iraq in particular – to combat other terrorist and weapons-of-mass-destruction (WMD) threats.

Military strategy vs. political science

The strategic shift from Afghanistan to Iraq created the impression that in spite of dire warnings about the political neglect of Afghanistan, when measured against the risks of distraction from other global threats, the US was to an extent willing to risk political (though not military) failure there. This was merely a tacit dispensation, and certainly not a reflection of anything approaching political apathy towards Central Asia. In Iraq, of course, political failure is not an option. It would fuel efforts by al-Qaeda and its followers to force the US from the Middle East and the Gulf. Further, the loss of prestige would compromise future counter-terrorist and counter-proliferation efforts by lowering the confidence of allies and potential partners in the United States' capacity to deliver.

A satisfactory result for Western policy requires more than unseating Saddam Hussein and neutralising Iraq's WMD. It also calls for spawning and nurturing a new Iraqi government that is stable, unthreatening to its neighbours as well as the US and capable of serving the needs of all of Iraq's people – including the Shia and the Kurds – so as to keep the country territorially intact. Only the US has the military power to do the former. Moreover, as Israel's main ally and security guarantor of last resort in the Middle East, only the US has overriding incentives and the ability to ensure that an effective government is in place. In the case of Iraq, military strategy and political science also cannot be operationally divorced. If the US undertakes military action, it is likely to involve overwhelming air and ground forces: indigenous groups appear unlikely to coalesce into anything comparable to the Northern Alliance, and Iraq's military remains considerably stronger than the al-Qaeda/Taliban force in Afghanistan. Yet the US cannot rely merely on 'constructive chaos' in the wake of an invasion to generate a sustainable government. A plan for both the establishment and maintenance of a government is required. In short, as much as the Bush administration might like to stand aloof from the 'granular' aspects of nation-building and economic reconstruction, at times Washington will find it necessary to execute military strategy and apply political science at the same time. In some cases, a refusal to engage in nation-building could constitute a gross case of strategic negligence.

Equally, the US cannot finesse political science when the use of US military power is simply not an option. This applies to one of the most strategically critical situations facing the US: the Israeli–Palestinian conflict. At the same time, while linkage need not be publicly underscored, effective

US Middle East policy will also need to be sensitive to the relationship between military action against Iraq and political mediation between the Israelis and the Palestinians. Heightened violence in the West Bank and Gaza poses political risks to the frontline states, and may make it more difficult for the US to win Saudi cooperation in a military campaign against Iraq, which is the top US priority. Further, should the US fail to lower Israeli–Palestinian tensions, the prospective loss of diplomatic leverage could make crisis stability in the Middle East all the more difficult to achieve. As the *intifada* remained robust in spite of – or perhaps because of – Israel's tough retaliatory policy, the Bush administration was inevitably drawn into a mediating role, whereby senior US officials were dispatched to broker cease-fires. The initial efforts fell short, however, because they did not come with any larger roadmap for returning to a position in which substantive peace negotiations were feasible. Missing was an affirmative basis for negotiations once cease-fires are in place. Washington hoped that the Israelis and the Palestinians themselves could provide direction. That hope proved unrealistic. Instead, it was Saudi Arabia that stepped into the breach, with Crown Prince Abdullah's plan for normalisation of Arab–Israeli relations in exchange for Israel's pullback to pre-1967 borders. While Saudi Arabia's skeletal peace proposal momentarily filled a diplomatic vacuum, it does not constitute a full-blown peace plan and neither Riyadh nor any other Arab capital is an acceptable mediator between Yasser Arafat and Ariel Sharon. The US has little choice but to assume that role. Otherwise, some Arab states may feel compelled to assume a provocative and destabilising stance, as Iran has done. President Bush appeared to understand these realities when, in early April 2002, he pushed Israel to withdraw from the Palestinian territories and dispatched Secretary of State Colin Powell to the Middle East with an extensive remit for deep and direct US engagement.

Outside the Middle East, Washington will face additional challenges where its application of force will be a catalyst for potentially destabilising political change. It may be hard to elude political science in Colombia and the northern Andes. As the Colombian rebels have abused and ultimately abandoned a three-year peace process, there is ample justification for the US to expand its support for Bogotá to include counter-insurgency as well as drug interdiction. At the same time, it remains to be seen whether Colombian President Andrés Pastrana's successor and regional leaders have the political means to sell their people on, for example, alternatives to coca production. To salvage its military and financial investment, the US may have to assume a more coordinative diplomatic role. There are, of course, areas in which limited applications of military power need not and indeed cannot be accompanied by an immersion in local politics. US military programmes in the Philippines, Yemen and Georgia – which involve training, advising and equipping indigenous forces rather than direct action – fall into this category.

Tactical foreign policy

The expression 'axis of evil' that President Bush promulgated in his 29 January 2002 State of the Union message alarmed the United States' European partners, Beijing and Moscow, among others. Even if it does reflect senior US officials' prevailing assessments of Iraq, North Korea and Iran, the decision to use the expression did not adequately take into account the fact that many of Washington's counter-terrorism coalition partners have serious questions about Washington's sweeping and aggressive posture towards provocative states, as opposed to non-state terrorist actors. The speech unhelpfully gave those partners – particularly European capitals – a focal point for doubt rather than unity. At the very least, by making it politically more difficult for potential allies to throw their support behind tough US strategic approaches to problematic states, the expression did not work well as tactical foreign policy. Furthermore, it seemed to underline the Bush administration's impatience with political science.

Dealing with Iraq, as noted, calls for military strategy as well as political science. What about North Korea and Iran? The Bush administration seemed, in early 2002, to be succumbing to the temptation to write off Pyongyang as a hopelessly opaque enigma, impervious to political suasion. Yet such a dispensation would throw out the baby, the bathwater and the bath itself. The 1994 Agreed Framework, though fraught in its implementation, probably has inhibited North Korea's missile and nuclear programmes. North Korea's unceasing need for international humanitarian assistance affords the US considerable leverage. Nevertheless, many senior officials of the administration believe that the US should not be helping to prop up the 'evil' North Korean regime through diplomatic deals and assistance. In this view, a far more effective and enduring strategy for ending the North Korea WMD threat is to isolate, starve and destroy the regime, as the sanctions programme has sought to do with Iraq. But in contrast with Iraq, US military options against North Korea are much more fraught. Although the US and its allies would certainly prevail in the end, North Korea could inflict very heavy damage and casualties on South Korea, including Seoul, which is within artillery range. Moreover, North Korea has a far more robust arsenal of ballistic missiles than Iraq as well as biological, chemical and possibly even nuclear weapons that it would presumably be prepared to use as a last resort if its survival were at risk. Finally, Washington would find it very difficult to convince its allies in the region, much less China, to support a high-risk strategy of pressure against Pyongyang. Accordingly, the Bush administration, like its predecessor, may find that it has little choice but to pursue diplomatic options with the North, no matter how distasteful and difficult.

The inclusion of Iran in the 'axis of evil' was unquestionably the most jarring aspect of Bush's speech. To most European countries – including the

United Kingdom, the United States' staunchest ally – reformist Iranian President Mohammad Khatami's re-election confirmed that engagement rather than confrontation was the best Western policy towards Iran. The Americans' threat assessment of Iran is different from the Europeans'. In Washington's view, the conservatives still hold the real political power in Iran; Iran is relentlessly pursuing WMD capability; and, in any case, on matters such as support for Hizbullah and armed Palestinian groups and opposition to Israel's existence, there is no daylight between the reformists and the conservatives. This analysis is probably correct. But the decision to demonise Tehran may have unduly limited the prospects for reformism – indisputably a popular movement in Iran that has retained momentum – to morph into a force that does diverge in material substantive terms from Iran's institutionally entrenched Islamic conservatives. Instead, although Bush made it clear subsequent to 29 January that Iran was not a candidate for US military action, his inclusion of Iran in the 'axis of evil' probably reinforced the conservatives' capacity to inhibit the reformists. This too may be bad political science. The problem is not, of course, irremediable. For example, initiatives aimed at producing Israeli–Palestinian peace could eventually lower tensions between the Israelis and the Palestinians and Tehran. If Iran responds by softening its stance on Israel or dialling back its support for Hizbullah or armed Palestinian groups, the US could drop Iran from the 'axis' without any chagrin. In the meantime, Washington can make up its political science deficit by recognising that the EU and European capitals may have a constructive role to play in maintaining a policy of 'critical engagement' with Tehran, and using their economic clout to encourage reformist transformation.

Legal challenges

Good political science also requires a solid legal framework. The 11 September attacks illuminated a variety of conceptually unfamiliar phenomena that taxed putative principles of international law and the law of armed conflict. These include 'terrorist-sponsored states' such as Afghanistan; unlawful combatants who nonetheless hold territory; and non-state actors who pose strategic military challenges to states. Indeed, non-state actors may be more likely than states to use WMD. Fashioning a definition of terrorism in an epoch of mass-casualty threats and foes decreasingly interested in negotiation appears less difficult than some have suggested; it would simply need to focus on means rather than motivation, and to sensibly confront the question of whether 'terrorists' can hold territory. The stiffer challenge is to articulate a jurisprudence to underpin the intuitively obvious notion that what is illegal if done by a state should also be illegal if done by a transnational non-state group or individual actor. Groups, networks and their individual members must be clearly punishable under international law.

The absence of a robust jurisprudence suited to the new threat environment became clear when the US detained al-Qaeda and Taliban members captured in Afghanistan at the US base at Guantanamo Bay, Cuba. Since the United States had suffered an attack on a civilian target without any military value, its refusal to accord them prisoner-of-war (POW) status was understandable. Further, it was technically correct for the US to classify Taliban detainees as 'battlefield detainees' or 'unlawful combatants' who were merely contemplated by exclusion but not specifically covered by the Geneva Conventions and the laws of war, and al-Qaeda detainees as unlawful combatants who were not complying with the laws of war and therefore were not entitled to POW status. Yet this dispensation was also politically unsatisfactory and legally inadequate in that it left a legal gap as to how, precisely, those apprehended in the counter-terrorism campaign should be treated in terms of interrogation, living conditions and legal process. Under customary international law, no detainee is supposed to be held in legal limbo. A decisive dispensation called for a considered legal judgment that the US was not prepared to make. In the event, US officials improvised answers to legal questions about what constituted proper treatment and legal process extemporaneously, and proffered vaguely construed solutions such as military tribunals – one minute to be closed, the next to be public. This uncertainty proved to be a public-relations problem for the Bush administration.

Similarly, the United States has justified military action in Afghanistan and potentially Iraq and elsewhere as a matter of self-defence under Article 51 of the UN Charter. This is a valid interpretation as far as it goes, but international actors have not fully appreciated its implications for the concept of sovereignty. To be sure, that concept has been diluted since the end of the Cold War by way of globalisation, supranational institutions like the EU and theories of humanitarian intervention. But even against this backdrop, the action of the US and its partners was relatively novel. In essence, they undertook military action against non-state actors who had first usurped sovereign authority that can be legitimately conferred only on a state and then used it illegally. A similar justification applied to US intervention in Panama in December 1989. In sponsoring the Bonn process and providing a peacekeeping force, the US-led coalition restored Afghanistan's legitimate sovereignty. The general point is perhaps uncontroversial: if the international community recognises and accords sovereignty, that community can also take it away or alter its terms. But the more incisive question of what constitutes legitimate sovereignty that cannot be interfered with – and what illegitimate sovereignty is therefore subject to outside intervention – remains unanswered.

It is in the interests of the US and its allies to fill these legal gaps. However vigorously they might argue that their soldiers are entitled to POW status while their al-Qaeda and Taliban adversaries are not, the captors of those soldiers are likely to do unto them as was done unto theirs. It is also central to eventual peace that the counter-terrorism coalition make a case to those adversaries that it is fair and principled, and honours the rule of law. Furthermore, any purported relaxation of the right of non-intervention (enshrined in Article 2(7) of the UN Charter) for the sake of battling transnational threats needs to be circumscribed such that it cannot be used capriciously or in ways that would be intolerably destabilising. It might be tempting to pronounce from an armchair that Robert Mugabe usurped Zimbabwe's sovereignty by rigging the presidential election and prescribe intervention on behalf of his wronged political opponents; but to use that rationale as a basis for intervention would also put at risk regimes – such as Pakistan's – that can be helpful in addressing the more salient terrorist threat.

Accordingly, it behoves coalition partners to establish equitable and practical principles for dealing with issues that fall between the cracks of the existing legal regime pertaining to intervention and armed conflict. The United States' well-known reasons for opposing the International Criminal Court remain formidable. Crusading European magistrates have sought to invest national courts with extra-territorial reach for the sake of implementing international law. A Belgian court, for example, is pursuing complaints lodged by Palestinians against Israeli Prime Minister Ariel Sharon for war crimes allegedly committed in Lebanon in 1982 when he was defence minister. A Belgian law allows prosecution in Belgium of foreign officials for human-rights violations committed outside Belgium. American officials – and presumably others – are loath to endorse an institution of universal jurisdiction that could similarly complicate its exercise of discretionary military or political power. Yet it is important for governments and lawyers to consider the related question of whether national legal authorities can acquire jurisdiction over transnational groups and non-state actors who are not acting on behalf of any state.

In the politically charged circumstances of the counter-terrorism mobilisation, such matters would best not be left to haphazard and piecemeal development via common law. A systematic debate makes more sense. Perhaps an international convention could be convened, bringing together official delegations from participating governments; lawyers from the UN and other multilateral institutions; international lawyers drawn from different nations; and the International Court of Justice acting in its advisory capacity. The convention's purpose would be to craft by consensus affirmative solutions to the legal problems posed by the counter-terrorism campaign on the basis of extant international treaties, agreements and case law and official interpretations of national law. Because the US will lead most operational aspects of that campaign, its input into its legal facets will take priority. The US Congress, federal judiciary and appropriate bar associations should take the lead in addressing these problems on the basis of the US constitution, American statutory and case law as well as international law. They might focus, in the first instance, on defining the power of US civilian courts and military tribunals to apply international law.

Beyond phrasemaking: political science as grand strategy

In revealing the pernicious cross-fertilisation of state and non-state actors, and the virulent resentments that the West's successes have generated in less accomplished or less fortunate societies, 11 September made grand strategy an obligation once again. The US, in particular, can no longer afford to have an itinerant foreign policy, excitable in crises but somnolent in their absence. At this stage, no country or supranational organisation can rival the US' 'hard' military and diplomatic power or its 'soft' economic and cultural power. US military spending exceeds that of the next 14 highest defence spenders combined. Based on voting shares, the US Treasury still effectively controls major decisions at the International Monetary Fund and the World Bank. In 2000, the US' GDP constituted 30% of the world's total. The US must apply both forms of power to try to eliminate the underlying reasons for the cultural antagonism that moved 19 young men – with the backing of a countless and faceless network of supporters – to commandeer four airliners in order to murder thousands of civilians and shock a superpower.

Though on balance unconstructive, the 'axis of evil' remark was not without utility. By projecting a vivid tripartite image of states perceived to be America's existential foes, it may have furnished US policymakers with a useful reminder of the need for a grand strategy that covers not only emergent terrorist threats but also the factors that underwrite their most dire capabilities. These factors include not only the development and potential proliferation of WMD but also the growing legions of young Arab and Muslim men predisposed to extremism by the tenuous economies of the Gulf, Central Asia and North Africa. If phrasemaking can inspire grand strategy, however, it does not constitute it. Military action, intelligence collection and analysis, law enforcement and counter-proliferation efforts can pre-empt or interdict terrorist operations. They cannot address the root cause of terrorism – namely, the unwillingness or inability of illiberal Muslim regimes to take care of their own people. The diplomatic application of political science is required to accomplish that far more profound objective. The first goal of that endeavour may be to help create the conditions whereby young Muslims see sufficient political hope in their home countries to give their governments a chance to do a better job, stay home and contribute to their nations' political and economic development.

Islamic terrorism is not merely a transnational problem; it is a diaspora problem. Angry young men dissatisfied with their own governments take flight, join the al-Qaeda-sponsored *jihad* and attack the 'far enemy' (the

United States) as a means of stunning its 'near enemies' (primarily, Saudi Arabia and Egypt) into positive action or rousing fellow citizens to upheaval. Demographic and economic trends would seem to reinforce these tendencies. Between now and 2015, the population of the Middle East is projected to grow by 32%, rising from 304 million to 400m (including Iran). The 2–5% population growth rates responsible for this enormous increase will keep the population relatively young, which correlates with political violence. High growth rates also practically mandate low or negative GDP growth, and perpetuate the low status of women, a low standard of living and low literacy rates. As some Middle Eastern governments try to placate Islamic pressure groups by permitting restrictions on the role of women in their societies, they will perpetuate high birth rates. At the same time, deteriorating educational systems will constrain literacy growth and yield to mosque-centred education, and declining per-capita GDP will be reflected in lower standards of living. Per-capita income in the Arab world did not grow at all from 1985–1995, when developing countries as a whole registered a 32% increase. Political consciousness in the region will grow as options for ruling élites shrink. The Middle East, apart from the oil sector, has become increasingly disengaged from the world economy, and has produced relatively little intra-regional trade.

The burden of coping with these negative trends rests on both sides. Arab leaders need to build domestic institutions for promoting capital and labour mobility, while permitting greater pluralism. For the US and its allies, as well as multilateral institutions over which they hold influence, applied political science is a strategic imperative. The goal should be to increase foreign assistance aimed at those who are most disadvantaged by economic and technological change, and to develop infrastructure and institutions that will attract investment. Technical assistance will be also be needed to help demographically besieged countries develop effective health care, environment and education policies. While the international financial institutions may be best equipped to provide such help, support and encouragement will be needed from their leading shareholders, such as the US, Japan and Germany. Meeting these demands is an enormous enterprise, and requires significant departures from current practices. The industrialised nations devote less than 0.25% of their aggregate GDP to foreign assistance; the United States, at 0.1%, is among the least generous. President Bush's March 2002 announcement in Monterrey, Mexico, that he would seek to increase the US foreign assistance budget by 50% by 2006, was a step in the right direction.

The US also may have to restrain any unilateralist instincts, especially in the economic realm. Baldly protectionist policies, such as the steel tariffs imposed by the US in March 2002, will not encourage Arab states that are (like Saudi Arabia) already reluctant to take the liberalising steps necessary to join the World Trade Organisation, which would facilitate global and regional economic integration. On the political side, Washington's management of transatlantic relations should take into account the potential political benefits of the EU expanding its economic ties with the Gulf states. Deeper transatlantic consultation and better coordinated Middle East policies may prove constructive.

It remains to be seen whether the US and its Western partners can make the necessary changes to their foreign policies, or Muslim states to their political cultures. It is also far from a foregone conclusion that the West will be able to change the fundamentally hostile apprehensions of most Muslims. In December 2001 and January 2002, the Gallup Organization surveyed 10,000 people in nine Islamic countries and found a collective perception that was as incoherent as it was strongly held. According to the survey, 67% of the respondents considered the 11 September attacks morally justifiable. Yet most did not believe that Arabs in general or al-Qaeda in particular had perpetrated the attacks, and appreciable numbers believed that Israel or the US itself was responsible. A decisive 77% thought that military action in Afghanistan was inappropriate. While this paints a daunting public-relations picture from a Western point of view, the alternative to attempting to change it is increasing mutual disengagement and heightened strategic instability. If these circumstances materialise, given the looming spectre of al-Qaeda and the probable resilience of radical Islamic terrorism beyond Osama bin Laden, both US security and Middle East regional security will be far more difficult to safeguard.

In the Third World, the strategic rescue of failed or failing states may await. Somalia's continued failure to re-materialise as a state, the fractured lawlessness of the Democratic Republic of Congo and Zimbabwe's tainted March 2002 elections may have had little to do with transnational terrorism. But the hardship endured by the populations of those nations and the desperation of their political leaders may make them vulnerable to terrorist co-optation – if not as active abettors, then perhaps as hosts. While this remains only a secondary threat to international security, it also suggests that the US and its allies should adopt a more anticipatory foreign policy that operates precisely at the level of political science. In Somalia, for example, the US has determined that the likelihood that indigenous groups would provide al-Qaeda sanctuary or operational help is sufficiently low to warrant only a preventive military posture there. To ensure that the threat stays at a low level, though, it may make sense for Washington to explore avenues of nation-building more intensively than it has since the frustrating American experience in Somalia during the early to mid-1990s. Finite diplomatic and economic resources needed for more immediate threats constitute a major constraint. Yet 11 September showed that mass dissatisfaction that prevails throughout entire regions could coalesce into transnational strategic threats. US policymakers might therefore consider that strategic inattention to such problems now may increase security burdens later, and might therefore assign a higher future value to present investments in peace and prosperity in sub-Saharan Africa and elsewhere.

Towards the end of political science

Critics of the Clinton administration derisively labelled a strategy keyed to peacekeeping, nation-building, conflict resolution and economic development 'foreign policy as social work'. They may have had a point before 11 September. But in the epoch of transnational terrorism and WMD, these activities are not non-strategic. On the contrary, they are essential for consolidating the gains of US-led counter-terrorism and counter-proliferation efforts. In the short term, it may be the case that the US must focus its energy and resources on urgent military action in Afghanistan and Iraq. After these keynotes are struck, however, the lion's share of day-to-day US counter-terrorism activity will occur at the level of intelligence and law enforcement. At that stage, the long-term priority will be to move from containment to victory. During the Cold War, that meant, at bottom, winning an ideological argument about what constituted the best political and economic system. History, in Fukuyama's interpretation, may then have ended. Political science did not. In the campaign against terrorism, victory means bringing the fruits of the democratic capitalist system to those who have not yet fully enjoyed them. That task is ultimately one not for generals but for political scientists. The United States, as the ranking superpower for the foreseeable future, must provide both.

IISS*maps*

Strategic Geography 2001/2002

Europe

The Americas

Middle East/Gulf

Central Asia and the Caucasus

Asia

Africa

Global Trends

international boundaries
province or state boundaries
disputed and other boundaries
roads
LOFA province or state
built-up areas
capital cities
cities/towns
attack(s)/incident(s) and skirmishes
Dar El Beida international airport/airfield
Bagram air base
rivers
lakes
mountain peaks (height in metres)

Europe Northern Ireland: low-level violence continues

The Good Friday Agreement was approved in May 1998 in simultaneous referendums in Northern Ireland (by 71%) and the Irish Republic (by 94%). The agreement provides for a devolved power-sharing government in Northern Ireland and cross-border agencies jointly run by the Northern Ireland assembly and the Irish parliament, while leaving the province's sovereign fate to its electoral majority. The peace process has faced a difficult year with hard-liners pressuring nationalists and unionists to abandon the agreement.

Republican Paramilitary Groups support unification of Ireland	Established	Strength	Status
Continuity Irish Republican Army (CIRA)/ Continuity Army Council	1994	50+	active
Irish National Liberation Army (INLA)/ People's Liberation Army/People's Republican Army/Catholic Reaction Force	1974	50	active
Irish Republican Army (IRA)/Provisional Irish Republican Army (PIRA – the Provos)	1969	250+	cease-fire
Real Irish Republican Army (RIRA)/ True IRA	1998	150+	active
Loyalist Paramilitary Groups support existing union between Northern Ireland and Great Britain			
Loyalist Volunteer Force (LVF)	1996	100	active
Orange Volunteers	1970s	20	cease-fire
Red Hand Defenders (RHD)	1998	20	active
Ulster Defence Association (UDA)/ Ulster Freedom Fighters (UFF)	1971	200+	active
Ulster Volunteer Force (UVF)/ Protestant Action Force/Protestant Action Group	1966	150+	cease-fire

Clashes during 2001
14 people were killed, two by the IRA and 12 by loyalist paramilitaries in Northern Ireland. Over 250 pipebomb attacks on Catholic homes were reported.

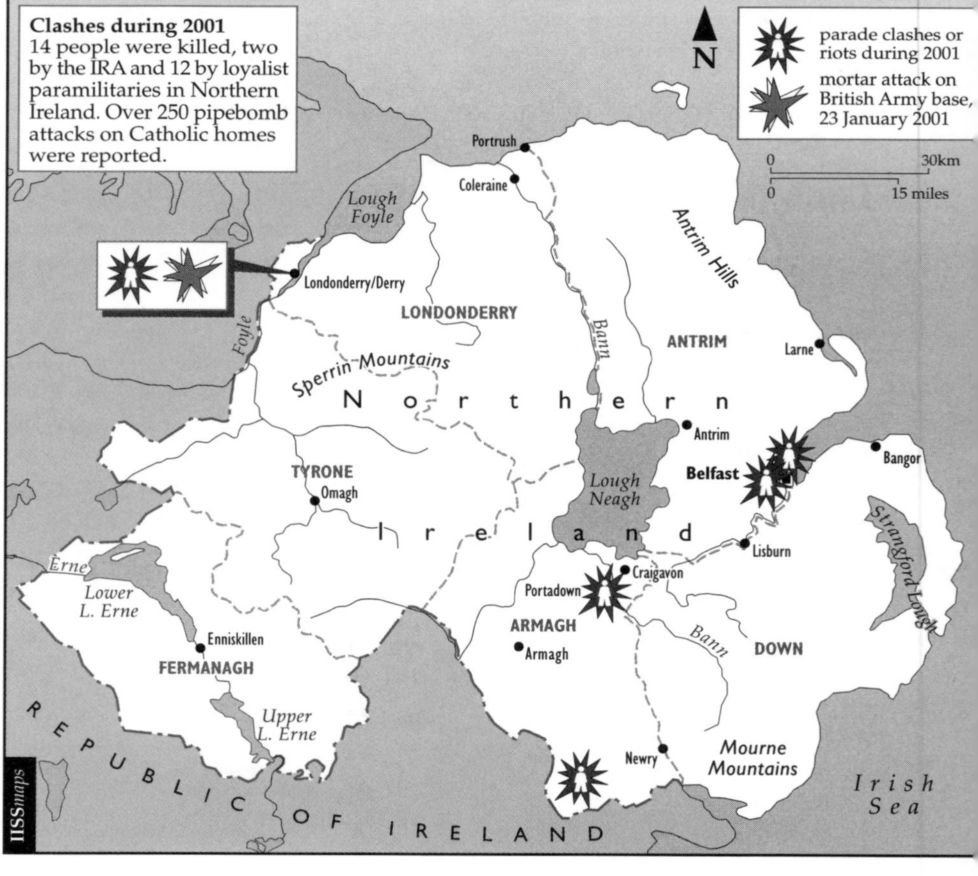

Vestminster elections Results by constituency, une 2001

Northern Ireland Assembly, June 2001

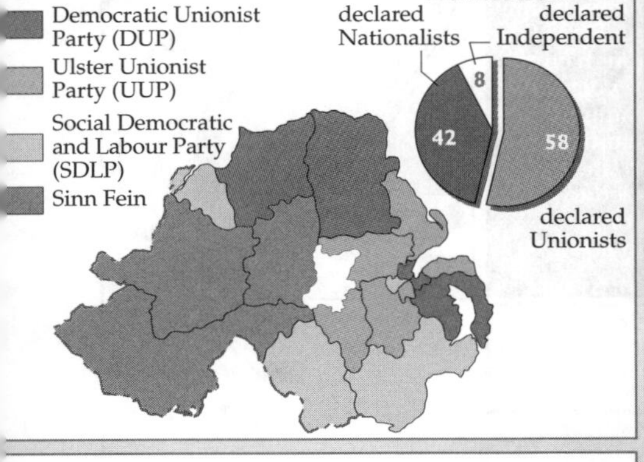

Protestant % of otal population by county, 1991

1991 Census
Total population: 1,577,836

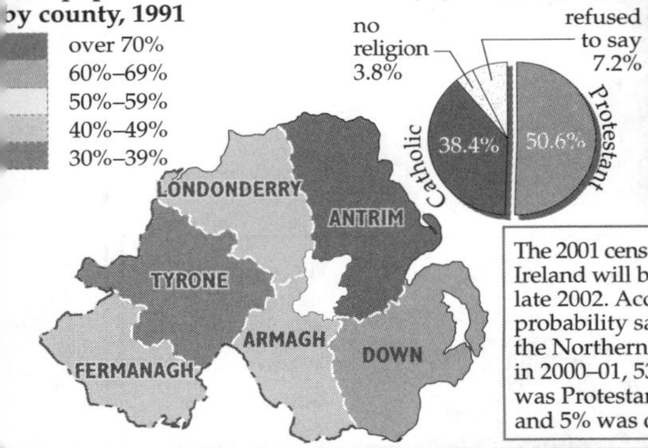

The 2001 census figures for Northern Ireland will be publicly available in late 2002. According to a large probability sample survey used by the Northern Ireland government, in 2000–01, 53% of the population was Protestant, 42% was Catholic and 5% was other or unknown.

Unemployment by religious group, 1971–1999

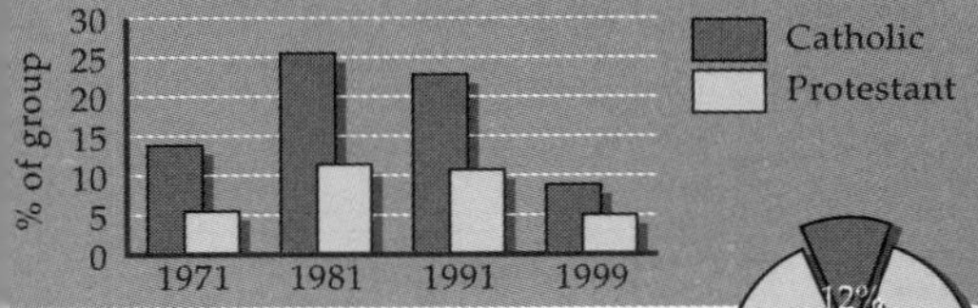

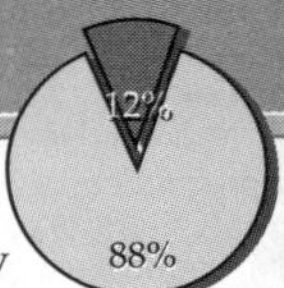

Police Service of Northern Ireland
As of early 2001 about 88% of the 8,500 officers of the Royal Ulster Constabulary (RUC) were Protestant. After the signing of the 1998 Good Friday Agreement, the Patten Commission was formed to make recommendations on the RUC's future. On the basis of this report and implementing legislation, the province's police force became known as the Police Service of Northern Ireland on 4 November 2001, with recruits to be drawn equally from the Catholic and Protestant communities.

Northern Ireland, 2001

4 March Car-bomb explodes outside BBC TV centre, West London. One man injured.

8 March IRA announces willingness to meet head of Independent International Commission on Decommissioning (IICD).

14 April Bomb explodes at Post Office delivery depot, North London. No one injured. RIRA believed responsible.

Bomb explodes in same Post Office building, North London. One man injured.

8 May David Trimble threatens to resign as First Minister unless IRA begins decommissioning.

19–20 June School-children face Loyalist protest entering a Catholic school.

1 July David Trimble resigns as First Minister.

9–14 July Talks between Tony Blair and Bertie Ahern at Weston Park, agree to produce document containing proposals for each party.

1 August Car-bomb defused at Belfast International Airport. RIRA believed responsible. British and Irish governments publish Implementation Plans for Good Friday Agreement.

2 August Republican paramilitaries carry out bomb attack, Ealing, London.

6 August Statement issued by head of IICD announcing IRA decommissioning proposal. UUP respond that proposal is insufficient.

14 August IRA withdraws decommissioning proposals.

3 September–5 November Catholic children en route to school face regular Loyalist protests in North Belfast.

12 October British government announces cease-fires of UDA, UFF and LVF have ended.

23 October IRA issues statement announcing the start of weapons decommissioning under verification of IICD. In response, several army bases agree to close, including watchtowers and listening posts along the border.

4 November Royal Ulster Constabulary title is changed to Police Service of Northern Ireland.

6 November David Trimble is re-elected as First Minister of Northern Ireland assembly.

18 November House of Commons votes to allow Sinn Fein allowances and use of facilities at Westminster.

Europe After Macedonia's essential harvest

Macedonia remains tense, over six months after the 13 August 2001 signing of a peace treaty and the disarming and disbanding of its chief Albanian insurgent group, the National Liberation Army. International monitors from the OSCE and the EU, and NATO through Task Force Fox have eased tensions to a certain degree. Although ethnic Albanians now have more of a representative voice after January 2002 constitutional revisions, and an amnesty for those rebels who surrendered their weapons under *Operation Essential Harvest* has been approved, the redeployment to the north of police units has led to some tension. The next test will come with the elections scheduled for late-2002. However, it is now in no group's interest to provoke renewed violence.

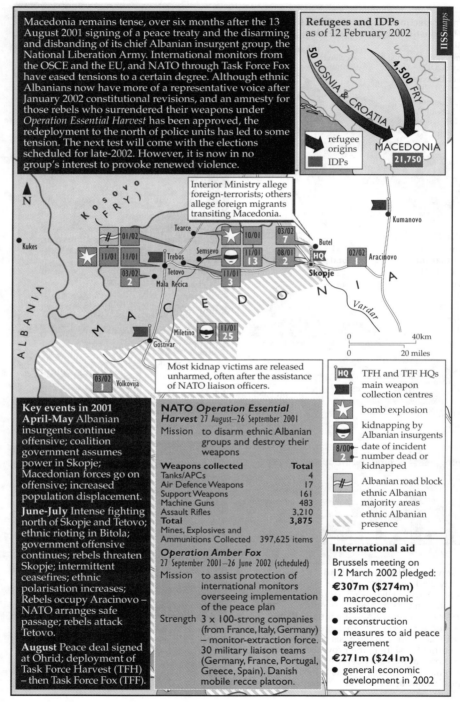

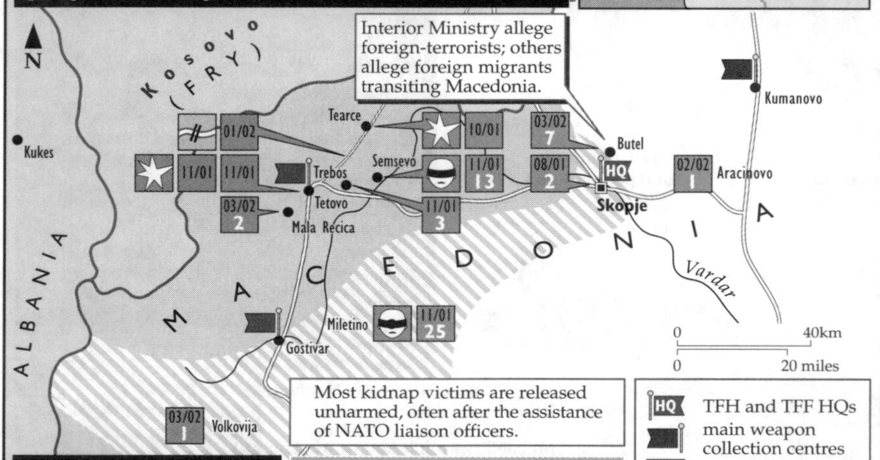

Key events in 2001

April-May Albanian insurgents continue offensive; coalition government assumes power in Skopje; Macedonian forces go on offensive; increased population displacement.

June-July Intense fighting north of Skopje and Tetovo; ethnic rioting in Bitola; government offensive continues; rebels threaten Skopje; intermittent ceasefires; ethnic polarisation increases; Rebels occupy Aracinovo – NATO arranges safe passage; rebels attack Tetovo.

August Peace deal signed at Ohrid; deployment of Task Force Harvest (TFH) – then Task Force Fox (TFF).

NATO *Operation Essential Harvest* 27 August–26 September 2001

Mission: to disarm ethnic Albanian groups and destroy their weapons

Weapons collected	Total
Tanks/APCs	4
Air Defence Weapons	17
Support Weapons	161
Machine Guns	483
Assault Rifles	3,210
Total	**3,875**

Mines, Explosives and Ammunitions Collected 397,625 items

Operation Amber Fox
27 September 2001–26 June 2002 (scheduled)

Mission: to assist protection of international monitors overseeing implementation of the peace plan

Strength: 3 x 100-strong companies (from France, Italy, Germany) – monitor-extraction force. 30 military liaison teams (Germany, France, Portugal, Greece, Spain). Danish mobile recce platoon.

International aid

Brussels meeting on 12 March 2002 pledged:

€307m ($274m)
- macroeconomic assistance
- reconstruction
- measures to aid peace agreement

€271m ($241m)
- general economic development in 2002

The Americas US homeland security: practical measures

The issues and numbers involved:

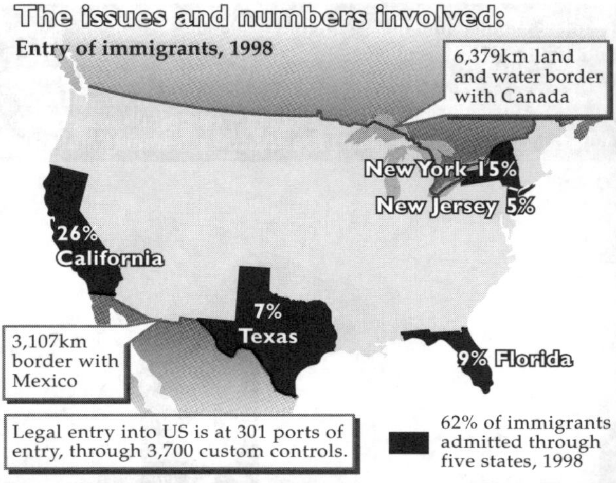

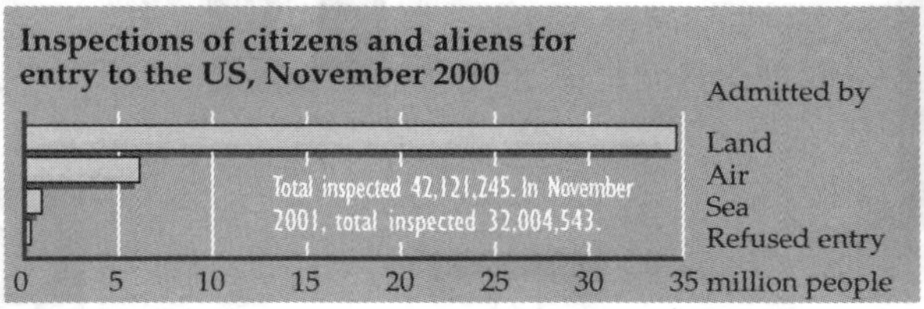

Since 11 September 2001, efforts have been made to improve homeland security in the US. This is a challenging task due to the volume of entries, the length of national borders and the dispersed responsibility for border controls. Responsibility is divided among numerous agencies, including the Immigration and Naturalization Service (INS) who examine people at ports of entry.

In October 2001 the Office of Homeland Security was established to implement a national strategy to secure the US against threats or attacks. The Council's responsibility includes coordinating efforts to improve border security.

During 2000

The US issued 7 million visas to foreigners.

The following passed through US border inspection systems:

489m people entered or left
127m vehicles
11.6m maritime containers
11.5m trucks
2.2m railroad cars
829,000 aircraft
211,000 vessels

40% of visas were overstayed
6–12 million illegal aliens resided in the US

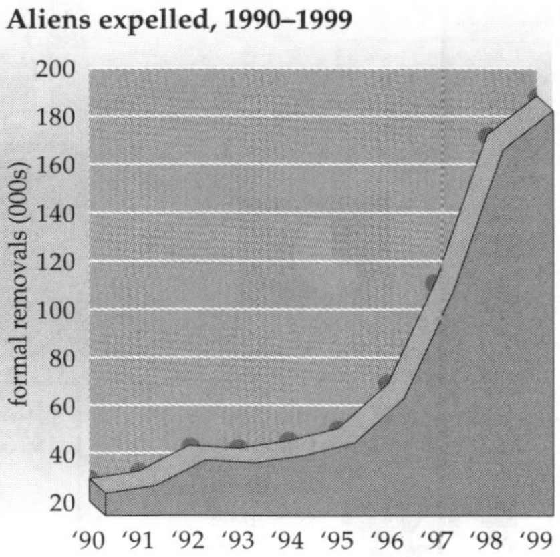

Some actions taken:

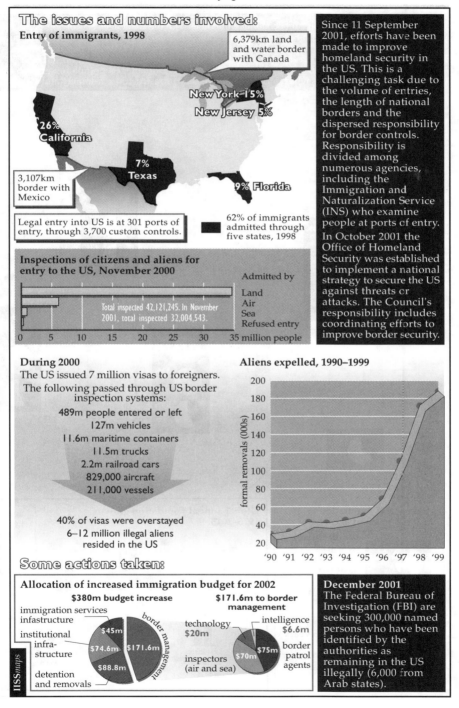

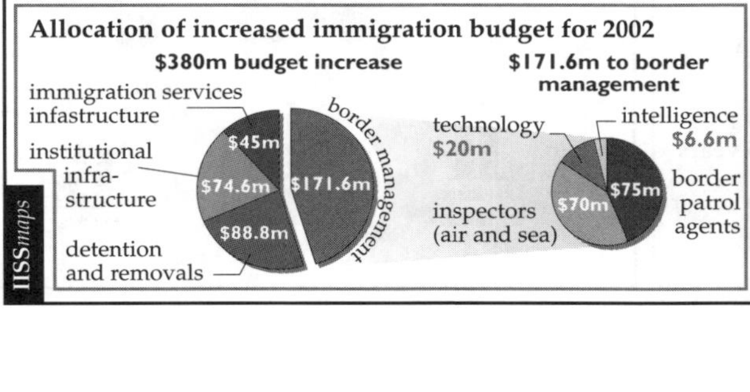

December 2001

The Federal Bureau of Investigation (FBI) are seeking 300,000 named persons who have been identified by the authorities as remaining in the US illegally (6,000 from Arab states).

Middle East/Gulf The Arab population boom

Arab States are facing significant economic difficulties with the challenges of growing populations. They are second only to Sub-Saharan Africa in rate of annual population growth and the current population is expected to have doubled in the next 30 years. Most Arab states also have disproportionately high percentages of under-25-year olds, with average figures at over 50%, compared to an average of 20% in the developed world. Unmanaged population growth can cause an array of problems which include straining state infrastructures, resources and technology.

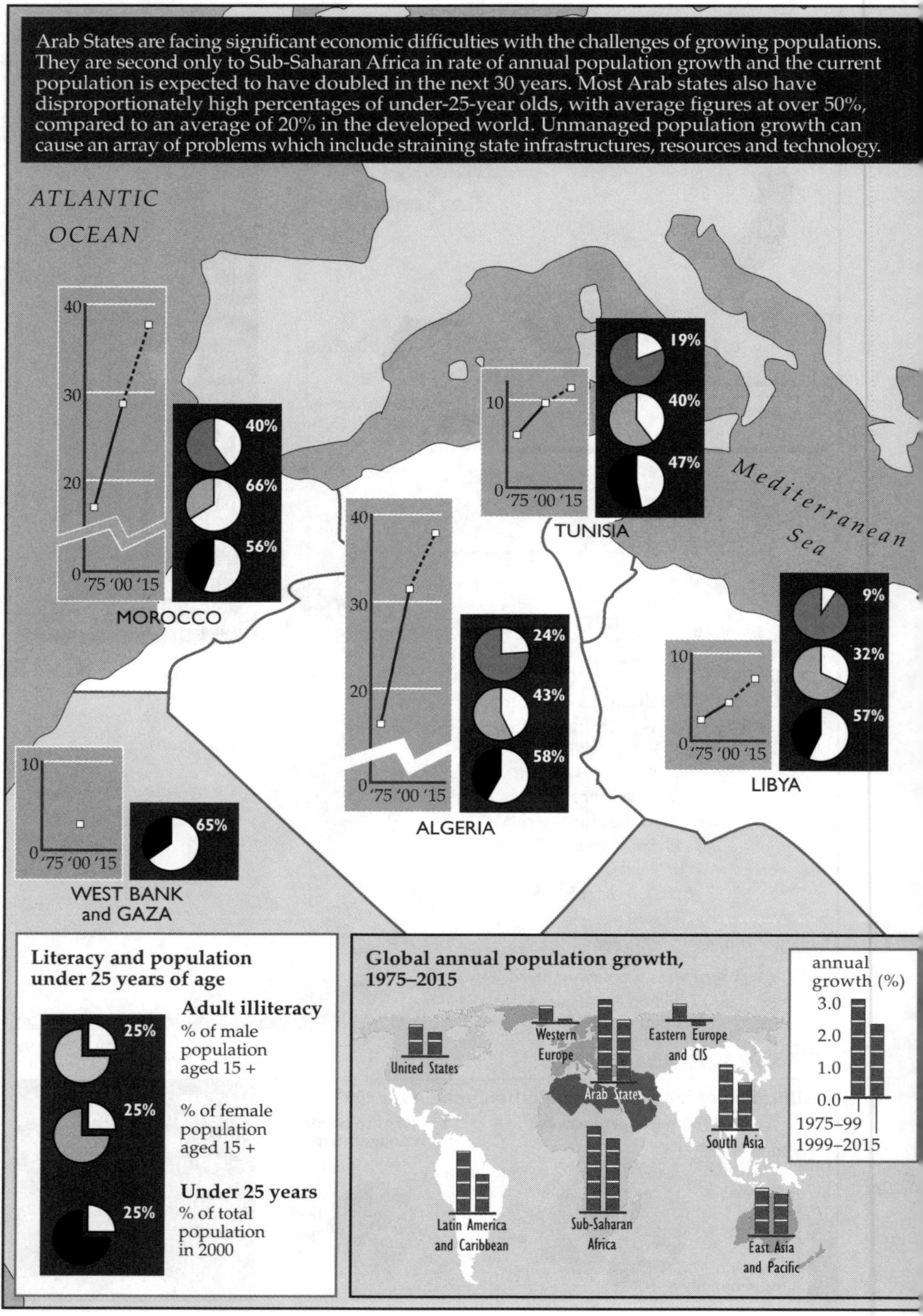

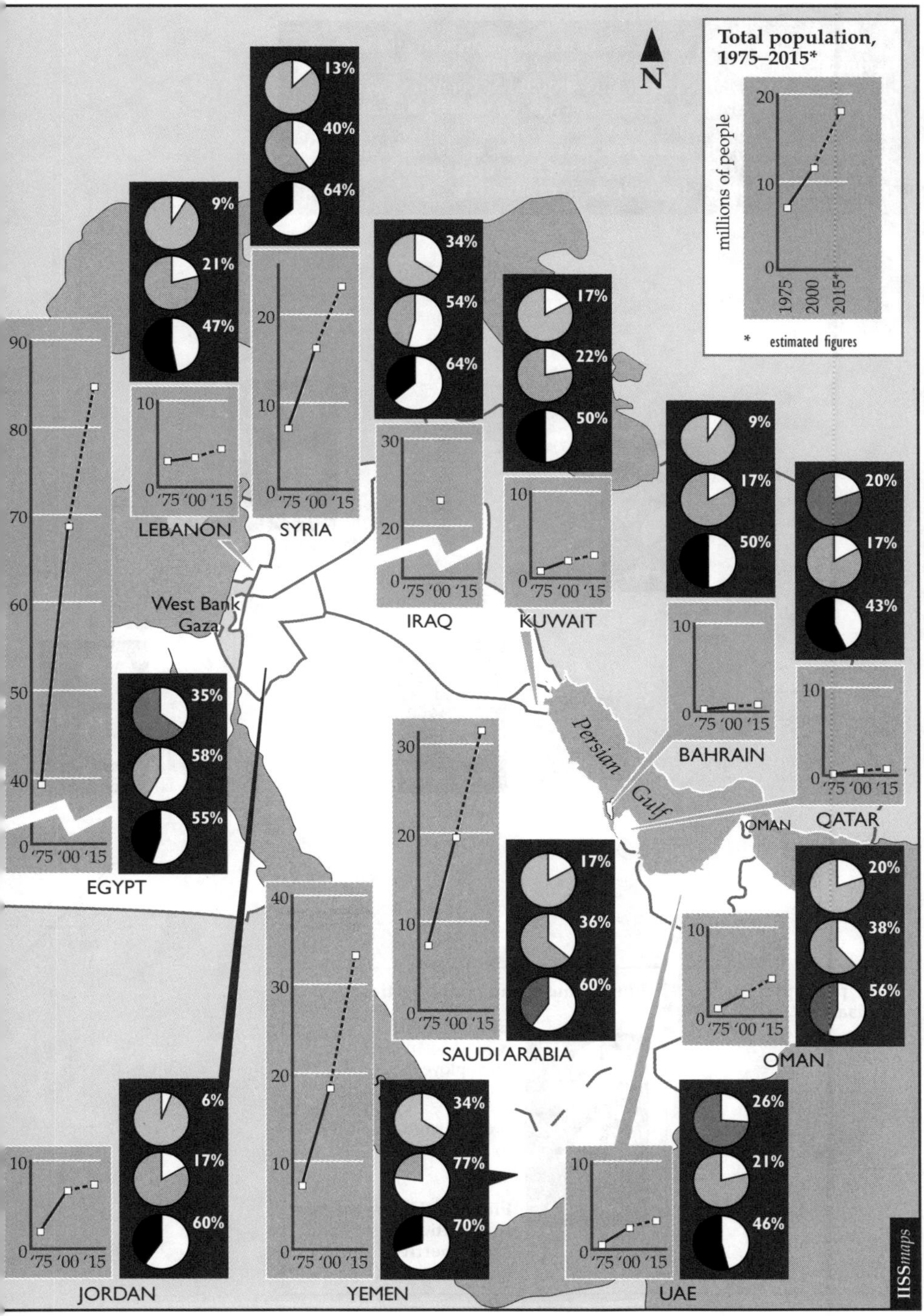
Total population, 1975–2015*
millions of people
20
10
0
1975
2000
2015*
* estimated figures
N
13%
40%
64%
SYRIA
9%
21%
47%
LEBANON
34%
54%
64%
IRAQ
17%
22%
50%
KUWAIT
9%
17%
50%
BAHRAIN
20%
17%
43%
QATAR
West Bank
Gaza
35%
58%
55%
EGYPT
Persian Gulf
OMAN
17%
36%
60%
SAUDI ARABIA
20%
38%
56%
OMAN
6%
17%
60%
JORDAN
34%
77%
70%
YEMEN
26%
21%
46%
UAE
'75 '00 '15
IISSmaps

Middle East/Gulf The Arab world: continuing economic troubles

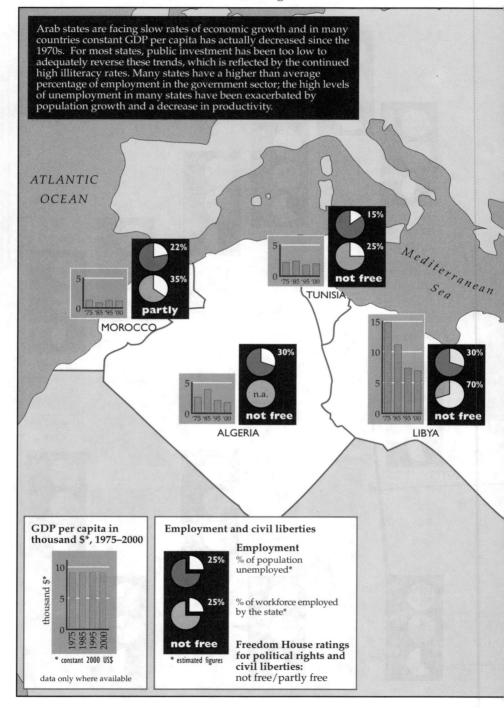

Arab states are facing slow rates of economic growth and in many countries constant GDP per capita has actually decreased since the 1970s. For most states, public investment has been too low to adequately reverse these trends, which is reflected by the continued high illiteracy rates. Many states have a higher than average percentage of employment in the government sector; the high levels of unemployment in many states have been exacerbated by population growth and a decrease in productivity.

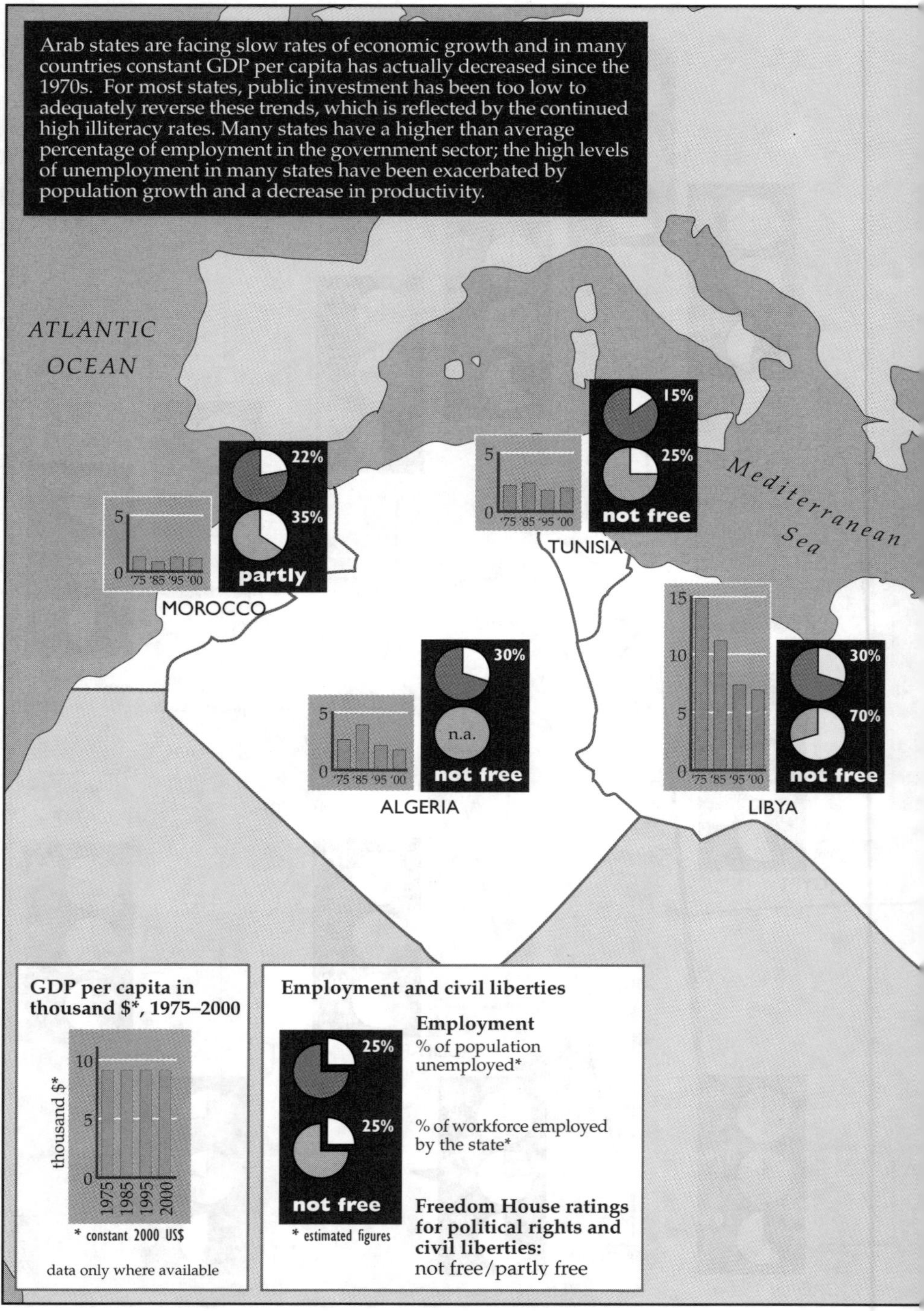

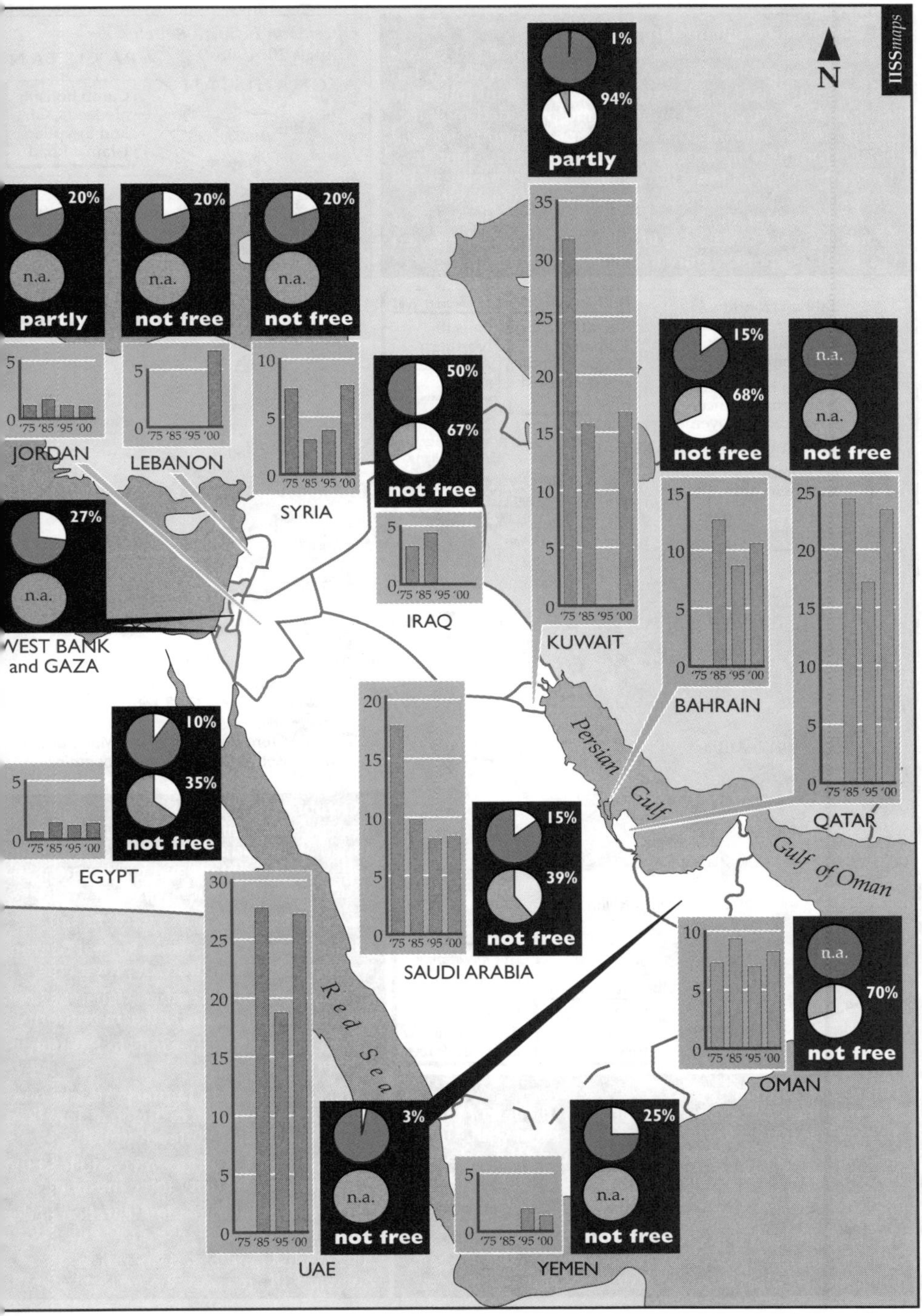
IISSmaps
N
JORDAN
20%
n.a.
partly
LEBANON
20%
n.a.
not free
SYRIA
20%
n.a.
not free
IRAQ
50%
67%
not free
KUWAIT
1%
94%
partly
BAHRAIN
15%
68%
not free
QATAR
n.a.
n.a.
not free
WEST BANK and GAZA
27%
n.a.
EGYPT
10%
35%
not free
SAUDI ARABIA
15%
39%
not free
OMAN
n.a.
70%
not free
UAE
3%
n.a.
not free
YEMEN
25%
n.a.
not free
'75 '85 '95 '00
Persian Gulf
Gulf of Oman
Red Sea

Central Asia and the Caucasus Afghanistan: from isolation to integration

Al-Qaeda and Afghanistan

After leaving Sudan in 1996, Osama bin Laden's al-Qaeda terrorist group relocated to Afghanistan. As in Sudan, bin Laden contributed funds to the leadership, bankrolled the Taliban's infrastructural projects, and provided military personnel for Taliban armed forces, presumably as a *quid pro quo* for allowing him to stay and protecting him. In 1998, after al-Qaeda was implicated in the bombing of US embassies in Nairobi and Dar es-Salaam (which killed over 200 people), the US initiated cruise missile strikes against four al-Qaeda bases in Afghanistan and a suspected chemical weapons facility in Khartoum, Sudan.

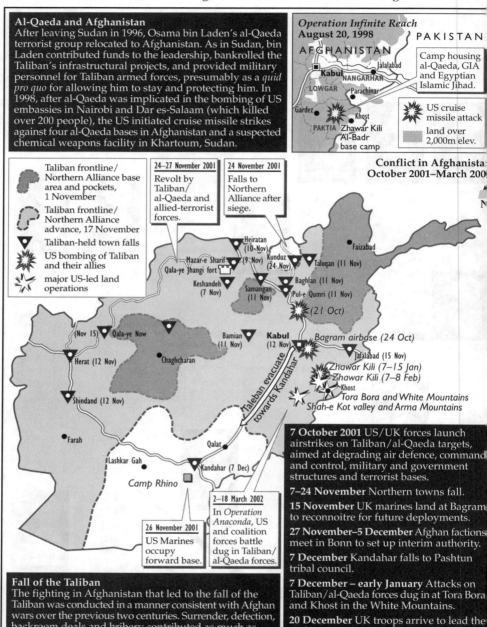

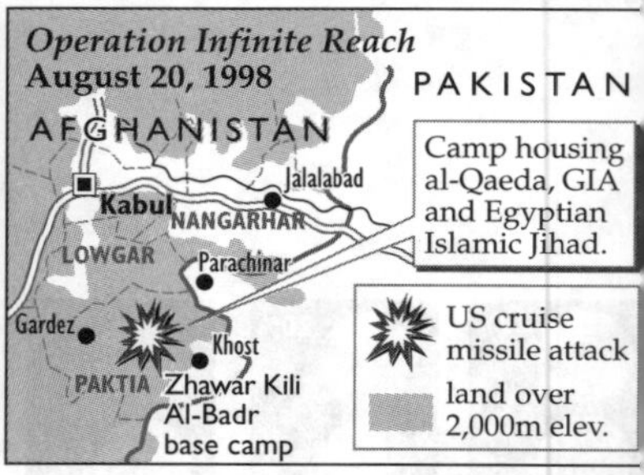

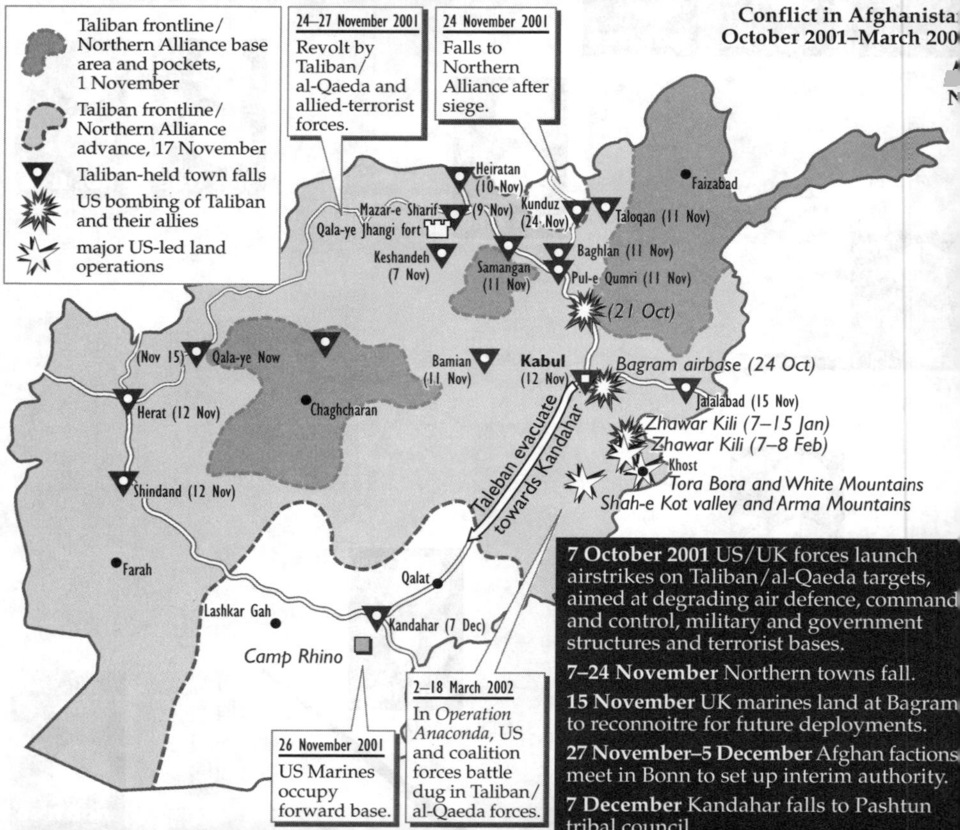

7 October 2001 US/UK forces launch airstrikes on Taliban/al-Qaeda targets, aimed at degrading air defence, command and control, military and government structures and terrorist bases.

7–24 November Northern towns fall.

15 November UK marines land at Bagram to reconnoitre for future deployments.

27 November–5 December Afghan factions meet in Bonn to set up interim authority.

7 December Kandahar falls to Pashtun tribal council.

7 December – early January Attacks on Taliban/al-Qaeda forces dug in at Tora Bora and Khost in the White Mountains.

20 December UK troops arrive to lead the multinational security force in Kabul.

22 December Interim administration under Hamid Karzai takes over in Kabul.

2002 US-led land based operations in Zhawar Kili area and Shah-e Kot valley.

Fall of the Taliban

The fighting in Afghanistan that led to the fall of the Taliban was conducted in a manner consistent with Afghan wars over the previous two centuries. Surrender, defection, backroom deals and bribery contributed as much as offensive military action. For those military operations that did take place, the turning point came when the US switched its bombing campaign to focus on hitting Taliban/al-Qaeda frontline forces. Northern Alliance gains in the period after this were extensive and swift.

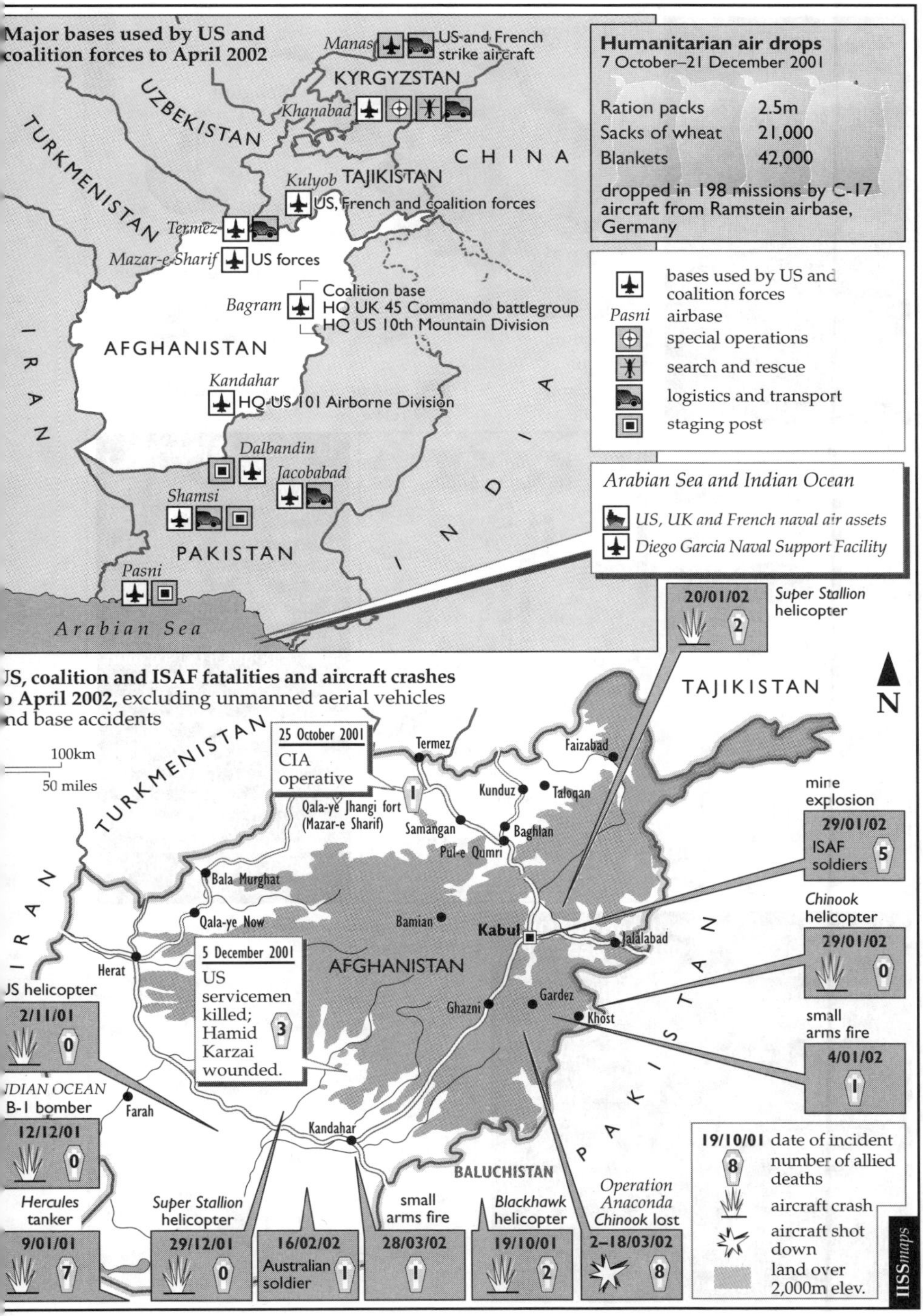
Major bases used by US and
coalition forces to April 2002
Manas
US and French
strike aircraft
KYRGYZSTAN
UZBEKISTAN
Khanabad
TURKMENISTAN
CHINA
Kulyob TAJIKISTAN
US, French and coalition forces
Termez
Mazar-e-Sharif
US forces
Bagram
Coalition base
HQ UK 45 Commando battlegroup
HQ US 10th Mountain Division
AFGHANISTAN
IRAN
Kandahar
HQ US 101 Airborne Division
INDIA
Dalbandin
Jacobabad
Shamsi
PAKISTAN
Pasni
Arabian Sea
Humanitarian air drops
7 October–21 December 2001
Ration packs 2.5m
Sacks of wheat 21,000
Blankets 42,000
dropped in 198 missions by C-17
aircraft from Ramstein airbase,
Germany
bases used by US and
coalition forces
Pasni
airbase
special operations
search and rescue
logistics and transport
staging post
Arabian Sea and Indian Ocean
US, UK and French naval air assets
Diego Garcia Naval Support Facility
US, coalition and ISAF fatalities and aircraft crashes
to April 2002, excluding unmanned aerial vehicles
and base accidents
100km
50 miles
TURKMENISTAN
25 October 2001
CIA
operative
1
Qala-ye Jhangi fort
(Mazar-e Sharif)
Termez
Faizabad
Kunduz
Taloqan
Samangan
Baghlan
Pul-e Qumri
TAJIKISTAN
N
Bala Murghat
Qala-ye Now
Bamian
Kabul
Jalalabad
Herat
5 December 2001
US
servicemen
killed;
Hamid
Karzai
wounded.
3
AFGHANISTAN
Gardez
Ghazni
Khost
IRAN
PAKISTAN
Farah
Kandahar
BALUCHISTAN
20/01/02
2
Super Stallion
helicopter
mine
explosion
29/01/02
ISAF
soldiers
5
Chinook
helicopter
29/01/02
0
small
arms fire
4/01/02
1
US helicopter
2/11/01
0
INDIAN OCEAN
B-1 bomber
12/12/01
0
Hercules
tanker
9/01/01
7
Super Stallion
helicopter
29/12/01
0
16/02/02
Australian
soldier
1
small
arms fire
28/03/02
1
Blackhawk
helicopter
19/10/01
2
Operation
Anaconda
Chinook lost
2–18/03/02
8
19/10/01 date of incident
8 number of allied
deaths
aircraft crash
aircraft shot
down
land over
2,000m elev.
IISSmaps

Central Asia and the Caucasus Afghanistan: from isolation to integration

Ethnic groups
A history of war and forced population movements has made Afghanistan a patchwork of differing ethnic groups speaking a variety of languages. These groups tend to have an external sponsor. The new interim administration has, allowing for politics, tried to combine ethnicity under the Afghan flag. The old Taliban administration was mainly Pashtun, while in the Northern Alliance, Tajiks, Uzbeks and Hazaras dominate.

Ethnic Groups

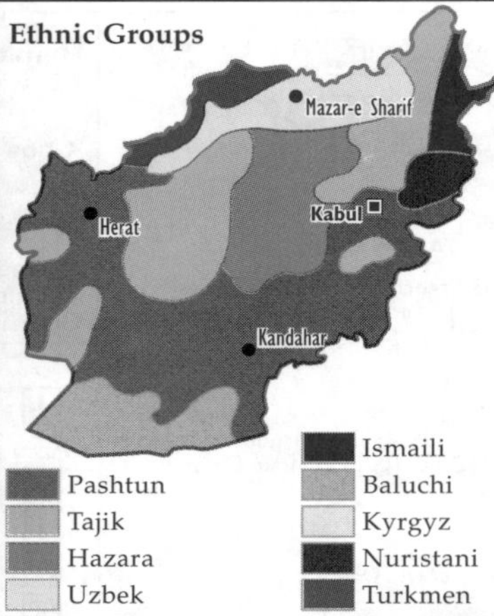

Religion

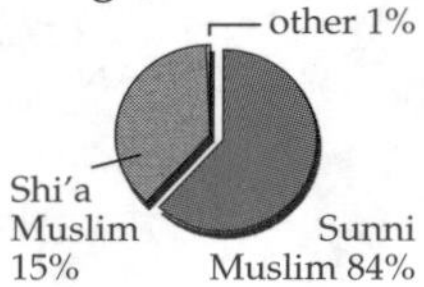

Ethnic composition

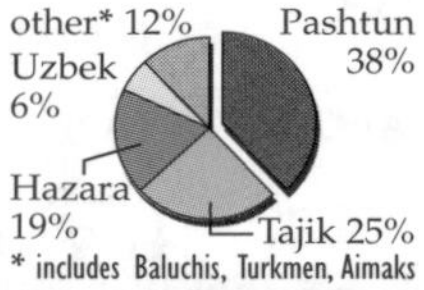

IDPs and refugees

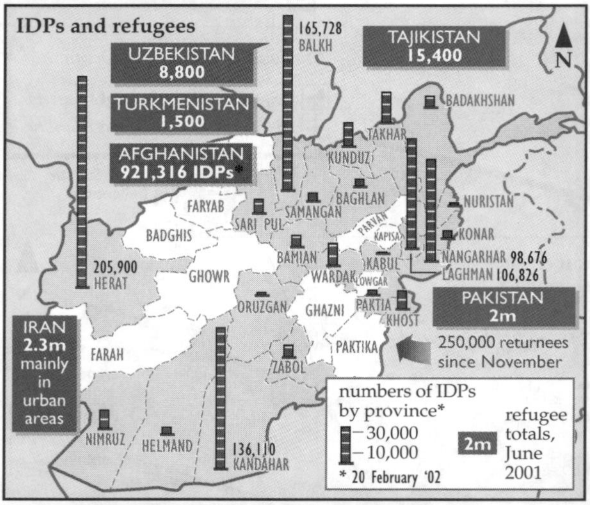

Internally-displaced persons (IDPs)
Although the US-led military action did not lead to the exodus feared by some, many Afghans have over the years sought refuge in surrounding countries, or other parts of the country as a result of war or political persecution and, in 2000, a severe drought leading to famine. With improved security and food provision, aid agencies and NGOs hope that many will return. A large number remain in surrounding countries. To encourage returnees, the UNHCR is offering cash and assistance.

Mines and unexploded ordnance (UXO)
No country is as laden with mines and other unexploded ordnance as Afghanistan. The country was heavily mined during the 1979 Soviet invasion, the factional fighting that followed, and the conflict from 7 October 2001 onwards. Landmines have proven particularly injurious, although other UXOs, such as cluster bomblets have also caused injuries. The UN's Mine Action Programme in Afghanistan (MAPA) suggests a mine/UXO casualty rate of 150–300 per month. The UN estimates that about 500 sq. km have been littered with unexploded ordnance (incl. 25,000 bomblets) since the start of the US-led military campaign; the cost of clearing Afghanistan of its mines and UXOs is estimated at $600m. The process would take roughly seven years.

Mines remaining to be cleared, as of August 2001

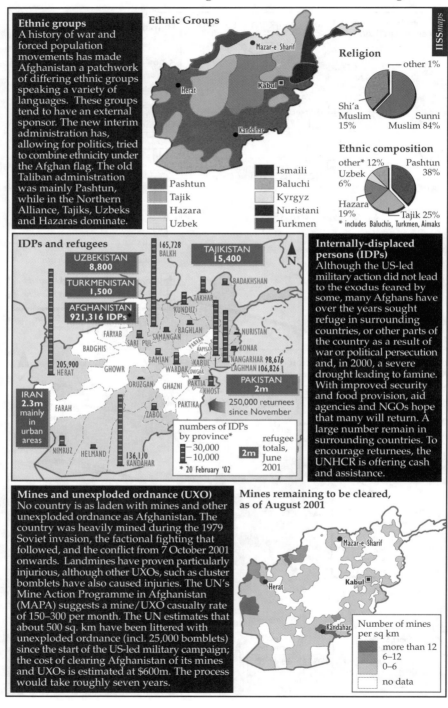

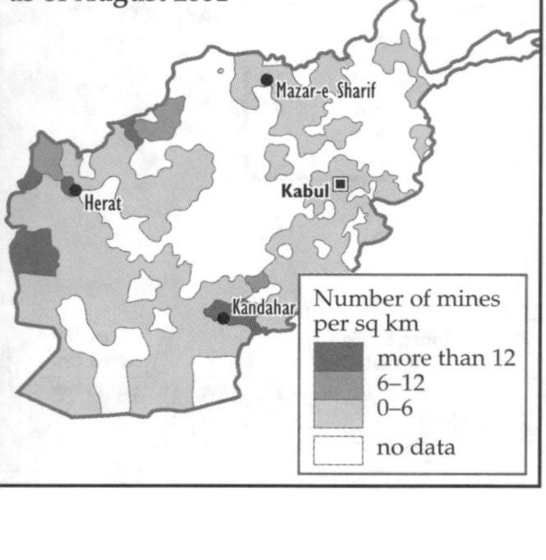

IISSmaps

Reconstruction

From 27 November–5 December 2001, Afghan factions met in Bonn with the aim of establishing a basis for governance. As a result, on 22 December, an interim administration assumed power in Kabul. This is the first step towards 'the creation of a broad-based…government', and is intended to be replaced after a *loya jirga*, or national assembly, is convened in June 2002 to establish a permanent multi-ethnic democratic government. In a bid to improve security in Kabul, an International Security Assistance Force (ISAF) was authorised to operate in the city. Throughout the country, however, disputes between warlords continue to hinder effective central authority.

Interim administration key facts

- 30 member interim administration
  - 11 Pashtuns
  - 8 Tajiks
  - 5 Hazara
  - 3 Uzbeks
  - 3 from other minorities
- Special independent commission to organise *loya jirga*, which will decide on a transitional government.This will oversee the writing of a constitution. A permanent government would be selected within two years
- Central Bank
- Supreme Court
- Judicial Commission to rebuild justice system

ISAF

On 20 December, the UN Security Council passed Resolution 1386, creating the International Security Assistance Force (ISAF), with the mandate of maintaining security 'so that the Afghan interim administration as well as the personnel of the United Nations can operate in a secure environment'.

ISAF participating nations' personnel

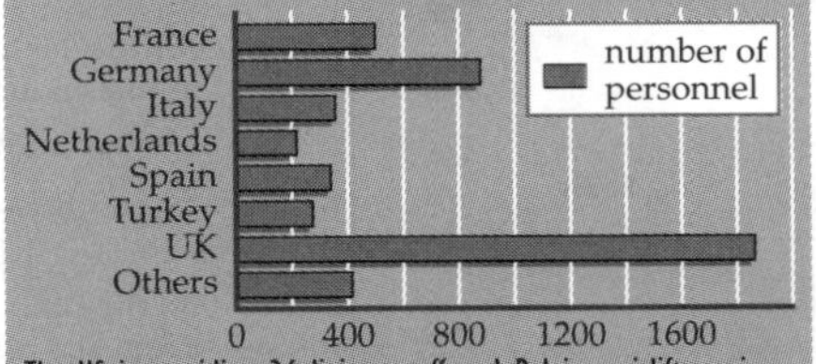

The US is providing 36 liaison staff and Belgium airlift services. Turkey may replace the UK as the lead contributor in mid-2002.

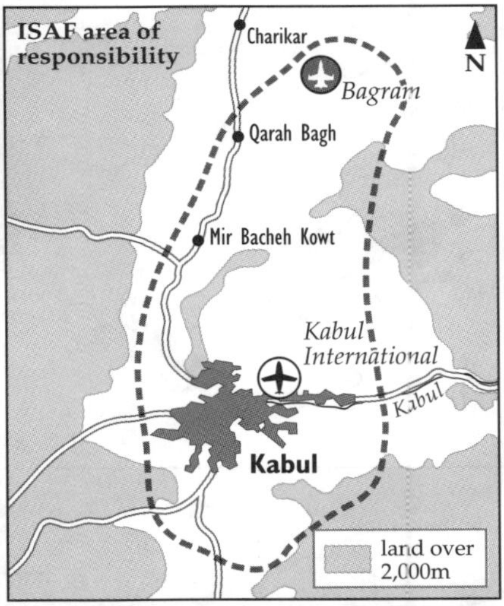

ISAF Composition

Strength	around 5,000 personnel
Force HQ	UK
Brigade HQ	UK
Two infantry battlegroups	UK, German-led battalion including Dutch, Austrians and Danes
Other infantry	France, Italy, Turkey
Recce squadron	France
Engineer group	UK, Greece, Italy, Spain
Explosive Ordnance Disposal	Denmark, France, Germany, Norway, Spain
Medical	UK, Germany, Portugal, Czech Republic
Logistics	UK, Bulgaria, France, New Zealand, Norway, Spain
Helicopter support	Germany, Spain
Military Police	UK, Germany, Romania
Other specialist troops	Finland, Italy, Sweden
Air transport support	UK, Belgium, Germany, Greece, Italy, Netherlands, Romania, Spain, Portugal

Central Asia and the Caucasus Georgia: internal disputes; external assistance

Recent disputes

Georgia is beset with secessionist disputes that date back to 1989, when South Ossetia agitated for greater autonomy. In 1991, fighting broke out, which eventually led to 1,000 deaths and a self-declaration of republican status. Although a ceasefire was declared in 1992, the dispute has yet to be resolved. Abkhaz secessionists fought for self-rule from 1992–1993. Following a 1993 treaty, the UN has maintained a monitoring force in Sukhumi, and Russian peacekeepers have been deployed under a CIS mandate. In recent statements, the US has stressed that it views Abkhazia as an integral part of Georgia.

Georgian relations with Russia remain tense, particularly in the light of the ongoing Chechen war and the remaining Russian military bases. Last year, after Russian pressure, Georgia acknowledged that Chechen guerillas may be sheltering in the eastern Pankisi gorge. Following 11 September, and allegations of an al-Qaeda presence in the Pankisi gorge, the Georgians have started to address this issue, although to the Russians' chagrin, they have chosen to accept further US, rather than Russian, military assistance to improve anti-terrorist capability.

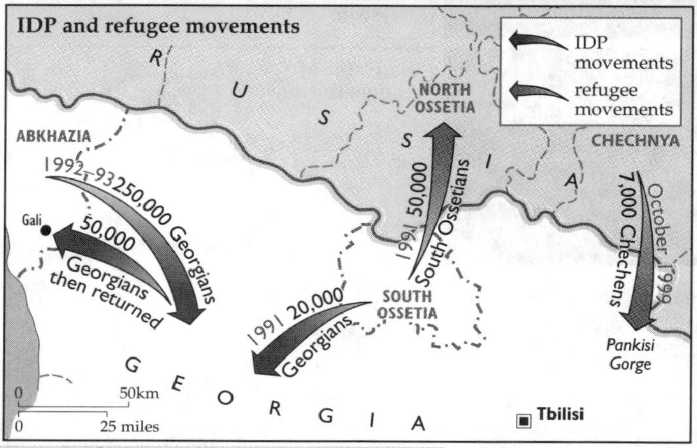

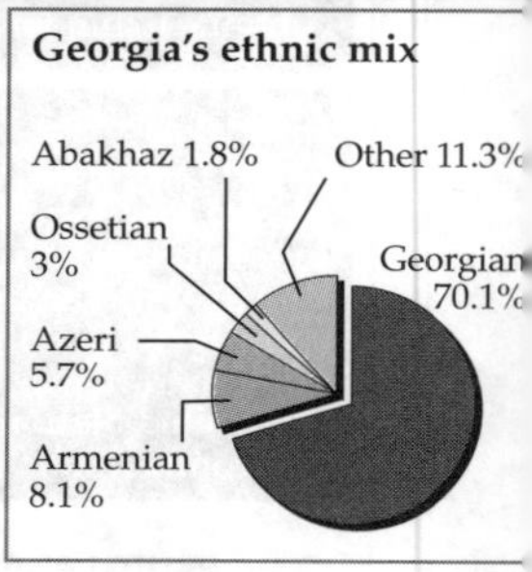

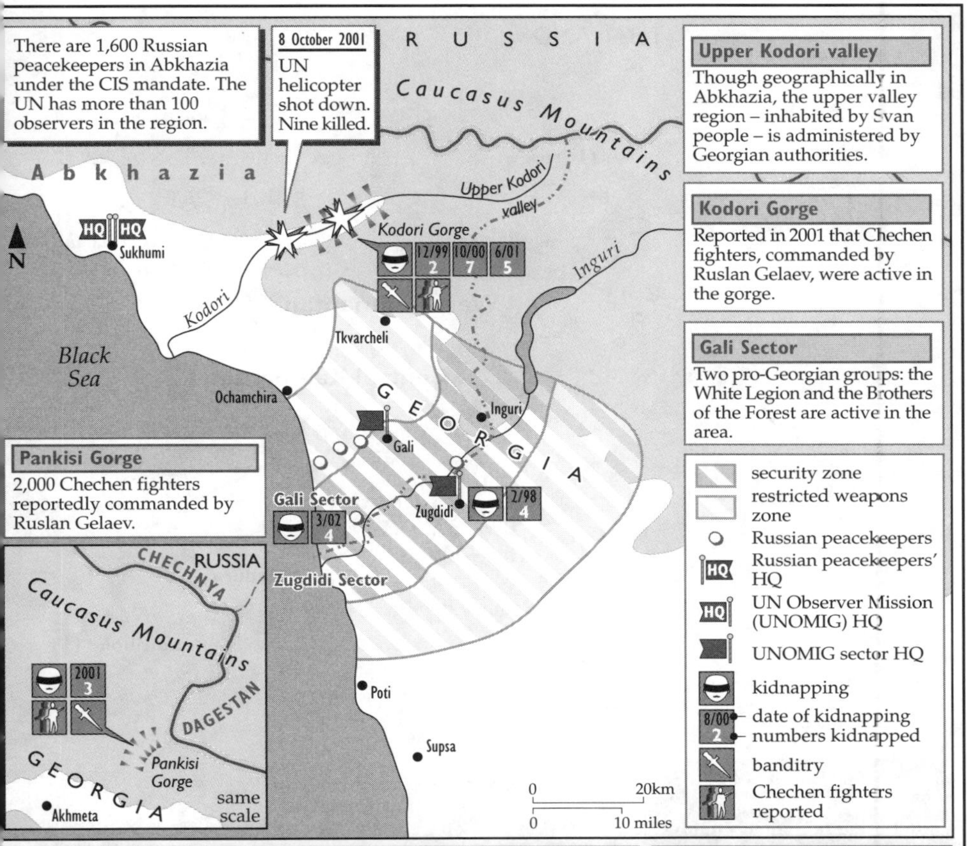
There are 1,600 Russian peacekeepers in Abkhazia under the CIS mandate. The UN has more than 100 observers in the region.
8 October 2001
UN helicopter shot down. Nine killed.
RUSSIA
Caucasus Mountains
Upper Kodori valley
Though geographically in Abkhazia, the upper valley region – inhabited by Svan people – is administered by Georgian authorities.
Abkhazia
Upper Kodori valley
HQ HQ
Sukhumi
N
Kodori Gorge
12/99 2
10/00 7
6/01 5
Kodori Gorge
Reported in 2001 that Chechen fighters, commanded by Ruslan Gelaev, were active in the gorge.
Inguri
Kodori
Tkvarcheli
Black Sea
Gali Sector
Two pro-Georgian groups: the White Legion and the Brothers of the Forest are active in the area.
Ochamchira
GEORGIA
Inguri
Gali
Pankisi Gorge
2,000 Chechen fighters reportedly commanded by Ruslan Gelaev.
Gali Sector
3/02 4
Zugdidi
2/98 4
Zugdidi Sector
RUSSIA
CHECHNYA
Caucasus Mountains
DAGESTAN
2001 3
Pankisi Gorge
GEORGIA
Akhmeta
same scale
Poti
Supsa
0 20km
0 10 miles
security zone
restricted weapons zone
Russian peacekeepers
Russian peacekeepers' HQ
UN Observer Mission (UNOMIG) HQ
UNOMIG sector HQ
kidnapping
8/00 2
date of kidnapping
numbers kidnapped
banditry
Chechen fighters reported

US military assistance

The US is keen to support Georgia as part of the war on terror and also because of its important commercial and strategic position *vis-à-vis* Caspian energy sources. Further, it is a useful transit route for military hardware to the nascent, and possibly long-term US military bases in Uzbekistan and Kyrgyzstan. The US–Georgian military training relationship dates back to 1996. The US has announced a substantial increase to the $11m initialed for Georgia's military in FY2002, and is to train Georgian troops for anti-terror operations, particularly aimed at the Pankisi gorge.

US assistance	date	detail
10 UH-1 *Huey* helicopters	Nov '01	delivered six operational and four for spares under a 1999 deal. Based in Tbilisi.
200 US military advisers	Feb '02	to train Georgian 11Bde in anti-terrorist actions. Costing $64m. Five US advisers flew to Tbilisi late February, remainder by late April.
$4.5m	FY2001	From the US Foreign Military Financing Budget (totalled $3.54bn).

Nuclear residues – how much is left?

The fate of unsecured, or 'orphan' sources of radiation in Georgia is of concern to the international community, particularly post-11 September. Georgia recognises the problem, and is cooperating with the International Atomic Energy Authority (IAEA) in the recovery of discovered sources. Most date from the Soviet era, and there is a severe dearth of relevant records. Georgia does not have nuclear power plants, but has research institutes in Tbilisi and Sukhumi. Another, in Mtskheta, closed in 1990. Georgia has also been used as a transshipment point for illicit materials from other countries.

Asia Indonesia: further violence and population movements

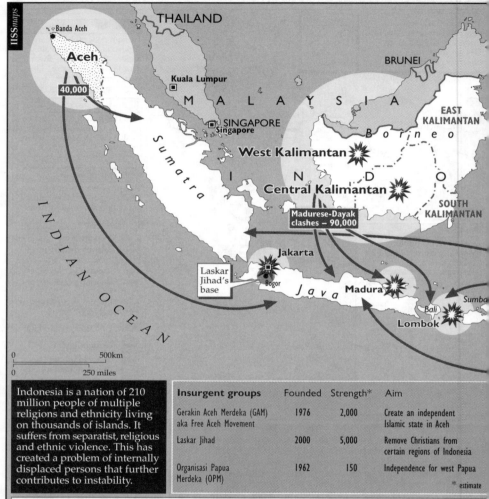

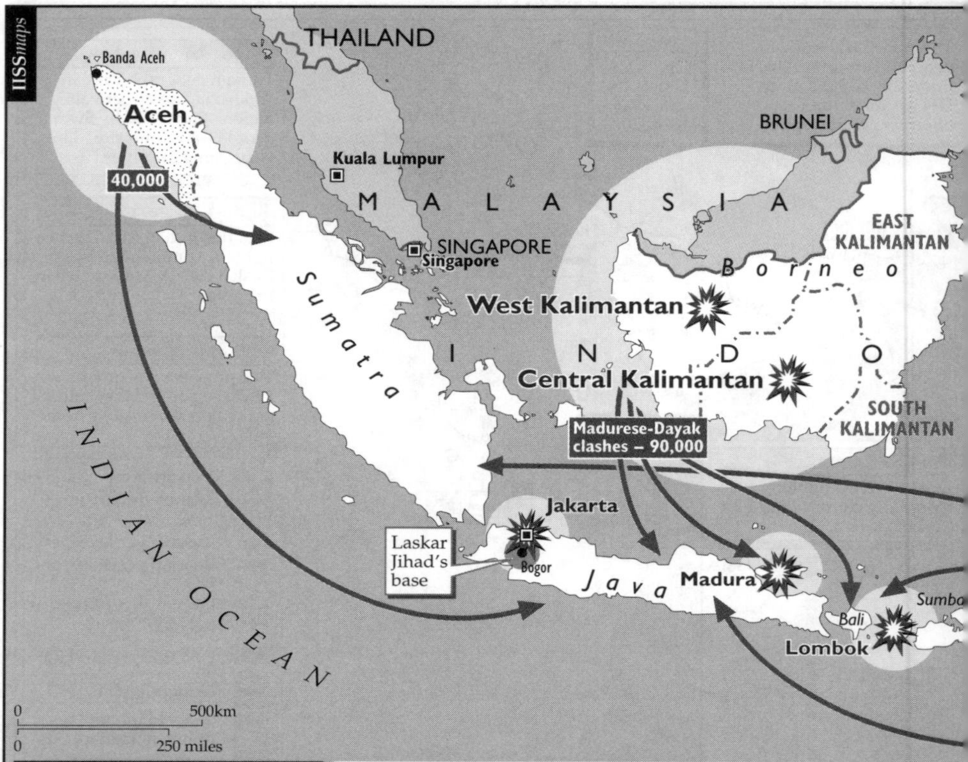

Indonesia is a nation of 210 million people of multiple religions and ethnicity living on thousands of islands. It suffers from separatist, religious and ethnic violence. This has created a problem of internally displaced persons that further contributes to instability.

Insurgent groups	Founded	Strength*	Aim
Gerakin Aceh Merdeka (GAM) aka Free Aceh Movement	1976	2,000	Create an independent Islamic state in Aceh
Laskar Jihad	2000	5,000	Remove Christians from certain regions of Indonesia
Organisasi Papua Merdeka (OPM)	1962	150	Independence for west Papua

* estimate

Aceh

In clashes between separatist rebels and government forces an estimated 1,000 people were killed in Aceh during 2001, despite President Megawati's decree providing for a measure of autonomy for the province, the right to adopt *sharia* law and a 70% share of the province's oil and gas revenues.

Officials believe that there are links between Abu Sayyaf rebels operating in the Philippines and the separatists in Aceh province.

Moluccas

Since January 1999 over 5,000 people are estimated to have been killed in the Moluccas. Laskar Jihad sent thousands of fighters there during 2000, causing a major escalation in violence. They have rejected the 12 February 2002 peace deal.

Sulawesi

1,000 people were killed in Muslim-Christian violence in Sulawesi, mainly in Poso after thousands of Laskar Jihad militants arrived on the island during November 2001.

Lombok

Christian-Muslims clashes. Fuelled, in January 2001 by a fued between two villages, Bangor and Parampuan.

Kalimantan

Scene of some of the worst ethnic violence against Muslims in Indonesia during the late 1990s. Violence has also occurred between the Dayak and Madurese minorities. 40% of West Kalimantan's population are Dayaks.

Irian Jaya

The movement for independence began in 1969, when Irian Jaya became an eastern province of Indonesia in a UN-endorsed process that was opposed by many west Papuans.

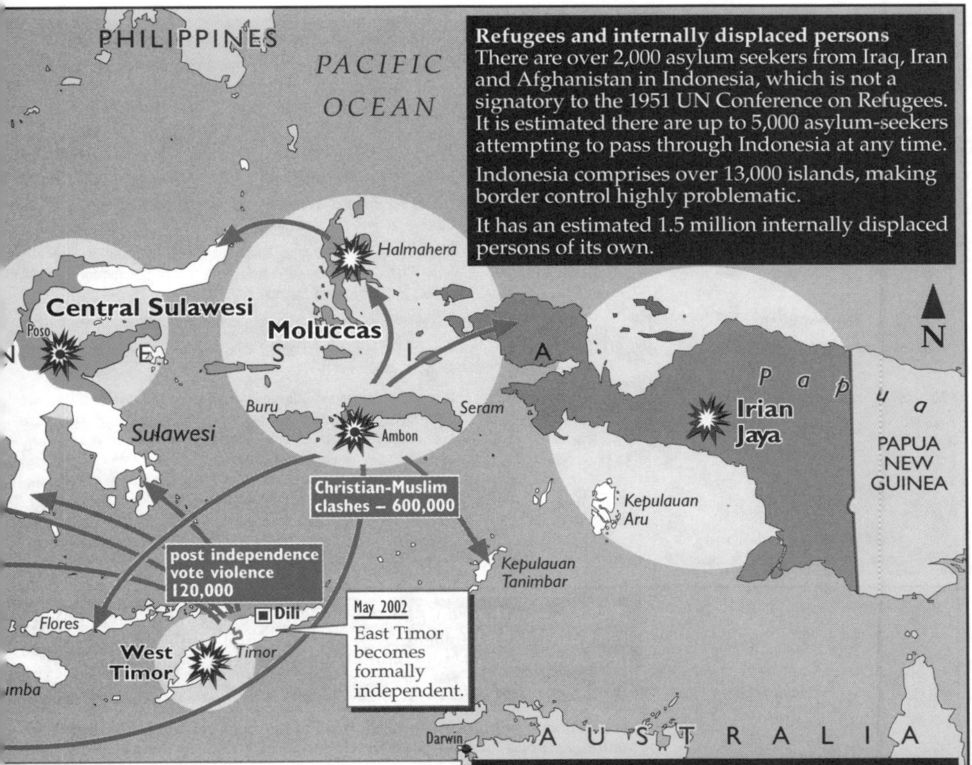

Refugees and internally displaced persons

There are over 2,000 asylum seekers from Iraq, Iran and Afghanistan in Indonesia, which is not a signatory to the 1951 UN Conference on Refugees. It is estimated there are up to 5,000 asylum-seekers attempting to pass through Indonesia at any time.

Indonesia comprises over 13,000 islands, making border control highly problematic.

It has an estimated 1.5 million internally displaced persons of its own.

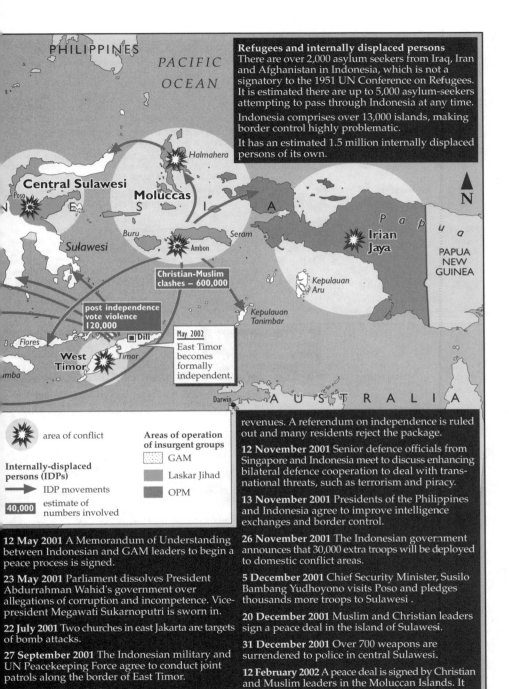

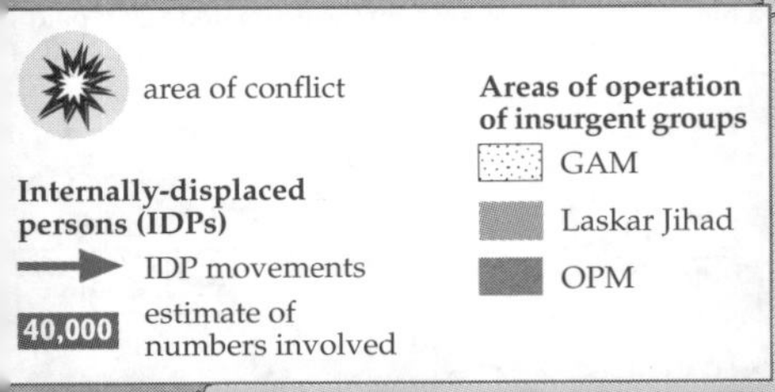

12 May 2001 A Memorandum of Understanding between Indonesian and GAM leaders to begin a peace process is signed.

23 May 2001 Parliament dissolves President Abdurrahman Wahid's government over allegations of corruption and incompetence. Vice-president Megawati Sukarnoputri is sworn in.

22 July 2001 Two churches in east Jakarta are targets of bomb attacks.

27 September 2001 The Indonesian military and UN Peacekeeping Force agree to conduct joint patrols along the border of East Timor.

23 October 2001 Parliament passes an autonomy bill to give Irian Jaya larger shares of resource revenues. A referendum on independence is ruled out and many residents reject the package.

12 November 2001 Senior defence officials from Singapore and Indonesia meet to discuss enhancing bilateral defence cooperation to deal with trans-national threats, such as terrorism and piracy.

13 November 2001 Presidents of the Philippines and Indonesia agree to improve intelligence exchanges and border control.

26 November 2001 The Indonesian government announces that 30,000 extra troops will be deployed to domestic conflict areas.

5 December 2001 Chief Security Minister, Susilo Bambang Yudhoyono visits Poso and pledges thousands more troops to Sulawesi .

20 December 2001 Muslim and Christian leaders sign a peace deal in the island of Sulawesi.

31 December 2001 Over 700 weapons are surrendered to police in central Sulawesi.

12 February 2002 A peace deal is signed by Christian and Muslim leaders in the Moluccan Islands. It calls for groups to surrender weapons and requires active groups from outside the region to leave.

Asia A closer US–Philippines relationship

Insurgent group	Founded	Strength	Active area	Objectives (where known) and detail
New People's Army (NPA)	1969	8,000+	Rural Luzon, Visayas and Mindanao	To overthrow Philippines government. Armed wing of Communist Party of the Philippines (CPP). Ended peace talks with government after 199 Philippine–US agreement to resume military exercises
Moro National Liberation Front (MNLF)	1970s		Sulu Islands, Tawi-Tawi and Marawi area, Zamboanga peninsula	Signed abortive Tripoli peace deal in 1976; another in 1996. Led by Nu Misuari who signed 1996 deal and became governor of the ARMM. Misua was deposed in April 2001 with a 15-member council assuming leadershi
Bangsa Moro Army	1970s	10,000+	Southern Philippines	Muslim separatist movement. Armed wing of MNLF. Reneged on a 1996 peace deal with the government
Moro Islamic Liberation Front (MILF)	1978	15,000+	Southern Philippines, Manila, Mindanao	Independent Islamic state in Bangsamoro and neighbouring islands. (Spli from MNLF in 1977; signed ceasefire with Manila government on 7 Augus 2000.) Led by Hashim Salamat
Moro Islamic Reformist Group	1978	200+	Southern Philippines	Independent Islamic state in southern Philippines. Split from MNLF
Alex Boncayao Brigade (ABB)	1980s	500	Manila, central Philippines	Urban hit squad of CPP. Claimed alliance with the Revolutionary Proletaria Army in 1997
Abu Sayyaf Group (ASG)	1991	500+	Southern Philippines, Jolo, Basilan, offshore activities	Ostensibly independent Islamic state in west Mindanao and Sulu, now often kidnap for ransom and murder. Group named after former bin Laden comrade. Reported links with al-Qaeda cover finance, training, equipment and connections with Ramzi Youssef, the 1993 World Trade Center bomber. Group presently split into two virtually independent sections: first based on Jolo, affiliated with renegade MNLF chairman Nu Misuari, and led by Galib Andang ('Commander Robot'); second based on Basilan led by Aldam Tilao ('Abu Sabaya'). Other factions, inactive in recent years, based near Zamboanga. Many members ex-MNLF.

AFP Armed Forces of the Philippines
CPP Communist Party of the Philippines

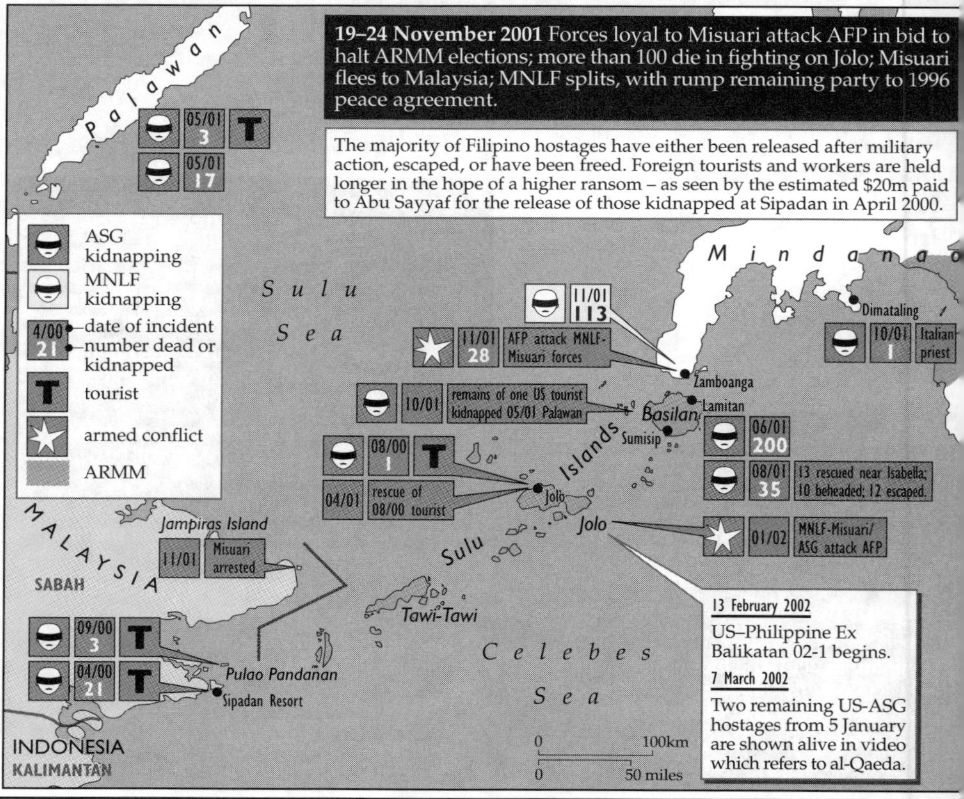
19–24 November 2001 Forces loyal to Misuari attack AFP in bid to halt ARMM elections; more than 100 die in fighting on Jolo; Misuari flees to Malaysia; MNLF splits, with rump remaining party to 1996 peace agreement.
The majority of Filipino hostages have either been released after military action, escaped, or have been freed. Foreign tourists and workers are held longer in the hope of a higher ransom – as seen by the estimated $20m paid to Abu Sayyaf for the release of those kidnapped at Sipadan in April 2000.
Palawan
05/01 3
05/01 17
ASG kidnapping
MNLF kidnapping
4/00 21 date of incident number dead or kidnapped
tourist
armed conflict
ARMM
Sulu Sea
Mindanao
11/01 113
11/01 28 AFP attack MNLF-Misuari forces
Dimataling
10/01 1 Italian priest
Zamboanga
10/01 remains of one US tourist kidnapped 05/01 Palawan
Basilan
Lamitan
Sumisip
06/01 200
08/01 35 13 rescued near Isabella; 10 beheaded; 12 escaped.
08/00 1
04/01 rescue of 08/00 tourist
Sulu Islands
Jolo
01/02 MNLF-Misuari/ ASG attack AFP
MALAYSIA
SABAH
Jampiras Island
11/01 Misuari arrested
Tawi-Tawi
09/00 3
04/00 21
Pulao Pandanan
Sipadan Resort
Celebes Sea
INDONESIA
KALIMANTAN
0 100km
0 50 miles
13 February 2002
US–Philippine Ex Balikatan 02-1 begins.
7 March 2002
Two remaining US-ASG hostages from 5 January are shown alive in video which refers to al-Qaeda.

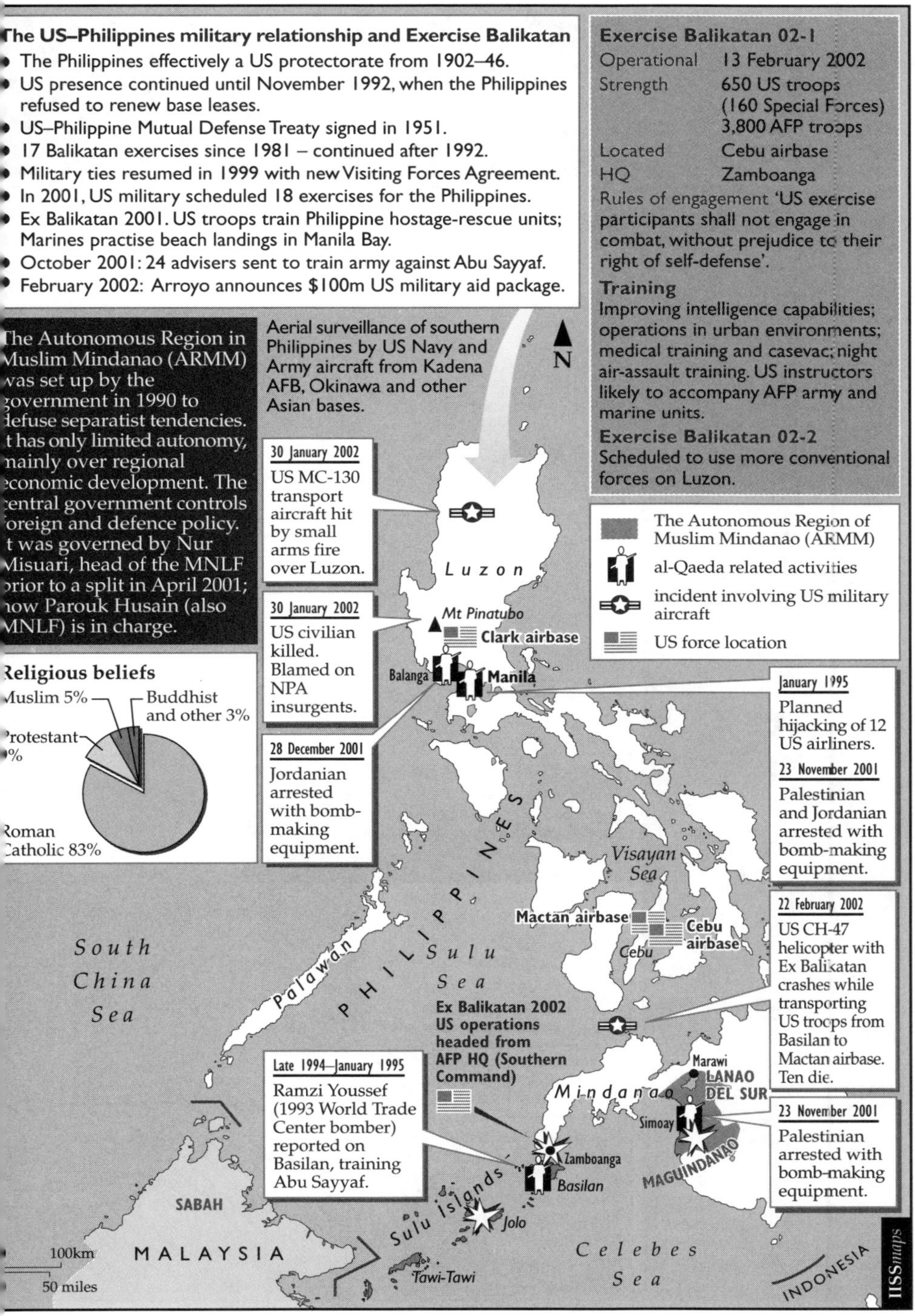

The US–Philippines military relationship and Exercise Balikatan
The Philippines effectively a US protectorate from 1902–46.
US presence continued until November 1992, when the Philippines refused to renew base leases.
US–Philippine Mutual Defense Treaty signed in 1951.
17 Balikatan exercises since 1981 – continued after 1992.
Military ties resumed in 1999 with new Visiting Forces Agreement.
In 2001, US military scheduled 18 exercises for the Philippines.
Ex Balikatan 2001. US troops train Philippine hostage-rescue units; Marines practise beach landings in Manila Bay.
October 2001: 24 advisers sent to train army against Abu Sayyaf.
February 2002: Arroyo announces $100m US military aid package.
Exercise Balikatan 02-1
Operational 13 February 2002
Strength 650 US troops (160 Special Forces) 3,800 AFP troops
Located Cebu airbase
HQ Zamboanga
Rules of engagement 'US exercise participants shall not engage in combat, without prejudice to their right of self-defense'.
Training
Improving intelligence capabilities; operations in urban environments; medical training and casevac; night air-assault training. US instructors likely to accompany AFP army and marine units.
Exercise Balikatan 02-2
Scheduled to use more conventional forces on Luzon.
The Autonomous Region in Muslim Mindanao (ARMM) was set up by the government in 1990 to defuse separatist tendencies. It has only limited autonomy, mainly over regional economic development. The central government controls foreign and defence policy. It was governed by Nur Misuari, head of the MNLF prior to a split in April 2001; now Parouk Husain (also MNLF) is in charge.
Aerial surveillance of southern Philippines by US Navy and Army aircraft from Kadena AFB, Okinawa and other Asian bases.
N
30 January 2002
US MC-130 transport aircraft hit by small arms fire over Luzon.
30 January 2002
US civilian killed. Blamed on NPA insurgents.
28 December 2001
Jordanian arrested with bomb-making equipment.
The Autonomous Region of Muslim Mindanao (ARMM)
al-Qaeda related activities
incident involving US military aircraft
US force location
Religious beliefs
Muslim 5%
Buddhist and other 3%
Protestant
Roman Catholic 83%
Luzon
Mt Pinatubo
Clark airbase
Balanga
Manila
January 1995
Planned hijacking of 12 US airliners.
23 November 2001
Palestinian and Jordanian arrested with bomb-making equipment.
PHILIPPINES
Visayan Sea
Mactan airbase
Cebu airbase
Cebu
22 February 2002
US CH-47 helicopter with Ex Balikatan crashes while transporting US troops from Basilan to Mactan airbase. Ten die.
South China Sea
Palawan
Sulu Sea
Ex Balikatan 2002 US operations headed from AFP HQ (Southern Command)
Late 1994–January 1995
Ramzi Youssef (1993 World Trade Center bomber) reported on Basilan, training Abu Sayyaf.
Mindanao
Marawi
LANAO DEL SUR
Simoay
MAGUINDANAO
23 November 2001
Palestinian arrested with bomb-making equipment.
Zamboanga
Basilan
Sulu Islands
Jolo
SABAH
MALAYSIA
Tawi-Tawi
Celebes Sea
INDONESIA
100km
50 miles
IISSmaps

Africa Continued ethnic and economic problems in Nigeria

Nigeria is Sub-Saharan Africa's most populous state and its leading oil producer. During 1999 Nigeria made the transition to an elected civilian government. However, corruption, ethnic violence, high levels of external debt and government overspending remain rife. Oil accounts for nearly 80% of government revenues, 90–95% of export revenues and 46% of GDP. This overdependence on the oil sector has meant that Nigeria has fallen short of its potential economic strength, especially in the agricultural sector. Regional economic difficulties have also fuelled tensions between various ethnic groups, heightened since 2000 when a number of states began to adopt *sharia* law.

Key dates

29 May 1999 Olusegun Obasanjo sworn in as Nigeria's elected President.

June 1999 Re-admitted as a member of the Commonwealth after being suspended in November 1995. EU restores full economic cooperation.

November 1999 Troops attack the village of Odi after the killing of 12 soldiers.

15 October 2000 Violence erupts after six Yorubas killed by policemen in Ilorin.

12 October 2001 16 soldiers killed by militia in Zaki Biam after being sent to quell violence between two local tribes – Tivs and Jukuns.

October 2001 Clashes between Nigerian soldiers and communities in Benue state leave 200 dead. Zaki Biam claimed to have been damaged by army shelling.

24 October 2001 13 people killed during student protest in Makurdi.

7 December 2001 President Obasanjo endorses a law revising the election timetable. All polls are to be held on same day in March 2003.

10–11 December 2001 Nigerian government and community leaders from Delta Region convene in Port Harcourt for a conference aimed at creating an improved environment for development.

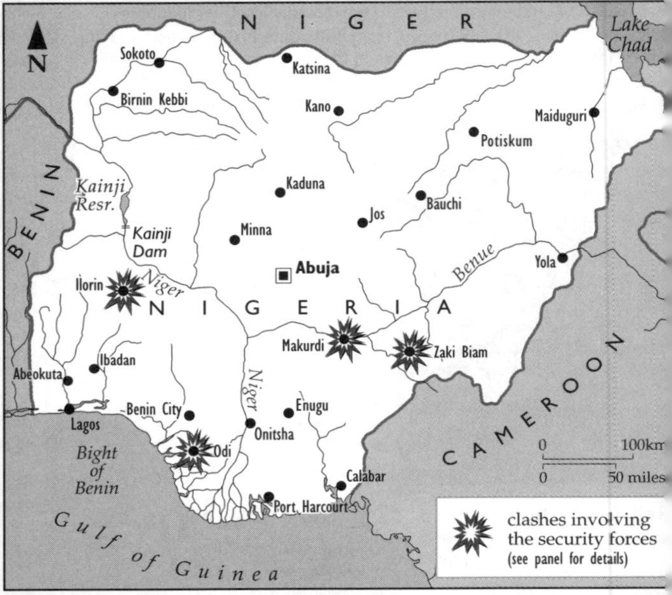

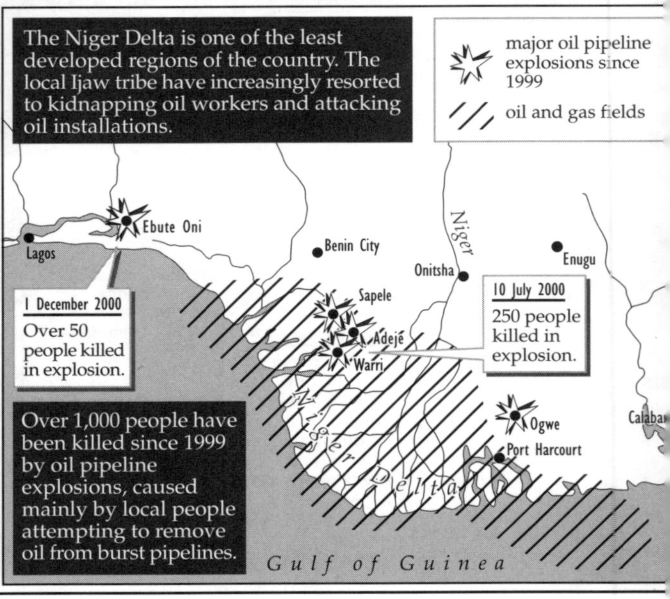

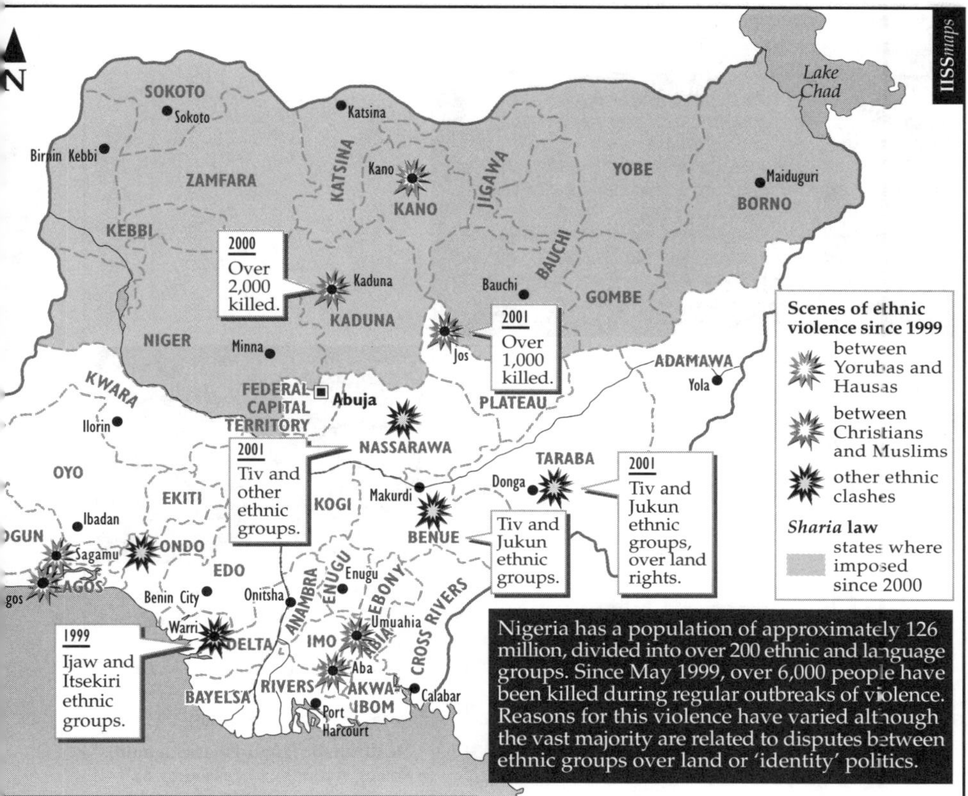

IISSmaps
N
Lake Chad
SOKOTO
Sokoto
Katsina
Birnin Kebbi
ZAMFARA
KATSINA
Kano
KANO
JIGAWA
YOBE
Maiduguri
BORNO
KEBBI
2000
Over 2,000 killed.
Kaduna
KADUNA
Bauchi
BAUCHI
GOMBE
NIGER
Minna
Jos
2001
Over 1,000 killed.
ADAMAWA
Yola
KWARA
FEDERAL CAPITAL TERRITORY
Abuja
PLATEAU
Ilorin
NASSARAWA
2001
Tiv and other ethnic groups.
TARABA
OYO
EKITI
KOGI
Makurdi
Donga
2001
Tiv and Jukun ethnic groups, over land rights.
Ibadan
BENUE
Tiv and Jukun ethnic groups.
OGUN
Sagamu
ONDO
EDO
Enugu
ENUGU
EBONYI
ANAMBRA
LAGOS
Lagos
Benin City
Onitsha
Warri
DELTA
IMO
Umuahia
ABIA
CROSS RIVERS
1999
Ijaw and Itsekiri ethnic groups.
Aba
RIVERS
AKWA-IBOM
Calabar
BAYELSA
Port Harcourt
Scenes of ethnic violence since 1999
between Yorubas and Hausas
between Christians and Muslims
other ethnic clashes
Sharia law
states where imposed since 2000
Nigeria has a population of approximately 126 million, divided into over 200 ethnic and language groups. Since May 1999, over 6,000 people have been killed during regular outbreaks of violence. Reasons for this violence have varied although the vast majority are related to disputes between ethnic groups over land or 'identity' politics.
Growth has currently slowed down due to restricted oil production to meet OPEC quotas. These are expected to rise in 2003.
Annual growth
Nigeria
Sub-Saharan Africa
Real GDP growth, 2000–2003
annual % growth
0
1
2
3
4
5
2000
2001
2002
2003
Ethnic divisions
Tiv 2%
Other 12%
Ibibio 4%
Kanuri 4%
Ijaw 10%
Ibo (Igbo) 18%
Hausa and Fulani 29%
Yoruba 21%
Religious beliefs
Indigenous beliefs 10%
Christian 40%
Muslim 50%

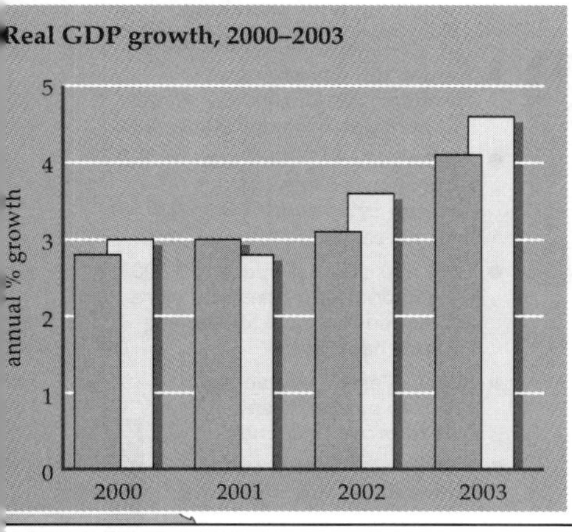

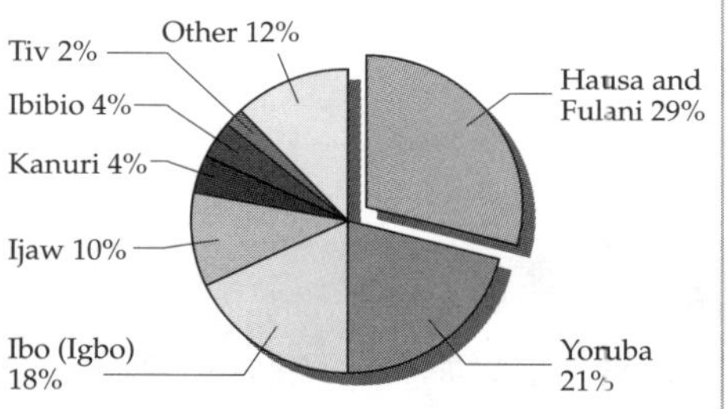

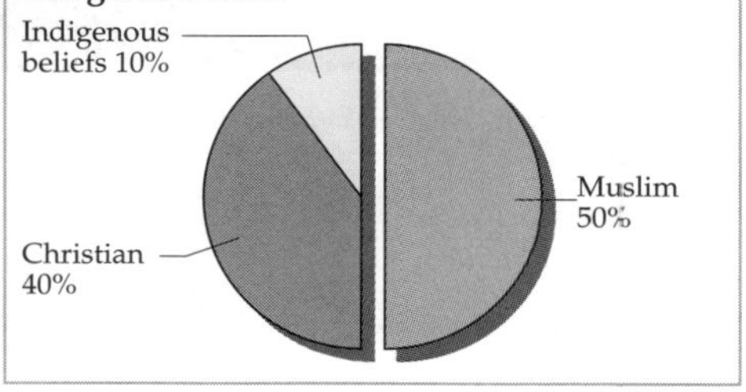

Africa Zimbabwe's election: free and fair?

Presidential election 9–11 March 2002

There has been disagreement over the election results, and the electoral processes used. Prior to late-10 March, the total voter turnout had been estimated at 2.4m; after 10 March the Registrar-General (Tobaiwa Mudede) raised the estimate to 2.9m. There are also discrepancies between the totals for constituency results, as released by the government's Electoral Supervisory Commission and the official constituency voting figures released by Mudede. In the aftermath of the election, Zimbabwe has been suspended from the Commonwealth, EU sanctions have been imposed, and the US does not recognise the result.

GDP and inflation

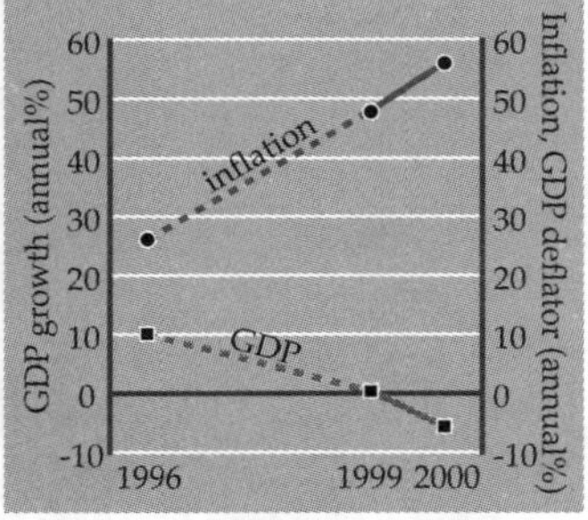

Election result 2002

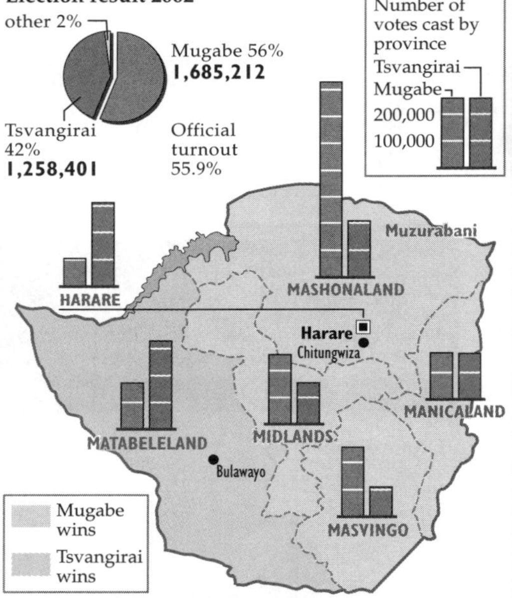

Electoral roll confusion

After four court orders, the Zimbabwe Civil Education Trust saw Zimbabwe's electoral roll, and reported the total of eligible voters as 5.2m. The electoral roll released just before the 2002 election contained 5,612,272 eligible voters.

A tale of two constituencies

Chitungwiza (MDC stronghold)

Polling stations	halved in places	
Election results	Mugabe	6,855
	Tsvangirai	16,901
Votes cast (Mudede total)		24,005

Muzurabani (Zanu-PF stronghold)

Polling stations	increased by 82% up to 51	
Election results	Mugabe	25,260
	Tsvangirai	3,463
Votes cast (Mudede total)		29,535

Speed of voting In the Harare township of Kuwadzana – less than 35 people per hour processed.

Meanwhile...

Zimbabwe's continuing economic crisis is now joined by a food crisis, largely as a result of a drop in agricultural production following the seizure of commercial white-owned farmland, compounded by drought. South Africa, and NGOs, have started to deliver food shipments to a country once able to export an agricultural surplus.

- Harare and Chitungwiza constituencies: 880,000 registered; 167 polling stations; 439,600 voted
- Additional 644 polling stations in rural areas; polling stations reduced by up to 50% in many urban areas
- Only 430 out of proposed 12,500 trained domestic observers were accredited for the 4,500 polling stations nationwide
- In urban areas, people had to produce passports and utility bills to prove residency
- Postal votes limited to the armed forces and diplomats.

Staple and cash crop production, 1997–01

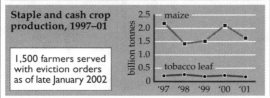

1,500 farmers served with eviction orders as of late January 2002

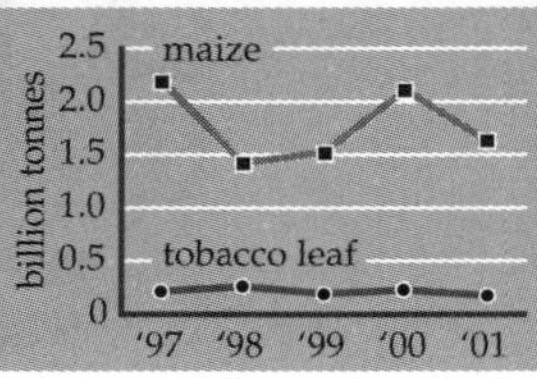

IISS*maps*

Global Trends Weapons of mass destruction: nuclear

On 5 December 2001, the US and Russia claimed that they had met the 1991 Strategic Arms Reduction Treaty I (START I) deadline. This reduced numbers of strategic nuclear warheads held by each side to 6,000 or below (Russia claimed to have 5,518 and the US 5,949).

Over the next decade the US aims to make further reductions of strategic warheads to 1,700–2,200 and the Russians to 1,500–2,200.

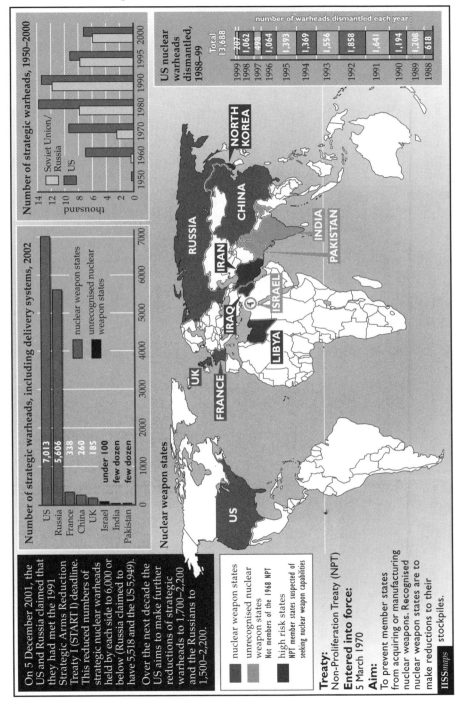

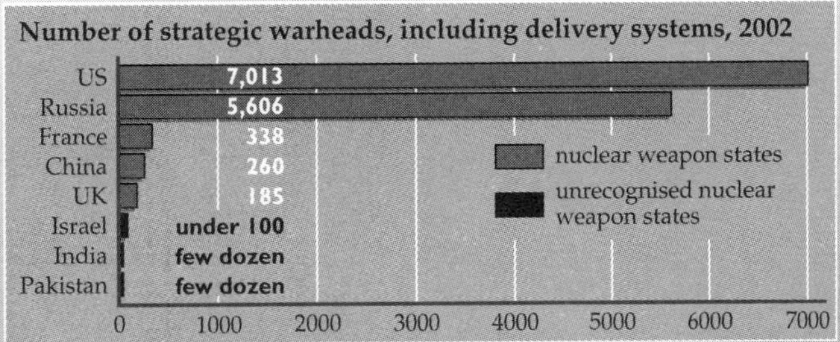

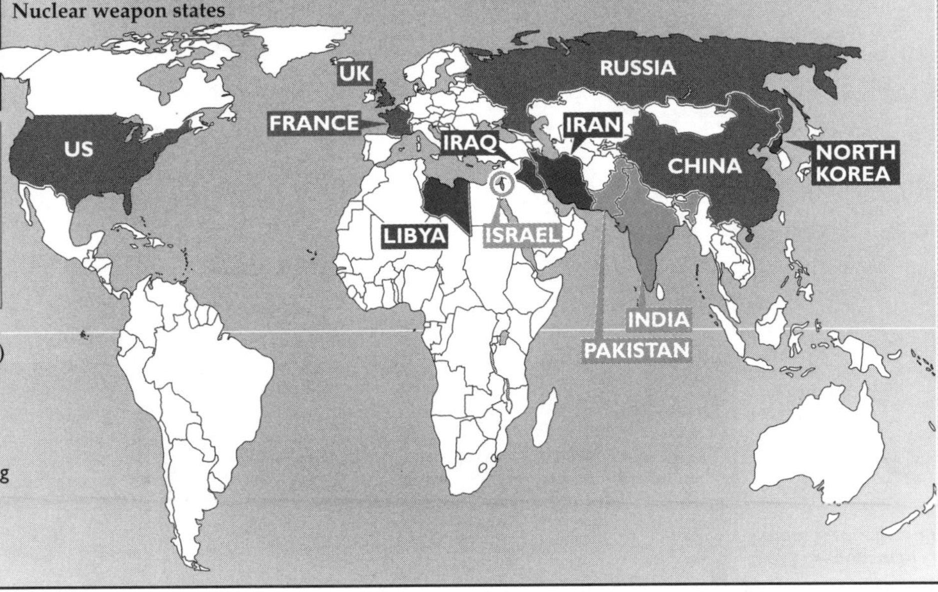

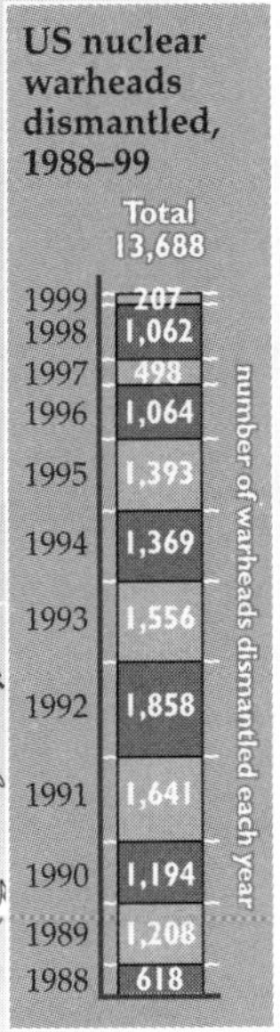

- nuclear weapon states
- unrecognised nuclear weapon states
  Not members of the 1968 NPT
- high risk states
  NPT member states suspected of seeking nuclear weapon capabilities

Treaty:
Non-Proliferation Treaty (NPT)

Entered into force:
5 March 1970

Aim:
To prevent member states from acquiring or manufacturing nuclear weapons. Recognised nuclear weapon states are to make reductions to their stockpiles.

IISS*maps*

Global Trends Weapons of mass destruction: biological

Biological weapons (BW) are any infectious microbial or biological agents or toxins such as a bacteria or viruses used intentionally to spread disease among humans, animals or plants. The Biological Weapons Convention (BWC) prohibits the development of such weapons and equipment for their delivery in quantities which have no justification for peaceful purposes.

In July 2001, the US rejected the draft protocol to the BWC which was to be presented at the fifth review conference. This would have established a verification system similar to that of the CWC. Alternative proposals were presented, including tightened national export controls, criminalising activity that violates the BWC, intensified non-proliferation activities, increased domestic preparedness, enhanced biodefence and counter-bioterrorism capabilities and measures designed to prevent disease outbreaks.

2002 US-sponsored Cooperative Threat Reduction Programme

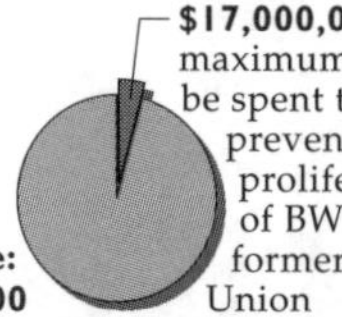

Biological weapon states

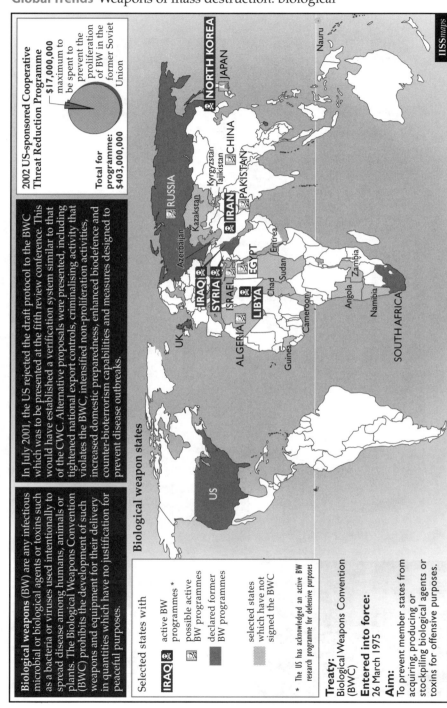

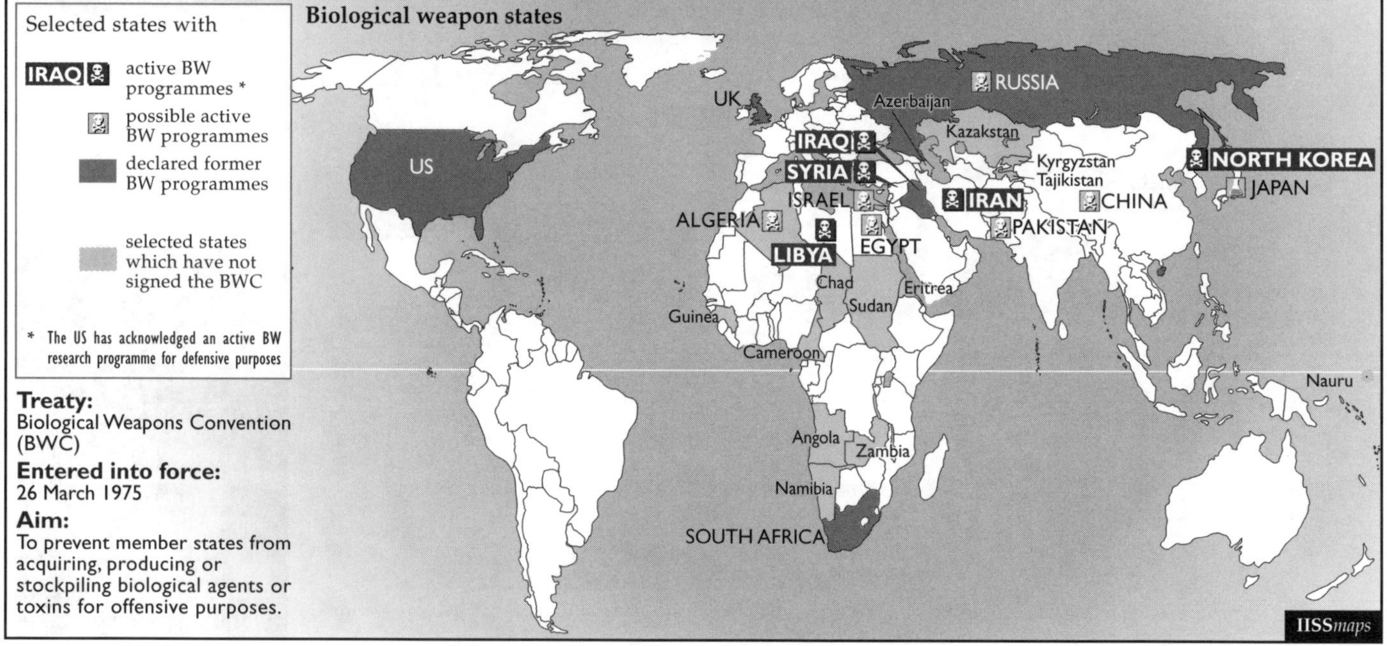

Treaty:
Biological Weapons Convention (BWC)

Entered into force:
26 March 1975

Aim:
To prevent member states from acquiring, producing or stockpiling biological agents or toxins for offensive purposes.

Global Trends Weapons of mass destruction: chemical

Chemical weapons (CW) are defined by the Chemical Weapons Convention (CWC) as including not only toxic chemicals but also ammunition and equipment for their disposal. Toxic chemicals refer to any chemical which may cause death, temporary loss of performance or permanent injury to people or animals.

Russia's declared CW stockpile is the largest in the world, at about 40,000 metric tons. It has requested an extension on the CWC deadline from 2007 to 2012 to destroy its stockpiles . As of 2000, $370 million had been pledged by the international community to assist destruction. $240 million of this has been allocated so far.

Verification of the CWC is carried out by the Organisation for the Prohibition of Chemical Weapons (OPCW). By 2001, the OPCW had conducted over 930 inspections in 49 countries.

2002 US-sponsored Cooperative Threat Reduction Programme

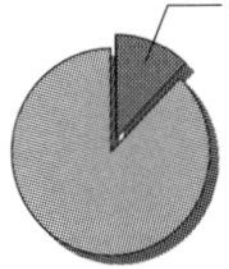

Chemical weapon states

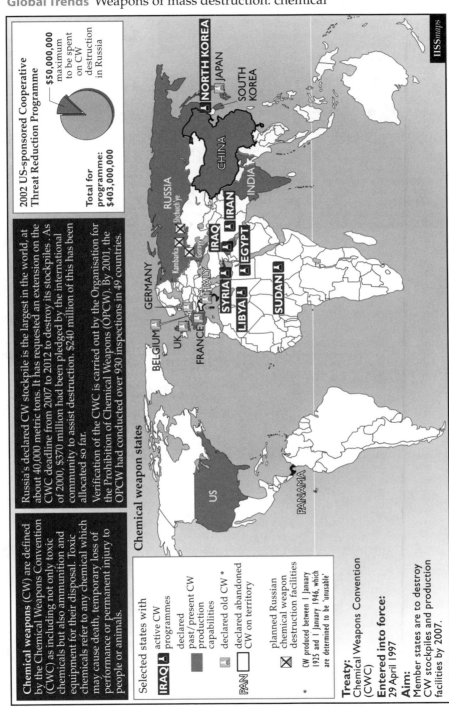

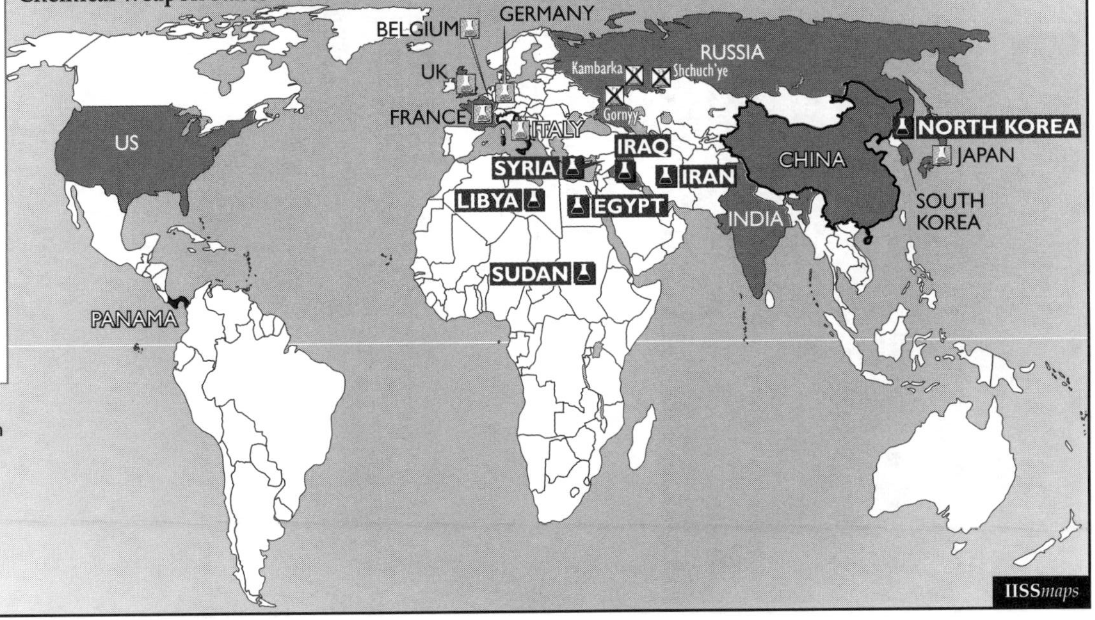

Selected states with

- IRAQ – active CW programmes
- declared past/present CW production capabilities
- declared old CW *
- PAN – declared abandoned CW on territory
- planned Russian chemical weapon destruction facilities

* CW produced between 1 January 1925 and 1 January 1946, which are determined to be 'unusable'

Treaty:
Chemical Weapons Convention (CWC)

Entered into force:
29 April 1997

Aim:
Member states are to destroy CW stockpiles and production facilities by 2007.

Global Trends Al-Qaeda's global network

Al-Qaeda ('the base') was founded in 1989 by Osama bin Laden. Bin Laden had fought against and facilitated transit of mujahideen to fight the Soviets in Afghanistan. He then used his new network to bring together mujahideen individuals and groups. When the Iraqi threat to Saudi Arabia arose in 1990–91, bin Laden offered a mujahideen army to deter Iraq – an offer that was rejected by the Saudis. Embittered by the US presence on Saudi territory, he moved his network to Sudan, where he remained until in 1996, relocating to Afghanistan.

As in Sudan, bin Laden contributed funds to the Taliban, bankrolled its infrastructural projects, and provided military personnel for Taliban armed forces, presumably as a *quid pro quo* for the Taliban's allowing him to stay there and protecting him. In 1998, after the bombing of US embassies in Nairobi and Dar es-Salaam, the US launched cruise missiles against four al-Qaeda bases in Afghanistan and a suspected chemical weapons facility in Khartoum, Sudan.

- US missile attacks against suspected al-Qaeda-related targets
- countries allegedly used by al-Qaeda financiers
- suspected al-Qaeda training or organisational bases – past or present
- IRAQ potential future al-Qaeda-related operational or reorganisation locations

Terrorist incidents linked to al-Qaeda

- successful operation
- unsuccessful operation
- possible/planned operation
- 11/09/01 date of incident
- 6 fatalities

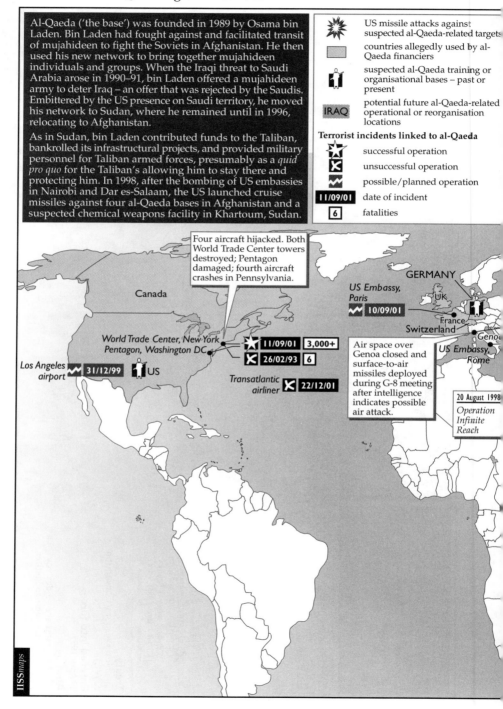

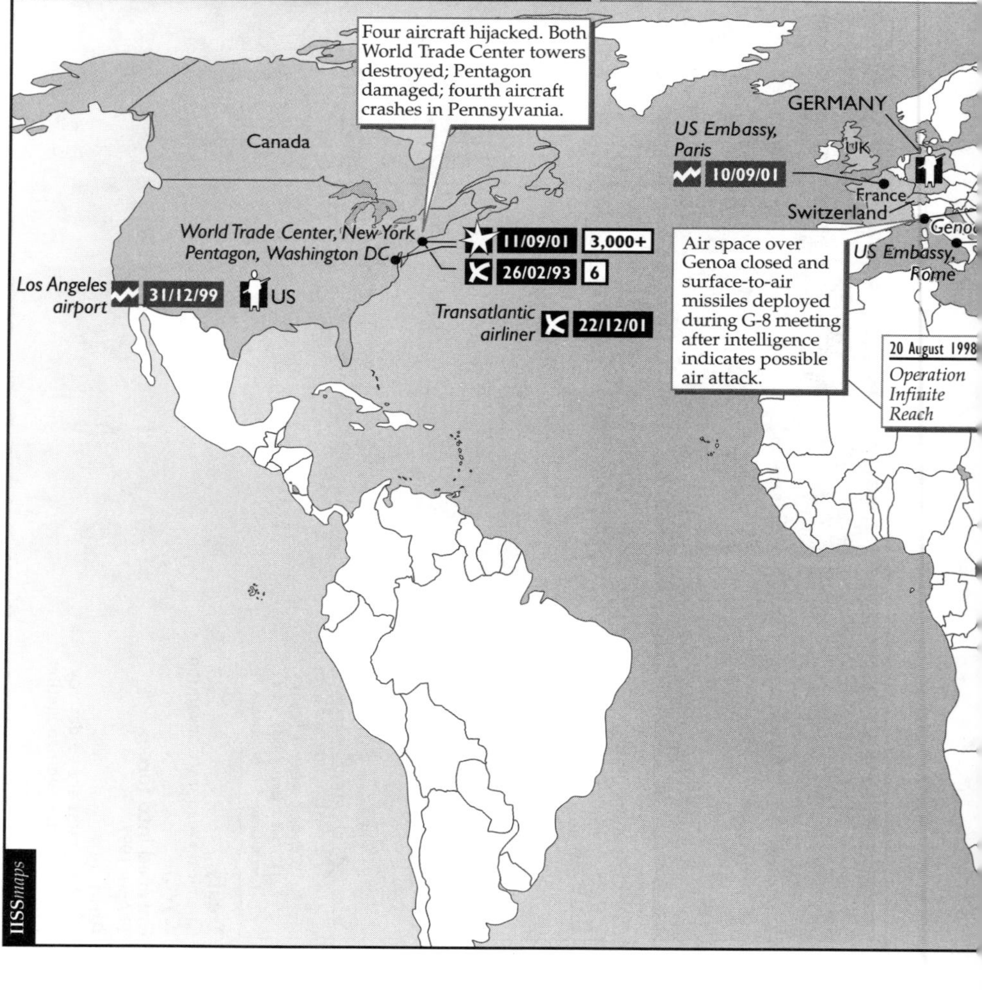

l-Qaeda structure

l-Qaeda represents a fusion of Saudi-born Wahhabi hinking and the expertise of primarily Egyptian errorist groups. It can function on its own, or through ssociated Islamic terrorist groups, such as Abu Sayyaf, he Islamic Movement of Uzbekistan and Pakistani roups. Thus, it is more correct to call it a network ather than an autonomous group. Osama bin Laden eads the network, with members of a *shura* (or council) ommanding other decision-making posts. Four ommittees (military, religio-political, finance and nedia) implement the decisions. In a bid to elicit wider upport – in terms of manpower and finances – from Muslims, bin Laden has dubbed his group the International Front for Jihad against the Jews and Crusaders'. This has enhanced al-Qaeda's resilience, s has its dispersed semi-autonomous cell structure nd wide links with global terror organizations.

Operational capabilities

Al-Qaeda cells can operate self-sufficiently to a degree, with links to the centre maintained by a few field commanders who can activate networks and give operational orders. Deployed assets have to be technologically literate, confident of operating in enemy territory, resourceful, highly motivated, and able to act on their own initiative. The lessons of 11 September, for which a sleeper cell trained and operated undetected for years, and the dispersed, self-sufficient and self-motivated nature of al-Qaeda cells, mean that the danger of future attacks remains real, even if military and law-enforcement operations have damaged al-Qaeda's major infrastructure and impaired its capacity to launch sophisticated operations such as the 11 September attacks.

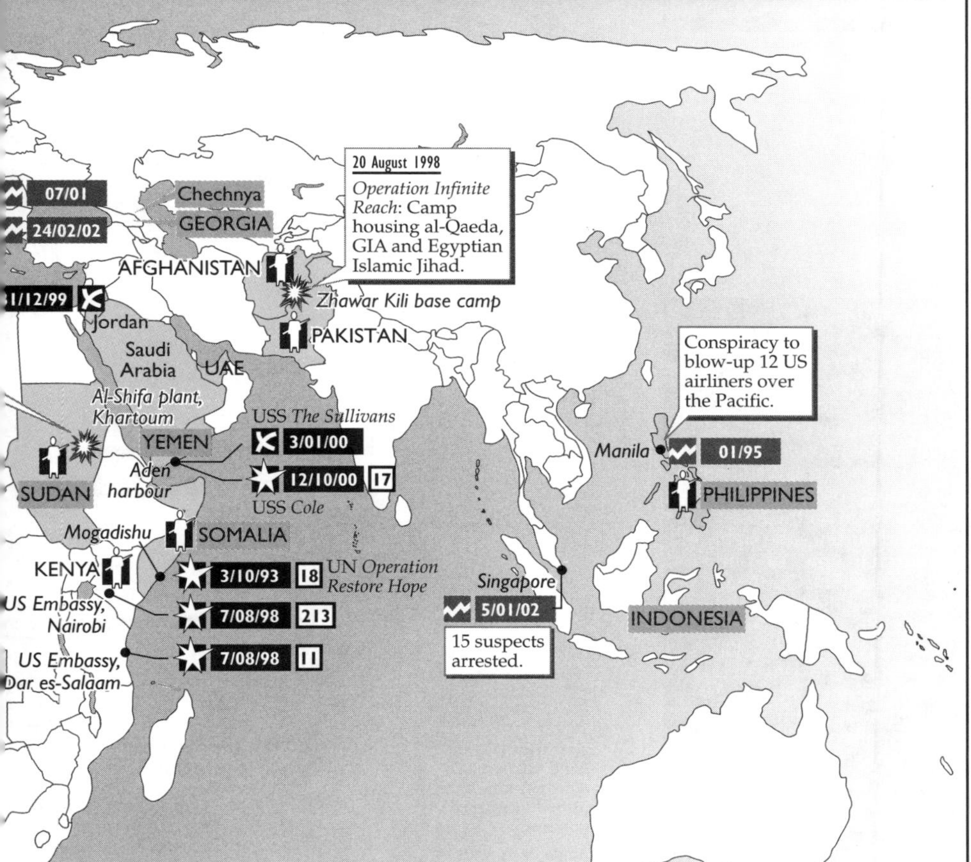

Global Trends Small arms, light weapons and child soldiers: restricting use

Small Arms

There is currently an estimated global stockpile of 550 million small arms and light weapons, of which 40–60% are illegal. The annual legal trade in these weapons is estimated at $7–10 billion. This money (together with that purchasing illicit weapons) has a disproportionate impact on global security, fuelling armed conflicts and adding to the burden of humanitarian aid. Since 1990, four million deaths have been directly attributed to these weapons and the fact that they are often easy to operate, and man-portable, increases likely use by children.

The United Nations 'Conference on the Illicit Trade in Small Arms and Light Weapons in all its Aspects' was held in New York, 9–20 July 2001. This was the first international meeting on the issue. Main topics discussed included reducing the volume and flow of such weapons, and halting illicit global trading. Agreement was difficult as many states rely on these weapons for legitimate defence and security needs. Although no legally binding document was signed, participants agreed to ensure that manufacturers mark weapons and maintain records to facilitate tracing.

Child Soldiers

There are an estimated 300,000 child soldiers fighting in armed conflicts across the world. A child soldier is defined as anyone under the age of 18 who volunteers or is forced to serve as a soldier in an armed conflict. The 1989 Convention on the Rights of a Child outlines the rights of children in times of conflict and peace. The Optional Protocol to the Convention adopted by the General Assembly on 25 May 2000 strengthens the convention by setting the age for compulsory recruitment or direct participation in hostilities at 18, calling upon states to raise the minimum age for voluntary recruitment to 16 and prohibiting armed groups from recruiting or using in hostilities anyone under 18. The protocol entered into force 12 February 2002.

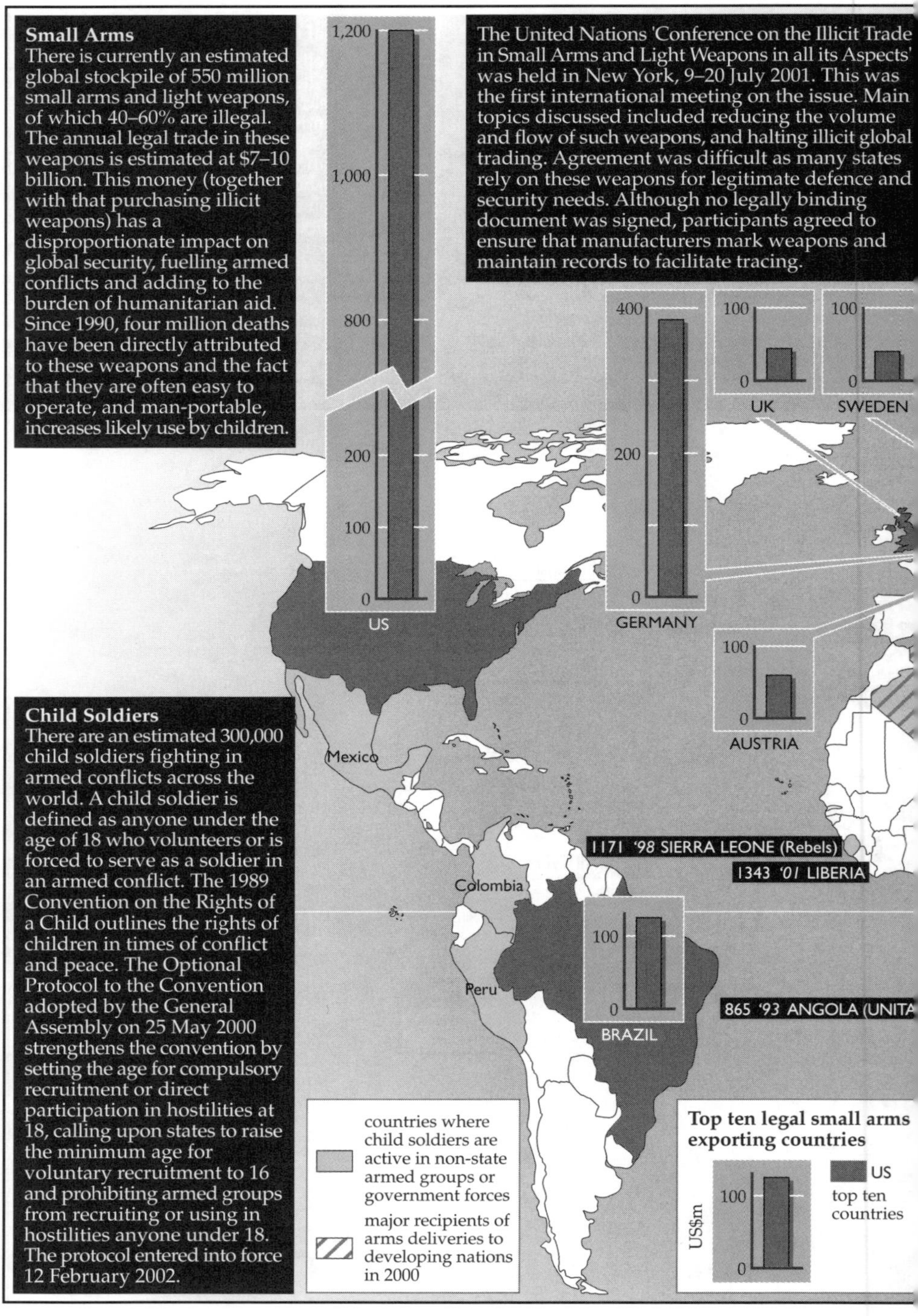

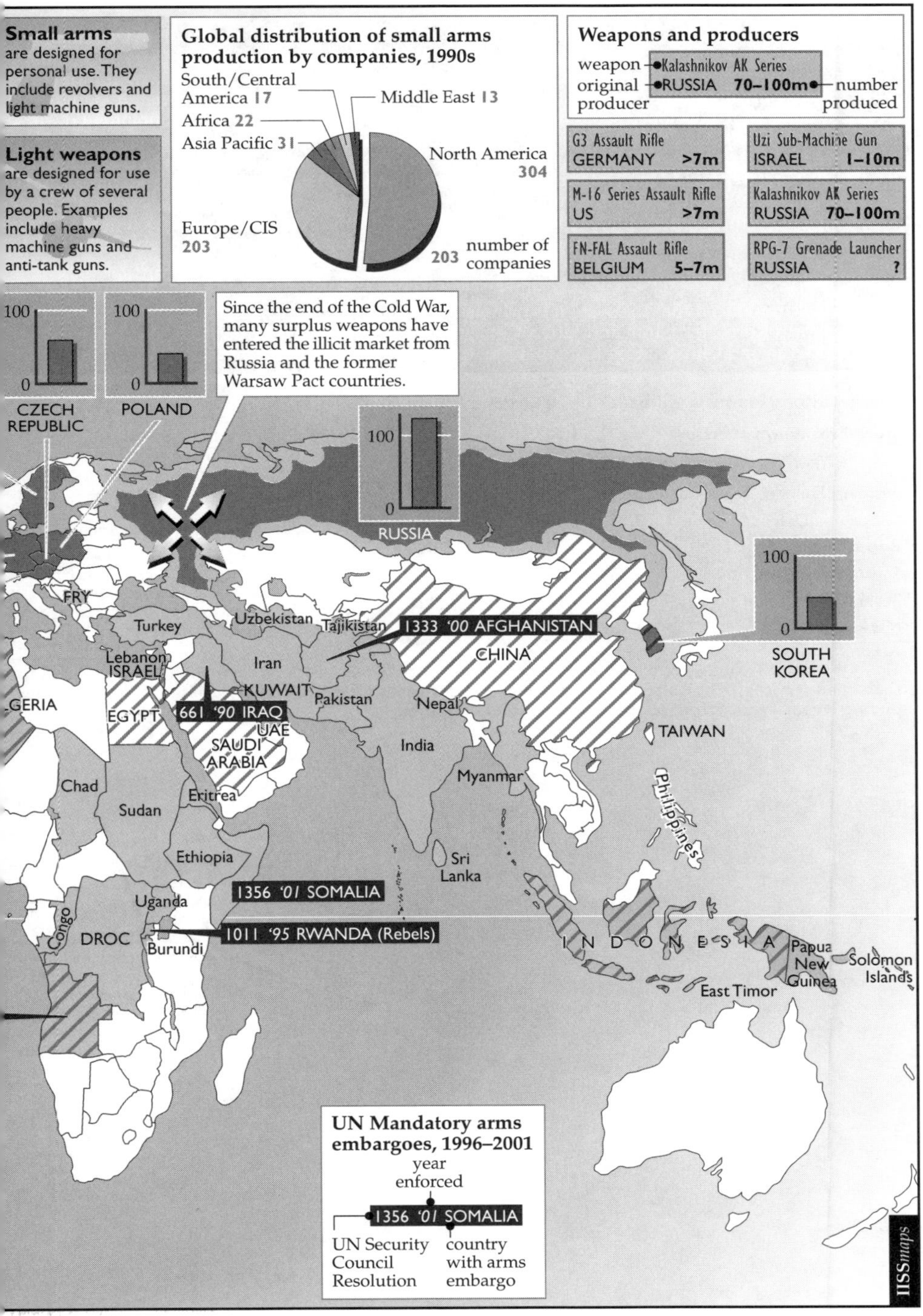
Small arms
are designed for personal use. They include revolvers and light machine guns.
Light weapons
are designed for use by a crew of several people. Examples include heavy machine guns and anti-tank guns.
Global distribution of small arms production by companies, 1990s
South/Central America 17
Middle East 13
Africa 22
Asia Pacific 31
North America 304
Europe/CIS 203
203 number of companies
Weapons and producers
weapon
Kalashnikov AK Series
original producer
RUSSIA 70–100m
number produced
G3 Assault Rifle
GERMANY >7m
Uzi Sub-Machine Gun
ISRAEL 1–10m
M-16 Series Assault Rifle
US >7m
Kalashnikov AK Series
RUSSIA 70–100m
FN-FAL Assault Rifle
BELGIUM 5–7m
RPG-7 Grenade Launcher
RUSSIA ?
100
0
CZECH REPUBLIC
100
0
POLAND
Since the end of the Cold War, many surplus weapons have entered the illicit market from Russia and the former Warsaw Pact countries.
100
0
RUSSIA
100
0
SOUTH KOREA
FRY
Turkey
Uzbekistan
Tajikistan
1333 '00 AFGHANISTAN
CHINA
Lebanon
ISRAEL
Iran
KUWAIT
Pakistan
Nepal
GERIA
EGYPT
661 '90 IRAQ
UAE
SAUDI ARABIA
India
TAIWAN
Chad
Sudan
Eritrea
Myanmar
Philippines
Ethiopia
Sri Lanka
1356 '01 SOMALIA
Uganda
Congo
DROC
1011 '95 RWANDA (Rebels)
Burundi
INDONESIA
Papua New Guinea
Solomon Islands
East Timor
UN Mandatory arms embargoes, 1996–2001
year enforced
1356 '01 SOMALIA
UN Security Council Resolution
country with arms embargo
IISSmaps

Global Trends The rejuvenated missile defence debate

The US missile defence system is intended to protect all US territory, and areas where US and allied forces are deployed, from attack by single- and limited multiple-warhead ballistic missiles, potentially carrying weapons of mass destruction. Although missile defence has been under discussion since the 1980s, it was only under the Clinton administration that attempts were made to generate deployable assets. Systems were developed separately by the different services, with most effort put into midcourse interceptions. On 1 May 2001, President George W. Bush stressed the overall objective of a layered defensive system, using complementary interceptors, sensors and battle management command and control systems to provide multiple engagement opportunities at the boost phase, midcourse, and terminal-phases of flight. This will combine – and refine – existing systems such as *Patriot*, with those in research and development under the framework of the former National Missile Defense project and other systems still at the conceptual stage. Such a wide suite of systems will enable the overall command and control system to determine which vehicle is best suited to engaging any particular target.

The US has announced that the system is primarily directed against 'rogue states', which generally include North Korea, Iraq, Iran and Libya. Concerns have been voiced at the plans, particularly from Europe, Russia and China, citing fears that the system could trigger an arms race.

Budget allocation by work breakdown structure ($ million)

Work breakdown structure	FY02	FY03	FY04	FY05	FY06	FY07
BMD System	846	1,101	1,252	1,200	1,182	1,219
Terminal Defence Segment	2,026	1,128	927	1,078	1,149	1,499
Midcourse Defence Segment	3,762	3,193	3,074	3,016	2,969	2,596
Boost Defence Segment	600	797	1,390	1,400	1,591	2,275
Sensor Segment	335	373	489	1,146	900	1,008
Technology	139	122	155	130	143	147
MDA Total	7,709	6,714	7,287	7,970	7,934	8,743

The BMD System segment comprises System Engineering and Integration (SE&I), BM/C2, Communications, Targets and Countermeasures, Test and Evaluation, Producibility and Manufacturing Technology, and Program Operations (which includes Management Headquarters and Pentagon Reservation).

Given the maturity of the terminal phase programmes, the MDA has transferred ownership of these back to the armed services. This also serves to free-up finance for other MDA projects, though the MDA still carries out incremental research, development, testing and evaluation.

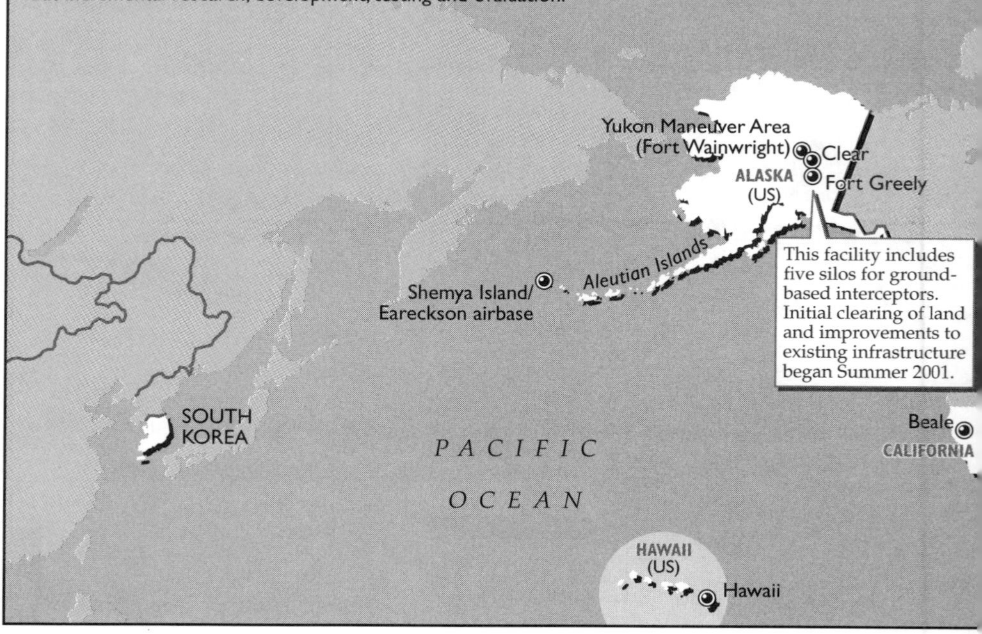

Missile Defense Agency (MDA), 2002 Budget

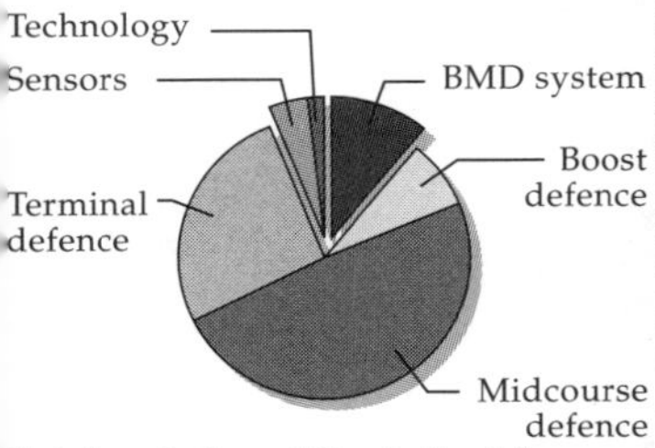

Total costs for a US missile defence system are estimated at over $150bn

Anti-Ballistic Missile (ABM) Treaty

Signed in 1972, this treaty bans missile-defence systems designed to protect national territory, although both the US and (then) Soviet Union were allowed two localised systems. Only the Soviets retained their (one) system. On 13 December 2001, President George W. Bush announced that the US intended to withdraw from the treaty, subject to a six-month timetable.

Integrated Flight Tests (IFT) of the ground-based midcourse system

The estimated cost of each IFT is $100 million. Some argue that the tests have been designed to succeed and therefore do not provide accurate indications of operational capabilities.

2 October '99 First successful IFT of the Exo-atmospheric Kill Vehicle (EKV), developed by US defence contractor Raytheon.

18 January '00 IFT fails when the infrared sensor on the EKV malfunctions.

7 July '00 IFT, which was delayed twice from the original test date, fails.

14 July '01 First IFT since George W. Bush took office succeeds.

3 December '01 IFT, identical to July test, succeeds.

15 March '02 Fourth successful IFT.

Phases	Planned	Aim
Phase-One	2005	20 GBIs installed at a single site in Alaska intended to defend the US against tens of warheads with simple penetration aids.
Phase-Two		Increase the number of interceptors in Alaska to 100. At this stage modernised facilities in Fylingdales are intended to be utilised.
Phase-Three	2015	Capacity to counter modernised missile warheads with decoys and multiple entry vehicles. This may consist of up to 125 interceptors in Alaska and a possible additional 125 at another site.

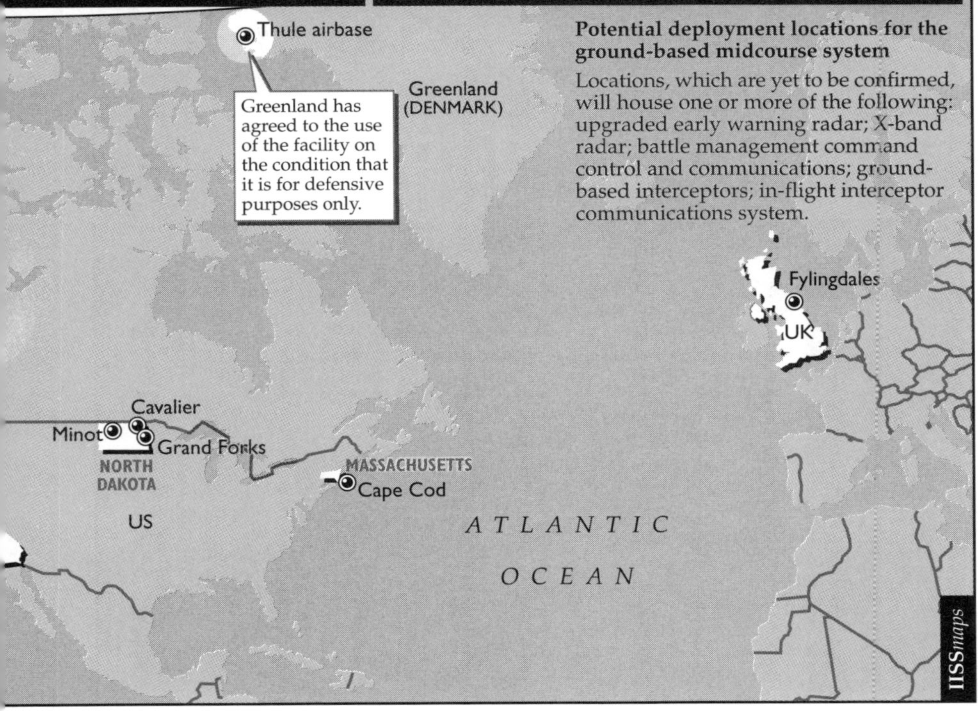

Potential deployment locations for the ground-based midcourse system

Locations, which are yet to be confirmed, will house one or more of the following: upgraded early warning radar; X-band radar; battle management command control and communications; ground-based interceptors; in-flight interceptor communications system.

Global Trends The rejuvenated missile defence debate

Ballistic-missile ranges (US definition)

Short-range (SRBM)	up to 600km
Medium-range (MRBM)	up to 1,300km
Intermediate range (IRBM)	up to 3,500 km
Inter-continental (ICBM)	from 5,500–10,000km

Summary of ballistic missile defence projects

System	System mobility	Presently aimed at
Boost phase defence systems		
Airborne laser*	strategic	all ranges
Space laser+	strategic	all ranges
Space/sea-based hit-to-kill+	strategic	all ranges
Midcourse defence systems		
Ground-based interceptors* utilising former National Missile Defense structure	fixed-site	all ranges especially ICBM
Sea-based interceptors Navy Theatre-Wide*	strategic	all ranges
Terminal defence systems		
Theater High Altitude Area Defense (THAAD)*	tactical	IRBM/ MRBM
Medium-range Extended Air Defense System (MEADS)* (with Germany and Italy)	tactical	MRBM/ SRBM
Patriot PAC-3* (nearing deployment)	tactical	SRBM

In December 2001, the Navy Area-Missile-Defense System was cancelled, after escalating costs were not matched by performance.

* in development
\+ conceptual

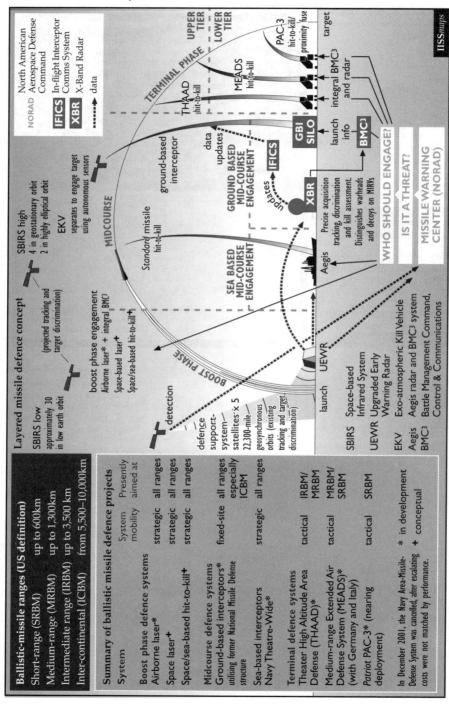

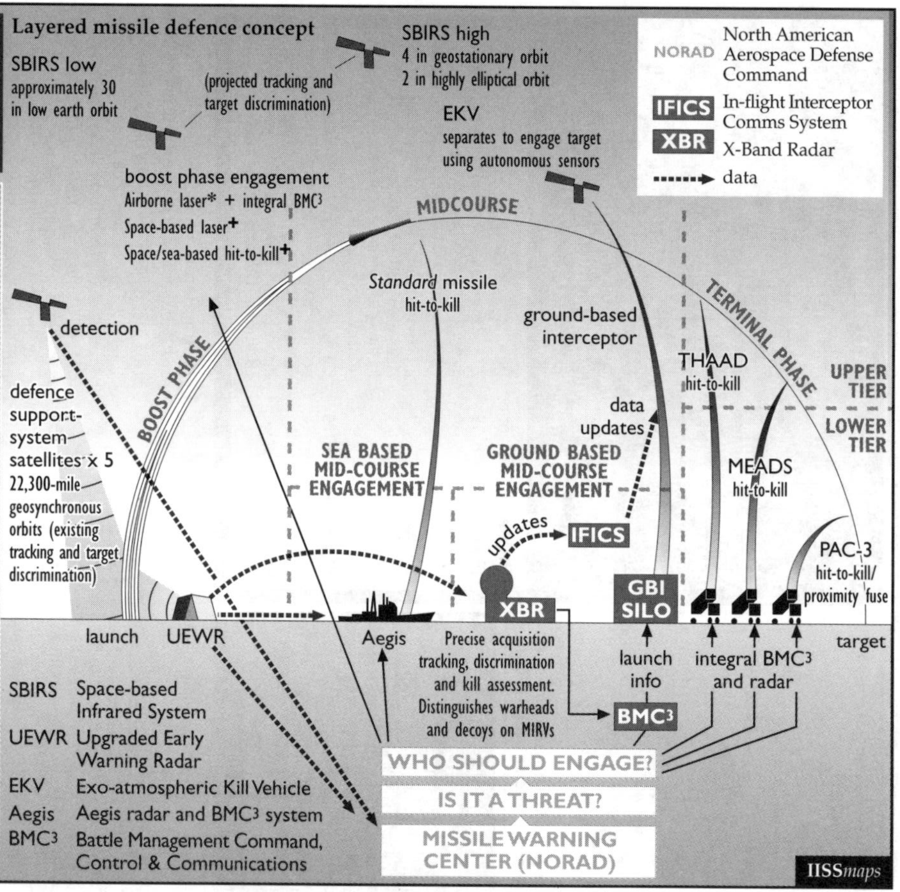